Everyman, I will go with thee,
and be thy guide

Edmund Spenser

THE FAERIE QUEENE
BOOKS I-III

Edited by
DOUGLAS BROOKS-DAVIES
University of Manchester

EVERYMAN
J. M. DENT · LONDON
CHARLES E. TUTTLE
VERMONT

First published as an Everyman Classic, 1987
Reprinted 1989
Reissued 1991
New edition 1993

© Introduction and other critical apparatus,
J. M. Dent, 1993

J. M. Dent
Orion Publishing Group
Orion House, 5 Upper St Martin's Lane,
London WC2H 9EA
and
Charles E. Tuttle Co. Inc.
28 South Main Street,
Rutland, Vermont 05701, USA

Typeset in Sabon by Deltatype Ltd, Ellesmere Port, Cheshire
Printed in Great Britain by
The Guernsey Press Co. Ltd, Guernsey, Channel Islands

British Library Cataloguing-in-Publication-Data
is available upon request.

ISBN 0 460 87391 1

CONTENTS

THE FAERIE QUEENE

To all those students who have read Spenser with me,
in gratitude

NOTE ON THE AUTHOR AND EDITOR

EDMUND SPENSER was born in London, probably in 1552. He was educated at Merchant Taylors' School, and Pembroke Hall, Cambridge. By 1579 he was employed in the Earl of Leicester's household and had become acquainted with Sir Philip Sidney, and in the same year married Machabyas Chylde. The year 1580 saw him in Ireland as secretary to Lord Grey, the new Lord Deputy, and from this time he regarded Ireland as his home, though his attachment to Elizabeth and her court remained strong. The success of *The Faerie Queene*, Books I–III (1590) can be measured in part from the grant by the queen of an annual pension of £50 in 1591, and the mid-1590s saw Spenser in a remarkable frenzy of creativity: *Amoretti and Epithalamion* appeared in 1595 as the formalised narrative of his courtship and marriage to his second wife, Elizabeth Boyle; *Colin Clout's Come Home Againe* was published the same year, and three more books of *The Faerie Queene*, together with *Prothalamion* and the *Fowre Hymnes*, appeared the year after. In 1598 Spenser's estate at Kilcolman, near Cork, was attacked by the Earl of Tyrone's forces, and a few months later he was sent to London with dispatches for the Privy Council, arriving on Christmas Eve. He died in Westminster on 13 January 1599, and is buried in the Abbey.

DOUGLAS BROOKS-DAVIES was, until 1993, Senior Lecturer in English Literature at the University of Manchester. He is currently Honorary Research Fellow there, and a freelance scholar. His many publications include *Spenser's 'Faerie Queene': A Critical Commentary on Books I and II* (1977); *The Mercurian Monarch* (1983); *Pope's 'Dunciad' and the Queen of Night* (1985); *Dickens' 'Great Expectations': A Critical Study* (1989); *Oedipal 'Hamlet'* (1989); and *Silver Poets of the Sixteenth Century* (Everyman, 1992). He was a major contributor to *The Spenser Encyclopedia* (1990) and is working on an edition of Spenser's minor poems.

CHRONOLOGY OF SPENSER'S LIFE

Year   Age   Life

1552   ?Born, probably in London; nothing known with certainty
             of his family origins

CHRONOLOGY OF HIS TIMES

Year	Artistic Events	Historical Events
1551		Council of Trent (second session–1552)
1552		Second Edwardian Prayer Book; Calvin's *Concerning Predestination*
1553	Gavin Douglas, *Aeneid* transln; Thomas Wilson, *Art of Rhetoric*	Death of Edward VI; Lady Jane Grey proclaimed queen; accession of Mary Tudor (Catholic); arrest of Protestant bishops
1554	Philip Sidney born	Lady Jane Grey executed; full restoration of Roman Catholicism in England; Mary marries Philip of Spain
1555		John Knox unites Scots Protestants
1556		Philip II succeeds to Spanish throne
1557	Surrey's *Aeneid* transln; *Tottel's Miscellany* of poems by Surrey, Wyatt, etc.	Incorporation of Stationers' Company
1558		Death of Mary I; accession of Elizabeth I; John Knox, *First Blast of the Trumpet against the Monstrous Regiment of Women*
1559	*Mirror for Magistrates*	Elizabeth I crowned; English Church re-established with Act of Supremacy and Elizabethan Prayer Book
1560		Geneva Bible
1561		Knox establishes constitution of Scottish Church
1562	Sackville and Norton, *Gorboduc* (first English blank verse tragedy)	John Hawkins starts Africa–America slave trade; Europe: Council of Trent resits

Year Age Life

?–1569	17	Merchant Taylors' School, London, under the headship of the celebrated humanist and scholar, Richard Mulcaster
1569	17	English translation of Jan van der Noot's Dutch Protestant *A Theatre for Worldlings* published including epigrams translated by Spenser from Petrarch, sonnets translated by him from Du Bellay and four sonnet paraphrases from the Book of Revelation. 20 May: matriculates at Cambridge; sizar (i.e., poor scholar) at Pembroke Hall, Cambridge; becomes friend of Gabriel Harvey (college fellow, 1570)
1573	21	Graduates B.A.

Year	Artistic Events	Historical Events
1563	John Foxe, *Book of Martyrs* (Protestant martyrology)	Council of Trent finishes
1564	Shakespeare, Marlowe born; John Dee, *Monas Hieroglyphica*	Calvin, Michelangelo die
1565	Arthur Golding's transln of Ovid's *Metamorphoses*, Books I–IV published	Hawkins's second South America voyage (1564–5)
1566	Nicholas Udall, *Ralph Roister Doister* (first English comedy) published	James VI of Scotland (future James I) born; Nostradamus, astrologer, dies
1567	Full text of Golding's Ovid published	Mary Queen of Scots abdicates, flees to England 1568; Hawkins's third voyage (to West Indies and Guinea)
1568	John Heywood's interlude, *The Four P's*	Douai College (seminary for training English Catholic priests) founded; Bishops' Bible
1570	Roger Ascham, *The Schoolmaster*	Papal bull *Regnans in Excelsis* excommunicates Elizabeth I
1571		Cecil becomes Lord Burghley; London Royal Exchange opened; Turks capture Cyprus from Venetians
1572	Ben Jonson (dramatist) born	Drake attacks Spaniards in South America; 23–4 August: French Protestants murdered in Paris (St Bartholomew Massacre); John Knox dies
1573		Drake views Pacific from Panama; Tasso, *Aminta*

Year *Age*   *Life*

1576   24   Graduates M.A.
1578   26   Employed as secretary to John Young, Bishop of
                Rochester, formerly Master of Pembroke

1579   27   Early October: employed by Earl of Leicester; acquainted
                with Philip Sidney, John Dyer and Daniel Rogers.
                27 October: an 'Edmounde Spenser' (presumably the poet)
                marries Machabyas Chylde at Westminster (they will have
                two children, Sylvanus and Katherine). 5 December: *The
                Shepheards Calendar* entered in the Stationers' Register
1580   28   June: the Gabriel Harvey–Spenser *Familiar Letters*
                published; contain first reference to *The Faerie Queene*.
                Appointed private secretary to Arthur, Lord Grey of
                Wilton, Lord Deputy of Ireland. 12 August: probably
                arrives in Ireland with Grey; works as Clerk of the Privy
                Council at Dublin Castle; will remain in Ireland, with
                occasional trips to England
1581   29   March: succeeds the poet Lodowick Bryskett as Clerk of
                the Chancery for Faculties while remaining under Grey.
                December: leases castle and manor at Enniscorthy, County
                Wexford for brief period; subsequently leases dissolved
                monastery at New Ross, County Wexford; a house in
                Dublin; and New Abbey, County Kildare (lease for the
                latter forfeited 1590 after failure to pay rent)
1583   31   Appointed Commissioner of Musters for County Kildare

1585   33   Prebendary of Effin (non-resident living attached to
                Limerick cathedral)
1586   34   Assigned Kilcolman Castle with 3,000 acres (confiscated
                along with another 245,000 acres from the Irish Earl
                Desmond); undertakes to assist in colonisation of Munster
                by populating it with English immigrants; takes possession
                1588(?); granted full perpetual lease to the property 1590

Year	Artistic Events	Historical Events
1575	Comedy *Gammer Gurton's Needle* (acted 1566) published; John Marston born	Elizabeth I offered (and declines) sovereignty of Netherlands
1578	Holinshed, *Chronicles*; Lyly, *Euphues, or the Anatomy of Wit*	English College moved from Douai to Rheims
1579	North's *Plutarch's Lives* transln; John Fletcher (dramatist) born	The Duc d'Alençon courts Elizabeth
1580	Philip Sidney, *Apology for Poetry* (publ. 1595); Lyly, *Euphues and His England*	Francis Drake returns from circumnavigation of globe (began 1575)
1581	Sidney completes *Arcadia*	Act against English Catholics; Tasso, *Gerusalemme Liberata*
1583		Discovery of Throckmorton plot against Elizabeth in favour of Mary Queen of Scots
1584	Peele, *The Arraignment of Paris*; Bruno, *Lo Spaccio della Bestia Trionfante* published in London (followed by *De gli Heroici Furori*, 1585)	Ralegh discovers Virginia; English acts against Jesuits and seminary priests
1586	Camden, *Britannia*	Sidney dies; trial of Mary Queen of Scots

Year   Age   Life

1589	37	Succeeds Bryskett as Clerk of the Council in Munster. October: Spenser to England with Sir Walter Ralegh ready to present *The Faerie Queene*, Books I–III (the 1590 *FQ*) to Queen Elizabeth. 1 December: *The Faerie Queene*, Books I–III entered in Stationers' Register
1590	38	January: *The Faerie Queene*, Books I–III published by William Ponsonby in London. 29 December: *Complaints. Containing sundrie small Poemes of the Worlds Vanitie* entered in Stationers' Register
1591	39	Returns to Ireland having been granted considerable annual pension of £50 by queen (February). *Complaints* and *Daphnaida* published by William Ponsonby. 27 December: date of Dedicatory Epistle to Sir Walter Ralegh of *Colin Clouts Come Home Againe* (not published until 1595)
1594	42	Queen's Justice for Cork. 11 June: marries Elizabeth Boyle (they have one child, Peregrine, who will die in 1642). 19 November: *Amoretti and Epithalamion* entered in Stationers' Register
1595	43	Publication of: *Colin Clouts Come Home Againe* (published with *Astrophel. A Pastoral Elegie upon the Death of the most Noble and Valorous Knight, Sir Philip Sidney*); *Amoretti and Epithalamion*. Ponsonby published both sets of works
1596	44	Publication of: *The Faerie Queene*, Books IV–VI (published with Books I–III); *Fowre Hymnes*; *Prothalamion*, all by Ponsonby. *A Vewe of the Present State of Ireland* written (unpublished). King James VI of Scotland claims Spenser slandered his mother, Mary Queen of Scots, in figure of Duessa in *FQ*, Book V

Year	Artistic Events	Historical Events
1587	Marlowe's *Dr Faustus*, *Tamburlaine* acted	Mary Queen of Scots executed; English expedition against Cadiz; Knox, *History of the Reformation in Scotland* published
1588	Anti-episcopal *Marprelate Tracts* published (–1590); Lyly, *Endimion*	Spanish Armada; William Morgan's Welsh translation of the Bible
1589	Puttenham, *Art of English Poesie*	
1590	Marlowe, *Tamburlaine*, *Jew of Malta*, Sidney, *Arcadia* printed	
1591	Harington's transln of Ariosto, *Orlando Furioso*; Sidney, *Astrophil and Stella*; Shakespeare, 2 and 3 *Henry VI*	Death of Spanish mystic, St John of the Cross
1592	Shakespeare, 1 *Henry VI*; Marlowe, *Edward II*; *Dr Faustus* printed; Kyd, *Spanish Tragedy*	Presbyterianism established in Scotland; remains of Pompeii discovered; Montaigne dies
1593	Marlowe, *Massacre at Paris*; Shakespeare, *Venus and Adonis*, *Richard III*, *Comedy of Errors*	Marlowe dies
1594	Hooker, *Ecclesiastical Polity*, I–IV (completed 1597); Shakespeare, *Titus Andronicus*, *Taming of the Shrew*, *Two Gentlemen of Verona*	Palestrina dies
1595	Shakespeare, *Love's Labour's Lost*, *Midsummer Night's Dream*, *Richard II*	Robert Southwell (poet and priest) martyred
1596	Shakespeare, *Merchant of Venice*, *King John*	English attack Cadiz

Year   Age   Life

1598   46   Named Sheriff-designate for County Cork. October: Kilcolman attacked and burned by forces led by Earl of Tyrone. 24 December: brings dispatches from Governor of Munster to Privy Council in London

1599   47   13 January: dies at Westminster; funeral in Westminster Abbey paid for by Earl of Essex

1609   Publication of: *The Faerie Queene* including *Two Cantos of Mutabilitie*
1611   Publication of folio works: *The Faerie Queene; The Shepheards Calendar; Together with the Other Works of England's Arch-Poet, Edm. Spenser*

Year	Artistic Events	Historical Events
1597	Shakespeare, *Romeo and Juliet*; Joseph Hall, *Virgidemiae* (*Harvest of Rods*)	
1598	Part of Chapman's *Iliad* transln printed; Jonson, *Every Man in His Humour*; Marlowe/Chapman, *Hero and Leander*; Shakespeare, 1 *Henry IV*, *Much Ado about Nothing*; John Stow, *Survey of London*; Francis Meres, *Palladis Tamia*, *Wit's Reflections*	Philip II of Spain dies
1599	Jonson, *Every Man out of His Humour*; Shakespeare, *Henry V*, *Julius Caesar*; James VI, *Basilikon Doron* (defending kingly Divine Right)	Oliver Cromwell born; Juan de Mariana, *De Rege et Regis Institutione* (defends tyrannicide); Essex appointed Deputy in Ireland
1600	Shakespeare, *As You Like It*, *Merry Wives of Windsor*, *Twelfth Night*; Fairfax's transln of Tasso, *Jerusalem Delivered*; Dekker, *Shoemaker's Holiday*; Jonson, *Cynthia's Revels*	East India Company founded; James VI appoints bishops in Scotland; Giordano Bruno burnt by Inquisition for heresy
1601	Shakespeare, *Hamlet*, *Troilus and Cressida*; Jonson, *The Poetaster*	Essex executed for attempted rebellion
1602	Marston, *Antonio's Revenge*	Bodleian Library founded
1603	Shakespeare, *All's Well That Ends Well*; Jonson, *Sejanus*	Elizabeth dies, James VI succeeds as James I, grants tolerance to Catholics

INTRODUCTION

The Faerie Queene is one of the great monuments to the Reformation on the one hand and the English Renaissance on the other. Born of icon smashing and the attempts under Elizabeth I, after her excommunication in 1570, to stifle and oppose both native and European Catholicism, it is itself nevertheless an icon: a shimmering multifaceted reflection of the queen to whom it is dedicated. This queen is head of the English Church (by the Settlement of 1559) and of the militant Protestant Order of the Garter (Una in Book I). She is the embodiment of temperance, that ability not only to control opposites through the exercise of reason but also mystically to transform opposites into a new whole (Belphoebe and Alma in Book II). And she is a warrior man–woman who redeems female history from the erasures it has been placed under by successive generations of males intent on building empire in their image (Britomart in Book III).

As an icon it has its roots in the word-portrait Spenser painted of Eliza in the April eclogue of *The Shepheards Calendar* (1579) as 'The flowre of Virgins . . . Yclad in scarlot like a mayden Queene,/ And Ermines white./Upon her head a Cremosin coronet . . .' Although not the first adulatory image of her, it was early enough to be a formative influence on the cult which developed in the 1580s and 1590s, forming Elizabeth into Cynthia, Diana, Venus, Dido, Astraea, Judith, to name but a few of the biblical and classical figures with whom she was identified: a powerful and various Virgin Queen whose portrait could only be painted or engraved according to a strict formula so that in the end she disappeared into facelessness under her own authoritarian strictures, merely leaving wig, cosmetic mask and allegorical jewels and clothes as signs of her former self – a kind of Miss Havisham aping the youth and beauty of Estella.

The Faerie Queene is not a simple poem. Its length guarantees this for one thing (by 1596 it comprised six books each of twelve cantos, with each canto containing between forty and fifty nine-line stanzas); but so also did its gestation period. Begun, apparently, by 1579 (Spenser's friend Gabriel Harvey mentions 'your *Faerie Queene*' in a letter to him published in *Three Proper Wittie Familiar Letters*, 1580), it eventually appeared in two instalments (1590, 1596) with the author's announced intention of extending it to a twelve-book epic on the model of the *Aeneid* (Letter to Ralegh appended to the 1590 text; the plan was abandoned, and the Letter omitted from the 1596 edition). It even insisted on posthumous birth, the *Two Cantos of Mutabilitie* – presumably part of a putative Book VII – being published in the 1609 edition, a decade after Spenser's death.

It is perhaps symbolic that the *Two Cantos* tell of Mutability's claim to supremacy and of her defeat by God, who controls time and can impose eternal rest at the end of time. For, in a sense, most of Spenser's poetry is impelled by the beliefs (Spenser would have recognised them as Platonic and Christian) that temporal process operates in the service of God and that we shall eventually see him 'face to face' (1 Corinthians 13:12). In other words, it enacts the metaphor that one's life is a journey towards light, the divine One, characterised by the givens of decay, a corrupted will, and partial understanding (our inheritance from the Fall: Genesis 3); that it is a pilgrimage through a wasteland of temptation, shadow and darkness in which the devil often masquerades as his opposite. Hence *The Faerie Queene* is, in essence, a quest poem obsessed with the gap between desire and attainment, governed by the oppositions of good and evil, light and dark. It is predicated upon the Tudor belief that the court is the centre of virtue, patronage, taste and religion, and that the centre of the court is the sovereign who reigns on earth as a manifestation of God's blazing light. Thus, as the Letter to Ralegh explains, each titular knight of *The Faerie Queene*'s books sets out from court on his/her adventure to avenge a particular wrong: Duessa, Orgoglio, Archimago and others in Book I; the witch Acrasia, Phaedria, Maleger (and others) in Book II; Malecasta, Proteus, Busirane (and others) in Book III. In Book I Holiness and Protestant national identity, in the figure of St George, the knight of the Red Cross, prevail over the Catholic Antichrist; in Book II Temperance vanquishes its opposite; in Book III Chastity succeeds in banishing the forces of sexual torment.

In order to encode his story as a narrative occupying the shadowy margins of the known and unknown, Spenser invented a pseudo-language comprising a mixture of current and archaic words together with neologisms; placed the tale in the half-mediaeval, half-dream, land of faerie; invented a super-heroine, Queen Gloriana, for it; and wrote the whole as a chivalric romantic epic on the model of Virgil and his Italian successors. He had to imitate Virgil's *Aeneid* in praise of Augustus not only to prove that, as a native Englishman, he could assert English as a poetic medium in accordance with Renaissance theories of imitation and arguments over the literary efficacy of the vernacular tongue, but also because Elizabeth, via the well-known story of Brutus (see the notes to Book II canto x in this volume), claimed ancestry from Aeneas and his Trojan forefathers and hence equality with Augustus. Of the Italian successors, Ariosto is perhaps the most important because his *Orlando Furioso* offered for imitation a post-Virgilian vernacular epic set in the time of Charlemagne which thus shadowed the achievements of the Holy Roman Emperor Charles v whom, even more than his secular predecessor as first presider over the Roman empire, Augustus, Elizabeth sought to rival in her claim to be supreme Protestant emperor in Europe and just inheritor of Christendom. And *The Faerie Queene* had to be chivalric because the 1570s saw the revival of the mediaeval courtly code in the form of tilts held annually to celebrate Elizabeth's accession day, 17 November (hence the 'Annual feaste' at Gloriana's court, during which, the Letter to Ralegh tells us, the knights leave on their adventures).

All the above was the 'official' interpretation; but there is an alternative reading.

England in the sixteenth century was in as great a state of crisis as the England of today and for similar reasons, though for our purposes it is perhaps the religious situation that is most relevant. Catholic, then with allegiance to the Pope forbidden under Henry VIII; devoutly Protestant under Edward vi; zealously Catholic under Mary; ineluctably Protestant under Elizabeth: how did those who lived from one of these reigns into the other (and Spenser could well have been baptised a Catholic) know where Truth was supposed to lie? Assuming that they had the leisure to care, this state control and manipulation of faith must have led to private revolt or cynicism. And what about the fundamental matter of transubstantiation – the Catholic position that in the Mass Christ is really present, blood changed to wine, bread to flesh, versus the new, Protestant, insistence that communion is a memorial act, the bread and wine being symbols only? Did not that reflect on the position of the monarch, insisting on a shift away from the belief in the Divine Right of kings to the Machiavellian view that leaders prevail through brute strength, opportunism, cunning and the mere symbolism of their office? For faith cannot be revised without fracturing every other certainty. If, by the exploration and exploitation of the New World, myths become fact, they cease to be myths (Spenser does not quite grasp this in the proem to *The Faerie Queene*, Book II when he celebrates 'The *Amazons* huge river now found true'; yet the poem's fantasy element constantly attests to the power of the unknowable). If wine can no longer be blood – if it is now symbol not transubstantiated mystery

– it is mere liquid fermented from grapes to be played around with by furtive choristers. If the queen succeeds to the throne amid adulation but is forced (or decides she is forced) to execute her relative and rival, Mary Queen of Scots (just as much a crowned and anointed queen as she herself), then how can the court believe in her authority as deriving from anything other than Machiavellian pragmatism?

Therefore, from the considerable distance of Ireland, as one of the agents of Elizabeth's policy of colonial oppression there, Spenser paused from secretarial and other duties, over a period of many years, to write *The Faerie Queene*. He dedicated it to an empress. But in his daily life he saw (and, if he is a poet worth reading, he sympathised profoundly with) the wretched state of those over whom she ruled, and so he thought of secrets, those things that secretaries know but are not supposed officially to reveal. He thought of the Irish faith and of the queen's (and his) opposite, Protestant, one. He thought of things as they ought to be, and of things as they were: the Virgin Queen who had succeeded in usurping the place of the Virgin Mary in her people's affections, yet who grew embarrassingly and vulgarly jealous whenever one of her favourites fell in love and married (Leicester; Ralegh). He thought of secularisation; of what happens when faith dies in a welter of bickering and schism. And as a result he wrote a double poem, a dream work of things as they might be; a nightmare of things as they were. Some modern critics would call it self-deconstructing, but terminology does not matter. I call it double because it constantly charts the gap between desire and the goal of desire.

Spenser wrote and published it in fragments – to announce himself publicly (and to gain attention from the queen, which he did in the not inconsiderable form of a pension of £50 a year) but also to register that its vision was provisional, even anti- holistic: to affirm that parts are separate testaments to the fragmentariness of experience. And although he seems to have had time to continue it beyond Book VI and the two surviving mutability cantos, he did not. He was tired, preoccupied, disenchanted (all readers of Book VI have noticed how in it courtly forms and displays disappear as epic converts to its generic opposite, pastoral, culminating in Spenser's evocation of himself as his own discarded radical shepherd *persona*, Colin Clout, in canto x). Yet simultaneously he bound – or attempted to bind – the whole poem together with an astonishing numerological virtuosity which insists that its books march solidly to the scale of the planetary week (Book of the Sun, Book of the Moon, Book of Mars and Minerva, etc.) and that its narrative harmonies are those of the God-ordained universe (see Fowler, *Spenser and the Numbers of Time*, 1964).

He conceived of it as an Arthurian epic with his Arthur the embodiment of the ultimate virtue, Magnificence (Letter to Ralegh), and his role the redemptive one of Providence and/or grace (his appearance in the eighth canto of each book – except the third – alludes to the redemptive symbolism of the number in Christian mythography from I Peter 3:20–1). Arthur, the great Cambro-British world conqueror, was another of Elizabeth's supposed ancestors, so the poem's Arthurianism functions to consolidate the Elizabethan imperial myth of the 1590s. Or does it? Spenser's Arthur is prince, not king, and although the Letter explains this away as necessary to the portrayal of his private virtues, assuring us that this Arthur will be succeeded by King Arthur demonstrating 'the polliticke vertues', this young knight recalls the queen's uncle, Prince Arthur, elder brother to her father Henry VIII, who died in 1502 at the age of sixteen amid considerable mourning. And Arthur's ghostly evocativeness is supported by the uncanniness of his narrative role. Redemptive he may be, but his is the absent presence lamented by sonneteers like Sidney and Spenser himself: there and not-there, by Book III he has diminished into a love-sick melancholic chasing the wrong girl. While even his tale to Book I's heroine, Una, of his vision of the faerie queen who visited him one night and has left him pursuing her ever since (I. ix. 13–15) is too similar to the Red Cross knight's dream of a false Una sent by Archimago in canto i for us not to feel that he, too, is contaminated by the darkness of the world's riddles, the distance between signifier and signified. Moreover, while the deferral of his arrival in the poem (to canto vii of Book I) is reminiscent of ceremonial delay (after false images the true solar prince emerges out of darkness in triumph), it is also suggestive of comic travesty: the deflation of heroic pretension in Rabelais as it was to be followed by Cervantes and, a century and a half after that, by Sterne (*Tristram Shandy*'s hero is not born until volume III) and Smollett (who delays the appearance of his eponymous hero in *Humphry Clinker* until a third of the way through the novel).

And as with Arthur, so with Gloriana, by whom 'I meane glory in my generall intention, but in my particular I conceive the most excellent and glorious person of our soveraine the Queene' (Letter to Ralegh): Elizabeth as manifestation of divine light and hence (according to the neo-Platonist Marsilio Ficino's *Commentary* on Plato's *Symposium*) essential Beauty itself, the goal of eros or desire. But although we hear of her in the Letter (and that was curiously placed, too, for a dedicatory explanation of the text: at the end of the third and final book in 1590; removed altogether in 1596), we never see her. Maybe we would have done at the poem's end, in Book XII or XXIV (that ambiguity, too, remains unresolved in the Letter), but Spenser seems to have done his best to ensure that it did not, in any formal sense, end.

Then, within the books themselves there are doubling riddles. Why at the threshold of Book I, after our introduction to Una/Oneness/ Truth/the queen as the sole head and governor of the Church (the multiplicity of her signifieds may reflect the Apuleian adage that the goddess has many names, but it sits rather strangely on the shoulders of a woman called One), do we meet Error as a snake woman eaten by her offspring in imitation of the story that the mother pelican, if she can obtain no other food for her young, pierces her breast with her beak and feeds them with her blood? The pelican was associated with Elizabeth as nursing mother of her realm (to quote the Isaian text – 49:23 – used in the coronation liturgy), so is Error here Una's opposite, the queen perceived as terrible mother? The identification would not have surprised Jung. It does not surprise us once we begin to recognise other clues to the poem's double vision, its secret other text. For example, Una's appearance dressed in black and white, the personal colours of Elizabeth which were also the colours favoured by Mary Queen of Scots (compare Elizabeth's 'Sieve' portrait with the 1583 portrait of Mary and the young James): the reading of Una by a Stuart loyalist would have been very different from that of an ideal Protestant supporter of Elizabeth. Or consider the usurping sun queen Lucifera (I. iv), whose name seems to signify that she is a proud Lucifer (Satan) and thus a Mary Queen of Scots figure in opposition to all that good queen Gloriana/Elizabeth stands for. Yet she, like Una and like the Virgin Queen herself, is called 'a mayden Queene' (I. iv. 8; see the notes at the end of this volume); and Lucifera is a name of Diana, the Virgin Queen's main mythological *persona* (Cicero, *On the Nature of the Gods*, II. 27). What, too, of the rigorous condemnation of Catholicism (through the figures of Duessa and Orgoglio particularly) while Red Cross, at the moment of his purgation in the House of Holiness, undergoes a ritual penance that could have come straight out of any treatise written by a believer in the old faith?

Similar riddles are posed by Books II and III. Acrasia, for example, labelled 'Intemperance' by her name, is the destructive venerean witch who, at the centre of her bower in II. xii, nevertheless recalls the bride of the Song of Solomon as 'a garden enclosed' and hence one imagistic strand associated with the Virgin Queen via the iconography of the Virgin Mary. Why? To say that she is a 'parody' of the queenly ideal, another 'terrible mother', is too simple. Spenser seems much more interested in exploring the dynamics of the process by which an ideal collapses into its opposite through the limitations of human perception (in this case, that of the peeping Sir Guyon whose creation she is as he gazes, lusts and then destroys). As with Guyon so with all of us, says Spenser: we produce the queen as the image of our desires in all their forms, while her production of herself into hieratic image is inevitably subject to contamination by the viewer/consumer. While in Book III, Britomart (Britomartis was the name of a nymph associated, and occasionally identified, with Diana; the name also means 'British Mars') marches through the text in armour that, although it reputedly belonged to the (fabulous) Saxon queen Angela who named the Angles and hence England, is sufficiently similar to the armour of male knights to make her so convincing a transvestite that Malecasta (the unchaste queen of canto i) creeps into her bed and starts to think about plundering her body in the time-honoured masculine way. The comedy is considerable – if the predictable stuff of Greek romance and picaresque novel – and, like the mad King Lear, raises all sorts of questions about woman's 'real' role. If, for instance, she overrides natural law to become queen – the begetter of John Knox's *First Blast . . . against the Monstrous Regiment of Women* – does she have to assume masculine traits? Does she, in Spenser's *reductio ad absurdum* here, have to mimic all the swaggering male postures? Then again, the fact that this transvestite knight, *persona* of Virgin Queen Elizabeth, is passionately in love with the image of Arthegall poses several questions. After all, the queen was long past marriage, yet Spenser climaxes the three-book *Faerie Queene* of 1590 with a legend of chastity, not virginity; with an image of love's triumph, not, for example, of the victory of Diana over Actaeon or an equivalent icon of virginal femininity's triumph over the male. Finally, given the primacy of the Trojan-British myth, it is at least a matter of curiosity that, after the solemn mythologising of British history in II. x and iii. iii, its Trojan roots should be mocked in III. ix when Sir Paridell, descendant of the Paris who abducted Trojan Helen and thus started the Trojan war (the subject of the *Iliad* and the *Aeneid* and the legendary origin of Britain and of Queen Elizabeth, the Virgin Queen), champions the memory of his lustful ancestor, then proceeds to seduce and abduct the wife of his host Malbecco whose name is Hellenore: Helen yet once more. So the Spenser who laments male appropriation of heroic deeds and asks why the ancient glory of women has been erased from modern records (III. ii, III. iv) and who even dares reverse the Genesis-given *fiat* that women should give birth in pain as a punishment for Eve's part in the Fall (Chrysogone in III. vi), doubles back to remind us that Tudor history, originating with Troy, is bound up with that of a whore, the same whore who generated the major epic texts of western civilisation, including Spenser's own. Britomart may counter Paridell by voicing the conventional history, but Paridell has been heard.

Thematic analysis

BOOK I

1. *Subject*: Holiness: i.e., devotion to God that ideally culminates in spiritual perfection. On earth it marks you out as one of the saints (God's elect); posthumously, you will be one of the elect in heaven, maybe even a canonical saint. Hence the titular knight of Book I is revealed, in a Protestant revision of a Catholic legend, to be St George (see I. x. 66).

2. *Allegorical method*: more than any other book in *The Faerie Queene*, Book I depends on the three-fold (four-fold if you count the literal level) scheme followed for biblical interpretation by the Church Fathers and used, for example, by Dante in the *Divine Comedy*. *Allegory* in this convention signifies historical allegory (narrative events corresponding to events in national history); *tropology* signifies moral allegory; *anagogy* signifies the allegorical level that is concerned with spiritual mysteries, God's providential plan for humanity. The levels do not operate continuously or, necessarily, simultaneously.

3. *Sources*: best understood in relation to 2. above. They are, mainly, (i) the St George legend (in which the knight kills the dragon that has been terrorising a city and demanding human sacrifice; the knight arrives when it is the turn of the king's daughter to be devoured and he encounters her waiting with her lamb); (ii) the Bible in the Protestant Geneva translation of 1560 (many times reprinted), especially the Song of Songs and Revelation. The Geneva version contained marginal glosses offering various allegorical readings of its texts. The Song, a series of love songs between bride and bridegroom embodying their passion and desperate quest for each other, was anagogised in Geneva (and other versions) as signifying Christ's love for his Church 'which he hath sanctified and appointed to be his spouse, holy, chaste'. In Song 3:2 the bride rises to 'go about . . . by the open places, [to] seeke him that my soule loveth'. Compare Una, abandoned by Red Cross, searching for him between cantos ii and vii. *Anagogically* she thus represents the Church, appearing as the

bride of her knight/Christ in canto xii. *Allegorically* she is the English church (and Elizabeth 1 as the head of that church). Slightly more complicatedly, she represents the Truth embodied in the English Church (as subscribing Elizabethans understood it). Red Cross separates from her, having been deceived into believing her to be false, and succumbs to Duessa (twoness, duplicity: canto ii). He is *allegorically* England (figured in her national saint) tied to a corrupt Catholicism, moving towards, and awaiting the revelation of, the true faith. This movement is paralleled by Red Cross's *tropological* development, his journey as embodiment of fallen man through error (canto i), pride (worldly and spiritual: cantos iv, vii–viii), lust (his attraction to Duessa throughout, but especially at the beginning of canto vii, when he strips off his armour – the armour of the Christian man, as the Letter to Ralegh tells us – to make love to her), despair (canto ix), repentance (canto x) and consequential fitness to battle with the dragon of the sins (canto xi).

The Book of Revelation – a vision of the end of the world culminating in the marriage between Christ (the Lamb) and the New Jerusalem, the heavenly city of the elect (the Church transferred to heaven) – supports the allegorical levels suggested by the Song. Una is again the bride, Red Cross her espoused Christ; but Revelation's insistence on the defeat of the dragon Satan (chaps 12, 20, etc.) focuses Book I's various dragons more precisely, while its Whore of Babylon (chap. 17) is a prototype for Duessa (one of the Geneva glosses announces allegorically that she is 'the spiritual Babylon, which is Rome'), and the woman clothed with the sun of chap. 12 ('a type of the true and holy Church': Geneva gloss) adds another layer to Una's significance (note the connection between Una and the sun at I. iii. 4; I. vi. 4; I. xii. 23).

4. *Structure*: this operates through Spenser's characteristic method of analogical (or parallel) patterning. Just as characters correspond (Una:Duessa; Red Cross:Archimago; etc.), so canto i is answered by xi and xii (forest displaced by the restored Eden when Una's parents are released; dragon of error defeated again in the dragon of xi); cantos vi and vii form a parallel core pair (Una in the forest encounters the wood folk in their pagan ignorance; Duessa and Red Cross embrace in a shady grove and engender the Catholic – specifically papal – ignorance of the giant Orgoglio); and canto iv, with Lucifera's palace of pride, is answered by canto x, Dame Caelia's humble house of holiness.

BOOK II

1. *Subject*: Temperance: i.e., control of the passions by reason; or, as equated with virtue and defined by Aristotle, *Nicomachean Ethics*, II. vi. 16, it is the midpoint between extremes of excess and defect (the paradigm is enacted in canto ii: Perissa (excess) / Medina (middle) / Elissa (defect)). The book's concerns are the passions traditionally allocated to the extreme parts of the tripartite soul: concupiscence (which can be subdivided into lust and avarice) on the one side, irascibility on the other. The main episodes and characters of the book fall into place around this scheme.

However, important as it is as a basis of moral behaviour (and thus the foundation from which the moral and spiritual edifice of *The Faerie Queene* can arise: Book II, as it were, begins at the beginning, whereas Book I has given us an overview of the difficulties besetting the Christian's – and Christianity's – life on earth and its *telos*), Aristotelian (classical) temperance has, of necessity, been redefined by Christianity. The passions are not, now, subject simply to the willed assertion of reason's controlling power, for Christianity states that they were corrupted by the fall of man with Original Sin (this is what the bloody-handed babe Ruddimane signifies in cantos i and ii), our willingness to battle with which is signalled first by baptism (note the frequency with which water flows through the book), then by faith and by God's willingness to impart grace to us (the angel who appears at the beginning of canto viii). The *Palmer* is the symbol of faith and also of Christian experience, wisdom and suffering in the book. When he advises, Guyon is (just about) safe; when he is absent, Guyon is endangered. In other words, Christian truth supplements and transcends the moral knowledge available to the ancients. The titular knight, Guyon, recalls chivalric romance heroes (e.g., Guy of Warwick) and the river of paradise, Gihon, identified with temperance (see Book II, proem note).

2. *Allegorical method*: essentially tropological (moral), with the characters representing the various passions (see notes to cantos iv, ix, etc.).

3. *Structure*: even more symmetrical than Book I in order to enact the mediating principle of rational control. The origin and goal of the book's journey is Acrasia (the witch of intemperance who is based on the Circe of *Odyssey*, X): she killed Mortdant (an Adamic figure who has succumbed to lust as Adam succumbed to Eve: canto i); she has Verdant (a recycled Mortdant, renewed as lust renews with every

generation) entrapped in her bower in canto xii (the bower parallels the Eden of Book I's end). Guyon has to avenge the one by freeing the other. On his way, he has to learn the virtue he practises by encountering various excesses: anger in the form of Furor and Pyrochles; lust and sloth in the form of Cymochles and Phaedria. More seriously, he encounters avarice, the other side of lust, in Mammon (more seriously, because worship of gold can be understood as idolatry: Mammon is the god of this world, and his hellish cave is, in effect, a reminder that Judas set pieces of silver above Christ).

In contrast to the negatives, the narrative erects three female positives: Medina (the middle way; Aristotle's reason); Belphoebe (who reconciles opposites within herself to become an embodiment of self-transcendence: she is the queen in her private capacity as 'a most vertuous and beautifull Lady', according to the Letter to Ralegh, icon of virtue to the realm; that realm's history – seen in terms of a constant battle of reason over passions, kings over unruliness – is the subject of canto x); and Alma (the rational soul herself, mistress of the temperate castle of the body which is, as all bodies are, subject to the attacks of the senses and original sin (Maleger, canto xi)).

Note: canto i (Acrasia/Mortdant/Amavia) corresponds to xii (Acrasia/Verdant): both represent concupiscence in the form of lust. Phaedria's island (canto vi; lust) glances back to i, anticipates xii, but balances canto vii (avarice). Within the book's second half, with avarice (vii) balancing lust (xii), Alma's temperate castle is central (ix, x: the virtuous middle way between extremes), cantos viii and xi containing battles.

BOOK III

1. *Subject*: Chastity: i.e., that aspect of temperance relating to sexual behaviour and attitudes which in Elizabethan thought comprised both virginity and marital fidelity. The book's titular knight, Britomart, embodies the virginal ideal in her name (see above); matrimonial chastity is her destiny (marriage with Arthegall). Book III (1590 edition) ends with an epithalamic vision to answer the betrothal of Una and Red Cross at the end of Book I: Amoret (in a sense a sexual double for Britomart) embraces her husband Scudamour (double, momentarily, for Arthegall), and they melt into a hermaphroditic union that sums up all the attempts at reconciliation and self-transcendence that have occurred, or been hinted at, in the previous books.

2. *Method*: The most Ariostan of the books in its episodic structure and characterisation (Britomart is, in addition to her other precursor selves, Ariosto's Bradamante; Florimell his fleeing Angelica: *Orlando Furioso*, canto i, etc.), it is also the most mythic of the three, the least obviously allegorically reductive. It is concerned with sexuality, but on a less didactic, more shadowy – even psychological and anthropological – level than Books I or II, its main symbols in this respect being Venus and Adonis (subject of the tapestry in canto i, mysterious centre of the book in the Garden of Adonis in canto vi); Narcissus (embodied in Marinell, beloved of Florimell who refuses to marry her but who, wounded by Britomart, lies in a stupor of self-involvement; the symbolism is implied at III. iv. 29); Proteus, god of Marinell's element, the sea [Latin *mare*], symbol of passion, moral fluidity, and the depths of the imagination, as well as Venus's life-source (she was born from the waves, and her emblem is the fish: thus Florimell, having fled the forester, finds herself, in canto viii, in a boat – cf. Venus in her traditional scallop shell; and when her sleeping companion attempts to rape her and, in doing so, covers her with fish scales, the moment is at once sexually suggestive and also mythologically apt); and the three maidens Amoret, Belphoebe, and Florimell, who represent the three Graces who were the traditional handmaids of Venus.

3. *Structure*: episodic but also symmetrical. The tapestry of Venus and Adonis (among others) in Malecasta's palace (i) is answered by the tapestries and triumph of Cupid in Busirane's castle (xi, xii), and both reflect into canto vi (the Garden of Adonis, which is itself the opposite of Acrasia's Bower of Bliss in II. xii). Less symmetrically, Britomart's love quest, as a result of which she discovers from Merlin her destiny as mother of a progeny which will culminate in the birth of an imperial, virginal, Queen Elizabeth (canto iii), is answered in the second half by cantos ix and x, which tell of the seduction of Malbecco's wife by Paridell, the firing of Malbecco's castle (so that it goes up in flames like ancient Troy), and the abandoning of Hellenore to a life among the satyrs where, marginalised and bestialised, she can fulfil her sexual appetite and be happier than she ever was married to a husband whose avarice was the visible sign of his constant and ubiquitous jealousy.

This revision of the tale of Helen of Troy is orthodox in being anti-Helen, heterodox in suggesting sympathy for her plight. As such it belongs to Spenser's avowed defence of women's function in history, confirming that the best way to begin to understand Book III is as a defence of chastity illuminating Elizabeth I's special role as Virgin

Queen married to her realm which expands to become a considera-
tion of women's role in social history and myth. Thus the women of
Book III emerge as strong and merciful but also as oppressed and
pursued victims, the legitimate game of any man's lust and hence
iconisable into fetishistic doll (the patriarchal forces operating here
are so strong that women betray women to gratify male desire, and so
the witch produces a false Florimell for her son) or the victim of
bondage to a monstrous phallus (Busirane with Amoret). Such
considerations led Spenser into a genuinely revisionist stance which
embraced the recognitions that, if life begins with and belongs to
woman, she has the right to be a virgin (and not be raped) or to marry
(and not be tyrannised over); that lust is no more despicable in a
woman than in a man; that she has the right to rule – and not as a
substitute man.

But the message of the three-book *Faerie Queene* is more complex
and radical than this. It is, that the male gaze perverts, that the male
libido insists on inscribing itself with destructive force on the female
body. This is what Busirane, rewriting the case of Guyon in II. xii,
signifies. By allowing Britomart to triumph over him, Spenser's epic
celebrates the image of the strong woman for whom sexual desire –
eros – is welcome and enjoyable without compromising herself or
denying the male, and in doing so offers a corrective lens for male
vision. It also leaves the reader with a fragmented Arthur who is the
ultimate image of male failure in respect of women. He will be whole
only when he learns how to view woman as she wants to be seen and
can thus forget his misleading dream of Gloriana as a demon of the
night.

DOUGLAS BROOKS-DAVIES

SUGGESTIONS FOR FURTHER READING

Editions: J. C. Smith ed., *Spenser's 'Faerie Queene'*, 2 vols, 1909; E. A. Greenlaw, F. M. Padelford, C. G. Osgood *et al*., eds, *The Works of Edmund Spenser: A Variorum Edition*, 11 vols, 1932–57; A. C. Hamilton ed., *Spenser: 'The Faerie Queene'*, 1977; T. P. Roche and C. P. O'Donnell eds, *Spenser: 'The Faerie Queen'*, 1978.

Background reading: Essential background material will be found in: Plato's *Symposium* (for Spenser's theory of love, which he inherited direct from Plato and also through the medium of Renaissance commentators: e.g., Marsilio Ficino's *Commentary on Plato's 'Symposium'*, trans. Sears Jayne; 1944; repr. 1985); Virgil's *Aeneid* and Ariosto's *Orlando Furioso* (for the epic and romance sources); Ovid's *Metamorphoses* (for many of Spenser's mythological tales); the Bible (especially Genesis; the Song of Songs; Isaiah; Revelation); Geoffrey of Monmouth's *History of th. Kings of Britain* (source for much of Spenser's view of British history and its myths). For symbolism and ideological backgrounds the following are especially recommended: D. C. Allen, *Mysteriously Meant: The Rediscovery of Pagan Symbolism and Allegorical Interpretation in the Renaissance*, 1970; Eamon Duffy, *The Stripping of the Altars: Traditional Religion in England 1400–1580*, 1992 (impact of Reformation and strength of residual Catholicism); Erwin Panofsky, *Studies in Iconology*, 1939; Roy Strong, *The Cult of Elizabeth*, 1977; Edgar Wind, *Pagan Mysteries in the Renaissance*, rev. ed. 1967; Jean Wilson ed., *Entertainments for Elizabeth I*, 1980 (courtly texts sharing assumptions with *FQ*).

Critical reading on 'The Faerie Queene': There is an overabundance of material, so the following list is very selective and personal.

1. *General Criticism*
The primary resource is now A. C. Hamilton *et al*., eds, *The Spenser Encyclopedia*, 1990, which will answer or offer pointers to answers to most enquiries.
General or introductory studies include:
Alpers, P., *The Poetry of 'The Faerie Queene'*, 1967
——, *Edmund Spenser: A Critical Anthology*, 1969
Bayley, P. C., *Edmund Spenser: Prince of Poets*, 1971

——, *Spenser: 'The Faerie Queene': A Casebook*, 1977

Bennett, J. W., *The Evolution of 'The Faerie Queene'*, 1942

Berger, H., Jr, *The Allegorical Temper*, 1957 (on Book II)

——, *Spenser: A Collection of Critical Essays*, 1968

——, *Revisionary Play: Studies in the Spenserian Dynamics*, 1988 (collects some of Berger's idiosyncratic and suggestive essays on *FQ*)

Bieman, E., *Plato Baptized: Towards the Interpretation of Spenser's Mimetic Fictions*, 1989

Brooks-Davies, D., *Spenser's 'Faerie Queene': A Critical Commentary on Books 1 and 2*, 1977 (stanza-by-stanza reading emphasising iconography)

Cullen, P., *Infernal Triad: The Flesh, the World, and the Devil in Spenser and Milton*, 1974

Evans, M., *Spenser's Anatomy of Heroism: A Commentary on 'The Faerie Queene'*, 1970

Fowler, A. D. S., *Edmund Spenser*, 1977

Giamatti, A. B., *Play of Double Senses: Spenser's 'Faerie Queene'*, 1975

Hamilton, A. C., *The Structure of Allegory in 'The Faerie Queene'*, 1961

——, *Essential Articles for the Study of Edmund Spenser*, 1972

Hankins, J. E., *Source and Meaning in Spenser's Allegory: A Study of 'The Faerie Queene'*, 1971

Hough, G., *A Preface to 'The Faerie Queene'*, 1962

Jones, H. S. V., *A Spenser Handbook*, 1930

Krier, T. M., *Gazing on Secret Sights: Spenser, Classical Imitation, and the Decorums of Vision*, 1990

Lewis, C. S., *Spenser's Images of Life*, ed. A. Fowler, 1967

McCaffrey, I. G., *Spenser's Allegory: The Anatomy of Imagination*, 1976

Nelson, W., *The Poetry of Edmund Spenser*, 1963 (best single introduction)

Nohrnberg, J., *The Analogy of 'The Faerie Queene'*, 1976 (monumental reading of imagery, structure, etc. Best single overall book on *FQ*)

Roche, T. P., Jr, *The Kindly Flame: A Study of the Third and Fourth Books of Spenser's 'Faerie Queene'*, 1964

Tonkin, H., *The Faerie Queene*, 1989 (good basic introduction)

Waller, G. F., *English Poetry of the Sixteenth Century*, 1986 (contains new historicist approach to *FQ*)

——, *Edmund Spenser: A Literery Life*, 1993

2. *More Specialised Studies*

Brooks-Davies, D., *The Mercurian Monarch: Magical Politics from Spenser to Pope*, 1983 (first chapter on magic, alchemy, etc. in *FQ*)

Dundas, J., *The Spider and the Bee: The Artistry of Spenser's 'Faerie Queene'*, 1985 (imagery, rhetoric, etc.)

Ellrodt, R., *Neoplatonism in the Poetry of Spenser*, 1960

Fowler, A. D. S., *Spenser and the Numbers of Time*, 1964 (iconography, astrology, numerology in *FQ*)

Goldberg, J., *Endlesse Work: Spenser and the Structures of Discourse*, 1981 (modernist/post-modernist)

Hume, A., *Edmund Spenser: Protestant Poet*, 1984 (religion)

King, J. N., *Spenser's Poetry and the Reformation Tradition*, 1990 (religion)

Leslie, M., *Spenser's 'Fierce Warres and Faithfull Loves': Martial and Chivalric Symbolism in 'The Faerie Queene'*, 1983 (includes Garter symbolism)

Lotspeich, H. G., *Classical Mythology in the Poetry of Edmund Spenser*, 1932 (alphabetical handbook of references)

Miller, D. L., *The Poem's Two Bodies: The Poetics of the 1590 'Faerie Queene'*, 1989 (post-modernist reading)

Norbrook, D., *Poetry and Politics in the English Renaissance*, 1984 (includes new historicist reading of Spenser)

Quilligan, M., *Milton's Spenser: The Politics of Reading*, 1983 (rhetoric and reader-response theory)

Smith, C. G., *Spenser's Proverb Lore*, 1970 (alphabetical list of proverbs)

Suzuki, M., *Metamorphoses of Helen: Authority, Difference, and the Epic*, 1989 (feminist, with a section on *FQ*)

Wells, R. H., *Spenser's 'Faerie Queene' and the Cult of Elizabeth*, 1983 (icons of the queen in *FQ*)

Yates, F. A., *Astraea: The Imperial Theme in the Sixteenth Century*, 1975 (iconography of empire in *FQ* and other texts)

——, *The Occult Philosophy in the Elizabethan Age*, 1979 (includes suggestive magical reading of *FQ*)

NOTE: For those with access to a major library, *Spenser Studies: A Renaissance Poetry Annual* contains excellent articles representing the varying persuasions of current Spenser critics.

NOTE ON THE TEXT

There is no surviving manuscript of any part of *The Faerie Queene*. Books I–III were first published in 1590 by Spenser's printer–publisher William Ponsonby; three issues of the text have been identified. In 1596 Ponsonby published a second edition containing six books: it reprinted Books I–III from 1590 with a few changes in substantives and accidentals; revised the dedication to the queen and altered the ending to Book III by removing the closure of Amoret's and Scudamour's embrace (Scudamour now leaves Busirane's castle before being reunited with her in order that his and Amoret's tale can continue into Book IV). In addition, it contained the first printing of Books IV–VI. (The *Cantos of Mutabilitie* were first published in the 1609 edition.) The Letter to Ralegh, which appeared at the end of the 1590 edition, was not published in 1596 and neither were the commendatory verses and (for the most part) the dedicatory sonnets.

The present edition offers the three-book 1590 *Faerie Queene* (minus the verses and sonnets just mentioned) in a form amenable to the modern reader. Since it is not designed as a full textual edition with appendix of variants, I have opted to ignore the bibliographical rigours demanded by modern textual criticism. While recognising that *1590* is likely to be closest in spelling and accidentals to the lost manuscript(s), I assume that most substantive alterations for *1596* were authorial, and that spelling and accidentals even in *1590* were as likely to be compositorial as authorial. Hence, for the most part, the present edition follows the revised 1596 text of the three-book *Faerie Queene* with the main exception that it retains the original 1590 ending. It is thus, in effect, *The Faerie Queene* as Spenser first presented it to his monarch, but incorporating his second thoughts. For further textual information see: *FQ* ed. Smith; *Variorum* edition; *FQ* ed. Roche (as in Suggestions for Further Reading). Also W. P. Williams in *Spenser Encyclopedia*, pp. 90–3, 259; and H. Yamashita, H. Sato, T. Suzuki, A. Takano eds, *A Textual Companion to 'The Faerie Queene' 1590* (Kenyusha Books, Tokyo; electronic version 1992).

THE FAERIE QUEENE

TO THE MOST MIGHT-
IE AND MAGNIFI-
CENT EMPRESSE ELI-
ZABETH, BY THE
GRACE OF GOD QVEENE
OF ENGLAND, FRANCE
AND IRELAND DE-
FENDER OF THE FAITH
&c.
Her most humble
Seruant:

Ed. Spenser

Dedication to the 1590 three-book *Faerie Queene*

TO
THE MOST HIGH,
MIGHTIE
And
MAGNIFICENT
EMPRESSE RENOVV-
MED FOR PIETIE, VER-
TVE, AND ALL GRATIOVS
GOVERNMENT ELIZABETH BY
THE GRACE OF GOD QVEENE
OF ENGLAND FRAVNCE AND
IRELAND AND OF VIRGI-
NIA, DEFENDOVR OF THE
FAITH, &c. HER MOST
HVMBLE SERVAVNT
EDMVND SPENSER
DOTH IN ALL HV-
MILITIE DEDI-
CATE, PRE-
SENT
AND CONSECRATE THESE
HIS LABOVRS TO LIVE
VVITH THE ETERNI-
TIE OF HER
FAME.

Dedication to the 1596 six-book *Faerie Queene*

THE FIRST BOOKE OF THE
FAERIE QUEENE.
Contayning,
THE LEGENDE OF THE KNIGHT
OF THE RED CROSSE.
Or
OF HOLINESSE.

Lo I the man, whose Muse whilome did maske,
  As time her taught in lowly Shepeards weeds,
  Am now enforst a farre unfitter taske,
  For trumpets sterne to chaunge mine Oaten reeds,
  And sing of Knights and Ladies gentle deeds;
  Whose prayses having slept in silence long,
  Me, all too meane, the sacred Muse areeds
  To blazon broad emongst her learned throng:
Fierce warres and faithfull loves shall moralize my song.

Helpe then, ô holy Virgin chiefe of nine,
  Thy weaker Novice to performe thy will,
  Lay forth out of thine everlasting scryne
  The antique rolles, which there lye hidden still,
  Of Faerie knights and fairest *Tanaquill*,
  Whom that most noble Briton Prince so long
  Sought through the world, and suffered so much ill,
  That I must rue his undeserved wrong:
O helpe thou my weake wit, and sharpen my dull tong.

And thou most dreaded impe of highest *Jove*,
  Faire *Venus* sonne, that with thy cruell dart
  At that good knight so cunningly didst rove,
  That glorious fire it kindled in his hart,
  Lay now thy deadly Heben bow apart,
  And with thy mother milde come to mine ayde:
  Come both, and with you bring triumphant *Mart*,
  In loves and gentle jollities arrayd,
After his murdrous spoiles and bloudy rage allayd.

And with them eke, ô Goddesse heavenly bright,
  Mirrour of grace and Majestie divine,
  Great Lady of the greatest Isle, whose light
  Like *Phœbus* lampe throughout the world doth shine,
  Shed thy faire beames into my feeble eyne,
  And raise my thoughts too humble and too vile,

To thinke of that true glorious type of thine,
The argument of mine afflicted stile:
The which to heare voichsafe, ô dearest dred a-while.

Canto I

The Patrone of true Holinesse
Foule Errour doth defeate:
Hypocrisie him to entrappe,
Doth to his home entreate.

1

A gentle Knight was pricking on the plaine,
   Y cladd in mightie armes and silver shielde,
   Wherein old dints of deepe wounds did remaine,
   The cruell markes of many' a bloudy fielde;
   Yet armes till that time did he never wield:
   His angry steede did chide his forming bitt,
   As much disdayning to the curbe to yield:
   Full jolly knight he seemed, and faire did sitt,
As one for knightly giusts and fierce encounters fitt.

2

And on his brest a bloudie Crosse he bore,
   The deare remembrance of his dying Lord,
   For whose sweete sake that glorious badge he wore,
   And dead as living ever him ador'd:
   Upon his shield the like was also scor'd,
   For soveraine hope, which in his helpe he had:
   Right faithfull true he was in deede and word,
   But of his cheere did seeme too solemne sad,
Yet nothing did he dread, but ever was ydrad.

3

Upon a great adventure he was bond,   *Gloriana*
   That greatest *Gloriana* to him gave,
   That greatest Glorious Queene of *Faerie* lond,
   To winne him worship, and her grace to have,
   Which of all earthly things he most did crave;
   And ever as he rode, his hart did earne
   To prove his puissance in battell brave
   Upon his foe, and his new force to learne;
Upon his foe, a Dragon horrible and stearne.

4

A lovely Ladie rode him faire beside,   *biblical*
   Upon a lowly Asse more white then snow,
   Yet she much whiter, but the same did hide
   Under a vele, that wimpled was full low,
   And over all a blacke stole she did throw,

As one that inly mournd: so was she sad,
And heavie sat upon her palfrey slow;
Seemed in heart some hidden care she had,
And by her in a line a milke white lambe she lad.

5

So pure an innocent, as that same lambe,
    She was in life and every vertuous lore,
    And by descent from Royall lynage came
    Of ancient Kings and Queenes, that had of yore
    Their scepters stretcht from East to Westerne shore,
    And all the world in their subjection held;
    Till that infernall feend with foule uprore
    Forwasted all their land, and them expeld:
Whom to avenge, she had this Knight from far compeld.

6

Behind her farre away a Dwarfe did lag,
    That lasie seemd in being ever last,
    Or wearied with bearing of her bag
    Of needments at his backe.   Thus as they past,
    The day with cloudes was suddeine overcast,
    And angry *Jove* an hideous storme of raine
    Did poure into his Lemans lap so fast,
    That every wight to shrowd it did constrain,
And this faire couple eke to shroud themselves were fain.

Storm

7

Enforst to seeke some covert night at hand,
    A shadie grove not far away they spide,
    That promist ayde the tempest to withstand;
    Whose loftie trees yclad with sommers pride,
    Did spred so broad, that heavens light did hide,
    Not perceable with power of any starre:
    And all within were pathes and alleies wide,
    With footing worne, and leading inward farre:
Faire harbour that them seemes; so in they entred arre.

8

And foorth they passe, with pleasure forward led,
    Joying to heare the birdes sweete harmony,
    Which therein shrouded from the tempest dred,
    Seemd in their song to scorne the cruell sky.
    Much can they prayse the trees so straight and hy,
    The sayling Pine, the Cedar proud and tall,

The vine-prop Elme, the Poplar never dry,
   The builder Oake, sole king of forrests all,
The Aspine good for staves, the Cypresse funerall.

9

The Laurell, meed of mightie Conquerours   *the grave*
   And Poets sage, the Firre that weepth still,
   The Willow worne of forlorne Paramours,
   The Eugh obedient to the benders will,
   The Birch for shaftes, the Sallow for the mill,
   The Mirrhe sweete bleeding in the bitter wound,
   The warlike Beech, the Ash for nothing ill,
   The fruitfull Olive, and the Platane round,
The carver Holme, the Maple seeldom inward sound.

10

Led with delight, they thus beguile the way,
   Untill the blustring storme is overblowne;
   When weening to returne, whence they did stray,   *path lost*
   They cannot finde that path, which first was showne,
   But wander too and fro in wayes unknowne,
   Furthest from end then, when they neerest weene,
   That makes them doubt, their wits be not their owne:
   So many pathes, so many turnings seene,
That which of them to take, in diverse doubt they been.

11

At last resolving forward still to fare,
   Till that some end they finde or in or out,
   That path they take, that beaten seemd most bare,
   And like to lead the labyrinth about;
   Which when by tract they hunted had throughout,
   At length it brought them to a hollow cave,
   Amid the thickest woods.   The Champion stout
   Eftsoones dismounted from his courser brave,
And to the Dwarfe a while his needlesse spere he gave.

12

'Be well aware,' quoth then that Ladie milde,
   'Least suddaine mischiefe ye too rash provoke: *♀ warns*
   The danger hid, the place unknowne and wilde,
   Breedes dreadfull doubts: oft fire is without smoke,
   And perill without show: therefore your hardy stroke,
   Sir knight with-hold, till further triall made.'
   'Ah Ladie' (said he) 'shame were to revoke

The forward footing for an hidden shade:
Vertue gives her selfe light, through darkenesse for to wade.'

13

'Yea but' (quoth she) 'the perill of this place
    I better wot then you, though nowe too late,
    To wish you backe returne with foule disgrace,
    Yet wisedome warnes, whilest foot is in the gate,
    To stay the steppe, ere forced to retrate.
    This is the wandring wood, this *Errours den*,
    A monster vile, whom God and man does hate:
    Therefore I read beware.'   'Fly, fly' (quoth then
The fearefull Dwarfe) 'this is no place for living men.'

14

But full of fire and greedy hardiment,
    The youthfull Knight could not for ought be staide,
    But forth unto the darksom hole he went,
    And looked in: his glistring armor made
    A litle glooming light, much like a shade,
    By which he saw the ugly monster plaine,
    Halfe like a serpent horribly displaide,
    But th' other halfe did womans shape retaine,
Most lothsom, filthie, foule, and full of vile disdaine.

15

And as she lay upon the durtie ground,
    Her huge long taile her den all overspred,
    Yet was in knots and many boughtes upwound,
    Pointed with mortall sting.   Of her there bred
    A thousand yong ones, which she dayly fed,
    Sucking upon her poisonous dugs; eachone
    Of sundrie shapes, yet all ill favoured:
    Soone as that uncouth light upon them shone,
Into her mouth they crept, and suddain all were gone.

16

Their dam upstart, out of her den effraide,
    And rushed forth, hurling her hideous taile
    About her cursed head, whose folds displaid
    Were stretcht now forth at length without entraile.
    She lookt about, and seeing one in mayle
    Armed to point, sought backe to turne againe;
    For light she hated as the deadly bale,
    Ay wont in desert darknesse to remaine,
Where plaine none might her see, nor she see any plaine.

17

Which when the valiant Elfe perceiv'd, he lept
  As Lyon fierce upon the flying pray,
  And with his trenchand blade her boldly kept   *knight attacks*
  From turning backe, and forced her to stay:
  Therewith enrag'd she loudly gan to bray,
  And turning fierce, her speckled taile advaunst,
  Threatning her angry sting, him to dismay:
  Who nought aghast, his mightie hand enhaunst:
The stroke down from her head unto her shoulder glaunst.

18

Much daunted with that dint, her sence was dazd,
  Yet kindling rage, her selfe she gathered round,
  And all attonce her beastly bodie raizd
  With doubled forces high above the ground:
  Tho wrapping up her wrethed sterne arownd,
  Lept fierce upon his shield, and her huge traine
  All suddenly about his body wound,
  That hand or foot to stirre he strove in vaine:
God helpe the man so wrapt in *Errours* endlesse traine.

19

His Lady sad to see his sore constraint,
  Cride out, 'Now now Sir knight, shew what ye bee,
  Add faith unto your force, and be not faint:
  Strangle her, else she sure will strangle thee.'
  That when he heard, in great perplexitie,
  His gall did grate for griefe and high disdaine,
  And knitting all his force, got one hand free,
  Wherewith he grypt her gorge with so great paine,
That soone to loose her wicked bands did her constraine.

20

Therewith she spewd out of her filthie maw   *gruesome*
  A floud of poyson horrible and blacke,   *poison*
  Full of great lumps of flesh and gobbets raw,
  Which stunck so vildly, that it forst him slacke
  His grasping hold, and from her turne him backe:
  Her vomit full of bookes and papers was,
  With loathly frogs and toades, which eyes did lacke,
  And creeping sought way in the weedy gras:
Her filthie parbreake all the place defiled has.

21

As when old father *Nilus* gins to swell
  With timely pride above the *Aegyptian* vale,
  His fattie waves do fertile slime outwell,
  And overflow each plaine and lowly dale:
  But when his later spring gins to avale,
  Huge heapes of mudd he leaves, wherein there breed
  Ten thousand kindes of creatures, partly male
  And partly female of his fruitfull seed;
Such ugly monstrous shapes elsewhere may no man reed.

22

The same so sore annoyed has the knight,
  That welnigh choked with the deadly stinke,
  His forces faile, ne can no lenger fight.
  Whose corage when the feend perceiv'd to shrinke,
  She poured forth out of her hellish sinke
  Her fruitfull cursed spawne of serpents small,
  Deformed monsters, fowle, and blacke as inke,
  Which swarming all about his legs did crall,
And him encombred sore, but could not hurt at all.

23

As gentle Shepheard in sweete even-tide,
  When ruddy *Phœbus* gins to welke in west,
  High on an hill, his flocke to vewen wide,
  Markes which do byte their nasty supper best;
  A cloud of combrous gnattes do him molest,
  All striving to infixe their feeble stings,
  That from their noyance he no where can rest,
  But with his clownish hands their tender wings
He brusheth oft, and oft doth mar their murmurings.

24

Thus ill bestedd, and fearefull more of shame,
  Then of the certaine perill he stood in,
  Halfe furious unto his foe he came,
  Resolv'd in minde all suddenly to win,
  Or soone to lose, before he once would lin;
  And strooke at her with more then manly force,
  That from her body full of filthie sin
  He raft her hatefull head without remorse;
A streame of cole black bloud forth gushed from her corse.

25

Her scattred brood, soone as their Parent deare
    They saw so rudely falling to the ground,
    Groning full deadly, all with troublous feare,
    Gathred themselves about her body round,
    Weening their wonted entrance to have found
    At her wide mouth: but being there withstood
    They flocked all about her bleeding wound,
    And sucked up their dying mothers blood,
Making her death their life, and eke her hurt their good.

26

That detestable sight him much amazde,
    To see th' unkindly Impes of heaven accurst,
    Devoure their dam; on whom while so he gazd,
    Having all satisfide their bloudy thurst,
    Their bellies swolne he saw with fulnesse burst,
    And bowels gushing forth: well worthy end
    Of such as drunke her life, the which them nurst;
    Now needeth him no lenger labour spend,
His foes have slaine themselves, with whom he should contend.

27

His Ladie seeing all, that chaunst, from farre
    Approcht in hast to greet his victorie,
    And said, 'Faire knight, borne under happie starre,
    Who see your vanquisht foes before you lye:
    Well worthie be you of that Armorie,
    Wherein ye have great glory wonne this day,
    And proov'd your strength on a strong enimie,
    Your first adventure: many such I pray,
And henceforth ever wish, that like succeed it may.'

knight has won
& proud.

28

Then mounted he upon his Steede againe,
    And with the Lady backward sought to wend;
    That path he kept, which beaten was most plaine,
    Ne ever would to any by-way bend,
    But still did follow one unto the end,
    The which at last out of the wood them brought.
    So forward on his way (with God to frend)
    He passed forth, and new adventure sought;
Long way he travelled before he heard of ought.

29

At length they chaunst to meet upon the way
　　An aged Sire, in long blacke weedes yclad,
　　His feete all bare, his beard all hoarie gray,
　　And by his belt his booke he hanging had;
　　Sober he seemde, and very sagely sad,
　　And to the ground his eyes were lowly bent,
　　Simple in shew, and voyde of malice bad,
　　And all the way he prayed, as he went,
And often knockt his brest, as one that did repent.

30

He faire the knight saluted, louting low,
　　Who faire him quited, as that courteous was:
　　And after asked him, if he did know
　　Of straunge adventures, which abroad did pas.
　　'Ah my dear Sonne' (quoth he) 'how should, alas,
　　Silly old man, that lives in hidden cell,
　　Bidding his beades all day for his trespas,
　　Tydings of warre and worldly trouble tell?
With holy father sits not with such things to mell.

31

'But if of daunger, which hereby doth dwell,
　　And homebred evil ye desire to heare,
　　Of a straunge man I can you tidings tell,
　　That wasteth all this countrey farre and neare.'
　　'Of such' (said he) 'I chiefly do inquere,
　　And shall you well reward to shew the place,
　　In which that wicked wight his dayes doth weare:
　　For to all knighthood it is foule disgrace,
That such a cursed creature lives so long a space.'

32

'Far hence' (quoth he) 'in wastfull wildernesse
　　His dwelling is, by which no living wight
　　May ever passe, but thorough great distresse.'
　　'Now' (sayd the Lady) 'draweth toward night,
　　And well I wote, that of your later fight
　　Ye all forwearied be: for what so strong,
　　But wanting rest will also want of might?
　　The Sunne that measures heaven all day long,
At night doth baite his steedes the *Ocean* waves emong.

33

'Then with the Sunne take Sir, your timely rest,
    And with new day new worke at once begin:
    Untroubled night they say gives counsell best.'
    'Right well Sir knight ye have advised bin,'
    (Quoth then that aged man;) 'the way to win
    Is wisely to advise: now day is spent;
    Therefore with me ye may take up your In
    For this same night.' The knight was well content:
So with that godly father to his home they went.

34

A litle lowly Hermitage it was,
    Downe in a dale, hard by a forests side,
    Far from resort of people, that did pas
    In travell to and froe: a litle wyde
    There was an holy Chappell edifyde,
    Wherein the Hermite dewly wont to say
    His holy things each morne and eventyde:
    Thereby a Christall streame did gently play,
Which from a sacred fountaine welled forth alway.

35

Arrived there, the little house they fill,
    Ne looke for entertainement, where none was:
    Rest is their feast, and all things at their will;
    The noblest mind the best contentment has.
    With faire discourse the evening so they pas:
    For that old man of pleasing wordes had store,
    And well could file his tongue as smooth as glas;
    he told of Saintes and Popes, and evermore
He strowd an *Ave-Mary* after and before.

36

The drouping Night thus creepeth on them fast,
    And the sad humor loading their eye liddes,
    As messenger of *Morpheus* on them cast
    Sweet slombring deaw, the which to sleep them biddes.
    Unto their lodgings then his guests he riddes:
    Where when all drownd in deadly sleepe he findes,
    He to his study goes, and there amiddes
    His Magick bookes and artes of sundry kindes,
He seeks out mighty charmes, to trouble sleepy mindes.

37

Then choosing out few wordes most horrible,
  (Let none them read) therefore did verses frame,
  With which and other spelles like terrible,
  He bad awake blacke *Plutoes* griesly Dame,
  And cursed heaven, and spake reprochfull shame
  Of highest God, the Lord of life and light;
  A bold bad man, that dar'd to call by name
  Great *Gorgon* Prince of darknesse and dead night,
At which *Cocytus* quakes, and *Styx* is put to flight.

38

And forth he cald out of deepe darknesse dred
  Legions of Sprights, the which like little flyes
  Fluttring about his ever damned hed,
  A-waite whereto their service he applyes,
  To aide his friends, or fray his enimies:
  Of those he chose out two, the falsest twoo,
  And fittest for to forge true-seeming lyes;
  The one of them he gave a message too,
The other by him selfe staide other worke to doo.

39

He making speedy way through spersed ayre,
  And through the world of waters wide and deepe,
  To *Morpheus* house doth hastily repaire.
  Amid the bowels of the earth full steepe,
  And low, where dawning day doth never peepe,
  His dwelling is; there *Tethys* his wet bed
  Doth ever wash, and *Cynthia* still doth steepe
  In silver deaw his ever-drouping hed,
Whiles sad Night over him her mantle black doth spred.

40

Whose double gates he findeth locked fast,
  The one faire fram'd of burnisht Yvory,
  The other all with silver overcast;
  And wakeful dogges before them farre doe lye,
  Watching to banish Care their enimy,
  Who oft is wont to trouble gentle sleepe.
  By them the Sprite doth passe in quietly,
  And unto *Morpheus* comes, whom drowned deepe
In drowsie fit he findes: of nothing he takes keepe.

41

And more, to lulle him in his slumber soft,
　　A trickling streame from high rocke tumbling downe
　　And ever-drizling raine upon the loft,
　　Mixt with a murmuring winde, much like the sowne
　　Of swarming Bees, did cast him in a swowne:
　　No other noyse, nor peoples troublous cryes,
　　As still are wont t' annoy the walled towne,
　　Might there be heard: but carelesse Quiet lyes,
Wrapt in eternall silence farre from enemyes.

42

The messenger approching to him spake,
　　But his wast wordes returnd to him in vaine:
　　So sound he slept, that nought mought his awake.
　　Then rudely he him thrust, and pusht with paine,
　　Whereat he gan to stretch: but he againe
　　Shooke him so hard, that forced him to speake.
　　As one then in a dreame, whose dryer braine
　　Is tost with troubled sights and fancies weake,
He mumbled soft, but would not all his silence breake.

43

The Sprite then gan more boldly him to wake,
　　And threatned unto him the dreaded name
　　Of *Hecate*: whereat he gan to quake,
　　And lifting up his lumpish head, with blame
　　Halfe angry asked him, for what he came.
　　'Hither' (quoth he) 'me *Archimago* sent,
　　He that the stubborne Sprites can wisely tame,
　　He bids thee to him send for his intent
A fit false dreame, that can delude the sleepers sent.'

44

The God obayde, and calling forth straight way
　　A diverse dreame out of his prison darke,
　　Delivered it to him, and downe did lay
　　His heavie head, devoide of carefull carke,
　　Whose sences all were straight benumbd and starke.
　　He backe returning by the Yvorie dore,
　　Remounted up as light as chearefull Larke,
　　And on his litle winges the dreame he bore
In hast unto his Lord, where he him left afore.

45

Who all this while with charmes and hidden artes,
  Had made a Lady of that other Spright,
  And fram'd of liquid ayre her tender partes
  So lively, and so like in all mens sight,
  That weaker sence it could have ravisht quight:
  The maker selfe for all his wondrous witt,
  Was nigh beguiled with so goodly sight:
  Her all in white he clad, and over it
Cast a black stole, most like to seeme for *Una* fit.

46

Now when that ydle dreame was to him brought,
  Unto that Elfin knight he bad him fly,
  Where he slept soundly void of evill thought,
  And with false shewes abuse his fantasy,
  In sort as he him schooled privily:
  And that new creature borne without her dew,
  Full of the makers guyle, with usage sly
  He taught to imitate that Lady trew,
Whose semblance she did carrie under feigned hew.

47

Thus well instructed, to their worke they hast,
  And comming where the knight in slomber lay,
  The one upon his hardy head him plast,
  And made him dreame of loves and lustful play,
  That nigh his manly hart did melt away,
  Bathed in wanton blis and wicked joy:
  Then seemed him his Lady by him lay,
  And to him playnd, how that false winged boy,
Her chast hart had subdewd, to learne Dame pleasures toy.

48

And she her selfe of beautie soveraigne Queene,
  Fayre *Venus* seemde unto his bed to bring
  Her, whom he waking evermore did weene
  To be the chastest flowre, that ay did spring
  On earthly braunch, the daughter of a king,
  Now a loose Leman to vile service bound:
  And eke the *Graces* seemed all to sing,
  Hymen iō Hymen, dauncing all around,
Whylst freshest *Flora* her with Yvie girlond crownd.

49

In this great passion of unwonted lust,
 Or wonted feare of doing ought amis,
 He started up, as seeming to mistrust
 Some secret ill, or hidden foe of his:
 Lo there before his face his Lady is,
 Under blake stole hyding her bayted hooke,
 And as halfe blushing offred him to kis,
 With gentle blandishment and lovely looke,
Most like that virgin true, which for her knight him took.

50

All cleane dismayd to see so uncouth sight,
 And half enraged at her shamelesse guise,
 He thought have slaine her in his fierce despight:
 But hasty heat tempring with sufferance wise,
 He stayde his hand, and gan himselfe advise
 To prove his sense, and tempt her faigned truth.
 Wringing her hands in wemens pitteous wise,
 Tho can she weepe, to stirre up gentle ruth,
Both for her noble bloud, and for her tender youth.

51

And said, 'Ay Sir, my liege Lord and my love,
 Shall I accuse the hidden cruell fate,
 And mightie causes wrought in heaven above,
 Or the blind God that doth me thus amate,
 For hoped love to winne me certaine hate?
 Yet thus perforce he bids me do, or die.
 Die is my dew: yet rew my wretched state
 You, whom my hard avenging destinie
Hath made judge of my life or death indifferently.

52

'You owne deare sake forst me at first to leave
 My Fathers kingdom,' There she stopt with teares;
 Her swollen hart her speech seemd to bereave,
 And then againe begun, 'My weaker yeares
 Captiv'd to fortune and frayle wordly feares,
 Fly to your faith for succour and sure ayde:
 Let me not dye in languor and long teares.'
 'Why Dame' (quoth he) 'what hath ye thus dismayd?
What frayes ye, that were wont to comfort me affrayd?'

53

'Love of your selfe,' she said, 'and deare constraint
　　Lets me not sleepe, but wast the wearie night
　　In secret anguish and unpittied plaint,
　　Whiles you in carelesse sleepe are drowned quight.'
　　Her doubtfull words made that redoubted knight
　　Suspect her truth: yet since no' untruth he knew,
　　Her fawning love with foule disdainefull spight
　　He would not shend, but said, 'Deare dame I rew,
That for my sake unknowne such griefe unto you grew.

54

'Assure your selfe, it fell not all to ground;
　　For all so deare as life is to my hart,
　　I deeme your love, and hold me to you bound;
　　Ne let vaine feares procure your needlesse smart,
　　Where cause is none, but to your rest depart.'
　　Not all content, yet seemd she to appease
　　Her mournefull plaintes, beguiled of her art,
　　And fed with words, that could not chuse but please,
So slyding softly forth, she turnd as to her ease.

55

Long after lay he musing at her mood,
　　Much griev'd to thinke that gentle Dame so light,
　　For whose defence he was to shed his blood.
　　At last dull wearines of former fight
　　Having yrockt a sleepe his irkesome spright,
　　That troublous dreame gan freshly tosse his braine,
　　With bowres, and beds, and Ladies deare delight:
　　But when he saw his labour all was vaine,
With that misformed spright he backe returnd againe.

Canto II

The guilefull great Enchaunter parts
The Redcross Knight from Truth:
Into whose stead faire falshood steps,
And workes him woefull ruth.

1

By this the Northerne wagoner had set
  His sevenfold teme behind the stedfast starre,
  That was in Ocean waves yet never wet,
  But firme is fixt, and sendeth light from farre
  To all, that in the wide deepe wandring arre:
  And chearefull Chaunticlere with his note shrill
  Had warned once, that *Phœbus* fiery carre
  In hast was climbing up the Easterne hill,
Full envious that night so long his roome did fill.

2

When those accursed messengers of hell,
  That feigning dreame, and that faire-forged Spright
  Came to their wicked maister, and gan tell
  Their bootlelesse paines, and ill succeeding night:
  Who all in rage to see his skilfull might
  Deluded so, gan threaten hellish paine
  And sad *Proserpines* wrath, them to affright.
  But when he saw his threatning was but vaine,
He cast about, and searcht his baleful bookes againe.

3

Eftsoones he tooke that miscreated faire,
  And that false other Spright, on whom he spred
  A seeming body of the subtile aire,
  Like a young Squire, in loves and lusty-hed
  His wanton dayes that ever loosely led,
  Without regard of armes and dreaded fight:
  Those two he tooke, and in a secret bed,
  Covered with darknesse and misdeeming night,
Them both together laid, to joy in vaine delight.

4

Forthwith he runnes with feigned faithfull hast
  Unto his guest, who after troublous sights
  And dreames, gan now to take more sound repast,
  Whom suddenly he wakes with fearfull frights,
  As one aghast with feends or damned sprights,

And to him cals, 'Rise rise unhappy Swaine,
  That here wex old in sleepe, whiles wicked wights
  Have knit themselves in *Venus* shameful chaine;
Come see, where your false Lady doth her honor staine.'

5

All in amaze he suddenly up start
  With sword in hand, and with the old man went;
  Who soone him brought into a secret part,
  Where that false couple were full closely ment
  In wanton lust and lewd embracement:
  Which when he saw, he burnt with gealous fire,
  The eye of reason was with rage yblent,
  And would have slaine them in his furious ire,
But hardly was restreined of that aged sire.

6

Returning to his bed in torment great,
  And bitter anguish of his guiltie sight,
  He could not rest, but did his stout heart eat,
  And wast his inward gall with deepe despight,
  Yrkesome of life, and too long lingring night.
  At last faire *Hesperus* in highest skie
  Had spent his lampe, and brought forth dawning light,
  Then up he rose, and clad him hastily;
The Dwarfe him brought his steed: so both away do fly.

7

Now when the rosy-fingred Morning faire,
  Weary of aged *Tithones* saffron bed,
  Had spred her purple robe through deawy aire,
  And the high hils *Titan* discovered,
  The royall virgin shooke off drowsy-hed;
  And rising forth out of her baser bowre,
  Lookt for her knight, who far away was fled,
  And for her Dwarfe, that wont to wait each houre;
Then gan she waile and weepe, to see that woeful stowre.

8

And after him she rode with so much speede
  As her slow beast could make; but all in vaine:
  For him so far had borne his light-foot steede,
  Pricked with wrath and fiery fierce disdaine,
  That him to follow was but fruitlesse paine;
  Yet she her weary limbes would never rest,

But every hill and dale, each wood and plaine
  Did search, sore grieved in her gentle brest,
He so ungently left her, whom she loved best.

9

But subtill *Archimago*, when his guests
  He saw divided into double parts,
  And *Una* wandring in woods and forrests,
  Th' end of his drift, he praisd his divelish arts,
  That had such might over true meaning harts;
  Yet rests not so, but other meanes doth make,
  How he may worke unto her further smarts:
  For her he hated as the hissing snake,
And in her many troubles did most pleasure take.

10

He then devisde himselfe how to disguise;
  For by his mighty science he could take
  As many formes and shapes in seeming wise,
  As ever *Proteus* to himselfe could make:
  Sometime a fowle, sometime a fish in lake,
  Now like a foxe, now like a dragon fell,
  That of himselfe he ofte for feare would quake,
  And oft would flie away. O who can tell
The hidden power of herbes, and might of Magicke spell?

11

But now seemde best the person to put on
  Of that good knight, his late beguiled guest:
  In mighty armes he was yclad anon:
  And silver shield, upon his coward brest
  A bloudy crosse, and on his craven crest
  A bounch of haires discolourd diversly:
  Full jolly knight he seemde, and well addrest,
  And when he sate upon his courser free,
Saint George himself ye would have deemed him to be.

12

But he the knight, whose semblaunt he did beare,
  The true *Saint George* was wandred far away,
  Still flying from his thoughts and gealous feare;
  Will was his guide, and griefe led him astray.
  At last him chaunst to meete upon the way
  A faithlesse Sarazin, all arm'd to point,
  In whose great shield was writ with letters gay

Sans foy: full large of limbe and every joint
He was, and cared not for God or man a point.

13

Hee had a faire companion of his way,
  A goodly Lady clad in scarlot red,
  Purfled with gold and pearle of rich assay,
  And like a *Persian* mitre on her hed
  She wore, with crownes and owches garnished,
  The which her lavish lovers to her gave;
  Her wanton palfrey all was overspred
  With tinsell trappings, woven like a wave,
Whose bridle rung with golden bels and bosses brave.

14

With faire disport and courting dalliaunce
  She intertainde her lover all the way:
  But when she saw the knight his speare advaunce,
  She soone left off her mirth and wanton play,
  And bad her knight addresse him to the fray:
  His foe was nigh at hand.   He prickt with pride
  And hope to winne his Ladies hearte that day,
  Forth spurred fast: adowne his coursers side
The red bloud trickling staind the way, as he did ride.

15

The knight of the *Redcrosse* when him he spide,
  Spurring so hote with rage dispiteous,
  Gan fairely couch his speare, and towards ride:
  Soone meete they both, both fell and furious,
  That daunted with their forces hideous,
  Their steeds do stagger, and amazed stand,
  And eke themselves too rudely rigorous,
  Astonied with the stroke of their owne hand,
Do backe rebut, and each to other yeeldeth land.

16

As when two rams stird with ambitious pride,
  Fight for the rule of the rich fleeced flocke,
  Their horned fronts so fierce on either side
  Do meete, that with the terrour of the shocke
  Astonied both, stand sencelesse as a blocke,
  Forgetfull of the hanging victory:
  So stood these twaine, unmoved as a rocke,
  Both staring fierce, and holding idely,
The broken reliques of their former cruelty.

17

The *Sarazin* sore daunted with the buffe
  Snatcheth his sword, and fiercely to him flies;
  Who well it wards, and quyteth cuff with cuff:
  Each others equall puissaunce envies,
  And through their iron sides with cruell spies
  Does seeke to perce: repining courage yields
  No foote to foe. The flashing fier flies,
  As from a forge out of their burning shields,
And streams of purple bloud new dies the verdant fields.

18

'Curse on that Cross' (quoth then the *Sarazin*)
  'That keepes thy body from the bitter fit;
  Dead long ygoe I wote thou haddest bin,
  Had not that charme from thee forwarned it:
  But yet I warne thee now assured sitt,
  And hide thy head.' Therewith upon his crest
  With rigor so outrageous he smitt,
  That a large share it hewd out of the rest,
And glauncing downe his shield, from blame him fairely blest.

19

Who thereat wondrous wroth, the sleeping spark
  Of native vertue gan eftsoones revive,
  And at his haughtie helmet making mark,
  So hugely stroke, that it the steele did rive,
  And cleft his head. He tumbling downe alive,
  With bloudy mouth his mother earth did kis,
  Greeting his grave: his grudging ghost did strive
  With the fraile flesh; at last it flitted is,
Whither the soules do fly of men that live amis.

20

The Lady when she saw her champion fall,
  Like the old ruines of a broken towre,
  Staid not to waile his woefull funerall,
  But from him fled away with all her powre;
  Who after her as hastily gan scowre,
  Bidding the Dwarfe with him to bring away
  The *Sarazins* shield, signe of the conqueroure.
  Her soone he overtooke, and bad to stay.
For present cause was none of dread her to dismay.

21

Shee turning backe with ruefull countenaunce,
　Cride, 'Mercy mercy Sir vouchsafe to show
　On silly Dame, subject to hard mischaunce,
　And to your mighty will.'　Her humblesse low
　In so ritch weedes, and seeming glorious show,
　Did much emmove his stout heroicke heart,
　And said, 'Deare dame, your sudden overthrow
　Much rueth me; but now put feare apart,
And tell, both who ye be, and who that tooke your part.'

22

Melting in teares, then gan shee thus lament;
　'The wretched woman, whom unhappy howre
　Hath now made thrall to your commandement,
　Before that angry heavens list to lowre,
　And fortune false betraide me to thy powre,
　Was, (O what now availeth that I was!)
　Borne the sole daughter of an Emperour,
　He that the wide West under his rule has,
And high hath set his throne, where *Tiberis* doth pas.

23

'He in the first flowre of my freshest age,
　Betrothed me unto the onley haire
　Of a most mighty king, most rich and sage;
　Was never Prince so faithfull and so faire,
　Was never Prince so meeke and debonaire;
　But ere my hoped day of spousall shone,
　My dearest Lord fell from high honours staire,
　Into the hands of his accursed fone,
And cruelly was slaine, that shall I ever mone.

24

'His blessed body, spoild of lively breath,
　Was afterward, I know not how, convaid
　And fro me hid: of whose most innocent death
　When tidings came to mee unhappy maid,
　O how great sorrow my sad soule assaid.
　Then forth I went his woefull corse to find,
　And many yeares throughout the world I straid,
　A virgin widow, whose deepe wounded mind
With love, long time did languish as the striken hind.

25

'At last it chaunced this proud *Sarazin*,
  To meete me wandring, who perforce me led
  With him away, but yet could never win
  The Fort, that Ladies hold in soveraigne dread.
  There lies he now with foule dishonour dead,
  Who whiles he liv'de, was called proud *Sans foy*,
  The eldest of three brethren, all three bred
  Of one bad sire, whose youngest is *Sans joy*,
And twixt them both was borne the bloudy bold *Sans loy*.

26

'In this sad plight, friendlesse, unfortunate,
  Now miserable I *Fidessa* dwell,
  Craving of you in pitty of my state,
  To do none ill, if please ye not do well.'
  He in great passion all this while did dwell,
  More busying his quicke eyes, her face to view,
  Then his dull eares, to heare what shee did tell;
  And said, 'Faire Lady hart of flint would rew
The undeserved woes and sorrowes, which ye shew.

27

'Henceforth in safe assurance may ye rest,
  Having both found a new friend you to aid,
  And lost an old foe, that did you molest;
  Better new friend then an old foe is said.'
  With chaunge of cheare the seeming simple maid
  Let fall her eyen, as shamefast to the earth,
  And yeelding soft, in that she nought gain-said,
  So forth they rode, he feining seemely merth,
And she coy lookes: so dainty they say maketh derth.

28

Long time they thus together traveiled,
  Till weary of their way, they came at last,
  Where grew two goodly trees, that faire did spred
  Their armes abroad, with gray mosse overcast,
  And their greene leaves trembling with every blast,
  Made a calme shadow far in compasse round:
  The fearefull Shepheard often there aghast
  Under them never sat, ne wont there sound
His mery oaten pipe, but shund th' unlucky ground.

29

But this good knight soone as he them can spie,
  For the coole shade him thither hastly got:
  For golden *Phœbus* now ymounted hie,
  From fiery wheeles of his faire chariot
  Hurled his beame so scorching cruell hot,
  That living creature mote it not abide;
  And his new Lady it endured not.
  There they alight, in hope themselves to hide
From the fierce heat, and rest their weary limbs a tide.

30

Faire seemely pleasaunce each to other makes,
  With goodly purposes there as they sit:
  And in his falsed fancy he her takes
  To be the fairest wight, that lived yit;
  Which to expresse, he bends his gentle wit,
  And thinking of those braunches greene to frame
  A girlond for her dainty forehead fit,
  He pluckt a bough; out of whose rift there came
Smal drops of gory bloud, that trickled down the same.

31

Therewith a piteous yelling voyce was heard,
  Crying, 'O spare with guilty hands to teare
  My tender sides in this rough rynd embard,
  But fly, ah fly far hence away, for feare
  Least to you hap that happened to me heare,
  And to this wretched Lady, my deare love,
  O too deare love, love bought with death too deare.'
  Astond he stood, and up his haire did hove,
And with that suddein horror could no member move.

32

At last whenas the dreadfull passion
  Was overpast, and manhood well awake,
  Yet musing at the straunge occasion,
  And doubting much his sence, he thus bespake;
  'What voyce of damned Ghost from *Limbo* lake,
  Or guilefull spright wandring in empty aire,
  Both which fraile men doe oftentimes mistake,
  Sends to my doubtful eares these speaches rare,
And ruefull plaints, me bidding guiltlesse bloud to spare?'

33

Then groning deep, 'Nor damned Ghost,' (quoth he,)
  'Nor guileful sprite to thee these words doth speake,
  But once a man *Fradubio*, now a tree,
  Wretched man, wretched tree; whose nature weake,
  A cruell witch her cursed will to wreake,
  Hath thus transformed, and plast in open plaines,
  Where *Boreas* doth blow full bitter bleake,
  And scorching Sunne does dry my secret vaines:
For though a tree I seeme, yet cold and heat me paines.'

34

'Say on *Fradubio* then, or man or tree.'
  Quoth then the knight, 'by whose mischievous arts
  Art thou misshaped thus, as now I see?
  He oft finds med'cine, who his griefe imparts;
  But double griefs afflict concealing harts,
  As raging flames who striveth to suppresse.'
  'The author then' (said he) 'of all my smarts,
  Is one *Duessa* a false sorceresse,
That many errant knights hath brought to wretchednesse.

35

'In prime of youthly yeares, when corage hot
  The fire of love and joy of chevalree
  First kindled in my brest, it was my lot
  To love this gentle Lady, whome ye see,
  Now not a Lady, but a seeming tree;
  With whome as once I rode accompanyde,
  Me chaunced of a knight encountred bee,
  That had a like faire Lady by his syde,
Lyke a faire Lady, but did fowle *Duessa* hyde.

36

'Whose forged beauty he did take in hand,
  All other Dames to have exceeded farre;
  I in defence of mine did likewise stand,
  Mine, that did then shine as the Morning starre:
  So both to battell fierce arraunged arre,
  In which his harder fortune was to fall
  Under my speare: such is the dye of warre:
  His Lady left as a prise martiall,
Did yield her comely person, to be at my call.

37

'So doubly lov'd of Ladies unlike faire,
   Th' one seeming such, the other such indeede,
   One day in doubt I cast for to compare,
   Whether in beauties glorie did exceede;
   A Rosy girlond was the victors meede:
   Both seemde to win, and both seemed won to bee,
   So hard the discord was to be agreede.
   Frælissa was as faire, as faire mote bee,
And ever false *Duessa* seemde as faire as shee.

38

'The wicked witch now seeing all this while
   The doubtfull ballaunce equally to sway,
   What not by right, she cast to win by guile,
   And by her hellish science raisd streight way
   A foggy mist, that overcast the day,
   And a dull blast, that breathing on her face.
   Dimmed her former beauties shining ray,
   And with foule ugly forme did her disgrace:
Then was she fayre alone, when none was faire in place.

39

'Then cride she out 'fye, fye, deformed wight,
   Whose borrowed beautie now appeareth plaine
   To have before bewitched all mens sight;
   O leave her soone, or let her soone be slaine.'
   Her loathly visage viewing with disdaine,
   Eftsoones I thought her such as she me told,
   And would have kild her; but with faigned paine,
   The false witch did my wrathful hand with-hold:
So left her, where she now is turnd to treen mould.

40

'Thens, forth I tooke *Duessa* for my Dame,
   And in the witch unweeting joyd long time,
   Ne ever wist, but that she was the same,
   Till on a day (that day is every Prime,
   When Witches wont do penance for their crime)
   I chaunst to see her in her proper hew,
   Bathing her selfe in origane and thyme:
   A filthy foule old woman I did vew,
That ever to have toucht her, I did deadly rew.

41

'Her neather partes misshapen, monstruous,
    Were hidd in water, that I could not see,
    But they did seeme more foule and hideous,
    Then womans shape man would beleeve to bee.
    Thens forth her most beastly companie
    I gan refraine, in minde to slip away,
    Soone as appeard safe opportunitie:
    For danger great, if not assur'd decay
I saw before mine eyes, if I were knowne to stray.

42

'The divelish hag by chaunges of my cheare
    Perceiv'd my thought, and drownd in sleepie night,
    With wicked herbs and ointments did besmeare
    My bodie all, through charmes and magicke might,
    That all my senses were bereaved quight:
    Then brought she me into this desert waste,
    And by my wretched lovers side me pight.
    Where now enclosd in wooden wals full faste,
Banisht from living wights, our wearie dayes we waste.'

43

'But how long time,' said then the Elfin knight,
    'Are you in this misformed house to dwell?'
    'We may not chaunge' (quoth he) 'this evil plight,
    Till we be bathed in a living well;
    That is the terme prescribed by the spell.'
    'O how,' said he, 'mote I that well out find,
    That may restore you to your wonted well?'
    'Time and suffised fates to former kynd
Shall us restore, none else from hence may us unbynd.'

44

The false *Duessa* now *Fidessa* hight,
    Heard how in vaine *Fradubio* did lament,
    And knew well all was true.   But the good knight
    Full of sad feare and ghastly dreriment,
    When all this speech the living tree had spent,
    The bleeding bough did thrust into the ground,
    That from the bloud he might be innocent,
    And with fresh clay did close the wooden wound:
Then turning to his Lady, dead with feare her found.

45

Her seeming dead he found with feigned feare,
　　As all unweeting of that well she knew,
　　And paynd himselfe with busie care to reare
　　Her out of carelesse swowne.　Her eylids blew
　　And dimmed sight with pale and deadly hew
　　At last she up gan lift: with trembling cheare
　　Her up he tooke, too simple and too trew,
　　And oft her kist.　At length all passed feare,
He set her on her steede, and forward forth did beare.

Canto III

Forsaken Truth long seekes her love,
And makes the Lyon mylde,
Marres blind Devotions mart, and fals
In hand of leachour vylde.

1

Nought is there under heav'ns wide hollownesse,
   That moves more deare compassion of mind,
   Then beautie brought t'unworthy wretchednesse
   Through envies snares or fortunes freakes unkind:
   I, whether lately through her brightnesse blind,
   Or through alleageance, and fast fealtie,
   Which I do owe unto all woman kind,
   Feele my hart perst with so great agonie,
When such I see, that all for pittie I could die.

2

And now it is empassioned so deepe,
   For fairest *Unaes* sake, of whom I sing,
   That my fraile eyes these lines with teares do steepe,
   To thinke how she through guilefull handeling,
   Though true as touch, though daughter of a king,
   Though faire as ever living wight was faire,
   Though nor in word nor deede ill meriting,
   Is from her knight divorced in despaire
And her due loves deriv'd to that vile witches share.

3

Yet she most faithfull Ladie all this while
   Forsaken, wofull, solitarie mayd,
   Far from all peoples preace, as in exile,
   In wildernesse and wastfull deserts strayd,
   To seeke her knight; who subtily betrayd
   Through that late vision, which th' Enchaunter wrought,
   Had her abandond. She of nought affrayd,
   Through woods and wastnesse wide him daily sought;
Yet wished tydings none of him unto her brought.

4

One day nigh wearie of the yrkesome way,
   From her unhastie beast she did alight,
   And on the grasse her daintie limbes did lay
   In secrete shadow, far from all mens sight:
   From her faire head her fillet she undight,

And laid her stole aside.   Her angels face
As the great eye of heaven shyned bright,
And made a sunshine in the shadie place;
Did ever mortall eye behold such heavenly grace.

5

It fortuned out of the thickest wood
A ramping Lyon rushed suddainly,
Hunting full greedie after salvage blood;
Soone as the royall virgin he did spy,
With gaping mouth at her ran greedily,
To have attonce devour'd her tender corse:
But to the pray when as he drew more ny,
His bloudie rage asswaged with remorse,
And with the sight amazd, forgat his furious forse.

6

In stead thereof he kist her wearie feet,
And lickt her lilly hands with fawning tong,
As he her wronged innocence did weet.
O how can beautie maister the most strong,
And simple truth subdue a avenging wrong?
Whose yeelded pride and proud submission,
Still dreading death, when she had marked long,
Her hart gan melt in great compassion,
And drizling teares did shed for pure affection.

7

'The Lyon Lord of everie beast in field'
Quoth she, 'his princely puissance doth abate,
And mightie proud to humble weake does yield,
Forgetfull of the hungry rage, which late
Him prickt, in pittie of my sad estate:
But he my Lyon, and my noble Lord
How does he find in cruell hart to hate
Her that him lov'd and ever most adord,
As the God of my life? why hath he me abhord?'

8

Redounding teares did choke th' end of her plaint,
Which softly ecchoed from the neighbour wood;
And sad to see her sorrowfull constraint
The kingly beast upon her gazing stood;
With pittie calmd, downe fell his angry mood.
At last in close hart shutting up her paine,

Arose the virgin borne of heavenly brood,
  And to her snowy Palfrey got againe,
To seeke her strayed Champion, if she might attaine.

9

The Lyon would not leave her desolate,
  But with her went along, as a strong gard
  Of her chast person, and a faithfull mate
  Of her sad troubles and misfortunes hard:
  Still when she slept, he kept both watch and ward,
  And when she wakt, he waited diligent,
  With humble service to her will prepard:
  From her faire eyes he tooke commaundement,
And ever by her lookes conceived her intent.

10

Long she thus traveiled through deserts wyde,
  By which she thought her wandring knight shold pas,
  Yet never shew of living wight espyde;
  Till that at length she found the troden gras,
  In which the tract of peoples footing was,
  Under the steepe foot of a mountaine hore;
  The same she followes, till at last she has
  A damzell spyde slow footing her before,
That on her shoulders sad a pot of water bore.

11

To whom approching she to her gan call,
  To weet, if dwelling place were nigh at hand;
  But the rude wench her answer'd nought at all,
  She could not heare, nor speake, nor understand;
  Till seeing by her side the Lyon stand,
  With suddaine feare her pitcher downe she threw,
  And fled away: for never in that land
  Face of faire Ladie she before did vew,
And that dread Lyons looke her cast in deadly hew.

12

Full fast she fled, ne ever lookt behynd,
  As if her life upon the wager lay,
  And home she came, whereas her mother blynd
  Sate in eternall night: nought could she say,
  But suddaine catching hold did her dismay
  With quaking hands, and other signes of feare:
  Who full of ghastly fright and cold affray,

Gan shut the dore.   By this arrived there
Dame *Una* wearie Dame, and entrance did requere.

13

Which when none yelded, her unruly Page
  With his rude clawes the wicket open rent,
  And let her in; where of his cruell rage
  Nigh dead with feare, and faint astonishment,
  Shee found them both in darksome corner pent;
  Where that old woman day and night did pray
  Upon her beades devoutly penitent;
  Nine hundred *Pater nosters* every day,
And thrise nine hundred *Aves* she was wont to say.

14

And to augment her painefull pennance more,
  Thrise every weeke in ashes shee did sit,
  And next her wrinkled skin, rough sackcloth wore,
  And thrise three times did fast from any bit:
  But now for feare her beads she did forget.
  Whose needlesse dread for to remove away,
  Faire *Una* framed words and count'nance fit:
  Which hardly doen, at length she gan them pray,
That in their cotage small, that night she rest her may.

15

The day is spent, and commeth drowsie night,
  When every creature shrowded is in sleepe;
  Sad *Una* downe her laies in wearie plight,
  And at her feet the Lyon watch doth keepe:
  In stead of rest, she does lament, and weepe
  For the late losse of her deare loved knight,
  And sighes, and grones, and evermore does steepe
  Her tender brest in bitter teares all night,
All night she thinks too long, and often lookes for light.

16

Now when *Aldeboran* was mounted hie
  Above the shynie *Cassiopeias* chaire,
  And all in deadly sleepe did drowned lie
  One knocked at the dore, and in would fare:
  He knocked fast, and often curst, and sware,
  That readie entrance was not at his call:
  For on his backe a heavy load he bare
  Of nightly stelths and pillage severall,
Which he had got abroad by purchas criminall.

17

He was to weete a stout and sturdie thiefe,
    Wont to robbe Churches of their ornaments,
    And poore mens boxes of their due reliefe,
    Which given was to them for good intents;
    The holy Saints of their rich vestiments
    He did disrobe, when all men carelesse slept,
    And spoild the Priests of their habiliments,
    Whiles none the holy things in safety kept;
Then he by cunning sleights in at the window crept.

18

And all that he by right or wrong could find,
    Unto this house he brought, and did bestow
    Upon the daughter of this woman blind,
    Abessa daughter of *Corceca* slow,
    With whom he whoredome usd, that few did know,
    And fed her fat with feast of offerings,
    And plentie, which in all the land did grow;
    Ne spared he to give her gold and rings:
And now he to her brought part of his stolen things.

19

Thus long the dore with rage and threats he bet,
    Yet of those fearfull women none durst rize,
    The Lyon frayed them, him in to let:
    He would no longer stay him to advize,
    But open breakes the dore in furious wize,
    And entring is; when that disdainfull beast
    Encountring fierce, him suddaine doth surprize,
    And seizing cruell clawes on trembling brest,
Under his Lordly foot him proudly hath supprest.

20

Him booteth not resist, nor succour call,
    His bleeding hart is in the vengers hand,
    Who streight him rent in thousand peeces small,
    And quite dismembred hath: the thirsty land
    Drunke up his life; his corse left on the strand.
    His fearfull friends weare out the wofull night,
    Ne dare to weepe, nor seeme to understand
    The heavie hap, which on them is alight,
Affraid least to themselves the like mishappen might.

21

Now when broad day the world discovered has,
　　Up *Una* rose, up rose the Lyon eke,
　　And on their former journey forward pas,
　　In wayes unknowne, her wandring knight to seeke,
　　With paines farre passing that long wandring *Greeke,*
　　That for his love refused deitie;
　　Such were the labours of this Lady meeke,
　　Still seeking him, that from her still did flie,
Then furthest from her hope, when most she weened nie.

22

Soone as she parted thence, the fearfull twaine,
　　That blind old woman and her daughter deare
　　Came forth, and finding *Kirkrapine* there slaine,
　　For anguish great they gan to rend their heare,
　　And beat their brests, and naked flesh to teare,
　　And when they both had wept and wayld their fill,
　　Then forth they ran, like two amazed deare,
　　Halfe mad through malice, and revenging will,
To follow her, that was the causer of their ill.

23

Whom overtaking, they gan loudly bray,
　　With hollow howling, and lamenting cry,
　　Shamefully at her rayling all the way,
　　And her accusing of dishonesty,
　　That was the flowre of faith and chastity;
　　And still amidst her rayling, she did pray,
　　That plagues, and mischiefes, and long misery
　　Might fall on her, and follow all the way,
And that in endlesse error she might ever stray.

24

But when she saw her prayers nought prevaile,
　　She backe returned with some labour lost;
　　And in the way as she did weepe and waile,
　　A knight her met in mighty armes embost,
　　Yet knight was not for all his bragging bost,
　　But subtill *Archimag*, that *Una* sought
　　By traynes into new troubles to have tost:
　　Of that old woman tydings he besought,
If that of such a Ladie shee could tellen ought.

25

Therewith she gan her passion to renew,
   And cry, and curse, and raile, and rend her heare,
Saying, that harlot she too lately knew,
   That causd her shed so many a bitter teare,
   And so forth told the story of her feare:
Much seemed he to mone her haplesse chaunce,
   And after for that Ladie did inquire;
   Which being taught, he forward gan advaunce
His fair enchaunted steed, and eke his charmed launce.

26

Ere long he came, where *Una* traveild slow,
   And that wilde Champion wayting her besyde:
Whom seeing such, for dread hee durst not show
   Himselfe too nigh at hand, but turned wyde
   Unto an hill; from whence when she him spyde,
By his like seeming shield, her knight by name
   She weend it was, and towards him gan ryde:
   Approching nigh, she wist it was the same,
And with faire fearefull humblesse towards him shee came.

27

And weeping said, 'Ah, my long lacked Lord,
   Where have ye bene thus long out of my sight?
Much feared I to have bene quite abhord,
   Or ought have done, that ye displeasen might,
   That should as death unto my deare hart light:
For since mine eye your joyous sight did mis,
   My chearefull day is turnd to chearelesse night,
   And eke my night of death the shadow is;
But welcome now my light, and shining lampe of blis.'

28

He thereto meeting said, 'My dearest Dame,
   Farre be it from your thought, and fro my will,
To thinke that knighthood I so much should shame,
   As you to leave, that have me loved still,
   And chose in Faery court of meere goodwill,
Where noblest knights were to be found on earth:
   The earth shall sooner leave her kindly skill
   To bring forth fruit, and make eternall derth,
Then I leave you, my liefe, yborne of heavenly berth.

29

'And sooth to say, why I left you so long,
  Was for to seeke adventure in strange place,
  Where *Archimago* said a felon strong
  To many knights did daily worke disgrace;
  But knight he now shall never more deface:
  Good cause of mine excuse, that mote ye please
  Well to accept, and evermore embrace
  My faithfull service, that by land and seas
Have vowd you to defend, now then your plaint appease.'

30

His lovely words her seemd due recompence
  Of all her passed paines: one loving howre
  For many yeares of sorrow can dispence:
  A dram of sweet is worth a pound of sowre:
  Shee has forgot, how many a wofull stowre
  For him she late endur'd; she speakes no more
  Of past: true is, that true love hath no powre
  To looken backe; his eyes be fixt before.
Before her stands her knight, for whom she toyld so sore.

31

Much like, as when the beaten marinere,
  That long hath wandred in the *Ocean* wide,
  Ofte soust in swelling *Tethys* saltish teare,
  And long time having tand his tawney hide
  With blustring breath of heaven, that none can bide,
  And scorching flames of fierce *Orions* hound,
  Soone as the port from farre he had espide,
  His cheareful whistle merrily doth sound,
And *Nereus* crownes with cups; his mates him pledge around.

32

Such joy made *Una*, when her knight she found;
  And eke th' enchaunter joyous seemd no lesse,
  Then the glad marchant, that does vew from ground
  His ship farre come from watrie wildernesse,
  He hurles out vowes, and *Neptune* oft doth blesse:
  So forth they past, and all the way they spent
  Discoursing of her dreadful late distresse,
  In which he askt her, what the Lyon ment:
Who told her all that fell in journey as she went.

33

They had not ridden farre, when they might see
  One pricking towards them with hastie heat,
  Full strongly armd, and on a courser free,
  That through his fiercenesse fomed all with sweat,
  And the sharpe yron did for anger eat,
  When his hot ryder spurd his chauffed side;
  His looke was sterne, and seemed still to threat
  Cruell revenge, which he in hart did hyde,
And on his shield *Sans loy* in bloody lines was dyde.

34

When nigh he drew unto this gentle payre
  And saw the Red-crosse, which the knight did beare,
  He burnt in fire, and gan eftsoones prepare
  Himselfe to battell with his couched speare.
  Loth was that other, and did faint through feare,
  To taste th' untryed dint of deadly steele;
  But yet his Lady did so well him cheare,
  That hope of new good hap he gan to feele;
So bent his speare, and spurnd his horse with yron heele.

35

But that proud Paynim forward came so fierce,
  And full of wrath, that with his sharp-head speare
  Through vainely crossed shield he quite did pierce,
  And had his staggering steed not shrunke for feare,
  Through shield and bodie eke he should him beare:
  Yet so great was the puissance of his push,
  That from his saddle quite he did him beare:
  He tombling rudely downe to ground did rush,
And from his gored wound a well of bloud did gush.

36

Dismounting lightly from his loftie steed,
  He to him lept, in minde to reave his life,
  And proudly said, 'Lo there the worthie meed
  Of him that slew *Sansfoy* with bloudie knife;
  Henceforth his ghost freed from repining strife,
  In peace may passen over *Lethe* lake,
  When mourning altars purgd with enemies life,
  The black infernall *Furies* doen aslake:
Life from *Sansfoy* thou tookst, *Sansloy* shall from thee take.'

37

Therewith in haste his helmet gan unlace,
    Till *Una* cride, 'O hold that heavie hand,
    Deare Sir, what ever that thou be in place:
    Enough is, that thy foe doth vanquisht stand
    Now at thy mercy: Mercie not withstand:
    For he is one the truest knight alive,
    Though conquered now he lie on lowly land,
    And whilest him fortune favours, faire did thrive
In bloudie field: therefore of life him not deprive.'

38

Her piteous words might not abate his rage,
    But rudely rending up his helmet, would
    Have slaine him straight: but when he sees his age,
    And hoarie head of *Archimago* old,
    His hastie hand he doth amazed hold,
    And halfe ashamed, wondred at the sight:
    For the old man well knew he, though untold,
    In charmes and magicke to have wondrous might,
Ne ever wont in field, ne in round lists to fight:

39

And said, 'Why *Archimago*, lucklesse syre,
    What doe I see? what hard mishap is this,
    That hath thee hither brought to taste mine yre?
    Or thine the fault, or mine the error is,
    In stead of foe to wound my friend amis?'
    He answered nought, but in a traunce still lay,
    And on those guilefull dazed eyes of his
    The cloud of death did sit. Which doen away,
He left him lying so, ne would no lenger stay.

40

But to the virgin comes, who all this while
    Amased stands, her selfe so mockt to see
    By him, who has the guerdon of his guile,
    For so misfeigning her true knight to bee:
    Yet is she now in more perplexitie,
    Left in the hand of that same Paynim bold,
    From whom her booteth not at all to flie;
    Who by her cleanly garment catching hold,
Her from her Palfrey pluckt, her visage to behold.

41

But her fierce servant full of kingly awe
  And high disdaine, whenas his soveraine Dame
  So rudely handled by her foe he sawe,
  With gaping jawes full greedy at him came,
  And ramping on his shield, did weene the same
  Have reft away with his sharpe rending clawes:
  But he was stout, and lust did now inflame
  His corage more, that from his griping pawes
He hath his shield redeem'd, and foorth his swerd he drawes.

42

O then too weake and feeble was the forse
  Of salvage beast, his puissance to withstand:
  For he was strong, and of so mightie corse,
  As ever wielded speare in warlike hand,
  And feates of armes did wisely understand,
  Eftsoones he perced through his chaufed chest
  With thrilling point of deadly yron brand,
  And launcht his Lordly hart: with death opprest
He roar'd aloud, whiles life forsooke his stubborne brest.

43

Who now is left to keepe the forlorne maid
  From raging spoile of lawlesse victors will?
  Her faithfull gard remov'd her hope dismaid,
  Her selfe a yeelded pray to save or spill.
  He now Lord of the field, his pride to fill,
  With foule reproches, and disdainfull spight
  Her vildly entertaines, and will or nill,
  Beares her away upon his courser light:
Her prayers nought prevaile, his rage is more of might.

44

And all the way, with great lamenting paine,
  And piteous plaints she filleth his dull eares,
  That stony hart could riven have in twaine,
  And all the way she wets with flowing teares:
  But he enrag'd with rancor, nothing heares.
  Her servile beast yet would not leave her so,
  But followes her farre off, ne ought he feares,
  To be partaker of her wandring woe,
More mild in beastly kind, then that her beastly foe.

Canto IV

To sinfull house of Pride Duessa
Guydes the faithfull knight;
Where brothers death to wreak Sansjoy
Doth chalenge him to fight.

I

Young knight, what ever that dost armes professe,
   And through long labours huntest after fame,
   Beware of fraud, beware of ficklenesse,
   In choice, and change of thy deare loved Dame,
   Least thou of her beleeve too lightly blame,
   And rash misweening doe thy hart remove:
   For unto knight there is no greater shame,
   Then lightnesse and inconstancie in love;
That doth this *Redcrosse* knights ensample plainly prove.

2

Who after that he had faire *Una* lorne,
   Through light misdeeming of her loialtie,
   And false *Duessa* in her sted had borne,
   Called *Fidess'*, and so supposd to bee;
   Long with her traveild, till at last they see
   A goodly building, bravely garnished,
   The house of mightie Prince it seemd to bee:
   And towards it a broad high way that led,
All bare through peoples feet, which thither traveiled.

3

Great troupes of people traveild thitherward
   Both day and night, of each degree and place,
   But few returned, having scaped hard,
   With balefull beggerie, or foule disgrace,
   Which ever after in most wretched case,
   Like loathsome lazars, by the hedges lay.
   Thither *Duessa* bad him bend his pace:
   For she is wearie of the toilesome way,
And also nigh consumed is the lingring day.

4

A stately Pallace built of squared bricke,
   Which cunningly was without morter laid,
   Whose wals were high, but nothing strong, nor thick,
   And golden foile all over them displaid,
   That purest skye with brightnesse they dismaid:

High lifted up were many loftie towres,
  And goodly galleries farre over laid,
  Full of faire windowes, and delightful bowres;
And on the top a Diall told the timely howres.

5

It was a goodly heape for to behould,
  And spake the praises of the workmans wit;
  But full great pittie, that so faire a mould
  Did on so weake foundation ever sit:
  For on a sandie hill, that still did flit,
  And fall away, it mounted was full hie,
  That every breath of heaven shaked it:
  And all the hinder parts, that few could spie,
Were ruinous and old, but painted cunningly.

6

Arrived there they passed in forth right;
  For still to all the gates stood open wide,
  Yet charge of them was to a Porter hight
  Cald *Malvenù*, who entrance none denide:
  Thence to the hall, which was on every side
  With rich array and costly arras dight:
  Infinite sorts of people did abide
  There waiting long, to win the wished sight
Of her, that was the Lady of that Pallace bright.

7

By them they passe, all gazing on them round,
  And to the Presence mount; whose glorious vew
  Their frayle amazed senses did confound:
  In living Princes court none ever knew
  Such endlesse richesse, and so sumptuous shew;
  Ne *Persia* selfe, the nourse of pompous pride
  Like ever saw. And there a noble crew
  Of Lords and Ladies stood on every side,
Which with their presence faire, the place much beautifide.

8

High above all a cloth of State was spred,
  And a rich throne, as bright as sunny day
  On which there sate most brave embellished
  With royall robes and gorgeous array,
  A mayden Queene, that shone as *Titans* ray,
  In glistring gold, and peerelesse pretious stone:

Yet her bright blazing beautie did assay
To dim the brightnesse of her glorious throne,
As envying her selfe, that too exceeding shone.

9

Exceeding shone, like *Phœbus* fairest childe,
That did presume his fathers firie wayne,
And flaming mouthes of steedes unwonted wilde
Through highest heaven with weaker hand to rayne;
Proud of such glory and advancement vaine,
While flashing beames do daze his feeble eyen,
He leaves the welkin way most beaten plaine,
And rapt with whirling wheeles, inflames the skyen,
With fire not made to burne, but fairely for to shyne.

10

So proud she shyned in her Princely state,
Looking to heaven; for earth she did disdayne,
And sitting high; for lowly she did hate:
Lo underneath her scornefull feete, was layne
A dreadfull Dragon with an hideous trayne,
And in her hand she held a mirrhour bright,
Wherein her face she often vewed fayne,
And in her selfe-lov'd semblance took delight;
For she was wondrous faire, as any living wight.

11

Of griesly *Pluto* she the daughter was,
And sad *Prosperina* the Queene of hell;
Yet did she thinke her pearelesse worth to pas
That parentage, with pride so did she swell,
And thundring *Jove*, that high in heaven doth dwell,
And wield the world, she claymed for her syre,
Or if that any else did *Jove* excell:
For to the highest she did still aspyre,
Or if ought higher were then that, did it desyre.

12

And proud *Lucifera* men did her call,
That made her selfe a Queene, and crownd to be,
Yet rightfull kingdome she had none at all,
Ne heritage of native soveraintie,
But did usurpe with wrong and tyrannie
Upon the scepter, which she now did hold:
Ne ruld her Realmes with lawes, but pollicie,

And strong advizement of six wisards old,
That with their counsels bad her kingdome did uphold.

13

Soone as the Elfin knight in presence came,
  And false *Duessa* seeming Lady faire,
  A gentle Husher, *Vanitie* by name
  Made rowme, and passage for them did prepaire:
  So goodly brought them to the lowest staire
  Of her high throne, where they on humble knee
  Making obeyssance, did the cause declare,
  Why they were come, her royall state to see,
To prove the wide report of her great Majestee.

14

With loftie eyes, halfe loth to looke so low,
  She thanked them in her disdainefull wise,
  Ne other grace vouchsafed them to show
  Of Princesse worthy, scarse them bad arise.
  Her Lordes and Ladies all this while devise
  Themselves to setten forth to straungers sight:
  Some frounce their curled haire in courtly guise,
  Some prancke their ruffes, and others trimly dight
Their gay attire: each others greater pride does spight.

15

Goodly they all that knight do entertaine,
  Right glad with him to have increast their crew:
  But to *Duess'* each one himselfe did paine
  All kindnesse and faire courtesie to shew;
  For in that court whylome her well they knew:
  Yet the stout Faerie mongst the middest crowd
  Thought all their glorie vaine in knightly vew,
  And that great Princesse too exceeding prowd,
That to strange knight no better countenance allowd.

16

Suddein upriseth from her stately place
  The royall Dame, and for her coche doth call:
  All hurtlen forth, and she with Princely pace,
  As faire *Aurora* in her purple pall,
  Out of the East the dawning day doth call:
  So forth she comes: her brightnesse brode doth blaze;
  The heapes of people, thronging in the hall,
  Do ride each other, upon her to gaze:
Her glorious glitterand light doth all mens eyes amaze.

17

So forth she comes, and to her coche does clyme,
 Adorned all with gold and girlonds gay,
 That seemd as fresh as *Flora* in her prime,
 And strove to match, in royall rich array,
 Great *Junoes* golden chaire, the which they say
 The Gods stand gazing on, when she does ride
 To *Joves* high house through heavens bras-paved way
 Drawne of faire Pecocks, that excell in pride,
And full of *Argus* eyes their tailes dispredden wide.

18

But this was drawne of six unequall beasts,
 On which her six sage Counsellours did ryde,
 Taught to obey their bestiall beheasts,
 With like conditions to their kinds applyde:
 Of which the first, that all the rest did guyde,
 Was sluggish *Idlenesse* the nourse of sin;
 Upon a slouthfull Asse he chose to ryde,
 Arayd in habit blacke, and amis thin,
Like to an holy Monck, the service to begin.

19

And in his hand his Portesse still he bare,
 That much was worne, but therein little red,
 For of devotion he had little care,
 Still drownd in sleepe, and most of his days ded;
 Scarse could he once uphold his heavie hed,
 To looken, whether it were night or day:
 May seeme the wayne was very evill led,
 When such an one had guiding of the way,
That knew not, whether right he went, or else astray.

20

From worldly cares himselfe he did esloyne,
 And greatly shunned manly exercise,
 From every worke he chalenged essoyne,
 For contemplation sake: yet otherwise,
 His life he led in lawlesse riotise;
 By which he grew to grievous malady;
 For in his lustlesse limbs through evill guise
 A shaking fever raignd continually:
Such one was *Idlenesse*, first of this company.

21

And by his side rode loathsome *Gluttony*,
 Deformed creature, on a filthie swyne,
 His belly was up-blowne with luxury,
 And eke with fatnesse swollen were his eyne,
 And like a Crane his necke was long and fyne,
 With which he swallowd up excessive feast,
 For want whereof poore people oft did pyne;
 And all the way, most like a brutish beast,
He spued up his gorge, that all did him deteast.

22

In greene vine leaves he was right fitly clad;
 For other clothes he could not weare for heat,
 And on his head an yvie girland had,
 From under which fast trickled downe the sweat:
 Still as he rode, he somewhat still did eat,
 And in his hand did beare a bouzing can,
 Of which he supt so oft, that on his seat
 His dronken corse he scarse upholden can,
In shape and life more like a monster, then a man.

23

Unfit he was for any worldly thing,
 And eke unhable once to stirre or go,
 Not meet to be of counsell to a king,
 Whose mind in meat and drinke was drowned so,
 That from his friend he seldome knew his fo:
 Full of diseases was his carcas blew,
 And a dry dropsie through his flesh did flow:
 Which by misdiet daily greater grew:
Such one was *Gluttony*, the second of that crew.

24

And next to him rode lustfall *Lechery*,
 Upon a bearded Goat, whose rugged haire,
 And whally eyes (the signe of gelosy,)
 Was like the person selfe, whom he did beare:
 Who rough, and blacke, and filthy did appeare,
 Unseemely man to please faire Ladies eye;
 Yet he of Ladies oft was loved deare,
 When fairer faces were bid standen by:
O who does know the bent of womens fantasy?

25

In a greene gowne he clothed was full faire,
    Which underneath did hide his filthinesse,
    And in his hand a burning hart he bare,
    Full of vaine follies, and new fanglenesse:
    For he was false, and fraught with ficklenesse,
    And learned had to love with secret lookes,
    And well could daunce, and sing with ruefulnesse,
    And fortunes tell, and read in loving bookes,
And thousand other wayes, to bait his fleshly hookes.

26

Inconstant man, that loved all he saw,
    And lusted after all, that he did love,
    Ne would his looser life be tide to law,
    But joyd weake wemens hearts to tempt and prove
    If from their loyall loves he might them move;
    Which lewdnesse fild him with reprochfull paine
    Of that fowle evill, which all men reprove,
    That rots the marrow, and consumes the braine:
Such one was *Lecherie*, the third of all this traine.

27

And greedy *Avarice* by him did ride,
    Upon a Camell loaden all with gold;
    Two iron coffers long on either side,
    With precious mettall full, as they might hold,
    And in his lap an heape of coine he told;
    For of his wicked pelfe his God he made,
    And unto hell him selfe for money sold;
    Accursed usurie was all his trade,
And right and wrong ylike in equall ballaunce waide.

28

His life was nigh unto deaths dore yplast,
    And thred-bare cote, and cobled shoes he ware,
    Ne scarse good morsell all his life did tast,
    But both from backe and belly still did spare,
    To fill his bags, and richesse to compare;
    Yet chylde ne kinsman livng had he none
    To leave them to; but thorough daily care
    To get, and nightly feare to lose his owne,
He led a wretched life unto himselfe unknowne.

29

Most wretched wight, whom nothing might suffise,
  Whose greedy lust did lacke in greatest store,
  Whose need had end, but no end covetise,
  Whose wealth was want, whose plenty made him pore,
  Who had enough, yet wished ever more;
  A vile disease, and eke in foote and hand
  A grievous gout tormented him full sore,
  That well he could not touch, nor go, nor stand:
Such one was *Avarice*, the fourth of this faire band.

30

And next to him malicious *Envie* rode,
  Upon a ravenous wolfe, and still did chaw
  Betweene his cankred teeth a venemous tode,
  That all the poison ran about his chaw;
  But inwardly he chawed his owne maw
  At neighbours wealth, that made him ever sad;
  For death it was, when any good he saw,
  And wept, that cause of weeping none he had,
But when he heard of harme, he wexed wondrous glad.

31

All in a kirtle of discolourd say
  He clothed was, ypainted full of eyes;
  And in his bosome secretly there lay
  An hatefull Snake, the which his taile uptyes
  In many folds, and mortall sting implyes.
  Still as he rode, he gnasht his teeth, to see
  Those heapes of gold with griple Covetyse,
  And grudged at the great felicitie
Of proud *Lucifera*, and his owne companie.

32

He hated all good workes and vertuous deeds,
  And him no lesse, that any like did use,
  And who with gracious bread the hungry feeds,
  His almes for want of faith he doth accuse;
  So every good to bad he doth abuse:
  And eke the verse of famous Poets witt
  He does backebite, and spightfull poison spues
  From leprous mouth on all, that ever writt:
Such one vile *Envie* was, that fifte in row did sitt.

33

And him beside rides fierce revenging *Wrath*,
  Upon a Lion, loth for to be led;
  And in his hand a burning brond he hath,
  The which he brandisheth about his hed;
  His eyes did hurle forth sparkles fiery red,
  And stared sterne on all, that him beheld,
  As ashes pale of hew and seeming ded;
  And on his dagger still his hand he held,
Trembling through hasty rage when choler in him sweld.

34

His ruffin raiment all was staind with blood,
  Which he had spilt, and all to rags yrent,
  Through unadvized rashnesse woxen wood;
  For of his hands he had no governement,
  Ne car'd for bloud in his avengement:
  But when the furious fit was overpast,
  His cruell facts he often would repent;
  Yet wilfull man he never would forecast,
How many mischieves should ensue his heedlesse hast.

35

Full many mischiefes follow cruell *Wrath*;
  Abhorred bloudshed, and tumultuous strife,
  Unmanly murder, and unthrifty scath,
  Bitter despight, with rancours rusty knife,
  And fretting griefe the enemy of life;
  All these, and many evils moe haunt ire,
  The swelling Splene, and Frenzy raging rife,
  The shaking Palsey, and Saint *Fraunces* fire:
Such one was *Wrath*, the last of this ungodly tire.

36

And after all, upon the wagon beame
  Rode *Sathan*, with a smarting whip in hand,
  With which he forward lasht the laesie teme,
  So oft as *Slowth* still in the mire did stand.
  Huge routs of people did about them band,
  Showting for joy, and still before their way
  A foggy mist had covered all the land;
  And, underneath their feet, all scattered lay
Dead sculs and bones of men, whose life had gone astray.

37

So forth they marchen in this goodly sort,
   To take the solace of the open aire,
   And in fresh flowring fields themselves to sport;
   Emongst the rest rode that false Lady faire,
   The fowle *Duessa*, next unto the chaire
   Of proud *Lucifer*, as one of the traine:
   But that good knight would not so nigh repaire,
   Him selfe estraunging from their joyaunce vaine,
Whose fellowship seemed far unfit for warlike swaine.

38

So having solaced themselves a space
   With pleasaunce of the breathing fields yfed,
   They backe returned to the Princely Place;
   Whereas an errant knight in armes ycled,
   And heathnish shield, wherein with letters red
   Was writ *Sans joy*, they new arrived find:
   Enflam'd with fury and fiers hardy-hed,
   He seemd in hart to harbour thoughts unkind,
And nourish bloudy vengeaunce in his bitter mind.

39

Who when the shamed shield of slaine *Sans foy*
   He spide with that same Faery champions page,
   Bewraying him, that did of late destroy
   His eldest brother, burning all with rage
   He to him leapt, and that same envious gage
   Of victors glory from him snacht away:
   But th' Elfin knight, which ought that warlike wage,
   Disdaind to loose the meed he wonne in fray,
And him rencountring fierce, reskewd the noble pray.

40

Therewith they gan to hurtlen greedily,
   Redoubted battaile ready to darrayne,
   And clash their shields, and shake their swerds on hy,
   That with their sturre they troubled all the traine;
   Till that great Queene upon eternall paine
   Of high displeasure, that ensewen might,
   Commaunded them their fury to refraine,
   And if that either to that shield had right,
In equall lists they should the morrow next it fight.

41

'Ah dearest Dame,' (quoth then the Paynim bold,)
    'Pardon the errour of enraged wight,
    Whom great griefe made forget the raines to hold
    Of reasons rule, to see this recreaunt knight,
    No knight, but treachour full of false despight
    And shameful treason, who through guile hath slayn
    The prowest knight, that ever field did fight,
    Even stout *Sans foy* (O who can then refrayn?)
Whose shield he beares renverst, the more to heape disdayn.

42

'And to augment the glorie of his guile,
    His dearest love the faire Fidessa loe
    Is there possessed of the traytour vile,
    Who reapes the harvest sowen by his foe,
    Sowen in bloudy field, and bought with woe:
    That brothers hand shall dearely well requight
    So be, ô Queene, you equall favour showe.'
    Him litle answerd th' angry Elfin knight;
He never meant with words, but swords to plead his right.

43

But threw his gauntlet as a sacred pledge,
    His cause in combat the next day to try:
    So been they parted both, with harts on edge,
    To be aveng'd each on his enimy.
    That night they pas in joy and jollity,
    Feasting and courting both in bowre and hall;
    For Steward was excessive *Gluttonie*
    That of his plenty poured forth to all;
Which doen, the Chamberlain *Slowth* did to rest them call.

44

Now whenas darkesome night had all displayd
    Her coleblacke curtein over brightest skye,
    The warlike youthes on dayntie couches layd,
    Did chace away sweet sleepe from sluggish eye,
    To muse on meanes of hoped victory.
    But whenas *Morpheus* had with leaden mace
    Arrested all that courtly company,
    Up-rose *Duessa* from her resting place,
And to the Paynims lodging comes with silent pace.

45

Whom broad awake she finds, in troublous fit,
 Forecasting, how his foe he might annoy,
 And him amoves with speaches seeming fit:
 'Ah deare *Sans joy*, next dearest to *Sans foy*,
 Cause of my new griefe, cause of my new joy,
 Joyous, to see his ymage in mine eye,
 And greev'd to thinke how foe did him destroy,
 That was the flowre of grace and chevalrye;
Lo his *Fidessa* to thy secret faith I flye.'

46

With gentle wordes he can her fairely greet,
 And bad say on the secret of her hart.
 Then sighing soft, 'I learne that litle sweet
 Oft tempred is' (quoth she) 'with muchell smart:
 For since my brest was launcht with lovely dart
 Of deare *Sansfoy*, I never joyed howre,
 But in eternall woes my weaker hart
 Have wasted, loving him with all my powre,
And for his sake have felt full many an heavie stowre.

47

'At last when perils all I weened past,
 And hop'd to reape the crop of all my care,
 Into new woes unweeting I was cast,
 By this false faytor, who unworthie ware
 His worthy shield, whom he with guilefull snare
 Entrapped slew, and brought to shamefull grave.
 Me silly maid away with him he bare,
 And ever since hath kept in darksom cave,
For that I would not yeeld, that so *Sans-foy* I gave.

48

'But since faire Sunne hath sperst that lowring clowd,
 And to my loathed life now shewes some light,
 Under your beams I will me safely shrowd,
 From dreaded storme of his disdainfull spight:
 To you th' inheritance belonges by right
 Of brothers prayse, to you eke longs his love.
 Let not his love, let not his restlesse spright
 Be unreveng'd, that calles to you above
From wandring *Stygian* shores, where it doth endlesse move.'

49

Thereto said he, 'faire Dame be nought dismaid
    For sorrowes past; their griefe is with them gone:
    Ne yet of present perill be affraid;
    For needlesse feare did never vantage none,
    And helplesse hap it booteth not to mone.
    Dead is *Sans-foy*, his vitall paines are past,
    Though greeved ghost for vengeance deep do grone:
    He lives that shall him pay his dewties last,
And guiltie Elfin bloud shall sacrifice in hast.'

50

'O but I feare the fickle freakes' (quoth shee)
    'Of fortune false, and oddes of armes in field.'
    'Why dame' (quoth he) 'what oddes can ever bee,
    Where both do fight alike, to win or yield?'
    'Yea but' (quoth she) 'he beares a charmed shield,
    And eke enchaunted armes, that none can perce,
    Ne none can wound the man, that does them wield.'
    'Charmd or enchaunted' (answered he then ferce)
'I no whitt reck, ne you the like need to reherce.

51

'But faire *Fidessa*, sithens fortunes guile,
    Or enimies powre hath now captived you,
    Returne from whence ye came, and rest a while
    Till morrow next, that I the Elfe subdew,
    And with *Sans foyes* dead dowry you endew.'
    'Ay me, that is a double death' (she said)
    'With proud foes sight my sorrow to renew:
    Where ever yet I be, my secret aid
Shall follow you.' So passing forth she him obaid.

Canto V

The faithfull knight in equall field
Subdewes his faithlesse foe,
Whom false Duessa saves, and for
His cure to hell does goe.

1

The noble hart, that harbours vertuous thought,
  And is with child of glorious great intent,
  Can never rest, untill it forth have brought
  Th' eternall brood of glorie excellent:
  Such restlesse passion did all night torment
  The flaming corage of that Faery knight,
  Devizing, how that doughtie turnament
  With greatest honour he atchieven might;
Still did he wake, and still did watch for dawning light.

2

At last the golden Orientall gate,
  Of greatest heaven gan to open faire,
  And *Phœbus* fresh, as bridegrome to his mate,
  Came dauncing forth, shaking his deawie haire:
  And hurld his glistring beams through gloomy aire.
  Which when the wakeful Elfe perceiv'd streight way,
  He started up, and did him selfe prepaire,
  In sun-bright armes, and battalious array:
For with that Pagan proud he combat will that day.

3

And forth he comes into the commune hall,
  Where earely waite him many a gazing eye,
  To weet what end to straunger knights may fall.
  There many Minstrales maken melody,
  To drive away the dull melancholy,
  And many Bardes, that to the trembling chord
  Can tune their timely voyces cunningly,
  And many Chroniclers, that can record
Old loves, and warres for Ladies doen by many a Lord.

4

Soone after comes the cruell Sarazin,
  In woven maile all armed warily,
  And sternly lookes at him, who not a pin
  Does care for looke of living creatures eye.
  They bring them wines of *Greece* and *Araby*,

And daintie spices fetcht from furthest *Ynd*,
To kindle heat of corage privily:
And in the wine a solemne oth thy bynd
T' observe the sacred lawes of armes, that are assynd.

5

At last forth comes that far renowmed Queene,
   With royall pomp and Princely majestie;
   She is ybrought unto a paled greene,
   And placed under stately canapee,
   The warlike feates of both those knights to see.
   On th' other side in all mens open vew
   Duessa placed is, and on a tree
   Sans-foy his shield is hangd with bloudy hew:
Both those the lawrell girlonds to the victor dew.

6

A shrilling trompett sownded from on hye,
   And unto battaill bad them selves addresse:
   Their shining shieldes about their wrests they tye,
   And burning blades about their heads do blesse,
   The instruments of wrath and heavinesse:
   With greedy force each other doth assayle,
   And strike so fiercely, that they do impresse
   Deepe dinted furrowes in the battred mayle;
The yron walles to ward their blowes are weak and fraile.

7

The Sarazin was stout, and wondrous strong,
   And heaped blowes like yron hammers great:
   For after bloud and vengeance he did long.
   The knight was fiers, and full of youthly heat:
   And doubled strokes, like dreaded thunders threat:
   For all for prayse and honour he did fight.
   Both stricken strike, and beaten both do beat,
   That from their shields forth flyeth firie light,
And helmets hewen deepe, shew marks of eithers might.

8

So th' one for wrong, the other strives for right:
   As when a Gryfon seized of his pray,
   A Dragon fiers encountreth in his flight,
   Through widest ayre making his ydle way,
   That would his rightfull ravine rend away:

With hideous horrour both together smight,
And souce so sore, that they the heavens affray:
The wise Southsayer seeing so sad sight,
Th' amazed vulgar tels of warres and mortall fight.

9

So th' one for wrong, the other strives for right,
    And each to deadly shame would drive his foe:
    The cruell steele so greedily doth bight
    In tender flesh, that streames of bloud down flow
    With which the armes, that earst so bright did show,
    Into a pure vermillion now are dyde:
    Great ruth in all the gazers harts did grow,
    Seeing the gored woundes to gape so wyde,
That victory they dare not wish to either side.

10

At last the Paynim chaunst to cast his eye,
    His suddein eye, flaming with wrathfull fyre,
    Upon his brothers shield, which hong thereby:
    Therewith redoubled was his raging yre,
    And said, 'Ah wretched sonne of wofull syre,
    Doest thou sit wayling by blacke *Stygian* lake,
    Whilest here thy shield is hangd for victors hyre,
    And sluggish german doest thy forces slake,
To after-send his foe, that him may overtake?

11

'Goe caytive Elfe, him quickly overtake,
    And soone redeeme from his long wandring woe;
    Goe guiltie ghost, to him my message make,
    That I his shield have quit from dying foe.'
    Therewith upon his crest he stroke him so,
    That twise he reeled, readie twise to fall;
    End of the doubtfull battell deemed tho
    The lookers on, and lowd to him gan call
The false *Duessa*, 'Thine the shield, and I, and all.'

12

Soone as the Faerie heard his Ladie speake,
    Out of his swowning dreame he gan awake,
    And quickning faith, that earst was woxen weake,
    The creeping deadly cold away did shake:
    Tho mov'd with wrath, and shame, and Ladies sake,
    Of all attonce he cast avengd to bee,

And with so' exceeding furie at him strake,
That forced him to stoupe upon his knee;
Had he not stouped so, he should have cloven bee.

13

And to him said, 'Goe now proud Miscreant,
Thy selfe thy message doe to german deare,
Alone he wandring thee too long doth want:
Goe say, his foe thy shield with his doth beare.'
Therewith his heavie hand he high gan reare,
Him to have slaine; when loe a darkesome clowd
Upon him fell: he no where doth appeare,
But vanisht is. The Elfe him cals alowd,
But answer none receives: the darknes him does shrowd.

14

In haste *Duessa* from her place arose,
And to him running said, 'O prowest knight,
That ever Ladie to her love did chose,
Let now abate the terrour of your might,
And quench the flame of furious despight,
And bloudie vengeance; lo th' infernall powres
Covering your foe with cloud of deadly night,
Have borne him hence to *Plutoes* balefull bowres.
The conquest yours, I yours, the shield, and glory yours.'

15

Not all so satisfide, with greedy eye
He sought all round about, his thirstie blade
To bath in bloud of faithlesse enemy;
Who all that while lay hid in secret shade:
He standes amazed, how he thence should fade.
At last the trumpets Triumph sound on hie,
And running Heralds humble homage made,
Greeting him goodly with new victorie,
And to him brought the shield, the cause of enmitie.

16

Wherewith he goeth to that soveraine Queene,
And falling her before on lowly knee,
To her makes present of his service seene:
Which she accepts, with thankes, and goodly gree,
Greatly advauncing his gay chevalree.
So marcheth home, and by her takes the knight,
Whom all the people follow with great glee,

Shouting, and clapping all their hands on hight,
That all the aire is fils, and flyes to heaven bright.

17

Home is he brought, and laid in sumptous bed:
  Where many skilfull leaches him abide,
  To salve his hurts, that yet still freshly bled.
  In wine and oyle they wash his woundes wide,
  And softly can embalme on every side.
  And all the while, most heavenly melody
  About the bed sweet musicke did divide,
  Him to beguile of griefe and agony:
And all the while *Duessa* wept full bitterly.

18

As when a wearie traveiler, that strayes
  By muddy shore of broad seven-mouthed *Nile*,
  Unweeting of the perillous wandring wayes,
  Doth meete a cruell craftie Crocodile,
  Which in false griefe hyding his harmefull guile,
  Doth weepe full sore, and sheddeth tender teares:
  The foolish man, that pitties all this while
  His mournefull plight, is swallowd up unwares,
Forgetfull of his owne, that mindes an others cares.

19

So wept *Duessa* until eventide,
  That shyning lampes in *Joves* high house were light:
  Then forth she rose, ne lenger would abide,
  But comes unto the place, where th' Hethen knight
  In slombring swownd nigh voyd of vitall spright,
  Lay cover'd with inchaunted cloud all day:
  Whom when she found, as she him left in plight,
  To wayle his woefull case she would not stay,
But to the easterne coast of heaven makes speedy way.

20

Where griesly *Night*, with visage deadly sad,
  That *Phœbus* chearefull face durst never vew,
  And in a foule blacke pitchie mantle clad,
  She findes forth comming from her darkesome mew,
  Where she all day did hide her hated hew.
  Before the dore her yron charet stood,
  Alreadie harnessed for journey new;

And coleblacke steedes yborne of hellish brood,
That on their rustie bits did champ, as they were wood.

21

Who when she saw *Duessa* sunny bright,
  Adornd with gold and jewels shining cleare,
  She greatly grew amazed at the sight,
  And th' unacquainted light began to feare:
  For never did such brightnesse there appeare,
  And would have backe retyred to her cave,
  Untill the witches speech she gan to heare,
  Saying, 'yet, ô thou dreaded Dame, I crave
Abide, till I have told the message, which I have.'

22

She stayd, and foorth *Duessa* gan proceede.
  'O thou most auncient Grandmother of all,
  More old then *Jove*, whom thou at first didst breede,
  Or that great house of Gods cælestiall,
  Which wast begot in *Dæmogorgons* hall,
  And sawst the secrets of the world unmade,
  Why suffredst thou thy Nephewes deare to fall
  With Elfin sword, most shamefully betrade?
Lo where the stout *Sansjoy* doth sleepe in deadly shade.

23

'And him before, I saw with bitter eyes
  The bold *Sansfoy* shrinke underneath his speare;
  And now the pray of fowles in field he lyes,
  Nor wayld of friends, nor layd on groning beare,
  That whylome was to me too dearely deare.
  O what of Gods then boots it to be borne,
  If old *Aveugles* sonnes so evill heare?
  Or who shall not great *Nightes* children scorne,
When two of three her Nephewes are so fowle forlorne?

24

'Up then, up dreary Dame, of darknesse Queene,
  Go gather up the reliques of thy race,
  Or else goe them avenge, and let be seene,
  That dreaded *Night* in brightest day hath place,
  And can the children of faire light deface.'
  Her feeling speeches some compassion moved
  In hart, and chaunge in that great mothers face:
  Yet pittie in her hart was never proved
Till then: for evermore she hated, never loved

25

And said, 'Deare daughter rightly may I rew
  The fall of famous children borne of mee,
  And good successes which their foes ensew:
  But who can turne the streame of destinee,
  Or breake the chayne of strong necessitee,
  Which fast is tyde to *Joves* eternall seat?
  The sonnes of Day he favoureth, I see,
  And by my ruines thinkes to make them great:
To make one great by others losse, is bad excheat.

26

'Yet shall they not escape so freely all;
  For some shall pay the price of others guilt:
  And he the man that made *Sansfoy* to fall,
  Shall with his owne bloud price that he hath spilt.
  But what art thou, that telst of Nephews kilt?'
  'I that do seeme not I, *Duessa* am,'
  (Quoth she) 'how ever now in garments gilt,
  And gorgeous gold arayd I to thee came;
Duessa I, the daughter of Deceipt and Shame.'

27

Then bowing downe her aged backe, she kist
  The wicked witch, saying, 'In that faire face
  The false resemblance of Deceipt, I wist,
  Did closely lurke; yet so true-seeming grace
  It carried, that I scarse in darkesome place
  Could it discerne, though I the mother bee
  Of falshood, and roote of *Duessaes* race.
  O welcome child, whom I have longd to see,
And now have seene unwares. Lo now I go with thee.'

28

Then to her yron wagon she betakes,
  And with her beares the fowle welfavourd witch:
  Through mirkesome aire her readie way she makes.
  Her twyfold Teme, of which two blacke as pitch,
  And two were browne, yet each to each unlich,
  Did softly swim away, ne ever stampe,
  Unlesse she chaunst their stubborne mouths to twitch;
  Then foming tarre, their bridles they would champe,
And trampling the fine element, would fiercely rampe.

29

So well they sped, that they be come at length
    Unto the place, whereas the Paynim lay,
    Devoid of outward sense, and native strength,
    Coverd with charmed cloud from vew of day,
    And sight of men, since his late luckelesse fray.
    His cruell wounds with cruddy bloud congealed,
    They binden up so wisely, as they may,
    And handle softly, till they can be healed:
So lay him in her charet, close in night concealed.

30

And all the while she stood upon the ground,
    The wakefull dogs did never cease to bay,
    As giving warning of th' unwonted sound,
    With which her yron wheeles did them affray,
    And her darke griesly looke them much dismay;
    The messenger of death, the ghastly Owle
    With drearie shriekes did also her bewray;
    And hungry Wolves continually did howle,
At her abhorred face, so filthy and so fowle.

31

Thence turning backe in silence soft they stole,
    And brought the heavie corse with easy pace
    To yawning gulfe of deepe *Avernus* hole.
    By that same hole an entrance dark and bace
    With smoake and sulphure hiding all the place,
    Descends to hell: there creatures never past,
    That backe returned without heavenly grace;
    But dreadfull *Furies*, which their chaines have brast,
And damned sprights sent forth to make ill men aghast.

32

By that same way the direfull dames doe drive
    Their mournefull charet, fild with rusty blood,
    And downe to *Plutoes* house are come bilive:
    Which passing through, on every side them stood
    The trembling ghosts with sad amazed mood,
    Chattring their yron teeth, and staring wide
    With stonie eyes; and all the hellish brood
    Of feends infernall flockt on every side,
To gaze on earthly wight, that with the Night durst ride.

33

They pas the bitter waves of *Acheron*,
　Where many soules sit wailing woefully,
　And come to fiery flood of *Phlegeton*,
　Whereas the damned ghosts in torments fry,
　And with sharpe shrilling shriekes doe bootlesse cry,
　Cursing high *Jove*, the which them thither sent,
　The house of endlesse paine is built thereby,
　In which ten thousand sorts of punishment
The cursed creatures doe eternally torment.

34

Before the threshold dreadfull *Cerberus*
　His three deformed heads did lay along,
　Curled with thousand adders venemous,
　And lilled forth his bloudie flaming tong:
　At them he gan to reare his bristles strong,
　And felly gnarre, untill dayes enemy
　Did him appease; then downe his taile he hong
　And suffered them to passen quietly:
For she in hell and heaven had power equally.

35

There was *Ixion* turned on a wheele,
　For daring tempt the Queene of heaven to sin;
　And *Sisyphus* an huge round stone did reele
　Against an hill, ne might from labour lin;
　There thirstie *Tantalus* hong by the chin;
　And *Tityus* fed a vulture on his maw;
　Typhœus joynts were stretched on a gin,
　Theseus condemned to endlesse slouth by law,
And fifty sisters water in leake vessels draw.

36

They all beholding worldly wights in place,
　Leave off their worke, unmindfull of their smart,
　To gaze on them; who forth by them doe pace,
　Till they be come unto the furthest part:
　Where was a Cave ywrought by wonderous art,
　Deepe, darke, uneasie, dolefull, comfortlesse,
　In which sad *Æsculapius* farre a part
　Emprisond was in chaines remedilesse,
For that *Hippolytus* rent corse he did redresse.

37

Hippolytus a jolly huntsman was,
　　That wont in charet chace the foming Bore;
　　He all his Peeres in beautie did surpas,
　　But Ladies love as losse of time forbore:
　　His wanton stepdame loved him the more,
　　But when she saw her offred sweets refused
　　Her love she turnd to hate, and him before
　　His father fierce of treason false accused,
And with her gealous termes his open eares abused.

38

Who all in rage his Sea-god syre besought,
　　Some cursed vengeance on his sonne to cast:
　　From surging gulf two monsters straight were brought,
　　With dread whereof his chacing steedes aghast,
　　Both charet swift and huntsman overcast.
　　His goodly corps on ragged cliffs yrent,
　　Was quite desmembred, and his members chast
　　Scattered on every mountaine, as he went,
That of *Hippolytus* was left no moniment.

39

His cruell stepdame seeing what was donne,
　　Her wicked dayes with wretched knife did end,
　　In death avowing th' innocence of her sonne.
　　Which hearing his rash Syre, began to rend
　　His haire, and hasty tongue that did offend:
　　Tho gathering up the relicks of his smart
　　By *Dianes* meanes, who was *Hippolyts* frend,
　　Them brought to *Aesculape*, that by his art
Did heale them all againe, and joyned every part.

40

Such wondrous science in mans wit to raine
　　When *Jove* avizd, that could the dead revive,
　　And fates expired could renew again,
　　Of endlesse life he might him not deprive,
　　But unto hell did thrust him downe alive,
　　With flashing thunderbolt ywounded sore:
　　Where long remaining, he did alwaies strive
　　Himselfe with salves to health for to restore,
And slake the heavenly fire, that raged evermore.

41

There auncient Night arriving, did alight
　　From her high wearie waine, and in her armes
　　To *Aesculapius* brought the wounded knight:
　　Whom having softly disarayd of armes,
　　Tho gan to him discover all his harmes,
　　Beseeching him with prayer, and with praise,
　　If either salves, or oyles, or herbs, or charmes
　　A fordonne wight from dore of death mote raise,
He would at her request prolong her nephews daies.

42

'Ah Dame' (quoth he) 'tho temptest me in vaine,
　　To dare the thing, which daily yet I rew,
　　And the old cause of my continued paine
　　With like attempt to like end to renew.
　　Is not enough, that thrust from heaven dew
　　Here endlesse penance for one fault I pay,
　　But that redoubled crime with vengeaunce new
　　Thou biddest me to eeke? Can Night defray
The wrath of thundring *Jove*, that rules both night and day?'

43

'Not so' (quoth she) 'but sith that heavens king
　　From hope of heaven hath thee excluded quight,
　　Why fearest thou, that canst not hope for thing,
　　And fearest not, that more thee hurten might,
　　Now in the powre of everlasting Night?
　　Goe to then, ô thou far renowmed sonne
　　Of great *Apollo*, shew thy famous might
　　In medicine, that else hath to thee wonne
Great paines, and greater praise, both never to be donne.'

44

Her words prevaild:　　And then the learned leach
　　His cunning hand gan to his wounds to lay,
　　And all things else, the which his art did teach:
　　Which having seene, from thence arose away
　　The mother of dread darknesse, and let stay
　　Aveugles sonne there in the leaches cure,
　　And backe returning tooke her wonted way,
　　To runne her timely race, whilst *Phœbus* pure
In westerne waves his wearie wagon did recure.

45

The false *Duessa* leaving noyous Night,
   Returnd to stately pallace of dame Pride;
   Where when she came, she found the Faery knight
   Departed thence, albe his woundes wide
   Not throughly heald, unreadie were to ride.
   Good cause he had to hasten thence away;
   For on a day his wary Dwarfe had spide
   Where in a dongeon deepe huge numbers lay
Of caytive wretched thrals, that wayled night and day.

46

A ruefull sight, as could be seene with eie;
   Of whom he learned had in secret wise
   The hidden cause of their captivitie,
   How mortgaging their lives to *Covetise*,
   Through wastfull Pride, and wanton Riotise,
   They were by law of that proud Tyrannesse
   Provokt with *Wrath* and *Envies* false surmise,
   Condemned to that Dongeon mercilesse,
Where they should live in woe, and die in wretchednesse.

47

There was that great proud king of *Babylon*,
   That would compell all nations to adore,
   And him as onely God to call upon,
   Till through celestiall doome throwne out of dore,
   Into an Oxe he was transform'd of yore:
   There also was king *Crœsus*, that enhaunst
   His heart too high through his great riches store;
   And proud *Antiochus*, the which advaunst
His cursed hand against God, and on his altars daunst.

48

And them long time before, great *Nimrod* was,
   That first the world with sword and fire warrayd;
   And after him old *Ninus* farre did pas
   In princely pompe, of all the world obayd;
   There also was that mightie Monarch layd
   Low under all, yet above all in pride,
   That name of native syre did fowle upbrayd,
   And would as *Ammons* sonne be magnifide,
Till scornd of God and man a shamefull death he dide.

49

All these together in one heape were throwne,
  Like carkases of beasts in butchers stall.
  And in another corner wide were strowne
  The antique ruines of the *Romaines* fall:
  Great *Romulus* the Grandsyre of them all,
  Proud *Tarquin*, and too lordly *Lentulus*,
  Stout *Scipio*, and stubborne *Hanniball*,
  Ambitious *Sylla*, and sterne *Marius*,
High *Cæsar*, *great Pompey*, and fiers *Antonius*.

50

Amongst these mighty men were wemen mixt,
  Proud wemen, vaine, forgetfull of their yoke:
  The bold *Semiramis*, whose sides transfixt
  With sonnes own blade, her fowle reproches spoke;
  Faire *Sthenobœa*, that her selfe did choke
  With wilfull cord, for wanting of her will;
  High minded *Cleopatra*, that with stroke
  Of Aspes sting her selfe did stoutly kill:
And thousands moe the like, that did that dongeon fill.

51

Besides the endlesse routs of wretched thralles,
  Which thither were assembled day by day,
  From all the world after their wofull falles,
  Through wicked pride, and wasted wealthes decay.
  But most of all, which in that Dongeon lay,
  Fell from high Princes courts, of Ladies bowres,
  Where they in idle pompe, or wanton play,
  Consumed had their goods, and thriftlesse howres,
And lastly throwne themselves into these heavy stowres.

52

Whose case when as the carefull Dwarfe had tould,
  And made ensample of their mournefull sight
  Unto his maister, he no lenger would
  There dwell in perill of like painefull plight,
  But early rose, and ere that dawning light
  Discovered had the world to heaven wyde,
  He by a privie Posterne tooke his flight,
  That of no envious eyes he mote be spyde:
For doubtlesse death ensewd, if any him descryde.

53

Scarse could he footing find in that fowle way,
    For many corses, like great Lay-stall
    Of murdred men which therein strowed lay,
    Without remorse, of decent funerall:
    Which all through that great Princesse pride did fall
And came to shamefull end. And them beside
    Forth ryding underneath the castell wall,
    A donghill of dead carkases he spide,
The dreadfull spectacle of that sad house of *Pride*.

Canto VI

From lawlesse lust by wondrous grace
Fayre Una is releast:
Whom salvage nation does adore,
And learnes her wise beheast.

1

As when a ship, that flyes faire under saile,
   An hidden rocke escaped hath unwares,
   That lay in waite her wrack for to bewaile,
   The Marriner yet halfe amazed stares
   At perill past, and yet in doubt ne dares
   To joy at his fool-happie oversight:
   So doubly is distrest twixt joy and cares
   The dreadlesse courage of this Elfin knight,
Having escapt so sad ensamples in his sight.

2

Yet sad he was that his too hastie speed
   The fayre *Duess'* had forst him to leave behind;
   And yet more sad, that *Una* his deare dreed
   Her truth hath staind with treason so unkind;
   Yet crime in her could never creature find,
   But for his love, and for her own selfe sake,
   She wandred had from one to other *Ynd*.
   Him for to seeke, ne ever would forsake,
Till her unwares the fiers *Sansloy* did overtake.

3

Who after *Archimagoes* fowle defeat,
   Led her away into a forest wilde,
   And turning wrathfull fire to lustfull heat,
   With beastly sin thought her to have defilde,
   And made the vassall of his pleasures vilde.
   Yet first he cast by treatie, and by traynes,
   Her to perswade, that stubborne fort to yilde:
   For greater conquest of hard love he gaynes,
That workes it to his will, then he that it constraines.

4

With fawning wordes he courted her a while,
   And looking lovely, and oft sighing sore,
   Her constant hart did tempt with diverse guile:
   But wordes, and lookes, and sighes she did abhore,
   As rocke of Diamond stedfast evermore.

Yet for to feed his fyrie lustfull eye,
   He snatcht the vele, that hong her face before;
   Then gan her beautie shine, as brightest skye,
And burnt his beastly hart t'efforce her chastitye.

5

So when he saw his flatt'ring arts to fayle,
   And subtile engines bet from batteree,
   With greedy force he gan the fort assayle,
   Whereof he weend possessed soone to bee,
   And win rich spoile of ransackt chastetee.
   Ah heavens, that do this hideous act behold,
   And heavenly virgin thus outraged see,
   How can ye vengeance just so long withhold,
And hurle not flashing flames upon that Paynim bold?

6

The pitteous mayden carefull comfortlesse,
   Does throw out thrilling shriekes, and shrieking cryes,
   The last vaine helpe of womens great distresse,
   And with loud plaints importuneth the skyes,
   That molten starres do drop like weeping eyes;
   And *Phœbus* flying so most shamefull sight,
   His blushing face in foggy cloud implyes,
   And bides for shame.   What wit of mortall wight
Can now devise to quit a thrall from such a plight?

7

Eternall providence exceeding thought,
   Where none appeares can make her selfe a way:
   A wondrous way it for this Lady wrought,
   From Lyons clawes to pluck the griped pray.
   Her shrill outcryes and shriekes so loud did bray,
   That all the woodes and forestes did resownd;
   A troupe of *Faunes* and *Satyres* far away
   Within the wood were dauncing in a rownd,
Whiles old *Sylvanus* slept in shady arber sownd.

8

Who when they heard that pitteous strained voice,
   In hast forsooke their rurall meriment,
   And ran towards the far rebownded noyce,
   To weet, what wight so loudly did lament.
   Unto the place they come incontinent:
   Whom when the raging Sarazin espide,

A rude, mishapen, monstrous rablement,
  Whose like he never saw, he durst not bide,
But got his ready steed, and fast away gan ride.

9

The wyld woodgods arrived in the place,
  There find a virgin dolefull desolate,
  With ruffled rayments, and faire blubbred face,
  As her outrageous foe had left her late,
  And trembling yet through feare of former hate;
  All stand amazed at so uncouth sight,
  And gin to pittie her unhappie state,
  All stand astonied at her beautie bright,
In their rude eyes unworthie of so wofull plight.

10

She more amaz'd, in double dread doth dwell;
  And every tender part for feare does shake:
  As when a greedie Wolfe through honger fell
  A seely Lambe farre from the flock does take,
  Of whom he meanes his bloudie feast to make,
  A Lyon spyes fast running towards him,
  The innocent pray in hast he does forsake,
  Which quit from death yet quakes in every lim
With chaunge of feare, to see the Lyon looke so grim.

11

Such fearefull fit assaid her trembling hart,
  Ne word to speake, ne joynt to move she had:
  The salvage nation feele her secret smart,
  And read her sorrow in her count'nance sad:
  Their frowning forheads with rough hornes yclad,
  And rusticke horror all a side doe lay,
  And gently grenning, shew a semblance glad
  To comfort her, and feare to put away,
Their backward bent knees teach her humbly to obay.

12

The doubtfull Damzell dare not yet commit
  Her single person to their barbarous truth,
  But still twixt feare and hope amazd does sit,
  Late learnd what harme to hastie trust ensu'th,
  They in compassion of her tender youth,
  And wonder of her beautie soveraine,
  Are wonne with pitty and unwonted ruth,

And all prostrate upon the lowly plaine,
Doe kisse her feet, and fawne on her with count'nance faine.

13

Their harts she ghesseth by their humble guise,
   And yieldes her to extremitie of time;
   So from the ground she fearelesse doth arise,
   And walketh forth without suspect of crime:
   They all as glad, as birdes of joyous Prime,
   Thence lead her forth, about her dauncing round,
   Shouting, and singing all a shepheards ryme,
   And with greene braunches strowing all the ground,
Do worship her, as Queene, with olive girlond cround.

14

And all the way their merry pipes they sound,
   That all the woods with doubled Eccho ring,
   And with their horned feet do weare the ground,
   Leaping like wanton kids in pleasant Spring.
   So towards old *Sylvanus* they her bring;
   Who with the noyse awaked, commeth out
   To weet the cause, his weake steps governing,
   And aged limbs on Cypresse stadle stout,
And with an yvie twyne his wast is girt about.

15

Far off he wonders, what them makes so glad,
   Or *Bacchus* merry fruit they did invent,
   Or *Cybeles* franticke rites have made them mad;
   They drawing nigh, unto their God present
   That flowre of faith and beautie excellent.
   The God himselfe vewing that mirrhour rare,
   Stood long amazd, and burnt in his intent;
   His owne faire *Dryope* now he thinkes not faire,
And *Pholoe* fowle, when her to this he doth compaire.

16

The woodborne people fall before her flat,
   And worship her as Goddesse of the wood;
   And old *Sylvanus* selfe bethinkes not, what
   To thinke of wight so faire, but gazing stood,
   In doubt to deeme her borne of earthly brood;
   Sometimes Dame *Venus* selfe he seemes to see,
   But *Venus* never had so sober mood;
   Sometimes *Diana* he her takes to bee,
But misseth bow, and shaftes, and buskins to her knee.

17

By vew of her he ginneth to revive
  His ancient love, and dearest *Cyparisse*
  And calles to mind his pourtraiture alive,
  How faire he was, and yet not faire to this,
  And how he slew with glauncing dart amisse
  A gentle Hynd, the which the lovely boy
  Did love as life, above all worldly blisse;
  For griefe whereof the lad n'ould after joy,
But pynd away in anguish and selfe-wild annoy.

18

The wooddy Nymphes, faire *Hamadryades*
  Her to behold do thither runne apace,
  And all the troupe of light-foot *Naiades*,
  Flocke all about to see her lovely face:
  But when they vewed have her heavenly grace,
  They envie her in their malitious mind,
  And fly away for feare of fowle disgrace:
  But all the *Satyres* scorne their woody kind,
And henceforth nothing faire, but her on earth they find.

19

Glad of such lucke, the luckelesse lucky maid,
  Did her content to please their feeble eyes,
  And long time with that salvage people staid,
  To gather breath in many miseries.
  During which time her gentle wit she plyes,
  To teach them truth, which worshipt her in vaine,
  And made her th' Image of Idolatryes;
  But when their bootlesse zeale she did restraine
From her own worship, they her Asse would worship fayn.

20

It fortuned a noble warlike knight
  By just occasion to that forrest came,
  To seeke his kindred, and the lignage right,
  From whence he tooke his well deserved name:
  He had in armes abroad wonne muchell fame,
  And fild far landes with glorie of his might,
  Plaine, faithfull, true, and enimy of shame,
  And ever lov'd to fight for Ladies right,
But in vaine glorious frayes he litle did delight.

21

A Satyres sonne yborne in forrest wyld,
　By straunge adventure as it did betyde,
　And there begotten of a Lady myld,
　Fayre *Thyamis* the daughter of *Labryde*,
　That was in sacred bands of wedlocke tyde
　To *Therion*, a loose unruly swayne;
　Who had more joy to raunge the forrest wyde,
　And chase the salvage beast with busie payne,
Then serve his Ladies love, and wast in pleasures vayne.

22

The forlorne mayd did with loves longing burne,
　And could not lacke her lovers company,
　But to the woods she goes, to serve her turne,
　And seeke her spouse, that from her still does fly,
　And followes other game and venery:
　A Satyre chaunst her wandring for to find,
　And kindling coles of lust in brutish eye,
　The loyall links of wedlocke did unbind,
And made her person thrall unto his beastly kind.

23

So long in secret cabin there he held
　Her captive to his sensuall desire,
　Till that with timely fruit her belly sweld,
　And bore a boy unto that salvage sire:
　Then home he suffred her for to retire,
　For ransome leaving him the late borne childe;
　Whom till to ryper yeares he gan aspire,
　He noursled up in life and manners wilde,
Emongst wilde beasts and woods, from lawes of men exilde.

24

For all he taught the tender ymp, was but
　To banish cowardize and bastard feare;
　His trembling hand he would him force to put
　Upon the Lyon and the rugged Beare,
　And from the she Beares teats her whelps to teare;
　And eke wyld roring Buls he would him make
　To tame, and ryde their backes not made to beare;
　And the Robuckes in flight to overtake,
That everie beast for feare of him did fly and quake.

25

Thereby so fearelesse, and so fell he grew,
  That his own sire, and maister of his guise
  Did often tremble at his horrid vew,
  And oft for dread of hurt would him advise,
  The angry beasts not rashly to despise,
  Nor too much to provoke; for he would learne
  The Lyon stoup to him in lowly wise,
  (A lesson hard) and make the Libbard sterne
Leave roaring, when in rage he for revenge did earne.

26

And for to make his powre approved more,
  Wyld beasts in yron yokes he would compell;
  The spotted Panther, and the tusked Bore,
  The Pardale swift, and the Tigre cruell;
  The Antelope, and Wolfe both fierce and fell;
  And them constraine in equall teme to draw.
  Such joy he had, their stubborne harts to quell,
  And sturdie courage tame with dreadfull aw,
That his beheast they feared, as a tyrans law.

27

His loving mother came upon a day
  Unto the woods, to see her little sonne;
  And chaunst unwares to meet him in the way,
  After his sportes, and cruell pastime donne,
  When after him a Lyonesse did runne,
  That roaring all with rage, did lowd requere
  Her children deare, whom he away had wonne:
  The Lyon whelpes she saw how he did beare,
And lull in rugged armes, withouten childish feare.

28

The fearefull Dame all quaked at the sight,
  And turning backe, gan fast to fly away,
  Untill with love revokt from vaine affright,
  She hardly yet perswaded was to stay,
  And then to him these womanish words gan say;
  'Ah *Satyrane*, my dearling, and my joy,
  For love of me leave off this dreadfull play;
  To dally thus with death, is no fit toy,
Go find some other play-fellowes, mine own sweet boy.'

29

In these and like delights of bloudy game
    He trayned was, till ryper yeares he raught,
    And there abode, whilst any beast of name
    Walkt in that forest, whom he had not taught
    To feare his force: and then his courage haught
    Desird of forreine foemen to be knowne,
    And far abroad for strange adventures sought:
    In which his might was never overthrowne,
But through all Faery lond his famous worth was blown.

30

Yet evermore it was his manner faire,
    After long labours and adventures spent,
    Unto those native woods for to repaire,
    To see his sire and ofspring auncient.
    And now he thither came for like intent;
    Where he unwares the fairest *Una* found,
    Straunge Lady, in so straunge habiliment,
    Teaching the Satyres, which her sat around,
Trew sacred lore, which from her sweet lips did redound.

31

He wondred at her wisedome heavenly rare,
    Whose like in womens wit he never knew;
    And when her curteous deeds he did compare,
    Gan her admire, and her sad sorrowes rew,
    Blaming of Fortune, which such troubles threw,
    And joyd to make proofe of her crueltie
    On gentle Dame, so hurtlesse, and so trew:
    Thenceforth he kept her goodly company,
And learnd her discipline of faith and veritie.

32

But she all vowd unto the *Redcrosse* knight,
    His wandring perill closely did lament,
    Ne in this new acquaintaunce could delight,
    But her deare heart with anguish did torment,
    And all her wit in secret counsels spent,
    How to escape.   At last in privie wise
    To *Satyrane* she shewed her intent;
    Who glad to gain such favour, gan devise,
How with that pensive Maid he best might thence arise.

33

So on a day when Satyres all were gone,
  To do their service to *Sylvanus* old,
  The gentle virgin left behind alone
  He led away with courage stout and bold.
  Too late it was, to Satyres to be told,
  Or ever hope recover her againe:
  In vaine he seekes that having cannot hold.
  So fast he carried her with carefull paine,
That they the woods are past, and come now to the plaine.

34

The better part now of the lingring day,
  They traveild had, whenas they far espide
  A wearie wight forwandring by the way
  And towards him they gan in hast to ride,
  To weet of newes, that did abroad betide,
  Or tydings of her knight of the *Redcrosse*.
  But he them spying, gan to turne aside,
  For feare as seemd, or for some feigned losse;
More greedy they of newes, fast towards him do crosse.

35

A silly man, in simple weedes forworne,
  And soild with dust of the long dried way;
  His sandales were with toilesome travell torne,
  And face all tand with scorching sunny ray,
  As he had traveild many a sommers day,
  Through boyling sands of *Arabie* and *Ynde*;
  And in his hand a *Jacobs* staffe, to stay
  His wearie limbes upon: and eke behind,
His scrip did hang, in which his needments he did bind.

36

The knight approching nigh, of him inquerd
  Tidings of warre, and of adventure new;
  But warres, nor new adventures none he herd.
  Then *Una* gan to aske, if ought he knew,
  Or heard abroad of that her champion trew,
  That in his armour bare a croslet red.
  'Aye me, Deare dame' (quoth he) 'well may I rew
  To tell the sad sight, which mine eies have red:
These eyes did see that knight both living and eke ded.'

37

That cruell word her tender hart so thrild,
   That suddein cold did runne through every vaine,
   And stony horrour all her sences fild
   With dying fit, that downe she fell for paine.
   The knight her lightly reared up againe,
   And comforted with curteous kind reliefe:
   Then wonne from death, she bad him tellen plaine
   The further processe of her hidden griefe;
The lesser pangs can beare, who hath endur'd the chief.

38

Then gan the Pilgrim thus, 'I chaunst this day,
   This fatall day, that shall I ever rew,
   To see two knights in travell on my way
   (A sory sight) arraung'd in battell new,
   Both beathing vengeaunce, both of wrathfull hew:
   My fearefull flesh did tremble at their strife,
   To see their blades so greedily imbrew,
   That drunke with bloud, yet thristed after life:
What more? the *Redcrosse* knight was slaine with Paynim knife.'

39

'Ah dearest lord' (quoth she) 'how might that bee,
   And he the stoutest knight, that ever wonne?'
   'Ah dearest dame' (quoth he) 'how might I see
   The thing, that might not be, and yet was donne?'
   'Where is' (said *Satyrane*) 'that Paynims sonne,
   That him of life, and us of joy hath reft?'
   'Not far away' (quoth he) 'he hence doth wonne
   Foreby a fountaine, where I late him left
Washing his bloudy wounds, that through the steele were cleft.'

40

Therewith the knight thence marched forth in hast,
   Whiles *Una* with huge heavinesse opprest,
   Could not for sorrow follow him so fast;
   And soone he came, as he the place had ghest,
   Whereas that *Pagan* proud him selfe did rest,
   In secret shadow by a fountaine side:
   Even he it was, that earst would have supprest
   Faire *Una*: whom when *Satyrane* espide,
With fowle reprochfull words he boldly him defide.

41

And said, 'Arise thou cursed Miscreaunt,
  That hast with knightlesse guile and trecherous train
  Faire knighthood fowly shamed, and doest vaunt
  That good knight of the *Redcrosse* to have slain:
  Arise, and with like treason now maintain
  Thy guilty wrong, or else thee guilty yield.'
  The Sarazin this hearing, rose amain,
  And catching up in hast his three square shield,
And shining helmet, soone him buckled to the field.

42

And drawing nigh him said, 'Ah misborne Elfe,
  In evill houre thy foes thee hither sent,
  Another wrongs to wreake upon thy selfe:
  Yet ill thou blamest me, for having blent
  My name with guile and traiterous intent;
  That *Redcrosse* knight, perdie, I never slew,
  But had he beene, where earst his armes were lent,
  Th' enchaunter vaine his errour should not rew:
But thou his errour shalt, I hope now proven trew.'

43

Therewith they gan, both furious and fell,
  To thunder blowes, and fiersly to assaile
  Each other bent his enimy to quell,
  That with their force they perst both plate and maile,
  And made wide furrowes in their fleshes fraile,
  That it would pitty any living eie.
  Large floods of bloud adowne their sides did raile;
  But floods of bloud could not them satisfie:
Both hungred after death: both chose to win, or die.

44

So long they fight, and full revenge pursue,
  That fainting each, themselves to breathen let,
  And oft refreshed, battell oft renue:
  As when two Bores with rancling malice met,
  Their gory sides fresh bleeding fiercely fret,
  Till breathlesse both them selves aside retire,
  Where foming wrath, their cruell tuskes they whet,
  And trample th' earth, the whiles they may respire;
Then backe to fight againe, new breathed and entire.

45

So fiersly, when these knights had breathed once,
  They gan to fight returne, increasing more
  Their puissant force, and cruell rage attonce,
  With heaped strokes more hugely, then before,
  That with their drerie wounds and bloudy gore,
  They both deformed, scarsely could be known.
  By this sad *Una* fraught with anguish sore,
  Led with their noise, which through the aire was thrown,
Arriv'd, where they in erth their fruitles bloud had sown.

46

Whom all so soone as that proud Sarazin
  Espide, he gan revive the memory
  Of his lewd lusts, and late attempted sin,
  And left the doubtfull battell hastily,
  To catch her, newly offred to his eie:
  But *Satyrane* with strokes him turning, staid,
  And sternely bad him other businesse plie,
  Then hunt the steps of pure unspotted Maid:
Wherewith he all enrag'd these bitter speaches said.

47

'O foolish faeries sonne, what furie mad
  Hath thee incenst, to hast thy dolefull fate?
  Were it not better, I that Lady had,
  Then that thou hadst repented it too late?
  Most sencelesse man he, that himselfe doth hate,
  To love another.   Lo then for thine ayd
  Here take thy lovers token on thy pate.'
  So they to fight; the whiles the royall Mayd
Fledd farre away, of that proud Paynim sore afrayd.

48

But that false *Pilgrim*, which that leasing told,
  Being in deed old *Archimage*, did stay
  In secret shadow, all this to behold,
  And much rejoyced in their bloudy fray:
  But when he saw the Damsell passe away
  He left his stond, and her pursewd apace,
  In hope to bring her to her last decay.
  But for to tell her lamentable cace,
And eke this battels end, will need another place.

Canto VII

The Redcrosse knight is captive made
By yaunt proud opprest,
Prince Arthur meets with Una great-
ly with those newes distrest.

I

What man so wise, what earthly wit so ware,
　As to descry the crafty cunning traine,
　By which deceipt doth maske in visour faire,
　And cast her colours dyed deepe in graine,
　To seeme like Truth, whose shape she well can faine,
　And fitting gestures to her purpose frame,
　The guiltlesse man with guile to entertaine?
　Great maistresse of her art was that false Dame,
The false *Duessa*, choked with *Fidessaes* name.

2

Who when returning from the drery *Night*,
　She fownd not in that perilous house of *Pryde*,
　Where she had left, the noble *Redcrosse* knight,
　Her hoped pray; she would no lenger bide,
　But forth she went, to seeke him far and wide.
　Ere long she fownd, whereas he wearie sate,
　To rest him selfe, foreby a fountaine side,
　Disarmed all of yron-coted Plate,
And by his side his steed the grassy forage ate.

3

He feedes upon the cooling shade, and bayes
　His sweatie forehead in the breathing wind,
　Which through the trembling leaves full gently playes
　Wherein the cherefull birds of sundry kind
　Doe chaunt sweet musick, to delight his mind:
　The Witch approching gan him fairely greet,
　And with reproch of carelesnesse unkind
　Upbrayd, for leaving her in place unmeet,
With fowle words tempring faire, soure gall with hony sweet.

4

Unkindnesse past, they gan of solace treat,
　And bathe in pleasaunce of the joyous shade,
　Which shielded them against the boyling heat,
　And with greene boughes decking a gloomy glade,
　About the fountaine like a girlond made;

Whose bubbling wave did ever freshly well,
　　Ne ever would through fervent sommer fade:
　　The sacred Nymph, which therein wont to dwell,
Was out of *Dianes* favor, as it then befell.

5

The cause was this: one day when *Phœbe* fayre
　　With all her band was following the chace,
　　This Nymph, quite tyr'd with heat of scorching ayre
　　Sat downe to rest in middest of the race:
　　The goddesse wroth gan fowly her disgrace,
　　And bad the waters, which from her did flow,
　　Be such as she her selfe was then in place.
　　Thenceforth her waters waxed dull and slow,
And all that drunke thereof, did faint and feeble grow.

6

Hereof this gentle knight unweeting was,
　　And lying downe upon the sandie graile,
　　Drunke of the streame, as cleare as cristall glas;
　　Eftsoones his manly forces gan to faile,
　　And mightie strong was tirnd to feeble fraile.
　　His chaunged powres at first them selves not felt,
　　Till crudled cold his corage gan assaile,
　　And cheareful bloud in faintnesse chill did melt,
Which like a fever fit through all his body swelt.

7

Yet goodly court he made still to his Dame,
　　Pourd out in loosenesse on the grassy grownd,
　　Both carelesse of his health, and of his fame:
　　Till at the last he heard a dreadfull sownd,
　　Which through the wood loud bellowing, did rebownd,
　　That all the earth for terrour seemd to shake,
　　And trees did tremble.　Th' Elfe therewith astownd,
　　Upstarted lightly from his looser make,
And his unready weapons gan in hand to take.

8

But ere he could his armour on him dight,
　　Or gett his shield, his monstrous enimy
　　With sturdie steps came stalking in his sight,
　　An hideous Geant horrible and hye,
　　That with his talnesse seemed to threat the skye,
　　The ground eke groned under him for dreed;

His living like saw never living eye,
    Ne durst behold: his stature did exceed
The hight of three the tallest sonnes of mortall seed.

9

The greatest Earth his uncouth mother was,
    And blustering *Æolus* his boasted sire,
    Who with his breath, which through the world doth pas,
    Her hallow womb did secretly inspire,
    And fild her hidden caves with stormie yre,
    That she conceiv'd; and trebling the dew time,
    In which the wombes of women doe expire,
    Brought forth this monstrous masse of earthly slime,
Puft up with emptie wind, and fild with sinfull crime.

10

So growen great through arrogant delight
    Of th' high descent, whereof he was yborne,
    And through presumption of his matchlesse might,
    All other powres and knighthood he did scorne.
    Such now he marcheth to this man forlorne,
    And left to losse: his stalking steps are stayde
    Upon a snaggy Oke, which he had torne
    Out of his mothers bowelles, and it made
His mortall mace, wherewith his foemen he dismayde.

11

That when the knight he spide, he gan advance
    With huge force and insupportable mayne,
    And towardes him with dreadfull fury praunce;
    Who haplesse, and eke hopelesse, all in vaine
    Did to him pace, sad battaile to darrayne,
    Disarmd, disgrast, and inwardly dismayde,
    And eke so faint in every joynt and vaine,
    Through that fraile fountaine, which him feeble made,
That scarsely could he weeld his bootlesse single blade.

12

The Geaunt strooke so maynly mercilesse,
    That could have overthrowne a stony towre,
    And were not heavenly grace, that him did blesse,
    He had beene pouldred all, as this as flowre:
    But he was wary of that deadly stowre,
    And lightly lept from underneath the blow:
    Yet so exceeding was the villeins powre,

That with the wind it did him overthrow,
And all his sences stound, that still he lay full low.

13

As when that divelish yron Engin wrought
  In deepest Hell, and framd by *Furies* skill,
  With windy Nitre and quick Sulphur fraught,
  And ramd with bullet round, ordaind to kill,
  Conceiveth fire, the heavens it doth fill
  With thundring noyse, and all the ayre doth choke
  That none can breath, nor see, nor heare at will,
  Through smouldry cloud of duskish stincking smoke,
That th' onely breath him daunts, who hath escapt the stroke.

14

So daunted when the Geaunt saw the knight,
  His heavie hand he heaved up on hye,
  And him to dust thought to have battred quight,
  Untill *Duessa* loud to him gan crye;
  'O great *Orgoglio*, greatest under skye,
  O hold thy mortall hand for Ladies sake,
  Hold for my sake, and do him not to dye,
  But vanquisht thine eternall bondslave make,
And me thy worthy meed unto thy Leman take.'

15

He hearkned, and did stay from further harmes,
  To gayne so goodly guerdon as she spake:
  So willingly she came into his armes,
  Who her as willingly to grace did take,
  And was possessed of his new found make.
  Then up he tooke the slombred sencelesse corse,
  And ere he could out of his swowne awake,
  Him to his castle brought with hastie forse,
And in a Dongeon deepe him threw without remorse.

16

From that day forth *Duessa* was his deare,
  And highly honourd in his haughtie eye,
  He gave her gold and purple pall to weare,
  And triple crowne set on her head full hye,
  And her endowd with royall majestye:
  Then for to make her dreaded more of men,
  And peoples harts with awfull terrour tye,
  A monstrous beast ybred in filthy fen
He chose, which he had kept long time in darksome den.

17

Such one it was, as that renowmed Snake
   Which great *Alcides* in *Stremona* slew,
   Long fostred in the filth of *Lerna* lake,
   Whose many heads out budding ever new,
   Did breed him endlesse labour to subdew:
   But this same Monster much more ugly was;
   For seven great heads out of his body grew,
   An yron brest, and backe of scaly bras,
And all embrewd in bloud, his eyes did shine as glas.

18

His tayle was stretched out in wondrous length,
   That to the house of heavenly gods it raught,
   And with extorted powre, and borrow'd strength,
   The ever-burning lamps from thence it brought,
   And prowdly threw to ground, as things of nought;
   And underneath his filthy feet did tread
   The sacred things, and holy heasts foretaught.
   Upon this dreadfull Beast with sevenfold head
He set the false *Duessa*, for more aw and dread.

19

The wofull Dwarfe, which saw his maisters fall,
   Whiles he had keeping of his grasing steed,
   And valiant knight become a caytive thrall,
   When all was past, tooke up his forlorne weed,
   His mightie armour, missing most at need;
   His silver shield, now idle maisterlesse;
   His poynant speare, that many made to bleed,
   The ruefull moniments of heavinesse,
And with them all departes, to tell his great distresse.

20

He had not travaild long, when on the way
   He wofull Ladie, wofull *Una* met,
   Fast flying from the Paynims greedy pray,
   Whilest *Satyrane* him from pursuit did let:
   Who when her eyes she on the Dwarfe had set,
   And saw the signes, that deadly tydings spake,
   She fell to ground for sorrowfull regret,
   And lively breath her sad brest did forsake,
Yet might her pitteous hart be seene to pant and quake.

21

The messenger of so unhappie newes,
　　Would faine have dyde: dead was his hart within,
　　Yet outwardly some little comfort shewes:
　　At last recovering hart, he does begin
　　To rub her temples, and to chaufe her chin,
　　And every tender part does tosse and turne:
　　So hardly he the flitted life does win,
　　Unto her native prison to retourne:
Then gins her grieved ghost thus to lament and mourne.

22

'Ye dreary instruments of dolefull sight,
　　That doe this deadly spectacle behold,
　　Why doe ye lenger feed on loathed light,
　　Or liking find to gaze on earthly mould,
　　Sith cruell fates the carefull threeds unfould,
　　The which my life and love together tyde?
　　Now let the stony dart of senselesse cold
　　Perce to my hart, and pas through every side,
And let eternall night so sad sight fro me hide.

23

'O lightsome day, the lampe of highest *Jove*,
　　First made by him, mens wandring wayes to guyde,
　　When darkenesse he in deepest dongeon drove,
　　Henceforth thy hated face for ever hyde,
　　And shut up heavens windowes shyning wyde:
　　For earthly sight can nought but sorrow breed,
　　And late repentance, which shall long abyde.
　　Mine eyes no more on vanitie shall feed,
But seeled up with death, shall have their deadly meed.'

24

Then downe againe she fell unto the ground;
　　But he her quickly reared up againe:
　　Thrise did she sinke adowne in deadly swownd,
　　And thrise he her reviv'd with busie paine:
　　At last when life recover'd had the raine,
　　And over-wrestled his strong enemie,
　　With foltring tong, and trembling every vaine,
　　'Tell on' (quoth she) 'the wofull Tragedie,
The which these reliques sad present unto mine eie.

25

'Tempestuous fortune hath spent all her spight,
   And thrilling sorrow throwne his utmost dart;
   Thy sad tongue cannot tell more heavy plight,
   Then that I feele, and harbour in mine hart:
   Who hath endur'd the whole, can beare each part.
   If death it be, it is not the first wound,
   That launched hath my brest with bleeding smart.
   Begin, and end the bitter balefull stound;
If lesse, then that I feare, more favour I have found.'

26

Then gan the Dwarfe the whole discourse declare,
   The subtill traines of *Archimago* old;
   The wanton loves of false *Fidessa* faire,
   Bought with the bloud of vanquisht Paynim bold:
   The wretched payre transform'd to treen mould;
   The house of Pride, and perils round about;
   The combat, which he with *Sansjoy* did hould;
   The lucklesse conflict with the Gyant stout,
Wherein captiv'd, of life or death he stood in doubt.

27

She heard with patience all unto the end,
   And strove to maister sorrowfull assay,
   Which greater grew, the more she did contend,
   And almost rent her tender hart in tway;
   And love fresh coles unto her fire did lay:
   For greater love, the greater is the losse.
   Was never Ladie loved dearer day,
   Then she did love the knight of the *Redcrosse*;
For whose deare sake so many troubles her did tosse.

28

At last when fervent sorrow slaked was,
   She up arose, resolving him to find
   Alive or dead: and forward forth doth pas,
   All as the Dwarfe the way to her assynd:
   And evermore in constant carefull mind
   She fed her wound with fresh renewed bale;
   Long tost with stormes, and bet with bitter wind,
   High over hills, and low adowne the dale,
She wandred many a wood, and measurd many a vale.

29

At last she chaunced by good hap to meet
  A goodly knight, faire marching by the way
  Together with his Squire, arayed meet:
  His glitterand armour shined farre away,
  Like glauncing light of *Phœbus* brightest ray;
  From top to toe no place appeared bare,
  That deadly dint of steele endanger may:
  Athwart his brest a bauldrick brave he ware,
That shynd, like twinkling stars, with stons most pretious rare.

30

And in the midst thereof one pretious stone
  Of wondrous worth, and eke of wondrous mights,
  Shapt like a Ladies head, exceeding shone,
  Like *Hesperus* emongst the lesser lights,
  And strove for to amaze the weaker sights;
  Thereby his mortall blade full comely hong
  In yvory sheath, ycarv'd with curious slights;
  Whose hilts were burnisht gold, and handle strong
Of mother pearle, and buckled with a golden tong.

31

His haughtie helmet, horrid all with gold,
  Both glorious brightnesse, and great terrour bred;
  For all the crest a Dragon did enfold
  With greedie pawes, and over all did spred
  His golden wings: his dreadfull hideous hed
  Close couched on the bever, seem'd to throw
  From flaming mouth bright sparkles fiery red,
  That suddeine horror to faint harts did show;
And scaly tayle was stretcht adowne his back full low.

32

Upon the top of all his loftie crest,
  A bounch of haires discolourd diversly,
  With sprincled pearle, and gold full richly drest,
  Did shake, and seem'd to daunce for jollity,
  Like to an Almond tree ymounted hye
  On top of greene *Selinis* all alone,
  With blossoms brave bedecked daintily;
  Whose tender locks do tremble every one
At every little breath, that under heaven is blowne.

33

His warlike shield all closely cover'd was,
  Ne might of mortall eye be ever seene;
  Not made of steele, nor of enduring bras,
  Such earthly mettals soon comsumed bene:
  But all of Diamond perfect pure and cleene
  It framed was, one massie entire mould,
  Hewen out of Adamant rocke with engines keene,
  That point of speare it never percen could,
Ne dint of direfull sword divide the substance would.

34

The same to wight he never wont disclose,
  But when as monsters huge he would dismay,
  Or daunt unequall armies of his foes,
  Or when the flying heavens he would affray;
  For so exceeding shone his glistring ray,
  That *Phœbus* golden face it did attaint,
  As when a cloud his beames doth over-lay;
  And silver *Cynthia* wexed pale and faint,
As when her face is staynd with magicke arts constraint.

35

No magicke arts hereof had any might,
  Nor bloudie wordes of bold Enchaunters call,
  But all that was not such, as seemd in sight,
  Before that shield did face, and suddeine fall:
  And when him list the raskall routes appall,
  Men into stones therewith he could transmew,
  And stones to dust, and dust to nought at all;
  And when him list the prouder lookes subdew,
He would them gazing blind, or turne to other hew.

36

Ne let it seeme, that credence this exceedes,
  For he that made the same, was knowne right well
  To have done much more admirable deedes.
  It *Merlin* was, which whylome did excell
  All living wightes in might of magicke spell:
  Both shield, and sword, and armour all he wrought
  For this young Prince, when first to armes he fell;
  But when he dyde, the Faerie Queene it brought
To Faerie lond, where yet it may be seene, if sought.

37

A gentle youth, his dearely loved Squire
  His speare of heben wood behind him bare,
  Whose harmefull head, thrice heated in the fire,
  Had riven many a brest with pikehead square;
  A goodly person, and could menage faire,
  His stubborne steed with curbed canon bit,
  Who under him did trample as the aire,
  And chauft, that any on his backe should sit;
The yron rowels into frothy fome he bit

38

When as this knight nigh to the Ladie drew,
  With lovely court he gan her entertaine;
  But when he heard her answers loth, he knew
  Some secret sorrow did her heart distraine:
  Which to allay, and calme her storming paine,
  Faire feeling words he wisely gan display,
  And for her humor fitting purpose faine,
  To tempt the cause it selfe for to bewray;
Wherewith enmov'd, these bleeding words she gan to say.

39

'What worlds delights, or joy of living speach
  Can heart, so plungd in sea of sorrowes deepe,
  And heaped with so huge misfortunes, reach?
  The carefull cold beginneth for to creepe,
  And in my heart his yron arrow steepe,
  Soone as I thinke upon my bitter bale:
  Such helplesse harmes yts better hidden keep,
  The rip up griefe, where if may not availe,
My last left comfort is, my woes to weepe and waile.'

40

'Ah Ladie deare,' quoth then the gentle knight,
  'Well may I weene your griefe is wondrous great;
  For wondrous great griefe groneth in my spright,
  Whiles thus I heare you of your sorrowes treat.
  But wofull Ladie let me you intrete,
  For to unfold the anguish of your hart:
  Mishaps are maistred by advice discrete,
  And counsell mittigates the greatest smart;
Found never helpe, who never would his hurts impart.'

41

'O but' (quoth she) 'great griefe will not be tould,
  And can more easily be thought, then said.'
  'Right so;' (quoth he) 'but he, that never would,
  Could never: will to might gives greatest aid.'
  'But griefe' (quoth she) 'does greater grow displaid.'
  If then it find not helpe, and breedes despaire.'
  'Despaire breeds not' (quoth he) 'where faith is staid.'
  'No faith so fast' (quoth she) 'but flesh does paire.'
Flesh may empaire' (quoth he) 'but reason can repaire.'

42

His goodly reason, and well guided speach
  So deepe did settle in her gracious thought,
  That her perswaded to disclose the breach,
  Which love and fortune in her heart had wrought,
  And said; 'faire Sir, I hope good hap hath brought
  You to inquire the secrets of my griefe,
  Or that your wisedome will direct my thought,
  Or that your prowesse can me yield reliefe:
Then heare the story sad, which I shall tell you briefe.

43

'The forlorne Maiden, whom your eyes have seene
  The laughing stocke of fortunes mockeries,
  Am th' only daughter of a King and Queene,
  Whose parents deare, whilest equal destinies
  Did runne about, and their felicities
  The favourable heavens did not envy,
  Did spred their rule through all the territories,
  Which *Phison* and *Euphrates* floweth by,
And *Gehons* golden waves doe wash continually.

44

'Till that their cruell cursed enemy,
  An huge great Dragon horrible in sight,
  Bred in the loathly lakes of *Tartary*,
  With murdrous ravine, and devouring might
  Their kingdome spoild, and countrey wasted quight:
  Themselves, for feare into his jawes to fall,
  He forst to castle strong to take their flight,
  Where fast embard in mighty brasen wall,
He has them now foure yeres besiegd to make them thrall.

45

'Full many knights adventurous and stout
  Have enterprizd that Monster to subdew;
  From every coast that heaven walks about,
  Have thither come the noble Martiall crew,
  That famous hard atchievements still pursew,
  Yet never any could that girlond win,
  But all still shronke, and still he greater grew:
  All they for want of faith, or guilt of sin,
The pitteous pray of his fierce crueltie have bin.

46

'At last yledd with far reported praise,
  Which flying fame throughout the world had spred,
  Of doughtie knights, whom Faery land did raise,
  That noble order hight of Maidenhed,
  Forthwith to court of *Gloriane* I sped,
  Of *Gloriane* great Queene of glory bright,
  Whose kingdomes seat *Cleopolis* is red,
  There to obtaine some such redoubted knight,
That Parents deare from tyrants powre deliver might.

47

'It was my chance (my chance was faire and good)
  There for to find a fresh unproved knight,
  Whose manly hands inbrew'd in guiltie blood
  Had never bene, ne ever by his might
  Had throwne to ground the unregarded right:
  Yet of his prowesse proofe he since hath made
  (I witnesse am) in many a cruell fight;
  The groning ghosts of many one dismaide
Have felt the bitter dint of his avenging blade.

48

'An ye the forlorne reliques of his powre,
  His byting sword, and his devouring speare,
  Which have endured many a dreadfull stowre,
  Can speake his prowesse, that did earst you beare,
  And well could rule: now he hath left you heare,
  To be the record of his ruefull losse,
  And of my dolefull disaventurous deare:
  O heavie record of the good *Redcrosse*,
Where have you left your Lord, that could so well you tosse?

49

'Well hoped I, and faire beginnings had,
   That he my captive langour should redeeme,
   Till all unweeting, an Enchaunter bad
   His sence abusd, and made him to misdeeme
   My loyalty, not such as it did seeme;
   That rather death desire, then such despight.
   Be judge ye heavens, that all things right esteeme,
   How I him lov'd, and love with all my might.
So thought I eke of him, and think I thought aright.

50

'Thenceforth me desolate he quite forsooke,
   To wander, where wilde fortune would me lead,
   And other bywaies he himselfe betooke,
   Where never foot of living wight did tread,
   That brought not backe the balefull body dead;
   In which him chaunced false *Duessa* meete,
   Mine onely foe, mine onely deadly dread,
   Who with her witchcraft and misseeming sweete,
Inveigled him to follow her desires unmeete.

51

'At last by subtill sleights she him betraid
   Unto his foe, a Gyant huge and tall,
   Who him disarmed, dissolute, dismaid,
   Unwares surprised, and with mighty mall
   The monster mercilesse him made to fall,
   Whose fall did never foe before behold;
   And now in darkesome dungeon, wretched thrall,
   Remedilesse, for aie he doth him hold;
This is my cause of griefe, more great, then may be told.'

52

Ere she had ended all, she gan to faint:
   But he her comforted and faire bespake,
   'Certes, Madame, ye have great cause of plaint,
   That stoutest heart, I weene, could cause to quake.
   But be of cheare, and comfort to you take:
   For till I have acquit your captive knight,
   Assure your selfe, I will you not forsake.'
   His chearefull words reviv'd her chearelesse spright,
So forth they went, the Dwarfe them guiding ever right.

Canto VIII

Faire virgin to redeeme her deare
Brings Arthure to the fight:
Who slayes that Gyant, wounds the beast,
And strips Duessa quight.

1

Ay me, how many perils doe enfold
  The righteous man, to make his daily fall:
  Were not, that heavenly grace doth him uphold,
  And stedfast truth acquite him out of all.
  Her love is firme, her care continuall,
  So oft as he through his own foolish pride,
  Or weaknesse is to sinfull bands made thrall:
  Els should this *Redcrosse* knight in bands have dyde,
For whose deliverance she this Prince doth thither guide.

2

They sadly traveild thus, untill they came
  Nigh to a castle builded strong and hie:
  Then cryde the Dwarfe, 'lo yonder is the same,
  In which my Lord my liege doth lucklesse lie,
  Thrall to that Gyants hatefull tyrannie:
  Therefore, deare Sir, your mightie powres assay.'
  The noble knight alighted by and by
  From loftie steede, and bad the Ladie stay,
To see what end of fight should him befall that day.

3

So with the Squire, th' admirer of his might,
  He marched forth towardes that castle wall;
  Whose gates he found fast shut, ne living wight
  To ward the same, nor answere commers call.
  Then tooke that Squire an horne of bugle small,
  Which hong adowne his side in twisted gold,
  And tassels gay.   Wyde wonders over all
  Of that same hornes great virtues weren told,
Which had approved bene in uses manifold.

4

Was never wight, that heard that shrilling sound,
  But trembling feare did feel in every vaine;
  Three miles it might be easie heard around,
  And Ecchoes three answerd it selfe againe:
  No false enchauntment, nor deceiptfull traine

Might once abide the terror of that blast,
But presently was voide and wholly vaine:
No gate so strong, no locke so firme and fast,
But with that percing noise flew open quite, or brast.

5

The same before the Geants gate he blew,
  That all the castle quaked from the ground,
  And every dore of freewill open flew.
  The Gyant selfe dismaied with that sownd,
  Where he with his *Duessa* dalliaunce fownd,
  In hast came rushing forth from inner bowre,
  With staring countenance sterne, as one astownd,
  And staggering steps, to weet, what suddein stowre
Had wrought that horror strange, and dar'd his dreaded powre.

6

And after him the proud *Duessa* came,
  High mounted on her manyheaded beast,
  And every head with fyrie tongue did flame,
  And every head was crowned on his creast,
  And bloudie mouthed with late cruell feast.
  That when the knight beheld, his mightie shild
  Upon his manly arme he soone addrest,
  And at him fiercely flew, with courage fild,
And eger greedinesse through every member thrild.

7

Therewith the Gyant buckled him to fight,
  Inflamd with scornefull wrath and high disdaine,
  And lifting up his dreadfull club on hight,
  All arm'd with ragged snubbes and knottie graine,
  Him thought at first encounter to have slaine.
  But wise and warie was that noble Pere,
  And lightly leaping from so monstrous maine,
  Did faire avoide the violence him nere;
It booted nought, to thinke, such thunderbolts to beare.

8

Ne shame he thought to shonne so hideous might:
  The idle stroke, enforcing furious way,
  Missing the marke of his misaymed sight
  Did fall to ground, and with his heavy sway
  So deeply dinted in the driven clay,
  That three yardes deepe a furrow up did throw:

The sad earth, wounded with so sore assay,
  Did grone full grievous underneath the blow,
And trembling with strange feare, did like an earthquake show.

9

As when almightie *Jove* in wrathfull mood,
  To wreake the guilt of mortall sins is bent,
  Hurles forth his thundring dart with deadly food,
  Enrold in flames, and smouldring dreriment,
  Through riven cloudes and molten firmament;
  The fierce threeforked engin making way,
  Both loftie towres and highest trees hath rent,
  And all that might his angrie passage stay,
And shooting in the earth, casts up a mount of clay.

10

His boystrous club, so buried in the ground,
  He could not rearen up againe so light,
  But that the knight him at avantage found,
  And whiles he strove his combred clubbe to quight
  Out of the earth, with blade all burning bright
  He smote off his left arme, which like a block
  Did fall to ground, depriv'd of native might:
  Large streames of bloud out of the truncked stocke
Forth gushed, like fresh water streame from riven rocke.

11

Dismaied with so desperate deadly wound,
  And eke impatient of unwonted paine,
  He loudly brayd with beastly yelling sound,
  That all the fields rebellowed againe;
  As great a noyse, as when in Cymbrian plaine
  An heard of Bulles, whom kindly rage doth sting,
  Doe for the milkie mothers want complaine,
  And fill the fields with troublous bellowing,
The neighbour woods around with hollow murmur ring.

12

That when his deare *Duessa* heard, and saw
  The evil stownd, that daungerd her estate,
  Unto his aide she hastily did draw
  Her dreadfull beast, who swolne with bloud of late,
  Came ramping forth with proud presumpteous gate,
  And threatned all his heads like flaming brands.
  But him the Squire made quickly to retrate,

Encountring fierce with single sword in hand,
And twixt him and his Lord did like a bulwarke stand.

13

The proud *Duessa* full of wrathfull spight,
  And fierce disdaine, to be affronted so,
  Enforst her purple beast with all her might
  That stop out of the way to overthroe,
  Scorning the let of so unequall foe:
  But nathemore would that courageous swayne
  To her yeeld passage, against his Lord to goe,
  But with outrageous strokes did him restraine,
And with his bodie bard the way atwixt them twaine.

14

Then tooke the angrie witch her golden cup,
  Which still she bore, replete with magick artes;
  Death and despeyre did many thereof sup,
  And secret poyson through their inner parts,
  Th' eternall bale of heavie wounded harts;
  Which after charmes and some enchauntments said,
  She lightly sprinkled on his weaker parts;
  Therewith his sturdie courage soon was quayd,
And all his senses were with suddein dread dismayd.

15

So downe he fell before the cruell beast,
  Who on his neck his bloudie clawes did seize,
  That life nigh crusht out of his panting brest:
  No powre he had to stirre, nor will to rize.
  That when the carefull knight gan well avise,
  He lightly left the foe, with whom he fought,
  And to the beast gan turne his enterprise;
  For wondrous anguish in his hart it wrought,
To see his loved Squire into such thraldome brought.

16

And high advauncing his bloud-thirstie blade,
  Stroke one of those deformed heads so sore,
  That of his puissauce proud ensample made;
  His monstrous scalpe downe to his teeth it tore,
  And that misformed shape mis-shaped more:
  A sea of bloud gusht from the gaping wound,
  That her gay garments staynd with filthy gore,
  And overflowed all the field around;
That over shoes in bloud he waded on the ground.

17

Thereat he roared for exceeding paine,
    That to have heard, great horror would have bred,
    And scourging th' emptie ayre with his long traine,
    Through great impatience of his grieved hed
    His gorgeous ryder from her loftie sted
    Would have cast downe, and trod in durtie myre,
    Had not the Gyant soone her succoured;
    Who all enrag'd with smart and frantick yre,
Came hurtling in full fierce, and forst the knight retyre.

18

The force, which wont in two to be disperst,
    In one alone left hand he now unites,
    Which is through rage more strong then both were erst;
    With which his hideous club aloft he dites,
    And at his foe with furious rigour smites,
    That strongest Oake might seeme to ovethrow:
    The stroke upon his shield so heavie lites,
    That to the ground it doubleth him full low:
What mortall wight could ever beare so monstrous blow?

19

And in his fall his shield, that covered was,
    Did loose his vele by chaunce, and open flew:
    The light whereof, that heavens light did pas,
    Such blazing brightnesse through the aier threw,
    That eye mote not the same endure to vew.
    Which when the Gyaunt spyde with staring eye,
    He downe let fall his arme, and soft withdrew
    His weapon huge, that heaved was on hye
For to have slaine the man, that on the ground did lye.

20

And eke the fruitfull-headed beast, amaz'd
    At flashing beames of that sunshiny shield,
    Became starke blind, and all his sences daz'd,
    That downe he tumbled on the durtie field,
    And seem'd himselfe as conquered to yield.
    Whom when his maistresse proud perceiv'd to fall,
    Whiles yet his feeble feet for faintnesse reeld,
    Unto the Gyant loudly she gan call,
'O helpe *Orgoglio,* helpe, or else we perish all.'

21

At her so pitteous cry was much amoov'd,
    Her champion stout, and for to ayde his frend,
    Againe his wonted angry weapon proov'd:
    But all in vaine: for he has read his end
    In that bright shield, and all their forces spend
    Themselves in vaine: for since that glauncing sight,
    He hath no powre to hurt, nor to defend;
    As where th' Almighties lightning brond does light,
It dimmes the dazed eyen, and daunts the senses quight.

22

Whom when the Prince, to battell new addrest,
    And threatning high his dreadfull stroke did see,
    His sparkling blade about his head he blest,
    And smote off quite his right leg by the knee,
    That downe he tombled; as an aged tree,
    High growing on the top of rocky clift,
    Whose hartstrings with keene steele nigh hewen be,
    The mightie trunck halfe rent, with ragged rift
Doth roll adowne the rocks, and fall with fearefull drift.

23

Or as a Castle reared high and round,
    By subtile engins and malitious slight
    Is undermined from the lowest ground,
    And her foundation forst, and feebled quight,
    At last downe falles, and with her heaped hight
    Her hastie ruine does more heavie make,
    And yields it selfe unto the victours might;
    Such was this Gyaunts fall, that seemd to shake
The stedfast globe of earth, as it for feare did quake.

24

The knight then lightly leaping to the pray,
    With mortall steeled him smot againe so sore,
    That headlesse his unweldy bodie lay,
    All wallowd in his owne fowle bloudy gore,
    Which flowed from his wounds in wondrous store.
    But soone as breath out of his breast did pas,
    That huge great body, which the Gyaunt bore,
    Was vanisht quite, and of that monstrous mas
Was nothing left, but like an emptie bladder was.

25

Whose grievous fall, when false *Duessa* spide,
  Her golden cup she cast unto the ground,
  And crowned mitre rudely threw aside;
  Such percing griefe her stubborne hart did wound,
  That she could not endure that dolefull stound,
  But leaving all behind her, fled away:
  The light-foot Squire her quickly turnd around,
  And by hard meanes enforcing her to stay,
So brought unto his Lord, as his deserved pray.

26

The royall Virgin, which beheld from farre,
  In pensive plight, and sad perplexitie,
  The whole atchievement of this doubtfull warre,
  Came running fast to greet his victorie,
  With sober gladnesse, and myld modestie,
  And with sweet joyous cheare him thus bespake;
  'Faire braunch of noblesse, flowre of chevalrie,
  That with your worth the world amazed make,
How shall I quite the paines, ye suffer for my sake?

27

'And you fresh budd of vertue springing fast,
  Whom these sad eyes saw nigh unto deaths dore,
  What hath poore Virgin for such perill past,
  Wherewith you to reward? Accept therefore
  My simple selfe, and service evermore;
  And he that high does sit, and all things see
  With equall eyes, their merites to restore,
  Behold what ye this day have done for mee,
And what I cannot quite, requite with usuree.

28

'But sith the heavens, and your faire handeling
  Have made you maister of the field this day,
  Your fortune maister eke with governing,
  And well begun end all so well, I pray,
  Ne let that wicked woman scape away;
  For she it is, that did my Lord bethrall,
  My dearest Lord, and deepe in dongeon lay,
  Where he his better dayes hath wasted all.
O heare, how piteous he to you for ayd does call.'

29

Forthwith he gave in charge unto his Squire,
   That scarlot whore to keepen carefully;
   Whiles he himselfe with greedie great desire
   Into the Castle entred forcibly,
   Where living creature none he did espye;
   Then gan he lowdly through the house to call:
   But no man car'd to answere to his crye.
   There raignd a solemne silence over all,
Nor voice was heard, nor wight was seene in bowre or hall.

30

At last with creeping crooked pace forth came
   An old old man, with beard as white as snow,
   That on a staffe his feeble steps did frame,
   And guide his wearie gate both too and fro:
   For his eye sight him failed long ygo,
   And on his arme a bounch of keyes he bore,
   The which unused rust did overgrow:
   Those were the keyes of every inner dore,
But he could not them use, but kept them still in store.

31

But very uncouth sight was to behold,
   How he did fashion his untoward pace,
   For as he forward moov'd his footing old,
   So backward still was turnd his wrincled face,
   Unlike to men, who ever as they trace,
   Both feet and face one way are wont to lead.
   This was the auncient keeper of that place,
   And foster father of the Gyant dead;
His name *Ignaro* did his nature right aread.

32

His reverend haires and holy gravitie
   The knight much honord, as beseemed well,
   And gently askt, where all the people bee,
   Which in that stately building wont to dwell.
   Who answerd him full soft, he could not tell.
   Againe he askt, where that same knight was layd,
   Whom great *Orgoglio* with his puissaunce fell
   Had made his caytive thrall; againe he sayde,
He could not tell: ne ever other answere made.

33

Then asked he, which way he in might pas:
  He could not tell, againe he answered.
  Thereat the courteous knight displeased was,
  And said, 'Old sire, it seemes thou hast not red
  How ill it sits with that same silver hed
  In vaine to mocke, or mockt in vaine to bee:
  But if thou be, as thou art pourtrahed
  With natures pen, in ages grave degree,
Aread in graver wise, what I demaund of thee.'

34

His answere likewise was, he could not tell.
  Whose sencelesse speach, and doted ignorance,
  When as the noble Prince had marked well,
  He ghest his nature by his countenance,
  And calmd his wrath with goodly temperance.
  Then to him stepping, from his arme did reach
  Those keyes, and made himselfe free enterance.
  Each dore he opened without any breach;
There was no barre to stop, nor foe him to empeach.

35

There all within full rich arayd he found,
  With royall arras and resplendent gold,
  And did with store of every thing abound,
  That greatest Princes presence might behold.
  But all the floore (too filthy to be told)
  With bloud of guiltlesse babes, and innocents trew,
  Which there were slaine, as sheepe out of the fold,
  Defiled was, that dreadfull was to vew,
And sacred ashes over it was strowed new.

36

And there beside of marble stone was built
  An Altare, carv'd with cunning imagery,
  On which true Christians bloud was often spilt,
  And holy Martyrs often doen to dye,
  With cruell malice and strong tyranny:
  Whose blessed sprites from underneath the stone
  To God for vengeance cryde continually,
  And with great griefe were often heard to grone,
That hardest heart would bleede, to hear their piteous mone.

37

Through every rowme he sought, and every bowr,
    But no where could he find that wofull thrall:
    At last he came unto an yron doore,
    That fast was lockt, but key found not at all
    Emongst that bounch, to open it withall;
    But in the same a little grate was pight,
    Through which he sent his voyce, and lowd did call
    With all his powre, to weet, if living wight
Were housed therewithin, whom he enlargen might.

38

Therewith an hollow, dreary, murmuring voyce
    These piteous plaints and dolours did resound;
    'O who is that, which brings me happy choyce
    Of death, that here lye dying every stound,
    Yet live perforce in balefull darkenesse bound?
    For now three Moones have changed thrice their hew,
    And have beene thrice hid underneath the ground,
    Since I the heavens chearefull face did vew,
O welcome thou, that doest of death bring tydings trew.'

39

Which when that Champion heard, with percing point
    Of pitty deare his hart was thrilled sore,
    And trembling horrour ran through every joynt,
    For ruth of gentle knight so fowle forlore:
    Which shaking off, he rent that yron dore,
    With furious force, and indignation fell;
    Where entred in, his foot could find no flore,
    But all a deepe descent, as darke as hell,
That breathed ever forth a filthie banefull smell.

40

But neither darkenesse fowle, nor filthy bands,
    Nor noyous smell, his purpose could withhold,
    (Entire affection hateth nicer hands)
    But that with constant zeale, and courage bold,
    After long paines and labours manifold,
    He found the meanes that Prisoner up to reare;
    Whose feeble thighes, unhable to uphold
    His pined corse, him scarse to light could beare,
A ruefull spectacle of death and ghastly drere.

41

His sad dull eyes deepe sunck in hollow pits,
　　Could not endure th' unwonted sunne to view;
　　His bare thin cheekes for want of better bits,
　　And empty sides deceived of their dew,
　　Could make a stony hart his hap to rew;
　　His rawbone armes, whose mighty brawned bowrs
　　Were wont to rive steele plates, and helmets hew,
　　Were cleane consum'd, and all his vitall powres
Decayd, and all his flesh shronk up like withered flowres.

42

Whom when his Lady saw, to him she ran
　　With hasty joy: to see him made her glad,
　　And sad to view his visage pale and wan,
　　Who earst in flowres of freshest youth was clad.
　　Tho when her well of teares she wasted had,
　　She said, 'Ah dearest Lord, what evill starre
　　On you hath fround, and pourd his influence bad,
　　That of your selfe ye thus berobbed arre,
And this misseeming hew your manly looks doth marre?

43

'But welcome now my Lord, in wele or woe,
　　Whose presence I have lackt too long a day;
　　And fie on Fortune mine avowed foe,
　　Whose wrathful wreakes them selves doe now alay.
　　And for these wrongs shall treble penaunce pay
　　Of treble good: good growes of evils priefe.'
　　The chearelesse man, whom sorrow did dismay,
　　Had no delight to treaten to his griefe.
His long endured famine needed more reliefe.

44

'Faire Lady,' then said that victorious knight,
　　'The things, that grievous were to do, or beare,
　　Them to renew, I wote, breeds no delight;
　　Best musicke breeds delight in loathing eare:
　　But th' onely good, that growes of passed feare,
　　Is to be wise, and ware of like agein.
　　This dayes ensample hath this lesson deare
　　Deepe written in my heart with yron pen,
That blisse may not abide in state of mortall men.

45

'Henceforth sir knight, take to you wonted strength,
　And maister these mishaps with patient might;
　Loe where your foe lyes stretcht in monstrous length,
　And loe that wicked woman in your sight,
　The roote of all your care, and wretched plight,
　Now in your powre, to let her live, or dye.'
　'To do her dye' (quoth *Una*) 'were despight,
　And shame t'avenge so weake an enimy;
But spoile her of her scarlot robe, and let her fly.'

46

So as she bad, that witch they disaraid,
　And robd of royall robes, and purple pall,
　And ornaments that richly were displaid;
　Ne spared they to strip her naked all.
　Then when they had despoiled her tire and call,
　Such as she was, their eyes might her behold,
　That her misshaped parts did them appall,
　A loathly, wrinckled hag, ill favoured, old,
Whose secret filth good manners biddeth not be told.

47

Her craftie head was altogether bald,
　And as in hate of honorable eld,
　Was overgrowne with scurfe and filthy scald;
　Her teeth out of her rotten gummes were feld,
　And her sowre breath abhominably smeld;
　Her dried dugs, like bladders lacking wind,
　Hong downe, and filthy matter from them weld;
　Her wrizled skin as rough, as maple rind,
So scabby was, that would have loathd all womankind.

48

Her neather parts, the shame of all her kind,
　My chaster Muse for shame doth blush to write;
　But at her rompe she growing had behind
　A foxes taile, with dong all fowly dight;
　And eke her feete most monstrous were in sight;
　For one of them was like an Eagles claw,
　With griping talaunts armd to greedy fight,
　The other like a Beares uneven paw:
More ugly shape yet never living creature saw.

49

Which when the knights beheld, amazd they were,
  And wondred at so fowle deformed wight.
  'Such then' (said *Una*) 'as she seemeth here,
  Such is the face of falshood, such the sight
  Of fowle *Duessa*, when her borrowed light
  Is laid away, and counterfesaunce knowne.'
  Thus when they had the witch disrobed quight,
  And all her filthy feature open showne,
They let her goe at will, and wander wayes unknowne.

50

She flying fast from heavens hated face,
  And from the world that her discovered wide,
  Fled to the wastfull wildernesse apace,
  From living eyes her open shame to hide,
  And lurkt in rocks and caves long unespide.
  But that faire crew of knights, and *Una* faire
  Did in that castle afterwards abide,
  To rest them selves, and weary powres repaire,
Where store they found of all, that dainty was and rare.

Canto IX

His loves and lignage Arthure tells
The knights knit friendly bands:
Sir Trevisan flies from Despayre,
Whom Redcrosse knight withstands.

I

O goodly golden chaine, wherewith yfere
  The vertues linked are in lovely wize:
  And noble minds of yore allyed were,
  In brave poursuit of chevalrous emprize,
  That none did others safety despize,
  Nor aid envy to him, in need that stands,
  But friendly each did others prayse devize
  How to advaunce with favourable hands,
As this good Prince redeemd the *Redcrosse* knight from bands.

2

Who when their powres, empaird through labour long,
  With dew repast they had recured well,
  And that weake captive wight now wexed strong,
  Them list no lenger there at leasure dwell,
  But forward fare as their adventures fell,
  But ere they parted, *Una* faire besought
  That straunger knight his name and nation tell;
  Least so great good, as he for her had wrought,
Should die unknown, and buried be in thankles thought.

3

'Faire virgin' (said the Prince) 'ye me require
  A thing without the compas of my wit:
  For both the lignage and the certain Sire,
  From which I sprong, from me are hidden yit.
  For all so soone as life did me admit
  Into this world, and shewed heavens light,
  From mothers pap I taken was unfit:
  And streight deliver'd to a Faery knight,
To be upbrought in gentle thewes and martiall might.

4

'Unto Old *Timon* he me brought bylive,
  Old *Timon* who in youthly yeares hath beene
  In warlike feates th' expertest man alive,
  And is the wisest now on earth I weene;
  His dwelling is low in a valley greene,

Under the foot of *Rauran* mossy hore,
From whence the river *Dee* as silver cleene
His tombling billowes rolls with gentle rore:
There all my dayes he traind me up in vertuous lore.

5

'Thither the great Magicien *Merlin* came,
  As was his use, ofttimes to visit me:
For he had charge my discipline to frame,
  And Tutors nouriture of oversee.
  Him oft and oft I askt in privitie,
  Of what loines and what lignage I did spring:
  Whose aunswere bad me still assured bee,
  That I was soone and heire unto a king,
As time in her just terme the truth to light should bring.'

6

'Well worthy impe,' said then the Lady gent,
  'And Pupill fit for such a Tutours hand.
  But what adventure, or what high intent
  Hath brought you hither into Faery land,
  Aread Prince *Arthur*, crowne of Martiall band?'
  'Full hard it is' (quoth he) 'to read aright
  The course of heavenly cause, or understand
  The secret meaning of th' eternall might,
That rules mens wayes, and rules the thoughts of living wight.

7

'For whither he through fatal deepe foresight
  Me hither sent, for cause to me unghest,
  Or that fresh bleeding wound, which day and night
  Whilome doth rancle in my riven brest,
  With forced fury following his behest,
  Me hither brought by wayes yet never found,
  You to have helpt I hold my selfe yet blest.'
  'Ah curteous knight' (quoth she) 'what secret wound
Could ever find, to grieve the gentlest hart on ground?'

8

'Dear Dame' (quoth he) 'you sleeping sparkes awake,
  Which troubled once, into huge flames will grow,
  Ne ever will their fervent fury slake,
  Till living moysture into smoke do flow,
  And wasted life do lye in ashes low.

Yet sithens silence lesseneth not my fire,
    But told it flames, and hidden it does glow,
    I will revele, what ye so much desire:
Ah Love, lay down thy bow, the whilst I may respire.

9

'It was in freshest flowre of youthly yeares,
    When courage first does creepe in manly chest,
    Then first the coale of kindly heat appeares
    To kindle love in every living brest;
    But me had warnd old *Timons* wise behest,
    Those creeping flames by reason to subdew,
    Before their rage grew to so great unrest,
    As miserable lovers use to rew,
Which still wex old in woe, whiles woe still wexeth new.

10

'That idle name of love, and lovers life,
    As losse of time, and vertues enimy
    I ever scornd, and joyd to stirre up strife,
    In middest of their mournfull Tragedy,
    Ay wont to laugh, when them I heard to cry,
    And blow the fire, which them to ashes brent:
    Their God himselfe, grieve'd at my libertie,
    Shot many a dart at me with fiers intent,
But I them warded all with wary government.

11

'But all in vaine: no fort can be so strong,
    Ne fleshly brest can armed be so sound,
    But will at last be wonne with battrie long,
    Or unawares at disavantage found;
    Nothing is sure, that growes on earthly ground:
    And who most trustes in arme of fleshly might,
    And boasts, in beauties chaine not to be bound,
    Doth soonest fall in disaventrous fight,
And yeeldes his caytive neck to victours most despight.

12

'Ensample make of him your haplesse joy,
    And of my selfe now mated, as ye see;
    Whose prouder vaunt that proud avenging boy
    Did soone pluck downe, and curbd my libertie.
    For on a day prickt forth with jollitie
    Of looser life, and heat of hardiment,

Raunging the forest wide on courser free,
The fields, the floods, the heavens, with one consent
Did seeme to laugh on me, and favour mine intent.

13

'For-wearied with my sports, I did alight
   From loftie steed, and downe to sleepe me layd;
   The verdant gras my couch did goodly dight,
   And pillow was my helmet faire displayd:
   Whiles every sence the humour sweet embayd,
   And slombring soft my hart did steale away,
   Me seemed, by my side a royall Mayd
   Her daintie limbes full softly down did lay:
So faire a creature yet saw never sunny day.

14

'Most goodly glee and lovely blandishment
   She to me made, and bade me love her deare,
   For dearely sure her love was to me bent,
   As when just time expired should appeare.
   But whether dreames delude, or true it were,
   Was never hart so ravisht with delight,
   Ne living man like words did ever heare,
   As she to me delivered all that night;
And at her parting said, She Queene of Faeries hight.

15

'When I awoke, and found her place devoyd,
   And nought but pressed gras, where she had lyen,
   I sorrowed all so much, as earst I joyd,
   And washed all her place with watry eyen.
   From that day forth I lov'd that face divine;
   From that day forth I cast in carefull mind,
   To seeke her out with labour, and long tyne,
   And never vowd to rest, till her I find,
Nine monethes I seeke in vaine yet ni'll that vow unbind.'

16

Thus as he spake, his visage wexed pale,
   And chaunge of hew great passion did bewray;
   Yett still he strove to cloke his inward bale,
   And hide the smoke, that did his fire display,
   Till gentle *Una* thus to him gan say;
   'O happy Queene of Faeries, that hast found
   Mongst many, one that with his prowesse may
   Defend thine honour, and thy foes confound:

True Loves are often sown, but seldom grow on ground.'

17
'Thine O then,' said the gentle *Redcrosse* knight,
   'Next to that Ladies love, shalbe the place,
   O fairest virgin, full of heavenly light,
   Whose wondrous faith, exceeding earthly race,
   Was firmest fixt in mine extremest case.
   And you, my Lord, the Patrone of my life,
   Of that great Queene may well gaine worthy grace:
   For onely worthy you through prowes priefe
Yf living man mote worthy be, to be her liefe.'

18
So diversly discoursing of their loves,
   The golden Sunne his glistring head gan shew,
   And sad remembraunce now the Prince amoves,
   With fresh desire his voyage to pursew:
   Als *Una* earnd her traveill to renew.
   Then those two knights, fast friendship for to bynd,
   And love establish each to other trew,
   Gave goodly gifts, the signes of gratefull mynd,
And eke as pledges firme, right hands together joynd.

19
Prince *Arthur* gave a boxe of Diamond sure,
   Embowd with gold and gorgeous ornament,
   Wherein were closd few drops of liquor pure,
   Of wondrous worth, and vertue excellent,
   That any wound could heale incontinent:
   Which to requite, the *Redcrosse* knight him gave
   A booke, wherein his Saveours testament
   Was writ with golden letters rich and brave;
A worke of wondrous grace, and hable soules to save.

20
Thus beene they parted, *Arthur* on his way
   To seeke his love, and th' other for to fight
   With *Unaes* foe, that all her realme did pray.
   But she now weighing the decayed plight,
   And shrunken synewes of her chosen knight,
   Would not a while her forward course pursew,
   Ne bring him forth in face of dreadfull fight,
   Till he recovered had his former hew:
For him to be yet weake and wearie well she knew.

21

So as they traveild, lo they gan espy
   An armed knight towards them gallop fast,
   That seemed from some feared foe to fly,
   Or other griesly thing that him agast.
   Still as he fled, his eye was backward cast,
   As if his feare still followed him behind;
   Als flew his steed as he his bandes had brast,
   And with his winged heeles did tread the wind,
As he had beene a fole of *Pegasus* his kind.

22

Nigh as he drew, they might perceive his head
   To bee unarmd, and curld uncombed heares
   Upstaring stiffe, dismaid with uncouth dread;
   Nor drop of bloud in all his face appeares
   Nor life in limbe: and to increase his feares,
   In fowle reproch of knighthoodes faire degree,
   About his neck an hempen rope he weares,
   That with his glistring armes does ill agree;
But he of rope or armes has now no memoree.

23

The *Redcrosse* knight toward him crossed fast,
   To weet, what mister wight was so dismayd:
   There him he finds all sencelesse and aghast,
   That of him selfe he seemd to be afrayd;
   Whom hardly he from flying forward stayd,
   Till he these wordes to him deliver might;
   'Sir knight, aread who hath ye thus arayd,
   And eke from whom make ye this hasty flight.
For never knight I saw in such misseeming plight.'

24

He answerd nought at all, but adding new
   Feare to his first amazment, staring wide
   With stony eyes, and hartlesse hollow hew,
   Astonisht stood, as one that had aspide
   Infernall furies, with their chaines untide
   Him yet againe, and yet againe bespake
   The gentle knight; who nought to him replide,
   But trembling every joynt did inly quake,
And foltring tongue at last these words seemd forth to shake.

25

'For Gods deare love, Sir knight, do me not stay;
  For loe he comes, he comes fast after mee.'
  Eft looking backe would faine have runne away;
  But he him forst to stay, and tellen free
  The secrete cause of his perplexitie:
  Yet nathemore by his bold hartie speach
  Could his bloud-frosen hart emboldened bee,
  But through his boldnes rather feare did reach,
Yet forst, at last he made through silence suddein breach.

26

'And am I now in safetie sure' (quoth he)
  'From him, that would have forced me to dye?
  And is the point of death now turnd fro mee,
  That I may tell this haplesse history?'
  'Fear nought:' (quoth he) 'no daunger now is nye.'
  'Then shall I you recount a ruefull cace,'
  (Said he) 'the which with this unlucky eye
  I late beheld, and had not greater grace
Me reft from it, had bene partaker of the place.

27

'I lately chaunst (Would I had never chaunst)
  With a faire knight to keepen companee,
  Sir *Terwin* hight, that welll himselfe advaunst
  In all affaires, and was both bold and free,
  But not so happie as mote happie bee:
  He lov'd as was his lot, a Ladie gent,
  That him againe lov'd in the least degree:
  For she was proud, and of too high intent,
And joyd to see her lover languish and lament.

28

'From whom returning sad and comfortlesse,
  As on the way together we did fare,
  We met that villen (God from him me blesse)
  That cursed wight, from whom I scapt whyleare,
  A man of hell, that cals himselfe *Despaire*:
  Who first us greets, and after faire areeds
  Of tydings strange, and of adventures rare:
  So creeping close, as Snake in hidden weedes,
Inquireth of our states, and of our knightly deedes.

29

'Which when he knew, and felt our feeble harts
 Embost with bale, and bitter byting griefe,
 Which love had launched with his deadly darts,
 With wounding words and termes of foule repriefe,
 He pluckt from us all hope of due reliefe,
 That earst us held in love of lingring life;
 Then hopelesse hartlesse, gan the cunning thiefe
 Perswade us die, to stint all further strife:
To me he lent this rope, to him a rustie knife.

30

'With which sad instrument of hastie death,
 That wofull lover, loathing lenger light,
 A wide way made to let forth living breath.
 But I more fearefull, or more lucky wight,
 Dismayd with that deformed dismall sight,
 Fled fast away, halfe dead with dying feare:
 Ne yet assur'd of life by you, Sir knight,
 Whose like infirmitie like chaunce may beare:
But God you never let his charmed speaches heare.'

31

'How may a man' (said he) 'with idle speach
 Be wonne to spoyle the Castle of his health?'
 'I wote' (quoth he) 'whom triall late did teach,
 That like would not for all this worldes wealth:
 His subtill tongue, like dropping honny, mealt'h
 Into the hart, and searcheth every vaine,
 That ere one be aware, by secret stealth
 His powre is reft, and weaknesse doth remaine.
O never Sir desire to try his guilefull traine.'

32

'Certes' (quoth he) 'hence shall I never rest,
 Till I that treachours art have heard and tride;
 And you Sir knight, whose name mote I request,
 Of grace do me unto his cabin guide.'
 'I that hight *Trevisan*' (quoth he) 'will ride
 Against my liking backe, to doe you grace:
 But nor for gold nor glee will I abide
 By you, when ye arrive in that same place;
For lever had I die, then see his deadly face.'

33

Ere long they come, where that same wicked wight
  His dwelling has, low in an hollow cave,
  Farre underneath a craggy clift ypight,
  Darke, dolefull, drearie, like a greedie grave,
  That still for carrion carcases doth crave:
  On top whereof aye dwelt the ghstly Owle,
  Shrieking his balefull note, which ever drave
  Far from that haunt all other chearefull fowle;
And all about it wandring ghostes did waile and howle.

34

And all about old stockes and stubs of trees,
  Whereon nor fruit, nor leafe was ever seene,
  Did hang upon the ragged rocky knees;
  On which had many wretches hanged beene,
  Whose carcases were scattered on the greene,
  And throwne about the cliffs.   Arrived there,
  That bare-head knight, for dread and dolefull teene,
  Would faine have fled, ne durst approchen neare,
But th' other forst him stay, and comforted in feare.

35

That darkesome cave they enter, where they find
  That cursed man, low sitting on the ground,
  Musing full sadly in his sullein mind;
  His griesie lockes, long growen and unbound,
  Disordred hong about his shoulders round,
  And hid his face; though which his hollow eyne
  Lookt deadly dull, and stared as astound;
  His raw-bone cheekes through penurie and pine,
Were shronke into his jaws, as he did never dine.

36

His garment nought but many ragged clouts,
  With thornes together pind and patched was,
  The which his naked sides he wrapt abouts;
  And him beside there lay upon the gras
  A drearie corse, whose life away did pas,
  All wallowd in his own yet luke-warme blood,
  That from his wound yet welled fresh alas;
  In which a rusty knife fast fixed stood,
And made an open passage for the gushing flood.

37

Which piteous spectacle, approving trew
  The wofull tale that *Trevisan* had told,
  When as the gentle *Redcrosse* knight did vew,
  With firie zeale he burnt in courage bold,
  Him to avenge, before his bloud were cold,
  And to the villein said, 'Thou damned wight,
  The authour of this fact we here behold,
  What justice can but judge against thee right,
With thine owne bloud to price his bloud, here shed in sight?'

38

'What franticke fit' (quoth he) 'hath thus distraught
  Thee, foolish man, so rash a doome to give?
  What justice ever other judgement taught,
  But he should die, who merites not to live?
  None else to death this man despayring drive,
  But his owne guiltie mind deserving death.
  Is then unjust to each his due to give?
  Or let him die, that loatheth living breath!
Or let him die at ease, that liveth here uneath?

39

'Who travels by the wearie wandring way,
  To come unto his wished home in haste,
  And meetes a flood, that doth his passage stay,
  Is not great grace to helpe him over past,
  Or free his feet, that in the myre sticke fast?
  Most envious man, that grieves at neighbours good,
  And fond, that joyest in the woe thou hast,
  Why wilt not let him passe, that long hath stood
Upon the banke, yet wilt thy selfe not passe the flood?

40

'He there does now enjoy eternall rest
  And happy ease, which thou doest want and crave,
  And further from it daily wanderest:
  What if some little paine the passage have,
  That makes fraile flesh to feare the bitter wave?
  Is not short paine well borne, that brings long ease,
  And layes the soule to sleepe in quiet grave?
  Sleepe after toyle, port after stormie seas,
Ease after warre, death after life does greatly please.'

41

The knight much wondred at his suddeine wit,
    And sayd, 'The terme of life is limited,
    Ne may a man prolong, nor shorten it:
    The souldier may not move from watchfull sted,
    Nor leave his stand, untill his Captaine bed.'
    'Who life did limit by almightie doome,'
    (Quoth he) 'knowes best the termes established;
    And he, that points the Centonell his roome,
Doth license him depart at sound of morning droome.'

42

'Is not his deed, what ever thing is donne,
    In heaven and earth? did not he all create
    To die againe? all ends that was begonne.
    Their times in his eternall booke of fate
    Are written sure, and have their certein date.
    Who then can strive with strong necessitie,
    That holds the world in his still chaunging state,
    Or shunne the death ordaynd by destinie?
When houre of death is come, let none aske whence, nor why.

43

'The lenger life, I wote the greater sin,
    The greater sin, the greater punishment:
    All those great battels, which thou boasts to win,
    Through strife, and bloud-shed, and avengement,
    Now praysd, hereafter deare thou shalt repent:
    For life must life, and bloud must bloud repay.
    Is not enough thy evil life forespent?
    For he, that once hath missed the right way,
The further he doth goe, the further he doth stray.

44

'Then do no further goe, no further stray,
    But here lie downe, and to thy rest betake,
    Th' ill to prevent, that life ensewen may.
    For what hath life that may it loved make,
    And gives not rather cause it to forsake?
    Feare, sicknesse, age, losse, labour, sorrow, strife,
    Payne, hunger, cold, that makes the hart to quake;
    And ever fickle fortune rageth rife,
All which, and thousands mo do make a loathsome life.

45

'Thou wretched man, of death has greatest need,
  If in true ballance thou wilt weigh thy state:
  For never knight, that dared warlike deede,
  More lucklesse disaventures did amate:
  Witnesse the dongeon deepe, wherein of late
  Thy life shut up, for death so oft did call;
  And though good lucke prolonged hath thy date,
  Yet death then, would the like mishaps forestall,
Into the which hereafter thou maiest happen fall.

46

'Why then doest thou, O man of sin, desire
  To draw thy dayes forth to their last degree?
  Is not the measure of thy sinfull hire
  High heaped up with huge iniquitie,
  Against the day of wrath, to burden thee?
  Is not enough, that to this Ladie milde
  Thou falsed hast thy faith with perjurie,
  And sold thy selfe to serve *Duessa* vilde,
With whom in all abuse thou hast thy selfe defilde?

47

'Is not he just, that all this doth behold
  From highest heaven, and beares an equall eye?
  Shall he thy sins up in his knowledge fold,
  And guiltie be of thine impietie?
  Is not his law, Let every sinner die:
  Die shall all flesh? What then must needs be donne,
  Is it not better to doe willinglie,
  Then linger, till the glas be all out ronne?
Death is the end of woes: die soone, O faeries sonne.'

48

The knight was much enmoved with his speach,
  That as a swords point through his hart did perse,
  And in his conscience made a secret breach,
  Well knowing true all that he did reherse,
  And to his fresh remembrance did reverse
  The ugly vew of his deformed crimes,
  That all his manly powres it did disperse,
  As he were charmed with inchaunted rimes,
That oftentimes he quakt, and fainted oftentimes.

49

In which amazement, when the Miscreant
  Perceived him to waver weake and fraile,
  Whiles trembling horror did his conscience dant
  And hellish anguish did his soule assaile,
  To drive him to despaire, and quite to quaile,
  He shew'd him painted in a table plaine,
  The damned ghosts, that doe in torments waile,
  And thousand feends that doe them endlesse paine
With fire and brimstone, which for ever shall remaine.

50

The sight whereof so throughly him dismaid,
  That nought but death before his eyes he saw,
  And ever burning wrath before him laid,
  By righteous sentence of th' Almighties law:
  Then gan villein him to overcraw,
  And brought unto him swords, ropes, poison, fire,
  And all that might him to perdition draw;
  And bad him choose, what death he would desire:
For death was due to him, that had provokt Gods ire.

51

But when as none of them he saw him take,
  He to him raught a dagger sharpe and keene,
  And gave it him in hand: his hand did quake,
  And tremble like a leafe of Aspin greene,
  And troubled bloud through his pale face was seene
  To come, and goe with tydings from the hart,
  As it a running messenger had beene.
  At last resolv'd to worke his finall smart,
He lifted up his hand, that backe againe did start.

52

Which when as Una saw, through every vaine
  The crudled cold ran to her well of life,
  As in a swowne: but soone reliv'd againe,
  Out of his hand she snatcht the cursed knife,
  And threw it to the ground, enraged rife,
  And to him said, 'Fie, fie, faint harted knight,
  What meanest thou by this reprochfull strife?
  Is this the battell which thou vauntst to fight
With that fire-mouthed Dragon, horrible and bright?

53

'Come, come away, fraile, feeble, fleshly wight,
  Ne let vaine words bewitch thy manly hart,
  Ne divelish thoughts dismay thy constant spright.
  In heavenly mercies hast thou not a part?
  Why shouldst thou then despeire, that chosen art?
  Where justice growes, there grows eke greater grace,
  The which doth quench the brond of hellish smart,
  And that accurst hand-writing doth deface.
Arise, Sir knight arise, and leave this cursed place.'

54

So up he rose, and thence amounted streight.
  Which when the carle beheld, and saw his guest
  Would safe depart, for all his subtill sleight,
  He chose an halter from among the rest,
  And with it hung himselfe, unbid unblest.
  But death he could not worke himselfe thereby;
  For thousand times he so himselfe had drest,
  Yet nathelesse it could not doe him die,
Till he should die his last, that is eternally.

Canto X

Her faithfull knight faire Una brings
To house of Holinesse,
Where he is taught repentance, and
The way to hevenly blesse.

I

What man is he, that boasts of fleshly might,
    And vaine assurance of mortality,
    Which all so soone as it doth come to fight,
    Against spirituall foes, yeelds by and by,
    Or from the field most cowardly doth fly?
    Ne let the man ascribe it to his skill,
    That thorough grace hath gained victory.
    If any strength we have, it is to ill,
But all the good is Gods, both power and eke will.

2

By that, which lately hapned, *Una* saw
    That this her knight was feeble, and too faint;
    And all his sinews woxen weake and raw,
    Through long enprisonment, and hard constraint,
    Which he endured in his late restraint,
    That yet he was unfit for bloudie fight:
    Therefore to cherish him with diets daint,
    She cast to bring him, where he chearen might,
Till he recovered had his late decayed plight.

3

There was an auntient house not farre away,
    Renowmd throughout the world for sacred lore,
    And pure unspotted life: so well they say
    It governd was, and guided evermore,
    Through wisedome of a matrone grave and hore;
    Whose onely joy was to relieve the needes
    Of wretched soules, and helpe the helpelesse pore:
    All night she spent in bidding of her bedes,
And all the day in doing good and godly deedes.

4

Dame *Cælia* men did her call, as thought
    From heaven to come, or thither to arise,
    The mother of three daughters, well upbrought
    In goodly thewes, and godly exercise:
    The eldest two, most sober, chast, and wise,

Fidelia and Speranza virgins were,
  Though spousd, yet wanting wedlocks solemnize;
  But faire Charissa to a lovely fere
Was lincked, and by him had many pledges dere.

5

Arrived there, the dore they find fast lockt;
  For it was warely watched night and day,
  For feare of many foes: but when they knockt,
  The Porter opened unto them streight way:
  He was an aged syre, all hory gray,
  With lookes full lowly cast, and gate full slow,
  Wont on a staffe his feeble steps to stay,
  Hight Humiltá. They passe in stouping low;
For streight and narrow was the way, which he did show.

6

Each goodly thing is hardest to begin,
  But entred in a spatious court they see,
  Both plaine, and pleasant to be walked in,
  Where them does meete a francklin faire and free,
  And entertaines with comely court glee,
  His name was Zele, that him right well became,
  For in his speeches and behaviour hee
  Did labour lively to expresse the same,
And gladly did them guide, till to the Hall they came.

7

There fairely them receives a gentle Squire,
  Of milde demeanure, and rare courtesie,
  Right cleanly clad in comely sad attire;
  In word and deede that shew'd great modestie,
  And knew his good to all of each degree,
  Hight Reverence.   He them with speeches meet
  Does faire entreat; no courting nicetie,
  But simple true, and eke unfained sweet,
As might become a Squire so great persons to greet.

8

And afterwardes them to his Dame he leades,
  That aged Dame, the Ladie of the place:
  Who all this while was busie at her beades:
  Which doen, she up arose with seemely grace,
  And toward them full matronely did pace.
  Where when that fairest Una she beheld,

Whom well she knew to spring from heavenly race,
  Her heart with joy unwonted inly sweld,
As feeling wondrous comfort in her weaker eld.

9

And her embracing said, 'O happie earth,
  Whereon thy innocent feet doe ever tread,
  Most vertuous virgin borne of heavenly berth,
  That to redeeme thy woefull parents head,
  From tyrants rage, and ever-dying dread,
  Hast wandred through the world now long a day;
  Yet ceasest not thy wearie soles to lead,
  What grace hath thee now hither brought this way?
Or doen thy feet unweeting hither stray?

10

'Strange thing it is an errant knight to see
  Here in this place, or any other wight,
  That hither turnes his steps.   So few there bee,
  That chose the narrow path, or seeke the right:
  All keepe the broad high way, and take delight
  With many rather for to go astray,
  And be partakers of their evill plight,
  Then with a few to walke the rightest way;
O foolish men, why haste ye to your own decay?'

11

'Thy selfe to see, and tyred limbes to rest,
  O matrone sage' (quoth she) 'I hither came,
  And this good knight his way with me addrest,
  Ledd with thy prayses and broad-blazed fame,
  That up to heven is blowne.'   The auncient Dame,
  Him goodly greeted in her modest guise,
  And entertaynd them both, as best became,
  With all the court'sies that she could devise,
Ne wanted ought, to shew her bounteous or wise.

12

Thus as they gan of sundry things devise,
  Loe two most goodly virgins came in place,
  Ylinked arme in arme in lovely wise,
  With countenance demure, and modest grace,
  They numbred even steps and equall pace:
  Of which the eldest, that *Fidelia* hight,
  Like sunny beames threw from her Christall face,

That could have dazd the rash beholders sight,
And round about her head did shine like heavens light.

13

She was araied all in lilly white,
  And in her right hand bore a cup of gold,
  With wine and water fild up to the hight,
  In which a Serpent did himselfe enfold,
  That horrour made to all, that did behold;
  But she no whit did chaunge her constant mood:
  And in her other hand she fast did hold
  A booke, that was both signd and seald with blood,
Wherein darke things were writ, hard to be understood.

14

Her younger sister, that *Speranza* hight,
  Was clad in blew, that her beseemed well;
  Not all so chearefull seemed she of sight,
  As was her sister; whether dread did dwell,
  Or anguish in her hart, is hard to tell:
  Upon her arme a silver anchor lay,
  Whereon she leaned ever, as befell:
  And ever up to heaven, as she did pray,
Her stedfast eyes were bent, ne swarved other way.

15

They seeing *Una*, towards her gan wend,
  Who them encounters with like courtesie;
  Many kind speeches they betwene them spend,
  And greatly joy each other for to see:
  Then to the knight with shamefast modestie
  They turne themselves, at *Unaes* meeke request,
  And him salute with well beseeming glee;
  Who faire them quites, as him beseemed best,
And goodly gan discourse of many a noble gest.

16

Then *Una* thus; 'But she your sister deare;
  The deare *Charissa* where is she become?
  Or wants she health, or busie is elsewhere?'
  'Ah no,' said they, 'but forth she may not come:
  For she of late is lightned of her wombe,
  And hath encreast the world with one sonne more,
  That her to see should be but troublesome.'
  'Indeede' (quoth she) 'that should her trouble sore,
But thankt be God, and her encrease so evermore.'

17

Then said the aged *Cælia*, 'Deare dame,
    And you good Sir, I wote that of youre toyle,
    And labours long, through which ye hither came,
    Ye both forwearied be: therefore a whyle
    I read you rest, and to your bowres recoyle.'
    Then called she a Groome, that forth him led
    Into a goodly lodge, and gan despoile
    Of puissant armes, and laid in easie bed;
His name was meeke *Obedience* rightfully ared.

18

Now when their wearie limbes with kindly rest,
    And bodies were refresht with dew repast,
    Faire *Una* gan *Fidelia* faire request,
    To have her knight into her schoolehouse plaste,
    That of her heavenly learning he might taste,
    And heare the wisedom of her words divine.
    She graunted, and that knight so much agraste,
    That she him taught celestiall discipline,
And opened his dull eyes, that light mote in them shine.

19

And that her sacred Booke, with bloud ywrit,
    That none could read except she did them teach,
    She unto him disclosed every whit,
    And heavenly documents thereout did preach,
    That weaker wit of man could never reach,
    Of God, of grace, of justice, of free will,
    That wonder was to heare her goodly speach:
    For she was able, with her words to kill,
And raise againe to life the hart, that she did thrill.

20

And when she list poure out her larger spright,
    She would commaund the hastie Sunne to stay,
    Or backward turne his course from heavens hight;
    Sometimes great hostes of men she could dismay,
    Dry-shod to passe, she parts the flouds in tway;
    And eke huge mountaines from their native seat
    She would commaund, themselves to beare away,
    And throw in raging sea with roaring threat.
Almightie God her gave such powre, and puissance great.

21

The faithfull knight now grew in litle space,
    By hearing her, and by her sisters lore,
    To such perfection of all heavenly grace,
    That wretched world he gan for to abhore,
    And mortall life gan loath, as thing forlore,
    Greev'd with remembrance of his wicked wayes,
    And prickt with anguish of his sinnes so sore,
    That he desirde, to end his wretched dayes:
So much the dart of sinfull guilt the soule dismayes.

22

But wise *Speranza* gave him comfort sweet,
    And taught him how to take assured hold
    upon her silver anchor, as was meet;
    Else had his sinnes so great, and manifold
    Made him forget all that *Fidelia* told.
    In this distressed doubtfull agonie,
    When him his dearest *Una* did behold,
    Disdeining life, desiring leave to die,
She found her selfe assayld with great perplexitie.

23

And came to *Cælia* to declare her smart,
    Who well acquainted with that commune plight,
    Which sinfull horror workes in wounded hart,
    Her wisely comforted all that she might,
    With goodly counsell and advisement right;
    And streightway sent with carefull diligence,
    To fetch a Leach, the which had great insight
    In that disease of grieved conscience,
And well could cure the same; His name was *Patience*.

24

Who comming to that soule-diseased knight,
    Could hardly him intreat, to tell his griefe:
    Which knowne, and all that noyd his heavie spright
    Well searcht, eftsoones he gan apply reliefe
    Of salves and med'cines, which had passing priefe,
    And thereto added wordes of wondrous might:
    By which to ease he him recured briefe,
    And much asswag'd the passion of his plight,
That he his paine endur'd, as seeming now more light.

25

But yet the cause and root of all his ill,
  Inward corruption, and infected sin,
  Not purg'd nor heald, behind remained still,
  And festring sore did rankle yet within,
  Close creeping twixt the marrow and the skin.
  Which to extirpe, he laid him privily
  Downe in a darkesome lowly place far in,
  Whereas he meant his corrosives to apply,
And with streight diet tame his stubborne malady.

26

In ashes and sackcloth he did array
  His daintie corse, proud humors to abate,
  And dieted with fasting every day,
  The swelling of his wounds to mitigate,
  And made him pray both earely and eke late:
  And ever as superfluous flesh did rot
  Amendment readie still at hand did wayt,
  To pluck it out with pincers firie whot,
That soone in him was left no one corrupted jot.

27

And bitter Pena with an yron whip,
  Was wont him once to disple every day:
  And sharp Remorse his hart did prick and nip,
  That drops of bloud thence like a well did play;
  And sad *Repentance* used to embay
  His bodie in salt water smarting sore,
  The filthy blots of sin to wash away.
  So in short space they did to health restore
The man that would not live, but erst lay at deathes dore.

28

In which his torment often was so great,
  That like a Lyon he would cry and rore,
  And rend his flesh, and his owne synewes eat.
  His owne deare *Una* hearing evermore
  His ruefull shriekes and gronings, often tore
  Her guiltlesse garments and her golden heare,
  For pitty of his paine and anguish sore;
  Yet all with patience wisely she did beare;
For well she wist his crime could else be never cleare.

29

Whom thus recover'd by wise Patience
   And trew *Repentaunce* they to *Una* brought:
   Who joyous of his cured conscience,
   Him dearely kist, and fayrely eke besought
   Himselfe to chearish, and consuming thought
   To put away out of his carefull brest.
   By this *Charissa*, late in child-bed brought,
   Was woxen strong, and left her fruitfull nest;
To her fayre *Una* brought this unacquainted guest.

30

She was a woman in her freshest age,
   Of wondrous beauty, and of bounty rare,
   With goodly grace and comely personage,
   That was on earth not easie to compare;
   Full of great love, but *Cupids* wanton snare
   As hell she hated, chast in worke and will;
   Her necke and brests were ever open bare,
   That ay thereof her babes might sucke their fill;
The rest was all in yellow robes arayed still.

31

A multitude of babes about her hong,
   Playing their sports, that joyd her to behold,
   Whom still she fed, whiles they were weake and young,
   But thrust them forth still, as they wexed old:
   And on her head she wore a tyre of gold,
   Adornd with gemmes and owches wondrous faire,
   Whose passing price uneath was to be told;
   And by her side there sate a gentle paire
Of turtle doves, she sitting in an yvorie chaire.

32

The knight and *Una* entring faire her greet,
   And bid her joy of that her happie brood;
   Who them requites with court'sies seeming meet,
   And entertaines with friendly chearefull mood.
   Then *Una* her besought, to be so good,
   As in her vertuous rules to schoole her knight,
   Now after all his torment well withstood,
   In that sad house of *Penaunce*, where his spright
Had past the paines of hell, and long enduring night.

33

She was right joyous of her just request,
  And taking by the hand that Faeries sonne,
  Gan him instruct in every good behest,
  Of love, and righteousnesse, and well to donne,
  And wrath and hatred warely to shonne,
  That drew on men Gods hatred, and his wrath,
  And many soules in dolours had fordonne:
  In which when him she well instructed hath,
From thence to heaven she teacheth him the ready path.

34

Wherein his weaker wandring steps to guide,
  An auntient matrone she to her does call,
  Whose sober lookes her wisedome well describe:
  Her name was *Mercie*, well knowne over all,
  To be both gratious, and eke liberall:
  To whom the carefull charge of him she gave,
  To lead aright, that he should never fall
  In all his waes through this wide worldes wave,
That Mercy in the end his righteous soule might save.

35

The godly Matrone by the hand him beares
  Forth from her presence, by a narrow way,
  Scattred with bushy thornes, and ragged breares,
  Which still before him she remov'd away,
  That nothing might his ready passage stay:
  And ever when his feet emcombred were,
  Or gan to shrinke, of from the right to stray,
  She held him fast, and firmely did upbeare,
As carefull Nourse her child from falling oft does reare.

36

Eftsoones unto an holy Hospitall,
  That was fore by the way, she did him bring,
  In which seven Bead-men, that had vowed all
  Their life to service of high heavens king
  Did spend their dayes in doing godly thing:
  Their gates to all were open evermore,
  That by the wearie way were traveiling,
  And one sate wayting ever them before,
To call in commers-by that needy were and pore.

37

The first of them that eldest was, and best,
  Of all the house had charge and governement,
  As Guardian and Steward of the rest:
  His office was to give entertainement
  And lodging, unto all that came, and went:
  Not unto such, as could him feast againe,
  And double quite, for that he on them spent,
  But such, as want of harbour did constraine:
Those for Gods sake his dewty was to entertaine.

38

The second was as Almner of the place,
  His office was, the hungry for to feed,
  And thristy give to drinke, a worke of grace:
  He feard not once him selfe to be in need,
  Ne car'd to hoord for those, whom he did breede:
  The grace of God he layd up still in store,
  Which as a stocke he left unto his seede;
  He had enough, what need him care for more?
And had he lesse, yet some he would give to the pore.

39

The third had of their wardrobe custodie,
  In which were not rich tyres, nor garments gay,
  The plumes of pride, and winges of vanitie,
  But clothes meet to keepe keene cold away,
  And naked nature seemely to aray;
  With which bare wretched wights he dayly clad,
  The images of God in earthly clay;
  And if that no spare cloths to give he had,
His owne coate he would cut, and it distribute glad.

40

The fourth appointed by his office was,
  Poore prisoners to relieve with gratious ayd,
  And captives to redeeme with price of bras,
  From Turkes and Sarazins, which them had stayd;
  And though they faultie were, yet well he wayd,
  That God to us forgiveth every howre
  Much more then that, why they in bands were layd,
  And he that harrowd hell with heavie stowre,
The faultie soules from thence brought to his heavenly bowre.

41

The fift had charge sicke persons to attend,
    And comfort those, in point of death which lay;
    For them most needeth comfort in the end,
    When sin, and hell, and death do most dismay
    The feeble soule departing hence away.
    All is but lost, that living we bestow,
    If not well ended at our dying day.
    O man have mind of that last bitter throw;
Far as the tree does fall, so lyes it ever low.

42

The sixt had charge of them now being dead,
    In seemely sort their corses to engrave,
    And deck with dainty flowres their bridall bed,
    That to their heavenly spouse both sweet and brave
    They might appeare, when he their soules shall save.
    The wondrous workemanship of Gods owne mould,
    Whose face he made, all beast to feare, and gave
    All in his hand, even dead we honour should.
Ah dearest God me graunt, I dead be not defould.

43

The seventh now after death and buriall done,
    Had charge the tender Orphans of the dead
    And widowes ayd, least they should be undone:
    In face of judgement he their right would plead,
    Ne ought the powre of mighty men did dread
    In their defence, nor would for gold or fee
    Be wonne their rightfull causes downe to tread:
    And when they stood in most necessitee,
He did supply their want, and gave them ever free.

44

There when the Elfin knight arrived was,
    The first and chiefest of the seven, whose care
    Was guests to welcome, towardes him did pas:
    Where seeing *Mercie*, that his steps up bare,
    And alwayes led, to her with reverence rare
    He humbly louted in meeke lowlinesse,
    And seemely welcome for her did prepare:
    For of their order she was Patronesse,
Albe *Charissa* were their chiefest founderesse.

45

There she awhile him stayes, him selfe to rest,
  That to the rest more able he might bee:
  During which time, in every good behest
  And godly worke of Almes and charitee
  She him instructed with great industree;
  Shortly therein so perfect he became,
  That, from the first unto the last degree,
  His mortall life he learned had to frame
In holy righteousnesse, without rebuke or blame.

46

Thence forward by that painfull way they pas,
  Forth to an hill, that was both steepe and hy;
  On top whereof a sacred chappell was,
  And eke a litle Hermitage thereby,
  Wherein an aged holy man did lye,
  That day and night said his devotion,
  Ne other worldly business did apply;
  His name was heavenly *Contemplation*;
Of God and goodnes was his meditation.

47

Great grace that old man to him given had;
  For God he often saw from heavens hight,
  All were his earthly eyen both blunt and bad,
  And through great age had lost their kindly sight,
  Yet wondrous quick and persant was his spright,
  As Eagles eye, that can behold the Sunne:
  That hill they scale with all their powre and might,
  That his frayle thighes nigh wearie and fordonne
Gan faile, but by her helpe the top at last he wonne.

48

There they do finde that godly aged Sire,
  With snowy lockes adowne his shoulders shed,
  As hoarie frost with spangles doth attire
  The mossy braunches of an Oke halfe ded.
  Each bone might through his body well be red,
  And every sinew seene through his long fast:
  For nought he car'd his carcas long unfed;
  His mind was full of spiritual repast,
And pyn'd his flesh, to keepe his body low and chast.

49

Who, when these two approching he aspide,
  At their first presence grew agrieved sore,
  That forst him lay his heavenly thoughts aside;
  And had he not that Dame respected more,
  Whom highly he did reverence and adore,
  He would not once have moved for the knight.
  They him saluted standing far afore;
  Who well them greeting, humbly did requight,
And asked, to what end they clomb that tedious height.

50

'What end' (quoth she) 'should cause us take such paine,
  But that same end, which every living wight
  Should make his marke, high heaven to attaine?
  Is not from hence the way, that leadeth right
  To that most glorious house, that glistreth bright
  With burning starres, and everliving fire,
  Whereof the keyes are to thy hand behight
  By wise *Fidelia*? Shee doth thee require,
To shew it to this knight, according his desire.'

51

'Thrise happy man,' said then the father grave,
  'Whose staggering steps thy steady hand doth lead,
  And shewes the way, his sinfull soule to save.
  Who better can the way to heaven aread,
  Then thou thy selfe, that was both borne and bred
  In heavenly throne, where thousand Angels shine?
  Thou doest the prayers of the righteous sead
  Present before the majestie divine,
And his avenging wrath to clemencie incline.

52

'Yet since thou bidst, thy pleasure shalbe donne.
  Then come thou man of earth, and see the way,
  That never yet was seene of Faeries sonne,
  That never leads the traveiler astray,
  But after labours long, and sad delay,
  Brings them to joyous rest and endlesse blis.
  But first thou must a season fast and pray,
  Till from her bands the spright assoiled is,
And have her strength recur'd from fraile infirmitis.'

53

That done, he leads him to the highest Mount;
    Such one, as that same mighty man of God,
    That bloud-red billowes like a walled front
    On either side disparted with his rod,
    Till that his army dry-foot through them yod,
    Dwelt fortie dayes upon; where writ in stone
    With bloudy letters by the hand of God,
    The bitter doome of death and balefull mone
He did receive, whiles flashing fire about him shone.

54

Or like that sacred hill, whose head full hie,
    Adornd with fruitfull Olives all arownd,
    Is, as it were for endlesse memory
    Of that deare Lord, who oft thereon was fownd,
    For ever with a flowring girlond crownd:
    Or like that pleasaunt Mount, that is for ay
    Through famous Poets verse each where renownd,
    On which the thrise three learned Ladies play
Their heavenly notes, and make full many a lovely lay.

55

From thence far off he unto him did shew
    A litle path, that was both steepe and long,
    Which to a goodly Citie led his vew;
    Whose wals and towres were builded high and strong
    Of perle and precious stone, that earthly tong
    Cannot describe, nor wit of man can tell;
    Too high a ditty for my simple song;
    The Citie of the great king hight it well,
Wherein eternall peace and happinesse doth dwell.

56

As he thereon stood gazing, he might see
    The blessed Angels to and fro descend
    From highest heaven, in gladsome companee,
    And with great joy into that Citie wend,
    As commonly as friend does with his frend.
    Whereat he wondred much, and gan enquere,
    What stately building durst so high extend
    Her loftie towres unto the starry sphere,
And what unknowen nation there empeopled were.

57

'Faire knight' (quoth he) '*Hierusalem* that is,
  The new *Hierusalem*, that God has built
  For those to dwell in, that are chosen his,
  His chosen people purg'd from sinfull guilt
  With pretious bloud, which cruelly was spilt
  On cursed tree, of that unspotted lam,
  That for the sinnes of all the world was kilt:
  Now are they Saints all in that Citie sam,
More deare unto their God, then younglings to their dam.'

58

'Till now,' said then the knight, 'I weened well,
  That great *Cleopolis*, where I have beene,
  In which that fairest *Faerie Queene* doth dwell,
  The fairest Citie was, that might be seene;
  And that bright towre all built of christall cleene,
  Panthea, seemd the brightest thing that was:
  But now by proofe all otherwise I weene;
  For this great Citie that does far surpas,
And this bright Angels towre quite dims that towre of glas.'

59

'Most trew,' then said the holy aged man;
  'Yet is *Cleopolis* for earthly frame,
  The fairest peece, that eye beholden can:
  And well beseemes all knights of noble name,
  That covet in th' immortall booke of fame
  To be eternized, that same to haunt,
  And doen their service to that soveraigne Dame,
  That glorie does to them for guerdon graunt:
For she is heavenly borne, and heaven may justly vaunt.

60

'And thou faire ymp, sprong out from English race,
  How ever now accompted Elfins sonne,
  Well worthy doest thy service for her grace,
  To aide a virgin desolate foredonne.
  But when thou famous victorie hast wonne,
  And high emongst all knights hast hong thy shield,
  Thenceforth the suit of earthly conquest shonne,
  And wash thy hands from guilt of bloudy field:
For bloud can nought but sin, and wars but sorrowes yield.

61

'Then seeke this path, that I to thee presage,
   Which after all to heaven shall thee send;
   Then peaceably thy painefull pilgrimage
   To yonder same *Hierusalem* do bend,
   Where is for thee ordaind a blessed end:
   For thou emongst those Saints whom thou doest see,
   Shalt be a Saint, and thine owne nations frend
   And Patrone: thou Saint *George* shalt called bee,
Saint *George* of mery England, the signe of victoree.'

62

'Unworthy wretch' (quoth he) 'of so great grace,
   How dare I thinke such glory to attaine?'
   'These that have it attaind, were in like cace
   (Quoth he) as wretched, and liv'd in like paine.'
   'But deeds of armes must I at last be faine,
   And Ladies love to leave so dearely bought?'
   'What need of armes, where peace doth ay remaine,'
   (Said he) 'and battailes none are to be fought?
As for loose loves they are vaine, and vanish into nought.'

63

'O let me not' (quoth he) 'then turne againe
   Backe to the world, whose joyes so fruitlesse are;
   But let me here for aye in peace remaine,
   Or streight way on that last long voyage fare,
   That nothing may my present hope empare.'
   'That may not be' (said he) 'ne maist thou yit
   Forgo that royall maides bequeathed care,
   Who did her cause into thy hand commit,
Till from her cursed foe thou have her freely quit.

64

'Then shall I soone,' (quoth he) 'so God me grace,
   Abet that virgins cause disconsolate,
   And shortly backe returne unto this place,
   To walke this way in Pilgrims poore estate.
   But now aread, old father, why of late
   Didst thou behight me borne of English blood,
   Whom all a Faeries sonne doen nominate?'
   'That word shall I' (said he) 'avouchen good,
Sith to thee is unknowne the cradle of thy brood.

65

'For well I wote, thou springst from ancient race
  Of *Saxon* kings, that have with mightie hand
  And many bloudie battailes fought in place
  High reard their royall throne in *Britane* land,
  And vanquisht them, unable to withstand:
  From thence a Faerie thee unweeting reft,
  There as thou slepst in tender swadling band,
  And her base Elfin brood there for thee left.
Such men do Chaungelings call, so chaung'd Faeries theft.

66

'Thence she thee brought into this Faerie lond,
  And in an heaped furrow did thee hyde,
  Where thee a Ploughman all unweeting fond,
  As he his toylesome teme that way did guyde,
  And brought thee up in ploughmans state to byde,
  Whereof *Georgos* he thee gave to name;
  Till prickt with courage, and thy forces pryde,
  To Faery court thou cam'st to seek for fame,
And prove thy puissaunt armes, as seemes thee best became.'

67

'O holy Sire' (quoth he) 'how shall I quight
  The many favours I with thee have found,
  That hast my name and nation red aright,
  And taught the way that does to heaven bound?'
  This said, adowne he looked to the ground,
  To have returnd, but dazed were his eyne,
  Through passing brightnesse, which did quite confound
  His feeble sence, and too exceeding shyne.
So darke are earthly things compard to things divine.

68

At last whenas himselfe he gan to find,
  To *Una* back he cast him to retire;
  Who him awaited still with pensive mind.
  Great thankes and goodly meed to that good syre,
  He thence departing gave for his paines hyre.
  So came to *Una*, who him joyd to see,
  And after litle rest, gan him desire,
  Of her adventure mindfull for to bee.
So leave they take of *Cælia*, and her daughters three.

Canto XI

The knight with that old Dragon fights
Two dayes incessantly:
The third him overthrowes, and gayns
Most glorious victory.

I

High time now gan it wex for *Una* faire
   To thinke of those her captive Parents deare,
   And thier forwasted Kingdom to repaire:
   Whereto whenas they now approched neare,
   With hartie wordes her knight she gan to cheare,
   And in her modest manner thus bespake;
   'Deare knight, as deare, as ever knight was deare,
   That all these sorrowes suffer for my sake,
High heaven behold the tedious toyle, ye for me take.

2

'Now are we come unto my native soyle,
   And to the place, where all our perils dwell;
   Here haunts that feend, and does his dayly spoyle,
   Therefore henceforth be at your keeping well,
   And ever ready for your foeman fell.
   The sparke of noble courage now awake,
   And strive your excellent selfe to excell;
   That shall ye evermore renowmed make,
Above all knights on earth, that batteill undertake.'

3

And pointing forth, 'lo yonder is' (said she)
   'The brasen towre in which my parents deare
   For dread of that huge feend emprisond be,
   Whom I from far see on the walles appeare,
   Whose sight my feeble soule doth greatly cheare:
   And on top of all I do espye
   The watchman wayting tydings glad to heare,
   That O my parents might I happily
Unto you bring, to ease you of your misery.'

4

With that they heard a roaring hideous sound,
   That all the ayre with terrour filled wide,
   And seemd uneath to shake the stedfast ground.
   Eftsoones that dreadful Dragon they espide,
   Where stretcht he lay upon the sunny side

Of a great hill, himselfe like a great hill.
But all so soone, as he from far descride
Those glistring armes, that heaven with light did fill,
He rousd himselfe full blith, and hastned them untill.

5

Then bad the knight his Lady yede aloofe,
And to an hill her selfe withdraw aside,
From whence she might behold that battailles proof
And eke be safe from daunger far descryde:
She him obayd, and turned a little wyde.
Now O thou sacred Muse, most learned Dame,
Fayre ympe of *Phœbus*, and his aged bride,
The Nourse of time, and everlasting fame,
That warlike hands ennoblest with immortall name;

6

O gently come into my feeble brest,
Come gently, but not with that mighty rage,
Wherewith the martiall troupes thou doest infest,
And hartes of great Heroës doest enrage,
That nought their kindled courage may aswage,
Soone as thy dreadfull trompe begins to sownd;
The God of warre with his fiers equipage
Thou doest awake, sleepe never he so sownd,
And scared nations doest with horrour sterne astownd.

7

Faire Goddesse lay that furious fit aside,
Till I of warres and bloudy *Mars* do sing,
And Briton fields with Sarazin bloud bedyde,
Twixt that great faery Queene and Paynim king,
That with their horrour heaven and earth did ring,
A worke of labour long, and endlesse prayse:
But now a while let downe that haughtie string,
And to my tunes thy second tenor rayse,
That I this man of God his godly armes may blaze.

8

By this the dreadful Beast drew nigh to hand,
Halfe flying, and halfe footing in his hast,
That with his largenesse measured much land,
And made wide shadow under his huge wast;
As mountaine doth the valley overcast.
Approching nigh, he reared high afore

His body monstrous, horrible, and vast,
   Which to increase his wondrous greatnesse more,
Was swoln with wrath and poyson, and with bloudy gore.

9

And over, all with brasen scales was armd,
   Like plated coate of steele, so couched neare,
   That nought mote perce, ne might his corse be harmd
   With dint of sword, nor push of pointed speare;
   Which as an Eagle, seeing pray appeare,
   His aery plumes doth rouze, full rudely dight,
   So shakd he, that horrour was to heare,
   For as the clashing of an Armour bright,
Such noyse his rouzed scales did send unto the knight.

10

His flaggy wings when forth he did display,
   Were like two sayles, in which the hollow wynd
   Is gathered full, and worketh speedy way:
   And eke the pennes, that did his pineons bynd,
   Were like mayne-yards with flying canvas lynd,
   With which whenas him list the ayre to beat,
   And there by force unwonted passage find,
   The cloudes before him fled for terror great,
And all the heavens stood still amazed with his threat.

11

His huge long tayle wound up in hundred foldes,
   Does overspred his long bras-scaly backe,
   Whose wreathed boughts when ever he unfoldes,
   And thick entangled knots adown does slacke,
   Bespotted as with shields of red and blacke,
   It sweepeth all the land behind him farre,
   And of three furlongs does but litle lacke;
   And at the point two stings in-fixed arre,
Both deadly sharpe, that sharpest steele exceeden farre.

12

But stings and sharpest steele did far exceed
   The sharpnesse of his cruel rending clawes;
   Dead was it sure, as sure as death in deed,
   What ever thing does touch his ravenous pawes,
   Or what within his reach he ever drawes.
   But his most hideous head my toung to tell,
   Does tremble: for his deepe devouring jawes

  Wide gaped, like the griesly mouth of hell
Through which into his darke abisse all ravin fell.

13

And that more wondrous was, in either jaw
    Three ranckes of yron teeth enraunged were,
    In which yet trickling bloud and gobbets raw
    Of late devoured bodies did appeare,
    That sight thereof bred cold congealed feare:
    Which to increase, and all atonce to kill,
    A cloud of smoothering smoke and sulphur seare
    Out of his stinking gorge forth steemed still,
That all the ayre about with smoke and stench did fill.

14

His blazing eyes, like two bright shining shields,
    Did burne with wrath, and sparkled living fyre;
    As two broad Beacons, set in open fields,
    Send forth their flames far off to every shyre,
    And warning give that enemies conspyre,
    With fire and sword the region to invade;
    So flam'd his eyne with rage and rancorous yre:
    But farre within, as in a hollow glade,
Those glaring lampes were set, that made a dreadfull shade.

15

So dreadfully he towards him did pas,
    Forelifting up loft his speckled brest,
    And often bounding on the brused gras,
    As for great joyance of his newcome guest.
    Elftsoones he gan advance his haughtie crest,
    As chauffed Bore his bristles doth upreare,
    And shoke his scales to battell readie drest;
    That made the *Redcrosse* knight nigh quake for feare,
As bidding bold defiaunce to his foeman neare.

16

The knight gan fairely couch his steadie speare,
    And fiercely ran at him with rigorous might:
    The pointed steele, arriving rudely theare,
    His harder hide would neither perce, nor bight,
    But glauncing by forth passed forward right;
    Yet sore amoved with so puissaunt push,
    The wrathfull beast about him turned light,
    And him so rudely passing by, did brush
With his long tayle, that horse and man to ground did rush.

17

Both horse and man up lightly rose againe,
  And fresh encounter toward him addrest:
  But th' idle stroke yet backe recoyld in vaine,
  And found no place his deadly point to rest.
  Exceeding rage enflam'd the furious beast,
  To be avenged of so great despight;
  For never felt his imperceable brest
  So wondrous force, from hand of living wight;
Yet had he prov'd the powre of many a puissant knight.

18

Then with his waving wings displayed wyde,
  Himselfe up high he lifted from the ground,
  And with strong flight did forcibly divide
  The yielding aire, which nigh too feeble found
  Her flitting partes, and element unsound,
  To beare so great a weight: he cutting way
  With his broad sayles, about him soared round:
  At last low stouping with unweldie sway,
Snatcht up both horse and man, to beare them quite away.

19

Long he them bore above the subject plaine,
  So far as Ewghen bow a shaft may send,
  Till struggling strong did him at last constraine,
  To let them downe before his fightes end:
  As hagard hauke presuming to contend
  With hardie fowle, above his hable might,
  His wearie pounces all in vaine doth spend,
  To trusse the pray too heavie for his flight;
Which comming down to ground, does free it selfe by fight.

20

He so disseized of his gryping grosse,
  The knight his thrillant speare againe assayd
  In his bras-plated body to embosse,
  And three mens strength unto the stroke he layd;
  Wherewith the strife beame quaked, as affrayd,
  And glauncing from his scaly necke, did glyde
  Close under his left wing, then broad displayd.
  The percing steele there wrought a wound full wyde,
That with the uncouth smart the Monster lowdly cryde.

21

He cryde, as raging seas are wont to rore,
   When wintry storme his wrathful wreck does threat,
   The rolling billowes beate the ragged shore,
   As they the earth would shoulder from her seat,
   And greedie gulfe does gape, as he would eat
   His neighbour element in his revenge:
   Then gin the blustring brethren boldly threat
   To move the world from off his stedfast henge,
And boystrous battell make, each other to avenge.

22

The steely head stucke fast still in his flesh,
   Till with his cruell clawes he snatcht the wood,
   And quite a sunder broke. Forth flowed fresh
   A gushing river of blacke goarie blood,
   That drowned all the land whereon he stood;
   The streame thereof would drive a water-mill.
   Trebly augmented was his furious mood
   With bitter sense of his deepe rooted ill,
That flames of fire he threw forth from his large nosethrill.

23

His hideous tayle then hurled he about,
   And therewith all enwrapt the nimble thyes
   Of his froth-fomy steed, whose courage stout
   Striving to loose the knot, that fast him tyes,
   Himselfe in streighter bandes too rash implyes,
   That to the ground he is perforce constraynd
   To throw his rider: who can quickly ryse
   From off the earth, with durty bloud distaynd,
For that reprochfull fall right fowly he disdaynd.

24

And fiercely tooke his trenchand blade in hand,
   With which he stroke so furious and so fell,
   That nothing seemd the puissaunce could withstand:
   Upon his crest the hardned yron fell,
   But his more hardned crest was armd so well,
   That deeper dint therein it would not make;
   Yet so extremely did the buffe him quell,
   That from thenceforth he shund the like to take,
But when he saw them come, he did them still forsake.

25

The knight was wroth to see his stroke beguyld,
　　And smot againe with more outrageous might;
　　But backe againe the sparckling steele recoyld,
　　And left not any marke, where it did light;
　　As if in Adamant rocke it had beene pight,
　　The beast impatient of his smarting wound,
　　And of so fierce and forcible despight,
　　Thought with his wings to stye above the ground;
But his late wounded wing unserviceable found.

26

Then full of griefe and anguish vehement,
　　He lowdly brayd, that like was never heard,
　　And from his wide devouring oven sent
　　A flake of fire, that flashing in his beard,
　　Him all amazd, and almost made affeard:
　　The scorching flame sore swinged all his face,
　　And through his armour all his bodie seard,
　　That he could not endure so cruell cace,
But thought his armes to leave, and helmet to unlace.

27

Not that great Champion of the antique world,
　　Whom famous Poetes verse so much doth vaunt,
　　And hath for twelve huge labours high extold,
　　So many furies and sharpe fits did haunt,
　　When him the poysoned garment did enchaunt
　　With *Centaures* bloud, and bloudie verses charm’d,
　　As did this knight twelve thousand dolours daunt,
　　Whom fyrie steele now burnt, that earst him arm’d,
That erst him goodly armd, now most of all him harm’d.

28

Fant, wearie, sore, emboyled, grieved, brent
　　With heat, toyle, wounds, armes, smart, and inward fire
　　That never man such mischiefes did torment;
　　Death better were, death did he oft desire,
　　But death will never come, when needes require.
　　Whom so dismayd when that his foe beheld,
　　He cast to suffer him no more respire,
　　But gan his sturdie sterne about to weld,
And him so strongly stroke, that to the ground him feld.

29

It fortuned (as faire it then befell)
  Behind his backe unweeting, where he stood,
  Of auncient time there was a springing well,
  From which fast trickled forth a silver flood,
  Full of great vertues, and for med'cine good.
  Whylome, before that cursed Dragon got
  That happie land, and all with innocent blood
  Defyld those sacred waves, it rightly hot
The well of life ne yet his vertues had forgot.

30

For unto life the dead it could restore,
  And guilt of sinfull crimes cleane wash away,
  Those that with sicknesse were infected sore,
  It could recure, and aged long decay
  Renew, as one were borne that very day.
  Both *Silo* this, and *Jordan* did excell,
  And th' English *Bath*, and eke the german *Spau*,
  Ne can *Cephise*, nor *Hebrus* match this well:
Into the same the knight back overthrowen, fell.

31

Now gan the golden *Phœbus* for to steepe
  His fierie face in billowes of the west,
  And his faint steedes watred in Ocean deepe,
  Whiles from their journall labours they did rest,
  When that infernall Monster, having kest
  His wearie foe into that living well,
  Can high advance his broad discoloured brest,
  Above his wonted pitch, with countenance fell,
And clapt his yron wings, as victor he did dwell.

32

Which when his pensive Ladie saw from farre,
  Great woe and sorrow did her soule assay,
  As weening that the sad end of the warre,
  And gan to highest God entirely pray,
  That feared chance from her to turne away;
  With folded hands and knees full lowly bent
  All night she watcht, ne once adowne would lay
  Her daintie limbs in her sad dreriment,
But praying still did wake, and waking did lament.

33

The morrow next gan earely to appeare,
   That *Titan* rose to runne his daily race;
   But earely ere the morrow next gan reare
   Out of the sea faire *Titans* deawy face,
   Up rose the gentle virgin from her place,
   And looked all about, if she might spy
   Her loved knight to move his manly pace:
   For she had great doubt of his safety,
Since late she saw him fall before his enemy.

34

At last she saw, where he upstarted brave
   Out of the well, wherein he drenched lay;
   As Eagle fresh out of the Ocean wave,
   Where he hath left his plumes all hoary gray,
   And deckt himselfe with feathers youthly gay,
   Like Eyas hauke up mounts unto the skies,
   His newly-budded pineons to assay,
   And marveiles at himselfe, still as he flies:
So new this new-borne knight to battell new did rise.

35

Whom when the damned feend so fresh did spy,
   No wonder if he wondred at the sight,
   And doubted, whether his late enemy
   It were, or other new supplied knight.
   He, now to prove his late-renewed might,
   High brandishing his bright deaw-burning blade,
   Upon his crested scalpe so sore did smite,
   That to the scull a yawning wound it made:
The deadly dint his dulled senses all dismaid.

36

I wote not, whether the revenging steele
   Were hardned with that holy water dew,
   Wherein he fell, or sharper edge did feele,
   Or his baptized hands now greater grew;
   Or other secret vertue did ensew;
   Els never could the force of fleshly arme,
   Ne molten mettall in his bloud embrew:
   For till that stownd could never wight him harme,
By subtilty, nor slight, nor might, nor mighty charme.

37

The cruell wound enraged him so sore,
   That loud he yelded for exceeding paine;
   As hundred ramping Lyons seem'd to rore,
   Whom ravenous hunger did thereto constraine:
   Then gan he tosse aloft his stretched traine,
   And therewith scourge the buxome aire so sore,
   That to his force to yeelden it was faine;
   Ne ought his sturdie strokes might stand afore,
That high trees overthrew, and rocks in peeces tore.

38

The same advauncing high above his head,
   With sharpe intended sting so rude him smot,
   That to the earth him drove, as stricken dead,
   Ne living wight would have him life behot:
   The mortall sting his angry needle shot
   Quite through his shield, and in his shoulder seasd,
   Where fast it stucke, ne would thereout be got:
   The griefe thereof him wondrous sore diseasd,
Ne might his ranckling paine with patience be appeasd.

39

But yet more mindfull of his honour deare,
   Then of the grievous smart, which him did wring,
   From loathed soile he can him lightly reare,
   And strove to loose the far infixed sting:
   Which when in vaine he tryde with struggeling,
   Inflam'd with wrath, his raging blade he heft,
   And strooke so strongly, that the knotty string
   Of his huge taile he quite a sonder cleft,
Five joints thereof he hewd, and but the stump him left.

40

Hart cannot thinke, what outrage, and what cryes,
   With foule enfouldred smoake and flashing fire,
   The hell-bred beast threw forth unto the skyes,
   That all was covered with darknesse dire:
   Then fraught with rancour, and engorged ire,
   He cast at once him to avenge for all,
   And gathering up himselfe out of the mire,
   With his uneven wings did fiercely fall
Upon his sunne-bright shield, and gript it fast withall.

41

Much was the man encombred with his hold,
  In feare to lose his weapon in his paw,
  Ne wist yet, how his talants to unfold;
  Nor harder was from *Cerberus* greedie jaw
  To plucke a bone, then from his cruell claw
  To reave by strength, the griped gage away:
  Thrise he assayd it from his foot to draw,
  And thrise in vaine to draw it did assay,
It booted nought to thinke, to robbe him of his pray.

42

Tho when he saw no power might prevaile,
  His trustie sword he cald to his last aid,
  Wherewith he fiercely did his foe assaile,
  And double blowes about him stoutly laid,
  That glauncing fire out of the yron plaid;
  As sparckles from the Andvile use to fly,
  When heavie hammers on the wedge are swaid;
  Therewith at last he forst him to unty
One of his grasping feete, him to defend thereby.

43

The other foot fast fixed on his shield,
  Whenas no strength, nor stroks mot him constraine
  To loose, ne yet the warlike pledge to yield,
  He smot thereat with all his might and maine,
  That nought so wondrous puissaunce might sustaine;
  Upon the joynt the lucky steele did light,
  And made such way, that hewd it quite in twaine;
  The paw yet missed not his minisht might,
But hong still on the shield, as it at first was pight.

44

For griefe thereof, and divelish despight,
  From his infernall fournace forth he threw
  Huge flames, that dimmed all the heavens light,
  Enrold in duskish smoke and brimstone blew;
  As burning *Aetna* from his boyling stew
  Doth belch out flames, and rockes in peeces broke,
  And ragged ribs of mountaines molten new,
  Enwrapt in coleblacke clouds and filthy smoke,
That all the land with stench and heaven with horror choke.

45

The heate whereof, and harmefull pestilence
 So sore him noyd, that forst him to retire
 A little backward for his best defence,
 To save his bodie from the scorching fire,
 Which he from hellish entrailes did expire.
 It chaunst (eternall God that chaunce did guide)
 As he recoyled backward, in the mire
 His nigh forewearied feeble feet did slide,
And downe he fell, with dread of shame sore terrifide.

46

There grew a goodly tree him faire beside,
 Loaden with fruit and apples rosie red,
 As they in pure vermilion had been dide,
 Whereof great vertues over all were red:
 For happie life to all which thereon fed,
 And life eke everlasting did befall:
 Great God it planted in that blessed sted
 With his almightie hand, and did it call
The tree of life, the crime of our first fathers fall.

47

In all the world like was not to be found,
 Save in that soile, where all good things did grow,
 And freely sprong out of the fruitfull ground,
 As incorrupted Nature did them sow,
 Till that dread Dragon all did overthrow.
 Another like faire tree eke grew thereby,
 Whereof whoso did eat, eftsoones did know
 Both good and ill: O mornefull memory:
That tree through one mans fault hath doen us all to dy.

48

From that first tree forth flowd, as from a well,
 A trickling streame of Balme, most soveraine
 And daintie deare, which on the ground still fell,
 And overflowed all the fertill plaine,
 As it had deawed bene with timely raine:
 Life and long health that gratious ointment gave,
 And deadly woundes could heale, and reare againe
 The sencelesse corse appointed for the grave.
Into that same he fell: which did from death him save.

49

For nigh thereto the ever damned beast
   Durst not approch, for he was deadly made,
   And all that life preserved, did detest:
   Yet he it oft adventur'd to invade.
   By this the drouping day-light gan to fade,
   And yeeld his roome to sad succeeding night,
   Who with her sable mantle gan to shade
   The face of earth, and wayes of living wight,
And high her burning torch set up in heaven bright.

50

When gentle *Una* saw the second fall
   Of her deare knight, who wearie of long fight,
   And faint through losse of bloud, mov'd not at all,
   But lay as in a dreame of deepe delight,
   Besmeard with pretious Balme, whose vertuous might
   Did heale his wounds, and scorching heat alay,
   Againe she stricken was with sore affright,
   And for his safetie gan devoutly pray;
And watch the noyous night, and wait for joyous day.

51

The joyous day gan early to appeare,
   And faire *Aurora* from the deawy bed
   Of aged *Tithone* gan her selfe to reare,
   With rosie cheekes, for shame as blushing red;
   Her golden lockes for haste were loosely shed
   About her eares, when *Una* her did marke
   Clymbe to her charet, all with flowers spred,
   From heaven high to chase the chearelesse darke;
With merry note her loud salutes the mounting larke.

52

Then freshly up arose the doughtie knight,
   All healed of his hurts and woundes wide,
   And did himselfe to battell readie dight;
   Whose early foe awaiting him beside
   To have devourd, so soone as day he spyde,
   When now he saw himselfe so freshly reare,
   As if late fight had nought him damnifyde,
   He woxe dismayd, and gan his fate to feare;
Nathlesse with wonted rage he him advaunced neare.

53

And in his first encounter, gaping wide,
  He thought attonce him to have swallowd quight,
  And rusht upon him with outragious pride;
  Who him r'encountring fierce, as hauke in flight,
  Perforce rebutted backe.   The weapon bright
  Taking advantage of his open jaw,
  Ran through his mouth with so importune might,
  That deepe emperst his darksom hollow maw,
And back retyrd, his life bloud forth with all did draw.

54

So downe he fell, and forth his life did beath,
  That vanisht into smoke and cloudes swift;
  So downe he fell, that th' earth him underneath
  Did grone, as feeble so great load to lift;
  So downe he fell, as an huge rockie clift,
  Whose false foundation waves have washt away,
  With dreadfull poyse is from the mayneland rift,
  And rolling downe, great *Neptune* doth dismay;
So downe he fell, and like an heaped mountaine lay.

55

The knight himselfe even trembled at his fall,
  So huge and horrible a masse it seem'd;
  And his deare Ladie, that beheld it all,
  Durst not approch for dread, which she misdeem'd,
  But yet at last, whenas the direfull feend
  She saw not stirre, off-shaking vaine affright,
  She nigher drew, and saw that joyous end:
  Then God she praysd, and thankt her faithfull knight,
That had atchiev'd so great a conquest by his might.

Canto XII

Fayre Una to the Redcrosse knight
Betrouthed is with joy:
Though false Duessa it to barre
Her false sleights doe imploy.

I

Behold I see the haven nigh at hand
  To which I meane my wearie course to bend;
  Vere the maine shete, and beare up with the land,
  The which afore is fairely to be kend,
  And seemeth safe from stormes, that may offend;
  There this faire virgin wearie of her way
  Must landed bee, now at her journeyes end:
  There eke my feeble barke a while may stay,
Till merry wind and weather call her thence away.

2

Scarsely had *Phœbus* in the glooming East
  Yett harnessed his firie-footed teeme,
  Ne reard above the earth his flaming creast,
  When the last deadly smoke aloft did steeme,
  That signe of last outbreathed life did seeme,
  Unto the watchman on the castle wall;
  Who thereby dead that balefull Beast did deeme,
  And to his Lord and Ladie lowd gan call,
To tell, how he had seene the Dragons fatall fall.

3

Uprose with hastie joy, and feeble speed
  That aged Sire, the Lord of all that land,
  And looked forth, to weet, if true indeede
  Those tydinges were, as he did understand,
  Which whenas true by tryall he out fond,
  He bad to open wyde his brazen gate,
  Which long time had beene shut, and out of hond
  Proclaymed joy and peace through all his state;
For dead now was their foe, which them forrayed late.

4

Then gan triumphant Trompets sownd on hie,
  That sent to heaven the ecchoed report
  Of their new joy, and happie victorie
  Gainst him, that had them long opprest with tort,
  And fast imprisoned in sieged fort.

Then all the people, as in solemne feast,
To him assembled with one full consort,
Rejoycing at the fall of that great beast,
From whose eternall bondage now thy were releast.

5

Forth came that auncient Lord and aged Queene,
  Arayd in antique robes downe to the ground,
  And sad habiliments right well beseene;
  A noble crew about them waited round
  Of sage and sober Peres, all gravely gownd;
  Whom farre before did march a goodly band
  Of tall young men, all hable armes to sownd,
  But now they laurell braunches bore in hand;
Glad signe of victorie and peace in all their land.

6

Unto that doughtie Conquerour they came,
  And him before themselves prostrating low,
  Their Lord and Patrone loud did him proclame,
  And at his feet their laurell boughes did throw.
  Soone after them all dauncing on a row
  The comely virgins came, with girlands dight,
  As fresh as flowres in medow greene do grow,
  When morning deaw upon their leaves doth light:
And in their hands sweet Timbrels all upheld on hight.

7

And them before, the fry of children young
  Their wanton sports and childish mirth did play,
  And to the Maydens sounding tymbrels sung
  In well attuned notes, a joyous lay,
  And made delightful musicke all the way,
  Untill they came, where that faire virgin stood;
  As fare *Diana* in fresh sommers day,
  Beholds her Nymphes, enraung'd in shadie wood,
Some wrestle, some do run, some bathe in christall flood.

8

So she beheld those maydens meriment
  With chearefull vew; who when to her they came,
  Themselves to ground with gracious humblesse bent,
  And her ador'd by honorable name,
  Lifting to heaven her everlasting fame:
  Then on her head they set a girlond greene,

And crowned her twixt earnest and twixt game;
　　Who in her self-resemblance well beseene,
Did seeme such, as she was, a goodly maiden Queene.

9

And after, all the raskall many ran,
　　Heaped together in rude rablement,
　　To see the face of that victorious man:
　　Whom all admired, as from heaven sent,
　　And gazd upon with gaping wonderment.
　　But when they came, where that dead Dragon lay,
　　Stretcht on the ground in monstrous large extent,
　　The sight with idle feare did them dismay,
Ne durst approch him nigh, to touch, or once assay.

10

Some feard, and fled; some feard and well it faynd;
　　One that would wiser seeme, then all the rest,
　　Warnd him not touch, for yet perhaps remaynd
　　Some lingring life within his hollow brest,
　　Or in his wombe might lurke some hidden nest
　　Of many Dragonets, his fruitfull seed;
　　Another said, that in his eyes did rest
　　Yet sparckling fyre, and bad thereof take heed;
Another said, he saw him move his eyes indeed.

11

One mother, when as her foolhardie chyld
　　Did come too neare, and with his talants play,
　　Halfe dead through feare, her litle babe revyld,
　　And to her gossips gan in counsell say;
　　'How can I tell, but that his talants may
　　Yet scratch my sonne, or rend his tender hand?'
　　So diversly them selves in vaine they fray;
　　Whiles some more bold, to measure him nigh stand,
To prove how many acres he did spread of land.

12

Thus flocked all the folke him round about,
　　The whiles that hoarie king, with all his traine,
　　Being arrived, where that champion stout
　　After his foes defeasance did remaine,
　　Him goodly greetes, and faire does entertaine,
　　With princely gifts of yvorie and gold,
　　And thousand thankes him yeelds for all his paine.

Then when his daughter deare he does behold,
Her dearely doth imbrace, and kisseth manifold.

13

And after to his Pallace he them brings,
   With shaumes, and trompets, and with Clarions sweet;
   And all the way the joyous people sings,
   And with their garments strowes the paved street:
   Whence mounting up, they find purveyaunce meet
   Of all, that royall Princes court became,
   And all the floore was underneath their feet
   Bespred with costly scarlot of great name,
On which they lowly sit, and fitting purpose frame.

14

What needs me tell their feast and goodly guize,
   In which was nothing riotous nor vaine?
   What needs of daintie dishes to devize,
   Of comely services, or courtly trayne?
   My narrow leaves cannot in them containe
   The large discourse of royall Princes state.
   Yet was their manner then but bare and plaine:
   For th' antique world excesse and pride did hate;
Such proud luxurious pompe is swollen up but late.

15

Then when with meates and drinkes of every kinde
   Their fervent appetites they quenched had,
   That auncient Lord gan fit occasion finde,
   Of straunge adventures, and of perils sad,
   Which in his travell him befallen had,
   For to demaund of his renowmed guest:
   Who then with utt'rance grave, and count'nance sad,
   From point to point, as is before exprest,
Discourst his voyage long, according his request.

16

Great pleasure mixt with pittifull regard,
   That godly King and Queene did passionate,
   Whiles they his pittifull adventures heard,
   That oft they did lament his lucklesse state,
   And often blame the too importune fate,
   That heapd on him so many wrathfull wreakes:
   For never gentle knight, as he of late,
   So tossed was in fortunes cruell freakes;
And all the while salt teares bedeawd the hearers cheaks.

17

Then said that royall Pere in sober wise;
  'Deare Sonne, great beene the evils, which ye bore
  From first to last in your late enterprise,
  That I note, whether prayse, or pitty more:
  For never living man, I weene, so sore
  In sea of deadly daungers was distrest;
  But since now safe ye seised have the shore,
  And well arrived are, (high God be blest)
Let us devize of ease and everlasting rest.'

18

'Ah dearest Lord,' said then that doughty knight,
  'Of ease or rest I may not yet devize;
  For by the faith, which I to armes have plight,
  I bonden am streight after this emprize,
  As that your daughter can ye well advize,
  Backe to returne to that great Faerie Queene,
  And her to serve six yeares in warlike wize,
  Gainst that proud Paynim king, that works her teene:
Therefore I ought crave pardon, till I there have beene.'

19

'Unhappie falles that hard necessitie,'
  (Quoth he) 'the troubler of my happie peace,
  And vowed foe of my felicitie;
  Ne I against the same can justly preace:
  But since that band ye cannot now release,
  Nor doen undo; (for vowes may not be vaine)
  Soone as the terme of those six yeares shall cease,
  Ye then shall hither backe returne againe,
The marriage to accomplish vowd betwixt you twain.

20

'Which for my part I covet to performe,
  In sort as through the world I did proclame,
  That who so kild that monster most deforme,
  And him in hardly battaile overcame,
  Should have mine onely daughter to his Dame,
  And of my kingdome heire apparaunt bee:
  Therefore since now to thee perteines the same,
  By dew desert of noble chevalree,
Both daughter and eke kingdome, lo I yield to thee.'

21

Then forth he called that his daughter faire,
  The fairest *Un'* his onely daughter deare,
  His onely daughter, and his only heyre;
  Who forth proceeding with sad sober cheare,
  As bright as doth the morning starre appeare
  Out of the East, with flaming lockes bedight,
  To tell that dawning day is drawing neare,
  And to the world does bring long wished light;
So faire and fresh that Lady shewd her selfe in sight.

22

So faire and fresh, as freshest flowre in May;
  For she had layd her mournefull stole aside,
  And widow-like sad wimple throwne away,
  Wherewith her heavenly beautie she did hide,
  Whiles on her wearie journey she did ride;
  And on her now a garment she did weare,
  All lilly white, withoutten spot, or pride,
  That seemd like silke and silver woven neare,
But neither silke nor silver therein did appeare.

23

The blazing brightnesse of her beauties beame,
  And glorious light of her sunshyny face
  To tell, were as to strive against the streame.
  My ragged rimes are all too rude and bace,
  Her heavenly lineaments for to enchace.
  Ne wonder; for her own deare loved knight,
  All were she dayly with himselfe in place,
  Did wonder much at her celestiall sight:
Oft had he seene her faire, but never so faire dight.

24

So fairely dight, when she in presence came,
  She to her Sire made humble reverence,
  And bowed low, that her right well became,
  And added grace unto her excellence:
  Who with great wisedome, and grave eloquence
  Thus gan to say.   But eare he thus had said,
  With flying speede, and seeming great pretence,
  Came running in, much like a man dismaid,
A Messenger with letters, which his message said.

25

All in the open hall amazed stood,
  At suddeinnesse of that unwarie sight,
  And wondred at his breathlesse hastie mood.
  But he for nought would stay his passage right,
  Till fast before the king he did alight;
  Where falling flat, great humblesse he did make,
  And kist the ground, whereon his foot was pight;
  Then to his hands that writ he did betake,
Which he disclosing, read thus, as the paper spake.

26

'To thee, most mighty king of *Eden* faire,
  Her greeting sends in these sad lines addrest,
  The wofull daughter, and forsaken heire
  Of that great Emperour of all the West;
  And bids thee be advized for the best,
  Ere thou thy daughter linck in holy band
  Of wedlocke to that new unknowen guest:
  For he already plighted his right hand
Unto another love, and to another land.

27

'To me sad mayd, or rather widow sad,
  He was affiaunced long time before,
  And sacred pledges he both gave, and had,
  False erraunt knight, infamous, and forswore:
  Witnesse the burning Altars, which he swore,
  And guiltie heavens of his bold perjury,
  Which though he hath polluted oft of yore,
  Yet I to them for judgement just do fly,
And them conjure t'avenge this shamefull injury.

28

'Therefore since mine he is, or free or bond,
  Or false or trew, or living or else dead,
  Withhold, O soveraine Prince, your hasty hond
  From knitting league with him, I you aread;
  Ne weene my right with strength adowne to tread,
  Through weaknesse of my widowhed, or woe:
  For truth is strong, her rightfull cause to plead,
  And shall find friends, if need requireth soe,
So bids thee well to fare, Thy neither friend, nor foe, *Fidessa*.'

29

When he these bitter byting wordes had red,
　The tydings straunge did him abashed make,
　That still he sate long time astonished
　As in great muse, ne word to creature spake.
　At last his solemne silence thus he brake,
　With doubtfull eyes fast fixed on his guest;
　'Redoubted knight, that for mine only sake
　Thy life and honor late adventurest,
Let nought be hid from me, that ought to be exprest.

30

'What meane these bloudy vowes, and idle threats,
　Throwne out from womanish impatient mind?
　What heavens? what altars? what enraged heates
　Here heaped up with termes of love unkind,
　My conscience cleare with guilty bands would bind?
　High God be witnesse that I guiltlesse ame.
　But if your selfe, Sir knight, ye faultie find,
　Or wrapped be in loves of former Dame,
With crime do not it cover, but disclose the same.'

31

To whom the *Redcrosse* knight this answere sent,
　'My Lord, my King, be nought hereat dismayd,
　Till well ye wote by grave intendiment,
　What woman, and wherefore doth me upbrayd
　With breach of love, and loyalty betrayd.
　It was in my mishaps, as hitherward
　I lately traveild, that unwares I strayd
　Out of my way, through perils straunge and hard;
That day should faile me, ere I had them all declard.

32

'There did I find, or rather I was found
　Of this false woman, that *Fidessa* hight,
　Fidessa hight the falsest Dame on ground,
　Most false *Duessa*, royall richly dight,
　That easie was t' invegle weaker sight:
　Who by her wicked arts, and wylie skill,
　Too false and strong for earthly skill or might,
　Unwares me wrought unto her wicked will,
And to my foe betrayd, when least I feared ill.'

33

Then stepped forth the goodly royall Mayd,
    And on the ground her selfe prostrating low,
    With sober countenance thus to him say'd;
    'O pardon me, my soveraigne Lord, to show
    The secret treasons, which of late I know
    To have bene wrought by that false sorceresse.
    She onely she it is, that earst did throw
    This gentle knight into so great distresse,
That death him did awaite in dayly wretchednesse.

34

'And now it seemes, that she suborned hath
    This craftie messenger with letters vaine,
    To worke new woe and improvided scath,
    By breaking of the band betwixt us twaine;
    Wherein she used hath the practicke paine
    Of this false footman, clokt with simplenesse,
    Whom if ye please for to discover plaine,
    Ye shall him *Archimago* find, I ghesse,
The falsest man alive; who tries shall find no lesse.'

35

The king was greatly moved at her speach,
    And all with suddein indignation fraight,
    Bad on the Messenger rude hands to reach.
    Eftsoones the Gard, which on his state did wait,
    Attacht that faitor false, and bound his strait:
    Who seeming sorely chauffed at his band,
    As chained Beare, whom cruell dogs do bait,
    With idle force did faine them to withstand,
And often semblaunce made to scape out of their hand.

36

But they him layd full low in dungeon deepe,
    And bound him hand and foote with yron chains.
    And with continual watch did warely keepe;
    Who then would thinke, that by his subtile trains
    He could escape fowle death or deadly paines?
    Thus when that Princes wrath was pacifide,
    He gan renew the late forbidden banes,
    And to the knight his daughter deare he tyde,
With sacred rites and vowes for ever to abyde.

37

His owne two hands the holy knots did knit,
  That none but death for ever can devide;
  His owne two hands, for such a turne most fit,
  The housling fire did kindle and provide,
  And holy water thereon sprinckled wide;
  At which the bushy Teade a groome did light,
  And sacred lampe in secret chamber hide,
  Where it should not be quenched day nor night,
For feare of evill fates, but burnen ever bright.

38

Then gan they sprinckle all the posts with wine,
  And made great feast to solemnize that day;
  They all perfumde with frankincense divine,
  And precious odours fetcht from far away,
  That all the house did sweat with great aray:
  And all the while sweete Musicke did apply
  Her curious skill, the warbling notes to play,
  To drive away the dull Melancholy;
The whiles one sung a song of love and jollity.

39

During the which there was an heavenly noise
  Heard sound through all the Pallace pleasantly,
  Like as it had bene many an Angels voice,
  Singing before th' eternall majesty,
  In their trinall triplicities on hye;
  Yet wist no creature, whence that heavenly sweet
  Proceeded, yet each one felt secretly
  Himselfe thereby reft of his sences meet,
And ravished with rare impression in his sprite.

40

Great joy was made that day of young and old,
  And solemne feast proclaimd throughout the land,
  That their exceeding merth may not be told:
  Suffice it heare by signes to understand
  The usuall joyes at knitting of loves band.
  Thrise happy man the knight himselfe did hold,
  Possessed of his Ladies hart and hand,
  And ever, when his eye did her behold,
His heart did seeme to melt in pleasures manifold.

41

Her joyous presence and sweet company
  In full content he there did long enjoy,
  Ne wicked envie, ne vile gealosy
  His deare delights were able to annoy:
  Yet swimming in that sea of blisfull joy,
  He nought forgot, how he whilome had sworne,
  In case he could that monstrous beast destroy,
  Unto his Faerie Queene backe to returne:
The which he shortly did, and *Una* left to mourne.

42

Now strike your sailes ye jolly Mariners,
  For we be come unto a quiet rode,
  Where we must land some of our passengers,
  And light this wearie vessell of her lode.
  Here she a while may make her safe abode,
  Till she repaired have her tackles spent,
  And wants supplide. And then againe abroad
  On the long voyage whereto she is bent:
Well may she speede and fairely finish her intent.

FINIS LIB. I

THE SECOND BOOKE OF THE FAERIE QUEENE.
Contayning,
THE LEGENDE OF SIR GUYON.
Or
OF TEMPERAUNCE.

Right well I wote most mighty Soveraine,
　That all this famous antique history,
　Of some th' aboundance of an idle braine
　Will judged be, and painted forgery,
　Rather than matter of just memory,
　Sith none, that breatheth living aire, does know,
　Where is that happy land of Faery,
　Which I so much do vaunt, yet no where show,
But vouch antiquities, which no body can know.

But let that man with better sence advize,
　That of the world least part to us is red:
　And dayly how through hardy enterprize,
　Many great Regions are discovered,
　Which to late age were never mentioned.
　Who ever heard of th' Indian *Peru*?
　Or who in venturous vessell measured
　The *Amazons* huge river now found trew?
Or fruitfullest Virginia who did ever vew?

Yet all these were, when no man did them know;
　Yet have from wisest ages hidden beene:
　And later times things more unknowne shall show.
　Why then should witlesse man so much misweene
　That nothing is, but that which he hath seene?
　What if within the Moones faire shining spheare?
　What if in every other starre unseene
　Of other worldes he happily should heare?
He wonder would much more: yet such to some appeare.

Of Faerie lond yet if he more inquire,
　By certain signes here set in sundry place
　He may it find; ne let him then admire,
　But yield his sence to be too blunt and bace,

That no'te without an hound fine footing trace.
And thou, O fairest Princesse under sky,
In this faire mirrhour maist behold thy face,
And thine owne realmes in lond of Faery,
And in this antique Image thy great auncestry.

The which O pardon me thus to enfold
In covert vele, and wrap in shadowes light,
That feeble eyes your glory may behold,
Which else could not endure those beames bright,
But would be dazled with exceeding light.
O pardon, and vouchsafe with patient eare
The brave adventures of this Faery knight
The good Sir *Guyon* gratiously to heare,
In whom great rule of Temp'raunce goodly doth appeare.

Canto I

Guyon by Archimage abusd,
The Redcrosse knight awaytes,
Findes Mordant and Amavia slaine
With pleasures poisoned baytes.

1

That cunning Architect of cancred guile,
    Whom Princes late displeasure left in bands,
    For falsed letters and suborned wile,
    Soone as the *Redcrosse* knight he understands,
    To beene departed out of *Eden* lands,
    To serve againe his soveraine Elfin Queene,
    His artes he moves, and out of caytives hand
    Himselfe he frees by secret meanes unseene;
His shackles emptie lefte, him selfe escaped cleene.

2

And forth he fares full of malicious mind,
    To worken mischiefe, and avenging woe,
    Where ever he that godly knight may find,
    His onely hart sore, and his onely foe,
    Sith *Una* now he algates must forgoe,
    Whom his victorious hands did earst restore
    To native crowne and kingdome late ygoe;
    Where she enjoyes sure peace for evermore,
As wether-beaten ship arriv'd on happie shore.

3

Him therefore now the object of his spight
    And deadly food he makes: him to offend
    By forged treason, or by open fight
    He seekes, of all his drift the aymed end:
    Thereto his subtile engins he does bend,
    His practick wit, and his faire filed tong,
    With thousand other sleights: for well he kend,
    His credit now in doubtfull ballaunce hong;
For hardly could be hurt, who was already stong.

4

Still as he went, he craftie stales did lay,
    With cunning traines him to entrap unwares,
    And privie spials plast in all his way,
    To weete what course he takes, and how he fares;
    To ketch him at a vantage in his snares.

But now so wise and warie was the knight
By triall of his former harmes and cares,
That he descride, and shonned still his slight:
The fish that once was caught, new bait wil hardly bite.

5

Nath'lesse th' Enchaunter would not spare his paine,
In hope to win occasion to his will;
Which when he long awaited had in vaine,
He chaungd his minde from one to other ill:
For to all good he enimy was still.
Upon the way him fortuned to meet,
Faire marching underneath a shady hill,
A goodly knight, all armd in harnesse meete,
That from his head no place appeared to his feete.

6

His carriage was full comely and upright,
His countenaunce demure and temperate,
But yet so sterne and terrible in sight,
That cheard his friends, and did his foes amate:
He was an Elfin borne of noble state,
And mickle worship in his native land;
Well could he tourney and in lists debate,
And knighthood tooke of good Sir *Huons* hand,
When with king *Oberon* he came to Faerie land.

7

Him als accompanyd upon the way
A comely Palmer, clad in black attire,
Of ripest yeares, and haires all hoarie gray,
That with a staffe his feeble steps did stire,
Least his long way his aged limbes should tire:
And if by lookes one may the mind aread,
He seemd to be a sage and sober sire,
And ever with slow pace the knight did lead,
Who taught his trampling steed with equall steps to tread.

8

Such whenas *Archimago* them did view,
He weened well to worke some uncouth wile.
Eftsoones untwisting his deceiptfull clew,
He gan to weave a web of wicked guile,
And with faire countenance and flattering stile
To them approching, thus the knight bespake:

'Faire sonne of *Mars*, that seeke with warlike spoile,
  And great atchiev'ments great your selfe to make,
Vouchsafe to stay your steed for humble misers sake.'

9

He stayd his steed for humble misers sake,
  And bad tell on the tenor of his plaint;
  Who feigning then in every limb to quake
  Though inward feare, and seeming pale and faint
  With piteous mone his percing speach gan paint;
  'Deare Lady how shall I declare thy cace,
  Whom late I left in langourous constraint?
  Would God thy selfe now present were in place,
To tell this ruefull tale; thy sight could win thee grace.

10

'Or rather would, O would it so had chaunst,
  That you, most noble Sir, had present beene,
  When that lewd ribauld with vile lust advaunst
  Layd first his filthy hands on virgin cleene,
  To spoile her daintie corse so faire and sheene,
  As on the earth, great mother of us all,
  With living eye more faire was never seene,
  Of chastitie and honour virginall:
Witnesse ye heavens, whom she in vaine to help did call.'

11

'How many it be,' (said then the knight halfe wroth,)
  'That knight should knighthood ever so have shent?'
  'None but that saw' (quoth he) 'would weene for troth,
  How shamefully that Maid he did torment.
  Her looser golden lockes he rudely rent,
  And drew her on the ground, and his sharpe sword,
  Against her snowy brest he fiercely bent,
  And threatned death with many a bloudie word;
Toung hates to tell the rest, that eye to see abhord.'

12

Therewith amoved from his sober mood,
  'And lives he yet' (said he) 'that wrought this act,
  And doen the heavens afford him vitall food?'
  'He lives,' (quoth he) 'and boasteth of the fact,
  Ne yet hath any knight his courage crackt.'
  'Where may that treachour then' (said he) 'be found,
  Or by what meanes may I his footing tract?'

'That shall I shew' (said he) 'as sure, as hound
The stricken Deare doth chalenge by the bleeding wound.'

13

He staid not lenger talke, but with fierce ire
    And zealous hast away is quickly gone
    To seeke that knight, where him that craftie Squire
    Supposd to be.   They do arrive anone,
    Where sate a gentle Lady all alone,
    With garments rent, and haire discheveled,
    Wringing her hands, and making piteous mone;
    Her swollen eyes were much disfigured,
And her faire face with teares was fowly blubbered.

14

The knight approching nigh, thus to her said,
    'Faire Ladie, through foule sorrow ill bedight,
    Great pittie is to see you thus dismaid,
    And marre the blossome of your beautie bright:
    For thy appease your griefe and heavie plight,
    And tell the cause of your conceived paine.
    For if he live that hath you doen despight;
    He shall you doe due recompence againe,
Or else his wrong with greater puissance maintaine.'

15

Which when she heard, as in despightfull wise,
    She wilfully her sorrow did augment,
    And offred hope of comfort did despise:
    Her golden lockes most cruelly she rent,
    And scratcht her face with ghastly dreriment,
    Ne would she speake, ne see, ne yet be seene,
    But hid her visage, and her head downe bent,
    Either for grievous shame, or for great teene,
As if her hart with sorrow had transfixed beene.

16

Till her that Squire bespake, 'Madame my liefe,
    For Gods deare love be not so wilfull bent,
    But doe vouchsafe now to receive reliefe,
    The which good fortune doth to you present.
    For what bootes it to weepe and to wayment,
    When ill is chaunst, but doth the ill increase,
    And the weake mind with double woe torment?'
    When she her Squire heard speake, she gan appease
Her voluntarie paine, and feele some secret ease.

17

Eftsoone she said, 'Ah gentle trustie Squire,
  What comfort can I wofull wretch conceave?
  Or why should ever I henceforth desire,
  To see faire heavens face, and life not leave,
  Sith that false Traytour did my honour reave?'
  'False traytour certes' (saide the Faerie knight)
  'I read the man, that ever would deceave
  A gentle Ladie, or her wrong through might:
Death were too litle paine for such a foule despight.

18

'But now, faire Ladie, comfort to you make,
  And read, who hath ye wrought this shamefull plight;
  That short revenge the man may overtake,
  Where so he be, and soone upon him light.'
  'Certes" (saide she) 'I wote not how he hight,
  But under him a gray steede he did wield,
  Whose sides with dapled circles weren dight;
  Upright he rode, and in his silver shield
He bore a bloudie Crosse, that quartred all the field.'

19

'Now by my head' (said *Guyon*) 'much I muse,
  How that same knight should doe so foule amis,
  Or even gentle Damzell so abuse:
  For may I boldly say, he surely is
  A right good knight, and trew of word ywis:
  I present was, and can it witnesse well,
  When armes he swore, and streight did enterpris
  Th' adventure of the *Errant damozell*,
In which he hath great glorie wonne, as I heare tell.

20

'Nathlesse he shortly shall againe be tryde,
  And fairely quit him of th' imputed blame,
  Else be ye sure he dearely shall abyde,
  Or make you good amendment for the same:
  All wrongs have mends, but no amends of shame.
  Now therefore Ladie, rise out of your paine,
  And see the salving of your blotted name.'
  Full loth she seemd thereto, but yet did faine;
For she was inly glad her purpose so to gaine.

21

Her purpose was not such, as she did faine,
　　Ne yet her person such, as it was seene,
　　But under simple shew, and semblant plaine
　　Lurckt false *Duessa* secretly unseene,
　　As a chaste Virgin, that had wronged beene:
　　So had false *Archimago* her disguisd,
　　To cloke her guile with sorrow and sad teene;
　　And eke himselfe had craftily devisd
To be her Squire, and do her service well aguisd.

22

Her late forlorne and naked he had found,
　　Where she did wander in waste wildernesse,
　　Lurking in rockes and caves far under ground,
　　And with greene mosse cov'ring her nakednesse,
　　To hide her shame and loathly filthinesse;
　　Sith her Prince *Arthur* of proud ornaments
　　And borrow'd beautie spoyld.　Her nathelesse
　　Th' enchaunter finding fit for his intents,
Did thus revest, and deckt with due habiliments.

23

For all he did, was to deceive good knights,
　　And draw them from pursuit of praise and fame,
　　To slug in slouth and sensuall delights,
　　And end their daies with irrenowmed shame.
　　And now exceeding griefe him overcame,
　　To see the *Redcrosse* thus advaunced hye;
　　Therefore this craftie engine he did frame,
　　Against his praise to stirre up enmitye
Of such, as vertues like mote unto him allye.

24

So now he *Guyon* guides an uncouth way
　　Through woods and mountains, till they came at last
　　Into a pleasant dale, that lowly lay
　　Betwixt two hils, whose high heads overplast,
　　The valley did with coole shade overcast,
　　Through midst thereof a little river rold,
　　By which there sate a knight with helme unlast,
　　Himselfe refreshing with the liquid cold,
After his travell long, and labours manifold.

25

'Loe yonder he,' cryde *Archimage* alowd,
  'That wrought the shamefull fact, which I did shew;
  And now he doth himselfe in secret shrowd,
  To flie the vengeance for his outrage dew;
  But vaine: for ye shall dearely do him rew,
  So God ye speed, and send you good successe;
  Which we farre off will here abide to vew.'
  So they him left, inflam'd with wrathfulnesse,
That streight against that knight his speare he did addresse.

26

Who seeing him from farre so fierce to pricke,
  His warlike armes about him gan embrace,
  And in the rest his readie speare did sticke;
  Tho when as still he saw him towards pace,
  He gan rencounter him in equall race.
  They bene ymet, both readie to affrap,
  When suddenly that warriour gan abace
  His threatned speare, as if some new mishap
Had him betidde, or hidden daunger did entrap.

27

And cryde, 'Mercie Sir knight, and mercie Lord,
  For mine offence and heedlesse hardiment,
  That had almost committed crime abhord,
  And with reprochfull shame mine honour shent,
  Whiles cursed steele against that badge I bent,
  The sacred badge of my Redeemers death,
  Which on your shield is set for ornament:'
  But his fierce foe his steed could stay uneath,
Who prickt with courage kene, did cruell battell breath.

28

But when he heard him speake, streight way he knew
  His error, and himselfe inclyning sayd;
  'Ah deare Sir *Guyon*, well becommeth you,
  But me behoveth rather to upbrayd,
  Whose hastie hand so farre from reason strayd,
  That almost it did haynous violence
  On that faire image of that heavenly Mayd,
  That decks and armes your shield with faire defence:
Your court'sie takes on you anothers due offence.'

29

So bene they both attone, and doen upreare
    Their bevers bright, each other for to greete;
    Goodly comportance each to other beare,
    And entertaine themselves with court'sies meet.
    Then said the *Redcrosse* knight, 'Now mote I weet,
    Sir *Guyon*, why with so fierce saliaunce,
    And fell intent ye did at earst me meet;
    For sith I know your goodly governaunce,
Great cause, I weene, you guided, or some uncouth chaunce.'

30

'Certes' (said he) 'well mote I shame to tell
    The fond encheason, that me hither led.
    A false infamous faitour late befell
    Me for to meet, that seemed ill bested,
    And playnd of grievous outrage, which he red
    A knight had wrought against a Ladie gent;
    Which to avenge, he to this place me led,
    Where you he made the marke of his intent,
And now is fled; foule shame him follow, where he went.'

31

So can he turne his earnest unto game,
    Through goodly handling and wise temperance.
    By this his aged guide in presence came;
    Who soone as on that knight his eye did glance,
    Eft soones of him had perfect cognizance,
    Sith him in Faerie court he late avizd;
    And said, 'faire sonne, God give you happy chance,
    And that deare Crosse upon your shield devizd,
Wherewith above all knights ye goodly seeme aguizd.

32

'Joy may you have, and everlasting fame,
    Of late most hard atchiev'ment by you donne,
    For which enrolled is your glorious name
    In heavenly Registers above the Sunne,
    Where you a Saint with Saints your seat have wonne:
    But wretched we, where ye have left your marke,
    Must now anew begin, like race to runne;
    God guide thee, *Guyon*, well to end thy warke,
And to the wished haven bring thy weary barke.'

33

'Palmer,' (him answered the *Redcrosse* knight)
  'His be the praise, that this atchiev'ment wrought,
  Who made my hand the organ of his might;
  More then goodwill to me attribute nought:
  For all I did, I did but as I ought.
  But you, faire Sir, whose pageant next ensewes,
  Well mote yee thee, as well can wish your thought,
  That home ye may report thrise happy newes;
For well ye worthie bene for worth and gentle thewes.'

34

So courteous conge both did give and take,
  With right hands plighted, pledges of good will.
  Then *Guyon* forward gan his voyage make,
  With his blacke Palmer, that him guided still.
  Still he him guided over dale and hill,
  And with his steedie staffe did point his way:
  His race with reason, and with words his will,
  From foule intemperance he oft did stay,
And suffred not in wrath his hastie steps to stray.

35

In this faire wize they traveild long yfere,
  Through many hard assayes, which did betide;
  Of which he honour still away did beare,
  And spred his glorie through all countries wide.
  At last as chaunst them by a forest side
  To passe, for succour from the scorching ray.
  They heard a ruefull voice, that dearnly cride
  With percing shriekes, and many a dolefull lay;
Which to attend, a while their forward steps they stay.

36

'But if that carelesse heavens' (quoth she) 'despise
  The doome of just revenge, and take delight
  To see sad pageants of mens miseries,
  As bound by them to live in lives despight,
  Yet can they not warne death from wretched wight.
  Come then, come soone, come sweetest death to mee,
  And take away this long lent loathed light:
  Sharpe be thy wounds, but sweete the medicines bee,
That long captived soules from wearie thraldome free.

37

'But thou, sweete Babe, whom frowning froward fate
  Hath made sad witnesse of thy fathers fall,
  Sith heaven thee deignes to hold in living state,
  Long maist thou live, and better thrive withall,
  Then to thy lucklesse parents did befall:
  Live thou, and to thy mother dead attest,
  That cleare she dide from blemish criminall;
  Thy litle hands embrewd in bleeding brest
Loe I for pledges leave. So give me leave to rest.'

38

With that a deadly shrieke she forth did throw,
  That through the wood reechoed againe,
  And after gave a grone so deepe and low,
  That seemd her tender heart was rent in twaine,
  Or thrild with point of thorough piercing paine;
  As gentle Hynd, whose sides with cruell steele
  Through launched, forth her bleeding life does raine,
  Whiles the sad pang approching she does feele,
Brayes out her latest breath, and up her eyes doth seele.

39

Which when that warriour heard, dismounting straict
  From his tall steed, he rusht into the thicke,
  And soone arrived, where that sad pourtraict
  Of death and dolour lay, halfe dead, halfe quicke,
  In whose white alabaster brest did sticke
  A cruell knife, that made a griesly wound,
  From which forth gusht a streme of gorebloud thick,
  That all her goodly garments staind around,
And into a deepe sanguine dide the grassie ground.

40

Pittifull spectacle of deadly smart,
  Beside a bubbling fountaine low she lay,
  Which she increased with her bleeding hart,
  And the cleane waves with purple gore did ray;
  Als in her lap a lovely babe did play
  His cruell sport, in stead of sorrow dew;
  For in her streaming blood he did embay
  His litle hands, and tender jots embrew;
Pitifull spectacle, as ever eye did view.

41

Besides them both, upon the soiled gras
   The dead corse of an armed knight was spred,
   Whose armour all with bloud besprinckled was;
   His ruddie lips did smile, and rosy red
   Did paint his chearefull cheekes, yet being ded,
   Seemd to have beene a goodly personage,
   Now in his freshest flowre of lustie hed,
   Fit to inflame faire Lady with loves rage,
But that fiers fate did crop the blossome of his age.

42

Whom when the good Sir *Guyon* did behold,
   His hart gan wexe as starke, as marble stone,
   And his fresh bloud did frieze with fearefull cold,
   That all his senses seemd berefte attone:
   At last his mightie ghost gan deepe to grone,
   As Lyon grudging in his great disdaine,
   Mournes inwardly, and makes to himselfe mone;
   Till ruth and fraile affection did constraine,
His stout courage to stoupe, and shew his inward paine.

43

Out of her gored wound the cruell steele
   He lightly snatcht, and did the floudgate stop
   With his faire garment: then gan softly feele
   Her feeble pulse, to prove if any drop
   Of living bloud yet in her veynes did hop;
   Which when he felt to move, he hoped faire
   To call backe life to her forsaken shop;
   So well he did her deadly wounds repaire,
That at the last she gan to breath out living aire.

44

Which he perceiving greatly gan rejoice,
   And goodly counsell, that for wounded hart
   Is meetest med'cine, tempred with sweete voice;
   'Ay me, deare Lady, which the image art
   Of ruefull pitie, and impatient smart,
   What direfull chance, armd with revenging fate,
   Or cursed hand hath plaid this cruell part,
   Thus fowle to hasten your untimely date;
Speake, O dear Lady speake: help never comes too late.'

45

Therewith her dim eie-lids she up gan reare,
On which the drery death did sit, as sad
As lump of lead, and made darke clouds appeare;
But when as him all in bright armour clad
Before her standing she espied had,
As one out of a deadly dreame affright,
She weakely started, yet she nothing drad:
Streight downe again her selfe in great despight,
She groveling threw to ground, as hating life and light.

46

The gentle knight her soone with carefull paine
Uplifted light, and softly did uphold:
Thrise he her reard, and thrise she sunke againe,
Till he his armes about her sides gan fold,
And to her said; 'Yet if the stony cold
Have not all seized on your frozen hart,
Let one word fall that may your grief unfold,
And tell the secret of your mortall smart;
He oft finds present helpe, who does his griefe impart.'

47

Then casting up a deadly looke, full low
Shee sight from bottome of her wounded brest,
And after, many bitter throbs did throw
With lips full pale and foltring tongue opprest.
These words she breathed forth from riven chest;
'Leave, ah leave off, whatever wight thou bee,
To let a wearie wretch from her dew rest,
And trouble dying soules tranquilitee.
Take not away now got, which none would give to me.'

48

'Ah farre be it' (said he) 'Deare dame fro mee,
To hinder soule from her desired rest,
Or hold sad life in long captivitee:
For all I seeke, is but to have redrest
The bitter pangs, that doth your heart infest.
Tell then, O Lady tell, what fatall priefe
Hath with so huge misfortune you opprest?
That I may cast to compasse your reliefe,
Or die with you in sorrow, and partake your griefe.'

49

With feeble hands then stretched forth on hye,
  As heven accusing guiltie of her death,
  And with dry drops congealed in her eye,
  In these sad words she spent her utmost breath:
  'Heare then, O man, the sorrowes that uneath
  My tongue can tell, so far all sense they pas:
  Loe this dead corpse, that lies here underneath,
  The gentlest knight, that ever on greene gras
Gay steed with spurs did pricke, the good Sir *Mortdant* was.

50

'Was, (ay the while, that he is not so now)
  My Lord my love; my deare Lord, my deare love,
  So long as heavens just with equall brow,
  Vouchsafed to behold us from above,
  One day when him high courage did emmove,
  As wont ye knights to seeke adventures wilde,
  He pricked forth, his puissant force to prove,
  Me then he left enwombed of this child,
This lucklesse childe, whom thus ye see with bloud defild.

51

'Him fortuned (hard fortune ye may ghesse)
  To come, where vile *Acrasia* does wonne,
  Acrasia a false enchaunteresse,
  That many errant knights hath foule fordonne:
  Within a wandring Island, that doth ronne
  And stray in perilous gulfe, her dwelling is,
  Faire Sir, if ever there ye travell, shonne
  The cursed land where many wend amis,
And know it by the name; it hight the *Bowre of blis*.

52

'Her bliss is all in pleasure and delight,
  Wherewith she makes her lovers drunken mad,
  And then with words and weedes of wondrous might,
  On them she workes her will to uses bad:
  My liefest Lord she thus beguiled had;
  For he was flesh: (all flesh doth frailtie breed.)
  Whom when I heard to beene so ill bestad.
  Weake wretch I wrap my selfe in Palmers weed,
And cast to seeke him forth through daunger and great dreed.

53

'Now had faire *Cynthia* by even tournes
   Full measured three quarters of her yeare,
   And thrise three times had fild her crooked hornes,
   Whenas my wombe her burdein would forbeare,
   And bad me call *Lucina* to me neare.
   Lucina came: a manchild forth I brought:
   The woods, the Nymphes, my bowres, my midwives weare,
   Hard helpe at need. So deare thee babe I bought,
Yet nought too deare I deemd, while so my dear I sought.

54

'Him so I sought, and so at last I found,
   Where him that witch had thralled to her will,
   In chaines of lust and lewde desyres ybound,
   And so transformed from his former skill,
   That me he knew not, neither his owne ill;
   Till through wise handling and faire governance,
   I him recured to a better will,
   Purged from drugs of foule intemperance:
Then meanes I gan devise for his deliverance.

55

'Which when the vile Enchaunteresse perceiv'd,
   How that my Lord from her I would reprive,
   With cup thus charmd, him parting she deceiv'd;
   Sad verse, give death to him that death does give,
   And losse of love, to her that loves to live,
   So soone as Bacchus with the Nymphe does lincke,
   So parted we, and on our journey drive,
   Till comming to this well, he stoupt to drincke:
The charme fulfild, dead suddenly he downe did sincke.

56

'Which when I wretch,' Not one word more she sayd
   But breaking off, the end for want of breath,
   And slyding soft, as downe to sleepe her layd,
   And ended all her woe in quiet death.
   That seeing good Sir *Guyon* could uneath
   From teares abstaine, for griefe his hart did grate,
   And from so heavie sight his head did wreath,
   Accusing fortune, and too cruell fate,
Which plunged had faire Ladie in so wretched state.

57

Then turning to his Palmer said, 'Old syre
   Behold the image of mortalitie,
   And feeble nature cloth'd with fleshly tyre,
   When raging passion with fierce tyrannie
   Robs reason of her dew regalitie,
   And makes it servant to her basest part:
   The strong it weakens with infirmitie,
   And with bold furie armes the weakest hart;
The strong through pleasure soonest falles, the weake through smart.'

58

'But temperance' (said he) 'with golden squire
   Betwixt them both can measure out a meane,
   Neither to melt in pleasures whott desire,
   Nor fry in hartlesse griefe and dolefull teene.
   Thrise happie man, who fares them both atweene:
   But sith this wretched woman overcome
   Of anguish, rather then of crime hath beene,
   Reserve her cause to her eternall doome,
And in the meane vouchsafe her honorable toombe.'

59

'Palmer' (quoth he) 'death is an equall doome
   To good and bad, the common Inne of rest;
   But after death the tryall is to come,
   When best shall be to them, that lived best:
   But both alike, when death hath both supprest,
   Religious reverence doth buriall teene,
   Which who so wants, wants so much of his rest:
   For all so great shame after death I weene,
As selfe to dyen bad, unburied bad to beene.'

60

So both agree their bodies to engrave;
   The great earthes wombe they open to the sky,
   And with sad Cypresse seemely it embrave,
   Then covering with a clod their closed eye,
   They lay therein their corses tenderly,
   And bid them sleepe in everlasting peace,
   But ere they did their utmost obsequy,
   Sir *Guyon* more affection to increace,
Bynempt a sacred vow, which none should aye releace.

61

The dead knights sword out of his sheath he drew,
  With which he cut a locke of all their heare,
  Which medling with their blood and earth, he threw
  Into the grave, and gan deoutly sweare;
  'Such and such evill God on *Guyon* reare,
  And worse and worse young Orphane be thy paine,
  If I or thou dew vengeaunce doe forbeare,
  Till guiltie bloud her guerdon doe obtaine:'
So shedding many teares, they closd the earth againe.

Canto II

Babes bloudie hands may not be clensd,
The face of golden Meane.
Her sisters two Extremities:
Strive her to banish cleane.

I

Thus when Sir *Guyon* with his faithfull guide
   Had with dew rites and dolorous lament
   The end of their sad Tragedie uptyde,
   The litle babe up in his armes he hent;
   Who with sweet pleasance and bold blandishment
   Gan smyle on them, that rather ought to weepe,
   As carelesse of his woe, or innocent
   Of that was doen, that ruth emperced deepe
In that knightes hart, and wordes with bitter teares did steepe.

2

'Ah lucklesse babe, borne under cruell starre,
   And in dead parents balefull ashes bred,
   Full litle weenest thou, what sorrowes are
   Left thee for portion of thy livelyhed,
   Poore Orphane in the wild world scattered,
   As budding braunch rent from the native tree,
   And throwen forth, till it be withered:
   Such is the state of men: thus enter wee
Into this life with woe, and end with miseree.'

3

Then soft himselfe inclyning on his knee
   Downe to that well, did in the water weene
   (So love does loath disdainefull nicitee)
   His guiltie hands from bloudy gore to cleene.
   He washt them oft and oft, yet nought they beene
   For all his washing cleaner.   Still he strove,
   Yet still the litle hands were bloudie seene;
   The which him into great amaz'ment drove,
And into diverse doubt his wavering wonder clove.

4

He wist not whether blot of foule offence
   Might not be purgd with water nor with bath;
   Or that high God, in lieu of innocence,
   Imprinted had that token of his wrath,
   To shew how sore bloudguiltinesse he hat'th;

Or that the charme and venim, which they druncke.
   Their bloud with secret filth infected hath,
   Being diffused through the senseless truncke,
That through the great contagion direfull deadly stunck.

5

Whom thus at gaze, the Palmer gan to bord
   With goodly reason, and thus faire bespake;
   "Ye bene right hard amated, gratious Lord,
   And of your ignorance great marvell make,
   Whiles cause not well conceived ye mistake.
   But know, that secret vertues are infusd
   In every fountaine, and in every lake,
   Which who hath skill them rightly to have chusd,
To proofe of passing wonders hath full often usd.

6

'Of those some were so from their sourse indewd
   By great Dame Nature, from whose fruitfull pap
   Their welheads spring, and are with moisture deawd;
   Which feedes each living plant with liquid sap.
   And filles with flowres faire *Floraes* painted lap:
   But other some, by gift of later grace,
   Or by good prayers, or by other hap,
   Had vertue pourd into their waters bace,
And thenceforth were renowmd, and sought from place to place.

7
vidiuous well

'Such is this well, wrought by occasion straunge,
   Which to her Nymph befell. Upon a day,
   As she the woods with bow and shafts did raunge,
   The hartlesse Hind and Robucke to dismay,
Nymph   *Dan Faunus* chaunst to meet her by the way,
   And kindling fire at her faire burning eye,
   Inflamed was to follow beauties chace,
   And chaced her, that fast from him did fly;
As Hind from her, so she fled from her enimy.

8

'At last when fayling breath began to faint,
   And saw no meanes to scape, of shame affrayd,
   She set her downe to weepe for sore constraint,
   And to *Diana* calling lowd for ayde,
   Her deare besought, to let her dye a mayd.
   The goddesse heard, and suddeine where she sate,

Welling out streames of teares, and quite dismayd
　　With stony feare of that rude rustick mate,
Transformd her to a stone from stedfast virgins state.

9

'Lo now she is that stone, from whose two heads,
　　As from two weeping eyes, fresh streames do flow,
　　Yet colde through feare, and old conceived dreads;
　　And yet the stone her semblance seemes to show,
　　Shapt like a maid, that such ye may her know;
　　And yet her vertues in her water byde:
　　For it is chast and pure, as purest snow,
　　Ne lets her waves with any filth be dyde,
But ever like her selfe unstained hath beene tryde.

pure water can't be contam

10

'From thence it comes, that this babes bloudy hand
　　May not be clensd with water of this well:
　　Ne certes Sir strive you it to withstand,
　　But let them still be bloudy, as befell,
　　That they his mothers innoncence may tell,
　　As she bequeathd in her last testament;
　　That as a sacred Symbole it may dwell
　　In her sonnes flesh, to minde revengement,
And be for all chast Dames an endlesse moniment.'

11

He hearkned to his reason, and the childe
　　Uptaking, to the Palmer gave to beare;
　　But his sad fathers armes with blood defilde,
　　An heavie load himselfe did lightly reare,
　　And turning to that place, in which whyleare
　　He left his loftie steed with golden sell,
　　And goodly gorgeous barbes, him found not theare.
　　By other accident that earst befell,
He is convaide, but how or where, here fits not tell.

12

horse gone

Which when Sir *Guyon* saw, all were he wroth,
　　Yet algates mote he soft himselfe appease,
　　And fairely fare on foot, how ever loth;
　　His double burden did him sore disease.
　　So long they traveiled with litle ease,
　　Till that at last they to a Castle came,
　　Built on a rocke adjoyning to the seas;

It was an auncient worke of antique fame,
And wondrous strong by nature, and by skilful frame.

13

Therein three sisters dwelt of sundry sort,
  The children of one sire by mothers three;
  Who dying whylome did divide this fort
  To them by equall shares in equall fee:
  But strifull minde, and diverse qualitee
  Drew them in parts, and each made others foe:
  Still did they strive, and dayly disagree;
  The eldest did against the youngest goe,
And both against the middest meant to worken woe.

14

Where when the knight arriv'd, he was right well
  Receiv'd, as knight of so much worth became,
  Of second sister, who did far excell
  The other two; *Medina* was her name,
  A sober sad, and comely curteous Dame;
  Who rich arayd, and yet in modest guize,
  In goodly garments that her well became,
  Faire marching forth in honorable wize,
Him at the threshold met, and well did enterprize.

15

She led him up into a goodly bowre,
  And comely courted with meet modestie,
  Ne in her speach, ne in her haviour,
  Was lightnesse seene, or looser vanitie,
  But gratious womanhood, and gravitie,
  Above the reason of her youthly yeares:
  Her golden lockes she roundly did uptye
  In breaded tramels, that no looser heares
Did out of order stray about her daintie eares.

16

Whilest she her selfe thus busily did frame,
  Seemely to entertaine her new-come guest,
  Newes hereof to her other sisters came,
  Who all this while were at their wanton rest,
  Accourting each her frend with lavish fest:
  They were two knights of perelesse puissance,
  And famous far abroad for warlike gest,
  Which to these Ladies love did countenaunce,
And to his mistresse each himselfe strove to advaunce.

17

He that made love unto the eldest Dame,   *Love*
    Was hight Sir *Huddibras*, an hardy man;
    Yet not so good of deedes, as great of name,
    Which he by many rash adventures wan,
    Since errant armes to sew he first began;
    More huge in strength, then wise in workes he was,
    And reason with foole-hardize over ran;
    Sterne melancholy did his courage pas,
And was for terrour more, all armd in shyning bras.

18

But he that lov'd the youngest, was *Sans-loy*,
    He that faire *Una* late fowle outraged,
    The most unruly, and the boldest boy,
    That ever warlike weapons menaged,
    And all to lawlesse lust encouraged,
    Through strong opinion of his matchlesse might:
    Ne ought he car'd, whom he endamaged
    By tortious wrong, or whom bereav'd of right.
He now this Ladies champion chose for love to fight.

19

These two gay knights, vowd to so diverse loves,
    Each other does envie with deadly hate,   *knights opposed*
    And dayly warre against his foeman moves,
    In hope to win more favour with his mate,
    And th' others pleasing service to abate,
    To magnifie his owne.   But when they heard,
    How in that place straunge knight arrived late,
    Both knightes and Ladies forth right angry far'd,
And fiercely unto battell sterne themselves prepar'd.

20

But ere they could proceede unto the place,
    Where he abode, themselves at discord fell,
    And cruell combat joynd in middle space:
    With horrible assault, and furie fell,
    They heapt huge strokes, the scorned life to quell,
    That all on uprore from her settled seat
    The house was raysd, and all that in did dwell;
    Seemd that lowde thunder with amazement great
Did rend the ratling skyes with flames of fouldring heat.

2 fight

21

The noyse thereof cald forth that straunger knight,
  To weet, what dreadfull thing was there in hand;
  Where when as two brave knights in bloudy fight
  With deadly rancour he enraunged fond,
  His sunbroad shield about his wrest he bond,
  And shyning blade unsheathd, with which he ran
  Unto that stead, their strife to understond;
  And at his first arrivall, them began
With goodly meanes to pacifie, well as he can.

22

But they him spying, both with greedy forse
  Attonce upon him ran, and him beset
  With strokes of mortall steele without remorse,
  And on his shield like yron sledges bet:
  As when a Beare and Tygre being met
  In cruell fight on lybicke Ocean wide,
  Espye a traveiler with feet surbet,
  Whom they in equall pray hope to devide,
They stint their strife, and him assaile on every side.

23

But he, not like a wearie traveilere,
  Their sharp assault right boldly did rebut,
  And suffred not their blowes to byte him nere,
  But with redoubled buffes them backe did put:
  Whose grieved mindes, which choler did englut,
  Against themselves turning their wrathfull spight,
  Gan with new rage their shieldes to hew and cut;
  But still when *Guyon* came to part their fight,
With heavie load on him they freshly gan to smight.

24

As a tall ship tossed in troublous seas,
  Whom raging windes threatning to make the pray
  Of the rough rockes, doe diversly disease,
  Meetes two contrary billowes by the way,
  That her on either side do sore assay,
  And boast to swallow her in greedy grave;
  She scorning both their spights, does make wide way,
  And with her best breaking the fomy wave,
Does ride on both their backs, and faire her self doth save.

25

So boldly he him beares, and rusheth forth
  Betweene them both, by conduct of his blade.
  Wondrous great prowesse and heroick worth
  He shewd that day, and rare ensample made,
  When two so mighty warriours he dismade:
  Attonce he wards and strikes, he takes and payes,
  Now forst to yield, now forcing to invade,
  Before, behind, and round about him layes:
So double was his paines, so double be his prayse.

26

Straunge sort of fight, three valiaunt knights to see
  Three combats joyne in one, and to darraine
  A triple warre with triple enmitee,
  All for their Ladies froward love to gaine, *love prize*
  Which gotten was but hate. So love does raine
  In stoutest minds, and maketh monstrous warre;
  He maketh warre, he maketh peace againe,
  And yet his peace is but continuall jarre:
O miserable men, that to him subject arre.

27

Whilst thus they mingled were in furious armes,
  The faire *Medina* with her tresses torne,
  And naked brest, in pitty of their harmes,
  Emongst them ran, and falling them beforne,
  Besought them by the womb, which them had borne,
  And by the loves, which were to them most deare,
  And by the knighthood, which they sure had sworne, *M's appeal*
  Their deadly cruell discord to forbeare,
And to her just conditions of faire peace to heare.

28

But her two other sisters standing by,
  Her lowd gainsaid, and both their champions bad
  Pursew the end of their strong enmity,
  As ever of their loves they would be glad.
  Yet she with pitthy words and counsell sad,
  Still strove their stubborne rages to revoke,
  That at the last suppressing fury mad,
  They gan abstaine from dint of direfull stroke,
And hearken to the sober speaches, which she spoke.

M.'s appeal

29

'Ah puissaunt Lords, what cursed evill Spright,
  Or fell *Erinnys* in your noble harts,
  Her hellish brond hath kindled with despight,
  And stird you up to worke your wilfull smarts?
  Is this the joy of armes? be these the parts
  Of glorious knighthood, after bloud to thrust,
  And not regard dew right and just desarts?
  Vaine is the vaunt, and victory unjust,
That more to mighty hands, then rightfull cause doth trust.

30

'And were there rightfull cause of difference,
  Yet were not better, faire it to accord,
  Then with bloud guiltinesse to heape offence,
  And mortall vengeaunce joyne to crime abhord?
  O fly from wrath, fly, O my liefest Lord:
  Sad be the sights, and bitter fruits of warre,
  And thousand furies wait on wrathfull sword;
  Ne ought the praise of prowesse more doth marre,
Then fowle revenging rage, and base contentious jarre.

31

'But lovely concord, and most sacred peace
  Doth nourish vertue, and fast friendship breeds;
  Weake she makes strong, and strong thing does increace,
  Till it the pitch of highest prayse exceeds:
  Brave be her warres, and honorable deeds,
  By which she triumphes over ire and pride,
  And winnes an Olive girlond for her meeds:
  Be therefore, O my deare Lords, pacifide,
And this misseeming discord meekely lay aside.'

32

Her gracious wordes their rancour did appall,
  And suncke so deepe into their boyling brests,
  That downe they let their cruell weapons fall,
  And lowly did abase their lofty crests
  To her faire presence, and discrete behests.
  Then she began a treatie to procure,
  And stablish termes betwixt both their requests,
  That as a law for ever should endure;
Which to observe in word of knights they did assure.

33

Which to confirme, and fast to bind their league,
 After their wearie sweat and bloudy toile,
 She them besought, during their quiet treague,
 Into her lodging to repaire a while,
 To rest themselves, and grace to reconcile.
 They soone consent: so forth with her they fare,
 Where they are well receiv'd, and made to spoile
 Themselves of soiled armes, and to prepare
Their minds to pleasure, and their mouthes to dainty fare.

34

And those two froward sisters, their faire loves,
 Came with them eke, all were they wondrous loth,
 And fained cheare, as for the time behoves,
 But could not colour yet so well the troth,
 But that their natures bad appeard in both:
 For both did at their second sister grutch,
 And inly grieve, as doth an hidden moth
 The inner garment fret, not th' utter touch;
One thought their cheare too litle, th' other thought too mutch.

35

Elissa (so the eldest hight) did deeme
 Such entertainment base, ne ought would eat,
 Ne ought would speake, but evermore did seeme
 As discontent for want of merth or meat;
 No solace could her Paramour intreat
 Her once to show, ne court, nor dalliance,
 But with bent lowring browes, as she would threat,
 She scould, and frownd with froward countenaunce,
Unworthy of faire Ladies comely governaunce.

36

But young *Perissa* was of other mind,
 Full of disport, still laughing, loosely light,
 And quite contrary to her sisters kind;
 No measure in her mood, no rule of right,
 But poured out in pleasure and delight;
 In wine and meats she flowd above the bancke,
 And in excesse exceeded her owne might;
 In sumptuous tire she joyd her selfe to prancke,
But of her love too lavish (litle have she thancke.)

37

Fast by her side did sit the bold *Sans-loy*,
 Fit mate for such a mincing mineon,
 Who in her loosenesse tooke exceeding joy;
 Might not be found a franker franion,
 Of her lewd parts to make companion;
 But *Huddibras*, more like a Malecontent,
 Did see and grieve at his bold fashion;
 Hardly could he endure his hardiment,
Yet still he sat, and inly did him selfe torment.

lose ?

38

Betwixt them both the faire *Medina* sate
 With sober grace, and goodly carriage:
 With equall measure she did moderate
 The strong extremities of their outrage;
 That forward paire she ever would asswage,
 When they would strive dew reason to exceed;
 But that same froward twaine would accourage,
 And of her plenty adde unto their need:
So kept she them in order, and her selfe in heed.

THE MEAN

39

Thus fairely she attempered her feast,
 And pleasd them all with meete satietie,
 At last when lust of meat and drinke was ceast,
 She *Guyon* deare besought of curtesie,
 To tell from whence he came through jeopardie,
 And whither now on new adventure bound.
 Who with bold grace, and comely gravitie,
 Drawing to him the eyes of all around,
From lofty siege began these words aloud to sound.

40

'This thy demaund, O Lady, doth revive
 Fresh memory in me of that great Queene,
 Great and most glorious virgin Queene alive,
 That with her soveraigne powre, and scepter shene
 All Faery lond does peaceably sustene.
 In widest Ocean she her throne does reare,
 That over all the earth it may be seene;
 As morning Sunne her beames dispredden cleare,
And in her face faire peace, and mercy doth appeare.

FQ

41

'In her the richesse of all heavenly grace,
  In chiefe degree are heaped up on hye:
  And all that else this worlds enclosure bace,
  Hath great or glorious in mortall eye,
  Adornes the person of her Majestie;
  That men beholding so great excellence,
  And rare perfection in mortalitie,
  Do her adore with sacred reverence,
As th' Idole of her makers great magnificence.

42

'To her I homage and my service owe,
  In number of the noblest knights on ground,
  Mongst whom on me she deigned to bestowe
  Order of *Maydenhead*, the most renownd,
  That may this day in all the world be found,
  An yearely solemne feast she wontes to make
  The day that first doth lead the yeare around;
  To which all knights of worth and courage bold
Resort, to heare of straunge adventures to be told.

43

'There this old Palmer shewed himselfe that day,
  And to that mighty Princesse did complaine
  Of grievous mischiefes, which a wicked Fay
  Had wrought, and many whelmd in deadly paine,
  Whereof he crav'd redresse.   My Soveraine,
  Whose glory is in gracious deeds, and joyes
  Throughout the world her mercy to maintaine,
  Eftsoones devisd redresse for such annoyes;
Me all unfit for so great purpose she employes.

44

'Now hath faire *Phoebe* with her silver face
  Thrise seene the shadowes of the neather world,
  Sith last I left that honourable place,
  In which her royall presence is inrold;
  Ne ever shall I rest in house nor hold,
  Till I that false *Acrasia* have wonne;
  Of whose fowle deedes, too hideous to be told,
  I witnesse am, and this their wretched sonne,
Whose wofull parents she hath wickedly furdonne.'

45
'Tell on, faire Sir,' said she, 'that dolefull tale,
    From which sad ruth does seeme you to restraine,
    That we may pitty such unhappy bale,
    And learne from pleasures poyson to abstaine:
    Ill by ensample good doth often gayne.'
    Then forward he his purpose gan pursew,
    And told the storie of the mortall payne,
    Which *Mordant* and *Amavia* did rew;
As with lamenting eyes him selfe did lately vew.

46
Night was far spent, and now in *Ocean* deepe
    Orion, flying fast from hissing snake,
    His flaming head did hasten for to steepe,
    When of his pitteous tale he end did make;
    Whilest with delight of that he wisely spake,
    Those guestes beguiled, did beguile their eyes
    Of kindly sleepe, that did them overtake.
    At last when they had markt the chaunged skyes,
They wist their houre was spent; then each to rest him hyes.

Canto III

Vaine Braggadocchio getting Guyons
Horse is made the scorne
Of knighthood trew, and is of fayre
Belphœbe fowle forlorne.

1

Soone as the morrow faire with purple beames
   Disperst the shadowes of the mistie night,
   And *Titan* playing on the eastern streames,
   Gan cleare the deawy ayre with springing light,
   Sir *Guyon* mindfull of his vow yplight,
   Uprose from drowsie couch, and him addrest
   Unto the journey which he had behight:
   His puissant armes about his noble brest,
And many-folded shield he bound about his wrest.

2

Then taking *Congé* of that virgin pure,
   The bloudy-handed babe unto her truth
   Did earnestly commit, and her conjure,
   In vertuous lore to traine his tender youth,
   And all that gentle noriture ensu'th:
   And that so soone as ryper yeares he raught,
   He might for memorie of that dayes ruth,
   Be called *Ruddymane*, and thereby taught,
T' avenge his Parents death on them, that had it wrought.

3

So forth he far'd, as now befell, on foot,
   Sith his good steed is lately from him gone;
   Patience perforce; helplesse what may it boot
   To fret for anger, or for griefe to mone?
   His Palmer now shall foot no more alone:
   So fortune wrought, as under greene woodes syde
   He lately heard that dying Lady grone,
   He left his steed without, and speare besyde,
And rushed in on foot to ayd her, ere she dyde.

4

The whiles a losell wandring by the way,
   One that to bountie never cast his mind,
   Ne thought of honour ever did assay
   His baser brest, but in his kestrell kind
   A pleasing vaine of glory vaine did find,

To which his flowing toung, and troublous spright
  Gave him great ayd, and made him more inclind:
  He that brave steed there finding ready dight,
Purloynd both steed and speare, and ran away full light.

5

Now gan his hart all swell in jollitie,
  And of him selfe great hope and help conceiv'd,
  That puffed up with smoke of vanitie,
  And with selfe-loved personage deceiv'd,
  He gan to hope, of men to be receiv'd
  For such, as he him thought, or faine would bee:
  But for in court gay portaunce he perceiv'd,
  And gallant shew to be in greatest gree,
Eftsoones to court he cast t'avaunce his first degree.

6

And by the way he chaunced to espy
  One sitting idle on a sunny bancke,
  To him avaunting in great bravery,
  As Peacocke, that his painted plumes doth prancke,
  He smote his courser in the trembling flancke,
  And to him threatned his hart-thrilling speare:
  The seely man seeing him ryde so rancke,
  And ayme at him, fell flat to ground for feare,
And crying 'Mercy' lowd, his pitious handes gan reare.

7

Thereat the Scarcrow wexed wondrous prowd,
  Through fortune of his first adventure faire,
  And with big thundring voyce revyld him lowd;
  'Vile Caytive, vassall of dread and despaire,
  Unworthie of the commune breathed aire,
  Why livest thou, dead dog, a lenger day,
  And doest not unto death thy selfe prepaire?
  Dye, or thy selfe my captive yield for ay;
Great favour I thee graunt, for aunswere thus to stay.'

8

'Hold, O deare Lord, hold your dead-doing hand,'
  Then loud he cryde, 'I am your humble thrall.'
  'Ay wretch' (quoth he) 'thy destinies withstand
  My wrathfull will, and do for mercy call.
  I give thee life: therefore prostrated fall,
  And kisse my stirrup; that thy homage bee.'

The Miser threw him selfe, as an Offall,
　　Streight at his foot in base humilitee,
And cleeped him his liege, to hold of him in fee.

9

So happy peace they made and faire accord:
　　Eftsoones this liege-man gan to wexe more bold.
　　And when he felt the folly of his Lord,
　　In his owne kind he gan him selfe unfold:
　　For he was wylie witted, and growne old
　　In cunning sleights and practick knavery.
　　From that day forth he cast for to uphold
　　His idle humour with fine flattery,
And blow the bellowes to his swelling vanity.

10

Trompart fit man for *Braggadocchio*,
　　To serve at court in view of vaunting eye;
　　Vaine-glorious man, when fluttring wind does blow
　　In his light wings, is lifted up to skye:
　　The scorne of knighthood and trew chevalrye,
　　To thinke without desert of gentle deed,
　　And noble worth to be advaunced hye:
　　Such prayse is shame; but honour vertues meed
Doth beare the fairest flowre in honorable seed.

11

So forth they pas, a well consorted paire,
　　Till that at length with *Archimage* they meet:
　　Who seeing one that shone in armour faire,
　　On goodly courser thundring with his feet,
　　Eftsoones supposed him a person meet,
　　Of his revenge to make the instrument:
　　For since the *Redcrosse* knight he erst did weet,
　　To beene with *Guyon* knit in one consent,
The ill, which earst to him, he now to *Guyon* ment.

12

And comming close to *Trompart* gan inquere
　　Of him, what might warriour that mote bee,
　　That rode in golden sell with single spere,
　　But wanted sword to wreake his enmitee.
　　'He is a great adventurer,' (said he)
　　'That hath his sword through hard assay forgone,
　　And now hath vowd, till he avenged bee,

Of that despight, never to wearen none;
That speare is him enough to doen a thousand grone.'

13
Th' enchaunter greatly joyed in the vaunt,
    And weened well ere long his will to win,
    And both his foen with equall foyle to daunt.
    Tho to him louting lowly, did begin
    To plaine of wrongs, which had committed bin
    By *Guyon*, and by that false *Redcrosse* knight,
    Which two through treason and deceiptfull gin,
    Had slaine Sir *Mordant*, and his Lady bright:
That mote him honour win, to wreak so foule despight.

14
Therewith all suddeinly he seemd enraged,
    And threatned death with dreadfull countenaunce,
    As if their lives had in his hand beene gaged;
    And with stiffe force shaking his mortall launce,
    To let him weet his doughtie valiaunce,
    Thus said; 'Old man, great sure shalbe thy meed,
    If where those knights for feare of dew vengeaunce
    Doe lurke, thou certainly to me areed,
That I may wreake on them their hainous hatefull deed.'

15
'Certes, my Lord,' (said he) 'that shall I soone,
    And give you eke good helpe to their decay,
    But mote I wisely you advise to doon;
    Give no ods to your foes, but do purvay
    Your selfe of sword before that bloudy day:
    For they be two the prowest knights on ground,
    And oft approv'd in many hard assay,
    And eke of surest steele, that may be found,
Do arme your selfe against that day, them to confound.'

16
'Dotard' (said he) 'let be thy deepe advise;
    Seemes that through many yeares thy wits thee faile,
    And that weake eld hath left thee nothing wise,
    Else never should thy judgement be so fraile
    To measure manhood by the sword or maile.
    Is not enough foure quarters of a man,
    Withouten sword or shield, an hoste to quaile?
    Thou litle wotest, what this right hand can:
Speake they, which have beheld the battailes, which it wan.'

17

The man was much abashed at his boast;
    Yet well he wist, that who so would contend
    With either of those knights on even coast,
    Should need of all his armes, him to defend;
    Yet feared least his boldnesse should offend,
    When *Braggadocchio* said, 'Once I did sweare,
    When with one sword seven knights I brought to end,
    Thence forth in battell never sword to beare,
But it were that, which noblest knight on earth doth weare.'

18

'Perdie Sir knight,' said then th' enchaunter blive,
    'That shall I shortly purchase to your hond:
    For now the best and noblest knight alive
    Prince *Arthur* is, that wonnes in Faerie lond;
    He hath a sword, that flames like burning brond.
    The same by my device I undertake
    Shall by to morrow by thy side be fond.'
    At which bold word that boaster gan to quake,
And wondred in his mind, what mote that monster make.

19

He stayd not for more bidding, but away
    Was suddein vanished out of his sight:
    The Northerne winde his wings did broad display
    At his commaund, and reared him up light
    From off the earth to take his aerie flight.
    They lookt about, but nowhere could espie
    Tract of his foot: then dead through great affright
    They both nigh were, and each bad other flie:
Both fled attonce, ne ever backe returned eie.

20

Till that they come unto a forrest greene,
    In which they shrowd themselves from causeles feare;
    Yet feare them followes still, where so they beene,
    Each trembling leafe, and whistling wind they heare,
    As ghastly bug their haire on end does reare:
    Yet both doe strive their fearefulnesse to faine.
    At last they heard a horne, that thrilled cleare
    Throughout the wood, that ecchoed againe,
And made the forrest ring, as it would rive in twaine.

21

Eft through the thicke they heard one rudely rush;
  With noyse whereof he from his loftie steed
  Downe fell to ground, and crept into a bush,
  To hide his coward head from dying dreed.
  But *Trompart* stoutly stayd to taken heed,
  Of what might hap.   Eftsoone there stepped forth
  A goodly Ladie clad in hunters weed,
  That seemd to be a woman of great worth,
And by her stately portance, borne of heavenly birth.

22

Her face so faire as flesh it seemed not,
  But heavenly pourtraict of bright Angels hew,
  Cleare as the skie, withouten blame or blot,
  Through goodly mixture of complexions dew;
  And in her cheekes the vermeill red did shew
  Like roses in a bed of lillies shed,
  The which ambrosiall odours from them threw,
  And gazers sense with double pleasure fed,
Hable to heale the sicke, and to revive the ded.

23

In her faire eyes two living lamps did flame,
  Kindled above at th' heavenly makers light,
  And darted fyrie beames out of the same,
  So passing persant, and so wondrous bright,
  That quite bereav'd the rash beholders sight:
  In them the blinded god his lustfull fire
  To kindle oft assayd, but had no might;
  For with dredd Majestie, and awfull ire,
She broke his wanton darts, and quenched base desire.

24

Her ivorie forhead, full of bountie brave,
  Like a broad table did it selfe dispred,
  For Love his loftie triumphes to engrave,
  And write the battels of his great godhed:
  All good and honour might therein be red:
  For there their dwelling was.   And when she spake,
  Sweet words, like dropping honny she did shed,
  And twixt the perles and rubins softly brake
A silver sound, that heavenly musicke seemd to make.

25

Upon her eyelids many Graces sate.
　Under the shadow of her even browes,
　Working belgards, and amorous retrate,
　And every one her with a grace endowes:
　And every one with meekenesse to her bowes.
　So glorious mirrhour of celestiall grace,
　And soveraine moniment of mortall vowes,
　How shall fraile pen descrive her heavenly face,
For feare through want of skill her beautie to disgrace?

26

So faire, and thousand thousand times more faire
　She seemd, when she presented was to sight,
　And was yclad, for heat of scorching aire,
　All in a silken Camus lylly whight,
　Purfled upon with many a folded plight,
　Which all above besprinckled was throughout,
　With golden aygulets, that glistred bright,
　Like twinckling starres, and all the skirt about
Was hemd with golden fringe.

27

Below her ham her weed did somewhat traine,
　And her streight legs most bravely were embayld
　In gilden buskins of costly Cordwaine,
　All bard with golden bendes, which were entayld
　With curious antickes, and full faire aumayld:
　Before they fastned were under her knee
　In a rich Jewell, and therein entrayld
　The ends of all their knots, that none might see,
How they within their fouldings close enwrapped bee.

28

Like two faire marble pillours they were seene.
　Which doe the temple of the Gods support,
　Whom all the people decke with girlands greene,
　And honour in their festivall resort;
　Those same with stately grace, and princely port
　She taught to tread, when she her selfe would grace,
　But with the wooddie Nymphes when she did play,
　Or when the flying Libbard she did chace,
She could then nimbly move, and after fly apace.

29

And in her hand a sharpe bore-speare she held,
  And at her backe a bow and quiver gay,
  Stuft with steele-headed darts, wherewith she queld
  The salvage beastes in her victorious play,
  Knit with a golden bauldricke, which forelay
  Athwart her snowy brest, and did divide
  Her daintie paps; which like young fruit in May
  Now little gan to swell, and being tide,
Through her thin weed their places only signifide.

30

Her yellow lockes crisped, like golden wyre,
  About her shoulders weren loosely shed,
  And when the winde emongst them did inspyre,
  They waved like a penon wide dispred,
  And low behinde her backe were scattered:
  And whether art it were, or heedlesse hap,
  As through the flouring forrest rash she fled,
  In her rude haires sweet flowres themselves did lap,
And flourishing flesh leaves and blossomes did enwrap.

31

Such as *Diana* by the sandie shore
  Of swift *Eurotas*, or on *Cynthus* greene,
  Where all the Nymphes have her unwares forlore,
  Wandreth alone with bow and arrowes keene,
  To seeke her game: Or as that famous Queene
  Of *Amazons* whom *Pyrrhus* did destroy,
  The day that first of *Priame* she was seene,
  Did shew her selfe in great triumphant joy,
To succour the weake state of sad afflicted *Troy*.

32

Such when as hartlesse *Trompart* her did view,
  He was dismayed in his coward mind,
  And doubted, whether he himselfe should shew,
  Or fly away, or bide alone behind:
  Both feare and hope he in her face did find,
  When she at last him spying thus bespake;
  'Hayle Groome; didst thou see a bleeding Hind
  Whose right haunch earst my stedfast arrow strake?
If thou didst, tell me, that I may her overtake.'

33

Wherewith reviv'd, this answere forth he threw;
 'O Goddesse, (for such I thee take to bee)
 For neither doth thy face terrestriall shew,
 Nor voyce sound mortall; I avow to thee,
 Such wounded beast, as that, I did not see,
 Sith earst into this forrest wild I came.
 But mote thy goodlyhed forgive it mee,
 To weet, which of the gods I shall thee name,
That unto thee dew worship I may rightly frame.'

34

To whom she thus; but ere her words ensewed
 Unto the bush her eye did suddein glaunce,
 In which vaine *Braggadocchio* was mewed,
 And saw it stirre: she left her percing launce,
 And towards gan a deadly shafte advaunce,
 In mind to marke the beast. At which sad stowre,
 Trompart forth stept, to stay the mortall chaunce,
 Out crying, 'O what ever heavenly powre,
Or earthly wight thou be, withhold this deadly howre.

35

'O stay thy hand, for yonder is no game
 For thy fierce arrowes, them to exercize,
 But loe my Lord, my liege, whose warlike name,
 Is far renowmd through many bold emprize;
 And now in shade he shrowded yonder lies.'
 She staid: with that he crauld out of his nest,
 Forth creeping on his caitive hands and thies,
 And, standing stoutly up, his loftie crest
Did fiercely shake, and rowze, as comming late from rest.

36

As fearfull fowle, that long in secret cave
 For dread of soaring hauke her selfe hath hid,
 Nor caring how, her silly life to save,
 She her gay painted plumes disorderid,
 Seeing at last her selfe from daunger rid,
 Peepes foorth, and soone renews her native pride;
 She gins her feathers foule disfigured
 Proudly to prune, and set on every side,
She shakes off shame, ne thinks how erst she did her hide.

37

So when her goodly visage he beheld,
   He gan himselfe to vaunt: but when he vewed
   Those deadly tooles, which in her hand she held,
   Soone into other fits he was transmewed,
   Till she to him her gratious speach renewed;
   'All haile, Sir knight, and well may thee befall,
   As all the like, which honor have pursewed
   Through deeds of armes and prowesse martiall;
All vertue merits praise, but such the most of all.'

38

To whom he thus; 'O fairest under skie,
   True be thy words, and worthy of thy praise,
   That warlike feats doest highest glorifie.
   Therein have I spent all my youthly daies,
   And many battailes fought, and many fraies
   Throughout the world, wher so they might be found,
   Endevoring my dreadded name to raise
   Above the Moone, that fame may it resound
In her eternall trompe, with laurell girlond cround.

39

'But what art thou, O Ladie, which doest raunge
   In this wilde forrest, where no pleasure is,
   And doest not it for joyous court exchaunge,
   Emongst thine equall peres, where happy blis
   And all delight does raigne, much more then this?
   There thou maist love, and dearly loved bee,
   And swim in pleasure, which thou here doest mis;
   There maist thou best be seene, and best maist see:
The wood is fit for beasts, the court is fit for thee.'

40

'Who so in pompe of proud estate' (quoth she)
   'Does swim, and bathes himselfe in courtly blis,
   Does waste his dayes in darke obscuritee,
   And in oblivion ever buried is:
   Where ease abounds, yt's eath to doe amis;
   But who his limbs with labours, and his mind
   Behaves with cares, cannot so eas mis.
   Abroad in armes, at home in studious kind,
Who seekes with painfull toile, shall honor soonest find.

41

'In woods, in waves, in warres she wonts to dwell,
  And wil be found with perill and with paine;
  Ne can the man, that moulds in idle cell
  Unto her happie mansion attaine:
  Before her gate high God did Sweate ordaine,
  And wakefull watches ever to abide:
  But easie is the way, and passage plaine
  To pleasures pallace; it may soone be spide,
And day and night her dores to all stand open wide.

42

'In Princes court,' The rest she would have said,
  But that the foolish man, fild with delight
  Of her sweet words, that all his sence dismaid,
  And with her wondrous beautie ravisht quight,
  Gan burne in filthy lust, and leaping light,
  Thought in his bastard armes her to embrace.
  With that she swarving backe, her Javelin bright
  Against him bent, and fiercely did menace:
So turned her about, and fled away apace.

43

Which when the Peasant saw, amazd he stood,
  And grieved at her flight; yet durst he not
  Pursew her steps through wild unknowen wood;
  Besides he feard her wrath, and threatned shot
  Whiles in the bush he lay, not yet forgot:
  Ne car'd he greatly for her presence vaine,
  But turning said to *Trompart*, 'What foule blot
  Is this to knight, that Ladie should againe
Depart to woods untoucht, and leave so proud disdaine.'

44

'Perdie' (said *Trompart*) 'let her pas at will,
  Least by her presence daunger mote befall.
  For who can tell (and sure I feare it ill)
  But that she is some powre celestiall?
  For whiles she spake, her great words did apall
  My feeble courage, and my hart oppresse,
  That yet I quake and tremble over all.'
  'And I' (said *Braggadocchio*) 'thought no lesse,
When first I heard her horne sound with such ghastlinesse.

45

'For from my mothers wombe this grace I have
  Me given by eternall destinie,
  That earthly thing may not my courage brave
  Dismay with feare, or cause one foot to flie,
  But either hellish feends, or powres on hie:
  Which was the cause, when earst that horne I heard,
  Weening it had beene thunder in the skie,
  I hid my selfe from it, as one affeard;
But when I other knew, my selfe I boldly reard.

46

'But now for feare of worse, that may betide,
  Let us soone hence depart.'   They soone agree;
  So to his steed he got, and gan to ride,
  As one unfit therefore, that all might see
  He had not trayned bene in chevalree.
  Which well that valiant courser did discerne:
  For he despysd to tread in dew degree,
  But chaufd and fom'd, with courage fierce and sterne,
And to be easd of that base burden still did erne.

Canto IV

*Guyon does Furor bind in chaines,
And stops Occasion:
Delivers Phedon, and therefore
By Strife is rayld upon.*

I

In brave pursuit of honorable deed,
   There is I know not what great difference
   Betweene the vulgar and the noble seed,
   Which unto things of valorous pretence
   Seemes to be borne by native influence;
   As feates of armes, and love to entertaine,
   But chiefly skill to ride, seemes a science
   Proper to gentle bloud, some others faine
To menage steeds, as did this vaunter; but in vaine.

2

But he the rightfull owner of that steed
   Who well could menage and subdew his pride,
   The whiles on foot was forced for to yeed,
   With that blacke Palmer, his most trusty guide;
   Who suffred not his wandring feete to slide.
   But when strong passion, or weake fleshlinesse
   Would from the right way seeke to draw him wide,
   He would, through temperance and stedfastnesse,
Teach him the weake to strengthen, and the strong suppresse.

3

It fortuned forth faring on his way,
   He saw from farre, or seemed for to see
   Some troublous uprore or contentious fray,
   Whereto he drew in hast it to agree.
   A mad man, or that feigned mad to bee,
   Drew by the haire along upon the ground,
   A handsome stripling with great crueltee,
   Whom sore he bett, and gor'd with many a wound,
That cheekes with teares, and sides with bloud did all abound.

4

And him behind, a wicked Hag did stalke,
   In ragged robes, and filthy disaray,
   Her other leg was lame, that she no'te walke,
   But on a staffe her feeble steps did stay;
   Her lockes, that loathly were and hoarie gray,

Grew all afore, and loosely hong unrold,
But all behind was bald, and worne away,
That none thereof could ever taken hold,
And eke her face ill favour, full of wrinckles old.

5

And ever as she went, her toungue did walke
  In foule reproch, and termes of vile despight,
  Provoking him by her outrageous talke,
  To heape more vengeance on that wretched wight;
  Sometimes she raught him stones, wherwith to smite,
  Sometimes her staffe, though it her one leg were,
  Withouten which she could not goe upright;
  Ne any evill meanes she did forbeare,
That might him move to wrath, and indignation reare.

6

The noble *Guyon* mov'd with great remorse,
  Approching, first the Hag did thrust away,
  And after adding more impetuous forse,
  His mightie hands did on the madman lay,
  And pluckt him backe; who all on fire streight way,
  Against him turning all his fell intent,
  With beastly brutish rage gan him assay,
  And smot, and bit, and kickt, and scratcht, and rent,
And did he wist not what in his avengement.

7

And sure he was a man of mickle might,
  Had he had governance, it well to guide.
  But when the franticke fit inflamd his spright,
  His force was vaine, and strooke more often wide,
  Then at the aymed marke, which he had eide:
  And oft himselfe he chaunst to hurt unwares,
  Whilst reason blent through passion, nought descride,
  But as a blindfold Bull at randon fares,
And where he hits, nought knowes, and whom he hurts, nought
cares.

8

His rude assault and rugged handeling
  Straunge seemed to the knight, that aye with foe
  In faire defence and goodly menaging
  Of armes was wont to fight, yet nathemoe
  Was he abashed now not fighting so,

But more enfierced through his currish play,
Him sternely grypt, and haling to and fro,
To overthrow him strongly did assay,
But overthrew himselfe unwares, and lower lay.

9

And being downe the villein sore did beat,
  And bruze with clownish fistes his manly face:
  And eke the Hag with many a bitter threat,
  Still cald upon to kill him in the place.
  With whose reproch and odious menace
  The knight emboyling in his haughtie hart,
  Knit all his forces, and gan soone unbrace
  His grasping hold: so lightly did upstart,
And drew his deadly weapon, to maintaine his part.

10

Which when the Palmer saw, he loudly cryde,
  'Not so, O *Guyon*, never thinke that so
  That Monster can be maistred or destroyd:
  He is not, ah, he is not such a foe,
  As steele can wound, or strength can overthroe.
  That same is *Furor*, cursed cruel wight,
  That unto knighthood workes much shame and woe;
  And that same Hag, his aged mother, hight
Occasion, the root of all wrath and despight.

11

'With her, whoso will raging *Furor* tame,
  Must first begin, and well her amenage:
  First her restraine from her reprochfull blame,
  And evil meanes, with which she doth enrage
  Her franticke sonne, and kindles his courage,
  Then when she is withdrawen, or strong withstood,
  It's eath his idle furie to asswage,
  And calme the tempest of his passion wood;
The bankes are overflowen, when stopped is the flood.'

12

Therewith Sir *Guyon* left his first emprise,
  And, turning to that woman, fast her hent
  By the hoare lockes, that hong before her eyes,
  And to the ground her threw: yet n'ould she stent
  Her bitter rayling and foule revilement,
  But still provokt her sonne to wreake her wrong;

But nathelesse he did her still torment,
  And, catching hold of her ungratious tong,
Thereon an yron lock, did fasten firme and strong.

13

Then when as use of speach was from her reft,
  With her two crooked handes she signes did make,
  And beckned him, the last helpe she had left:
  But he that last left helpe away did take,
  And both her hands fast bound unto a stake,
  That she note stirre. Then gan her sonne to flie
  Full fast away, and did her quite forsake;
  But *Guyon* after him in hast did hie,
And soone him overtooke in sad perplexitie.

14

In his strong armes he stiffely him embraste,
  Who him gainstriving, nought at all prevaild:
  For all his power was utterly defaste,
  And furious fits at earst quite weren quaild:
  Oft he re'nforst, and oft his forces fayld,
  Yet yield he would not, nor his rancour slacke.
  Then him to ground he cast, and rudely hayld,
  And both his hands fast bound behind his backe,
And both his feet in fetters to an yron racke.

15

With hundred yron chaines he did him bind,
  And hundred knots that did him sore constraine:
  Yet his great yron teeth he still did grind,
  And grimly gnash, threatning revenge in vaine;
  His burning eyen, whom bloudie strakes did staine,
  Stared full wide, and threw forth sparkes of fire,
  And more for ranck despight then for great paine,
  Shakt his long lockes, colourd like copper-wire,
And bit his tawny beard to shew his raging ire.

16

Thus when as *Guyon Furor* had captiv'd,
  Turning about he saw that wretched Squire,
  Whom that mad man of life nigh late depriv'd
  Lying on ground, all soild with bloud and mire:
  Whom whenas he perceived to respire,
  He gan to comfort, and his wounds to dresse.
  Being at last recured, he gan inquire,
  What hard mishap him brought to such distresse.
And made that caitives thrall, the thrall of wretchednesse.

17

With hart then throbbing, and with watry eyes,
  'Faire Sir' (quoth he) 'what man can shun the hap,
  That hidden lyes unwares him to surpryse?
  Misfortune waites advantage to entrap
  The man most warie in her whelming lap.
  So me weake wretch, of many weakest one,
  Unweeting, and unware of such mishap,
  She brought to mischiefe through occasion,
Where this same wicked villein did me light upon.

18

'It was a faithlesse Squire, that was the sourse
  Of all my sorrow and of these sad teares,
  With whom from tender dug of commune nourse
  Attonce I was upbrought, and eft when yeares
  More rype us reason lent to chose our Peares,
  Our selves in league of vowed love wee knit:
  In which we long time without gealous feares,
  Or faultie thoughts continewd, as was fit;
And for my part I vow, dissembled not a whit.

19

'It was my fortune commune to that age,
  To love a Ladie faire of great degree,
  The which was borne of noble parentage,
  And set in highest seat of dignitee,
  Yet seemd no lesse to love, then loved to bee:
  Long I her serv'd, and found her faithfull still,
  Ne ever thing could cause us disagree:
  Love that two harts makes one, makes eke one will:
Each strove to please, and others pleasure to fulfill.

20

'My friend, hight *Philemon*, I did partake
  Of all my love and all my privitie;
  Who greatly joyous seemed for my sake,
  And gratious to that Ladie, as to mee,
  Ne ever wight, that mote so welcome bee,
  As he to her, withouten blot or blame,
  Ne ever thing, that she could think or see,
  But unto him she would impart the same:
O wretched man, that would abuse so gentle Dame.

21

'At last such grace I found, and meanes I wrought,
   That I that Ladie to my spouse had wonne;
   Accord of friends, consent of parents sought,
   Affiance made, my happinesse begonne,
   There wanted nought but few rites to be donne,
   Which mariage make; that day too farre did seeme:
   Most joyous man, on whom the shining Sunne,
   Did shew his face, my selfe I did esteeme,
And that my falser friend did no less joyous deeme.

22

'But ere that wished day his beame disclosd,
   He either envying my toward good,
   Or of him selfe to treason ill disposed,
   One day unto me came in friendly mood,
   And told for secret, how he understood
   That Ladie whom I had to me assynd,
   Had both distaind her honorable blood,
   And eke the faith, which she to me did bynd;
And therefore wisht me stay, till I more truth should fynd.

23

'The gnawing anguish and sharp gelosy,
   Which his sad spech infixed in my brest,
   Ranckled so sore, and festred inwardly,
   That my engreeved mind could find no rest,
   Till that the truth thereof I did out wrest,
   And him besought by that same sacred band
   Betwixt us both, to counsell me the best.
   He then with solemne oath and plighted hand
Assur'd, ere long the truth to let me understand.

24

'Ere long with like againe he boorded mee,
   Saying, he now had boulted all the floure,
   And that it was a groome of base degree,
   Which of my love was partner Paramoure:
   Who used in a darkesome inner bowre
   Her oft to meet: which better to approve,
   He promised to bring me at that howre,
   When I should see, that would me nearer move,
And drive me to withdraw my blind abused love.

25

'This gracelesse man for furtherance of his guile,
    Did court the handmayd of my Lady deare,
    Who glad t' embosome his affection vile,
    Did all she might, more pleasing to appeare.
    One day to worke her to his will more neare,
    He woo'd her thus: *Pryene* (so she hight,)
    What great despight doth fortune to thee beare,
    Thus lowly to abase thy beautie bright,
That it should not deface all others lesser light?

26

'But if she had her least helpe to thee lent,
    T'adorne thy forme according thy desart,
    Their blazing pride thou wouldest soone have blent,
    And staynd their prayses with thy least good part;
    Ne should faire *Claribell* with all her art,
    Tho' she thy Lady be, approch thee neare:
    For proofe thereof, this evening, as thou art,
    Aray thy selfe in her most gorgeous geare,
That I may more delight in thy embracement deare.

27

'The Maiden proud through prayse, and mad through love
    Him hearkned to, and soone her selfe arayd,
    The whiles to me the treachour did remove
    His craftie engin, and as he had sayd,
    Me leading, in a secret corner layd,
    The sad spectatour of my Tragedie;
    Where left, he went, and his owne false part playd,
    Disguised like that groome of base degree,
Whom he had feignd th' abuser of my love to bee.

28

'Eftsoones he came unto th' appointed place,
    And with him brought *Pryene*, rich arayd,
    In *Claribellaes* clothes.   Her proper face
    I not descerned in that darkesome shade,
    But weend it was my love, with whom he playd.
    Ah God, what horrour and tormenting griefe
    My hart, my hands, mine eyes, and all assayd?
    Me liefer were ten thousand deathes priefe,
Then wound of gealous worme, and shame of such repriefe.

29

'I home returning, fraught with fowle despight,
    And chawing vengeaunce all the way I went,
    Soone as my loathed love appeard in sight,
    With wrathfull hand I slew her innocent;
    That after soone I dearely did lament;
    For when the cause of that outrageous deede
    Demaunded, I made plaine and evident,
    Her faultie Handmayd, which that bale did breede,
Confest, how *Philemon* her wrought to chaunge her weede.

30

'Which when I heard, with horrible affright
    And hellish fury all enragd, I sought
    Upon my selfe that vengeable despight
    To punish: yet it better first I thought,
    To wreake my wrath on him that first it wrought.
    To *Philemon*, false faytour *Philemon*
    I cast to pay, that I so dearely bought;
    Of deadly drugs I gave him drinke anon,
And washt away his guilt with guiltie potion.

31

'Thus heaping crime on crime, and griefe on griefe,
    To losse of love adjoyning losse of frend,
    I meant to purge both with a third mischiefe,
    And in my woes beginner it to end:
    That was *Pryene*; she did first offend,
    She last should smart: with which cruell intent,
    When I at her my murdrous blade did bend,
    She fled away with ghastly dreriment,
And I pursewing my fell purpose, after went.

32

'Feare gave her wings, and rage enforst my flight;
    Through woods and plaines so long I did her chace,
    Till this mad man, whom your victorious might
    Hath now fast bound, me met in middle space,
    As I her, so he me pursewd apace,
    And shortly overtooke: I breathing yre,
    Sore chauffed at my stay in such a cace,
    And with my heat kindled his cruell fyre;
Which kindled once, his mother did more rage inspyre.

33

'Betwixt them both, they have me doen to dye,
   Through wounds, and strokes, and stubborne handeling,
   That death were better, then such agony,
   As griefe and furie unto me did bring;
   Of which in me yet stickes the mortall sting,
   That during life will never be appeasd.'
   When he thus ended had his sorrowing,
   Said *Guyon*, 'Squire, sore have ye beene diseasd;
But all your hurts may soone through temperance be easd.'

34

Then gan the Palmer thus, 'Most wretched man,
   That to affections does the bridle lend;
   In their beginning they are weake and wan,
   But soone through suff'rance growe to fearefull end;
   Whiles they are weake betimes with them contend:
   For when they once to perfect strength do grow,
   Strong warres they make, and cruell battry bend
   Gainst fort of Reason, it to overthrow:
Wrath, gelosie, griefe, love this Squire have layd thus low.

35

'Wrath, gealosie, griefe, love, do thus expell:
   Wrath is a fire, and gealosie a weede,
   Griefe is a flood, and love a monster fell;
   The fire of sparkes, the weede of little seede,
   The flood of drops, the Monster filth did breede:
   But sparks, seed, drops, and filth do thus delay;
   The sparks soone quench, the springing seed outweed,
   The drops dry up, and filth wipe cleane away:
So shall wrath, gealosie, griefe, love dye and decay.'

36

'Unlucky Squire' (saide *Guyon*) 'sith thou hast
   Falne into mischiefe through intemperaunce,
   Henceforth take heede of that thou now hast past,
   And guide thy wayes with warie governaunce,
   Least worse betide thee by some later chaunce.
   But read how art thou nam'd, and of what kin.'
   Phedon I hight' (quoth he) 'and do advaunce
   Mine auncestry from famous *Coradin*,
Who first to rayse our house to honour did begin.'

37

Thus as he spake, lo far away they spyd
  A varlet running towards hastily,
  Whose flying feet so fast their way applyde,
  That round about a cloud of dust did fly,
  Which mingled all with sweate, did him his eye.
  He soone approched, panting, breathlesse, whot,
  And all so soyld, that none could him descry;
  His countenance was bold, and bashed not
For Guyons lookes, but scornefull eyeglaunce at him shot.

38

Behind his backe he bore a brasen shield,
  On which was drawen faire, in colours fit,
  A flaming fire in midst of bloudy field,
  And round about the wreath this word was writ,
  Burnt I do burne.   Right well beseemed it,
  To be the shield of some redoubted knight;
  And in his hand two darts exceeding flit,
  And deadly sharpe he held, whose heads were dight
In poyson and in bloud, of malice and despight.

39

When he in presence came, to *Guyon* first
  He boldly spake, 'Sir knight, if knight thou bee,
  Abandon this forestalled place at erst,
  For feare of further harme, I counsell thee,
  Or bide the chaunce at thine owne jeoperdie.'
  The knight at his great boldnesse wondered,
  And though he scornd his idle vanitie,
  Yet mildly him to purpose answered;
For not to grow of nought he it conjectured.

40

'Varlet, this place most dew to me I deeme,
  Yielded by him, that held it forcibly.
  But whence should come that harme, which thou doest seeme
  To threat to him, that mind his chaunce t' abye?'
  'Perdy' (said he) 'here comes, and is hard by
  A knight of wondrous powre, and great assay,
  That never yet encountred enemy,
  But did him deadly daunt, or fowle dismay;
Ne thou for better hope, if thou his presence stay.'

41

'How hight he then' (said *Guyon*) 'and from whence?'
  '*Pyrochles* is his name, renowmed farre
  For his bold feates and hardy confidence,
  Full oft approv'd in many a cruell warre,
  The brother of *Cymochles*, both which arre
  The sonnes of old *Acrates* and *Despight*,
  Acrates sonne of *Phlegeton* and *Jarre*;
  But *Phlegeton* is sonne of *Herebus* and *Night*;
But *Herebus* sonne of *Aeternitie* is hight.

42

'So from immortall race he does proceede,
  That mortall hands may not withstand his might,
  Drad for his derring do, and bloudy deed;
  For all in bloud and spoile is his delight.
  His am I *Atin*, his in wrong and right,
  That matter make for him to worke upon,
  And stirre him up to strife and cruell fight.
  Fly therefore, fly this fearefull stead anon,
Least thy foolhardize worke thy sad confusion.'

43

'His be that care, whom most it doth concerne,'
  (Said he) 'but whither with such hasty flight
  Art thou now bound? for well mote I discerne
  Great cause, that carries thee so swifte and light.'
  'My Lord' (quoth he) 'me sent, and streight behight
  To seeke *Occasion*; where so she bee:
  For he is all disposd to bloudy fight,
  And breathes out wrath and hainous crueltie;
Hard is his hap, that first fals in his jeopardie.'

44

'Madman' (said then the Palmer) 'that does seeke
  Occasion to wrath, and cause of strife;
  She comes unsought, and shonned followes eke.
  Happy, who can abstaine, when Rancour rife
  Kindles Revenge, and threats his rusty knife;
  Woe never wants, where every cause is caught,
  And rash *Occasion* makes unquiet life.'
  'Then loe, where bound she sits, whom thou hast sought,'
(Said *Guyon*,) 'let that message to thy Lord be brought.'

45

That when the varlet heard and saw, streight way
  He wexed wondrous wroth, and said, 'Vile knight,
  That knights and knighthood doest with shame upbray,
  And shewst th' ensample of thy childish might,
  With silly weake old woman thus to fight.
  Great glory and gay spoile sure hast thou got
  And stoutly prov'd thy puissaunce here in sight;
  That shall *Pyrochles* well requite, I wot,
And with thy bloud abolish so reprochfull blot.'

46

With that one of his thrillant darts he threw,
  Headed with ire and vengeable despight;
  The quivering steele his aymed end wel knew,
  And to his brest it selfe intended right:
  But he was warie, and ere it empight
  In the meant marke, advaunst his shield atweene,
  On which it seizing, no way enter might,
  But backe rebounding, left the forckhead keene;
Eftsoones he fled away, and might no where be seene.

Canto V

1

Who ever doth to temperaunce apply
  His stedfast life, and all his actions frame,
  Trust me, shall find no greater enimy,
  Then stubborne perturbation, to the same;
  To which right well the wise do give that name,
  For it the goodly peace of stayed mindes
  Does overthrow, and troublous warre proclame:
  His owne woes author, who so bound it findes,
As did *Pyrochles*, and it wilfully unbindes.

2

After that varlets flight, it was not long,
  Ere on the plaine fast pricking *Guyon* spide
  One in bright armes embatteiled full strong,
  That, as the Sunny beames do glaunce and glide
  Upon the trembling wave, so shined bright,
  And round about him threw forth sparkling fire,
  That seemd him to enflame on every side:
  His steed was bloudy red, and fomed ire,
When with the maistring spur he did him roughly stire.

3

Approching nigh, he never stayd to greete,
  Ne chaffar words, prowd courage to provoke,
  But prickt so fiers, that underneath his feete
  The smouldring dust did round about him smoke,
  Both horse and man nigh able for to choke;
  And fayrly couching his steele-headed speare,
  Him first saluted with a sturdy stroke;
  It booted nought Sir *Guyon* comming neare
To thinke, such hideous puissaunce on foot to beare.

4

But lightly shunned it, and passing by
  With his bright blade did smite at him so fell,
  That the sharpe steele arriving forcibly
  On his broad shield, bit not, but glauncing fell
  On his horse necke before the quilted sell

And from the head the body sundred quight.
So him dismounted low, he did compell
On foot with him to matchen equall fight;
The truncked beast fast bleeding, did him fowly dight.

5

Sore bruzed with the fall, he slow uprose,
And all enraged, thus him loudly shent;
'Disleall knight, whose coward courage chose
To wreake it selfe on beast all innocent,
And shund the marke, at which it should be ment,
Thereby thine armes seem strong, but manhood fraile;
So hast thou oft with guile thine honor blent;
But litle may such guile thee now availe,
If wonted force and fortune do not much me faile.'

6

With that he drew his flaming sword, and strooke
At him so fiercely, that the upper marge
Of his sevenfolded shield away it tooke,
And glauncing on his helmet, made a large
And open gash therein: were not his targe,
That broke the violence of his intent,
The weary soule from thence it would discharge;
Nathelesse so sore a buff to him it lent,
That made him reele, and to his brest his bever bent.

7

Exceeding wroth was *Guyon* at that blow,
And much ashamd, that stroke of living arme
Should him dismay, and make him stoup so low,
Though otherwise it did him litle harme:
Tho hurling high his yron braced arme,
He smote so manly on his shoulder plate,
That all his left side it did quite disarme;
Yet there the steel stayd not, but inly bate
Deepe in his flesh, and opened wide a red floodgate.

8

Deadly dismayd, with horrour of that dint
Pyrochles was, and grieved eke entyre;
Yet nathemore did it his fury stint,
But added flame unto his former fire,
That welnigh molt his hart in raging yre;
Ne thenceforth his approved skill, to ward,

Or strike, or hurtle, round in warlike gyre,
  Remembred he, ne car'd for his saufgard,
But rudely rag'd, and like a cruell Tygre far'd.

9

He hewd, and lasht, and foynd, and thundred blowes,
  And every way did seeke into his life,
  Ne plate, ne male could ward so mighty throwes,
  But yielded passage to his cruell knife.
  But *Guyon*, in the heat of all his strife,
  Was warie wise, and closely did awayt
  Avauntage, whilest his foe did rage most rife;
  Sometimes a thwart, sometimes he strooke him strayt,
And falsed oft his blowes, t' illude him with such bayt.

10

Like as a Lyon, whose imperiall powre
  A prowd rebellious Unicorne defies,
  T' avoide the rash assault and wrathful stowre
  Of his fiers foe, him to a tree applies,
  And when him running in full course he spies,
  He slips aside; the whiles that furious beast
  His precious horne, sought of his enimies,
  Strikes in the stocke, ne thence can be releast,
But to the mighty victor yields a bounteous feast.

11

With such faire slight him *Guyon* often faild,
  Till at the last all breathlesse, wearie, faint
  Him spying, with fresh onsett he assaild,
  And kindling new his courage seeming queint,
  Strooke him so hugely, that through great constraint
  He made him stoup perforce unto his knee,
  And do unwilling worship to the Saint,
  That on his shield depainted he did see;
Such homage till that instant never learned hee.

12

Whom *Guyon* seeing stoup, pursewed fast
  The present offer to faire victory,
  And soone his dreadfull blade about he cast,
  Wherewith he smote his haughty crest so hye,
  That streight on ground made him full low to lye;
  Then on his brest his victor foote he thrust,
  With that he cryde, 'Mercy, do me not dye,

Ne deeme thy force by fortunes doome unjust,
That hath (maugre her spight) thus low me laid in dust.'

13

Eftsoones his cruell hand Sir *Guyon* stayd,
  Tempring the passion with advizement slow,
  And maistring might on enimy dismayd:
  For th' equall dye of warre he well did know;
  Then to him said, 'Live and allegaunce owe,
  To him that gives thee life and libertie,
  And henceforth by this dayes ensample trow,
  That hasty wroth, and heedlesse hazardrie
Do breede repentaunce late, and lasting infamie.'

14

So up he let him rise, who with grim looke
  And count'naunce sterne upstanding, gan to grind
  His grated teeth for great disdeigne, and shooke
  His sandy lockes, long hanging downe behind,
  Knotted in bloud, and dust, for griefe of mind,
  That he in ods of armes was conquered;
  Yet in himselfe some comfort he did find,
  That him so noble knight had maistered,
Whose bounty more then might, yet both he wondered.

15

Which *Guyon* marking said, 'Be nought agriev'd,
  Sir knight, that thus ye now subdewed arre:
  Was never man, who most conquestes atchiev'd,
  But sometimes had the worse, and lost by warre,
  Yet shortly gaynd, that losse exceeded farre:
  Losse is no shame, nor to be lesse then foe,
  But to be lesser, then himselfe, doth marre
  Both loosers lot, and victours prayse alsoe.
Vaine others overthrowes, who selfe doth overthrowe.

16

'Fly, O *Pyrochles*, fly the dreadfull warre,
  That in thy selfe thy lesser partes do move,
  Outrageous anger, and woe-working jarre,
  Direfull impatience, and hart murdring love;
  Those, those thy foes, those warriours far remove,
  Which thee to endlesse bale captived lead.
  But sith in might thou didst my mercy prove,
  Of curtesie to me the cause aread,
That thee against me drew with so impetuous dread.'

17

'Dreadlesse' (said he) 'that shall I soone declare:
  It was complaind, that thou hadst done great tort
  Unto an aged woman, poore and bare,
  And thralled her in chaines with strong effort,
  Voide of all succour and needfull comfort:
  That ill beseemes thee, such as I thee see,
  To worke such shame. Therefore I thee exhort,
  To chaunge thy will, and set *Occasion* free,
And to her captive sonne yield his first libertee.'

18

Thereat Sir *Guyon* smilde, 'And is that all'
  (Said he) 'that thee so sore displeased hath?
  Great mercy sure, for to enlarge a thrall,
  Whose freedom shall thee turne to greatest scath.
  Nath'lesse now quench thy whot emboyling wrath:
  Loe there they be; to thee I yield them free.'
  Thereat he wondrous glad, out of the path
  Did lightly leape, where he them bound did see,
And gan to breake the bands of their captivitee.

19

Soone as *Occasion* felt her selfe untyde,
  Before her sonne could well assoyled bee,
  She to her use returnd, and streight defyde
  Both *Guyon* and *Pyrochles*: th' one (said shee)
  Bycause he wonne; the other because hee
  Was wonne: So matter did she make of nought,
  To stirre up strife, and do them disagree:
  But soone as *Furor* was enlargd, she sought
To kindle his quencht fire, and thousand causes wrought.

20

It was not long, ere she inflam'd him so,
  That he would algates with *Pyrochles* fight,
  And his redeemer chalengd for his foe,
  Because he had not well mainteind his right,
  But yielded had to that same straunger knight:
  Now gan *Pyrochles* wex as wood, as hee,
  And him affronted with impatient might:
  So both together fiers engrasped bee,
Whyles *Guyon* standing by, their uncouth strife does see.

21

Him all that while *Occasion* did provoke
　Against *Pyrochles*, and new matter framed
　Upon the old, him stirring to be wroke
　Of his late wrongs, in which she oft him blamed
　For suffering such abuse, as knighthood shamed,
　And him dishabled quite.　But he was wise
　Ne would with vaine occasions be inflamed;
　　Yet others she more urgent did devise:
Yet nothing could him to impatience entise.

22

Their fell contention still increased more,
　And more thereby increased *Furors* might,
　That he his foe has hurt, and wounded sore,
　And him in bloud and durt deformed quight.
　His mother eke, more to augment his spight,
　Now brought to him a flaming fire brond,
　Which she in *Stygian* lake, ay burning bright,
　　Had kindled: that she gave into his hond,
That armd with fire more hardly he mote him withstond.

23

Tho gan that villein wex so fiers and strong,
　That nothing might sustaine his furious forse;
　He cast him downe to ground, and all along
　Drew him through durt and myre without remorse,
　And fowly battered his comely corse,
　That *Guyon* much disdeigned so loathly sight.
　At last he was compeld to cry perforse,
　　'Help, O Sir *Guyon*, helpe most noble knight,
To rid a wretched man from handes of hellish wight.'

24

The knight was greatly moved at his plaint,
　And gan him dight to succour his distresse,
　Till that the Palmer, by his grave restraint,
　Him stayd from yielding pitifull redresse;
　And said, 'Deare sonne, thy causelesse ruth represse,
　Ne let thy stout hart melt in pitty vayne:
　He that his sorrow sought through wilfulnesse,
　　And his foe fettred would release agayne,
Deserves to taste his follies fruit, repented payne.'

25

Guyon obayd; So him away he drew
　From needlesse trouble of renewing fight
　Already fought, his voyage to pursew.
　But rash *Pyrochles* varlet, *Atin* hight,
　When late he saw his Lord in heavie plight,
　Under Sir *Guyons* puissaunt stroke to fall,
　Him deeming dead, as then he seemd in sight,
　Fled fast away, to tell his funerall
Unto his brother, whom *Cymochles* men did call.

26

He was a man of rare redoubted might,
　Famous throughout the world for warlike prayse,
　And glorious spoiles, purchast in perilous fight:
　Full many doughtie knights he in his dayes
　Had doen to death, subdewde in equall frayes,
　Whose carkases, for terrour of his name,
　Of fowles and beastes he made the piteous prayes,
　And hong their conquered armes for more defame
On gallow trees, in honour of his dearest Dame.

27

His dearest Dame is that Enchaunteresse,
　The vile *Acrasia*, that with vaine delightes,
　And idle pleasures in her *Bowre of Blisse*,
　Does charme her lovers, and the feeble sprightes
　Can call out of the bodies of fraile wightes:
　Whom then she does transforme to monstrous hewes,
　And horribly misshapes with ugly sightes,
　Captiv'd eternally in yron mewes,
And darksom dens, where *Titan* his face never shewes.

28

There *Atin* found *Cymochles* sojourning,
　To serve his Lemans love: for he, by kind,
　Was given all to lust and loose living,
　When ever his fiers hands he free mote find:
　And now he has pourd out his idle mind
　In daintie delices, and lavish joyes,
　Having his warlike weapons cast behind,
　And flowes in pleasures, and vaine pleasing toyes,
Mingled emongst loose Ladies and lascivious boyes.

29

And over him, art striving to compaire
  With nature, did an Arber greene dispred,
  Framed of wanton Yvie, flouring faire,
  Through which the fragrant Eglantine did spred
  His pricking armes, entrayld with roses red,
  Which daintie odours round about them threw
  And all within with flowres was garnished,
  That when myld *Zephyrus* emongst them blew,
Did breath out bounteous smels, and painted colors shew.

30

And fast beside, there trickled softly downe
  A gentle streame, whose murmuring wave did play
  Emongst the pumy stones, and made a sowne,
  To lull him soft a sleepe, that by it lay;
  The wearie Traveiler, wandring that way,
  Therein did often quench his thristy heat,
  And then by it his wearie limbes display,
  Whiles creeping slomber made him to forget
His former paine, and wypt away his toylsom sweat.

31

And on the other side a pleasaunt grove
  Was shot up high, full of the stately tree,
  That dedicated is t' *Olympicke Jove*,
  And to his sonne *Alcides*, whenas hee
  Gaynd in *Nemea* goodly victoree;
  Therein the mery birds of every sort
  Chaunted alowd their chearefull harmonie:
  And made emongst them selves a sweet consort,
That quickned the dull spright with musicall comfort.

32

There he him found all carelesly displayd,
  In secret shadow from the sunny ray,
  On a sweet bed of lillies softly layd,
  Amidst a flocke of Damzels fresh and gay,
  That round about him dissolute did play
  Their wanton follies, and light meriment;
  Every of which did loosely disaray
  Her upper parts of meet habiliments,
And shewd them naked, deckt with many ornaments.

33

And every of them strove, with most delights,
    Him to aggrate, and greatest pleasures shew;
    Some framd faire lookes, glancing like evening lights,
    Others sweet words, dropping like honny dew;
    Some bathed kisses, and did soft embrew
    The sugred licour through his melting lips:
    One boastes her beautie, and does yeeld to vew
    Her daintie limbes above her tender hips;
Another her out boastes, and all for tryall strips.

34

He, like an Adder, lurking in the weeds,
    His wandring thought in deepe desire does steepe,
    And his fraile eye with spoyle of beautie feedes:
    Sometimes he falsely faines himselfe to sleepe,
    Whiles through their lids his wanton eies do peepe,
    To steale a snatch of amorous conceipt,
    Whereby close fire into his heart does creepe:
    So, he them deceives, deceiv'd in his deceipt,
Made drunke with drugs of deare voluptuous receipt.

35

Atin arriving there, when him he spide,
    Thus in still waves of deepe delight to wade,
    Fiercely approching, to him lowdly cride,
    '*Cymochles*; oh no, but *Cymochles* shade,
    In which that manly person late did fade,
    What is become of great *Acrates* sonne?
    Or where hath he hong up his mortall blade,
    That hath so many haughtie conquests wonne?
Is all his force forlorne, and all his glory donne?'

36

Then pricking him with his sharp-pointed dart,
    He saide; 'Up, up, thou womanish weake knight,
    That here in Ladies lap entombed art,
    Unmindfull of thy praise and prowest might,
    And weetlesse eke of lately wrought despight,
    Whiles sad *Pyrochles* lies on senselesse ground,
    And groneth out his utmost grudging spright,
    Through many a stroke and many a streaming wound,
Calling thy helpe in vaine, that here in joyes art dround.'

37

Suddeinly out of his delightfull dreame
   The man awoke, and would have questiond more;
   But he would not endure that wofull theame
   For to dilate at large, but urged sore
   With percing words, and pittifull implore,
   Him hastie to arise.   As one affright
   With hellish feends, or *Furies* mad uprore,
   He then uprose, inflamd with fell despight,
And called for his armes; for he would algates fight.

38

They bene ybrought; he quickly does him dight,
   And lightly mounted, passeth on his way,
   Ne Ladies loves, ne sweete entreaties might
   Appease his heat, or hastie passage stay;
   For he has vowd, to beene aveng'd that day,
   (That day it selfe him seemed all too long:)
   On him, that did *Pyrochles* deare dismay:
   So proudly pricketh on his courser strong,
And *Atin* aie him pricks with spurs of shame and wrong.

Canto VI

Guyon is of immodest Merth
Led into loose desire,
Fights with Cymochles, whiles his bro-
ther burnes in furious fire.

1

A harder lesson, to learne Continence
   In joyous pleasure, then in grievous paine:
   For sweetnesse doth allure the weaker sence
   So strongly, that uneathes it can refraine
   From that, which feeble nature covets faine;
   But griefe and wrath, that be her enemies,
   And foes of life, she better can abstaine;
   Yet vertue vauntes in both her victories,
And *Guyon* in them all shewes goodly maisteries.

2

Whom bold *Cymochles* travelling to find,
   With cruell purpose bent to wreake on him
   The wrath, which *Atin* kindled in his mind,
   Came to a river, by whose utmost brim
   Wayting to passe, he saw whereas did swim
   Along the shore, as swift as glaunce of eye,
   A litle Gondelay, bedecked trim
   With boughes and arbours woven cunningly,
That like a litle forrest seemed outwardly.

3

And therein sate a Ladie fresh and faire,
   Making sweet solace to herselfe alone;
   Sometimes she sung, as loud as larke in aire,
   Sometimes she laught, that nigh her breth was gone,
   Yet was there not with her else any one,
   That to her might move cause of meriment:
   Matter of merth enough, though there were none
   She could devise, and thousand waies invent,
To feede her foolish humour, and vaine jolliment.

4

Which when farre off *Cymochles* heard, and saw,
   He lowdly cald to such, as were a bord,
   The little barke unto the shore to draw,
   And him to ferrie over that deepe ford:
   The merry marriner unto his word

Soone hearkned, and her painted bote streightway
Turnd to the shore, where that same warlike Lord
She in receiv'd; but *Atin* by no way
She would admit, albe the knight her much did pray.

5

Eftsoones her shallow ship away did slide,
    More swift, then swallow sheres the liquid skie,
Withouten oare or Pilot it to guide,
    Or winged canvas with the wind to flie,
    Only she turn'd a pin, and by and by
It cut away upon the yielding wave,
    Ne cared she her course for to apply:
    For it was taught the way, which she would have,
And both from rocks and flats it selfe could wisely save.

6

And all the way, the wanton Damzell found
    New merth, her passenger to entertaine;
For she in pleasant purpose did abound,
    And greatly joyed merry tales to faine,
    Of which a store-house did with her remaine,
Yet seemed, nothing well they her became;
    For all her words she drownd with laughter vaine,
    And wanted grace in utt'ring of the same,
That turnd all her pleasance to a scoffing game.

7

And other whiles vaine toyes she would devize
    As her fantasticke wit did most delight,
Sometimes her head she fondly would aguize
    With gaudie girlonds, or fresh flowrets dight
    About her necke, or rings of rushes plight;
Sometimes to doe him laugh, she would assay
    To laugh at shaking of the leaves light,
    Or to behold the water worke, and play
About her little frigot, therein making way.

8

Her light behaviour, and loose dalliaunce
    Gave wondrous great contentment to the knight,
That of his way he had no sovenaunce,
    Nor care of vow'd revenge, and cruell fight,
    But to weake wench did yeeld his martiall might.
So easie was to quench his flamed mind

With one sweet drop of sensuall delight,
  So easie is, t' appease the stormie wind
Of malice in the calme of pleasant womankind.

f sensuality

9

Diverse discourses in their way they spent,
  Mongst which *Cymochles* of her questioned,
  Both what she was, and what that usage ment,
  Which in her cot she daily practised.
  'Vaine man' (said she) 'that wouldest be reckoned
  A straunger in thy home, and ignoraunt
  Of *Phædria* (for so my name is red)
  Of *Phædria*, thine owne fellow servaunt;
For thou to serve *Acrasia* thy selfe doest vaunt.

10

'In this wide Inland sea, that hight by name
  The *Idle lake*, my wandring ship I row,
  That knowes her port, and thither sailes by ayme,
  Ne care, ne feare, I how the wind do blow,
  Or whether swift I wend, or whether slow:
  Both slow and swift a like do serve my tourne,
  Ne swelling *Neptune*, ne lowd thundring *Jove*
  Can chaunge my cheare, or make me ever mourne;
My little boat can safely passe this perilous bourne.'

11

Whiles thus she talked, and whiles thus she toyd,
  They were farre past the passage, which he spake,
  And come unto an Island, waste and voyd,
  That floted in the midst of that great lake,
  There her small Gondelay her port did make,
  And that gay paire issewing on the shore
  Disburdned her.   Their way they forward take
  Into the land, that lay them faire before,
Whose pleasaunce she him shewd, and plentifull great store.

12

It was a chosen plot of fertile land,
  Emongst wide waves set, like a litle nest,
  As if it had by Natures cunning hand,
  Bene cloisely picked out from all the rest,
  And laid forth for ensample of the best:
  No daintie flowre or herbe, that growes on ground,
  No arboret with painted blossomes drest

And smelling sweet, but there it might be found
To bud out faire, and her sweet smels throw all around.

13

No tree, whose braunches did not bravely spring;
  No braunch, whereon a fine bird did not sit:
  No bird, but did her shrill notes sweetely sing;
  No song but did containe a lovely dit:
  Trees, braunches, birds, and songs were framed fit,
  For to allure fraile mind to carelesse ease.
  Carelesse the man soone woxe, and his weake wit
  Was overcome of thing, that did him please;
So pleased, did his wrathfull purpose faire appease.

14

Thus when she had his eyes and senses fed
  With false delights, and fild with pleasures vaine,
  Into a shady dale she soft him led,
  And laid him downe upon a grassie plaine;
  And her sweet selfe without dread, or disdaine,
  She set beside, laying his head disarm'd
  In her loose lap, it softly to sustaine,
  Where soone he slumbred, fearing not be harm'd,
The whiles with a loud lay she thus him sweetly charm'd.

15

'Behold, O man, that toilesome paines doest take,
  The flowres, the fields, and all that pleasant growes,
  How they them selves doe thine ensample make,
  Whiles nothing envious nature them forth throwes
  Out of her fruitfull lap; how, no man knowes,
  They spring, they bud, they blossome fresh and faire,
  And deck the world with their rich pompous showes;
  Yet no man for them taketh paines or care,
Yet no man to them can his carefull paines compare.

16

'The lilly, Ladie of the flowring field,
  The Flowre-deluce, her lovely Paramoure,
  Bid thee to them thy fruitlesse labours yield,
  And soone leave off this toylsome wearie stoure:
  Loe loe how brave she decks her bounteous boure,
  With silken curtens and gold coverlets,
  Therein to shroud her sumptuous Belamoure,
  Yet nether spinnes nor cardes, ne cares nor frets,
But to her mother Nature all her care she lets.

17

'Why then dost thou, O man, that of them all
   Art Lord, and eke of nature Soveraine,
   Wilfully make thy selfe a wretched thrall,
   And wast thy joyous houres in needlesse paine,
   Seeking for daunger and adventures vaine?
   What bootes it all to have, and nothing use?
   Who shall him rew, that swimming in the maine,
   Will die for thirst, and water doth refuse?
Refuse such fruitlesse toile, and present pleasures chuse.'

18

By this she had him lulled fast a sleepe,
   That of no worldly thing he care did take;
   Then she with liquors strong his eyes did steepe,
   That nothing should him hastily awake:
   So she him left, and did her selfe betake
   Unto her boat againe, with which she cleft
   The slouthfull wave of that great griesly lake;
   Soone shee that Island farre behind her left,
And now is come to that same place, where first she weft.

19

By this time was the worthy *Guyon* brought
   Unto the other side of that wide strond,
   Where she was rowing, and for passage sought:
   Him needed not long call, she soone to hond
   Her ferry, brought, where him she byding fond,
   With his sad guide; himselfe she tooke a boord,
   But the *Blacke Palmer* suffred still to stond,
   Ne would for price, or prayers once affoord,
To ferry that old man over the perlous foord.

20

Guyon was loath to leave his guide behind,
   Yet being entred, might not backe retyre;
   For the flit barke, obaying to her mind,
   Forth launched quickly, as she did desire,
   Ne gave him leave to bid that aged sire
   Adieu, but nimbly ran her wonted course
   Through the dull billowes thicke as troubled mire,
   Whom neither wind out of their seat could forse,
Nor timely tides did drive out of their sluggish sourse.

21

And by the way, as was her wonted guize,
  Her merry fit she freshly gan to reare,
  And did of joy and jollitie devize,
  Her selfe to cherish, and her guest to cheare:
  The knight was courteous, and did not forbeare
  Her honest merth and pleasaunce to partake;
  But when he saw her toy, and gibe, and geare,
  And passe the bonds of modest merimake,
Her dalliance he despis'd, and follies did forsake.

22

Yet she still followed her former stile,
  And said, and did all that mote him delight,
  Till they arrived in that pleasant Ile,
  Where sleeping late she left her other knight.
  But when as *Guyon* of that land had sight,
  He wist himselfe amisse, and angry said;
  'Ah Dame, perdie ye have not doen me right,
  Thus to mislead me, whiles I you obaid:
Me litle needed from my right way to have straid.'

23

'Faire Sir' (quoth she) 'be not displeasd at all;
  Who fares on sea, may not commaund his way,
  Ne wind and weather at his pleasure call:
  The sea is wide, and easie for to stray;
  The wind unstable, and doth never stay.
  But here a while ye may in safety rest,
  Till season serve new passage to assay;
  Better safe port, then be in seas distrest.'
Therewith she laught, and did her earnest end in jest.

24

But he halfe discontent, mote nathlesse
  Himselfe appease, and issewd forth on shore:
  The joyes whereof, and happy fruitfulnesse,
  Such as he saw she gan him lay before,
  And all though pleasant, yet she made much more:
  The fields did laugh, the flowres did freshly spring,
  The trees did bud, and earely blossomes bore,
  And all the quire of birds did sweetly sing,
And told that gardins pleasures in their caroling.

25

And she more sweet, then any bird on bough,
   Would oftentimes emongst them beare a part,   * sweet*
   And strive to passe (as she could well enough)
   Their native musicke by her skilful art:
   So did she all, that might his constant hart
   Withdraw from thought of warlike enterprize,
   And drowne in dissolute delights apart,
   Where noyse of armes, or vew of martiall guize
Might not revive desire of knightly exercize.

26

But he was wise, and warie of her will,
   And ever held his hand upon his hart:
   Yet would not seeme so rude, and thewed ill,
   As to despise so courteous seeming part,
   That gentle Ladie did to him impart,
   But fairely tempring fond desire subdewd,
   And ever her desired to depart.
   She list not heare, but her disports poursewd,   *perswasive*
And ever bad him stay, till time the tide renewd.

27

And now by this, *Cymochles* howre was spent,
   That he awoke out of his idle dreme,
   And shaking off his drowzie dreriment,
   Gan him avize, how ill did him beseeme;
   In slouthfull sleepe his molten hart to steme,
   And quench the brond of his conceived ire.
   Tho up he started, stird with shame extreme,
   Ne staied for his Damzell to inquire,
But marched to the strond, there passage to require.

28

And in the way he with Sir *Guyon* met,   *G+C meet*
   Accompanyde with *Phædria* the faire,
   Eftsoones he gan to rage, and inly fret,
   Crying, 'Let be that Ladie debonaire,
   Thou recreant knight, and soone thyselfe prepaire
   To battell, if thou meane her love to gaine:
   Loe, loe alreadie, how the fowles in aire
   Doe flocke, awaiting shortly to obtaine
Thy carcasse for their pray, the guerdon of thy paine.

fight

29

And therewithall he fiercely at him flew,
   And with importune outrage him assayld;
   Who soone prepard to field, his sword forth drew,
   And him with equall value countervayld:
   Their mightie strokes their haberjeons dismayld,
   And naked made each others manly spalles;
   The mortall steele despiteously entayld
   Deepe in their flesh, quite through the yron walles,
That a large purple streme adowne their giambeux falles.

30

Cymochles, that had never met before
   So puissant foe, with envious despight
   His proud presumed force increased more,
   Disdeigning to be held so long in fight;
   Sir *Guyon*, grudging not so much his might,
   As those unknightly raylings, which he spoke,
   With wrathfull fire his courage kindled bright,
   Thereof devising shortly to be wroke,
And doubling all his powres, redoubled every stroke.

31

Both of them high attonce their handes enhaunst,
   And both attonce their huge blowes down did sway;
   Cymochles sword on *Guyons* shield yglaunst,
   And thereof nigh one quarter sheard away;
   But *Guyons* angry blade so fiers did play
   On th' others helmet, which as *Titan* shone,
   That quite it clove his plumed crest in tway,
   And bared all his head unto the bone;
Wherewith astonisht, still he stood, as senselesse stone.

32

Still as he stood, faire *Phædria*, that beheld
   That deadly daunger, soone atweene them ran;
   And at their feet her selfe most humbly feld,
   Crying with pitteous voice, and count'nance wan;
   'Ah well away, most noble Lords, how can
   Your cruell eyes endure so pitteous sight,
   To shed your lives on ground? wo worth the man,
   That first did teach the cursed steele to bight
In his owne flesh, and make way to the living spright.

33

'If ever love of Ladie did empierce   *♀ as peace maker*
   Your yron brestes, or pittie could find place,
   Withhold your bloudie hands from battell fierce,
   And sith for me ye fight, to me this grace
   Both yeeld, to stay your deadly strife a space.'
   They stayd a while: and forth she gan proceed:
   'Most wretched woman, and of wicked race,   *// ♀ wicked*
   That am the authour of this hainous deed,
And cause of death betweene two doughtie knights doe breed.

34

'But if for me ye fight, or me will serve,
   Not this rude kind of battell, nor these armes
   Are meet, the which doe men in bale to sterve,
   And dolefull sorrow heape with deadly harmes:
   Such cruell game my scarmoges disarmes:
   Another warre, and other weapons I
   Doe love, where love does give his sweet alarmes,
   Without bloudshed, and where the enemy
Does yeeld unto his foe a pleasant victory.

35

'Debatefull strife, and cruell enmitie
   The famous name of knighthood fowly shend;
   But lovely peace, and gentle amitie,
   And in Amours the passing houres to spend,
   The mightie martiall hands doe most commend;
   Of love they ever greater glory bore,
   Then of their armes: *Mars* is *Cupidoes* frend,
   And is for *Venus* loves renowmed more,
Then all his wars and spoiles, the which he did of yore.'

36

Therewith she sweetly smyld.   They though full bent,
   To prove extremities of bloudie fight,
   Yet at her speach their rages gan relent,   *♀ calms*
   And calme the sea of their tempestuous spight,
   Such powre have pleasing words: such is the might
   Of courteous clemencie in gentle hart.
   Now after all was ceast, the Faery knight
   Besought that Damzell suffer him depart,
And yield him readie passage to that other part.

37

She no lesse glad, then he desirous was
  Of his departure thence; for of her joy
  And vaine delight she saw he light did pas,
  A foe of folly and immodest toy,
  Still solemne sad, or still disdainfull coy,
  Delighting all in armes and cruell warre,
  That her sweet peace and pleasures did annoy,
  Troubled with terrour and unquiet jarre,
That she well pleased was thence to amove him farre.

38

Tho him she brought abord, and her swift bote
  Forthwith directed to that further strand;
  The which on the dull waves did lightly flote
  And soone arrived on the shallow sand,
  Where gladsome *Guyon* sailed forth to land,
  And to that Damzell thankes gave for reward.
  Upon that shore he spied *Atin* stand,
  There by his maister left, when late he far'd
In *Phædrias* fit barke over that perlous shard.

39

Well could he him remember, sith of late
  He with *Pyrochles* sharp debatement made;
  Streight gan he him revile, and bitter rate,
  As shepheards curre, that in darke evenings shade
  Hath tracted forth some salvage beastes trade;
  'Vile Miscreant' (said he) 'whither dost thou flie
  The shame and death, which will thee soone invade?
  What coward hand shall doe thee next to die,
That art thus foully fled from famous enemie?'

40

With that he stiffely shooke his steele head dart:
  But sober *Guyon*, hearing him so raile,
  Though somewhat moved in his mightie hart,
  Yet with strong reason maistred passion fraile,
  And passed fairely forth.   He turning taile,
  Back to the strond retyrd, and there still stayd,
  Awaiting passage, which him late did faile;
  The whiles *Cymochles* with that wanton mayd
The hastie heat of his avowd revenge delayd.

41

Whylest there the varlet stood, he saw from farre
  An armed knight, that towards him fast ran,
  He ran on foot, as if in lucklesse warre
  His forelorne steed from him the victour wan;
  He seemed breathlesse, hartlesse, faint, and wan,
  And all his armour sprinckled was with bloud,
  And soyld with durtie gore, that no man can
  Discerne the hew thereof. He never stood,
But bent his hastie course towardes the idle flood.

42

The varlet saw, when to the flood he came,
  How without stop or stay he fiercely lept,
  And deepe him selfe beducked in the same,
  That in the lake his loftie crest was steept,
  Ne of his safetie seemed care he kept,
  But with his raging armes he rudely flasht
  The waves about, and all his armour swept,
  That all the bloud and filth away was washt,
Yet still he bet the water, and the billowes dasht.

43

Atin drew nigh, to weet what it mote bee;
  For much he wondred at that uncouth sight;
  Whom should he, but his owne deare Lord, there see,
  His owne deare Lord *Pyrochles*, in sad plight,
  Readie to drowne himselfe for fell despight.
  'Harrow now out, and well away,' he cryde,
  'What dismall day hath lent this cursed light,
  To see my Lord so deadly damnifyde?
Pyrochles, O *Pyrochles*, what is thee betyde?'

44

'I burne, I burne, I burne,' then loud he cryde,
  'Oh how I burne with implacable fire,
  Yet nought can quench mine inly flaming syde,
  Nor sea of licour cold, nor lake of mire:
  Nothing but death can doe me to respire.'
  'Ah be it' (said he) 'from *Pyrochles* farre
  After pursewing death once to require,
  Or think, that ought those puissant hands may marre:
Death is for wretches borne under unhappie starre.'

45

'Perdie, then is it fit for me' (said he)
  'That am, I weene, most wretched man alive,
  Burning in flames, yet no flames can I see,
  And dying daily, daily yet revive:
  O *Atin*, helpe to me last death to give.'
  The varlet at his plaint was grieved so sore,
  That his deepe wounded hart in two did rive,
  And his owne health remembring now no more,
Did follow that ensample, which he blam'd afore.

46

Into the lake he lept, his Lord to ayd,
  (So Love the dread of daunger doth despise)
  And of him catching hold him strongly stayd
  From drowning.   But more happie he, then wise
  Of that seas nature did him not avise.
  The waves thereof so slow and sluggish were,
  Engrost with mud, which did them foule agrise,
  That every weightie thing they did upbeare,
Ne ought mote ever sinke downe to the bottom there.

47

Whiles thus they strugled in that idle wave,
  And strove in vaine, the one himselfe to drowne,
  The other both from drowning for to save,
  Lo, to that shore one in an auncient gowne,
  Whose hoarie locks great gravitie did crowne,
  Holding in hand a goodly arming sword,
  By fortune came, led with the troublous sowne:
  Where drenched deepe he found in that dull ford
The carefull servant, striving with his raging Lord.

48

Him *Atin* spying, knew right well of yore,
  And loudly cald, 'Helpe helpe, O *Archimage*;
  To save my Lord, in wretched plight forlore;
  Helpe with thy hand, or with thy counsell sage:
  Weake hands, but counsell is most strong in age.'
  Him when the old man saw, he wondred sore,
  To see *Pyrochles* there so rudely rage:
  Yet sithens helpe, he saw, he needed more
Then pittie he in hast approched to the shore.

49

And cald, '*Pyrochles*, what is this, I see?
  What hellish furie hath at earst thee hent?
  Furious ever I thee knew to bee,
  Yet never in this straunge astonishment.'
  'These flames, these flames' (he cryde) 'do me torment.'
  'What flames' (quoth he) 'when I thee present see,
  In daunger rather to be drent, then brent?'
  'Harrow, the flames which me consume' (said hee)
'Ne can be quencht, within my secret bowels bee.

50

'That cursed man, that cruell feend of hell,
  Furor, oh *Furor* hath me thus bedight:
  His deadly wounds within my liver swell,
  And his whot fire burnes in mine entrails bright,
  Kindled through his infernall brond of spight,
  Sith late with him I batteil vaine would boste;
  That now I weene *Joves* dreaded thunder light
  Does scorch not halfe so sore, nor damned ghoste
In flaming *Phlegeton* does not so felly roste.'

51

Which when as *Archimago* heard, his griefe
  He knew right well, and him attonce disarmd:
  Then searcht his secret wounds, and made a priefe
  Of every place, that was with brusing harmd,
  Or with the hidden fire too inly warmd.
  Which done, he balmes and herbes thereto applyde,
  And evermore with mighty spels them charmd,
  That in short space he has them qualifyde,
And him restor'd to health, that would have algates dyde.

Canto VII

1

As Pilot well expert in perilous wave,
   That to a stedfast starre his course hath bent,
   When foggy mistes, or cloudy tempests have
   The faithfull light of that faire lampe yblent,
   And cover'd heaven with hideous dreriment,
   Upon his card and compas firmes his eye,
   The maisters of his long experiment,
   And to them does the steddy helme apply,
Bidding his winged vessell fairely forward fly.

2

So *Guyon* having lost his trusty guide,
   Late left beyond that *Ydle lake*, proceedes
   Yet on his way, of none accompanide;
   And evermore himselfe with comfort feedes,
   Of his own vertues, and prayse-worthy deedes.
   So long he yode, yet no adventure found,
   Which fame of her shrill trompet worthy reedes:
   For still he traveild through wide wastfull ground,
That nought but desert wildernesse shew'd all around.

3

At last he came unto a gloomy glade,
   Cover'd with boughes and shrubs from heavens light,
   Whereas he sitting found in secret shade
   An uncouth, salvage, and incivile wight,
   Of griesly hew, and fowle ill favour'd sight;
   His face with smoke was tand, and eyes were bleard,
   His head and beard with sout were ill bedight,
   His cole-blacke hands did seeme to have ben seard
In smithes fire-spitting forge, and nayles like clawes appeard.

4

His yron coate all overgrowne with rust,
   Was underneath enveloped with gold,
   Whose glistring glosse darkned with filthy dust,
   Well yet appeared, to have beene of old
   A worke of rich entayle, and curious mould,

Woven with antickes and wild Imagery:
And in his lap a masse of coyne he told,
And turned upsidowne, to feede his eye
And covetous desire with his huge threasury.

5

And round about him lay on every side
  Great heapes of gold, that never could be spent:
  Of which some were rude owre, not purifide
  Of *Mulcibers* devouring element;
  Some others were new driven, and distent
  Into great Ingoes, and to wedges square;
  Some in round plates withouten moniment;
  But most were stampt, and in their metall bare
The antique shapes of kinges and kesars straunge and rare.

6

Soone as he *Guyon* saw, in great affright
  And hast he rose, for to remove aside
  Those pretious hils from straungers envious sight,
  And downe them poured through an hole full wide,
  Into the hollow earth, them there to hide.
  But *Guyon* lightly to him leaping, stayd
  His hand, that trembled, as one terrifyde;
  And though him selfe were at the sight dismayd,
Yet him perforce restraynd, and to him doubtfull sayd.

7

'What art thou man, (if man at all thou art)
  That here in desert hast thine habitaunce,
  And these rich heapes of wealth doest hide apart
  From the worldes eye, and from her right usaunce?'
  Thereat with staring eyes fixed askaunce,
  In great disdaine, he answerd; 'Hardy Elfe,
  That darest vew my direfull countenaunce,
  I read thee rash, and heedlesse of thy selfe,
To trouble my still seate, and heapes of pretious pelfe.

8

'God of the world and worldlings I me call,
  Great *Mammon*, greatest god below the skye,
  That of my plenty poure out unto all,
  And unto none my graces do envye:
  Riches, renowme, and principality,
  Honour, estate, and all this worldes good,

For which men swinck and sweat incessantly,
　Fro me do flow into an ample flood,
And in the hollow earth have their eternall brood.

9

'Wherefore if me thou deigne to serve and sew,
　At thy commaund lo all these mountaines bee;
　Or if to thy great mind, or greedy vew
　All these may not suffise, there shall to thee
　Ten times so much be numbred francke and free.'
　'*Mammon*' (said he) 'thy godheades vaunt is vaine,
　And idle offers of thy golden fee;
　To them that covet such eye-glutting gaine,
Proffer thy giftes, and fitter servaunts entertaine.

10

'Me ill besits, that in der-doing armes,
　And honours suit my vowed dayes do spend,
　Unto thy bounteous baytes, and pleasing charmes,
　With which weake men thou witchest, to attend:
　Regard of worldly mucke doth fowly blend,
　And low abase the high heroicke spright,
　That joyes for crownes and kingdomes to contend;
　Faire shields, gay steedes, bright armes be my delight:
Those be the riches fit for an advent'rous knight.'

11

'Vaine glorious Elfe' (said he) 'doest not thou weet,
　That money can thy wantes at will supply?
　Sheilds, steeds, and armes, and all things for thee meet
　It can purvay in twinckling of an eye;
　And crownes and kingdomes to thee multiply.
　Do not I kings create, and throw the crowne
　Sometimes to him, that low in dust doth ly?
　And him that raignd, into his rowme thrust downe,
And whom I lust, do heape with glory and renowne?'

12

'All otherwise' (said he) 'I riches read,
　And deeme them roote of all disquietnesse;
　First got with guile, and then preserv'd with dread,
　And after spent with pride and lavishnesse,
　Leaving behind them griefe and heavinesse.
　Infinite mischiefes of them doe arize,
　Strife, and debate, bloudshed, and bitternesse,

Outrageous wrong, and hellish covetize,
That noble heart as great dishonour doth despize.

13

'Ne thine be kingdomes, ne the scepters thine;
  But realmes and rulers thou doest both confound,
  And loyall truth to treason doest incline;
  Witnesse the guiltlesse bloud pourd oft on ground,
  The crowned often slaine, the slayer cround,
  The sacred Diademe in peeces rent,
  And purple robe gored with many a wound;
  Castles surprizd, great cities sackt and brent:
So mak'st thou kings, and gaynest wrongfull governement.

14

'Long were to tell the troublous stormes, that tosse
  The private state, and make the life unsweet:
  Who swelling sayles in *Caspian* sea doth crosse,
  And in frayle wood on *Adrian* gulf doth fleet,
  Doth not, I weene, so many evils meet.'
  Then *Mammon* wexing wroth, 'And why then,' said,
  'Are mortall men so fond and undiscreet,
  So evill thing to seeke unto their ayd,
And having not complaine, and having it upbraid?'

15

'Indeede' (quoth he) 'through fowle intemperaunce,
  Frayle men are oft captiv'd to covetise:
  But would they thinke, with how small allowaunce
  Untroubled Nature doth her selfe suffise,
  Such superfluities they would despise,
  Which with sad cares empeach our native joyes:
  At the well head the purest streames arise:
  But mucky filth his braunching armes annoyes,
And with uncomely weedes the gentle wave accloyes.

16

'The antique world, in his first flowring youth,
  Fownd no defect in his Creatours grace,
  But with glad thankes, and unreproved truth,
  The gifts of soveraigne bountie did embrace:
  Like Angels life was then mens happy cace;
  But later ages pride, like corn-fed steed,
  Abusd her plenty, and fat swolne encreace
  To all licentious lust, and gan exceed
The measure of her meane, and naturall first need.

17

'Then gan a cursed hand the quiet wombe
  Of his great Grandmother with steele to wound,
  And the hid treasures in her sacred tombe,
  With Sacriledge to dig.   Therein he found
  Fountaines of gold and silver to abound,
  Of which the matter of his huge desire
  And pompous pride eftsoones he did compound;
  Then avarice gan through his veines inspire
His greedy flames, and kindled life-devouring fire.'

18

'Sonne' (said he then) 'let be thy bitter scorne,
  And leave the rudeness of that antique age
  To them, that liv'd therein in state forlorne;
  Thou that doest live in later times, must wage
  Thy workes for wealth, and life for gold engage.
  If then thee list my offred grace to use,
  Take what thou please of all this surplusage;
  If thee list not, leave have thou to refuse:
But thing refused, do not afterward accuse.'

19

'Me list not' (said the Elfin knight) 'receave
  Thing offred, till I know it well be got,
  Ne wote I, but thou didst these goods bereave
  From rightfull owner by unrighteous lot,
  Or that bloodguiltnesse or guile them blot.
  'Perdy' (quoth he) 'yet never eye did vew,
  Ne toung did tell, ne hand these handled not,
  But safe I have them kept in secret mew,
From heavens sight, and powre of al which them pursew.'

Guyon 20

'What secret place' (quoth he) 'can safely hold
  So huge a masse, and hide from heavens eye?
  Or where hast thou thy wonne, that so much gold
  Thou canst preserve from wrong and robbery?'
  'Come thou' (quoth he) 'and see.' // So by and by
  Through that thicke covert he him led, and found
  A darkesome way, which no man could descry,
  That deep descended through the hollow ground,
And was with dread and horrur compassed around.

tempted / going down

21

At length they came into a larger space,
　　That stretcht it selfe into an ample plaine,
　　Through which a beaten broad high way did trace,
　　That streight did lead to *Plutoes* griesly raine:
　　By that wayes side, there sate infernall Payne,
　　And fast beside him sat tumultuous Strife:
　　The one in hand an yron whip did straine,
　　The other brandished a bloudy knife,
And both did gnash their teeth, and both did threaten life.

22

On thother side in one consort there sate,
　　Cruell Revenge, and rancorous Despight,
　　Disloyall Treason, and hart-burning Hate,
　　But gnawing Gealousie out of their sight
　　Sitting alone, his bitter lips did bight,
　　And trembling Feare still to and fro did fly,
　　And found no place, where safe he shroud him might,
　　Lamenting Sorrow did in darknesse lye,
And Shame his ugly face did hide from living eye.

23

And over them sad horrour with grim hew,
　　Did alwayes sore, beating his yron wings;
　　And after him Owles and Night-ravens flew,
　　The hatefull messengers of heavy things,
　　Of death and dolour telling sad tidings;
　　Whiles sad Celeno, sitting on a clift,
　　A song of bale and bitter sorrow sings,
　　That hart of flint a sunder could have rift:
Which having ended, after him she flyeth swift.

24

All these before the gates of *Pluto* lay,
　　By whom they passing, spake unto them nought.
　　But th' Elfin knight with wonder all the way
　　Did feed his eyes, and fild his inner thought.
　　At last him to a litle dore he brought,
　　That to the gate of Hell, which gaped wide,
　　Was next adjoyning, ne them parted ought:
　　Betwixt them both was but a litle stride,
That did the house of Richesse from hell-mouth divide.

25

Before the dore sat selfe-consuming Care,
  Day and night keeping wary watch and ward,
  For feare least Force or Fraud should unaware
  Breake in, and spoile the treasure there in gard:
  Ne would he suffer Sleepe once thither-ward
  Approch, albe his drowsie den were next;
  For next to death is Sleepe to be compard:
  Therefore his house is unto his annext;
Here Sleep, ther Richesse, and Hel-gate them both betwext.

sleep

26

So soon as *Mammon* ther arriv'd, the dore
  To him did open, and affoorded way;
  Him followed eke Sir *Guyon* evermore,
  Ne darkenesse him, ne daunger might dismay.
  Soone as he entred was, the dore streight way
  Did shut, and from behind it forth there lept
  An ugly feend, more fowle then dismall day,
  The which with monstrous stalke behind him stept,
And ever as he went, dew watch upon him kept.

27

Well hoped he, ere long that hardy guest,
  If ever covetous hand, or lustfull eye,
  Or lips he layd on thing, that likt him best,
  Or ever sleepe his eye-strings did untye,
  Should be his pray.   And therefore still on hye
  He over him did hold his cruell clawes,
  Threatning with greedy gripe to do him dye
  And rend in peeces with his ravenous pawes,
If ever he transgrest the fatall *Stygian* lawes.

28

That houses forme within was rude and strong,
  Like an huge cave, hewne out of rocky clift,
  From whose rough vaut the ragged breaches hong
  Embost with massy gold of glorious gift,
  And with rich metall loaded every rift,
  That heavy ruine they did seeme to threat;
  And over them *Arachne*
  Her cunning web, and spred her subtile net,
Enwrapped in fowle smoke and clouds more black then Jet.

29

Both roofe, and floore, and wals were all of gold,
    But overgrowne with dust and old decay.
    And hid in darkenesse none could behold
    The hew thereof: for vew of chearefull day
    Did never in that house it selfe display,
    But a faint shadow of uncertain light;
    Such as a lamp, whose life does fade away:
    Or as the Moone cloathed with clowdy night,
Does show to him, that walkes in feare and sad affright.

30

In all that rowme was nothing to be seene,
    But huge great yron chests and coffers strong,
    All bard with double bends, that none could weene
    Them to efforce by violence or wrong;
    On every side they placed were along.
    But all the ground with sculs was scattered,
    And dead mens bones, which round about were flong,
    Whose lives, it seemed, whilome there were shed,
And their vile carcases now left unburied.

31

They forward passe, ne *Guyon* yet spoke word,
    Till that they came unto an yron dore,
    Which to them opened of his owne accord,
    And shewd of richesse such exceeding store,
    As eye of man did never see before;
    Ne ever could within one place be found,
    Though all the wealth, which is, or was of yore,
    Could gathered be through all the world around,
And that above were added to that under ground.

32

The charge thereof unto a covetous Spright
    Commaunded was, who thereby did attend,
    And warily awaited day and night,
    From other covetous feends it to defend,
    Who it to rob and ransacke did intend.
    Then *Mammon* turning to that warriour, said;
    'Loe here the worldes blis, loe here the end,
    To which all men doe ayme, rich to be made:
Such grace now to be happy, is before thee laid.'

33

'Certes' (said he) 'I n'ill thine offred grace,
  Ne to be made so happy do intend:
  Another blis before mine eyes I place,
  Another happinesse, another end.
  To them, that list, these base regardes I lend:
  But I in armes, and in atchievements brave,
  Do rather choose my flitting houres to spend,
  And to be Lord of those, that riches have,
Then them to have my selfe, and be their servile sclave.'

34

Thereat the feend his gnashing teeth did grate,
  And griev'd, so long to lacke his greedy pray;
  For well he weened, that so glorious bayte
  Would tempt his guest, to take thereof assay:
  Had he so doen, he had him snatcht away,
  More light then Culver in the Faulcons fist.
  Eternall God thee save from such decay.
  But whenas *Mammon* saw his purpose mist,
Him to entrap unwares another way he wist.

35

Thence forward he him led, and shortly brought
  Unto another rowme, whose dore forthright,
  To him did open, as it had been taught:
  Therein an hundred raunges weren pight,
  And hundred fornaces all burning bright:
  By every fornace many feends did bide,
  Deformed creatures, horrible in sight,
  And every feend his busie paines applide,
To melt the golden metall, ready to be tride.

36

One with great bellowes gathered filling aire,
  And with forst wind the fewell did inflame;
  Another did the dying bronds repaire
  With yron toungs, and sprinckled ofte the same
  With liquid waves, fiers *Vulcans* rage to tame,
  Who maistring them, renewd his former heat;
  Some scumd the drosse, that from the metall came;
  Some stird the molten owre with ladles great;
And every one did swincke, and every one did sweat.

37

But when as earthly wight they present saw,
   Glistring in armes and battailous aray,
   From their whot work they did themselves withdraw
   To wonder at the sight: for till that day,
   They never creature saw, that cam that way.
   Their staring eyes sparckling with fervent fire
   And ugly shapes did nigh the man dismay,
   That were it not for shame, he would retire,
Till that him thus bespake their soveraigne Lord and sire.

38

'Behold, thou Faeries sonne, with mortall eye,
   That living eye before did never see:
   The thing, that thou didst crave so earnestly,
   To weet, whence all the wealth late shewd by mee,
   Proceeded, lo now is reveald to thee.
   Here is the fountaine of the worldes good:
   Now therefore, if thou wilt enriched bee,
   Avise thee well, and chaunge thy wilfull mood,
Least thou perhaps hereafter wish, and be withstood.'

39

'Suffise it then, thou Money God' (quoth hee)
   'That all thine idle offers I refuse.
   All that I need I have; what needeth mee
   To covet more, then I have cause to use?
   With such vaine shewes thy worldlings vile abuse:
   But give me leave to follow mine emprise.'
   Mammon was much displeasd, yet no'te he chuse,
   But beare the rigour of his bold mesprise,
And thence him forward led, him further to entise.

40

He brought him through a darksome narrow strait,
   To a broad gate, all built of beaten gold:
   The gate was open, but therein did wait
   A sturdy villein, striding stiffe and bold,
   As if the highest God defie he would;
   In his right hand an yron club he held,
   But he himselfe was all of golden mould,
   Yet had both life and sence, and well could weld
That cursed weapon, when his cruell foes he queld.

41

Disdayne he called was, and did disdaine
  To be so cald, and who so did him call:
  Sterne was his looke, and full of stomacke vaine,
  His portaunce terrible, and stature tall,
  Far passing th' hight of men terrestriall;
  Like an huge Gyant of the *Titans* race,
  That made him scorne all creatures great and small,
  And with his pride all others powre deface:
More fit emongst black fiendes, then men to have his place.

42

Soone as those glitterand armes he did espye,
  That with their brightnesse made that darknesse light,
  His harmefull club he gan to hurtle hye,
  And threaten batteill to the Faery knight;
  Who likewise gan himselfe to batteill dight,
  Till *Mammon* did his hasty hand withhold,
  And counseld him abstaine from perilous fight:
  For nothing might abash the villein bold,
Ne mortall steele emperce his miscreated mould.

43

So having him with reason pacifide,
  And the fiers Carle commaunding to forbeare,
  He brought him in.   The rowme was large and wide,
  As it some Gyeld or solemne Temple weare:
  Many great golden pillours did upbeare
  The massy roofe, and riches huge sustayne,
  And every pillour decked was full deare
  With crownes and Diademes, and titles vaine,
Which mortall Princes wore, whiles they on earth did rayne.

44

A route of people there assembled were,
  Of every sort and nation under skye,
  Which with great uprore preaced to draw nere
  To th' upper part, where was advaunced hye
  A stately siege of soveraigne majestye;
  And thereon sat a woman gorgeous gay,
  And richly clad in robes of royaltye,
  That never earthly Prince in such aray
His glory did enhaunce, and pompous pryde display.

45

Her face right wondrous faire did seeme to bee,
  That her broad beauties beam gret brightnes threw *Beauty*
  Through the dim shade, that all men might it see:
  Yet was not that same her owne native hew,
  But wrought by art and counterfetted shew, *treachery*
  Thereby more lovers unto her to call:
  Nath'lesse most heavenly faire in deed and vew
  She by creation was, till she did fall;
Thenceforth she sought for helps, to cloke her crime withall.

46

There, as in glistring glory she did sit,
  She held a great gold chaine ylincked well,
  Whose upper end to highest heaven was knit,
  And lower part did reach to lowest Hell;
  And all that preace did round about her swell,
  To catchen hold of that long chaine, thereby
  To clime aloft, and others to excell:
  That was *Ambition*, rash desire to sty,
And every linck thereof a step of dignity.

47

Some thought to raise themselves to high degree,
  By riches and unrighteous reward,
  Some by close shouldring, some by flatteree;
  Others through friends, others for base regard;
  And all by wrong wayes for themselves prepard.
  Those that were up themselves, kept others low,
  Those that were low themselves, held others hard,
  Ne suffred them to rise or greater grow,
But every one did strive his fellow downe to throw.

48

Which whenas *Guyon* saw, he gan inquire,
  What meant that preace about that Ladies throne,
  And what she was that did so high aspire.
  Him *Mammon* answered; 'That goodly one,
  Whom all that folke with such contention,
  Doe flocke about, my deare, my daughter is;
  Honour and dignitie from her alone
  Derived are, and all this worldes blis
For which ye men do strive: few get, but many mis.

49

'And faire *Philotime* she rightly hight,
    The fairest wight that wonneth under skye,
    But that this darksome neather world her light
    Doth dim with horrour and deformitie,
    Worthy of heaven and hye felicitie,
    From whence the gods have her for envy thrust:
    But sith thou hast found favour in mine eye,
    Thy spouse I will her make, if that thou lust,
That she may thee advance for workes and merites just.'

50

'Gramercy *Mammon*' (said the gentle knight)
    'For so great grace and offred high estate;
    But I, that am fraile flesh and earthly wight,
    Unworthy match for such immortall mate
    My selfe well wote, and mine unequall fate;
    And were I not, yet is my trouth yplight,
    And love avowd to other Lady late,
    That to remove the same I have no might:
To chaunge love causelesse is reproch to warlike knight.'

51

Mammon emmoved was with inward wrath;
    Yet forcing it to faine, him forth thence led
    Through griesly shadowes by a beaten path,
    Into a gardin goodly garnished
    With hearbs and fruits, whose kinds mote not be red:
    Not such, as earth out of her fruitfull woomb
    Throwes forth to men, sweet and well savoured,
    But direfull deadly black both leafe and bloom,
Fit to adorne the dead, and deck the drery toombe.

52

There mournfull *Cypresse* grew in greatest store,
    And trees of bitter *Gall*, and *Heben* sad;
    Dead sleeping *Poppy*, and black *Hellebore*,
    Cold *Coloquintida*, and *Tetra* mad,
    Mortall *Samnitis*, and *Cicuta* bad,
    With which th' unjust *Atheniens* made to dy
    Wise *Socrates*, who thereof quaffing glad
    Pourd out his life, and last Philosophy
To the faire *Critias*, his dearest Belamy.

53

The *Gardin* of *Proserpina* this hight;
  And in the midst thereof a silver seat,
  With a thick Arber goodly over dight,
  In which she often usd from open heat
  Her selfe to shroud, and pleasures to entreat.
  Next thereunto did grow a goodly tree,
  With braunches broad dispred and body great,
  Clothed with leaves, that non the wood mote see
And loaden all with fruit as thicke as it might bee.

54

Their fruit were golden apples glistring bright,
  That goodly was their glory to behold,
  On earth like never grew, ne living wight
  Like ever saw, but they from hence were sold;
  For those, which *Hercules* with conquest bold
  Got from great *Atlas* daughters, hence began,
  And planted there, did bring forth fruit of gold:
  And those with which th' *Eubœan* young man wan
Swift *Atalanta*, when through craft he her out ran.

55

Here also sprong that goodly golden fruit,
  With which *Acontius* got his lover trew,
  Whom he had long time sought with fruitlesse suit:
  Here eke that famous golden Apple grew,
  The which emongst the gods false *Ate* threw;
  For which th' *Idæan* Ladies disagreed,
  Till partiall *Paris* dempt it *Venus* dew,
  And had of her, faire *Helen* for his meed,
That many noble *Greekes* and *Trojans* made to bleed.

56

The warlike Elfe, much wondred at this tree,
  So faire and great, that shadowed all the ground,
  And his broad braunches, laden with rich fee,
  Did stretch themselves without the utmost bound
  Of this great gardin, compast with a mound,
  Which over-hanging, they themselves did steepe,
  In a blacke flood which flow'd about it round;
  That is the river of *Cocytus* deepe,
In which full many soules do endlesse waile and weepe.

57

Which to behold, he clomb up to the banke,
　And looking downe, saw many damned wights,
　In those sad waves, which direfull deadly stanke,
　Plonged continually of cruell Sprights,
　That with their pitteous cryes, and yelling shrights,
　They made the further shore resounden wide:
　Emongst the rest of those same ruefull sights,
　One cursed creature, he by chaunce espide,
That drenched lay full deepe, under the Garden side.

58

Deepe was he drenched to the upmost chin,
　Yet gaped still, as coveting to drinke
　Of the cold liquor, which he waded in,
　And stretching forth his hand, did often thinke
　To reach the fruit, which grew upon the brincke:
　But both the fruit from hand, and floud from mouth,
　Did flie abacke, and made him vainely swinke:
　The whiles he sterv'd with hunger and with drouth
He daily dyde, yet never throughly dyen couth.

59

The knight him seeing labour so in vaine,
　Askt who he was, and what he ment thereby:
　Who groning deepe, thus answerd him againe,
　'Most cursed of all creatures under skye,
　Lo *Tantalus*, I here tormented lye:
　Of whom high *Jove* wont whylome feasted bee,
　Lo here I now for want of food doe dye:
　But if that thou be such, as I thee see,
Of grace I pray thee, give to eat and drinke to mee.'

60

'Nay, nay, thou greedie *Tantalus*' (quoth he)
　'Abide the fortune of thy present fate,
　And unto all that live in high degree,
　Ensample be of mind intemperate,
　To teach them how to use their present state.'
　Then gan the cursed wretch aloud to cry,
　Accusing highest *Jove* and gods ingrate,
　And eke blaspheming heaven bitterly,
As author of unjustice, there to let him dye.

61

He lookt a litle further, and espyde
  Another wretch, whose carkasse deepe was drent
  Within the river, which the same did hyde:
  But both his hands most filthy feculent,
  Above the water were on high extent,
  And faynd to wash themselves incessantly;
  Yet nothing cleaner were for such intent,
  But rather fowler seemed to the eye;
So lost his labour vaine and idle industry.

62

The knight him calling, asked who he was,
  Who lifting up his head, him answered thus:
  'I *Pilate* am the falsest Judge, alas,
  And most unjust, that by unrighteous
  And wicked doome, to Jewes despiteous
  Delivered up the Lord of life to die,
  And did acquite a murdrer felonous;
  The whiles my hands I washt in puritie,
The whiles my soule was soyld with foule iniquitie.

63

Infinite moe, tormented in like paine
  He there beheld, too long here to be told:
  Ne *Mammon* would there let him long remaine,
  For terrour of the tortures manifold,
  In which the damned soules he did behold,
  But roughly him bespake.   'Thou fearefull foole,
  Why takest not of that same fruit of gold
  Ne sittest downe on that same silver stoole,
To rest thy wearie person, in the shadow coole?'

64

All which he did, to doe him deadly fall
  In frayle intemperaunce through sinfull bayt;
  To which if he inclined had at all,
  That dreadfull feend, which did behinde him wayt,
  Would him have rent in thousand peeces strayt:
  But he was warie wise in all his way,
  And well perceived his deceiptfull sleight,
  Ne suffred lust his safetie to betray;
So goodly did beguile the Guyler of pray.

65

And now he has so long remained there,
  That vitall powres gan wexe both weake and wan,
  For want of food, and sleepe, which two upbeare,
  Like mightie pillours, this fraile life of man,
  That none without the same enduren can.
  For now three dayes of men were full outwrought,
  Since he this hardie enterprize began:
  For thy great *Mammon* fairely he besought,
Into the world to guide him backe, as he him brought.

66

The God, though loth, yet was constraind t' obay,
  For lenger time, then that, no living wight
  Below the earth might suffred be to stay:
  So backe againe, him brought to living light.
  But all so soone as his enfeebled spright
  Gan sucke this vitall aire into his brest,
  As overcome with two exceeding might,
  The life did flit away out of her nest,
And all his senses were with deadly fit opprest.

Canto VIII

Sir Cuyon laid in swowne is by
Acrates sonnes despoyld,
Whom Arthure soone hath reskewed
And Paynim brethren foyld.

I

And is there care in heaven? and is there love
  In heavenly spirits to these creatures bace,
  That may compassion of their evils move?
  There is: else much more wretched were the cace
  Of men, then beasts.   But O th' exceeding grace
  Of highest God, that loves his creatures so,
  And all his workes with mercy doth embrace,
  That blessed Angels, he sends to and fro,
To serve to wicked man, to serve his wicked foe.

2

How oft do they, their silver bowers leave,
  To come to succour us, that succour want?
  How oft do they with golden pineons, cleave
  The flitting skyes, like flying Pursuivant,
  Against foule feends to aide us militant?
  They for us fight, they watch and dewly ward,
  And their bright Squadrons round about us plant,
  And all for love, and nothing for reward:
O why should heavenly God to men have such regard?

3

During the while, that *Guyon* did abide
  In *Mammons* house, the Palmer, whom whyleare
  That wanton Mayd of passage had denide,
  By further search had passage found elsewhere,
  And being on his way, approched neare,
  Where *Guyon* lay in traunce, when suddenly
  He heard a voice, that called loud and cleare,
  'Come hither, come hither, O come hastily;'
That all the fields resounded with the ruefull cry.

4

The Palmer lent his eare into the noyce,
  To weet, who called so importunely:
  Againe he heard a more efforced voyce,
  That bad him come in haste.   He by and by
  His feeble feet directed to the cry;

Which to that shadie delve him brought at last,
Where *Mammon* earst did sunne his threasury:
There the good *Guyon* he found slumbring fast
In senselesse dreame; which sight at first him sore aghast.

5

Beside his head there sat a faire young man,
    Of wondrous beautie and of freshest yeares,
    Whose tender bud to blossome new began,
    And flourish faire above his equall peares;
    His snowy front curled with golden heares,
    Like *Phœbus* face adornd with sunny rayes,
    Divinely shone, and two sharpe winged sheares,
    Decked with diverse plumes, like painted Jayes,
Were fixed at his backe, to cut his ayerie wayes.

6

Like as *Cupido* on *Idæan* hill,
    When having laid his cruell bow away,
    And mortall arrowes, wherewith he doth fill
    The world with murdrous spoiles and bloudie pray,
    With his faire mother he him dights to play,
    And with his goodly sisters, *Graces* three;
    The Goddesse pleased with his wanton play,
    Suffers her selfe through sleepe beguild to bee,
The whiles the other Ladies mind their merry glee.

7

Whom when the Palmer saw, abasht he was
    Through feare and wonder, that he nought could say,
    Till him the child bespoke, 'Long lackt, alas,
    Hath bene thy faithfull aide in hard assay,
    Whiles deadly fit thy pupill doth dismay;
    Behold this heavie sight, thou reverend Sire,
    But dread of death and dolour doe away;
    For life ere long shall to her home retire,
And he that breathlesse seemes, shal corage bold respire.

8

'The charge, which God doth unto me arret,
    Of his deare safetie, I to thee commend;
    Yet will I not forgoe, ne yet forget
    The care thereof my selfe unto the end,
    But evermore him succour, and defend
    Against his foe and mine: watch thou I pray;

For evill is at hand him to offend.'
So having said, eftsoones he gan display
His painted nimble wings, and vanisht quite away.

9

The Palmer seeing his left empty place,
  And his slow eyes beguiled of their sight,
  Woxe sore affraid, and standing still a space,
  Gaz'd after him, as fowle escapt by flight;
  At last him turning to his charge behight,
  With trembling hand his troubled pulse gan try;
  Where finding life not yet dislodged quight,
  He much rejoyst, and courd it tenderly,
As chicken newly hatcht, from dreaded destiny.

10

At last he spide, where towards him did pace
  Two Paynim knights, al armd as bright as skie,
  And them beside an aged Sire did trace,
  And farre before a light-foot Page did flie,
  That breathed strife and troublous enmitie;
  Those were the two sonnes of *Acrates* old,
  Who meeting earst with *Archimago* slie,
  Foreby that idle strond, of him were told,
That he, which earst them combatted, was *Guyon* bold.

11

Which to avenge on him they dearely vowd,
  Where ever that on ground they mote him fynd;
  False *Archimage* provokt their courage prowd,
  And stryfull *Atin* in their subborne mynd
  Coles of contention and whot vengeaunce tynd.
  Now bene they come, whereas the Palmer sate,
  Keeping that slombred corse to him assynd;
  Well knew they both his person, sith of late
With him in bloudie armes they rashly did debate.

12

Whom when *Pyrochles* saw, inflam'd with rage,
  That sire he fo bespake, 'Thou dotard vile,
  That with thy brutenesse shendst thy comely age,
  Abandon soone, I read, the caitive spoile
  Of that same outcast carkasse, that erewhile
  Made it selfe famous through false trechery,
  And crownd his coward crest with knightly stile;

Loe where he now inglorious doth lye,
To prove he lived ill, that did thus foully dye.'

13

To whom the Palmer fearlesse answered;
   'Certes, Sir knight, ye bene too much to blame,
   Thus for to blot the honour of the dead,
   And with foule cowardize his carcasse shame,
   Whose living hands immortalizd his name.
   Vile is the vengeance on the ashes cold,
   And envie base, to barke at sleeping fame:
   Was never wight, that treason of him told;
Your selfe his prowesse prov'd, and found him fiers and bold.'

14

Then sayd *Cymochles*: 'Palmer, thou doest dote,
   Ne canst of prowesse, ne of knighthood deeme,
   Save as thou seest or hearst. But well I wote,
   That of his puissance tryall made extreme;
   Yet gold all is not, that doth golden seeme,
   Ne all good knights, that shake well speare and shield:
   The worth of all men by their end esteeme,
   And then due praise, or due reproch them yield;
Bad therefore I him deeme, that thus lies dead on field.'

15

'Good or bad' (gan his brother fierce reply)
   'What doe I recke, sith that he dyde entire?
   Or what doth his bad death now satisfy
   The greedy hunger of revenging ire,
   Sith wrathfull hand wrought not her owne desire?
   Yet since no way is left to wreake my spight,
   I will him reave of armes, the victors hire,
   And of that shield, more worthy of good knight;
For why should a dead dog be deckt in armour bright?'

16

'Faire Sir,' said then the Palmer suppliaunt,
   'For knighthoods love, doe not so foule a deed,
   Ne blame your honour with so shamefull vaunt
   Of vile revenge.   To spoile the dead of weed
   Is sacrilege, and doth all sinnes exceed;
   But leave these relicks of his living might,
   To decke his herce, and trap his tomb-blacke steed.'
   'What herce or steed' (said he) 'should he have dight,
But be entombed in the raven or the kight?'

17

With that, rude hand upon his shield he laid,
  And th' other brother gan his helme unlace,
  Both fiercely bent to have him disaraid;
  Till that they spide where towards them did pace
  An armed knight, of bold and bounteous grace,
  Whose squire bore after him an heben launce,
  And covered shield.   Well kend him so farre space
  Th' enchaunter by his armes and amenaunce,
When under him he saw his Lybian steed to praunce.

18

And to those brethren said, 'Rise rise by live,
  And unto battell doe your selves addresse;
  For yonder comes the prowest knight alive,
  Prince *Arthur*, flowre of grace and nobilesse,
  That hath to Paynim knights wrought great distresse,
  And thousand Sar'zins foully donne to dye.'
  That word so deepe did in their harts impresse,
  That both eftsoones upstarted furiously,
And gan themselves prepare to battell greedily.

19

But fierce *Pyrochles*, lacking his owne sword,
  The want thereof now greatly gan to plaine,
  And *Archimage* besought, him that afford,
  Which he had brought for *Braggadocchio* vaine.
  'So would I' (said th' enchaunter) 'glad and faine
  Beteeme to you this sword, you to defend,
  Or ought that else your honour might maintaine,
  But that this weapons powre I well have kend,
To be contrarie to the worke, which ye intend.

20

'For that same knights owne sword that is of yore,
  Which *Merlin* made by his almightie art
  For that his noursling, when he knighthood swore,
  Therewith to doen his foes eternall smart.
  The metall first he mixt with *Medæwart*,
  That no enchauntment from his dint might save;
  Then it in flames of *Aetna* wrought apart,
  And seven times dipped in the bitter wave
Of hellish *Styx*, which hidden vertue to it gave.

21

'The vertue is, that nether steele, nor stone
  The stroke thereof from entrance may defend;
  Ne ever may be used by his fone,
  Ne forst his rightful owner to offend,
  Ne ever will it breake, ne ever bend.
  Wherefore *Morddure* it rightfully is hight.
  In vaine therefore, *Pyrochles*, should I lend
  The same to thee, against his lord to fight,
For sure it would deceive thy labour, and thy might.'

22

'Foolish old man,' said then the Pagan wroth,
  'That weenest words or charmes may force withstond:
  Soone shalt thou see, and then beleeve for troth,
  That I can carve with this inchaunted brond
  His Lords owne flesh.'   Therewith out of his hond
  That vertuous steele he rudely snatcht away,
  And *Guyons* shield about his wrest he bond;
  So readie dight, fierce battaile to assay,
And match his brother proud in battailous array.

23

By this that straunger knight in presence came,
  And goodly salued them; who nought againe
  Him answered, as courtesie became,
  But with sterne lookes, and stomachous disdaine,
  Gave signes of grudge and discontentment vaine:
  Then turning to the Palmer, he gan spy
  Where at his feet, with sorrowfull demaine
  And deadly hew, an armed corse did lye,
In whose dead face he red great magnanimity.

24

Said he then to the Palmer, 'Reverend syre,
  What great misfortune hath betidd this knight?
  Or did his life her fatall date expyre,
  Or did he fall by treason, or by fight?
  How ever, sure I rew his pitteous plight.'
  'Not one, nor other,' (said the Palmer grave)
  'Hath him befalne, but cloudes of deadly night
  A while his heavie eylids cover'd have,
And all his senses drowned in deepe senselesse wave.

25

'Which, those his cruell foes, that stand hereby,
      Making advantage, to revenge their spight,
      Would him disarme, and treaten shamefully,
      Unworthy usage of redoubted knight.
      But you, faire Sir, whose honourable sight
      Doth promise hope of helpe, and timely grace,
      Mote I beseech to succour his sad plight,
      And by your powre protect his feeble cace.
First praise of knighthood is, foule outrage to deface.'

26

'Palmer,' (said he) 'no knight so rude, I weene,
      As to doen outrage to a sleeping ghost;
      Ne was there ever noble courage seene,
      That in advauntage would his puissaunce bost:
      Honour is least, where oddes appeareth most.
      May be, that better reason will asswage
      The rash revengers heat.   Words well dispost
      Have secret powre, t' appease inflamed rage:
If not, leave unto me thy knights last patronage.'

27

Tho turning to those brethren, thus bespoke,
      'Ye warlike payre, whose valorous great might
      It seemes, just wrongs to vengeance doe provoke,
      To wreake your wrath on this dead seeming knight,
      Mote ought allay the storme of your despight,
      And settle patience in so furious heat?
      Not to debate the chalenge of your right,
      But for his carkasse pardon I entreat,
Whom fortune hath alreadie laid in lowest seat.'

28

To whom *Cymochles* said; 'For what art thou,
      That mak'st thy selfe his dayes-man, to prolong
      The vengeance prest?   Or who shall let me now
      On this vile bodie from to wreake my wrong,
      And made his carkasse as the outcast dong?
      Why should not that dead carrion satisfie
      The guilt, which if he lived had thus long,
      His life for dew revenge should deare abie?
The trespasse still doth live, albe the person die.'

29

'Indeed' (then said the Prince) 'the evill donne
  Dyes not, when breath the bodie first doth leave,
  But from the grandsyre to the Nephewes sonne,
  And all his seed the curse doth often cleave,
  Till vengeance utterly the guilt bereave:
  So streightly God doth judge.   But gentle knight,
  That doth against the dead his hand upreare,
  His honour staines with rancour and despight,
And great disparagment makes to his former might.'

30

Pyrochles gan reply the second time,
  And to him said, 'Now felon sure I read,
  How that thou art partaker of his crime:
  Therefore by *Termagaunt* thou shalt be dead.'
  With that his hand, more sad then lomp of lead,
  Uplifting high, he weened with *Morddure*,
  His owne good sword *Morddure*, to cleave his head.
  The faithful steele such treason no'uld endure,
But swarving from the marke, his Lords life did assure.

31

Yet was the force so furious and so fell,
  That horse and man it made to reele aside:
  Nath'lesse the Prince would not forsake his sell:
  For well of yore he learned had to ride,
  But full of anger fiercely to him cride;
  'False traitour miscreaunt, thou broken hast
  The law of armes, to strike foe undefide.
  But thou thy treasons fruit, I hope, shalt taste
Right sowre, and feele the law, the which thou hast defast.'

32

With that his balefull speare, he fiercely bent
  Against the Pagans brest, and therewith thought
  His cursed life out of her lodge have rent:
  But ere the point arrived, where it ought,
  That seven fold shield, which he from *Guyon* brought,
  He cast betwene to ward the bitter stound:
  Through all those foldes the steelehead passage wrought
  And through his shoulder pierst; wherwith to ground
He groveling fell, all gored in his gushing wound.

33

Which when his brother saw, fraught with great griefe
  And wrath, he to him leaped furiously,
  And fowly said, 'By *Mahoune*, cursed theife,
  That direfull stroke thou dearely shalt aby.'
  Then hurling up his harmefull blade on hye,
  Smote him so hugely on his haughtie crest,
  That from his saddle forced him to fly:
  Else mote it needes downe to his manly brest
Have cleft his head in twaine, and life thence dispossest.

34

Now was the Prince in daungerous distresse,
  Wanting his sword, when he on foot should fight:
  His single speare could doe him small redresse,
  Against two foes of so exceeding might,
  The least of which was match for any knight.
  And now the other, whom he earst did daunt,
  Had reard him selfe againe to cruell fight,
  Three times more furious, and more puissaunt,
Unmindfull of his wound, of his fate ignoraunt.

35

So both attonce him charge on either side,
  With hideous strokes, and importable powre,
  That forced him his ground to traverse wide,
  And wisely watch to ward that deadly stowre:
  For in his shield, as thicke as stormie showre,
  Their strokes did raine, yet did he never quaile,
  Ne backward shrinke, but as a stedfast towre,
  Whom foe with double battry doth assaile,
Them on her bulwarke beares, and bids them nought availe.

36

So stoutly he withstood their strong assay,
  Till that at last, when he advantage spyde,
  His poinant speare he thrust with puissant sway
  At proud *Cymochles*, whiles his shield was wyde,
  That through his thigh the mortall steele did gryde:
  He swarving with the force, within his flesh
  Did breake the launce, and let the head abyde:
  Out of the wound the red bloud flowed fresh,
That underneath his feet soone made a purple plesh.

37

Horribly then he gan to rage, and rayle,
  Cursing his Gods, and him selfe damning deepe:
  Als when his brother saw the red bloud rayle
  Adowne so fast, and all his armour steepe,
  For every felnesse lowd he gan to weepe,
  And said, 'Caytive, curse on thy cruell hond,
  That twise hath sped; yet shall it not thee keepe
  From the third brunt of this my fatall brond:
Lo where the dreadfull Death behnd thy backe doth stond.'

38

With that he strooke, and thother strooke withall,
  That nothing seem'd mote beare so monstrous might:
  The one upon his covered shield did fall,
  And glauncing downe would not his owner byte:
  But th'other did upon his troncheon smyte,
  Which hewing quite a sunder, further way
  It made, and on his hacqueton did lyte,
  The which dividing with importune sway,
It seized in his right side, and there the dint did stay.

39

Wyde was the wound, and a large lukewarme flood,
  Red as the Rose, thence gushed grievously;
  That when the Paynim spyde the streaming blood,
  Gave him great hart, and hope of victory.
  On th' other side, in huge perplexity,
  The Prince now stood, having his weapon broke;
  Nought could he hurt, but still at ward did ly:
  Yet with his troncheon he so rudely stroke
Cymochles twise, that twise him forst his foot revoke.

40

Whom when the Palmer saw in such distresse,
  Sir Guyons sword he lightly to him raught,
  And said; 'faire Son, great God thy right hand blesse,
  To use that sword so wisely as it ought.
  Glad was the knight, and with fresh courage fraught,
  When as againe he armed felt his hond;
  Then like a Lion, which hath long time saught
  His robbed whelpes, and at the last them fond
Emongst the shepeheard swaynes, then wexeth wood and yond.

41

So fierce he laid about him, and dealt blowes
    On either side, that neither mayle could hold,
    Ne shield defend the thunder of his throwes:
    Now to *Pyrochles* many strokes he told;
    Eft to Cymochles twise so many fold:
    Then backe againe turning his busie hond,
    Them both attonce compeld with courage bold,
    To yield wide way to his hart-thrilling brond;
And though they both stood stiffe, yet could not both withstond.

42

As salvage Bull, whom two fierce mastives bayt,
    When rancour doth with rage him once engore,
    Forgets with warie ward them to awayt,
    But with his dreadfull hornes them drives afore,
    Of flings aloft, or treads downe in the flore,
    Breathing out wrath, and bellowing disdaine,
    That all the forrest quakes to heare him rore:
    But rag'd Prince *Arthur* twixt his foemen twaine,
That neither could his mightie puissaunce sustaine.

43

But ever at *Pyrochles* when he smit,
    Who *Guyons* shield cast ever him before,
    Whereon the Faery Queenes pourtract was writ,
    His hand relented, and the stroke forbore,
    And his deare hart the picture gan adore,
    Which oft the Paynim sav'd from deadly stowre.
    But him henceforth the same can save no more;
    For now arrived is his fatall howre,
That no'te avoyded be by earthly skill or powre.

44

For when *Cymochles* saw the fowle reproch,
    Which them appeached, prickt with guilty shame,
    And inward griefe, he fiercely gan approch,
    Resolv'd to put away that loathly blame,
    Or dye with honour and desert of fame;
    And on the hauberk stroke the Prince so sore,
    That quite disparted all the linked frame,
    And pierced to the skin, but bit no more,
Yet made him twise to reele, that never moov'd afore.

45

Whereat renfierst with wrath and sharp regret,
  He stroke so hugely with his borrowd blade,
  That it empierst the Pagans burganet,
  And cleaving the hard steele, did deepe invade
  Into his head, and cruell passage made
  Quite through his braine.   He tombling downe on ground,
  Breathd out his ghost which, to th' infernall shade
  Fast flying, there eternall torment found,
For all the sinnes, wherewith his lewd life did abound.

46

Which when his german saw, the stony feare,
  Ran to his hart, and all his sence dismayd,
  Ne thenceforth life ne corage did appeare,
  But as a man, whom hellish feends have frayd,
  Long trembling still he stood: at last thus sayd;
  'Traytour what hast thou doen? how ever may
  Thy cursed hand so cruelly have swayd
  Against that knight: Harrow and well away,
After so wicked deede why liv'st thou lenger day?'

47

With that all desperate as loathing light,
  And with revenge desiring soone to dye,
  Assembling all his force and utmost might,
  With his owne sword he fierce at him did flye,
  And strooke, and foynd, and lasht outrageously,
  Withouten reason or regard.   Well knew
  The Prince, with patience and sufferaunce sly
  So hasty heat soone cooled to subdew:
Tho when this breathlesse woxe, that batteil gan renew.

48

As when a windy tempest bloweth hye,
  That nothing may withstand his stormy stowre,
  The cloudes, as things affrayd, before him flye;
  But all so soone as his outrageous powre
  Is layd, they fiercely then begin to shoure,
  And as in scorne of his spent stormy spight,
  Now all attonce their malice forth do poure;
  So did Prince *Arthur* beare himselfe in fight,
And suffred rash *Pyrochles* wast his idle might.

49

At last when as the Sarazin perceiv'd,
   How that straunge sword refusd, to serve his need,
   But when he stroke most strong, the dint deceiv'd,
   He flong it from him, and devoyd of dreed,
   Upon him lightly leaping without heed,
   Twixt his two mighty armes engrasped fast,
   Thinking to overthrow and downe him tred:
   But him in strength and skill the Prince surpast,
And through his nimble sleight did under him down cast.

50

Nought booted it the Paynim then to strive;
   For as a Bittur in the Eagles claw,
   That may not hope by flight to scape alive,
   Still waites for death with dread and trembling aw;
   So he now subject to the victours law,
   Did not once move, nor upward cast his eye,
   For vile disdaine and rancour, which did gnaw
   His hart in twaine with sad melancholy,
As one that loathed life, and yet despisd to dye.

51

But full of Princely bounty and great mind,
   The Conquerour nought cared him to slay,
   But casting wrongs and all revenge behind,
   More glory thought to give life, then decay,
   And said, 'Paynim, this is thy dismall day;
   Yet if thou wilt renounce thy miscreaunce,
   And my trew liegeman yield thy selfe for ay,
   Life will I graunt thee for thy valiaunce,
And all thy wrongs will wipe out of my sovenaunce.'

52

'Foole' (said the Pagan) 'I thy gift defye,
   But use thy fortune, as it doth befall,
   And say, that I not overcome do dye,
   But in despight of life, for death doe call.'
   Wroth was the Prince, and sory yet withall,
   That he so wilfully refused grace;
   Yet sith his fate so cruelly did fall,
   His shining Helmet he gan soone unlace,
And left his headlesse body bleeding all the place.

53

By this Sir *Guyon* from his traunce awakt,
   Life having maistered her sencelesse foe;
   And looking up, whenas his shield he lakt,
   And sword saw not, he wexed wondrous woe:
   But when the Palmer, whom he long ygoe
   Had lost, he by him spide, right glad he grew,
   And said, 'Deare sir, whom wandring to and fro
   I long have lackt, I joy thy face to vew;
Firme is thy faith, whom daunger never fro me drew.

54

'But read, what wicked hand hath robbed mee
   Of my good sword and shield?'   The Palmer glad,
   With so fresh hew uprising him to see,
   Him answered; 'faire sonne, be no whit sad
   For want of weapons, they shall soone be had.'
   So gan he to discourse the whole debate,
   Which that straunge knight for him sustained had,
   And those two Sarazins confounded late,
Whose carcases on ground were horribly prostrate.

55

Which when he heard, and saw the tokens trew,
   His hart with great affection was embayd,
   And to the Prince bowing with reverence dew,
   As to the Patrone of his life, thus sayd;
   'My Lord, my liege, by whose most gratious ayd
   I live this day, and see my foes subdewd,
   What may suffice, to be for meede repayd
   Of so great graces, as ye have me shewd,
But to be ever bound.'

56

To whom the Infant thus, 'Faire Sir, what need
   Good turnes be counted, as a servile bond,
   To bind their doers, to receive their meed?
   Are not all knights by oath bound, to withstond
   Oppressours powre by armes and puissant hond?
   Suffise, that I have done my dew in place.'
   So goodly purpose they together fond,
   Of kindnesse and of curteous aggrace;
The whiles false *Archimage* and *Atin* fled apace.

Canto IX

The house of Temperance, in which
Doth sober Alma dwell,
Besiegd of many foes, whom straunger
Knightes to flight compell.

1

Of all Gods workes, which do this worlde adorne,
　　There is no one more faire and excellent,
　　Then is mans body both for powre and forme,
　　Whiles it is kept in sober government;
　　But none then it, more fowle and indecent,
　　Distempred through misrule and passions bace:
　　It growes a Monster, and incontinent
　　Doth loose his dignitie and native grace.
Behold, who list, both one and other in this place.

2

After the Paynim brethren conquer'd were,
　　The *Briton* Prince recov'ring his stolne sword,
　　And *Guyon* his lost shield, they both yfere
　　Forth passed on their way in faire accord,
　　Till him the Prince with gentle court did bord:
　　'Sir knight, mote I of you this curt'sie read,
　　To weet why on your shield so goodly scord
　　Beare ye the picture of that Ladies haed?
Full lively is the semblaunt, though the substance dead.'

3

'Faire Sir' (said he) 'if in that picture dead
　　Such life ye read, and vertue in vaine shew,
　　What mote ye weene, if the trew lively-head
　　Of that most glorious visage ye did vew?
　　But if the beautie of her mind ye knew,
　　That is her bountie and imperiall powre,
　　Thousand times fairer than her mortall hew,
　　O how great wonder would your thoughts devoure,
And infinite desire into your spirite poure!

4

'Shee is the mighty Queene of *Faerie*,
　　Whose faire retrait I in my shield do beare;
　　Shee is the flowre of grace and chastitie,
　　Throughout the world renowmed far and neare,

My liefe, my liege, my Soveraigne, my deare,
Whose glory shineth as the morning starre,
And with her light the earth enlumines cleare;
Far reach her mercies, and her prayses farre,
As well in state of peace, as puissance in warre.'

5

'Thrise happy man,' (said then the *Briton* knight)
'Whom gracious lot and thy great valiaunce
Have made thee soldier of that Princesse bright,
Which with her bounty and glad countenance
Doth blesse her servaunts, and them high advaunce.
How many straunge knight hope ever to aspire,
By faithful service, and meete amenance,
Unto such blisse? sufficient were that hire
For losse of thousand lives, to dye at her desire.'

6

Said *Guyon*, 'Noble Lord, what meed so great,
Or grace of earthly Prince so soveraine,
But by your wondrous worth and warlike feat
Ye well may hope, and easely attaine?
But were your will, her sold to entertaine,
And numbred be mongst knights of *Maydenhed*,
Great guerdon, well I wote, should you remaine,
And in her favor high be reckoned,
As *Arthegall*, and *Sophy* now beene honored.'

7

'Certes' (then said the Prince) 'I God avow,
That sith I armes and knighthood first did plight,
My whole desire hath beene, and yet is now,
To serve that Queene with all my powre and might.
Now hath the Sunne with his lamp-burning light,
Walkt round about the world, and I no lesse,
Sith of that Goddesse I have sought the sight,
Yet no where can her find: such happinesse
Heaven doth to me envy, and fortune favourlesse.'

8

'Fortune, the foe of famous chevisaunce
'Seldome' (said *Guyon*) 'yields to vertue aide,
But in her way throwes mischiefe and mischaunce,
Whereby her course is stopt, and passage staid.
But you, faire Sir, be not herewith dismaid,

But constant keepe the way, in which ye stand;
  Which were it not that I am else delaid
  With hard adventure, which I have in hand,
I labour would to guide you through all Faery land.'

9

'Gramercy Sir' (said he) 'but mote I weete
  What straunge adventure do ye now pursew?
  Perhaps my succour, or advizement meete
  Mote stead you much your purpose to subdew.'
  Then gan Sir *Guyon* all the story shew
  Of false *Acrasia*, and her wicked wiles,
  Which to avenge, the Palmer him forth drew
  From Faery court.   So talked they, the whiles
They wasted had much way, and measurd many miles.

10

And now faire *Phœbus* gan decline in hast
  His weary wagon to the Westerne vale,
  Whenas they spide a goodly castle, plast
  Foreby a river in a pleasaunt dale,
  Which choosing for that evenings hospitale,
  They thither marcht: but when they came in sight,
  And from their sweaty Coursers did avale,
  They found the gates fast barred long ere night,
And every loup fast lockt, as fearing foes despight.

11

Which when they saw, they weened fowle reproch
  Was to them doen, their entraunce to forstall,
  Till that the Squire gan nigher to approch;
  And wind his horne under the castle wall,
  That with the noise it shooke, as it would fall:
  Eftsoones forth looked from the highest spire
  The watch, and lowd unto the knights did call,
  To weete, what they so rudely did require.
Who gently answered, They entrance did desire.

12

'Fly fly, good knights,' (said he) 'fly fast away,
  If that your lives ye love, as meete ye should;
  Fly fast, and save your selves from neare decay,
  Here may ye not have entraunce, though we would:
  We would and would againe, if that we could;
  But thousand enemies about us rave,

And with long siege us in the castle hould:
Seven yeares this wize they us besieged have,
And many good knights slaine, that have us sought to save.'

13

Thus as he spoke, loe with outragious cry
 A thousand villeins round about them swarmd
 Out of the rockes and caves adjoyning nye,
 Vile caytive wretches, ragged, rude, deformd,
 All threatning death, all in straunge manner armd,
 Some with unweldy clubs, some with long speares,
 Some rusty knives, some staves in fi warmd.
 Sterne was their looke, like wild amazed steares,
Staring with hollow eyes, and stiffe upstanding heares.

14

Fiersly at first those knights they did assaile,
 And drove them to recoile: but when againe
 They gave fresh charge, their forces gan to faile,
 Unhable their encounter to sustaine;
 For with such puissaunce and impetuous maine
 Those Champions broke on them, that forst them fly,
 Like scattered Sheepe, whenas the Shepheards swaine
 A Lyon and a Tigre doth espye,
With greedy pace forth rushing from the forest nye.

15

A while they fled, but soone returnd againe
 With greater fury, then before was found;
 And evermore their cruell Capitaine
 Sought with his raskall routs t' enclose them round,
 And overrun to tread them to the ground.
 But soone the knights with their bright-burning blades
 Broke their rude troupes, and orders did confound,
 Hewing and slashing at their idle shades;
For though they bodies seeme, yet substance from them fades.

16

As when a swarme of Gnats at eventide
 Out of the fennes of Allan doe arise,
 Their murmuring small trompets sounden wide,
 Whiles in the aire their clustring army flies,
 That as a cloud doth seeme to dim the skies;
 Ne man nor beast may rest, or take repast,
 For their sharpe wounds, and noyous injuries,
 Till the fierce Northerne wind with blustring blast
Doth blow them quite away, and in the *Ocean* cast.

17

Thus when they had that troublous rout disperst,
  Unto the castle gate they come againe,
  And entraunce crav'd, which was denied erst.
  Now when report of that their perilous paine,
  And combrous conflict, which they did sustaine,
  Came to the Ladies eare, which there did dwell,
  Shee forth issewed with a goodly traine
  Of Squires and Ladies equipaged well,
And entertained them right fairely, as befell.

18

Alma she called was, a virgin bright;
  That had not yet felt *Cupides* wanton rage,
  Yet was shee woo'd of many a gentle knight,
  And many a Lord of noble parentage,
  That sought with her to lincke in marriage:
  For shee was faire, as faire mote ever bee,
  And in the flowre now of her freshest age;
  Yet full of grace and goodly modestee,
That even heven rejoyced her sweete face to see.

19

In robe of lilly white she was arayd,
  That from her shoulder to her heele downe raught,
  The traine whereof loose far behind her strayd,
  Braunched with gold and perle most richly wrought,
  And borne of two faire Damsels, which were taught
  That service well.   Her yellow golden heare
  Was trimly woven, and in tresses wrought,
  Ne other tyre she on her head did weare,
But crowned with a garland of sweete Rosiere.

20

Goodly she entertaind those noble knights,
  And brought them up into her castle hall;
  Where gentle court and gracious delight
  She to them made, with mildnesse virginall,
  Shewing her selfe both wise and liberall:
  There when they rested had a season dew,
  They her besought of favour speciall,
  Of that faire Castle to affoord them vew;
She graunted, and them leading forth, the same did shew.

21

First she them led, up to the Castle wall,
  That was so high, as foe might not it clime,
  And all so faire, and fensible withall,
  Not built of bricke, ne yet of stone and lime,
  But of thing like to that *Ægyptian* slime,
  Whereof king *Nine* whilome built *Babell* towre;
  But O great pitty, that no lenger time
  So goodly workemanship should not endure:
Soone it must turne to earth; no earthly thing is sure.

22

The frame thereof seemd partly circulare,
  And part triangulare, O worke divine;
  Those two the first and last proportions are,
  The one imperfect, mortall, fœminine;
  Th' other immortall, perfect, masculine,
  And twixt them both a quadrate was the base,
  Proportioned equally by seven and nine;
  Nine was the circle set in heavens place,
All which compacted made a goodly diapase.

23

Therein two gates were placed seemly well:
  The one before, by which all in did pas,
  Did th' other far in workmanship excell;
  For not of wood, nor of enduring bras,
  But of more worthy substance fram'd it was;
  Doubly disparted, it did locke and close,
  That when it locked, none might thorough pas,
  And when it opened, no man might it close,
Still open to their friends, and closed to their foes.

24

Of hewen stone the porch was fairely wrought,
  Stone more of valew, and more smooth and fine,
  Then Jet or Marble far from Ireland brought;
  Over the which was cast a wandring vine,
  Enchaced with a wanton yvie twine.
  And over it a faire Portcullis hong,
  Which to the gate directly did incline,
  With comely compasse, and compacture strong,
Nether unseemely short, nor yet exceeding long.

25

Within the Barbican a Porter sate,
  Day and night duely keeping watch and ward,
  Nor wight, nor word mote passe out of the gate,
  But in good order, and with dew regard;
  Utterers of secrets he from thence debard,
  Bablers of folly, and blazers of crime.
  His larumbell might lowd and wide be hard,
  When cause requird, but never out of time;
Early and late it rong, at evening and at prime.

26

And round about the porch on every side
  Twise sixteen warders sat, all armed bright
  In glistring steele, and strongly fortifide:
  Tall yeomen seemed they, and of great might,
  And were enraunged ready, still for fight.
  By them as *Alma* passed with her guestes,
  They did obeysaunce, as beseemed right,
  And then againe returned to their restes:
The Porter eke to her did lout with humble gestes.

27

Thence she them brought into a stately Hall,
  Wherein were many tables faire dispred,
  And ready dight with drapets festivall,
  Against the viaundes should be ministred.
  At th' upper end there sate, yclad in red
  Downe to the ground, a comely personage,
  That in his hand a white rod menaged.
  He Steward was hight *Diet*; rype of age,
And in demeanure sober, and in counsell sage.

28

And through the Hall there walked to and fro
  A jolly yeoman, Marshall of the same,
  Whose name was *Appetite*; he did bestow
  Both guestes and meate, when ever in they came,
  And knew them how to order without blame,
  As him the Steward bad.   They both attone
  Did dewty to their Lady, as became;
  Who passing by, forth led her guestes anone
Into the kitchen rowme, ne spard for nicenesse none.

29

It was a vaut ybuilt for great dispence,
  With many raunges reard along the wall;
  And one great chimney, whose long tonnell thence
  The smoke forth threw.   And in the midst of all
  There placed was a caudron wide and tall,
  Upon a mighty furnace, burning whot,
  More whot, then *Aetn'*, or flaming *Mongiball*:
  For day and night it brent, ne ceased not,
So long as any thing it in the caudron got.

30

But to delay the heat, least by mischaunce
  It might breake out, and set the whole on fire,
  There added was by goodly ordinaunce,
  An huge great paire of bellowes, which did styre
  Continually, and cooling breath inspyre.
  About the Caudron many Cookes accoyld,
  With hookes and ladles, as need did require;
  The whiles the viandes in the vessell boyld
They did about their businesse sweat, and sorely toyld.

31

The maister Cooke was cald *Concoction*,
  A carefull man, and full of comely guise:
  The kitchin Clerke, that hight *Digestion*,
  Did order all th' Achates in seemely wise,
  And set them forth, as well he could devise.
  The rest had severall offices assind,
  Some to remove the scum, as it did rise;
  Others to beare the same away did mind;
And others it to use according to his kind.

32

But all the liquour, which was fowle and wast,
  Not good nor serviceable else for ought,
  They in another great round vessell plast,
  Till by a conduit pipe it thence were brought:
  And all the rest, that noyous was, and nought,
  By secret wayes, that none might it espy,
  Was close convaid, and to the backgate brought,
  That cleped was *Port Esquiline*, whereby
It was avoided quite, and throwne out privily.

33

Which goodly order, and great workmans skill
   Whenas those knights beheld, with rare delight,
   And gazing wonder they their minds did fill;
   For never had they seene so straunge a sight.
   Thence backe againe faire *Alma* led them right,
   And soone into a goodly Parlour brought,
   That was with royall arras richly dight,
   In which was nothing pourtrahed, nor wrought,
Not wrought, nor pourtrahed, but easie to be thought.

34

And in the midst thereof upon the floure,
   A lovely bevy of faire Ladies sate,
   Courted of many a jolly Paramoure,
   The which them did in modest wise amate,
   And eachone sought his Lady to aggrate:
   And eke emongst them litle *Cupid* playd
   His wanton sports, being returned late
   From his fierce warres, and having from him layd
His cruell bow, wherewith he thousands hath dismayd.

35

Diverse delights they found them selves to please;
   Some song in sweet consort, some laught for joy,
   Some plaid with strawes, some idly sat at ease;
   But other some could not abide to toy,
   All pleasaunce was to them griefe and annoy:
   This frownd, that faund, the third for shame did blush,
   Another seemd envious, or coy,
   Another in her teeth did gnaw a rush:
But at these straungers presence every one did hush.

36

Soone as the gracious *Alma* came in place,
   They all attonce out of their seates arose,
   And to her homage made, with humble grace:
   Whom when the knights beheld, they gan dispose
   Themselves to court, and each a Damsell chose:
   The Prince by chaunce did on a Lady light,
   That was right faire and fresh as morning rose,
   But somwhat sad, and solemne eke in sight,
As if some pensive thought constraind her gentle spright.

37

In a long purple pall, whose skirt with gold,
   Was fretted all about, she was arayd;
   And in her hand a Poplar braunch did hold:
   To whom the Prince in curteous manner said;
   'Gentle Madame, why beene ye thus dismaid,
   And your faire beautie doe with sadnesse spill?
   Lives any that you hath thus ill apaid?
   Or doen you love, or doen you lacke your will?
What ever be the cause, it sure beseemes you ill.'

38

'Faire Sir,' (said she halfe in disdainefull wise,)
   'How is it, that this mood in me ye blame,
   And in your selfe do not the same advise?
   Him ill beseemes, anothers fault to name,
   That may unwares be blotted with the same:
   Pensive I yeeld I am, and sad in mind,
   Through great desire of glory and of fame;
   Ne ought I weene are ye therein behind,
That have twelve months sought one, yet no where can her find.'

39

The Prince was inly moved at her speach,
   Well weeting trew, what she had rashly told;
   Yet with faire semblaunt sought to hide the breach,
   Which chaunge of colour did perforce unfold,
   Now seeming flaming whot, now stony cold.
   Tho turning soft aside, he did inquire,
   What wight she was, that Poplar braunch did hold:
   It answered was, her name was *Prays-desire*,
That by well doing sought to honour to aspire.

40

The whiles, the *Faerie* knight did entertaine
   Another Damsell of that gentle crew,
   That was right faire, and modest of demaine,
   But that too oft she chaung'd her native hew:
   Straunge was her tyre, and all her garment blew,
   Close round about her tuckt with many a plight:
   Upon her fist the bird, which shonneth vew,
   And keepes in coverts close from living wight,
Did sit, as yet ashamd, how rude *Pan* did her dight.

41

So long as *Guyon* with her commoned,
  Unto the ground she cast her modest eye,
  And ever and anone with rosie red
  The bashfull bloud her snowy cheekes did dye,
  That her became, as polisht yvory,
  Which cunning Craftesman hand hath overlayd
  With faire vermilion or pure Castory.
  Great wonder had the knight, to see the mayd
So straungely passioned, and to her gently sayd,

42

'Faire Damzell, seemeth, by your troubled cheare,
  That either me too bold ye weene, this wise
  You to molest, or other ill to feare
  That in the secret of your hart close lyes,
  From whence it doth, as cloud from sea arise.
  If it be I, of pardon I you pray;
  But if ought else that I mote not devise,
  I will, if you please you it discure, assay
To ease you of that ill, so wisely as I may.'

43

She answerd nought, but more abasht for shame,
  Held downe her head, the whiles her lovely face
  The flashing bloud with blushing did inflame,
  And the strong passion mard her modest grace,
  That *Guyon* marvayld at her uncouth cace:
  Till *Alma* him bespake, 'why wonder yee,
  Faire Sir at that, which ye so much embrace?
  She is the fountaine of your modestee:
You shamefast are, but *Shamefastnesse* it selfe is shee.'

44

Thereat the Elfe did blush in privitee,
  And turned his face away; but she the same
  Dissembled faire, and faynd to oversee.
  Thus they awhile with court and goodly game,
  Themselves did solace each one with his Dame,
  Till that great Ladie thence away them sought,
  To vew her castles other wondrous frame.
  Up to a stately Turret she them brought,
Ascending by ten steps of Alabaster wrought.

45

That Turrets frame most admirable was,
  Like highest heaven compassed around,
  And lifted high above this earthly masse,
  Which it servew'd, as hils doen lower ground;
  But not on ground mote like to this be found,
  Not that, which antique *Cadmus* whylome built
  In *Thebes*, which *Alexander* did confound;
  Nor that proud towre of *Troy*, though richly guilt,
From which young *Hectors* bloud by cruell *Greekes* was spilt.

46

The roofe hereof was arched over head,
  And deckt with flowers and herbars daintly;
  Two goodly Beacons, set in watches stead,
  Therein gave light, and flamd continually:
  For they of living fire most subtilly
  Were made, and set in silver sockets bright,
  Cover'd with lids deviz'd of substance sly,
  That readily they shut and open might.
O who can tell the prayses of that makers might!

47

Ne can I tell, ne can I stay to tell
  This parts great workmanship, and wondrous powre,
  That all this other worlds worke doth excell,
  And likest is unto that heavenly towre,
  That God hath built for his owne blessed bowre.
  Therein were divers roomes, and divers stages,
  But three the chiefest, and of greatest powre,
  In which there dwelt three honorable sages,
The wisest men, I weene, that lived in their ages.

48

Not he, whom *Greece*, the Nourse of all good arts,
  By *Phœbus* doome the wisest thought alive,
  Might be compar'd to these by many parts:
  Nor that sage *Pylian* syre, which did survive
  Three ages, such as mortall men contrive,
  By whose advise old *Priams* cittie fell,
  With these in praise of pollicies mote strive.
  These three in these three roomes did sundry dwell,
And counselled faire *Alma*, how to governe well.

49

The first of them could things to come foresee:
   The next could of thinges present best advize;
   The third things past could keep in memoree,
   So that no time, nor reason could arize,
   But that the same could one of these comprize.
   For thy the first did in the forepart sit,
   That nought mote hinder his quicke prejudize:
   He had a sharpe foresight, and working wit,
That never idle was, ne once could rest a whit.

50

His chamber was dispainted all within,
   With sundry colours, in the which were writ
   Infinite shapes of things dispersed thin;
   Some such as in the world were never yit,
   Ne can devized be of mortall wit;
   Some daily seene and knowen by their names,
   Such as in idle fantasies doe flit:
   Infernall Hags, *Centaurs*, feendes, *Hippodames*,
Apes, Lions, Ægles, Owles, fooles, lovers, children, Dames.

51

And all the chamber filled was with flyes,
   Which buzzed all about, and made such sound,
   That they encombred all mens eares and eyes,
   Like many swarmes of Bees assembled round,
   After their hives with honny do abound:
   All those were idle thoughts and fantasies,
   Devices, dreames, opinions unsound,
   Shewes, visions, sooth-sayes, and prophesies;
And al that fained is, as leasings, tales, and lies.

52

Emongst them all sate he, which wonned there,
   That hight *Phantastes* by his nature trew;
   A man of yeares yet fresh, as mote appere,
   Of swarth complexion, and of crabbed hew,
   That him full of melancholy did shew;
   Bent hollow beetle browes, sharpe staring eyes,
   That mad or foolish seemd: one by his vew
   Mote deeme him borne with ill disposed skyes,
When oblique *Saturne* sate in the house of agonyes.

53

Whom *Alma* having shewed to her guestes,
   Thence brought them to the second roome, whose wals
   Were painted faire with memorable gestes,
   Of famous Wisards, and with picturals
   Of Magistrates, of courts, of tribunals,
   Of commen wealthes, of states, of pollicy,
   Of lawes, of judgements, and of decretals;
   All artes, all science, all Philosophy,
And all that in the world was aye thought wittily.

54

Of those that roome was full, and them among
   There sate a man of ripe and perfect age,
   Who did them meditate all his life long,
   That through continuall practise and usage,
   He now was growne right wise, and wondrous sage.
   Great pleasure had those stranger knights, to see
   His goodly reason, and grave personage.
   That his disciples both desir'd to bee;
But *Alma* thence them led to th' hindmost roome of three.

55

That chamber seemed ruinous and old,
   And therefore was removed far behind,
   Yet were the wals, that did the same uphold,
   Right firme and strong, though somewhat they declind;
   And therein sat an old oldman, halfe blind,
   And all decrepit in his feeble corse,
   Yet lively vigour rested in his mind,
   And recompenst them with a btter scorse:
Weake body well is chang'd for minds redoubled forse.

56

This man of infinite remembrance was,
   And things foregone through many ages held,
   Which he recorded still, as they did pas,
   Ne suffred them to perish through long eld,
   As all things else, the which this world doth weld,
   But laid them up in his immortall scrine,
   Where they for ever incorrupted dweld:
   The warres he well remembred of king *Nine*,
Of old *Assaracus*, and *Inachus* divine.

57

The yeares of *Nestor* nothing were to his,
 Ne yet *Mathusalem*, though longest liv'd;
 For he remembred both their infancies:
 Ne wonder then, if that he were depriv'd
 Of native strength now, that he them surviv'd.
 His chamber all was hangd about with rolles,
 And old records from auncient times deriv'd,
 Some made in books, some in long parchment scrolles,
That were all worm-eaten, and full of canker holes.

58

Amidst them all he in a chaire was set,
 Tossing and turning them withouten end;
 But for he was unhable them to fet,
 A litle boy did on him still attend,
 To reach, when ever he for ought did send;
 And oft when things were lost, or laid amis,
 That boy them sought, and unto him did lend.
 Therefore he *Anamnestes* cleped is,
And that old man *Eumnestes*, by their propertis.

59

The knights there entring, did him reverence dew
 And wondred at his endlesse exercise,
 Then as they gan his Librarie to vew,
 And antique Registers for to avise,
 There chaunced to the Princes hand to rize,
 An auncient booke, hight *Briton moniments*,
 That of this lands first conquest did devize,
 And old division into Regiments,
Till it reduced was to one mans governments.

60

Sir *Guyon* chaunst eke on another booke,
 That hight *Antiquitie* of *Faerie* lond,
 In which when as he greedily did looke;
 Th' off-spring of Elves and Faries there he fond,
 As it delivered was from hond to hond:
 Whereat they burning both with fervent fire,
 Their countries auncestry to understond,
 Crav'd leave of *Alma*, and that aged sire,
To read those bookes; who gladly graunted their desire.

Canto X

1

Who now shall give unto me words and sound,
   Equall unto this haughtie enterprise?
   Or who shall lend me wings, with which from ground
   My lowly verse may loftily arise,
   And lift it selfe unto the highest skies?
   More ample spirit, then hitherto was wount
   Here needes me, whiles the famous auncestries
   Of my most dreaded Soveraigne I recount,
By which all earthly Princes she doth farre surmount.

2

Ne under Sunne, that shines so wide and faire,
   Whence all that lives, does borrow life and light,
   Lives ought, that to her linage may compaire,
   Which though from earth it be derived right,
   Yet doth it selfe stretch forth to heavens hight,
   And all the world with wonder overspred;
   A labour huge, exceeding far my might:
   How shall fraile pen, with feare disparaged,
Conceive such soveraine glory and great bountihed?

3

Argument worthy of *Mæonian* quill;
   Or rather worthy of great *Phœbus* rote,
   Whereon the ruines of great *Ossa* hill,
   And triumphes of *Phlegræan Jove* he wrote,
   That all the Gods admird his loftie note.
   But if some relish of that heavenly lay
   His learned daughters would to me report,
   To decke my song withall, I would assay,
Thy name, O soveraine Queene, to blazon farre away.

4

Thy name O soveraine Queene thy realme and race,
   From this renowmed Prince derived arre,
   Who mightily upheld that royall mace,
   Which now thou bear'st, to thee descended farre
   From mightie kings and conquerours in warre,

Thy fathers and great Grandfathers of old,
Whose noble deeds above the Northerne starre
Immortall fame for ver hath enrold;
As in that old mans booke they were in order told.

5

The land, which warlike Britons now possesse,
    And therein have their mightie empire raysd,
    In antique times was salvage wildernesse,
    Unpeopled, unmanurd, unprov'd, unpraysd,
    Ne was it Island then, ne was it paysd
    Amid the *Ocean* waves, ne was it sought
    Of marchants farre for profits therein praysd,
    But was all desolate, and of some thought
By sea to have been from the *Celticke* mayn-land brought.

6

Ne did it then deserve a name to have,
    Till that the venturous Mariner that way
    Learning his ship from those white rocks to save,
    Which all along the Southerne sea-coast lay,
    Threatning unheedie wrecke and rash decay,
    For safeties sake that same his sea-marke made,
    And named it *Albion*.   But later day
    Finding in it fit ports for fishers trade,
Gan more the same frequent, and further to invade.

7

But farre in land a salvage nation dwelt,
    Of hideous Giants, and halfe beastly men,
    That never tasted grace, nor goodnes felt,
    But wild like beast lurking in loathsome den,
    And flying fast as Roebucke through the fen,
    All naked without shame, or care of cold,
    By hunting and by spoiling lived then;
    Of stature huge, and eke of courage bold,
That sonnes of men amazd their sternnesse to behold.

8

But whence they sprong, or how they were begot,
    Uneath is to assure; uneath to wene
    That monstrous error, which doth some assot,
    That *Dioclesians* fiftie daughters shene
    Into this land by chaunce have driven bene,
    Where companing with feends and filthy Sprights,

Through vaine illusion of their lust unclene,
They brought forth Giants and such dreadful wights,
As far exceeded men in their immeasurd mights.

9

They held this land, and with their filthinesse
  Polluted this same gentle soyle long time:
  That their owne mother loathd their beastlinesse,
  And gan abhorre her broods unkindly crime,
  All were they borne of her owne native slime,
  Untill that *Brutus* anciently deriv'd
  From royall stocke of old *Assaracs* line,
  Driven by fatall error, here arriv'd,
And them of their unjust possession depriv'd.

10

But ere he had established his throne,
  And spred his empire to the utmost shore,
  He fought great battels with his salvage fone;
  In which he them defeated evermore,
  And many Giants left on groning flore;
  That well can witnesse yet unto this day
  The westerne Hogh, besprincled with the gore
  Of mighty *Goëmot*, whom in stout fray
Corineus conquered, and cruelly did slay.

11

And eke that ample Pit, yet far renownd,
  For the large leape, which *Debon* did compell
  Coulin to make, being eight lugs of grownd;
  Into the which returning backe, he fell,
  But those three monstrous stones doe most excell
  Which that huge sonne of hideous *Albion*,
  Whose father *Hercules* in Fraunce did quell,
  Great *Godmer* threw, in fierce contention,
At bold *Cantus*; but of him was slaine anon.

12

In meed of these great conquests by them got,
  Corineus had that Province utmost west,
  To him assigned for his worthy lot,
  Which of his name and memorable gest
  He called *Cornewaile*, yet so called best:
  And Debons shayre was, that is *Devonshyre*:
  But *Canute* had his portion from the rest,

The which he cald *Canutium*, for his hyre;
Now *Cantium*, which Kent we commenly inquire.

13

Thus *Brute* this Realme unto his rule subdewd,
  And raigned long in great felicitie,
  Lov'd of his friends, and of his foes eschewd,
  He left three sonnes, his famous progeny,
  Borne of fayre *Inogene* of *Italy*;
  Mongst whom he parted his imperiall state,
  And *Locrine* left chiefe Lord of *Britany*.
  At last ripe age bad him surrender late
His life, and long good fortune unto finall fate.

14

Locrine was left the soveraine Lord of all;
  But *Albanact* had all the Northrene part,
  Which of himselfe *Albania* he did call;
  And *Camber* did possesse the Westerne quart,
  Which *Severne* now from *Logris* doth depart:
  And each his portion peaceably enjoyd,
  Ne was there outward breach, nor grudge in hart,
  That once their quiet government annoyd,
But each his paines to others profit still employd.

15

Until a nation straunge, with visage swart,
  And courage fierce, that all men did affray,
  Which through the world then swarmd in every part,
  And overflow'd all countries farre away,
  Like *Noyes* great flood, with their importune sway,
  This land invaded with like violence,
  And did themselves through all the North display:
  Until that *Locrine* for his Realmes defence,
Did head against them make, and strong munificence.

16

He then encountred, a confused rout,
  Foreby the River, that whylome was hight
  The auncient *Abus*, where with courage stout
  He them defeated in victorious fight,
  And chaste so fiercely after fearefull flight,
  That forst their Chieftaine for his safeties sake,
  (Their Chieftaine *Humber* named was aright)
  Unto the mighty streame him to betake,
Where he an end of battell, and of life did make.

17

The king returned proud of victorie,
  And insolent wox through unwonted ease,
  That shortly he forgot the jeopardie,
  Which in his land he lately did appease,
  And fell to vaine voluptuous disease;
  He lov'd faire Ladie *Estrild*, lewdly lov'd,
  Whose wanton pleasures him too much did please,
  That quite his hart from Guendolene remov'd,
From *Guendolene* his wife, though alwaies faithfull prov'd.

18

The noble daughter of *Corineus*
  Would not endure to be so vile disdaind,
  But gathering force, and courage valorous,
  Encountred him in battell well ordaind,
  In which him vanquisht she to fly constraind:
  But she so fast pursewd, that him she tooke,
  And threw in bands, where he till death remaind;
  Als his faire Leman, flying through a brooke,
She overhent, nought moved with her piteous looke.

19

But both her selfe, and eke her daughter deare,
  Begotten by her kingly Paramoure,
  The faire *Sabrina* almost dead with feare,
  She there attached, farre from all succoure;
  The one she slew in that impatient stoure,
  But the sad virgin innocent of all.
  Adowne the rolling river she did poure,
  Which of her name now *Severne* men do call:
Such was the end, that to disloyall love did fall.

20

Then for her sonne, which she to *Locrin* bore,
  Madan was young, unmeet the rule to sway,
  In her owne hand the crowne she kept in store,
  Till ryper years he raught, and stronger stay:
  During which time her powre she did display
  Through all this realme, the glorie of her sex,
  And first taught men a woman to obay:
  But when her sonne to mans estate did wex,
She it surrendred, ne her selfe would lenger vex.

21

Tho *Madan* raignd, unworthie of his race:
  For with all shame that sacred throne he fild:
  Next *Memprise*, as unworthy of that place,
  In which being consorted with *Manild*,
  For thirst of single kingdome him he kild.
  But *Ebranck* salved both their infamies
  With noble deedes, and warreyd on *Brunchild*
  In *Henault*, where yet of his victories
Brave moniments remaine, which yet that land envies.

22

An happie man in his first dayes he was,
  And happie father of faire progeny:
  For all so many weekes as the yeare has,
  So many children he did multiply;
  Of which were twentie sonnes, which did apply,
  Their minds to praise, and chevalrous desire:
  Those germans did subdew all Germany,
  Of whom it hight; but in the end their Sire
With foule repulse from Fraunce was forced to retire.

23

Which blot his sonne succeeding in his seat,
  The second *Brute*, the second both in name,
  And eke in semblaunce of his puissaunce great,
  Right well recur'd, and did away that blame
  With recompence of everlasting fame.
  He with his victour sword first opened,
  The bowels of wide Fraunce, a forlorne Dame,
  And taught her first how to be conquered;
Since which, with sundrie spoiles she hath been ransacked.

24

Let *Scaldis* tell, and let tell *Hania*,
  And let the marsh of *Esthambruges* tell,
  What colour were their waters that same day,
  And all the moore twixt *Eluersham* and *Dell*,
  With bloud of *Henalois* which therein fell.
  How oft that day did sad *Brunchildis* see
  The greene shield dyde in dolorous vermell?
  That not *Scuith guiridh* it mote seeme to bee,
But rather *y Scuith gogh*, signe of sad crueltee.

25

His sonne king *Leill*, by fathers labour long,
   Enjoyd an heritage of lasting peace,
   And built *Cairleill*, and built *Cairleon* strong.
   Next *Huddibras* his realme did not encrease,
   But taught the land from wearie warres to cease.
   Whose footsteps *Bladud* following, in arts
   Exceld at *Athens* all the learned preace,
   From whence he brought them to these salvage parts,
And with sweet science mollifide their stubborne harts.

26

Ensample of his wondrous faculty,
   Behold the boyling Bathes at *Cairbadon*,
   Which seeth with secret fire eternally,
   And in their entrails, full of quicke Brimston,
   Nourish the flames, which they are warm'd upon,
   That to their people wealth they forth do well,
   And health to every forreine nation:
   Yet he at last contending to excell
The reach of men, through flight into fond mischief fell.

27

Next him king *Leyr* in happie peace long raind,
   But had no issue male him to succeed,
   But three faire daughters, where were well uptraind,
   In all that seemed fit for kingly seed:
   Mongst who his realme he equally decreed
   To have divided.   Tho when feeble age
   Nigh to his utmost date he saw proceed,
   He cald his daughters; and with speeches sage
Inquyrd, which of them most did love her parentage.

28

The eldest *Gonorill* gan to protest
   That she much more then her owne life him lov'd;
   And *Regan* greater love to him profest
   Then all the world, when ever it were proov'd;
   But *Cordeill* said she lov'd him, as behoov'd:
   Whose simple answere, wanting colours faire
   To paint it forth, him to displeasance moov'd,
   That in his crowne he counted her no haire,
But twixt the other twaine his kingdom whole did shaire.

29

So wedded th' one to *Maglan* king of Scot
  And t'other to the king of *Cambria*,
  And twixt them shayrd his realme by equall lots:
  But without dowre the wise *Cordelia*,
  Was sent to *Aganip* of *Celtica*.
  Their aged Syre, thus eased of his crowne,
  A private life led in *Albania*,
  With *Gonorill*, long had in great renowne,
That nought him griev'd to bene from rule deposed downe.

30

But true it is, that when the oyle is spent,
  The light goes out, and weeke is throwne away;
  So when he had resigned his regiment,
  His daughter gan despise his drouping day,
  And wearie waxe of his continuall stay.
  Tho to his daughter *Regan* he repayrd,
  Who him at first well used every way;
  But when of his departure she despayrd,
Her bountie she abated, and his cheare empayrd.

31

The wretched man gan then avise too late,
  That love is not, where most it is profest,
  Too truely tryde in his extreamest state;
  At last resolv'd likewise to prove the rest,
  He to *Cordelia* him selfe addrest,
  Who with entire affection him receav'd,
  As for her Syre and king her seemed best;
  And after all an army strong she leav'd,
To war on those, which him had of his realme bereav'd.

32

So to his crowne she him restor'd againe,
  In which he dyde, made ripe for death by eld,
  And after wild, it should to her remaine:
  Who peaceably the same long time did weld:
  And all mens harts in dew obedience held:
  Till that her sisters children, woxen strong
  Through proud ambition, against her rebeld,
  And overcommen kept in prison long.
Till wearie of that wretched life, her selfe she hong.

33

Then gan the bloudie brethren both to raine:
 But fierce *Cundah* gan shortly to envie
 His brother *Morgan*, prickt with proud disdaine,
 To have a pere in part of soveraintie,
 And kindling coles of cruell enmitie,
 Raisd warre, and him in battell overthrew:
 Whence as he to those woodie hils did flie,
 Which hight of him *Glamorgan*, there him slew:
Then did he raigne alone, when he none equall knew.

34

His sonne *Rivallo* his dead roome did supply,
 In whose sad time bloud did from heaven raine.
 Next great *Gurgustus* then faire *Cæcily*
 In constant peace their kingdomes did containe,
 After whom *Lago*, and *Kinmarke* did raine,
 And *Gorbogud*, till farre in years he grew:
 Then his ambitious sonnes unto them twaine
 Arraught the rule, and from their father drew,
Stout *Ferrex* and sterne *Porrex* him in prison threw.

35

But O, the greedy thirst of royall crowne,
 That knowes no kinred, nor regardes no right,
 Stird *Porrex* up to put his brother downe;
 Who unto him assembling forreine might,
 Made warre on him, and fell him selfe in fight:
 Whose death t'avenge, his mother mercilesse,
 Most mercilesse of women, *Wyden* hight,
 Her other sonne fast sleeping did oppresse,
And with most cruell hand him murdred pittilesse.

36

Here ended *Brutus* sacred progenie,
 Which had seven hundred yeares this scepter borne,
 With high renowme, and great felicitie;
 The noble braunch from th' antique stocke was torne
 Through discord, and the royall throne forlorne:
 Thenceforth this Realme was into factions rent,
 Whilest each of *Brutus* boasted to be borne,
 That in the end was left no moniment
Of *Brutus*, nor of Britons glory auncient.

37

Then up arose a man of matchlesse might,
   And wondrous wit to menage high affaires,
   Who stird with pitty of the stressed plight
   Of this sad Realme, cut into sundry shaires
   By such, as claymd themselves *Brutes* rightfull haires,
   Gathered the Princes of the people loose,
   To taken counsell of their common cares;
   Who with wisedom won, him streight did choose
Their king, and swore him fealty to win or loose.

38

Then made he head against his enimies,
   And *Ymner* slew, of *Logris* miscreate;
   Then *Ruddoc* and proud *Stater*, both allyes,
   This of *Albanie* newly nominate,
   And that of *Cambry* king confirmed late,
   He overthrew through his owne valiaunce;
   Whose countries he redus'd to quiet state,
   And shortly brought to civil governaunce,
Now one, which earst were many, made through variaunce.

39

Then made he sacred lawes, which some men say
   Were unto him reveald in vision,
   By which he freed the Traveilers high way,
   The Churches part, and Ploughmans portion,
   Restraining stealth, and strong extortion;
   The gracious *Numa* of great *Britanie*:
   For till his dayes, the chiefe dominion
   By strength was wielded without pollicie;
Therefore he first wore crowne of gold for dignitie.

40

Donwallo dyde (for what may live for ay?)
   And left two sonnes, of pearelesse prowesse both;
   That sacked Rome too dearely did assay,
   The recompense of their perjured oth,
   And ransackt *Greece* well tryde, when they were wroth;
   Besides subjected *Fraunce* and *Germany*,
   Which yet their prayses speake, all be they loth,
   And inly tremble at the memory
Of *Brennus* and *Belinus*, kings of *Britany*.

41

Next them did *Gurgunt*, great *Bellinus* sonne,
   In rule succeede, and eke in fathers prase;
   He Easterland subdewd, and Danmarke wonne,
   And of them both did foy and tribute raise,
   The which was dew in his dead fathers daes:
   He also gave to fugitives of *Spayne*,
   Whom he at sea found wandring from their waes,
   A seate in Ireland safely to remayne,
Which they should hold of him, as subject to *Britayne*.

42

After him raigned *Guitheline* his hayre,
   The justest man and trewest in his dayes,
   Who had to wife Dame *Mertia* the fayre,
   A woman worthy of immortall prayse,
   Which for this Realme found many goodly layes,
   And wholesome Statutes to her husband brought;
   Her many deemd to have beene of the Fayes.
   As was *Aegerie*, that *Numa* tought:
Those yet of her be *Mertian* lawes both nam'd and thought.

43

Her sonne *Sisillus* after her did rayne,
   And then *Kilmarus*, and then *Danius*:
   Next whom *Morindus* did the crowne sustaine,
   Who, had he not with wrath outrageous,
   And cruell rancour dim'd his valorous
   And mightie deeds, should matched have the best:
   As well in that same field victorious
   Against the forreine *Morands* he exprest;
Yet lives his memorie, though carcas sleepe in rest.

44

Five sonnes he left begotten of one wife,
   All which successively by turnes did raine:
   First *Gorboman* a man of vertuous life;
   Next *Archigald*, who for his proud disdaine,
   Deposed was from Princedome soveraine,
   And pitteous *Elidure* put in his sted;
   Who shortly it to him restord againe,
   Till by his death he it recovered;
But *Peridure* and *Vigent* him disthronized.

45

In wretched prison long he did remaine,
  Till they outraigned had their utmost date,
  And then therein reseized was againe,
  And ruled long with honorable state,
  Till he surrendred Realme and life to fate.
Then all the sonnes of these five brethren raynd
  By dew successe, and all their Nephewes late,
  Even thrise eleven descents the crowne retaynd,
Till aged *Hely* by dew heritage it gaynd.

46

He had two sonnes whose eldest called *Lud*
  Left of his life most famous memory,
  And endlesse moniments of his great good:
  The ruin'd wals he did reædifye
  Of *Troynovant*, gainst force of enimy,
  And built that gate, which of his name is hight,
  By which he lyes entombed solemnly.
He left two sonnes, too young to rule aright
Androgeus and *Tenantius*, pictures of his might.

47

Whilst they were young, *Cassibalane* their Eme,
  Was by the people chosen in their sted,
  Who on him tooke the royall Diademe,
  And goodly well long time it governed,
  Till the prowd *Romanes* him disquieted,
  And warlike *Cæsar*, tempted with the name
  Of this sweet Island, never conquered,
  And envying the Britons blazed fame,
(O hideous hunger of dominion) hither came.

48

Yet twise they were repulsed backe againe,
  And twise renforst, backe to their ships to fly,
  The whiles with bloud they all the shore did staine,
  And the gray *Ocean* into purple dy:
  Ne had they footing found at last perdie,
  Had not *Androgeus*, false to native soyle,
  And envious of Uncles soveraintie,
  Betrayd his contrey unto forreine spoyle:
Nought else, but treason, from the first this land did foyle.

49

So by him *Cæsar* got the victory,
  Through great bloudshed, and many a sad assay,
  In which him selfe was charged heavily
  Of hardy *Nennius*, whom he yet did slay,
  But lost his sword, yet to be seene this day.
  Thenceforth this land was tributarie made
  T' ambitious *Rome*, and did their rule obay,
  Till *Arthur* all that reckoning defrayd;
Yet oft the Briton kings against them strongly swayd.

50

Next him *Tenantius* raigned, then *Kimbeline*,
  What time th' eternall Lord in fleshly slime
  Enwombed was, from wretched *Adams* line
  To purge away the guilt of sinfull crime:
  O joyous memorie of happy time,
  That heavenly grace so plenteously displayd;
  (O too high ditty for my simple rime.)
  Soone after this the *Romanes* him warrayd;
For that their tribute he refusd to let be payd.

51

Good *Claudius*, that next was Emperour,
  An army brought, and with him battell fought,
  In which the king was by a Treachetour
  Disguised slaine, ere any thereof thought:
  Yet creased not the bloudy fight for ought;
  For *Arvirage* his brothers place supplide,
  Both in his armes, and crowne, and by that draught
  Did drive the *Romanes* to the weaker side,
That they to peace agreed.   So all was pacifide.

52

Was never king more highly magnifide,
  Nor dred of *Romanes*, then was *Arvirage*,
  For which the Emperour to him allide
  His daughter *Genuiss'* in marriage:
  Yet shortly he renounst the vassalage
  Of *Rome* againe, who hither hastly sent
  Vespasian, that with great spoile and rage
  Forwasted all, till *Genuissa* gent
Perswaded him to ceasse, and her Lord to relent.

53

He dyde; and him succeeded *Marius*,
    Who joyd his dayes in great tranquillity,
    Then *Coyll*, and after him good *Lucius*,
    That first received Christianitie,
    The sacred pledge of Christes Evangely;
    Yet true it is, that long before that day
    Hither came *Joseph* of *Arimathy*,
    Who brought with him the holy grayle, (they say)
And preacht the truth, but since it greatly did decay.

54

This good king shortly without issew dide,
    Whereof great trouble in the kingdome grew,
    That did her selfe in sundry parts divide,
    And with her powre her owne selfe overthrew,
    Whilest *Romanes* dayly did the weake subdew:
    Which seeing stout *Bunduca*, up arose,
    And taking armes, the *Britons* to her drew;
    With whom she marched streight against her foes,
And them unwares besides the *Severne* did enclose.

55

There she with them a cruell battell tride,
    Not with so good successe, as she deserv'd;
    By reason that the Captaines on her side,
    Corrupted by *Paulinus*, from her swerv'd:
    Yet such, as were through former flight preserv'd,
    Gathing againe, her Host she did renew,
    And with fresh courage on the victour serv'd:
    But being all defeated, save a few,
Rather then fly, or be captiv'd her selfe she slew.

56

O famous moniment of womens prayse,
    Matchable either to *Semiramis*,
    Whom antique history so high doth raise,
    Or to *Hypsiphil'*, or to *Thomiris*:
    Her Host two hundred thousand numbred is;
    Who, whiles good fortune favoured her might,
    Triumphed oft against her enmis;
    And yet though overcome in haplesse fight,
She triumphed on death, in enemies despight.

57

Her reliques *Fulgent* having gathered,
   Fought with *Severus*, and him overthrew;
   Yet in the chace was slaine of them that fled,
   So made them victours whom he did subdew.
   Then gan *Carausius* tirannize anew,
   And gainst the *Romanes* bent their proper powre;
   But him *Allectus* treacherously slew,
   And tooke on him the robe of Emperoure:
Nath'lesse the same enjoyed but short happy howre:

58

For *Asclepiodate* him overcame,
   And left inglorious on the vanquisht playne,
   Without or robe, or rag, to hide his shame.
   Then afterwards he in his stead did rayne;
   But shortly was by *Coyll* in battell slaine;
   Who after long debate, since *Lucies* time,
   Was of the *Britons* first crownd Soveraine:
   Then gan this Realme renew her passed prime:
He of his name *Coylchester* built of stone and lime.

59

Which when the *Romanes* heard, they hither sent
   Constantius, a man of mickle might,
   With whom king *Coyll* made an agreement,
   And to him gave for wife his daughter bright,
   Faire *Helena*, the fairest living wight;
   Who in all godly thewes, and goodly prayse
   Did far excell, but was most famous hight
   For skill in Musicke of all in her dayes,
As well in curious instruments, as cunning layes.

60

Of whom he did great Constantine beget,
   Who afterward was Emperour of *Rome*;
   To which whiles absent he his mind did set,
   Octavius here lept into his roome,
   And it usurped by unrighteous doome:
   But he his title justifide by might,
   Slaying *Traherne*, and having overcome
   The *Romane* legion in dreadfull fight:
So settled he his kingdome, and confirmd his right.

61

But wanting issew male, his daughter deare
  He gave in wedlocke to *Maximian*,
  And him with her made of his kingdome heyre,
  Who soone by meanes thereof the Empire wan,
  Till murdred by the friends of *Gratian*;
  Then gan the *Hunnes* and *Picts* invade this land,
  During the raigne of *Maximinian*;
  Who dying left none heire them to withstand,
But that they overran all parts with easie hand.

62

The weary *Britons*, whose war-hable youth
  Was by *Maximian* lately led away,
  With wretched miseries and woefull ruth,
  Were to those Pagans made an open pray,
  And dayly spectacle of sad decay:
  Whom *Romane* warres, which now foure hundred yeares,
  And more had wasted, could not whit dismay;
  Till by consent of Commons and of Peares,
Thy crownd the second *Constantine* with joyous teares,

63

Who having oft in battell vanquished
  Those spoilefull Picts, and swarming Easterlings,
  Long time in peace his Realme established,
  Yet oft annoyd with sundry bordragings
  Of neighbour Scots, and forrein Scatterlings,
  With which the world did in those dayes abound:
  Which to outbarre, with painefull pyonings
  From sea to sea he heapt a mightie mound,
Which from *Alcluid* to *Panwelt* did that border bound.

64

Three sonnes he dying left, all under age;
  By meanes whereof, their uncle *Vortigere*
  Usurpt the crowne, during their pupillage;
  Which th' Infants tutors gathering to feare
  Them closely into *Armorick* did beare:
  For dread of whom, and for those Picts annoyes,
  He sent to *Germanie*, straunge aid to reare,
  From whence eftsoones arrived here three hoyes
Of *Saxons*, whom he for his safetie imployes.

65

Two brethren were their Capitans, which hight
  Hengist and *Horsus*, well approv'd in warre,
  And both of them men of renowmed might;
  Who making vantage of their civile jarre,
  And of those forreiners, which came from farre,
  Grew great, and got large portions of land,
  That in the Realme ere long they stronger arre,
  Then they which sought at first their helping hand,
And *Vortiger* enforst the kingdome to aband.

66

But by the helpe of *Vortimere* his sonne,
  He is againe unto his rule restord,
  And *Hengist* seeming sad, for that was donne,
  Received is to grace and new accord,
  Through his faire daughters face, and flattring word;
  Soone after which, three hundred Lordes he slew
  Of British bloud, all sitting at his bord;
  Whose dolefull moniments who list to rew,
Th' eternall markes of treason may at *Stonheng* vew.

67

By this the sonnes of *Constantine*, which fled,
  Ambrose and *Uther* did ripe yeares attaine,
  And here arriving, strongly challenged
  The crowne, which *Vortiger* did long detaine:
  Who flying from his guilt, by them was slaine,
  And *Hengist* eke soone brought to shamefull death.
  Thenceforth *Aurelius* peaceably did rayne,
  Till that through poyson stopped was his breath;
So now entombed lyes at Stoneheng by the heath.

68

After him *Uther*, which *Pendragon* hight,
  Succeding There abruptly it did end,
  Without full point, or other Cesure right,
  As if the rest some wicked hand did rend,
  Or th' Authour selfe could not at least attend
  To finish it: that so untimely breach
  The Prince him selfe halfe seemed to offend,
  Yet secret pleasure did offence empeach,
And wonder of antiquitie long stopt his speach.

69

At last quite ravisht with delight to heare
   The royall Ofspring of his native land,
   Cryde out, 'Deare countrey, O how dearely deare
   Ought thy remembraunce and perpetuall band
   Be to thy foster Childe, that from thy hand
   Did commun breath and nouritire receave?
   How brutish is it not to understand,
   How much to her we owe, that all us gave,
That gave unto us all, what ever good we have.'

70

But *Guyon* all this while his booke did read,
   Ne yet has ended: for it was a great
   And ample volume, that doth far excead
   My leasure, so long leaves here to repeat:
   It told, how first *Prometheus* did create
   A man, of many partes from beasts derived,
   And then stole fire from heven, to animate
   His worke, for which he was by *Jove* deprived
Of life him selfe, and hart-strings of an Ægle rived.

71

That man so made, he called *Elfe*, to weet
   Quick, the first author of all Elfin kind:
   Who wandring through the world with wearie feet,
   Did in the gardins of *Adonis* find
   A goodly creature, whom he deemed in mind
   To be no earthly wight, but either Spright,
   Or Angell, th' authour of all woman kind;
   Therefore a *Fay* he her according hight,
Of whom all *Faeryes* spring, and fetch their lignage right.

72

Of these a mightie people shortly grew,
   And puissant kings, which all the world warrayd,
   And to them selves all Nations did subdew:
   The first and eldest, which that scepter swayd,
   Was Elfin; him all *India* obayd.
   And all that now *America* men call:
   Next him was noble *Elfinan*, who layd
   Cleopolis foundation first of all:
But *Elfiline* enclosd it with a golden wall.

73

His sonne was *Elfinell*, who overcame
  The wicked *Gobbelines* in bloudy field:
  But *Elfant* was of most renowmed fame,
  Who all of Christall did *Panthea* build:
  Then *Elfar*, who two brethren gyants kild,
  The one of which had two heads, th' other three:
  Then *Elfinor*, who was in Magick skild;
  He built by art upon the glassy See
A bridge of bras, whose sound heavens thunder seem'd to bee.

74

He left three sonnes, the which in order raynd,
  And all their Ofspring, in their dew descents,
  Even seven hundred Princes, which maintaynd
  With mightie deedes their sundry governments;
  That were too long their infinite contents
  Here to record, ne much materiall:
  Yet should they be most famous moniments,
  And brave ensample, both of martiall
And civil rule to kings and states imperiall.

75

After all these *Elficleos* did rayne,
  The wise *Elficleos* in great Majestie,
  Who mightily that scepter did sustayne,
  And with rich spoiles and famous victorie,
  Did high advaunce the crowne of *Faery*:
  He left two sonnes, of which faire *Elferon*
  The eldest brother did untimely dy;
  Whose emptie place the mightie *Oberon*
Doubly supplide, in spousall, and dominion.

76

Great was his power and glorie over all,
  Which him before, that sacred seate did fill,
  That yet remaines his wide memoriall:
  He dying left the fairest *Tanaquill*,
  Him to succeede therein, by his last will:
  Fairer and nobler liveth none this howre,
  Ne like in grace, ne like in learned skill;
  Therefore they *Glorian* call that glorious flowre,
Long mayst thou *Glorian* live, in glory and great powre.

77

Beguild thus with delight of novelties,
  And naturall desire of countreys state,
  So long they red in those antiquities,
  That how the time was fled, they quite forgate,
  Till gentle *Alma* seeing it so late,
  Perforce their studies broke, and them besought
  To thinke, how supper did them long awaite.
    So halfe unwilling from their bookes them brought,
And fairely feasted, as so noble knights she ought.

Canto XI

I

What warre so cruel or what siege so sore,
　As that, which strong affections do apply
　Against the fort of reason evermore
　To bring the soule into captivitie:
　Their force is fiercer through infirmitie
　Of the fraile flesh, relenting to their rage,
　And exercise most bitter tyranny
　Upon the parts, brought into their bondage:
No wretchednesse is like to sinfull vellenage.

2

But in a body, which doth freely yeeld
　His partes to reasons rule obedient,
　And letteth her that ought the scepter weeld,
　All happy peace and goodly government
　Is setled there in sure establishment;
　There *Alma* like a virgin Queene most bright,
　Doth florish in all beautie excellent.
　And to her guestes doth bounteous banket dight,
Attempred goodly well for health and for delight.

3

Early before the Morne with cremosin ray
　The windowes of bright heaven opened had,
　Through which into the world the dawning day
　Might looke, that maketh every creature glad,
　Uprose Sir *Guyon*, in bright armour clad,
　And to his purposd journey him prepar'd:
　With him the Palmer eke in habit sad,
　Him selfe addrest to that adventure hard:
So to the rivers side they both together far'd.

4

Where them awaited ready at the ford
　The *Ferriman*, as *Alma* had behight,
　With his wel rigged boate:　　They goe abord,
　And he eftsoones gan launch his brake forthright.
　Ere long they rowed were quite out of sight,

And fast the land behind them fled away.
But let them pas, whiles wind and weather right
Doe serve their turnes: here I a while must stay,
To see a cruell fight doen by the Prince this day.

5

For all so soone, as *Guyon* thence was gon
Upon his voyage with his trustie guide,
That wicked band of villeins fresh begon
That castle to assaile on every side,
And lay strong siege about it far and wide.
So huge and infinite their numbers were,
That all the land they under them did hide;
So fowle and ugly, that exceeding feare
Their visages imprest, when they approched neare.

6

Them in twelve troupes their Captein did dispart
And round about in fittest steades did place,
Where each might best offend his proper part,
And his contrary object most deface,
As every one seem'd meetest in that cace.
Seven of the same against the Castle gate,
In strong entrenchments he did closely place,
Which with incessaunt force and endlesse hate,
They battred day and night, and entraunce did awate.

7

The other five, five sundry wayes he set,
Against the five great Bulwarkes of that pile,
And unto each a Bulwarke did arret,
T' assayle with open force or hidden guile,
In hope thereof to win victorious spoile.
They all that charge did fervently apply
With greedie malice and importune toyle,
And planted there their huge artillery,
With which they dayly made most dreadfull battery.

8

The first troupe was a monstrous rablement
Of fowle misshapen wights, of which some were
Headed like Owles, with beckes uncomely bent,
Others like Dogs, others like Gryphons dreare,
And some had wings, and some had clawes to teare,
And every one of them had Lynces eyes,

And every one did bow and arrowes beare:
   All those were lawlesse lustes, corrupt envies,
And covetous aspectes, all cruell enimies.

9

Those same against the bulwarke of the *Sight*
   Did lay strong siege, and battailous assault,
   Ne once did yield it respit day nor night,
   But soone as *Titan* gan his head exault,
   And soone againe as he his light with hault,
   Their wicked engins they against it bent:
   That is each thing, by which the eyes may fault,
   But two then all more huge and violent,
Beautie, and money, they want Bulwarke sorely rent.

10

The second Bulwarke was the *Hearing* sence,
   Gainst which the second troupe assignment makes;
   Deformed creatures, in straunge difference,
   Some having heads like Harts, some like to Snakes,
   Some like wilde Bores late rouzd out of the brakes;
   Slaunderous reproches and fowle infamies,
   Leasings, backbytings, and vaine-glorious crakes,
   Bad counsels, prayses, and false flatteries.
All those against that fort did bend their batteries.

11

Likewise that same third Fort, that is the *Smell*
   Of that third troupe was cruelly assayd:
   Whose hideous shapes were like to feends of hell,
   Some like to hounds, some like to Apes, dismayd,
   Some like to Puttockes, all in plumes arayd;
   All shap't according their conditions,
   For by those ugly formes weren pourtrayd,
   Foolish delights and fond abusions,
Which do that sence besiege with light illusions.

12

And that fourth band, which cruell battry bent,
   Against the fourth Bulwarke, that is the *Tast*,
   Was as the rest, a grysie rablement,
   Some mouth'd like greedy Oystriges, some fast
   Like loathly Toades, some fashioned in the wast
   Like swine; for so deformd is luxury,
   Surfeat, misdiet, and unthriftie wast,

Vaine feasts, and idle superfluity:
All those this sences Fort assayle incessantly.

13

But the fift troupe most horrible of hew,
    And fierce of force, was dreadfull to report:
    For some like Snailes, some did like spyders shew,
    And some like ugly Urchins thicke and short:
    Cruelly they assayled that fift Fort,
    Armed with darts of sensuall delight,
    With strings of carnall lust, and strong effort
    Of feeling pleasures, with which day and night
Against that same fift bulwarke they continued fight.

14

Thus these twelve troupes with dreadfull puissance
    Against that Castle restlesse siege did lay,
    And evermore their hideous Ordinance
    Upon the Bulwarkes cruelly did play,
    That now it gan to threaten neare decay:
    And evermore their wicked Capitaine
    Provoked them the breaches to assay,
    Sometimes with threats, somtimes with hope of gaine,
Which by the ransack of that peece they should attaine?

15

On th' other side, th' assieged Castles ward
    Their stedfast stonds did mightily maintaine,
    And many bold repulse, and many hard
    Atchievement wrought with perill and with paine,
    That goodly frame from ruine to sustaine:
    And those two brethren Giants did defend
    The walles so stoutly with their sturdie maine,
    That never entrance any durst pretend,
But they to direfull death their groning ghosts did send.

16

The noble virgin, Ladie of the Place,
    Was much dismayed with that dreadful sight:
    For never was she in so evill cace,
    Till that the Prince seeing her wofull plight,
    Gan her recomfort from so sad affright,
    Offring his service, and his dearest life
    For her defence, against that Carle to fight,
    Which was their chiefe and th' authour of that strife:
She him remercied as the Patrone of her life.

17

Eftsoones himselfe in glitterand armes he dight,
   And his well proved weapons to him hent;
   So taking courteous conge he behight,
   Those gates to be unbar'd, and forth he went.
   Faire mote he thee, the prowest and most gent,
   That ever brandished bright steele on hye:
   Whom soone as that unruly rablement
   With his gay Squire issuing did espy,
They reard a most outrageous dreadfull yelling cry.

18

And therewithall attonce at him let fly
   Their fluttering arrowes, thicke as flakes of snow,
   And round about him flocke impetuously,
   Like a great water flood, that tombling low
   From the high mountaines, threats to overflow
   With sudden fury all the fertile plaine,
   And the sad husbandmans long hope doth throw
   A downe the streame, and all his vowes make vaine,
Nor bounds nor banks his headlong ruine may sustaine.

19

Upon his shield their heaped hayle he bore,
   And with his sword disperst the raskall flockes,
   Which fled a sunder, and him fell before,
   As withered leaves drop from their dryed stockes,
   When the wroth Western wind does reave their locks;
   And under neath him his courageous steed,
   The fierce *Spumador* trode them downe like docks,
   The fierce *Spumador* borne of heavenly seed:
Such as *Laomedon* of *Phœbus* race did breed.

20

Which suddeine horrour and confused cry,
   When as their Captaine heard, in haste he yode,
   The cause to weet, and fault to remedy;
   Upon a Tygre swift and fierce he rode,
   That as the winde ran underneath his lode,
   Whiles his long legs nigh raught unto the ground;
   Full large he was of limbe, and shoulders brode,
   But of such subtile substance and unsound,
That like a ghost he seem'd, whose grave-clothes were unbound.

21

And in his hand a bended bow was seene,
  And many arrowes under his right side,
  All deadly daungerous, all cruell keene,
  Headed with flint, and fethers bloudie dide;
  Such as the Indians in their quivers hide;
  Those could he well direct and streight as line,
  And bid them strike the marke, which he had eyde,
  Ne was there salve, ne was there medicine,
That mote recure their wounds: so inly they did tine.

22

As pale and wan as ashes was his looke,
  His body leane and meagre as a rake,
  And skin all withered like a dryed rooke,
  Thereto as cold and drery as a Snake,
  That seemd to tremble evermore, and quake:
  All in a canvas thin he was bedight,
  And girded with a belt of twisted brake,
  Upon his head he wore an Helmet light,
Made of a dead mans skull, that seemd a ghastly sight.

23

Maleger was his name, and after him,
  There follow'd fast at hand two wicked Hags,
  With hoarie lockes all loose, and visage grim;
  Their feet unshod, their bodies wrapt in rags,
  And both as swift on foot, as chased Stags;
  And yet the one her other legge had lame,
  Which with a staffe, all full of litle snags
  She did support, and *Impotence* her name:
But th' other was *Impatience*, arm'd with raging flame.

24

Soone as the Carle from farre the Prince espyde,
  Glistring in armes and warlike ornament,
  His Beast he felly prickt on either syde,
  And his mischievous bow full readie bent,
  With which at him a cruell shaft he sent:
  But he was warie, and it warded well
  Upon his shield, that it no further went,
  But to the ground the idle quarrell fell:
Then he another and another did expell.

25

Which to prevent, the Prince his mortall speare
    Soone to hime raught, and fierce at him did ride,
    To be avenged of that shot whyleare:
    But he was not so hardy to abide
    That bitter stownd, but turning quicke aside
    His light-foot beast, fled fast away for feare:
    Whom to pursue the Infant after hide,
    So fast as his good Courser could him beare,
But labour lost it was, to weene approch him neare.

26

For as the winged wind his Tigre fled,
    That vew of eye could scarse him overtake,
    Ne scarse his feet on ground were seene to tred;
    Through hils and dales he speedie way did make,
    Ne hedge ne ditch his readie passage brake,
    And in his flight the villein turn'd his face
    (As wonts the *Tartar* by the *Caspian* lake,
    When as the *Russian* him in fight does chace)
Unto his Tygres taile, and shot at him apace.

27

Apace he shot, and yet he fled apace,
    Still as the greedy knight nigh to him drew,
    And oftentimes he would relent his pace,
    That him his foe more fiercely should pursew:
    But when his uncouth manner he did vew,
    He gan avize to follow him no more,
    But keepe his standing, and his shaftes eschew,
    Untill he quite had spent his perlous store,
And then assayle him fresh, ere he could shift for more.

28

But that lame Hag, still as abroad he strew
    His wicked arrowes, gathered them againe,
    And to him brought, fresh battell to renew:
    Which he espying, cast her to restraine
    From yielding succour to that cursed Swaine,
    And her attaching, thought her hands to tye;
    But soone as him dismounted on the plaine,
    That other Hag did far away espy
Binding her sister, she to him ran hastily.

29

And catching hold of him, as downe he lent,
  Him backward overthrew, and downe him stayd
  With their rude hands and griesly graplement,
  Till that the villein comming to their ayd,
  Upon him fell, and lode upon him layd:
  Full litle wanted, but he had him slaine,
  And of the battell balefull end had made,
  Had not his gentle Squire beheld his paine,
And commen to his reskew, ere his bitter bane.

30

So greatest and most glorious thing on ground
  May often need the helpe of weaker hand;
  So feeble is mans state, and life unsound,
  That in assuraunce it may never stand,
  Till it dissolved be from earthly band.
  Proofe be thou Prince, the prowest man alive,
  And noblest borne of all in *Britayne* land;
  Yet thee fierce Fortune did so nearely drive,
That had not grace thee blest, thou shouldest not survive.

31

The Squire arriving fiercely in his armes
  Snatcht first the one, and then the other Jade,
  His chiefest lets and authors of his harmes,
  And them perforce withheld with threatned blade,
  Least that his Lord they should behinde invade;
  The whiles the Prince prickt with reprochful shame,
  As one awakt out of long slombring shade,
  Reviving thought of glorie and of fame,
United all his powres to purge him selfe from blame.

32

Like as a fire, the which in hollow cave
  Hath long bene underkept and down supprest,
  With murmurous disdaine doth inly rave,
  And grudge in so streight prison to be prest,
  At last breakes forth with furious unrest,
  And strives to mount unto his native seat;
  All that did earst it hinder and molest,
  It now devoures with flames and scorching heat,
And carries into smoake with rage and horror great.

33

So mightily the *Briton* Prince him rouzd
  Out of his hold, and broke his caitive bands,
  And as a Beare whom angry curres have touzd,
  Having off-shakt them, and escapt their hands
  Becomes more fell, and all that him withstands
  Treads down and overthrowes. Now had the Carle
  Alighted from his Tigre, and his hands
  Discharged of his bow and deadly quar'le,
To seize upon his foe flat lying on the marle.

34

Which now him turnd to disavantage deare;
  For neither can he fly, nor other harme,
  But trust unto his strength and manhood meare,
  Sith now he is far from his monstrous swarme,
  And of his weapons did himselfe disarme.
  The knight yet wrothfull for his late disgrace,
  Fiercely advaunst his valorous right arme,
  And him so sore smott with his yron mace,
That groveling to the ground he fell, and fild his place.

35

Wel weened he, that field was then his owne,
  And all his labour brought to happie end,
  When suddein up the villeine overthrowne
  Out of his swowne arose, fresh to contend,
  And gan himselfe to second battell bend,
  As hurt he had not bene.   Thereby there lay
  An huge great stone, which stood upon one end,
  And had not bene removed many a day;
Some land-marke seem'd to be, or signe of sundry way.

36

The same he snatcht, and with exceeding sway
  Threw at his foe, who was right well aware
  To shunne the engin of his meant decay;
  It booted not to thinke that throw to beare,
  But ground he gave, and lightly lept areare:
  Eft fierce returning, as a Faulcon faire
  That once hath failed of her souse full neare,
  Remounts againe into the open aire,
And unto better fortune doth her selfe prepaire.

37

So brave returning, with his brandisht blade,
  He to the Carle him selfe againe addrest,
  And strooke at him so sternely, that he made
  An open passage through his riven brest,
  That halfe the steele behind his back did rest;
  Which drawing backe, he looked evermore
  When the hart bloud gush out of his chest,
  Or his dead corse should fall upon the flore;
But his dead corse upon the flore fell nathemore.

38

Ne drop of bloud appeared shed to bee,
  All were the wounde so wide and wonderous,
  That through his carcasse one might plainely see:
  Halfe in a maze with horror hideous,
  And halfe in rage to be deluded thus,
  Againe through both the sides he strooke him quight,
  That made his spright to grone full piteous;
  Yet nathermore forth fled his groning spright,
But freshly as at first, prepard himselfe to fight.

39

Thereat he smitten was with great affright,
  And trembling terror did his hart apall,
  Ne wist he, what to thinke of that same sight,
  Ne what to say, ne what to doe at all;
  He doubted, least it were some magicall
  Illusion, that did beguile his sense,
  Or wandring ghost, that wanted funerall,
  Or aerie spirit under false pretence,
Or hellish feend raysd up through divelish science.

40

His wonder far exceeded reasons reach,
  That he began to doubt his dazeled sight,
  And oft of terror did himselfe appeach:
  Flesh without bloud, a person without spright,
  Wounds without hurt, a body without might,
  That could doe harme, yet could not harmed bee,
  That could not die, yet seem'd a mortall wight,
  That was most strong in most infirmitee;
Like did he never heare, like did he never see.

41

A while he stood in this astonishment,
　　Yet would he not for all his great dismay
　　Give over to effect his first intent,
　　And th' utmost meanes of victorie assay,
　　Or th' utmost issew of his owne decay.
　　His owne good sword *Morddure*, that never fayld
　　At need, till now, he lightly threw away,
　　And his bright shield, that nought him now avayld,
And with his naked hands him forcibly assayld.

42

Twixt his two mightie armes him up he snatcht,
　　And crusht his carcasse so against his brest,
　　That the disdainfull soule he thence dispatcht,
　　And th' idle breath all utterly exprest:
　　Tho when he felt him dead, a downe he kest
　　The lumpish corse unto the senselesse grownd;
　　Adowne he kest it with so puissant wrest,
　　That backe againe it did alofte rebownd,
And gave against his mother earth a gronefull sownd.

43

As when *Joves* harnesse-bearing Bird from hie
　　Stoupes at a flying heron with proud disdaine,
　　The stone-dead quarrey fals so forciblie,
　　That it rebounds against the lowly plaine,
　　A second fall redoubling backe againe.
　　Then thought the Prince all perill sure was past,
　　And that he victor onely did remaine;
　　No sooner thought, then that the Carle as fast
Gan heap huge strokes on him, as ere he down was cast.

44

Nigh his wits end then woxe th' amazed knight,
　　And thought his labour lost, and travell vaine,
　　Against this lifelesse shadow so to fight:
　　Yet life he saw, and felt his mightie maine,
　　That whiles he marveild still, did still him paine;
　　For thy he gan some other wayes advize,
　　How to take life from that dead-living swaine,
　　Whom still he marked freshly to arize
From th' earth, and from her wombe new spirits to reprize.

45

He then remembred well, that had bene sayd,
How th' Earth his mother was, and first him bore;
She eke so often as his life decayd,
Did life with usury to him restore,
And raysd him up much stronger then before,
So soone as he unto her wombe did fall;
Therefore to ground he would him cast no more,
Ne him committ to grave terrestriall,
But beare him farre from hope of succour usuall.

46

Tho up he caught him twixt his puissant hands,
And having scruzd out of his carrion corse
The lothfull life, now loosd from sinfull bands,
Upon his shoulders carried him perforse
Above three furlongs, taking his full course,
Until he came unto a standing lake;
Him thereinto he threw without remorse,
Ne stird, till hope of life did him forsake;
So end of that Carles dayes, and his owne paines did make.

47

Which when those wicked Hags from farre did spy,
Like two mad dogs they ran about the lands,
And th' one of them with dreadfull yelling cry,
Throwing away her broken chaines and bands,
And having quencht her burning fier brands,
Hedlong her selfe did cast into that lake;
But *Impotence* with her owne wilfull hands,
One of *Malegers* cursed darts did take,
So riv'd her trembling hart, and wicked end did make.

48

Thus now alone he conquerour remaines;
Tho comming to his Squire, that kept his steed,
Thought to have mounted, but his feeble vaines
Him faild thereto, and served not his need,
Through losse of bloud, which from his wounds did bleed,
That he began to faint, and life decay:
But his good Squire him helping up with speed,
With stedfast hand upon his horse did stay,
And led him to the Castle by the beaten way.

49

Where many Groomes and Squiers readie were,
  To take him from his steed full tenderly,
  And eke the fairest *Alma* met him there
  With blame and wine and costly spicery,
  To comfort him in his infirmity;
  Eftesoones she causd him up to be convayd,
  And of his armes despoyled easily,
  In sumptuous bed she made him to be layd,
And al the while his wounds were dressing, by him stayd.

Canto XII

Guyon by Palmers governance,
Passing through perils great,
Doth overthrow the Bowre of blisse,
And Acrasie defeat.

I

Now gins this goodly frame of Temperance
    Fairely to rise, and her adorned hed
    To pricke of highest praise forth to advance,
    Formerly grounded and setteled
    On firme foundation of true bountihed;
    And this brave knight, that for this vertue fights,
    Now comes to point of that same perilous sted,
    Where Pleasure dwelles in sensuall delights,
Mongst thousand dangers, and ten thousand magick mights.

2

Two dayes now in that sea he sayled has,
    Ne ever land beheld, ne living wight,
    Ne ought save perill still as he did pas:
    Tho when appeared the third *Morrow* bright,
    Upon the waves to spred her trembling light,
    An hideous roaring farre away they heard,
    That all their senses filled with affright,
    And streight they saw the raging surges reard
Up to the skyes, that them of drowning made affeard.

3

Said then the Boteman, 'Palmer stere aright,
    And keepe an even course; for yonder way
    We needes must pas (God do us well acquight,)
    That is the *Gulfe of Greedinesse*, they say,
    That deepe engorgeth all this worldes pray:
    Which having swallowd up excessively,
    He soone in vomit up againe doth lay,
    And belcheth forth his superfluity,
That all the seas for feare do seeme away to fly.

4

'On th'other side an hideous Rocke is pight
    Of mightie *Magnes* stone, whose craggie clift
    Depending from on high, dreadfull to sight,
    Over the waves his rugged armes doth lift,
    And threatneth downe to throw his ragged rift

On who so cometh nigh; yet nigh it drawes
All passengers, that none from it can shift:
For whiles they fly that Gulfes devouring jawes,
They on this rock are rent, and sunck in helples wawes.'

5

Forward they passe, and strongly he them rowes,
    Untill they nigh unto that Gulfe arrive,
    Where streame more violent and greedy growes:
    Then he with all his puissance doth strive
    To strike his oares, and mightily doth drive
    The hollow vessell through the threatfull wave,
    Which gaping wide, to swallow them alive,
    In th' huge abysse of his engulfing grave,
Doth rore at them in vaine, and with great terrour rave.

6

They passing by, that griesly mouth did see,
    Sucking the seas into his entralles deepe,
    That seem'd more horrible then hell to bee,
    Or that darke dreadfull hole of *Tartare* steepe,
    Through which the damned ghosts doen often creepe
    Backe to the world, bad livers to torment:
    But nought that falles into this direfull deepe,
    Ne that approcheth nigh the wide descent,
May backe returne, but is condemned to be drent.

7

On th'other side, they saw that perilous Rocke,
    Threatning it selfe on them to ruinate,
    On whose sharp clifts the ribs of vessels broke,
    And shivered ships, which had beene wrecked late,
    Yet stuck, with carkasses exanimate
    Of such, as having all their substance spent
    In wanton joyes, and lustes intemperate,
    Did afterwards make shipwrack violent,
Both of their life, and fame for ever fowly blent.

8

For thy, this hight *The Rocke of* vile *Reproch*,
    A daungerous and detestable place,
    To which nor fish nor fowle did once approch,
    But yelling Meawes, with Seagulles hoarse and bace,
    And Cormoyrants with birds of ravenous race,
    Which still sate waiting on that wastfull clift,

For spoyle of wretches, whose unhappie cace,
  After lost credite and consumed thrift,
At last them driven hath to this despairefull drift.

9

The Palmer seeing them in safetie past,
  Thus saide: 'behold th' ensamples in our sights,
  Of lustfull luxurie and thriftlesse wast:
  What now is left of miserable wights,
  Which spent their looser daies in lewd delights,
  But shame and sad reproch, here to be red,
  By these rent reliques, speaking their ill plights?
  Let all that live, hereby be counselled,
To shunne *Rocke of Reproch*, and it as death to dred.'

10

So forth they rowed, and that *Ferryman*
  With his stiffe oares did brush the sea so strong,
  That the hoare waters from his frigot ran,
  And the light bubbles daunced all along,
  Whiles the salt brine out of the billowes sprong.
  At last farre off they many Islands spy,
  On every side floting the floods emong:
  Then said the knight, 'Lo I the land descry,
Therefore old Syre thy course do thereunto apply.'

11

'That may not be,' said then the *Ferryman*
  'Least we unweeting hap to be fordonne:
  For those same Islands, seeming now and than,
  Are not firme lande, nor any certein wonne,
  But straggling plots, which to and fro do ronne
  In the wide waters: therefore are they hight
  The *wandring Islands*.   Therefore doe them shonne;
  For they have ofte drawne many a wandring wight
Into most deadly daunger and distressed plight.

12

'Yet well they seeme to him, that farre doth vew,
  Both faire and fruitfull, and the ground dispred
  With grassie greene of delectable hew,
  And the tall trees with leaves apparelled,
  Are deckt with blossomes dyde in white and red,
  The mote the passengers thereto allure;
  But whosoever once hath fastened

His foot thereon, may never it recure,
But wandreth evermore uncertein and unsure.

13

'As th' Isle of *Delos* whylome men report
  Amid th' *Aegæn* sea long time did stray,
  Ne made for shipping any certaine port,
  Till that *Latona* traveiling that way,
  Flying from *Junoes* wrath and hard assay,
  Of her faire twins was there delivered,
  Which afterwards did rule the night and day;
  Thenceforth it firmely was established,
And for *Apolloes* honor highly herried.'

14

They to him hearken, as beseemeth meete,
  And passe on forward: so their way does ly,
  That one of those same Islands, which doe fleet
  In the wide sea, they needes must passen by,
  Which seemd so sweet and pleasant to the eye,
  That it would tempt a man to touchen there:
  Upon the banck they sitting did espy
  A daintie damzell, dressing of her heare,
By whom a little skippet floting did appeare.

15

She them espying, loud to them can call,
  Bidding them nigher draw unto the shore;
  For she had cause to busie them withall;
  And therewith loudly laught: But nathemore
  Would they once turne, but kept on as afore:
  Which when she saw, she left her lockes undight,
  And running to her boat withouten ore
  From the departing land it launched light,
And after them did drive with all her power and might.

16

Whom overtaking, she in merry sort
  Them gan to bord, and purpose diversly,
  Now faining dalliance and wanton sport,
  Now throwing forth lewd words immodestly;
  Till that the Palmer gan full bitterly
  Her to rebuke for being loose and light:
  Which not abiding, but more scornefully
  Scoffing at him, that did her justly wite,
She turnd her bote about, and from them rowed quite.

17

That was the wanton *Phædria* which late   *Phaedria*
    Did ferry him over the *Idle lake*:
    Whom nought regarding, they kept on their gate,
    And all her vaine allurements did forsake,
    When them the wary Boateman thus bespake;
    'Here now behoveth us well to avyse,
    And of our safetie good heede to take;
    For here before a perlous passage lyes,
Where many Mermayds haunt, making false melodies.

18

'But by the way, there is a great Quicksand,
    And a whirlpoole of hidden jeopardy,
    Therefore, Sir Palmer, keepe an even hand;
    For twixt them both the narrow way doth ly.'
    Scarse had he said, when hard at hand they spy
    That quicksand nigh with water covered;
    But by the checked wave they did descry
    It plaine, and by the sea discoloured:
It called was the quicksand of *Unthriftyhed*.

19

They passing by, a goodly Ship did see
    Laden from far with precious merchandize,
    And bravely furnished as ship might bee,
    Which through great disaventure, or mesprize,
    Her selfe had ronne into that hazardize;
    Whose mariners and merchants with much toyle,
    Labour'd in vaine, to have recur'd their prize,
    And the rich wares to save from pitteous spoyle,
But neither toyle nor travell might her backe recoyle.

20

On th' other side they see that perilous Poole,
    That called was the *Whirlepoole of decay*,
    In which full many had with haplesse doole
    Beene suncke, of whom no memorie did stay:
    Whose circled waters rapt with whirling sway,
    Like to a restlesse wheele, still running round,
    Did covet, as they passed by that way,
    To draw their boate within the utmost bound
Of his wide *Labyrinth*, and then to have them dround.

21

But th' heedful Boateman strongly forth did stretch
    His brawnie armes, and all his body straine,
    That th' utmost sandy breach they shortly fetch,
    Whiles the dred daunger does behind remaine.
    Suddeine they see from midst of all the Maine,
    The surging waters like a mountaine rise,
    And the great sea puft up with proud disdaine,
    To swell above the measure of his guise,
As threatning to devoure all, that his powre despise.

22

The waves come rolling, and the billowes rore
    Outragiously, as they enraged were,
    Or wrathfull *Neptune* did them drive before
    His whirling charet, for exceeding feare:
    For not one puffe of wind there did appeare,
    That all the three thereat woxe much afrayd,
    Unweeting what such horrour straunge did reare.
    Eftsoones they saw an hideous hoast arrayd,
Of huge Sea monsters, such as living sence dismayd.

23

Most ugly shapes, and horrible aspects,
    Such as Dame Nature selfe mote feare to see,
    Or shame, that ever should so fowle defects
    From her most cunning hand escaped bee;
    All dreadfull pourtraicts of deformitee:
    Spring-headed *Hydraes* and sea-shouldring Whales,
    Great whirlpooles, which all fishes make to flee,
    Bright Scolopendraes, arm'd with silver scales,
Mighty *Monoceroses*, with immeasured tayles.

24

The dreadful Fish, that hath deserv'd the name
    Of Death, and like him lookes in dreadfull hew,
    The griesly Wasserman, that makes his game
    The flying ships with swiftnesse to pursew,
    The horrible Sea-satyre, that doth shew
    His fearefull face in time of greatest storme,
    Huge *Ziffius*, whom Mariners eschew
    No lesse, then rockes, (as travellers informe,)
And greedy *Rosmarines* with visages deforme.

25

All these, and thousand thousands many more,
 And more deformed Monsters thousand fold,
 With dreadfull noise, and hollow rombling rore,
 Came rushing in the fomy waves enrold,
 Which seem'd to fly for feare them to behold:
 Ne wonder, if these did the knight appall;
 For all that here on earth we dreadfull hold,
 Be but as bugs to fearen babes withall,
Compared to the creatures in the seas entrall.

26

'Feare nought,' (then said the Palmer well aviz'd;)
 'For these same Monsters are not these in deed,
 But are into these fearefull shapes disguiz'd
 By that same witch, to worke us dreed,
 And draw from on this journey to proceede.
 Tho lifting up his vertuous staffe on hye,
 He smote the sea, which calmed was with speed,
 And all that dreadfull Armie fast gan flye
Into great *Tethys* bosome, where they hidden lye.

27

Quit from that daunger forth their course they kept;
 And as they went, they heard a ruefull cry
 Of one, that wayld and pittifully wept,
 That through the sea resounding plaints did fly:
 At last they in an Island did espy
 A seemely Maiden, sitting by the shore,
 That with great sorrow and sad agony,
 Seemed some great misfortune to deplore,
And lowd to them for succour called evermore.

28

Which *Guyon* hearing, streight his Palmer bad,
 To stere the boate towards that dolefull Mayd,
 That he might know, and ease her sorrow sad:
 Who him avizing better, to him sayd;
 'Faire Sir, be not displeasd, if disobayd:
 For ill it were to hearken to her cry;
 For she is inly nothing ill apayd,
 But onely womanish fine forgery,
Your stubborne hart t'affect with fraile infirmity.

29

'To which when she your courage hath inclind
    Through foolish pitty, then her guilefull bayt
    She will embosome deeper in your mind,
    And for your ruine at the last awayt.'
    The knight was ruled, and the Boateman strayt
    Held on his course with stayed stedfastnesse,
    Ne ever shruncke, ne ever sought to bayt
    His tyred armes for toylesome wearinesse,
But with his oares did sweepe the watry wildernesse.

30

And now they nigh approched to the sted
    Whereas those Mermayds dwelt: it was a still
    And calmy bay, on th' one side sheltered
    With the brode shadow of an hoarie hill,
    On th'other side an high rocke toured still,
    That twixt them both a pleasaunt port they made,
    And did like an halfe Theatre fulfill:
    There those five sisters had continuall trade,
And usd to bath themselves in that deceiptfull shade.

Mermaids

31

They were faire Ladies, till they fondly striv'd
    With th' *Heliconian* maides for maistery;
    Of whom they over-comen, were depriv'd
    Of their proud beautie, and th' one moyity
    Transform'd to fish, for their bold surquedry,
    But th' upper halfe their hew retained still,
    And their sweet skill in wonted melody;
    Which ever after they abusd to ill,
T' allure weake travellers, whom gotten they did kill.

beauty
deprived

32

So now to *Guyon*, as he passed by,
    Their pleasant tunes they sweetly thus applide;
    'O thou faire sonne of gentle Faery,
    That art in mighty armes most magnifide
    Above all knights, that ever battell tride,
    O turne thy rudder hither-ward a while:
    Here may thy storme-bet vessell safely ride;
    This is the Port of rest from troublous toyle,
The worlds sweet In, from paine and wearisome turmoyle.'

flattery
to lure

33

With that the rolling sea resounding soft,
   In his big base them fitly answered,
   And on the rocke the waves breaking aloft,
   A solemne Meane unto them measured,
   The whiles sweet *Zephirus* lowd whisteled
   His treble, a straunge kinde of harmony;
   Which *Guyons* senses softly tickeled,
   That he the boateman bad row easily,
And let him heare some part of their rare melody.

34

But him the Palmer from that vanity
   With temperate advice discounselled,
   That they it past, and shortly gan descry
   The land, to which their course they leveled;
   When suddeinly a grosse fog over spred
   With his dull vapour all that desert has,
   And heavens chearefull face enveloped,
   That all things one, and one as nothing was,
And this great Universe seemd one confused mas.

35

Thereat they greatly were dismayd, ne wist
   How to direct their way in darkenesse wide,
   But feard to wander in that wastfull mist,
   For tombling into mischiefe unespide.
   Worse is the daunger hidden, then descride.
   Suddeinly an innumerable flight
   Of harmefull fowles about them fluttering, cride,
   And with their wicked wings them oft did smight,
And sore annoyed, groping in that griesly night.

36

Even all the nation of unfortunate
   And fatall birds about them flocked were,
   Such as by nature men abhorre and hate,
   The ill-faste Owle, deaths dreadfull messengere,
   The hoars Night-raven, trump of dolefull drere,
   The lether-winged Bat, dayes enimy,
   The ruefull Strich, still waiting on the bere,
   The Whistler shrill, that who so heares, doth dy,
The hellish Harpies, prophets of sad destiny.

37

All those, and all that els does horrour breed,
    About them flew, and fild their sayles with feare:
    Yet stayd they not, but forward did proceed,
    Whiles th' one did row, and th' other stifly steare;
    Till that at last the weather gan to cleare,
    And the faire land it selfe did plainly show.
    Said then the Palmer, 'Lo where does appeare
    The sacred soile, where all our perils grow;
Therefore, Sir knight, your ready armes about you throw.'

38

He hearkned, and his armes about him tooke,
    The whiles the nimble boate so well her sped,
    That with her crooked keele the land she strooke,
    Then forth the noble *Guyon* sallied,
    And his sage Palmer, that him governed;
    But th' other by his boate behind did stay.
    They marched fairly forth, of nought ydred,
    Both firmely armd for every hard assay,
With constancy and care, gainst daunger and dismay.

39

Ere long they heard an hideous bellowing
    Of many beasts, that roard outrageously,
    As if that hungers point, or *Venus* sting
    Had them enraged with fell surquedry:
    Yet nought they feard, but past on hardily,
    Untill they came in vew of those wild beasts:
    Who all attonce, gaping full greedily,
    And rearing fercely their upstaring crests,
Ran towards, to devoure those unexpected guests.

40

But soone as they approcht with deadly threat,
    The Palmer over them his staffe upheld,
    His mighty staffe, that could all charmes defeat.
    Eftsoons their stubborne courages were queld,
    And high advaunced crests downe meekely feld,
    In stead of fraying, they them selves did feare,
    And trembled as them passing they beheld:
    Such wondrous powre did in that staffe appeare,
All monsters to subdew to him, that did it beare.

41

Of that same wood it fram'd was cunningly,
   Of which *Caduceus* whilome was made,
   Caduceus the rod of *Mercury*,
   With which he wonts the *Stygian* realmes invade,
   Through ghastly horrour and eternall shade;
   Th' infernall feends with it he can asswage,
   And *Orcus* tame, whom nothing can perswade,
   And rule the *Furyes*, when they most do rage:
Such vertue in his staffe had eke this Palmer sage.

42

Thence passing forth, they shortly do arrive,
   Whereas the Bowre of *Blisse* was situate;
   A place pickt out by choice of best alive,
   That natures worke by art can imitate:
   In which what ever in this worldly state
   Is sweet, and pleasing unto living sense,
   Or that may dayntiest fantasy aggrate,
   Was poured forth with plentifull dispence,
And made there to abound with lavish affluence.

43

Goodly it was enclosed round about,
   As well their entred guestes to keep within,
   As those unruly beasts to hold without;
   Yet was the fence thereof but weake and thin;
   Nought feard their force that fortilage to win,
   But wisedomes powre, and temperaunces might,
   By which the mightiest things efforced bin:
   And eke the gate was wrought of substaunce light,
Rather for pleasure, then for battery or fight.

44

Yt framed was of precious yvory,
   That seemd a worke of admirable wit;
   And therein all the famous history
   Of *Jason* and *Medæa* was ywrit;
   Her mighty charmes, her furious loving fit.
   His goodly conquest of the golden fleece,
   His falsed faith, and love too lightly flit,
   The wondred *Argo*, which in venturous peece
First through the *Euxine* seas bore all the flowr of *Greece*.

45

Ye might have seene the frothy billowes fry
   Under the ship, as thorough them she went,
   That seemd the waves were into yvory,
   Or yvory into the waves were sent;
   And other where the snowy substaunce sprent
   With vermell, like the boyes bloud therein shed,
   A piteous spectacle did represent,
   And otherwhiles with gold besprinkeled;
Yt seemd th' enchaunted flame, which did *Creusa* wed.

46

All this, and more might in that goodly gate
   Be red; that ever open stood to all,
   Which thither came: but in the Porch there sate
   A comely personage of stature tall,
   And semblaunce pleasing, more than naturall,
   That travellers to him seemd to entize;
   His looser garment to the ground did fall,
   And flew about his heeles in wanton wize,
Not fit for speedy pace, or manly exercize.

47

They in that place him *Genius* did call:
   Not that celestiall powre, to whom the care
   Of life, and generation of all
   That lives, pertaines in charge particulare,
   Who wondrous things concerning our welfare,
   And straunge phantomes doth let us oft forsee,
   And oft of secret ill bids us beware:
   That is our Selfe, whom though we do not see,
Yet each doth in him selfe it well perceive to bee.

48

Therefore a God him sage Antiquity
   Did wisely make, and good *Agdistes* call:
   But this same was to that quite contrary,
   The foe of life, that good envyes to all,
   That secretly doth us procure to fall,
   Through guilefull semblaunts, which he makes us see.
   He of this Gardin had the governall,
   And Pleasures porter was devizd to bee,
Holding a staffe in hand for mere formalitee.

49

With diverse flowres he daintily was deckt,
  And strowed round about, and by his side
  A mighty Mazer bowle of wine was set,
  As if it had to him bene sacrifide;
  Wherewith all new-come guests he gratifide:
  So did he eke Sir *Guyon* passing by:
  But he his idle curtesie defide,
  And overthrew his bowle disdainfully;
And broke his staffe with which he charmed semblants sly.

50

Thus being entred, they behold around
  A large and spacious plaine, on every side
  Strowed with pleasauns, whose faire grassy ground
  Mantled with greene, and goodly beautifide
  With all the ornaments of *Floraes* pride,
  Wherewith her mother Art, as halfe in scorne
  Of niggard Nature, like a pompous bride
  Did decke her, and too lavishly adorne,
When forth from virgin bowre she comes in th' early morne.

51

Thereto the Heavens alwayes Joviall,
  Lookt on them lovely, still in stedfast state,
  Ne suffred storme nor frost on them to fall,
  Their tender buds or leaves to violate,
  Nor scorching heat, nor cold intemperate
  T' afflict the creatures which therein did dwell,
  But the milde aire with season moderate
  Gently attempred, and disposd so well,
That still it breathed forth sweet spirit and holesome smell.

52

More sweet and holesome, then the pleasaunt hill
  Of *Rhodope*, on which the Nimphe, that bore
  A gyaunt babe, heselfe for griefe did kill;
  Or the Thessalian *Tempe*, where of yore
  Faire *Daphne Phœbus* hart with love did gore;
  Or *Ida*, where the Gods lov'd to repaire,
  When ever they their heavenly bowres forlore;
  Or sweet *Parnasse*, the haunt of Muses faire;
Or *Eden* selfe, if ought with *Eden* mote compaire.

53

Much wondred *Guyon* at the faire aspect
  Of that sweet place, yet suffred no delight
  To sincke into his sence, nor mind affect,
  But passed forth, and lookt still forward right,
  Bridling his will and maistering his might:
  Till that he came unto another gate;
  No gate, but like one, being goodly dight
  With boughes and braunches, which did broad dilate
Their clasping armes, in wanton wreathings intricate.

54

So fashioned a Porch with rare device,
  Archt over head with an embracing vine,
  Whose bounches hanging downe, seemd to entice
  All passers by, to tast their lushious wine,
  And did them selves into their hands incline,
  As freely offering to be gathered:
  Some deepe empurpled as the *Hyacint*,
  Some as the Rubine, laughing sweetly red,
Some like faire Emeraudes, not yet well ripened.

55

And them amongst, some were of burnisht gold,
  So made by art, to beautifie the rest,
  Which did themselves emongst the leaves enfold,
  As lurking from the vew of covetous guest,
  That the weake bowes, with so rich load opprest,
  Did bow adowne, as over-burdened.
  Under that Porch a comely dame did rest,
  Clad in faire weedes, but fowle disordered,
And garments loose, that seemd unmeet for womanhed.

56

In her left hand a Cup of gold she held,
  And with her right the riper fruit did reach,
  Whose sappy liquor, that with fulnesse sweld,
  Into her cup she scruzd, with daintie breach
  Of her fine fingers, without fowle empeach,
  That so faire wine-presse made the wine more sweet:
  Thereof she usd to give to drinke to each,
  Whom passing by she happened to meet:
It was her guise, all Straungers goodly so to greet.

57

So she to *Guyon* offred it to tast;
 Who taking it out of her tender hond,
 The cup to ground did violently cast,
 That all in peeces it was broken fond,
 And with the liquor stained all the lond:
 Whereat *Excesse* exceedingly was wroth,
 Yet no'te the same amend, ne yet withstond,
 But suffered him to passe, all were she loth;
Who nought regarding her displeasure forward goth.

58

There the most daintie Paradise on ground,
 It selfe doth offer to his sober eye,
 In which all pleasures plenteously abound,
 And none does others happinesse envye:
 The painted flowres, the trees upshooting hye,
 The dales for shade, the hilles for breathing space,
 The trembling groves, the Christall running by;
 And that, which all faire workes doth most aggrace,
The art, which all that wrought, appeared in no place.

59

One would have thought, (so cunningly, the rude,
 And scorned parts were mingled with the fine,)
 That nature had for wantonesse ensude
 Art, and that Art at nature did repine;
 So striving each th' other to undermine,
 Each did the others worke more beautifie;
 So diff'ring both in willes, agreed in fine:
 So all agreed through sweete diversitie,
This Gardin to adorne with all varietie.

60

And in the midst of all, a fortaine stood,   *fountain*
 Of richest substaunce, that on earth might bee,
 So pure and shiny, that the silver flood
 Through every channell running one might see;
 Most goodly it with curious imageree
 Was over-wrought, and shapes of naked boyes,
 Of which some seemd with lively jollitee,
 To fly about, playing their wanton toyes,
Whilest others did them selves embay in liquid joyes.

61

And over all, of purest gold was spred,
   A trayle of yvie in his native hew:
   For the rich mettall was so coloured,
   That wight, who did not well avis'd it vew,
   Would surely deeme it to bee yvie trew:
   Low his lascivious armes adown did creepe,
   That themselves dipping in the silver dew,
   Their fleecy flowres they fearefully did steepe,
Which drops of Christall seemd for wantones to weepe.

62

Infinit streames continually did well
   Out of this fountaine, sweet and faire to see,
   The which into an ample laver fell,
   And shortly grew into so great quantitie,
   That like a little lake it seemd to bee;
   Whose depth exceeded not three cubits hight,
   That through the waves one might the bottom see,
   All pav'd beneath with Jaspar shining bright,
That seemd the fountaine in that sea did sayle upright.

63

And all the margent round about was set,
   With shady Laurell trees, thence to defend
   The sunny beames, which on the billowes bet,
   And those which therein bathed, mote offend.
   As *Guyon* hapned by the same to wend,
   Two naked Damzelles he therein espyde,
   Which therein bathing, seemed to contend,
   And wrestle wantonly, ne car'd to hyde,
Their dainty partes from vew of any, which them eyde.

64

Sometimes the one would lift the other quight
   Above the waters, and then downe againe
   Her plong, as over maistered by might,
   Were both a while would covered remaine,
   And each the other from to rise restraine;
   The whiles their snowy limbes, as through a vele,
   So through the Christall waves appeared plaine:
   Then suddeinly both would themselves unhele,
And th' amarous sweet spoiles to greedy eyes revele.

65

As that faire Starre, the messenger of morne,
   His deawy face out of the sea doth reare:
Or as the *Cyprian* goddesse, newly borne
Of th' Ocean's fruitfull froth, did first appeare:
Such seemed they, and so their yellow heare
Christalline humor dropped downe apace.
   Whom such when *Guyon* saw, he drew him neare,
   And somewhat gan relent his earnest pace,
His stubborne brest gan secret plesaunce to embrace.

66

The wanton Maidens him espying, stood
   Gazing a while at his unwonted guise;
Then th' one her selfe low ducked in the flood,
Abasht, that her a straunger did a vise:
But th' other rather higher did arise,
And her two lilly paps aloft displayd,
   And all, that might his melting hart entise
   To her delights, she unto him bewrayd:
The rest hid underneath, him more desirous made.

67

With that, the other likewise up arose,
   And her faire lockes, which formerly were bownd
Up in one knot, she low adowne did lose:
Which flowing low and thick, her cloth'd arownd,
And th' yvorie in golden mantle gownd:
So that faire spectacle from him was reft,
   Yet that, which reft it no lesse faire was fownd:
   So hid in lockes and waves from lookers theft,
Nought but her lovely face she for his looking left.

68

Withall she laughed, and she blusht withall,
   That blushing to her laughter gave more grace,
And laughter to her blushing, as did fall:
Now when they spide the knight to slacke his pace,
Them to behold, and in his sparkling face
The secrete signes of kindled lust appeare,
   Their wanton meriments they did encreace,
   And to him beckned, to approch more neare,
And shewd him many sights, that courage cold could reare.

69

On which when gazing him the Palmer saw,
  He much rebukt those wandring eyes of his,
  And counseld well, him forward thence did draw.
  Now are they come nigh to the *Bowre of blis*
  Of her fond favorites so nam'd amis:
  When thus the Palmer; 'Now Sir, well avise;
  For here the end of all our travell is:
  Here wonnes *Acrasia*, whom we must surprise,
Else she will slip away, and all our drift despise.'

70

Eftsoones they heard a most melodious sound,
  Of all that mote delight a daintie eare,
  Such as attonce might not on living ground,
  Save in this Paradise, be heard elsewhere:
  Right hard it was, for wight which did it heare,
  To read, what manner musicke that mote bee:
  For all that pleasing is to living eare,
  Was there consorted in one harmonee,
Birdes, voyces, instruments, windes, waters, all agree.

Birds

71

The joyous birdes shrouded in chearefull shade
  Their notes unto the voyce attempred sweet;
  Th' Angelicall soft trembling voyces made
  To th' instruments divine respondence meet:
  The silver sounding instruments did meet
  With the base murmure of the waters fall:
  The waters fall with difference discreet,
  Now soft, now loud, unto the wind did call:
The gentle warbling wind low answered to all.

72

There, whence that Musick seemed heard to bee,
  Was the faire Witch her selfe now solacing,
  With a new Lover, whom through sorceree
  And witchcraft, she from farre did thither bring:
  There she had him now layd a slombering,
  In secret shade, after long wanton joyes:
  Whilst round about them pleasauntly did sing
  Many faire Ladies, and lascivious boyes,
That ever mixt their song with light licentious toyes.

73

And all that while, right over him she hong,
 With her false eyes fast fixed in his sight,
 As seeking medicine, whence she was stong,
 Or greedily depasturing delight:
 And oft inclining downe with kisses light,
 For feare of waking him, his lips bedewd,
 And through his humid eyes did sucke his spright,
 Quite molten into lust and pleasure lewd;
Wherewith she sighed soft, as if his case she rewd.

74

The whiles some one did chaunt this lovely lay;
 'Ah see, who so faire thing doest faine to see,
 In springing flowre the image of thy day;
 Ah see the Virgin Rose, how sweetly shee
 Doth first peepe forth with bashfull modestee,
 That fairer seemes, the lesse ye see her may;
 Lo see soone after, how more bold and free
 Her bared bosome she doth broad display;
Lo see soone after, how she fades, and falles away.

75

'So passeth, in the passing of a day,
 Of mortall life the leafe, the bud, the flowre,
 Ne more doth flourish after first decay,
 That earst was sought to decke both bed and bowre,
 Of many a Ladie, and many a Paramowre:
 Gather therefore the Rose, whilest yet is prime,
 For soone comes age, that will her pride deflowre:
 Gather the Rose of love, whilest yet is time,
Whilest loving thou mayst loved be with equall crime.'

76

He ceast, and then gan all the quire of birdes
 Their diverse notes t'attune unto his lay,
 As in approvance of his pleasing words.
 The constant paire heard all that he did say,
 Yet swarved not, but kept their forward way,
 Through many covert groves and thickets close,
 In which they creeping did at last display
 That wanton Ladie, with her lover lose,
Whose sleepie head she in her lap did soft dispose.

77

Upon a bed of Roses she was layd,
　As faint through heat, or dight to pleasant sin,
　And was arayd, or rather disarayd,
　All in a vele of silke and silver thin,
　That hid no whit her alablaster skin,
　But rather shewd more white, if more might bee:
　More subtile web *Arachne* can not spin,
　Nor the fine nets, which oft we woven see
Of scorched deaw, do not in th' aire more lightly flee.

78

Her snowy brest was bare to readie spoyle
　Of hungry eies, which n'ote therewith be fild,
　And yet through languour of her late sweet toyle,
　Few drops, more cleare then Nectar, forth distild,
　That like pure Orient perles adowne it trild,
　And her faire eyes sweet smyling in delight,
　Moystened their fierie beames, with which she thrild
　Fraile harts, yet quenched not; like starry light
Which sparckling on the silent waves, does seeme more bright.

79

The young man sleeping by her, seemd to bee
　Some goodly swayne of honorable place,
　That certes it great pittie was to see
　Him his nobilitie so foule deface;
　A sweet regard, and amiable grace,
　Mixed with manly sternnesse did appeare
　Yet sleeping, in his well proportiond face,
　And on his tender lips the downy heare
Did now but freshly spring, and silken blossoms beare.

80

His warlike armes, the idle instruments
　Of sleeping praise, were hong upon a tree,
　And his brave shield, full of old moniments,
　Was fowly ra'st, that none the signes might see;
　Ne for them, ne for honour cared hee,
　Ne ought, that did to his advauncement tend,
　But in lewd loves, and wastfull luxuree,
　His dayes, his goods, his bodie he did spend:
O horrible enchantment, that him so did blend.

81

The noble Elfe, and carefull Palmer drew
  So nigh them, minding nought, but lustfull game,
  That suddein forth they on them rusht, and threw
  A subtile net, which only for the same
  The skilfull Palmer formally did frame.
  So held them under fast, the whiles the rest
  Fled all away for feare of fowler shame.
  The faire Enchauntresse, so unwares opprest,
Tryde all her arts, and all her sleights, thence out to wrest.

82

And eke her lover strove: but all in vaine;
  For that same net so cunningly was wound,
  That neither guile, nor force might it distraine.
  They tooke them both, and both them strongly bound
  In captives bandes, which there they readie found:
  But her in chaines of adamant he tyde;
  For nothing else might keepe her safe and sound;
  But *Verdant* (so he hight) he soone untyde,
And counsell sage in steed thereof to him applyde.

83

But all those pleasant bowres, and Pallace brave,
  Guyon broke downe with rigour pittilesse;
  Ne ought their goodly workmanship might save
  Them from the tempest of his wrathfulnesse,
  But that their blisse he turn'd to balefulnesse:
  Their groves he feld, their gardins did deface,   *Destroys*
  Their arbers spoyle, their Cabinets suppresse,   *Bower*
  Their banket houses burne, their buildings race,
And of the fairest late, now made the fowlest place.

84

Then led they her away, and eke that knight
  They with them led, both sorrowfull and sad:
  The way they came, the same retourn'd they right,
  Till they arrived, where they lately had
  Charm'd those wild-beasts, that rag'd with furie mad.
  Which now awaking, fierce at them gan fly,
  As in their mistresse reskew, whom they lad;
  But them the Palmer soone did pacify.
Then *Guyon* askt, what meant those beastes, which there did ly.

85

Said he, 'These seeming beasts are men indeed,
  Whom this Enchauntresse hath transformed thus,
  Whylome her lovers, which her lustes did feed,
  Now turned into figures hideous,
  According to their mindes like monstruous.'
  'Sad end' (quoth he) 'of life intemperate,
  And mournefull meed of joyes delicious:
  But Palmer, if it mote thee so aggrate,
Let them returned be unto their former state.'

86

Streight way he with his vertuous staffe them strooke,
  And streight of beasts they comely men became;
  Yet being men they did unmanly looke,
  And stared ghastly, some for inward shame,
  And some for wrath, to see their captive Dame:
  But one above the rest in speciall
  That had an hog beene late, hight *Grille* by name,
  Repyned greatly, and did him miscall,
That had from hoggish forme him brought to naturall.

87

Saide *Guyon*, 'See the mind of beastly man,
  That hath so soone forgot the excellence
  Of his creation, when he life began,
  That now he chooseth with vile difference,
  To be a beast, and lacke intelligence.'
  To whom the Palmer thus, 'The donghill kind
  Delights in filth and foule incontinence:
  Let *Grill* be *Grill*, and have his hoggish mind,
But let us hence depart whilest wether serves and wind.'

THE THIRD BOOKE OF THE
FAERIE QUEENE.

Contayning,

THE LEGENDE OF BRITOMARTIS.

Or

OF CHASTITIE.

It falls me here to write of Chastity,
    That fairest vertue, farre above the rest;
    For which what needs me fetch from *Faery*
    Forreine ensamples, it to have exprest?
    Sith it is shrined in my Soveraines brest,
    And formd so lively in each perfect part,
    That to all Ladies, which have it profest,
    Need but behold the pourtraict of her hart,
If pourtrayd it might be by any living art.

But living art may not least part expresse,
    Nor life-resembling pencill it can paint,
    All were it *Zeuxis* or *Praxiteles*:
    His dædale hand would faile, and greatly faint,
    And her perfections with his error taint:
    Ne Poets wit, that passeth Painter farre
    In picturing the parts of beauty daint,
    So hard a workmanship adventure darre,
For feare through want of words her excellence to marre.

How then shall I, Apprentice of the skill
    That whylome in divinest wits did raine,
    Presume so high to stretch mine humble quill?
    Yet now my lucklesse lott doth me constraine
    Hereto performce.   But O dred Soveraine
    Thus farre forth pardon, sith that choicest wit
    Cannot your glorious portraict figure plaine
    That I in colour showes may shadow it,
And antique praises unto present persons fit.

But if in living colours, and right hew,
    Your selfe you covet to see pictured,
    Who can it doe more lively, or more trew,
    Then that sweete verse, with *Nectar* sprinckeled,

In which a gracious servaunt pictured
His *Cynthia*, his heavens fairest light?
That with his melting sweetnesse ravished,
And with the wonder of her beames bright,
My scenes lulled are in slomber of delight.

But let that same delitious Poet lend
A little leave unto a rusticke Muse
To sing his mistresse prayse, and let him mend,
If ought amis her liking may abuse:
Ne let his fairest *Cynthia* refuse,
In mirrours more then one her selfe to see,
But either *Gloriana* let her chuse,
Or in *Belphœbe* fashioned to bee:
In th' one her rule, in th' other her rare chastitee.

Canto I

Guyon encountreth Britomart,
Faire Florimell is chaced:
Duessaes traines and Malecastaes
Champions are defaced.

1

The famous Briton Prince and Faerie knight,
  After long wayes and perilous paines endured,
  Having their wearie limbes to perfect plight
  Restord, and sory wounds right well recured,
  Of the faire *Alma* greatly were procured,
  To make there lenger sojourne and abode;
  But when thereto they might not be allured,
  From seeking praise, and deeds of armes abrode,
They courteous conge tooke, and forth together yode.

2

But the captiv'd *Acrasia* he sent,
  Because of travell long, a nigher way,
  With a strong gard, all reskew to prevent,
  And her to Faerie court safe to convay,
  That her for witnesse of his hard assay
  Unto his *Faerie* Queene he might present:
  But he himselfe betooke another way,
  To make more triall of his hardiment,
And seek adventures, as he with Prince *Arthur* went.

3

Long so they travelled through wastefull wayes,
  Where daungers dwelt, and perils most did wonne,
  To hunt for glorie and renowmed praise.
  Full many Countries they did overronne,
  From the uprising to the setting Sunne,
  And many hard adventures did atchieve;
  Of all the which they honour ever wonne,
  Seeking the weake oppressed to relieve,
And to recover right for such, as wrong did grieve.

4

At last as through an open plaine they yode,
  They spide a knight, that towards pricked faire,
  And him beside an aged Squire there rode,
  That seemd to couch under his shield three-square,
  As if that age bad him that burden spare,

And yield it those, that stouter could it wield:
He them espying, gan himselfe prepare,
And on his arme addresse his goodly shield
That bore a Lion passant in a golden field.

5

Which seeing good Sir *Guyon*, deare besought
　The Prince of grace, to let him ronne that turne.
He graunted: then the Faery quickly raught
His poinant speare, and sharpely gan to spurne
His fomy steed, whose fierie feet did burne
The verdant grasse, as he thereon did tread;
Ne did the other backe his foote returne,
But fiercely forward came withouten dread,
And bent his dreadfull speare against the others head.

6

They bene ymet, and both their points arrived,
　But *Guyon* drove so furious and fell,
That seem'd both shield and plate it would have rived;
Nathelesse it bore his foe not from his sell,
But made him stagger, as he were not well:
But *Guyon* selfe, ere well he was aware,
Nigh a speares length behind his crouper fell,
Yet in his fall so well him selfe he bare,
That mischievous mischance his life and limbes did spare.

7

Great shame and sorrow of that fall he tooke;
　For never yet, sith warlike armes he bore
And shivering speare in bloudie field first shooke,
He found himselfe dishonored so sore.
Ah gentlest knight, that ever armour bore,
Let not thee grieve dismounted to have beene,
And brought to ground that never wast before;
For not thy fault, but secret powre unseene,
That speare enchaunted was, which layd thee on the greene.

8

But weenedst thou what wight thee overthrew,
　Much greater griefe and shamefuller regret
For thy hard fortune then thou wouldst renew,
That of a single damzell thou wert met
On equall plaine, and there so hard beset;
Even the famous *Britomart* it was,

Whom straunge adventure did from *Britaine* fet,
   To seeke her lover (love farre sought alas)
Whose image she had seene in *Venus* looking glas.

9

Full of disdainefull wrath he fierce uprose
   For to revenge that foule reprochfull shame,
   And snatching his bright sword began to close
   With her on foot, and stoutly forward came;
   Die rather would he, then endure that same.
   Which when his Palmer saw, he gan to feare
   His toward perill, and untoward blame,
   Which by that new rencounter he should reare;
For death sate on the point of that enchaunted speare.

10

And hasting towards him gan faire perswade,
   Not to provoke misfortune, nor to weene
   His speares default to mend with cruell blade;
   For by his mightie Science he had seene
   The secret vertue of that weapon keene,
   That mortall puissance mote not withstond:
   Nothing on earth mote alwaies happie beene.
   Great hazard were it, and adventure fond,
To loose long gotten honour with one evill hond.

11

By such good meanes he him discounselled,
   From prosecuting his revenging rage:
   And eke the Prince like treaty handeled,
   His wrathfull will with reason to asswage,
   And laid the blame, not to his carriage,
   But to his starting steed that swarv'd asyde,
   And to the ill purveyance of his page,
   That had his furnitures not firmely tyde:
So is his angry courage fairely pacifyde.

12

Thus reconcilement was betweene them knit,
   Through goodly temperance and affection chaste,
   And either vowd with all their power and wit
   To let not others honour be defaste,
   Of friend or foe, who ever it embaste,
   Ne armes to beare against the others syde:
   In which accord the Prince was also plaste,

And with that golden chaine of concord tyde.
So goodly all agreed, they forth yfere did ryde.

13

O goodly usage of those antique times,
   In which the sword was servant unto right;
   When not for malice and contentious crimes,
   But all for praise, and proofe of manly might,
   The martiall brood accustomed to fight:
   Then honour was the meed of victorie
   And yet the vanquished had no despight:
   Let later age that noble use envie
Vile rancour to avoid and cruel surquedrie.

14

Long they thus travelled in friendly wise,
   Through countries waste, and eke well edifyde,
   Seeking adventures hard, to exercise
   Their puissance, whylome full dernly tryde:
   At length they came into a forest wyde,
   Whose hideous horror and sad trembling sound
   Full griesly seem'd: Therein they long did ryde,
   Yet tract of living creature none they found,
Save Beares, Lions, and Buls, which romed them around.

15

All suddenly out of the thickest brush,
   Upon a milk-white Palfrey all alone,
   A goodly Ladie did foreby them rush,
   Whose face did seeme as cleare as Christall stone,
   And eke through feare as white as whales bone:
   Her garments all were wrought of beaten gold,
   And all her steed with tinsell trappings shone,
   Which fled so fast, that nothing mote him hold,
And scarse them leasure gave, her passing to behold.

16

Still as she fled, her eye she backward threw,
   As fearing evill, that pursewd her fast;
   And her faire yellow locks behind her flew,
   Loosely disperst with puff of every blast:
   All as a blazing starre doth farre outcast
   His hearie beames, and flaming lockes dispred,
   At sight whereof the people stand aghast:
   But the sage wisard telles, as he has red,
That it importunes death and dolefull drerihed.

17

So as they gazed after her a while,
  Lo where a griesly Foster forth did rush,
  Breathing out beastly lust her to defile:
  His tyreling jade he fiercely forth did push,
  Through thicke and thin, both over banke and bush
  In hope her to attaine by hooke or crooke,
  That from his gorie sides the bloud did gush.
  Large were his limbes, and terrible his looke,
And his clownish hand a sharp bore sheare he shooke.

18

Which outrage when those gentle knights did see,
  Full of great envie and fell gealosy,
  They stayd not to avise, who first should bee,
  But all spurd after fast, as they mote fly,
  To reskew her from shamefull villany.
  The Prince and *Guyon* equally bylive
  Her selfe pursewd, in hope to win thereby
  Most goodly meede, the fairest Dame alive:
But after the foule foster Timias did strive.

19

The whiles faire *Britomart*, whose constant mind,
  Would not so lightly follow beauties chace,
  Ne reckt of Ladies Love, did stay behind,
  And them awayted there a certaine space,
  To weet if they would turne backe to that place:
  But when she saw them gone, she forward went,
  As lay her journey, through that perlous Pace,
  With stedfast courage and stout hardiment:
Ne evil thing she feard, ne evill thing she ment.

20

At last as nigh out of the wood she came,
  A stately Castle farre away she spyde,
  To which her steps directly she did frame.
  That Castle was most goodly edifyde,
  And plaste for pleasure nigh that forrest syde:
  But faire before the gate a spatious plaine,
  Mantled with greene, it selfe did spredden wyde,
  On which she saw six knights, that did darraine
Fierce battell against one with cruell might and maine.

21

Mainly they all attonce upon him laid,
  And sore beset on every side around,
  That nigh he breathlesse grew, yet nought dismaid,
  Ne ever to them yielded foot of ground,
  All had he lost much bloud through many a wound,
  But stoutly dealt his blowes, and every way
  To which he turned in his wrathfull stound,
  Made them recoile, and fly from dred decay,
That none of all the sixe before, him durst assay.

22

Like dastard Curres, that having at a bay
  The salvage beast embost in wearie chace,
  Dare not adventure on the stubborne pray,
  Ne byte before, but rome from place to place,
  To get a snatch, when turned is his face.
  In such distresse and doubtfull jeopardy,
  When *Britomart* him saw, she ran a pace
  Unto his reskew, and with earnest cry,
Bad those same sixe forbeare that single enimy.

23

But to her cry they list not lenden eare,
  Ne ought the more their mightie strokes surceasse,
  But gathering him round about more neare,
  Their direfull rancour rather did encreasse;
  Till that she rushing through the thickest preasse,
  Perforce disparted their compacted gyre,
  And soone compeld to hearken unto peace:
  Tho gan she myldly of them to inquyre
The cause of their dissention and outrageous yre.

24

Whereto that single knight did answere frame;
  'These sixe would me enforce by oddes of might
  To chaunge my liefe, and love another Dame,
  That death me liefer were, then such despight,
  So unto wrong to yield my wrested right:
  For I love one, the truest one on ground,
  Ne list me chaunge; she th' *Errant Damzell* hight,
  For whose deare sake full many a bitter stownd,
I had endur'd, and tasted many a bloudy wound.'

25

'Certes' (said she) 'then beene ye sixe to blame,
    To weene your wrong by force to justifie:
    For knight to leave his Ladie were great shame
    That faithfull is, and better were to die.
    All losse is lesse, and lesse the infamie,
    Then losse of love to him that loves but one;
    Ne may love be compeld by maisterie;
    For soone as maisterie comes, sweet love anone
Taketh his nimble wings, and soone away is gone.'

26

Then spake one of those sixe, 'There dwelleth here
    Within this castle wall a Laide faire,
    Whose soveraine beautie hath no living pere,
    Thereto so bounteous and so debonaire,
    That never any mote with her compaire.
    She hath ordaind this law, which we approve,
    That every knight, which doth this way repaire,
    In case he have no Ladie, nor no love,
Shall doe unto her service, never to remove.

27

'But if he have a Ladie or a Love,
    Then must he her forgoe with foule defame,
    Or else with us by dint of sword approve,
    That she is fairer then our fairest Dame,
    As did this knight, before ye hither came.'
    'Perdie' (said *Britomart*) 'the choise is hard:
    But what reward had he that overcame?''
    'He should advaunced be to high regard,'
(Said they) 'and have our Ladies love for his reward.

28

'Therefore a read Sir, if thou have a love.'
    'Love have I sure,' (quoth she) 'but Lady none;
    Yet will I not fro mine own love remove,
    Ne to your Lady will I service done,
    But wreake your wrongs wrought to this knight alone,
    And prove his cause.' With that her mortall speare
    She mightily aventred towards one,
    And downe him smot, ere well aware he weare,
Then to the next she rode, and downe the next did beare.

29

Ne did she stay, till three on ground she layd,
   That none of them himselfe could reare againe;
   The fourth was by that other knight dismayd,
   All were he wearie of his former paine,
   That now there do but two of six remaine;
   Which two yield, before she did them smight.
   'Ah' (said she then) 'now may ye all see plaine,
   That truth is strong, and trew love most of might,
That for his trusty servaunts doth so strongly fight.'

30

'Too well we see,' (said they) 'and prove too well
   Our faulty weaknesse and your matchlesse might:
   For thy, faire Sir, yours be the Damozell,
   Which by her owne law to your lot doth light,
   And we your liege men faith unto you plight.'
   So underneath her feet their swords they mard,
   And after her besought, well as they might,
   To enter in, and reape the dew reward:
She graunted, and then in they all together far'd.

31

Long were it to describe the goodly frame,
   And stately port of *Castle Joyeous*,
   (For so that Castle hight by commune name)
   Where they were entertaind with curteous
   And comely glee of many gracious
   Faire Ladies, and of many a gentle knight,
   Who through a Chamber long and spacious,
   Eftsoones them brought unto their Ladies sight,
That of them cleeped was the *Lady of delight*.

32

But for to tell the sumptuous aray
   Of that great chamber, should be labour lost:
   For living wit, I weene, cannot display
   The royall riches and exceeding cost,
   Of every pillour and of every post;
   Which all of purest bullion frame were,
   And with great pearles and pretious stones embost,
   That the bright sliter of their beames cleare
Did sparckle forth great light, and glorious did appeare.

33

These stranger knights through passing, forth were led
   Into an inner rowme, whose royaltee
   And rich purveyance might uneath be red;
   Mote Princes place beseeme so deckt to bee.
   Which stately manner whenas they did see,
   The image of superfluous riotize,
   Exceeding much the state of meane degree,
   They greatly wondred, whence so sumptuous guize
Might be maintayned, and each gan diversely devize.

34

The wals were round about apparelled
   With costly clothes of *Arras* and of *Toure*,
   In which with cunning hand was pourtrahed
   The love of *Venus* and her Paramoure
   The faire *Adonis*, turned to a flowre,
   A worke of rare device and wondrous wit.
   First did it shew the bitter balefull stowre,
   Which her assayd with many a fervent fit,
When first her tender hart was with his beautie smit.

35

Then with what sleights and sweet allurements she
   Entyst the Boy, as well that art she knew,
   And wooed him her Paramoure to be;
   Now making girlonds of each flowre that grew,
   To crowne his golden lockes with honour dew;
   Now leading him into a secret shade
   From his Beauperes, and from bright heavens vew,
   Where him to sleepe she gently would perswade,
Or bathe him in a fountaine by some covert glade.

36

And whilst he slept, she over him would spred
   Her mantle, colour'd like the starry skyes,
   And her soft arme lay underneath his hed,
   And with ambrosiall kisses bathe his eyes;
   And whilst he bath'd, with her two crafty spyes,
   She secretly would search each daintie lim,
   And throw into the well sweet Rosemaryes,
   And fragrant violets, and Pances trim,
And ever with sweet Nectar she did sprinkle him.

37

So did she steale his heedeless hart away,
  And joyd his love in secret unespyde.
  But for she saw him bent to cruell play,
  To hunt the salvage beast in forrest wyde,
  Dreadfull of daunger that mote him betyde,
  She oft and oft adviz'd him to refraine
  From chase of greater beasts, whose brutish pryde
  Mote breede him scath unwares: but all in vaine;
For who can shun the chaunce, that dest'ny doth ordaine?

38

Lo, where beyond he lyeth languishing,
  Deadly engored of a great wilde Bore,
  And by his side the Goddesse groveling
  Makes for him endlesse mone, and evermore
  With her soft garment wipes away the gore,
  Which staines his snowy skin with hateful hew:
  But when she saw no helpe might him restore,
  Him to a dainty flowre she did transmew,
Which in that cloth was wrought, as if it lively grew.

39

So was that chamber clad in goodly wize,
  And round about it many beds were dight,
  As whilome was the antique worldes guize,
  Some for untimely ease, some for delight,
  As pleased them to use, that use it might;
  And all was full of Damzels, and of Squires,
  Dauncing and reveling both day and night,
  And swimming deepe in sensuall desires;
And *Cupid* still emongst them kindled lustfull fires.

40

And all the while sweet Musicke did divide
  Her looser notes with *Lydian* harmony;
  And all the while sweet birdes thereto applide
  Their daintie layes and dulcet melody,
  Ay caroling of love and jollity,
  That wonder was to heare their trim consort.
  Which when those knights beheld, with scornefull eye,
  They sdeigned such lascivious disport,
And loath'd the loose demeanure of that wanton sort.

41

Thence they were brought to that great Ladies vew,
 Whom they found sitting on a sumptuous bed,
 That glistred all with gold and glorious shew,
 As the proud *Persian* Queenes accustomed:
 She seemd a woman of great bountihed,
 And of rare beautie, saving that askaunce
 Her wanton eyes, ill signes of womanhed,
 Did roll too lightly, and too often glaunce,
Without regard of grace, or comely amenaunce.

42

Long worke it were, and needlesse to devize
 Their goodly entertainement and great glee:
 She caused them be led in curteous wize
 Into a bowre, disarmed for to bee
 And cheared well with wine and spiceree:
 The *Redcrosse* Knight was soon disarmed there,
 But the brave Mayd would not disarmed bee,
 But onely vented up her umbriere,
And so did let her goodly visage to appere.

43

As when faire *Cynthia*, a darkesome night,
 Is in a noyous cloud enveloped,
 Where she may find the substance thin and light,
 Breakes forth her silver beames, and her bright hed
 Discovers to the world discomfited;
 Of the poore traveller that went astray,
 With thousand blessings she is heried;
 Such was the beautie and the shining ray,
With which faire *Britomart* gave light unto the day.

44

And eke those six, which lately with her fought,
 Now were disarmd, and did them selves present
 Unto her vew, and company unsoght;
 For they all seemed curteous and gent,
 And all sixe brethren, borne of one parent,
 Which had them traynd in all civilitee,
 And goodly taught to tilt and turnament;
 Now were they liegmen to this Lady free,
And her knights service ought, to hold of her in fee.

45

The first of them by name *Gardante* hight,
  A jolly person, and of comely vew;
  The second was *Parlante*, a bold knight,
  And next to him *Jocante* did ensew;
  Basciante did him selfe most curteous shew;
  But fierce *Bacchante* seemed too fell and keene;
  And yet in armes *Noctante* greater grew:
  All were faire knights, and goodly well beseene,
But to faire *Britomart* they all but shadowes beene.

46

For she was full of amiable grace,
  And manly terrour mixed therewithall,
  That as the one stird up affections bace,
  So th' other did mens rash desires apall,
  And hold them backe, that would in errour fall;
  As he, that hath espide a vermeill Rose,
  To which sharp thornes and breres the way forstall,
  Dare not for dread his hardy hand expose,
But wishing it far off, his idle wish doth lose.

47

Whom when the Lady saw so faire a wight,
  All ignoraunt of her contrary sex,
  (For shee her weend a fresh and lusty knight)
  She greatly gan enamoured to wex,
  And with vaine thoughts her falsed fancy vex:
  Her fickle hart conceived hasty fire,
  Like sparkes of fire which fall in sclender flex,
  That shortly brent into extreme desire,
And ransackt all her veines with passion entire.

48

Eftsoones she grew to great impatience
  And into termes of open outrage brust,
  That plaine discovered her incontinence,
  Ne reckt she, who her meaning did mistrust;
  For she was given all to fleshly lust,
  And poured forth in sensuall delight,
  That all regard of shame she had discust,
  And meet respect of honor put to flight:
So shamelesse beauty soone becomes a loathly sight.

49

Faire Ladies, that to love captived arre,
  And chaste desires do nourish in your mind,
  Let not her fault your sweete affections marre,
  Ne blot the bounty of all womankind;
  'Mongst thousands good one wanton Dame to find:
  Emongst the Roses grow some wicked weeds;
  For this was not to love, but lust inclind;
  For love does alwayes bring forth bounteous deeds,
And in each gentle hart desire of honour breeds.

50

Nought so of love this looser Dame did skill,
  But as a coale to kindle fleshly flame,
  Giving the bridle to her wanton will,
  And treading under foote her honest name:
  Such love is hate, and such desire is shame.
  Still did she rove at her with crafty glaunce
  Of her false eyes, that at her hart did ayme,
  And told her meaning in her countenaunce;
But *Britomart* dissembled it with ignoraunce.

51

Supper was shortly dight and downe they sat,
  Where they were served with all sumptuous fare,
  Whiles fruitfull *Ceres*, and *Lyæus* fat
  Pourd out their plenty without spight or spare:
  Nought wanted there, that dainty was and rare;
  And aye the cups their bancks did overflow,
  And aye betweene the cups, she did prepare
  Way to her love, and secret darts did throw;
But *Britomart* would not such guilfull message know.

52

So when they slaked had the fervent heat
  Of appetite with meates of every sort,
  The Lady did faire *Britomart* entreat,
  Her to disarme, and with delightfull sport
  To loose her warlike limbs and strong effort,
  But when she mote not thereunto be wonne,
  (For she her sexe under that straunge purport
  Did use to hide, and plaine appaurance shonne:)
In plainer wise to tell her grievaunce she begonne.

53

And all attonce discovered her desire
   With sighes, and sobs, and plaints, and piteous griefe,
   The outward sparkes of her inburning fire;
   Which spent in vaine, at last she told her briefe,
   That but if she did lend her short reliefe,
   And doe her comfort, she mote algates dye.
   But the chaste damzell, that had never priefe
   Of such malengine and fine forgerie,
Did easily beleeve her strong extremitie.

54

Full easie was for her to have beliefe,
   Who by self-feeling of her feeble sexe,
   And by long triall of the inward griefe,
   Wherewith imperious love her hart did vexe,
   Could judge what paines do loving harts perplexe.
   Who meanes no guile, be guiled soonest shall,
   And to faire semblaunce doth light faith annexe;
   The bird, that knowes not the false fowlers call,
Into his hidden net full easily doth full.

55

For thy she would not in discourteise wise,
   Scorne the faire offer of good will profest;
   For great rebuke it is, love to despise,
   Or rudely sdeigne a gentle harts request;
   But with faire countenaunce, as beseemed best,
   Her entertayned; nath'lesse shee inly deemd
   Her love too light, to wooe a wandring guest:
   Which she misconstruing, thereby esteemd
That from like inward fire that outward smoke had steemd.

56

Therewith a while she her flit fancy fed,
   Till she mote winne fit time for her desire,
   But yet her wound still inward freshly bled,
   And through her bones the false instilled fire
   Did spred it selfe, and venime close inspire.
   Tho were the tables taken all away,
   And every knight, and every gentle Squire
   Gan choose his dame with *Basci*
With whom he ment to make his sport and courtly play.

57

Some fell to daunce, some fel to hazardry,
   Some to make love, some to make meriment,
   As diverse wits to diverse things apply;
   And all the while faire *Malecasta* bent
   Her crafty engins to her close intent.
   By this th' eternall lampes, wherewith high *Jove*
   Doth light the lower world, were halfe yspent,
   And the moist daughters of huge Atlas strove
Into the *Ocean* deepe to drive their weary drove.

58

High time it seemed then for ever wight
   Them to betake unto their kindly rest:
   Eftsoones long waxen torches weren light,
   Unto their bowres to guiden every guest:
   Tho when the Britonesse saw all the rest
   Avoided quite, she gan her selfe despoile,
   And safe commit to her soft fethered nest,
   Wher through long watch, and late dayes weary toile,
She soundly slept, and carefull thoughts did quite assoile.

59

Now whenas all the world in silence deepe
   Yshrowded was, and every mortall wight
   Was drowned in the depth of deadly sleepe,
   Faire *Malecasta*, whose engrieved spright
   Could find no rest in such perplexed plight,
   Lightly arose out of her wearie bed,
   And under the blacke vele of guilty Night,
   Her with a scarlot mantle covered
That was with gold and Ermines faire enveloped.

60

Then panting soft, and trembling ever joynt,
   Her fearfull feete towards the bowre she moved,
   Where she for secret purpose did appoynt
   To lodge the warlike mayd unwisely loved,
   And to her bed approching, first she prooved
   Whether she slept or wakt, with her soft hand
   She softly felt, if any member mooved,
   And lent her wary eare to understand,
If any puffe of breath, or signe of sence she fond.

61

Which whenas none she fond, with easie shift,
  For feare least her unwares she should abrayd,
  Th' embroderd quilt she lightly up did lift,
  And by her side her selfe she softly layd,
  Of every finest fingers touch affrayd;
  Ne any noise she made, ne word she spake,
  But inly sigh'd.   At last the royall Mayd
  Out of her quiet slomber did awake,
And chaunged her weary side, the better ease to take.

62

Where feeling one close couched by her side,
  She lightly lept out of her filed bed,
  And to her weapon ran, in minde to gride
  The loathed leachour.   But the Dame halfe ded
  Through suddein feare and ghastly drerihed,
  Did shrieke alowd, that through the house it rong,
  And the whole family therewith adred,
  Rashly out of their rouzed couches sprong,
And to the troubled chamber all in armes did throng.

63

And those six Knights that Ladies Champions,
  And eke the *Redcrosse* knight ran to the stownd,
  Half armd and halfe unarmd, with them attons:
  Where when confusedly they came, they fownd
  Their Lady lying on the sencelesse grownd;
  On th' other side they saw the warlike Mayd
  Al in her snow-white smocke, with locks unbownd,
  Threatning the point of her avenging blade,
That with so troublous terror they were all dismayde.

64

About their Lady first they flockt arownd,
  Whom having laid in comfortable couch,
  Shortly they reard out of her frosen swownd;
  And afterwards they gan with fowle reproch
  To stirre up strife, and trouble contecke broch:
  By by ensample of the last dayes losse,
  None of them rashly durst to her approch,
  Ne in so glorious spoile themselves embosse:
Her succourd eke the Champion of the bloudy Crosse.

65

But one of those six knights, *Gardante* hight,
　Drew out a deadly bow and arrow keene,
　Which forth he sent with felonous despight
　And fell intent against the virgin sheene:
　The mortall steele stayd not, till it was seene
　To gore her side, yet was the wound not deepe,
　But lightly rased her soft silken skin,
　That drops of purple bloud thereout did weepe,
Which did her lilly smock with staines of vermeil steepe.

66

Wherewith enrag'd she fiercely at them flew,
　And with her flaming sword about her layd,
　That none of them foule mischiefe could eschew,
　But with her dreadfull strokes were all dismayd:
　Here, there, and every where about her swayd
　Her wrathfull steele, that none mote it abide;
　And eke the *Redcrosse* knight gave her good aid,
　Ay joyning foot to foot, and side to side,
That in short space their foes they have quite terrifide.

67

Tho whenas all were put to shamefull flight,
　The noble *Britomartis* her arayd,
　And her bright armes about her body dight:
　For nothing would she lenger there be stayd,
　Where so loose life, and so ungentle trade
　Was usd of Knights and Ladies seeming gent:
　So earely ere the grosse Earthes gryesy shade
　Was all disperst out of the firmament,
They tooke their steeds, and forth upon their journey went.

Canto II

The Redcrosse knight to Britomart
Describeth Artegall:
The wondrous myrrhour, by which she
In love with him did fall.

I

Here have I cause, in men just blame to find,
  That in their proper prayse too partiall bee,
  And not indifferent to woman kind,
  To whom no share in armes and chevalrie
  They do impart, ne maken memorie
  Of their brave gestes and prowesse martiall:
  Scarse to the spare to one or two or three
  Rowme in their writs; yet the same writing small
Does all their deedes deface, and dims their glories all.

2

But by record of antique times I find,
  That women wont in warres to beare most sway,
  And to all great exploites them selves inclind,
  Of which they still the girlond bore away,
  Till envious Men fearing their rules decay,
  Gan coyne streight lawes to curb their liberty:
  Yet sith they warlike armes have layd away
  They have exceld in artes and pollicy,
That now we foolish men that prayse gin eke t' envy.

3

Of warlike puissaunce in ages spent,
  Be thou faire *Britomart*, whose prayse I write,
  But of all wisedom be thou precedent,
  O soveraigne Queene, whose prayse I would endite,
  Endite I would as dewtie doth excite;
  But ah my rimes too rude and rugged arre,
  When in so high an object they do lite,
  And striving, fit to make, I feare do marre:
Thy selfe thy prayses tell, and make them knowen farre.

4

She travelling with *Guyon* by the way,
  Of sundry things faire purpose gan to find,
  T' abridg their journey long, and lingring day;
  Mongst which it fell into that Faeries mind,
  To aske this Briton Mayd, what uncouth wind,

Brought her into those parts, and what inquest
    Made her dissemble her disguised kind:
    Faire Lady she him seemd, like Lady drest
But fairest knight alive, when armed was her brest.

5

Thereat she sighing softly, had no powre
    To speake a while, ne ready answere make,
    But with hart-thrilling throbs and bitter stowre,
    As if she had a fever fit, did quake,
    And every daintie limbe with horrour shake;
    And ever and anone the rosy red,
    Flasht through her face, as it had beene a flake
    Of lightning, through bright heaven fulmined;
At last the passion past she thus him answered.

6

'Faire Sir, I let you weete, that from the howre
    I taken was from nourses tender pap,
    I have been trained up in warlike stowre,
    To tossen speare and shield, and to affrap
    The warlike ryder to his most mishap;
    Sithence I loathed have my life to lead,
    As Ladies wont, in pleasures wanton lap,
    To finger the fine needle and nyce thread;
Me lever were with point of foemans speare be dead.

7

'All my delight on deedes of armes is set,
    To hunt out perils and adventures hard,
    By sea, by land, where so they may be met,
    Onely for honour and for high regard,
    Without respect of richesse or reward.
    For such intent into these parts I came,
    Withouten compasse, or withoutent card,
    Far fro my native soyle, that is by name
The greater *Britaine*, here to seek for prayse and fame.

8

'Fame blazed hath, that here in Faery lond
    Doe many famous Knightes and Ladies wonne,
    And many straunge adventures to be fond,
    Of which great worth and worship may be wonne;
    Which I to prove, I this voyage have begonne.
    But mote I weet of you, right curteous knight,

Tydings of one that hath unto me donne
Late foule dishonour and reprochfull spight,
The which I seeke to wreake, and *Arthegall* he hight.'

9

The word gone out, she backe againe would call,
  As her repenting so to have missayd,
  But that he, it uptaking ere the fall,
  Her shortly answered: 'Faire martiall Mayd
  Certes ye misavised beene, t' upbrayd
  A gentle knight with so unknightly blame:
  For weet ye well of all, that ever playd
  At tilt or tourney, or like warlike game,
The noble *Arthegall* hath ever borne the name.

10

'For thy great wonder were it, if such shame
  Should ever enter in his bounteous thought,
  Or ever do, that mote deserven blame:
  The noble courage never weeneth ought,
  That may unworthy of it selfe be thought.
  Therefore, faire Damzell, be ye well aware,
  Least that too farre ye have your sorrow sought:
  You and your countrey both I wish welfare,
And honour both; for each of other worthy are.'

11

The royall Mayd woxe inly wondrous glad,
  To heare her Love so highly magnifide,
  And joyd that ever she affixed had,
  Her hart on knight so goodly glorifide,
  How ever finely she it faind to hide:
  The loving mother, that nine monethes did beare,
  In the deare closet of her painefull side
  Her tender babe, it seeing safe appeare,
Doth not so much rejoyce, as she rejoyced theare.

12

But to occasion him to further talke,
  To feed her humour with his pleasing stile,
  Her list in strifull termes with him to balke,
  And thus replide: 'How ever, Sir, ye file
  Your curteous tongue, his prayses to compile,
  It ill beseemes a knight of gentle sort,
  Such as ye have him boasted, to beguile

A simple mayd, and worke so haynous tort,
In shame of knighthood, as I largely can report.

13

'Let be therefore my vengeaunce to disswade,
  And read where I that faytour false may find.'
  'Ah, but if reason faire might you perswade
  To slake your wrath, and mollifie your mind,'
  (Said he) 'perhaps ye should it better find:
  For hardy thing it is, to weene by might,
  That man to hard conditions to bind,
  Or ever hope to match in equall fight,
Whose prowesse paragon saw never living wight.

14

'Ne soothlich is it easie for to read,
  Where now on earth, or how he may be found;
  For he ne wonneth in one certine stead,
  But restlesse walketh all the world around,
  Ay doing things, that to his fame redound,
  Defending Ladies cause, and Orphans right,
  Whereso he heares, that any doth confound
  Them comfortlesse, through tyranny or might;
So is his soveraine honour raisde to heavens hight.'

15

His feeling words her feeble sence much pleased,
  And softly sunck into her molten hart;
  Hart that is inly hurt, is greatly eased
  With hope of thing, that may allegge his smart;
  For pleasing words are like to Magick art,
  That doth the charmed Snake in slomber lay:
  Such secrete ease felt gentle *Britomart*,
  Yet list the same efforce with faind gainesay;
So dischord oft in Musick makes the sweeter lay.

16

And said, 'Sir knight, these idle termes forbeare,
  And sith it is uneath to find his haunt,
  Tell me some markes, by which he may appeare,
  If chaunce I him encounter paravaunt;
  For perdie one shall other slay, or daunt:
  What shape, what shield, what armes, what steed, what sted,
  And what so else his person most may vaunt?'
  All which the *Redcrosse* knight to point ared,
And him in every part before her fashioned.

17

Yet him in every part before she knew,
   How ever list her now her knowledge faine,
   Sith him whilome in *Britaine* she did vew,
   To her revealed in a mirrhour plaine,
   Whereof did grow her first engraffed paine;
   Whose root and stalke so bitter yet did tast,
   That but the fruit more sweetnesse did containe,
   Her wretched dayes in dolour she mote wast,
And yield the pray of love to lothsome death at last.

18

By strange occasion she did him behold,
   And much more strangely gan to love his sight,
   As it in bookes hath written bene of old.
   In *Deheubarth* that now South-wales is hight,
   What time king *Ryence* raign'd, and dealed right,
   The great Magitian *Merlin* had deviz'd,
   By his deepe science, and hell-dreaded might,
   A looking glasse, right wondrously aguiz'd,
Whose vertues through the wyde worlde soone were solemniz'd.

19

It vertue had, to shew in perfect sight
   What ever thing was in the wold contaynd,
   Betwixt the lowest earth and hevens hight,
   So that it to the looker appertaynd;
   What ever foe had wrought, or frend had faynd,
   Therein discovered was, ne ought mote pas,
   Ne ought in secret from the same remaynd;
   Forthy it round and hollow shaped was,
Like to the world it selfe, and seemd a world of glas.

20

Who wonders not, that reades so wonderous worke?
   But who does wonder, that has red the Towre
   Wherein th' Ægyptian *Phao* long did lurke
   From all mens vew, that none might her discoure,
   Yet she might all men vew out of her bowre?
   Great *Ptolomæe* it for his lemans sake
   Ybuilded all of glasse, by Magicke powre,
   And also it impregnable did make;
Yet when his love was false, he with a peaze it brake.

21

Such was the glassie globe that *Merlin* made,
  And gave unto king *Ryence* for his gard,
  That never foes his kingdome might invade,
  But he it knew at home before he hard
  Tydings thereof, and so them still debar'd.
  It was a famous Present for a Prince,
  And worthy worke of infinite reward,
  That treasons cold bewray, and foes convince;
Happie this Realme had it remained ever since.

22

One day it fortuned, faire Britomart
  Into her fathers closet to repayre;
  For nothing he from her reserv'd apart,
  Being his onely daughter and his hayre:
  Where when she had espyde that mirrhour fayre,
  Her selfe a while therein she vewd in vaine;
  Tho her avizing of the vertues rare,
  Which thereof spoken were, she gan againe
Her to bethinke of, that mote to her selfe pertaine.

23

But as it falleth, in the gentlest harts
  Imperious Love hath highest set his throne,
  And tyrannizeth in the bitter smarts
  Of them that to him buxome are and prone:
  So thought this Mayd (as maydens use to done)
  Whom fortune for her husband would allot,
  Not that she lusted after any one;
  For she was pure from blame of sinfull blot,
Yet wist her life at last must lincke in that same knot.

24

Eftsoones there was presented to her eye
  A comely knight, all arm'd in complete wize,
  Through whose bright ventayle lifted up on hye
  His manly face, that did his foes agrize,
  And friends to termes of gentle truce entize,
  Lookt foorth, as *Phœbus* face out of the east,
  Betwixt two shadie mountaines doth arize;
  Portly his person was, and much increast
Through his Heroicke grace and honorable gest.

25

His crest was covered with a couchant Hound,
　　And all his armour seemd of antique mould,
　　But wondrous massie and assured sound,
　　And round about yfretted all with gold,
　　In which there written was with cyphers old,
　　Achilles armes, which Arthegall did win.
　　And on his shield enveloped sevenfold
　　He bore a crowned little Ermilin,
That deckt the azure field with her faire pouldred skin.

26

The Damzell well did vew his personage
　　And liked well, ne further fastned not,
　　But went her way; ne her unguilty age
　　Did weene, unwares, that her unlucky lot
　　Lay hidden in the bottome of the pot;
　　Of hurt unwist most daunger doth redound:
　　But the false Archer, which that arrow shot
　　So slyly, that she did not feele the wound,
Did smyle full smoothly at her weetlesse wofull stound.

27

Thenceforth the feather in her loftie crest,
　　Ruffed of love, gan lowly to availe,
　　And her proud portance, and her princely gest,
　　With which she earst tryumphed, now did quaile:
　　Sad, solemn, sowre, and full of fancies fraile
　　She woxe; yet wist she neither how, nor why,
　　She wist not, silly Mayd, what she did aile,
　　Yet wist, she was not well at ease perdy,
Yet thought it was not love, but some melancholy.

28

So soone as Night had with her pallid hew
　　Defast the beautie of the shining sky,
　　And reft from men the worlds desired vew,
　　She with her Nourse adowne to sleepe did lye;
　　But sleepe full farre away from her did fly:
　　In stead thereof sad sighes, and sorrowes deepe
　　Kept watch and ward about her warily,
　　That nought she did but wayle, and often steepe
Her daintie couch with teares, which closely she did weepe.

29

And if that any drop of slombring rest
   Did chaunce to sill into her wearie spright,
   When feeble nature felt her selfe opprest,
   Streight way with dreames, and with fantasticke sight
   Of dreadfull things the same was put to flight,
   That oft out of her bed she did astart,
   As one with vew of ghastly feends affright:
   Tho gan she to renew her former smart,
And thinke of that faire visage, written in her hart.

30

One night, when she was tost with such unrest,
   Her aged Nurse, whose name was *Glauce* hight,
   Feeling her leape out of her loathed nest,
   Betwixt her feeble armes her quickly keight,
   And downe againe in her warm bed her dight;
   'Ah my deare daughter, ah my dearest dread,
   What uncouth fit' (said she) 'what evill plight
   Hath thee opprest, and with sad drearyhead
Chaunged thy lively cheare, and living made thee dead?

31

'For not of nought these suddein ghastly feares
   All night afflict thy naturall repose,
   And all the day, when as thine equall peares
   Their fit disports with faire delight doe chose,
   Thou in dull corners doest thy selfe inclose,
   Ne tastest Princes pleasures, ne doest spred
   Abroad they fresh youthes fairest flowre, but lose
   Both leafe and fruit, both too untimely shed,
As one in wilfull bale for ever buried.

32

'The time, that mortall men their weary cares
   Do lay away, and all wilde beastes do rest,
   And every river eke his course forbeares,
   Then doth this wicked evill thee infest,
   And rive with thousand throbs thy thrilled brest;
   Like an huge *Aetn'* of deepe engulfed griefe,
   Sorrow is heaped in thy hollow chest,
   Whence forth it breakes in sighes and anguish rife,
As smoke and sulphure mingled with confused strife.

33

'Ay me, how much I feare, least love it bee;
  But if that love it be, as sure I read
  By knowen signes and passions, which I see,
  Be it worthy of thy race and royall sead,
  Then I avow by this most sacred head
  Of my deare foster child, to ease thy griefe,
  And win they will: Therefore away doe dread;
  For death nor daunger from thy dew reliefe
Shall me debarre, tell me therefore my liefest liefe.'

34

So having said, her twixt her armes twaine
  She straightly straynd, and colled tenderly,
  And every trembling joynt, and every vaine
  She softly felt, and rubbed busily,
  To doe the frosen cold away to fly;
  And her faire deawy eies with kisses deare
  She oft did bath, and oft againe did dry;
  And ever her importund, not to feare
To let the secret of her hart to her appeare.

35

The Damzell pauzd, and then thus fearefully;
  'Ah Nurse, what needeth thee to eke my paine?
  Is not enough, that I alone doe dye,
  But it must doubled be with death of twaine?
  For nought for me but death there doth remaine.'
  'O daughter deare' (said she) 'despaire no whit;
  For never sore, but might a salve obtaine:
  That blinded God, which hath ye blindly smit,
Another arrow hath your lovers hart to hit.'

36

'But mine is not' (quoth she) 'like others wound;
  For which no reason can find remedy.'
  'Was never such, but mote the like be found,'
  (Said she) 'and though no reason may apply
  Salve to your sore, yet love can higher stye,
  Then reasons reach, and oft hath wonders donne.'
  'But neither God of love nor God of sky
  Can doe' (said she) 'that, which cannot be donne.'
'Things oft impossible' (quoth she) 'seeme, ere begonne.'

37

'These idle words' (said she) 'doe nought asswage
  My stubborne smart, but more annoyance breed,
  For no no usuall fire, no usuall rage
  It is, O Nurse, which on my life doth feed,
  And suckes the bloud which from my hart doth bleed.
  But since thy faithful zeale lets me not hyde
  My crime, (if crime it be) I will it reed.
  Nor Prince, nor pere it is, whose love hath gryde
My feeble brest of late, and launched this wound wyde.

38

'Nor man it is, nor other living wight;
  For then some hope I might unto me draw,
  But th' only shade and semblant of a knight,
  Whose shape or person yet I never saw,
  Hath me subjected to loves cruell law:
  The same one day, as me misfortune led,
  I in my fathers wondrous mirrhour saw,
  And pleased with that seemingly goodly-hed,
Unwares the hidden hooke with baite I swallowed.

39

'Sithens it hath infixed faster hold
  Within my bleeding bowels, and so sore
  Now ranckleth in this same fraile fleshly mould,
  That all my entrailes flow with poysnous gore,
  And th' ulcer groweth daily more and more;
  Ne can my ronning sore find remedie,
  Other then my hard fortune to deplore,
  And languish as the leafe faln from the tree,
Till death make one end of my dayes and miserie.'

40

'Daughter' (said she) 'what need ye be dismayd,
  Or why make ye such Monster of your mind?
  Of much more uncouth thing I was affrayd;
  Of filthy lust, contrarie unto kind:
  But this affection nothing straunge I find;
  For who with reason can you aye reprove,
  To love the semblant pleasing most your mind,
  And yield your heart, whence ye cannot remove?
No guilt in you, but in the tyranny of love.

41

'Not so th' *Arabian Myrrhe* did set her mind;
　Nor so did *Biblis* spend her pining hart,
　But lov'd their native flesh against all kind,
　And to their purpose used wicked art:
　Yet playd *Pasiphaë* a more monstrous part,
　That lov'd a Bull, and learnd a beast to bee;
　Such shamefull lusts who loaths not, which depart
　From course of nature and of modestie?
Sweete love such lewdnes bands from his faire companie.

42

'But thine my Deare (welfare thy heart my deare)
　Though strange beginning had, yet fixed is
　On one, that worthy may perhaps appeare;
　And certes seemes bestowed not amis:
　Joy thereof have thou and eternall blis.'
　With that upleaning on her elbow weake,
　Her alablaster brest she soft did kis,
　Which all that while she felt to pant and quake,
As it an Earth-quake were; at last she thus bespake.

43

'Beldame, your words doe worke me litle ease;
　For though my love be not so lewdly bent,
　As those ye blame, yet may it nought appease
　My raging smart, ne ought my flame relent,
　But rather doth my helplesse griefe augment.
　For they, how ever shamefull and unkind,
　Yet did possesse their horrible intent:
　Short end of sorrowes they thereby did find;
So was their fortune good, though wicked were their mind.

44

'But wicked fortune mine, though mind be good,
　Can have no end, nor hope of my desire,
　But feed on shadowes whiles I die for food,
　And like a shadow wexe, whiles with entire
　Affection, I doe languish and expire.
　I fonder then *Cephisus* foolish child,
　Who having vewed in a fountaine shere
　His face, was with the love thereof beguild;
I fonder love a shade, the bodie farre exild.'

45

'Nought like' (quoth she) 'for that same wretched boy
  Was of himselfe the dle Paramoure,
  Both love and lover, without hope of joy,
  For which he faded to a watry flowre.
  But better fortune thine, and better howre,
  Which lov'st the shadow of a warlike knight;
  No shadow, but a bodie hath in powre:
  That bodie, wheresoever that it light,
May learned be by cyphers, or by Magicke might.

46

'But if thou may with reason yet represse
  The growing evill, ere it strength have got,
  And thee abandond wholly doe possesse,
  Against it strongly strive, and yield thee not,
  Till thou in open fielde adowne be smot.
  But if the passion mayster thy fraile might,
  So that needs love or death must be thy lot,
  Then I avow to thee, by wrong or right
To compasse thy desire, and find that loved knight.'

47

Her chearefull words much cheard the feeble spright
  Of the sicke virgin, that her downe she layd
  In her warme bed to sleepe, if that she might;
  And the old-woman carefully displayd
  The clothes about her round with busy ayd;
  So that at last a little creeping sleepe
  Surprisd her sence: She therewith well apayd,
  The drunken lampe down in the oyle did steepe,
And set her by to watch, and set her by to weepe.

48

Earely the morrow next, before that day
  His joyous face did to the world reveale,
  They both uprose and tooke their readie way
  Unto the Church, their prayers to appeale,
  With great devotion, and with litle zeale:
  For the faire Damzell from the holy herse
  Her love-sicke hart to other thoughts did steale;
  And that old Dame said many an idle verse,
Out of her daughters hart fond fancies to reverse.

49

Returned home, the royall Infant fell
  Into her former fit; for why no powre
  Nor guidance of her selfe in her did dwell.
  But th' aged Nurse her calling to her bowre,
  Had gathered Rew, and Savine, and the flowre
  Of *Camphora*, and Calamint, and Dill,
  All which she in a earthen Pot did poure,
  And to the brim with Colt wood did it fill,
And many drops of milke and bloud through it did spill.

50

Then taking thrise three haires from off her head,
  Them trebly breaded in a threefold lace,
  And round about the pots mouth bound the thread,
  And after having whispered a space
  Certaine sad words with hollow voice and bace,
  She to the virgin said, thrise said it;
  'Come daughter come, come; spit upon my face,
  Spit thrise upon me, thrise upon me spit;
Th' uneven number for this busines is most fit.'

51

That sayd, her round about she from her turnd,
  She turnd her contrarie to the Sunne,
  Thrise she her turnd contrary, and returnd,
  All contrary, for she the right did shunne,
  And ever what she did, was streight undonne.
  So thought she to undoe her daughters love:
  But love, that is in gentle brest begonne,
  No idle charmes so lightly may remove,
That well can witnesse, who by triall it does prove.

52

Ne ought it mote the noble Mayd avayle,
  Ne slake the furie of her cruell flame,
  But that she still did waste, and still did wayle,
  That through long languour, and hart-burning brame
  She shortly like a pyned ghost became,
  Which long hath waited by the Stygian strond.
  That when old *Glauce* saw, for feare least blame
  Of her miscarriage should in her be fond,
She wist not how t'amend, nor how it to withstond.

Canto III

Merlin bewrayes to Britomart,
The state of Artegall.
And shewes the famous Progeny
Which from them springen shall.

1

Most sacred fire, that burnest mightily
  In living brests, ykindled first above,
  Emongst th' eternall spheres and lamping sky,
  And thence pourd into men, which men call Love;
  Not that same, which doth base affections move
  In brutish minds, and filthy lust inflame,
  But that sweet fit that doth true beautie love,
  And choseth vertue for his dearest Dame,
Whence spring all noble deeds and never dying fame:

2

Well did Antiquitie a God thee deeme,
  That over mortall minds hast so great might,
  To order them, as best to thee doth seeme,
  And all their actions to direct aright;
  The fatall purpose of divine foresight
  Thou doest effect in destined descents,
  Through deepe impression of thy secret might,
  And stirredst up th' Heroes high intents,
Which the late world admyres for wondrous moniments.

3

But thy dread darts in none doe triumph more,
  Ne braver proofe in any, of thy powre
  Shewd'st thou, then in this royall Maid of yore,
  Making her seeke an unknowne Paramoure,
  From the worlds end, through many a bitter stowre:
  From whose two loynes thou afterwardes did rayse
  Most famous fruits of matrimoniall bowre,
  Which through the earth have spred their living prayse,
That fame in trompe of gold eternally displayes.

4

Begin then, O my dearest sacred Dame,
  Daughter of *Phœbus* and of *Memorie*,
  That doest ennoble with immortall name
  The warlike Worthies, from antiquitie,
  In thy great volume of Eternitie:

Begin, O *Clio*, and recount from hence
My glorious Soveraines goodly auncestrie,
  Till that by dew degrees, and long protense,
Thou have it lastly brought unto her Excellence.

5

Full many wayes within her troubled mind,
  Old *Glauce* cast to cure this Ladies griefe:
  Full many waies she sought, but none could find,
  Nor herbes, nor charmes, nor counsell, that is chiefe
  And choicest med'cine for sicke harts reliefe:
  For thy great care she tooke, and greater feare,
  Least that it should her turne to foule repriefe,
  And sore reproch, when so her father deare
Should of his dearest daughters hard misfortune heare.

6

At last she her avisd, that he which made
  That mirrhour, wherein the sicke Damosell
  So straungely vewed her straunge lovers shade,
  To weet, the learned Merlin, well could tell
  Under what coast of heaven the man did dwell,
  And by what means his love might best be wrought:
  For though beyond the *Africk Ismael*
  Or th' Indian *Peru* he were, she thought
Him forth through infinite endevour to have sought.

7

Forthwith themselves disguising both in straunge
  And base attyre, that none might them bewray,
  To *Maridunum*, that is now by chaunge
  Of name *Cayr-Merdin* cald, they tooke their way:
  There the wise *Merlin* whylome wont (they say)
  To make his wonne, low underneath the ground,
  In a deepe delve, farre from the vew of day,
  That of no living wight he mote be found,
When he so counseld with his sprights encompast round.

8

And if thou ever happen that same way
  To travell, goe to see that dreadful place:
  It is an hideous hollow cave (they say)
  Under a rocke that lyes a litle space
  From the swift *Barry*, tombling downe apace,
  Emongst the woodie hilles of *Dynevowre*:

But dare thou not, I charge, in any cace
To enter into the same baleful Bowre,
For feare the cruell Feends should thee unwares devowre.

9

But standing high aloft low lay thine eare,
 And there such ghastly noise of yron chaines
 And brasen Caudrons thou shalt rombling heare,
 Which thousand sprights with long enduring paines
 Doe tosse, that it will stonn thy feeble braines;
 And oftentimes great grones, and grstonds,
 When too huge toile and labour them constraines
 And oftentimes loud strokes and ringing sond
From under that deepe Rock most horribly rebond.

10

The cause some say is this: A litle while
 Before that *Merlin* dyde, he did intend,
 A brasen wall in compas to compile
 About *Cairmardin*, and did it commend
 Unto these Sprights, to bring to perfect end.
 During which worke the Ladie of the Lake,
 Whom long he lov'd, for him in hast did send,
 Who thereby forst his workemen to forsake,
Them bound till his returne, their labour not to slake.

11

In the meane time, through that false Ladies traine,
 He was surprisd, and buried under beare,
 Ne ever to his worke returnd againe:
 Nath'lesse those feends may not their work forbeare,
 So greatly his commaundement they feare,
 But there doe toyle and travell day and night,
 Untill that brasen wall they up doe reare:
 For *Merlin* had in Magicke more insight,
Then ever him before or after living wight.

12

For he by words could call out of the sky
 Both Sunne and Moone, and make them him obay:
 The land to sea, and sea to maineland dry,
 And darkesome night he eke could turne to day:
 Huge hostes of men he could alone dismay,
 And hostes of men of meanest things could frame,
 When so him list his enimies to fray:

That to this day for terror of his fame,
The feends do quake, when any him to them does name.

13

And sooth, men say that he was not the sonne
   Of mortall Syre, or other living wight,
   But wondrously begotten, and begonne
   By false illusion of a guilefull Spright,
   On a faire Ladie Nonne, that whilome hight
   Matilda, daughter to Pubidius,
   Who was the Lord of Mathravall by right,
   And coosen unto king Ambrosius:
Whence he indued was with skill so marvellous.

14

They were ariving, staid a while without,
   Ne durst adventure rashly in to wend,
   But of their first intent gan make new dout
   For dread of daunger which it might protend:
   Untill the hardie Mayd (with love to frend)
   First entering, the dreadfull Mage there found
   Deepe busied bout worke of wondrous end,
   And writing strange characters in the ground,
With which the stubborne feends he to his service bound.

15

He nought was moved at their entrance bold:
   For of their comming well he wist afore,
   Yet list them bid their businesse to unfold,
   As if ought in this world in secrete store
   Were from him hidden, or unknowne of yore.
   Then Glauce thus, 'Let not it thee offend,
   That we thus rashly through thy darkesome dore
   Unwares have prest: for either fatall end,
Or other mightie cause us two did hither send.'

16

He bad tell on;   And then she thus began.
   'Now have three Moones with borrow'd brothers light
   Thrise shined faire, and thrise seem'd dim and wan,
   Sith a sore evill, which this virgin bright
   Tormenteth, and doth plonge in dolefull plight
   First rooting tooke; but what thing it mote bee,
   Or whence it sprong, I cannot read aright:
   But this I read, that but if remedee
Thou her afford, full shortly I her dead shall see.'

17

Therewith th' Enchaunter softly gan to smyle
  At her smooth speeches, weeting inly well
  That she to him dissembled womanish guyle,
  And to her said, 'Beldame, by that ye tell,
  More neede of leach-craft hath your Damozell,
  Then of my skill: who helpe may have elsewhere,
  In vaine seekes wonders out of Magicke spell.'
  Th' old woman wox half blanck, those wordes to heare;
And yet was loth to let her purpose plaine appeare.

18

And to him said, 'If any leaches skill,
  Or other learned meanes could have redrest
  This is my deare daughters deepe engraffed ill,
  Certes I should be loth thee to molest:
  But this sad evill, which dost her infest,
  Doth course of naturall cause farre exceed,
  And housed is within her hollow brest,
  That either seemes some cursed witches deed,
Or evill spright, that in her doth such torment breed.'

19

The wisard could no lenger beare her bord,
  But brusting forth in laughter, to her sayd;
  '*Glauce*, what needs this colourable word
  To cloke the cause, that hath it selfe bewrayd?
  Ne ye faire *Britomartis*, thus arayd,
  More hidden are, then Sunne in cloudy vele;
  Whom thy good fortune, having fate obayd,
  Hath hither brought, for succour to appele:
The which the powres to thee are pleased to revele.'

20

The doubtfull Mayd, seeing her selfe descryde,
  Was all abasht, and her pure yvory
  Into a cleare Carnation suddeine dyde;
  As faire *Aurora* rising hastily,
  Doth by her blushing, tell that she did lye
  All night in old *Tithonus* frosen bed,
  Whereof she seemes ashamed inwardly.
  But her olde Nourse was nought dishartened,
But vauntage made of that, which *Merlin* had ared.

21

And sayd, 'Sith then thou knowest all our griefe,
　(For what doest not thou know?) of grace I pray,
　Pitty our plaint, and yield us meet reliefe.'
　With that the Prophet still awhile did stay,
　And then his spirite thus gan forth display;
　'Most noble Virgin, that by fatall lore
　Hast learn'd to love, let no whit thee dismay
　The hard begin, that meets thee in the dore,
And with sharpe fits thy tender hart oppresseth sore.

22

'For so must all things excellent begin,
　And eke enrooted deepe must be that Tree,
　Whose big embodied braunches shall not lin,
　Till they to heavens hight forth stretched bee.
　For from thy wombe a famous Progenie
　Shall spring, out of the auncient *Trojan* blood,
　Which shall revive the sleeping memorie
　Of those same antique Peres, the heavens brood,
Which *Greeke* and *Asian* rivers stained with their blood.

23

'Renowmed kings, and sacred Emperours,
　Thy fruitfull Offspring, shall from thee descend;
　Brave Captaines, and most mighty warriours,
　That shall their conquests through all lands extend,
　And their decayed kingdomes shall amend:
　The feeble Britons, broken with long warre,
　They shall upreare, and mightily defend
　Against their forrein foe, that comes from farre,
Till universall peace compound all civill jarre.

24

'It was not, *Britomart*, thy wandring eye,
　Glauncing unwares in charmed looking glas,
　But the streight course of heavenly destiny,
　Led with eternall providence, that has
　Guided thy glaunce, to bring his will to pas:
　Ne is thy fate, ne is thy fortune ill,
　To love the prowest knight that ever was.
　Therefore submit thy wayes unto his will,
And do by all dew meanes thy destiny fulfill.'

25

'But read' (said *Glauce*) 'thou Magitian
   What meanes shall she out seeke, or what wayes take?
   How shall she know, how shall she find the man?
   Or what needs her to toyle, sith fates can make
   Way for themselves, their purpose to partake?'
   Then *Merlin* thus; 'Indeed the fates are firme,
   And may not shrinck, though all the world do shake:
   Yet ought mens good endevours them confirme,
And guide the heavenly causes to their constant terme.

26

'The man whom heavens have ordaynd to bee
   The spouse of *Britomart*, is *Arthegall*:
   He wonneth in the land of *Fayeree*,
   Yet is no *Fary* borne, ne sib at all
   To Elfes, but sprong of seed terrestriall,
   And whilome by false *Faries* stolne away,
   Whiles yet in infant cradle he did crall;
   Ne other to himselfe is knowne this day,
But that he by an Elfe was gotten of a *Fay*.

27

'But sooth he is the sonne of *Gorlois*,
   And brother unto *Cador* Cornish king,
   And for his warlike feates renowmed is,
   From where the day out of the sea doth spring,
   Until the closure of the Evening.
   From thence, him firmely bound with faithfull band,
   To this his native soyle thou backe shalt bring,
   Strongly to aide his countrey, to withstand
The powre of forrein Paynims, which invade thy land.

28

'Great aid thereto his mighty puissaunce,
   And dreaded name shall give in that sad day:
   Where also proofe of they prow valiaunce
   Thou then shalt make, t'increase thy lovers pray.
   Long time ye both in armes shall beare great sway,
   Till thy wombes burden thee from them do call,
   And his last fate him from thee take away,
   Too rathe cut off by practise criminall
Of secrete foes, that him shall make in mischiefe fall.

29

'With thee yet shall he leave for memory
  Of his late puissaunce, his Image dead,
  That living him in all activity
  To thee shall represent. He from the head
  Of his coosin *Constantius* without dread
  Shall take the crowne, that was his fathers right,
  And therewith crowne himself in th' others stead:
  Then shall he issew forth with dreadfull might,
Against his Saxon foes in bloudy field to fight.

30

'Like as a Lyon, that in drowsie cave
  Hath long time slept, himselfe so shall he shake,
  And comming forth, shall spred his banner brave
  Over the troubled South, that it shall make
  The warlike *Mertians* for feare to quake:
  Thrise shall he fight with them, and twise shall win,
  But the third time shall faire accordaunce make:
  And if he then with victorie can lin,
He shall his dayes with peace bring to his earthly In.

31

'His sonne, hight *Vortipore*, shall him succeede
  In kingdome, but not in felicity:
  Yet shall he long time warre with happy speed,
  And with great honour many battels try:
  But at the last to th' importunity
  Of froward fortune shall be forst to yield.
  But his sonne *Malgo* shall full mightily
  Avenge his fathers losse with speare and shield,
And his proud foes discomfit in victorious field.

32

'Behold the man, and tell me *Britomart*,
  If ay more goodly creature thou didst see;
  How like a Gyaunt in each manly part
  Beares he himselfe with portly majestee,
  That one of th' old *Heroes* seemes to bee:
  He the six Islands, comprovinciall
  In auncient times unto great Britainee,
  Shall to the same reduce, and to him call
Their sundry kings to do their homage severall.

33

'All which his sonne *Careticus* awhile
  Shall well defend, and *Saxons* powre suppresse,
  Untill a straunger king from unknowne soyle
  Arriving, him with multitude oppresse;
  Great *Gormond*, having with huge mightinesse
  Ireland subdewd, and therein fixt his throne,
  Like a swift Otter, fell through emptinesse,
  Shall overswim the sea with many one
Of his *Norveyses*, to assist the Britons fone.

34

'He in his furie all shall overrunne,
  And holy Church with faithlesse hands deface,
  That they sad people utterly fordonne,
  Shall to the utmost mountaines fly apace:
  Was never so great wast in any place,
  Nor so fowle outrage doen by living men:
  For all thy Cities, they shall sacke and race,
  And the greene grasse, that groweth, they shall bren,
That even the wilde beast shall dy in starved den.

35

'Whiles thus thy Britons do in languour pine,
  Proud *Etheldred* shall from the North arise,
  Serving th' ambitious will of *Augustine*,
  And passing *Dee* with hardy enterprise,
  Shall backe repulse the valiaunt *Brockwell* twise,
  And *Bangor* with massacred Martyrs fill;
  But the third time shall rew his foolhardise:
  For *Cadwan* pittying his peoples ill,
Shall stoutly him defeat, and thousand *Saxons* kill.

36

'But after him, *Cadwallin* mightily
  On his sonne *Edwin* all those wrongs shall wreake;
  Ne shall availe the wicked sorcery
  Of false *Pellite*, his purposes to breake,
  But him shall slay, and on a gallowes bleake
  Shall give th' enchaunter his unhappy hire;
  Then shall the Britons, late dismayd and weake,
  From their long vassalage gin to respire,
And on their Paynim foes avenge their ranckled ire.

37

'Ne shall he yet his wrath so mitigate,
  Till both the sonnes of *Edwin* he have slaine,
  Offricke and *Osricke*, twinnes unfortunate,
  Both slaine in battell upon Layburne plaine,
  Together with the king of *Louthiane*,
  Hight *Adin*, and the king of *Orkeny*,
  Both joynt partakers of their fatall paine:
  But *Penda*, fearefull of like desteny,
Shall yield him selfe his liegeman, and sweare fealty.

38

'Him shall he make his fatall Instrument
  T' afflict the other *Saxons* unsubdewd;
  He marching forth with fury insolent
  Against the good king *Oswald*, who indewd
  With heavenly powre, and by Angels reskewd,
  All holding crosses in their hands on hye,
  Shall him defeate withouten bloud imbrewd:
  Of which, that field for endlesse memory,
Shall *Hevenfield* be cald to all posterity.

39

'Where at *Cadwallin* wroth shall forth issew,
  And an huge hoste into Northumber lead,
  With which he godly *Oswald* shall subdew,
  And crowne with martyrdome his sacred head.
  Whose brother *Oswin*, daunted with like dread,
  With price of silver shall his kingdome buy,
  And *Penda*, seeking him adowne to tread,
  Shall tread adowne, and doe him fowly dye,
But shall with gifts his Lord *Cadwallin* pacify.

40

'Then shall *Cadwallim* dye, and then the raine
  Of *Britons* eke with him attonce shall dye;
  Ne shall the good *Cadwallader* with paine,
  Or powre, be hable it to remedy,
  When the full time prefixt by destiny,
  Shalbe expird of *Britons* regiment.
  For heven it selfe shall their successe envy,
  And them with plagues and murrins pestilent
Consume, till all their warlike puissaunce be spent.

41

Yet after all these sorrowes, and huge hills
  Of dying people, during eight yeares space,
  Cadwallader not yielding to his ills,
  From *Armoricke*, where long in wretched cace
  He liv'd, retourning to his native place,
  Shalbe by vision staide from his intent:
  For th' heavens have decreed, to displace
  The *Britons*, for their sinnes dew punishment,
And to the *Saxons* over-give their government.

42

'Then woe, and woe, and everlasting woe,
  Be to the Briton babe that shalbe borne,
  To live in thraldome of his fathers foe;
  Late King, now captive, late Lord, now forlorne,
  The worlds reproch, the cruell victors scorne,
  Banisht from Princely bowre to wastfull wood:
  O who shall helpe me to lament, and mourne
  The royal seed, the antique *Trojan* blood,
Whose Empire lenger here then ever any stood.'

43

The Damzell was full deepe empassioned,
  Both for his griefe, and for her peoples sake,
  Whose future woes so plaine he fashioned,
  And sighing sore, at length him thus bespake;
  'Ah but will heavens fury never slake,
  Nor vengeaunce huge relent it selfe at last?
  Will not long misery late mercy make,
  But shall their name for ever be defast,
And quite from of the earth their memory be raste?'

44

'Nay but the terme' (said he) 'is limited,
  That in this thraldome *Britons* shall abide,
  And the just revolution measured,
  That they as Straungers shalbe notifide.
  For twise foure hundredth yeares shal be supplide,
  Ere they to former rule restor'd shalbee,
  And their importune fates all satisfide:
  Yet during this their most obscuritee,
Their beames shall oft breake forth, that men them faire may see.

45

'For *Rhodoricke*, whose surname shal be Great,
    Shall of him selfe a brave ensample shew,
    That Saxon kings his friendship shall intreat;
    And *Howell Dha* shall goodly well indew
    The salvage minds with skill of just and trew;
    Then *Griffyth Conan* also shall up reare
    His dreaded head, and the old sparkes renew
    Of native courage, that his foes shall feare,
Least back againe the kingdom he from them should beare.

46

'Ne shall the Saxons selves all peaceably
    Enjoy the crowne, which they from Britons wonne
    First ill, and after ruled wickedly:
    For ere two hundred yeares be full outronne,
    There shall a Raven far from rising Sunne,
    With his wide wings upon them fiercely fly,
    And bid his faithlesse chickens overronne
    The fruitfull plaines, and with fell cruelty
In their avenge, tread downe the victours surquedry.

47

'Yet shall a third both these and thine subdew.
    There shall a Lyon from the sea-bord wood
    Of *Neustria* come roring, with a crew
    Of hungry whelpes, his battailous bold brood,
    Whose clawes were newly dipt in cruddy blood,
    That from the Daniske Tyrants head shall rend
    Th' usurped crowne, as if that he were wood,
    And the spoile of the countrey conquered
Emongst his young ones shall divide with bountyhed.

48

'Tho when the terme is full accomplishid,
    There shall a sparke of fire, which hath long-while
    Bene in his ashes raked up and hid,
    Bee freshly kindled in the fruitfull Ile
    Of *Mona*, where it lurked in exile;
    Which shall breake forth into bright burning flame,
    And reach into the house, that beares the stile
    Of royall majesty and soveraigne name;
So shall the Briton bloud their crowne againe reclame.

49

'Thenceforth eternall union shall be made
   Betweene the nations different afore,
   And sacred Peace shall lovingly perswade
   The warlike minds, to learne her goodly lore,
   And civile armes to exercise no more:
   Then shall a royall virgin raine, which shall
   Stretch her white rod over the *Belgicke* shore,
   And the great Castle smite so sore with all,
That it shall make him shake, and shortly learne to fall.

50

'But yet the end is not.' There *Merlin* stayd,
   As overcomen of the spirites powre,
   Or other ghastly spectacle dismayd,
   That secretly he saw, yet note discoure:
   Which suddein fit, and halfe extatick stoure
   When the two fearefull women saw, they grew
   Greatly confused in behavioure;
   At last the fury past, to former hew
He turnd againe, and chearfull looks as earst did shew.

51

Then, when them selves they well instructed had
   Of all that needed them to be inquird,
   They both conceiving hope of comfort glad,
   With lighter hearts unto their home retird;
   Where they in secret counsell close conspird,
   How to effect so hard an enterprize,
   And to possesse the purpose they desird:
   Now this, now that twixt them they did devise,
And diverse plots did frame, to maske in strange disguise.

52

At last the Nourse in her foolhardy wit
   Conceiv'd a bold devise, and thus bespake;
   'Daughter, I deeme that counsel aye most fit,
   That of the time doth dew advauntage take;
   Ye see that good king *Uther* now doth make
   Strong warre upon the Paynim brethren, hight
   Octa and *Oza*, whom he lately brake
   Beside *Cayr Verolame* in victorious fight,
That now all *Britanie* doth burne in armes bright.

53

'That therefore nought our passage may empeach,
  Let us in feigned armes our selves disguize,
  And our weake hands (whom need new strength shall teach)
  The dreadful speare and shield to exercize:
  Ne certes daughter that same warlike wize
  I weene, would you misseeme; for ye bene tall,
  And large of limbe, t' atchieve an hard emprize,
  Ne ought ye want, but skill, which practize small
Will bring, and shortly make you a mayd Martiall.

54

'And sooth, it ought to courage much inflame,
  To heare so often, in that royall hous,
  From whence to none inferiour ye came,
  Bards tell of many women valorous
  Which have full many feats adventurous
  Performd, in paragone of proudest men:
  The bold *Bunduca*, whose victorious
  Exploits made *Rome* to quake, stout *Guendolen*,
Renowmed *Martia*, and redoubted *Emmilen*.

55

'And that, which more than all the rest may sway,
  Late dayes ensample, which these eyes beheld,
  In the last field before *Menevia*
  Which *Uther* with those forrein Pagans held,
  I saw a *Saxon* Virgin, the which feld
  Great *Ulfin* thrise upon the bloudy plaine,
  And had not *Carados* her hand withheld
  From rash revenge, she had him surely slaine,
Yet *Carados* himselfe from her escapt with paine.'

56

'Ah read,' (quoth *Britomart*) 'how is she hight?'
  'Faire *Angela*' (quoth she) 'men do her call,
  No whit lesse faire then terrible in fight:
  She hath the leading of a Martiall
  And mighty people, dreaded more then all
  The other *Saxons*, which do for her sake
  And love, themselves of her name *Angles* call.
  Therefore faire Infant her ensample make
Unto thy selfe, and equall courage to thee take.'

57

Her harty words so deepe into the mynd
  Of the young Damzell sunke, that great desire
  Of warlike armes in her forthwith they tynd,
  And generous stout courage did inspire,
  That she resolv'd, unweeting to her Sire,
  Advent'rous knighthood on her selfe to don,
  And counseld with her Nourse, her Maides attire
  To turne into a massy habergeon,
And bad her all things put in readinesse anon.

58

Th' old woman nought, that needed did omit;
  But all things did conveniently purvay.
  It fortuned (so time their turne did fit)
  A band of Britons ryding on forray
  Few dayes before, had gotten a great pray
  Of Saxon goods, emongst the which was seene
  A goodly Armour, and full rich aray,
  Which long'd to *Angela*, the Saxon Queene,
All fretted round with gold, and goodly wel beseene.

59

The same, with all the other ornaments,
  King *Ryence* caused to be hanged hy
  In his chiefe Church, for endlesse moniments
  Of his successe and gladfull victory:
  Of which her selfe avising readily,
  In th' evening late old *Glauce* thither led
  Faire *Britomart*, and that same Armory
  Downe taking, her therein appareled,
Well as she might, and with brave bauldrick garnished.

60

Beside those armes there stood a mightie speare,
  Which *Bladud* made by Magick art of yore,
  And usd the same in battell aye to beare;
  Sith which it had bin here preserv'd in store,
  For his great vertues proved long afore:
  For never wight so fast in sell could sit,
  But him perforce unto the ground it bore:
  Both speare she tooke and shield which hong by it.
Both speare and shield of great powre, for her purpose fit.

61

Thus when she had the virgin all arayd,
  Another harnesse, which did hang thereby,
  About her selfe she dight, that the young Mayd
  She might in equall armes accompany,
  And as her Squire attend her carefully:
  Tho to their ready Steeds they clombe full light,
  And through back wayes, that none might them espy,
  Covered with secret cloud of silent night,
Themselves they forth convayd, and passed forward right.

62

Ne rested they, till that to Faery lond
  They came, as *Merlin* them directed late:
  Where meeting with this *Redcrosse* knight, she fond
  Of diverse things discourses to dilate,
  And most of *Arthegall*, and his estate.
  At last their wayes so fell, that they mote part:
  Then each to other well affectionate,
  Friendship professed with unfained hart,
The *Redcrosse* knight diverst, but forth rode *Britomart*.

Canto IV

Bold Marinell of Britomart
Is throwne on the Rich strond:
Faire Florimell of Arthur is
Long followed, but not fond.

1

Where is the Antique glory now become,
    That whilome wont in women to appeare?
    Where be the brave atchievements doen by some?
    Where be the battels, where the shield and speare,
    And all the conquests, which them high did reare,
    That matter made for famous Poets verse,
    And boastful men so aft abasht to heare?
    Bene they all dead, and laid in dolefull herse?
Or doen they onely sleepe, and shall againe reverse?

2

If they be dead, then woe is me therefore:
    But if they sleepe, O let them soone awake:
    For all too long I burne with envy sore,
    To heare the warlike feates, which *Homere* spake
    Of bold *Penthesilee*, which made a lake
    Of *Greekish* bloud so oft in *Trojan* plaine:
    But when I read, how stout *Debora* strake
    Proud *Sisera*, and how *Camill'* hath slaine
The huge *Orsilochus*, I swell with great disdaine.

3

Yet these, and all that else had puissaunce,
    Cannot with noble *Britomart* compare,
    Aswell for glory of great valiaunce,
    As for pure chastitie and vertue rare,
    That all her goodly deeds do well declare.
    Well worthy stock, from which the branches sprong,
    That in late yeares so faire a blossome bare,
    As thee, O Queene, the matter of my song,
Whose lignage from this Lady I derive along.

4

Who when, through speaches with the *Redcrosse* knight,
    She learned had th' estate of *Arthegall*,
    And in each point her selfe informd aright,
    A friendly league of love perpetuall
    She with him bound, and *Congé* tooke withall.

Then he forth on his journey did proceede,
To seeke adventures, which mote him befall,
And win him worship through his warlike deed,
Which alwayes of his paines he made the chiefest meed.

5

But *Britomart* kept on her former course,
Ne ever dofte her armes, but all the way
Grew pensive through that amorous discourse,
By which the *Redcrosse* knight did earst display
Her lovers shape and chevalrous aray;
A thousand thoughts she fashioned in her mind,
And in her feigning fancie did pourtray
Him such, as fittest she for love could find,
Wise, warlike, personable, curteous, and kind.

6

With such selfe-pleasing thoughts her wound she fed,
And thought so to beguile her grievous smart;
But so her smart was much more grievous bred,
And the deepe wound more deep engord her hart,
That nought but death her dolour mote depart.
So forth she rode, without repose or rest,
Searching all lands and each remotest part,
Following the guidance of her blinded guest,
Till that to the sea-coast at length she her addrest.

7

There she alighted from her light-foot beast,
And sitting downe upon the rocky shore,
Bad her old Squire unlace her lofty creast;
Tho having vewd a while the surges hore,
That gainst the craggy clifts did loudly rore,
And in their raging surquedry disdaynd,
That the fast earth affronted them so sore,
And their devouring covetize restraynd,
Thereat she sighed deepe, and after thus complaynd.

8

'Huge sea of sorrow, and tempestuous griefe,
Wherein my feeble barke is tossed along,
Far from the hoped haven of reliefe,
Why do thy cruell billowes beat so strong,
And thy moyst mountaines each on others throng,
Threatning to swallow up my fearefull life?

O do thy cruell wrath and spightfull wrong
At length allay, and stint thy stormy strife,
Which in these troubled bowels raignes, and rageth rife.

9

'For else my feeble vessell crazd, and crackt
　Through thy strong buffets and outrageous blowes,
　Cannot endure, but needes it must be wrackt
　On the rough rocks, or on the sandy shallowes,
　The whiles that love it steres, and fortune rowes;
　Love my lewd Pilot hath a restlesse mind
　And fortune Boteswaine no assurance knowes,
　But saile withouten starres gainst tide and wind:
How can they other do, sith both are bold and blind?

10

'Thou God of winds, that raignest in the seas,
　That raignest also in the Continent,
　At last blow up some gentle gale of ease,
　The which may bring my ship, ere it be rent,
　Unto the gladsome port of her intent:
　Then when I shall my selfe in safety see,
　A table, for eternall moniment
　Of thy great grace and my great jeopardee,
Great *Neptune*, I avow to hallow unto thee.

11

Then sighing softly sore, and inly deepe,
　She shut up all her plaint in privy griefe;
　For her great courage would not let her weepe,
　Till that old *Glauce* gan with sharpe repriefe,
　Her to restrain, and give her good reliefe,
　Through hope of those, which *Merlin* had her told
　Should of her name and nation be chiefe,
　And fetch their being from the sacred mould
Of her immortall womb, to be in heaven enrold.

12

Thus as she her recomforted, she spyde
　Where far away one all in armour bright,
　With hasty gallop towards her did ryde;
　Her dolour soone she ceast, and on her dight
　Her Helmet, to her Courser mounting light:
　Her former sorrow into suddein wrath,
　Both coosen passions of distroubled spright,

Converting, forth she beates the dustie path;
Love and despight attonce her courage kindled hath.

13

As when a foggy mist hath overcast
　　The face of heaven, and the cleare aire engrost,
　　The world in darkenesse dwels, till that at last
　　The watry Southwinde from the seabord cost
　　Upblowing, doth disperse the vapour lo'st,
　　And poures it selfe forth in a stormy showre;
　　So the faire *Britomart*, having disclo'st
　　Her clowdy care into a wrathfull stowre,
The mist of griefe dissolv'd, did into vengeance powre.

14

Eftsoones her goodly shield addressing faire,
　　That mortall speare she in her hand did take,
　　And unto battell did her selfe prepaire.
　　The knight approching, sternely her bespake;
　　'Sir knight, that doest thy voyage rashly make
　　By this forbidden way in my despight,
　　Ne doest by others death ensample take,
　　I read thee soone retyre, whiles thou hast might,
Least afterwards it be too late to take thy flight.'

15

Ythrild with deepe disdaine of his proud threat,
　　She shortly thus; 'Fly they, that need to fly;
　　Words fearen babes.　　I meane not thee entreat
　　To passe; but maugre thee will passe or dy.'
　　Ne lenger stayd for th' other to reply,
　　But with sharpe speare the rest made dearly knowne.
　　Strongly the straunge knight ran, and sturdily
　　Strooke her full on the brest, that made her downe
Decline her head, and touch her crouper with her crowne.

16

But she againe him in the shield did smite
　　With so fierce furie and great puissaunce,
　　That through his three square scuchin percing quite,
　　And through his mayled hauberque, by mischaunce
　　The wicked steele through his left side did glaunce;
　　Him so transfixed she before her bore
　　Beyond his croupe, the length of all her launce,
　　Till sadly soucing on the sandie shore,
He tombled on an heape, and wallowed in his gore.

17

Like as the sacred Oxe, that carelesse stands,
  With gilden hornes and flowry girlonds crownd,
  Proud of his dying honor and deare bands,
  Whiles th' altars fume with frankincense arownd,
  All suddenly with mortall stroke astownd,
  Doth groveling fall, and with his streaming gore
  Distaines the pillours and the holy grownd,
  And the faire flowres, that decked him afore;
So fell proud *Marinell* upon the pretious shore.

18

The martiall Mayd stayd not him to lament,
  But forward rode, and kept her readie way
  Along the strond, which as she over-went,
  She saw bestowed all with rich aray
  Of pearles and pretious stones of great assay,
  And all the gravell mixt with golden owre;
  Whereat she wondred much, but would not stay
  For gold, or perles, or pretious stones an howre,
But them despised all; for all was in her powre.

19

Whiles thus he lay in deadly stonishment,
  Tydings hereof came to his mothers eare;
  His mother was the blacke-browd *Cymoent*,
  The daughter of great *Nereus*, which did beare
  This warlike sonne unto an earthly peare,
  The famous *Dumarin*; who on a day
  Finding the Nymph a sleepe in secret wheare,
  As he by chaunce did wander that same way,
Was taken with her love, and by her closely lay.

20

There he this knight of her begot, whom borne
  She of his father *Marinell* did name,
  And in a rocky cave as wight forlorne,
  Long time she fostred up, till he became
  A mightie man at armes, and mickle fame
  Did get through great adventures by him donne:
  For never man he suffred by that same
  Rich strond to travell, whereas he did wonne,
But that he must do battell with the Sea-nymphes sonne.

21

An hundred knights of honorable name
  He had subdew'd, and then his vassals made,
  That through all Farie lond his noble fame
  Now blazed was, and feare did all invade,
  That none durst passen through that perilous glade.
  And to advance his name and glory more,
  Her Sea-god syre she dearely did perswade,
  T' endow her sonne with threasure and rich store,
Bove all the sonnes, that were of earthly wombes ybore.

22

The God did graunt his daughters deare demaund,
  To doen his Nephew in all riches flow;
  Eftsoones his heaped waves he did commaund,
  Out of their hollow bosome forth to throw
  All the huge threasure, which the sea below
  Had in his greedie gulfe devoured deepe,
  And him enriched through the overthrow
  And wreckes of many wretches, which did weepe,
And often waile their wealth, which he from them did keepe.

23

Shortly upon that shore there heaped was,
  Exceeding riches and all pretious things,
  The spoyle of all the world, that it did pas
  The wealth of th' East, and pompe of *Persian* kings;
  Gold, amber, yvorie, perles, owches, rings,
  And all that else was pretious and deare,
  The sea unto him voluntary brings,
  That shortly he a great Lord did appeare,
As was in all the lond of Faery, or elsewhere.

24

Thereto he was a doughtie dreaded knight,
  Tryde often to the scath of many deare,
  That none in equall armes him matchen might,
  The which his mother seeing, gan to feare
  Least his too haughtie hardines might reare
  Some hard mishap, in hazard of his life:
  For thy she oft him counseld to forbeare
  The bloudie battell and to stirre up strife,
But after all his warre, to rest his wearie knife.

25

And for his more assurance, she inquir'd
  One day of *Proteus* by his mightie spell
  (For *Proteus* was with prophecie inspir'd)
  Her deare sonnes destinie to her to tell,
  And the sad end of her sweet *Marinell*.
  Who through foresight of his eternall skill,
  Bad her from womankind to keepe him well:
  For of a woman he should have much ill,
A virgin strange and stout him should dismay, or kill.

26

For thy she gave him warning every day,
  The love of women not to entertaine;
  A lesson too too hard for living clay,
  From love in course of nature to refraine:
  Yet he his mothers lore did well retaine,
  And ever from faire Ladies love did fly;
  Yet many Ladies faire did oft complaine,
  That they for love of him would algates dy:
Dy, who so list for him, he was loves enimy.

27

But ah, who can deceive his destiny,
  Or weene by warning to avoyd his fate?
  That when he sleepes in most security,
  And safest seemes, him soonest doth amate,
  And findeth dew effect or soone or late.
  So feeble is the powre of fleshly arme.
  His mother bad him womens love to hate,
  For she of womans force did feare no harme;
So weening to have arm'd him, she did quite disarme.

28

This was that woman, this that deadly wound,
  That *Proteus* prophecide should him dismay,
  The which his mother vainely did expound,
  To be hart-wounding love, which should assay
  To bring her sonne unto his last decay.
  So ticle be the termes of mortall state,
  And full of subtile sophismes, which do play
  With double senses, and with false debate,
T' approve the unknowen purpose of eternall fate.

29

Too trew the famous *Marinell* it fownd,
    Who through late triall, on that wealthy Strond
    Inglorious now lies in senselesse swownd,
    Through heavy stroke of *Britomartis* hond.
    Which when his mother deare did understond,
    And heavy tydings heard, whereas she playd
    Amongst her watry sisters by a pond,
    Gathering sweete daffadillyes, to have made
Gay girlonds, from the Sun their forheads faire to shade;

30

Eftsoones both flowres and girlonds farre away
    She flong, and her faire deawy lockes yrent,
    To sorrow huge she turnd her former play,
    And gamesom merth to grievous dreriment:
    She threw her selfe downe on the Continent,
    Ne word did speake, but lay as in a swowne;
    Whiles all her sisters did for her lament,
    With yelling outcries, and with shrieking sowne;
And every one did teare her girlond from her crowne.

31

Soone as she up out of her deadly fit
    Arose, she bad her charet to be brought,
    And all her sisters, that with her did sit,
    Bad eke attonce their charets to be sought;
    Tho full of bitter griefe and pensife thought,
    She to her wagon clombe; clombe all the rest,
    And forth together went, with sorrow fraught.
    The waves obedient to their beheast,
Them yielded readie passage, and their rage surceast.

32

Great *Neptune* stood amazed at their sight,
    Whiles on his broad round backe they softly slid
    And eke himselfe mournd at their mournful plight,
    Yet wist not what their wailing ment, yet did
    For great compassion of their sorrow bid
    His mightie waters to them buxome bee:
    Eftsoones the roaring billowes still abid,
    And all the griesly Monsters of the See
Stood gaping at their gate, and wondred them to see.

33

A teme of Dolphins raunged in aray,
 Drew the smooth charet of sad *Cymoent*:
 They were all taught by *Triton*, to obay
 To the long traines at her commaundement:
 As swift as swallowes, on the waves they went,
 That their broad flaggie finnes no fome did reare,
 Ne bubbling roundell they behind them sent;
 The rest of other fishes drawen weare,
Which with their finny oars the swelling sea did sheare.

34

Soone as they bene arriv'd upon the brim
 Of the *Rich strond*, their charets they forlore,
 And let their temed fishes softly swim
 Along the margent of the fomy shore,
 Least they their finnes should bruze, and surbate sore
 Their tender feet upon the stony ground:
 And comming to the place, where all in gore
 And cruddy bloud enwallowed they found
The lucklesse *Marinell*, lying in deadly swound;

35

His mother swowned thrise, and the third time
 Could scarce recovered be out of her paine;
 Had she not bene devoyd of mortall slime,
 Shee should not then have been reliv'd againe,
 But soone as life recovered had the raine,
 She made so piteous mone and deare wayment,
 That the hard rocks could scarse from tears refraine,
 And all her sister Nymphes with one consent
Supplide her sobbing breaches with sad complement.

36

'Deare image of my selfe' (she said) 'that is
 The wretched sonne of wretched mother borne,
 Is this thine high advauncement, O is this
 Th' immortall name, with which thee yet unborne
 Thy Grandsire *Nereus* promist to adorne?
 Now lyest thou of life and honor reft;
 Now lyest thou a lumpe of earth forlorne,
 Ne of thy late life memory is left,
Ne can thy irrevocable destiny be weft?

37

'Fond *Proteus*, father of false prophecis,
 And they more fond, that credit to thee give,
 Not this the worke of womans hand ywis,
 That so deepe wound through these deare members drive.
 I feared love: but they that love do live,
 But they that die, do neither love nor hate.
 Nath'lesse to thee thy folly I forgive,
 And to my selfe, and to accursed fate
The guilt I doe ascribe: deare wisedome bought too late.

38

'O what availes it of immortall seed
 To beene ybred and never borne to die?
 Farre better I it deeme to die with speed,
 Then waste in woe and wailefull miserie:
 Who dyes the utmost dolor doth abye,
 But who that lives is left to waile his losse:
 So life is losse, and death felicitie.
 Sad life worse then glad death: and greater crosse
To see friends grave, then dead the grave self to engrosse.

39

'But if the heavens did his dayes envie,
 And my short blisse maligne, yet mote they well
 Thus much afford me, ere that he did die
 That the dim eyes of my deare *Marinell*
 I mote have closed, and him bed farewell,
 Sith other offices for mother meet
 They would not graunt.
 Yet maulgre them farewell, my sweetest sweet;
Farewell my sweetest sonne, sith we no more shall meet.'

40

Thus when they all had sorrowed their fill,
 They softly gan to search his griesly wound:
 And that they might him handle more at will,
 They him disarm'd, and spredding on the ground
 Their watchet mantles frindgd with silver round,
 They softly wipt away the gelly blood
 From th' orifice; which having well upbound,
 They pourd in soveraine balme and Nectar good,
Good both for earthly med'cine, and for heavenly food.

41

Tho when the lilly handed *Liagore*,
  (This *Liagore* whylome had learned skill
  In leaches craft, by great *Apolloes* lore,
  Sith her whylome upon high *Pindus* hill
  He loved, and at last her wombe did fill
  With heavenly seed, whereof wise *Pæon* sprong)
  Did feele his pulse, shee knew there staied still
  Some little life his feeble sprites emong;
Which to his mother told, despeire she from her flong.

42

Tho up him taking in their tender hands,
  They easily unto her charet beare:
  Her teme at her commaundement quiet stands,
  Whiles they the corse into her wagon reare,
  And strow with flowres the lamentable beare:
  Then all the rest into their coches clim,
  And through the brackish waves their passage sheare;
  Upon great *Neptunes* necke they softly swim,
And to her watry chamber swiftly carry him.

43

Deepe in the bottome of the sea, her bowre
  Is built of hollow billowes heaped hye,
  Like to thicke cloudes, that threat a stormy showre,
  And vauted all within, like to the sky,
  In which the Gods do dwell eternally;
  There they him laid in easie couch well dight;
  And sent in haste for *Tryphon*, to apply
  Salves to his wounds, and medicines of might;
For *Tryphon* of sea gods the soveraine leach is hight.

44

The whiles the *Nymphes* sit all about him round,
  Lamenting his mishap and heavy plight;
  And ofte his mother vewing his wide wound,
  Cursed the hand, that did so deadly smight
  Her dearest sonne, her dearest harts delight.
  But none of all those curses overtooke
  The warlike Maid, th' ensample of that might,
  But fairely well she thriv'd, and well did brooke
Her noble deeds, ne her right course for ought forsooke.

45

Yet did false *Archimage* her still pursew,
    To bring to passe his mischievous intent,
    Now that he had her singled from the crew
    Of courteous knights, the Prince, and Faery gent,
    Whom late in chace of beautie excellent
    She left, pursewing that same foster strong;
    Of whose foule outrage they impatient,
    And full of fiery zeale, him followed long,
To reskew her from shame, and to revenge her wrong.

46

Through thick and thin, through mountaines and through plains,
    Those two great champions did attonce pursew
    The fearefull damzell, with incessant paines:
    Who from them fled, as light-foot hare from vew
    Of hunter swift, and scent of houndes trew.
    At last they came unto a double way,
    Where, doubtfull which to take, her to reskew,
    Themselves they did dispart, each to assay
Whether more happie were, to win so goodly pray.

47

But *Timias*, the Princes gentle Squire,
    That Ladies love unto his Lord forlent,
    And with proud envy, and indignant ire,
    After that wicked foster fiercely went.
    So beene they three three sondry wayes ybent.
    But fairest fortune to the Prince befell,
    Whose chaunce it was, that soone he did repent,
    To take that way, in which that Damozell
Was fledd afore, affraid of him, as feend of hell.

48

At last of her farre off he gained vew:
    Then gan he freshly pricke his fomy steed,
    And ever as he nigher to her drew,
    So evermore he did increase his speed,
    And of each turning still kept warie heed:
    Aloud to her he oftentimes did call,
    To doe away vaine doubt, and needlesse dreed:
    Full myld to her he spake, and oft let fall
Many meeke wordes, to stay and comfort her withall.

49

But nothing might relent her hastie flight;
   So deepe the deadly feare of that foule swaine
   Was earst impressed in her gentle spright;
   Like as a fearefull Dove, which through the raine,
   Of the wide aire her way does cut amaine,
   Having farre off espyde a Tassell gent,
   Which after her his nimble wings doth straine,
   Doubleth her hast for feare to be for-hent,
And with her pineons cleaves the liquid firmament.

50

With no lesse haste, and eke with no lesse dreed,
   That fearefull Ladie fledd from him, that ment
   To her no evill thought nor evill deed;
   Yet former feare of being fowly shent,
   Carried her forward with her first intent:
   And though oft looking backward, well she vewd,
   Her selfe freed from that foster insolent,
   And that it was a knight, which now her sewd,
Yet she no lesse the knight-feard, then that villein rude.

51

His uncouth shield and straunge armes her dismay'd,
   Whose like in Faery lond were seldom seene,
   That fast she from him fled, no lesse afrayd,
   Then of wilde beastes if she had chased beene:
   Yet he her followd still with courage keene,
   So long that now the golden *Hesperus*
   Was mounted high in top of heaven sheene,
   And warnd his other brethren joyeous,
To light their blessed lamps in *Joves* eternall hous.

52

All suddenly dim woxe the dampish ayre,
   And griesly shadowes covered heaven bright,
   That now with thousand starres was decked fayre:
   Which when the Prince beheld, a lothfull sight,
   And that perforce, for want of lenger light,
   He mote surcease his suit, and lose the hope
   Of his long labour, he gan fowly wyte
   His wicked fortune, that had turnd aslope,
And cursed night, that reft from him so goodly scope.

53

Tho when her wayes he could no more descry,
   But to and fro at disaventure strayd;
   Like as a ship, whose Lodestarre suddenly
   Covered with cloudes, her Pilot hath dismayd;
   His wearisome pursuit perforce he stayd,
   And from his loftie steed dismounting low,
   Did let him forage. Downe himselfe he layd
   Upon the grassie ground, to sleepe a throw;
The cold earth was his couch, the hard steele his pillow.

54

But gentle Sleepe envyde him any rest;
   In stead thereof sad sorrow, and disdaine
   Of his hard hap did vexe his noble brest,
   And thousand fancies bet his idle braine
   With their light wings, the sights of semblants vaine:
   Oft did he wish that Lady faire mote bee
   His Faery Queene, for whom he did complaine:
   Or that his Faery Queene, were such, as shee:
And ever hastie Night he blamed bitterlie.

55

'Night thou foule Mother of annoyance sad,
   Sister of heavie death, and nourse of woe,
   Which wast begot in heaven, but for thy bad
   And brutish shape thrust downe to hell below,
   Where by the grim floud of *Cocytus* slow
   Thy dwelling is, in *Herebus* blacke hous,
   (Black *Herebus* thy husband is the foe
   Of all the Gods) where thou ungratious,
Halfe of thy dayes doest lead in horrour hideous.

56

'What had th' eternall Maker need of thee
   The world in his continuall course to keepe,
   That doest all things deface, ne lettest see
   The beautie of his worke? Indeed in sleepe
   The slouthfull bodie, that doth love to steepe
   His lustlesse limbes, and drowne his baser mind,
   Doth praise thee oft, and oft from *Stygian* deepe
   Calles thee, his goddesse in his error blind,
And great Dame Natures handmaide, chearing every kind.

57

'But well I wote, that to an heavy hart
　　Thou art the root and nurse of bitter cares,
　　Breeder of new, renewer of old smarts:
　　In stead of rest thou lendest rayling teares,
　　In stead of sleepe thou sendest troublous feares,
　　And dreadfull visions, in the which alive
　　The drearie image of sad death appeares:
　　So from the wearie spirit thou doest drive
Desired rest, and men of happinesse deprive.

58

'Under thy mantle black there hidden lye
　　Light-shonning theft, and traiterous intent,
　　Abhorred bloudshed, and vile felony,
　　Shamefull deceipt, and daunger imminent;
　　Foule horror, and eke hellish dreriment:
　　All these I wote in they protection bee,
　　And light doe shonne, for fear of being shent:
　　For light ylike is loth'd of them and thee,
And all that lewdnesse love, doe hate the light to see.

59

'For day discovers all dishonest wayes,
　　And sheweth each thing, as it is indeed:
　　The prayses of high God he faire displayes,
　　And his large bountie rightly doth areed.
　　Dayes dearest children be the blessed seed,
　　Which darknesse shall subdew, and heaven win:
　　Truth is his daughter; he her first did breed,
　　Most sacred virgin without spot of sin.
Our life is day, but death with darknesse doth begin.

60

'O when will day then turne to me againe.
　　And bring with him his long expected light?
　　O *Titan*, haste to reare thy joyous waine:
　　Speed thee to spred abroad thy beames bright,
　　And chase away this too long lingring night,
　　Chace her away, from whence she came, to hell.
　　She, she it is, that hath me done despight:
　　There let her with the damned spirits dwell,
And yeeld her roome to day, that can it governe well.'

61

Thus did the Prince that wearie night outweare,
  In restlesse anguish and unquiet paine:
  And earely, ere the morrow did upreare
  His deawy head out of the *Ocean* maine,
  He up arose, as halfe in great disdaine,
  And clombe unto his steed.   So forth he went,
  With heavie looke and lumpish pace, that plaine
  In him bewraid great grudge and maltalent:
His steed eke seemd t' apply his steps to his intent.

Canto V

Prince Arthur heares of Florimell:
Three fosters Timias wound,
Belphebe finds him almost dead,
And reareth out of sownd.

1

Wonder it is to see in diverse minds,
  How diversly love doth his pageants play,
  And shewes his powre in variable kinds:
  The baser wit, whose idle thoughts alway
  Are wont to cleave unto the lowly clay,
  It stirreth up to sensuall desire,
  And in lewd slouth to wast his carelesse day:
  But in brave sprite it kindles goodly fire,
That to all high desert and honour doth aspire.

2

Ne suffereth it uncomely idlenesse,
  In his free thought to build her sluggish nest:
  Ne suffereth it thought of ungentlenesse,
  Ever to creepe into his noble brest,
  But to the highest and the worthiest
  Lifteth it up, that else would lowly fall:
  It lets not fall, it lets it not to rest.
  It lets not scarse this Prince to breath at all,
But to his first poursuit him forward still doth call.

3

Who long time wandred through the forrest wyde,
  To finde some issue thence, till that at last
  He met a Dwarfe, that seemed terrifyde
  With some late perill, which he hardly past,
  Or other accident, which him aghast;
  Of whom he asked, whence he lately came,
  And whither now he traveiled so fast:
  For sore he swat, and ronning through that same
Thicke forest, was bescratcht and both his feet nigh lame.

4

Panting for breath, and almost out of hart,
  The Dwarfe him answerd, 'Sir, ill mote I stay
  To tell the same. I lately did depart
  From Faery court, where I have many a day
  Served a gentle Lady of great sway,

And high accompt through out all Elfin land,
Who lately left the same, and tooke this way:
Her now I seeke, and if ye understand
Which way she fared hath, good Sir tell out of hand.'

5

'What mister wight' (said he) 'and how arayd?'
'Royally clad' (quoth he) 'in cloth of gold,
As meetest may beseeme a noble mayd;
Her faire lockes in rich circlet be enrold,
A fairer wight did never Sunne behold,
And on a Palfrey rides more white then snow,
Yet she her selfe is whiter manifold:
The surest signe, whereby ye may her know,
Is that she is the fairest wight alive, I trow.'

6

'Now certes swaine' (said he) 'such one I weene,
Fast flying through this forest from her fo,
A foule ill favoured foster, I have seene;
Her selfe, well as I might, I reskewd tho,
But could not stay; so fast she did forego,
Carried away with wings of speedy feare.'
'Ah dearest God' (quoth he) 'that is great woe,
And wondrous ruth to all, that shall it heare.
But can ye read Sir, how I may her find, or where?'

7

'Perdy me lever were to weeten that,'
(Said he) 'then ransome of the richest knight,
Or all the good that ever yet I gat:
But froward fortune, and too forward Night
Such happinesse did, maulgre, to me spight,
And fro me reft both life and light attone.
But Dwarfe aread, what is that Lady bright,
That through this forest wandreth thus alone;
For of her errour straunge I have great ruth and mone.'

8

'That Lady is' (quoth he) 'where so she bee,
The bountiest virgin, and most debonaire,
That ever living eye I weene did see;
Lives none this day, that may with her compare
In stedfast chastitie and vertue rare,
The goodly ornaments of beautie bright;

And is ycleped *Florimell* the faire,
  Faire *Florimell* belov'd of many a knight,
Yet she loves none but one, that *Marinell* is hight.

9

'A Sea-nymphes sonne, that *Marinell* is hight,
  Of my deare Dame is loved dearely well;
  In other none, but him, she sets delight,
  All her delight is set on *Marinell*;
  But he sets nought at all by *Florimell*:
  For Ladies love his mother long ygoe
  Did him, they say, forwarne through sacred spell.
  But fame now flies, that of a forreine foe
He is yslaine, which is the ground of all our woe.

10

'Five days there be, since he (they say) was slaine,
  And foure since *Florimell* the Court for-went,
  And vowed never to returne againe,
  Till him alive or dead she did invent.
  Therefore, faire Sir, for love of knighthood gent,
  And honour of trew Ladies, if ye may
  By your good counsell, or bold hardiment,
  Or succour her, or me direct the way;
Do one or other good, I you most humbly pray.

11

'So may ye gaine to you full great renowne,
  Of all good Ladies through the worlde so wide,
  And haply in her hart finde highest rowme,
  Of whom ye seeke to be most magnifide:
  At least eternall meede shall you abide.'
  To whom the Prince; 'Dwarfe, comfort to thee take,
  For till thou tidings learne, what her betide,
  I here avow thee never to forsake.
Ill weares he armes, that nill them use for Ladies sake.'

12

So with the Dwarfe he back return'd againe,
  To seeke his Lady, where he mote her find;
  But by the way he greatly gan complaine
  The want of his good Squire late left behind,
  For whom he wondrous pensive grew in mind,
  For doubt of daunger, which mote him betide;
  For him he loved above all mankind,

Having him trew and faithfull ever tride,
And bold, as ever Squire that waited by knights side.

13

Who all this while full hardly was assayd
    Of deadly daunger, which to him betid;
    For whiles his Lord pursewd that noble Mayd,
    After that foster fowle he fiercely rid,
    To bene avenged of the shame, he did
    To that faire Damzell: Him he chaced long
    Through the thick woods, wherein he would have hid
    His shamefull head from his avengement strong,
And oft him threatned death for his outrageous wrong.

14

Nathlesse the villen sped him selfe so well,
    Whether through swiftnesse of his speedy beast,
    Or knowledge of those woods, where he did dwell,
    That shortly he from daunger was releast,
    And out of sight escaped at the least;
    Yet not escaped from the dew reward
    Of his bad deeds, which daily he increast,
    Ne ceased not, till him oppressed hard
The heavie plague, that for such leachours is prepard.

15

For soone as he was vanisht out of sight,
    His coward courage gan emboldned bee,
    And cast t' avenge him of that fowle despight,
    Which he had borne of his bold enimee.
    Tho to his brethren came: for they were three
    Ungratious children of one graceless sire,
    And unto them complained, how that he
    Had used bene of that foolehardy Squire;
So them with bitter words he stird to bloudy ire.

16

Forthwith themselves with their sad instruments
    Of spoyle and murder they gan arme bylive,
    And with him forth into the forest went,
    To wreake the wrath, which he did earst revive
    In their sterne brests, on him which late did drive
    Their brother to reproch and shamefull flight:
    For they had vow'd, that never he alive
    Out of that forest should escape their might;
Vile rancour their rude harts had fild with such despight.

17

Within that wood there was a covert glade,
  Foreby a narrow foord, to them well knowne,
  Through which it was uneath for wight to wade;
  And now by fortune it was overflowne:
  By that same way they knew that Squire unknowne
  Mote algates passe; for thy themselves they set
  There in await, with thicke woods over growne,
  And all the while their malice they did whet
With cruell threats, his passage through the ford to let.

18

It fortuned, as they devised had,
  The gentle Squire came ryding that same way,
  Unweeting of their wile and treason bad,
  And through the ford to passen did assay;
  But that fierce foster, which late fled away,
  Stoutly forth stepping on the further shore,
  Him boldly bad his passage there to stay,
  Till he had made amends, and full restore
For all the damage, which he had him doen afore.

19

With that at him a quiv'ring dart he threw,
  With so fell force and villeinous despighte,
  That through his haberjeon the forkehead flew,
  And through the linked mayles empierced quite,
  But had no powre in his soft flesh to bite:
  That stroke the hardy Squire did sore displease;
  But more that him he could not come to smite;
  For by no meanes the high banke he could sease,
But labour'd long in that deepe ford with vaine disease.

20

And still the foster with his long bore-speare
  Him kept from landing at his wished will;
  Anone one sent out of the thicket neare
  A cruell shaft, headed with deadly ill,
  And fethered with an unlucky quill;
  The wicked steele stayd not, till it did light
  In his left thigh, and deepely did it thrill:
  Exceeding griefe that wound in him empight,
But more that with his foes he could not come to fight.

21

At last through wrath and vengeaunce making way,
    He on the bancke arrivd with mickle paine,
    Where the third brother him did sore assay,
    And drove at him with all his might and maine
    A forrest bill, which both his hands did straine;
    But warily he did avoide the blow,
    And with his speare requited him againe,
    That both his sides were thrilled with the throw,
And a large streame of bloud out of the wound did flow.

22

He tombling downe, with gnashing teeth did bite
    The bitter earth, and bad to let him in
    Into the balefull house of endlesse night,
    Where wicked ghosts do waile their former sin.
    Tho gan the battell freshly to begin;
    For nathemore for that spectacle bad,
    Did th' other two their cruell vengeaunce blin,
    But both attonce on both sides him bestad,
And load upon him layd, his life for to have had.

23

Tho when that villain he aviz'd, which late
    Affrighted had the fairest *Florimell*,
    Full of fiers fury and indignant hate,
    To him he turned, and with rigour fell
    Smote him so rudely on the Pannikell,
    That to the chin he cleft his head in twaine:
    Downe on the ground his carkas groveling fell;
    His sinfull soule with desperate disdaine,
Out of her fleshly ferme fled to the place of paine.

24

That seeing now the only last of three,
    Who with that wicked shaft him wounded had,
    Trembling with horrour, as that did foresee
    The fearefull end of his avengement sad,
    Through which he follow should his brethren bad,
    His bootelesse bow in feeble had upcaught,
    And therewith shot an arrow at the lad;
    Which faintly fluttering, scarce his helmet raught,
And glauncing fell to ground, but him annoyed naught.

25

With that he would have fled into the wood;
  But *Timias* him lightly overhent,
  Right as he entring was into the flood,
  And strooke at him with force so violent,
  That headlesse him into the foord he sent:
  The carkas with the streame was carried downe,
  But th' head fell backeward on the Continent.
  So mischief fel upon the meaners crowne;
They three be dead with shame, the Squire lives with renowne.

26

He lives, but takes small joy of his renowne;
  For of that cruell wound he bled so sore,
  That from his steed he fell in deadly swowne;
  Yet still the bloud forth gusht in so great store,
  That he lay wallowd all in his owne gore.
  Now God thee keepe, thou gentlest Squire alive,
  Else shall thy loving Lord thee see no more,
  But both of comfort him thou shalt deprive,
And eke thy selfe of honour, which thou didst atchive.

27

Providence hevenly passeth living thought,
  And doth for wretched mens reliefe make way;
  For loe great grace or fortune thither brought
  Comfort to him, that comfortlesse now lay.
  In those same woods, ye well remember may,
  How that a noble hunteresse did wonne,
  She, that base *Braggadochio* did affray,
  And made him fast out of the forrest runne;
Belphœbe was her name, as faire as *Phœbus* sunne.

28

She on a day, as she pursewd the chace
  Of some wild beast, which with her arrowes keene
  She wounded had, the same along did trace
  By tract of bloud, which she had freshly seene,
  To have besprinckled all the grassy greene;
  By the great persue, which she there perceav'd,
  Well hoped she the beast engor'd had beene,
  And made more hast, the life to have bereav'd:
But ah, her expectation greatly was deceav'd.

29

Shortly she came, whereas that wofull Squire,
　　With bloud deformed, lay in deadly swownd;
　　In whose faire eyes, like lamps of quenched fire,
　　The Christall humour stood congealed rownd;
　　His locks, like faded leaves fallen to grownd,
　　Knotted with bloud, in bounches rudely ran,
　　And his sweete lips, on which before that stownd
　　The bud of youth to blossome faire began,
Spoild of their rosie red, were woxen pale and wan.

30

Saw never living eye more heavy sight,
　　That could have made a rocke of stone to rew,
　　Or rive in twaine: which when that Lady bright
　　Besides all hope with melting eyes did vew,
　　All suddeinly abasht she chaunged hew,
　　And with sterne horrour backward gan to start:
　　But when she better him beheld, she grew
　　Full of soft passion and unwonted smart:
The point of pitty perced through her tender hart.

31

Meekely she bowed downe, to weete if life
　　Yet in his frosen members did remaine,
　　And feeling by his pulses beating rife,
　　That the weake soule her seat did yet retaine,
　　She cast to comfort him with busie paine:
　　His double folded necke she reard upright,
　　And rubd his temples, and each trembling vaine;
　　His mayled haberjeon she did undight,
And from his head his heavy burganet did light.

32

Into the woods thenceforth in hast she went,
　　To seeke for hearbes that mote him remedy;
　　For she of hearbes had great intendiment,
　　Taught of the Nymphe, which from her infancy
　　Her nourced had in trew Nobility:
　　There, whether it divine *Tobacco* were,
　　Or *Panachæa*, or *Polygony*,
　　Shee found, and brought it to her patient deare
Who al this while lay bleeding out his hart-bloud neare.

33

The soveraigne weede betwixt two marbles plaine
   She pownded small, and did in peeces bruze,
   And then atweene her lilly handes twaine,
   Into his wound the juice thereof did scruze,
   And round about, as she could well it uze,
   The flesh therewith shee suppled and did steepe,
   T' abate all spasme, and soke the swelling bruze,
   And after having searcht the intuse deepe,
She with her scarfe did bind the wound from cold to keepe.

34

By this he had sweet life recur'd againe,
   And groning inly deepe, at last his eyes,
   His watry eyes, drizling like deawy raine,
   He up gan lift toward the azure skies,
   From whence descend all hopelesse remedies:
   Therewith he sigh'd, and turning him aside,
   The goodly Mayd full of divinities,
   And gifts of heavenly grace he by him spide,
Her bow and gilden quiver lying him beside.

35

'Mercy deare Lord' (said he) 'what grace is this,
   That thou hast shewed to me sinfull wight,
   To send thine Angell from her bowre of blis,
   To comfort me in my distressed plight?
   Angell, or Goddesse do I call thee right?
   What service may I do unto thee meete,
   That hast from darkenesse me returnd to light,
   And with thy heavenly salves and med'cines sweete,
Hast drest my sinfull wounds? I kisse thy blessed feete.'

36

Thereat she blushing said, 'Ah gentle Squire,
   Nor Goddesse I, nor Angell, but the Mayd,
   And daughter of a woody Nymphe, desire
   No service, but thy safety and ayd;
   Which if thou gaine, I shalbe well apayd.
   We mortall wights, whose lives and fortunes bee
   To commun accidents still open layd,
   Are bound with commun bond of fraïltee,
To succour wretched wights, whom we captived see.'

37

By this her Damzels, which the former chace
    Had undertaken after her, arriv'd,
    As did *Belphœbe*, in the bloudy place,
    And thereby deemd the beast had bene depriv'd
    Of life, whom late their Ladies arrow ryv'd:
    For thy the bloudy tract they followd fast,
    And every one to runne the swiftest stryv'd;
    But two of them the rest far overpast,
And where their Lady was, arrived at the last.

38

Where when they saw that goodly boy, with blood
    Defowled, and their Lady dresse his wownd,
    They wondred much, and shortly understood,
    How him in deadly cace their Lady fownd,
    And reskewed out of the heavy stownd.
    Eftsoones his warlike courser, which was strayd
    Farre in the woods, whiles that he lay in swownd,
    She made those Damzels search, which being stayd,
They did him set thereon, and forth with them convayd.

39

Into that forest farre they thence him led,
    Where was their dwelling, in a pleasant glade,
    With mountaines round about environed,
    And mighty woods, which did the valley shade,
    And like a stately Theatre it made,
    Spreading it selfe into a spatious plaine.
    And in the midst a little river plaide
    Emongst the pumy stones, which seemd to plaine
With gentle murmure, that his course they did restraine.

40

Beside the same a dainty place there lay,
    Planted with mirtle trees and laurells greene,
    In which the birds song many a lovely lay
    Of gods high prayse, and of their loves sweet teene,
    As it an earthly Paradize had beene:
    In whose enclosed shadow there was pight
    A faire Pavilion, scarcely to be seene,
    The which was all within most richly dight,
That greatest Princes liking it mote well delight.

41

Thither they brought that wounded Squire, and layd
   In easie couch his feeble limbes to rest,
   He rested him a while, and then the Mayd
   His readie wound with better salves new drest;
   Daily she dressed him, and did the best
   His grievous hurt to garish, that she might,
   That shortly she his dolour hath redrest,
   And his foule sore reduced to faire plight:
It she reduced, but himselfe destroyed quight.

42

O foolish Physick, and unfruitfull paine,
   That heales up one and makes another wound:
   She his hurt thigh to him recurd againe,
   But hurt his hart, the which before was sound,
   Through an unwary dart, which did rebound
   From her faire eyes and gracious countenaunce.
   What bootes it him from death to be unbound,
   To be captived in endlesse duraunce
Of sorrow and despaire without aleggeaunce?

43

Still as his wound did gather, and grow hole,
   So still his hart woxe sore, and health decayd:
   Madnesse to save a part, and lose the whole.
   Still whenas he beheld the heavenly Mayd,
   Whiles dayly plaisters to his wound she layd,
   So still his Malady the more increast,
   The whiles her matchlesse beautie him dismayd,
   Ah God, what other could he do at least,
But love so faire a Lady, that his life releast?

44

Long while he strove in his courageous brest
   With reason dew the passion to subdew,
   And love for to dislodge out of his nest:
   Still when her excellencies he did vew,
   Her soveraigne bounty, and celestiall hew,
   The same to love he strongly was constraind:
   But when his meane estate he did revew,
   He from such hardy boldnesse was restraind,
And of his lucklesse lot and cruell love thus plaind.

45

'Unthankfull wretch' (said he) 'is this the meed,
  With which her soveraigne mercy thou doest quight?
  Thy life she saved by her gratious deed,
  But thou doest weene with villeinous despight,
  To blot her honour, and her heavenly light.
  Dye rather, dye, then so disloyally
  Deeme of her high desert, or seeme so light:
  Faire death it is to shonne more shame, to dy:
Dye rather, dy, then ever love disloyally.

46

'But if to love disloyalty it bee,
  Shall I then hate her that from deathes dore
  Me brought? ah farre be such reproch fro mee.
  What can I lesse do, then her love therefore,
  Sith I her dew reward cannot restore:
  Dye rather, dye, and dying do her serve,
  Dying her serve, and living her adore;
  Thy life she gave, thy life she doth deserve:
Dye rather, dye, then ever from her service swerve.

47

'But foolish boy, what bootes thy service bace
  To her, to whom the heavens doe serve and sew?
  Thou a meane Squire of meeke and lowly place,
  She heavenly borne and of celestiall hew.
  How then? of all love taketh equall vew:
  Ahd doth not highest God vouchsafe to take
  The love and service of the basest crew?
  If she will not, dye meekly for her sake;
Dye rather, dye, then ever so faire love forsake.'

48

Thus warreid he long time against his will,
  Till that through weaknesse he was forst at last,
  To yield himselfe unto the mighty ill:
  Which as a victour proud, gan ransack fast
  His inward parts, and all his entrayles wast,
  That neither bloud in face nor life in hart
  It left, but both did quite drye up and blast;
  As percing levin, which the inner part
Of every thing consumes, and calcineth by art.

49

Which seeing faire *Belphœbe* gan to feare,
　　Least that his wound were inly well not healed,
　　Of that the wicked steele empoysned were:
　　Litle shee weend, that love he close concealed;
　　Yet still he wasted, as the snow congealed,
　　When the bright sunne his beams thereon doth beat;
　　Yet never he his hart to her revealed,
　　But rather chose to dye for sorrow great,
Then with dishonorable termes her to entreat.

50

She gracious Lady, yet no paines did spare,
　　To do him ease, or do him remedy:
　　Many Restoratives of vertues rare,
　　And costly Cordialles she did apply,
　　To mitigate his stubborne mallady:
　　But that sweet Cordiall, which can restore
　　A love-sick hart, she did to him envy;
　　To him, and to all th' unworthy world forlore
She did envy that soveraiyne salve, in secret store.

51

That dainty Rose, the daughter of her Morne,
　　More deare then life she tendered, whose flowre
　　The girlond of her honour did adorne:
　　Ne suffred she the Middayes scorching powre,
　　Ne the sharp Northerne wind thereon on showre,
　　But lapped up her silken leaves most chaire,
　　When so the froward skye began to lowre:
　　But soone as calmed was the Christall aire,
She did it faire dispred, and led to florish faire.

52

Eternall God in his almighty powre,
　　To make ensample of his heavenly grace,
　　In Paradize whilome did plant this flowre,
　　Whence he it fetcht out of her native place,
　　And did in stocke of earthly flesh enrace,
　　That mortall men her glory should admire:
　　In gentle Ladies brest, and bounteous race
　　Of woman kind it fairest flowre doth spire,
And beneath fruit of honour and all chast desire.

53

Faire ympes of beautie, whose bright shining beames
  Adorne the world with like to heavenly light,
  And to your willes both royalties and Realmes
  Subdew, through conquest of your wondrous might,
  With this faire flowre your goodly girlonds dight,
  Of chastity and vertue virginall,
  That shall embellish more your beautie bright,
  And crowne your heades with heavenly coronall,
Such as the Angels weare before Gods tribunall.

54

To your faire selves a faire ensample frame,
  Of this faire virgin, this *Belphœbe* faire,
  To whom in perfect love, and spotlesse fame
  Of chastitie, none living may compaire:
  Ne poysnous Envy justly can empaire
  The prayse of her fresh flowring Maidenhead;
  For thy she standeth on the highest staire
  Of th' honorable stage of womanhead,
That Ladies all may follow her ensample dead.

55

In so great prayse of stedfast chastity,
  Nathlesse she was so curteous and kind,
  Tempred with grace, and goodly modesty,
  That seemed those two vertues strove to find
  The higher place in her Heroick mind:
  So striving each did other more augment,
  And both encreast the prayse of woman kind,
  And both encreast her beautie excellent;
So all did make in her a perfect complement.

Canto VI

*The birth of faire Belphœbe and
Of Amoret is told.
The Gardins of Adonis fraught
With pleasures manifold.*

1

Well may I weene, faire Ladies, all this while
  Ye wonder, how this noble Damozell
  So great perfections did in her compile,
  Sith that in salvage forests she did dwell,
  So farre from court and royall Citadell,
  The great schoolmistresse of all curtesy:
  Seemeth that such wild woods should far expell
  All civil usage and gentility,
And gentle sprite deforme with rude rusticity.

2

But to this faire *Belphœbe* in her berth
  The hevens so favourable were and free,
  Looking with myld aspect upon the earth,
  In th' *Horoscope* of her nativitee,
  That all the gifts of grace and chastitee
  On her they poured forth of plenteous horne;
  Jove laught on *Venus* from his soveraigne see,
  And *Phœbus* with faire beames did her adorne,
And all the *Graces* rockt her cradle being borne.

3

Her berth was of the wombe of Morning dew,
  And her conception of the joyous Prime,
  And all her whole creation did her shew
  Pure and unspotted from all loathly crime,
  That is ingenerate in fleshly slime.
  So was this virgin borne, so was she bred,
  So was she trayned up from time to time,
  In all chaste vertue, and true bounti-hed,
Till to her dew perfection she was ripened.

4

Her mother was the faire *Chrysogonee*,
  The daughter of *Amphisa*, who by race
  A Faerie was, yborne of high degree,
  She bore *Belphœbe*, she bore in like cace
  Faire *Amoretta* in the second place:

These two were twinnes, and twixt them two did share
The heritage of all celestiall grace.
That all the rest it seem'd they robbed bare
Of bountie, and of beautie, and all vertues rare.

5

It were a goodly storie, to declare,
  By what straunge accident faire *Chrysogone*
Conceiv'd these infants, and how them she bare,
  In this wilde forrest wandring all alone,
  After she had nine moneths fulfild and gone:
For not as other wemens commune brood,
  They were enwombed in the sacred throne
Of her chaste bodie, nor with commune food,
As other wemens babies, they sucked vitall blood.

6

But wondrously they were begot, and bred
  Through influence of th' heavens fruitfull ray,
As it in antique bookes is mentioned.
  It was upon a Sommers shynie day,
  When *Titan* faire his beames did display,
In a fresh fountaine, farre from all mens vew,
  She bath'd her brest, the boyling heat t' allay;
She bath'd with roses red, and violets blew,
And all the sweetest flowres, that in the forrest grew.

7

Till faint through irkesome wearinesse, adowne
  Upon the grassie ground her selfe she layd
To sleepe, the whiles a gentle slombring swowne
  Upon her fell all naked bare displayd;
  The sunne-beames bright upon her body playd,
Being through former bathing mollifide,
  And pierst into her wombe, where they embayd
With so sweete sence and secret powre unspide,
That in her pregnant flesh they shortly fructifide.

8

Miraculous may seeme to him that reades
  So straunge emsample of conception;
But reason teacheth that the fruitfull seades
  Of all things living, through impression
  Of the sunbeames in moyst complexion,
Doe life conceive and quickned are by kynd:

So after *Nilus* inundation,
Infinite shapes of creatures men doe fynd,
Informed in the mud, on which the Sunne hath shynd.

9

Great father he of generation
  Is rightly cald, th' authour of life and light;
  And his faire sister for creation
  Ministreth matter fit, which tempred right
  With heate and humour, breedes the living wight.
  So sprong these twinnes in womb of *Chrysogone*,
  Yet wist she nought thereof, but sore affright,
  Wondred to see her belly so upblone,
Which still increast, till she her terme had full outgone.

10

Whereof conceiving shame and foule disgrace,
  Albe her guiltlesse conscience her cleard,
  She fled into the wildernesse a space,
  Till that unweeldy burden she had reard,
  And shund dishonor, which as death she feard:
  Where wearie of long travell, downe to rest
  Her selfe she set, and comfortably cheard;
  There a sad cloud of sleepe her overkest,
And seized every sense with sorrow sore opprest.

11

It fortuned, faire *Venus* having lost
  Her little sonne, the winged god of love,
  Who for some light displeasure, which him crost,
  Was from her fled, as flit as ayerie Dove,
  And left her blisfull bowre of joy above,
  (So from her often he had fled away,
  When she for ought him sharpely did reprove,
  And wandred in the world in strange aray,
Disguiz'd in a thousand shapes, that none might him bewray.)

12

Him for to seeke, she left her heavenly hous,
  The house of goodly formes and faire aspects,
  Whence all the world derives the glorious
  Features of beautie, and all shapes select,
  With which high God his workmanship hath deckt;
  And searched every way, through which his wings
  Had borne him, or his tract she mote detect:

She promist kisses sweet, and sweeter things
Unto the man, that of him tydings to her brings.

13

First she him sought in Court, where most he used
   Whylome to haunt, but there she found him not;
   But many there she found, which sore accused
   His falsehood, and with foule infamous blot
   His cruell deedes and wicked wyles did spot:
   Ladies and Lords she everywhere mote heare
   Complayning, how with his empoysned shot
   Their wofull harts he wounded had whyleare,
And so had left them languishing twixt hope and feare.

14

She then the Citties sought from gate to gate,
   And every one did aske, did he him see;
   And every one her answerd, that too late
   He had him seene, and felt the crueltie
   Of his sharpe darts and whot artillerie;
   And every one threw forth reproches rife
   Of his mischievous deedes, and said, That hee
   Was the disturber of all civill life,
The enimy of peace, and authour of all strife.

15

Then in the countrey she abroad him sought,
   And in the rurall cottages inquired,
   Where also many plaints to her were brought,
   How he their heedelesse harts with love had fyred,
   And his false venim through their veines inspyred;
   And eke the gentle shepheard swaynes, which sat
   Keeping their fleecie flockes, as they were hyred,
   She sweetly heard complaine, both how and what
Her sonne had to them doen; yet she did smile thereat.

16

But when in none of all these she him got,
   She gan avize, where else he mote him hyde:
   At last she her bethought that she had not
   Yet sought the salvage woods and forrests wyde,
   In which full many lovely Nymphes abyde,
   Mongst whom might be that he did closely lye,
   Or that the love of some of them him tyde:
   For thy she thither cast her course t' apply,
To search the secret haunts of *Dianes* company.

17

Shortly unto the wasteful woods she came,
　Whereas she found the Goddesse with her crew,
　After late chace of their embrewed game,
　Sitting beside a fountaine in a rew,
　Some of them washing with the liquid dew
　From off their dainty limbs the dustie sweat
　And soyle which did deforme their lively hew;
　Others lay shaded from the scorching heat;
The rest upon her person gave attendance great.

18

She having hong upon a bough on high
　Her bow and painted quiver, had unlaste
　Her silver buskins from her nimble thigh,
　And her lancke loynes ungirt, and brests unbraste,
　After her heat the breathing cold to taste;
　Her golden lockes, that late in tresses bright
　Embreaded were for hindring of her haste,
　Now loose about her shoulders hong undight,
And were with sweet *Ambrosia* all besprinckled light.

19

Soone as she *Venus* saw behinde her backe,
　She was asham'd to be so loose surprized,
　And woxe halfe wroth against her damzels slacke,
　That had not her thereof before avized,
　But suffred her so carelesly disguized
　Be overtaken.　Soone her garments loose
　Upgath'ring, in her bosome she comprized
　Well as she might, and to the Goddesse rose,
Whiles all her Nymphes did like a girlond her enclose.

20

Goodly she gan faire *Cytherea* greet,
　And shortly asked her, what cause her brought
　Into that wildenesse for her unmeet,
　From her sweete bowres, and beds with pleasures fraught:
　That suddein change she strange adventure thought.
　To whom halfe weeping, she thus answered,
　That she her dearest sonne *Cupido* sought,
　Who in his frowardnesse from her was fled,
That she repented sore, to have him angered.

21

Thereat *Diana* gan to smile, in scorne
  Of her vaine plaint, and to her scoffing sayd;
  'Great pittie sure, that ye be so forlorne
  Of your gay sonne, that gives ye so good ayd
  To your disports: ill mote ye bene apayd.'
  But she was more engrieved, and replide;
  'Faire sister, ill beseemes it to upbrayd
  A dolefull heart with so disdainfull pride;
The like that mine, may be your paine another tide.

22

'As you in woods and wanton wildernesse
  Your glory set, to chace the salvage beasts,
  So my delight is all in joyfulnesse,
  In beds, in bowres, in banckets, and in feasts:
  And ill becomes you, with your loftie creasts,
  To scorne the joy, that *Jove* is glad to seeke;
  We both are bound to follow heavens beheasts,
  And tend our charges with obeisance meeke:
Spare, gentle sister, with reproch my paine to eeke.

23

'And tell me, if that ye my sonne have heard,
  To lurke emongst your Numphes in secret wize;
  Or keepe their cabins: much I am affeard,
  Least he like one of them him selfe disguize,
  And turne his arrowes to their exercize:
  So may he long himselfe full easie hide:
  For he is faire and fresh in face and guize,
  As any Nymph (let not it be envyde.)
So saying every Nymph full narrowly shee eyde.

24

But *Phœbe* therewith sore was angered,
  And sharply said; 'Goe Dame, goe seeke your boy,
  Where you him lately left, in *Mars* his bed;
  He comes not here, we scorne his foolish joy,
  Ne lend we leisure to his idle toy:
  But if I catch him in this company,
  By *Stygian* lake I vow, whose sad annoy
  The Gods doe dread, he dearly shall abye:
Ile clip his wanton wings, that he no more shall fly.'

25

Whom whenas *Venus* saw so sore displeased,
  She inly sory was, and gan relent,
  What she had said: so her she soone appeased,
  With sugred words and gentle blandishment,
  Which as a fountaine from her sweete lips went,
  And welled goodly forth, that in short space
  She was well pleasd, and forth her damzells sent,
  Through all the woods, to search from place to place,
If any tract of him or tydings they mote trace.

26

To search the God of love her Nymphes she sent
  Throughout the wandring forest every where:
  And after them her selfe eke with her went
  To seeke the fugitive, both farre and nere,
  So long they sought, till they arrived were
  In that same shadie covert, whereas lay
  Faire *Crysogone* in slombry traunce whilere:
  Who in her sleepe (a wondrous thing to say)
Unwares had borne two babes, as faire as springing day.

27

Unwares she them conceiv'd, unwares she bore:
  She bore withouten paine, that she conceiv'd
  Withouten pleasure: ne her need implore
  Lucinaes aide: which when they both perceived,
  They were through wonder nigh of sence bere
  And gazing each on other, nought bespake:
  At last they both agreed, her seeming grieved
  Out of her heavy swowne not to awake,
But from her loving side the tender babes to take.

28

Up they them tooke, each one a babe uptooke,
  And with them carried, to be fostered;
  Dame *Phœbe* to a Nymph her babe betooke,
  To be upbrought in perfect Maydenhed,
  And of her selfe her name *Belphœbe* red:
  But *Venus* hers thence farre away convayd,
  To be upbrought in goodly womanhed,
  And in her litle loves stead, which was stayd,
Her *Amoretta* cald, to comfort her dismayd.

29

She brought her to her joyous Paradize,
    Wher most she wonnes, when she on earth does dwel.
    So faire a place, as Nature can devize:
    Whether in *Paphos*, or *Cytheron* hill,
    Or it in *Gnidus* be, I wote not wel;
    But well I wote by tryall, that this same
    All other pleasant places doth excell,
    And called is by her lost lovers name,
The *Gardin* of *Adonis*, far renowmd by fame.

30

In that same Gardin all the goodly flowres,
    Wherewith dame Nature doth her beautifie,
    And decks the girlonds of her paramoures,
    Are fetcht: there is the first seminarie
    Of all things, that are borne to live and die,
    According to their kindes. Long worke it were,
    Here to account the endlesse progenie
    Of all the weedes that bud and blossome there;
But so much as doth need, must needs be counted here.

31

It sited was in fruitfull soyle of old,
    And gift in with two walles on either side;
    The one of yron, the other of bright gold,
    That none might thorough breake, nor over-stride:
    And double gates it had, which opened wide,
    By which both in and out men moten pas;
    Th' one faire and fresh, the other old and dride:
    Old *Genius* the porter of them was,
Old *Genius*, the which a double nature has.

32

He letteth in, he letteth out to wend,
    All that to come into the world desire;
    A thousand thousand naked babes attend
    About him day and night, which doe require,
    That he with fleshly weedes would them attire:
    Such as him list, such as eternall fate
    Ordained hath, he clothes with sinful mire,
    And sendeth forth to live in mortall state,
Till they againe returne backe by the hinder gate.

33

After that they againe returned beene,
   They in that Gardin planted be againe;
   And grow a fresh, as they had never seene
   Fleshly corruption, nor mortall paine.
   Some thousand yeares so doen they there remaine;
   And then of him are clad with other hew,
   Or sent into the chaungefull world againe,
   Till thither they returne, where first they grew:
So like a wheele around they runne from old to new.

34

Ne needs there Gardiner to set, or sow,
   To plant or prune: for of their owne accord
   All things, as they created were, doe grow,
   And yet remember well the mightie word,
   Which first was spoken by th' Almightie lord,
   That bad them to increase and multiply:
   Ne doe they need with water of the ford,
   Or of the clouds to moysten their roots dry;
For in themselves eternall moisture they imply.

35

Infinite shapes of creatures there are bred,
   And uncouth formes, which none yet ever knew,
   And every sort is in a sundry bed
   Set by it selfe, and ranckt in comely rew:
   Some fit for reasonable soules t' indew,
   Some made for beasts, some made for birds to weare,
   And all the fruitful spawne of fishes hew
   In endlesse rancks along enraunged were,
That seem'd the *Ocean* could not containe them there.

36

Daily they grow, and daily forth are sent
   Into the world, it to replenish more;
   Yet is the stocke not lessened, nor spent,
   But still remaines in everlasting store,
   As it at first created was of yore.
   For in the wide wombe of the world there lyes,
   In hateful darkenesse and in deepe horrore,
   An huge eternall *Chaos*, which supplyes
The substances of natures fruitfull progenyes.

37

All things from thence doe their first being fetch,
   And borrow matter, whereof they are made,
   Which when as forme and feature it does ketch,
   Becomes a bodie, and doth then invade
   The state of life, out of the griesly shade.
   That substance is eterne, and bideth so,
   Ne when the life decayes, and forme does fade,
   Doth it consume, and into nothing go,
But chaunged is, and often altred to and fro.

38

The substance is not chaunged, nor altered,
   But th' only forme and outward fashion;
   For every substance is conditioned
   To change her hew, and sundry formes to don,
   Meet for her temper and complexion:
   For formes are variable and decay,
   By course of kind, and by occasion;
   And that faire flowre of beautie fades away,
As doth the lilly fresh before the sunny ray.

39

Great enimy to it, and to all the rest,
   That in the *Gardin* of *Adonis* springs,
   Is wicked *Time*, who with his scyth addrest,
   Does mow the flowring herbes and goodly things,
   And all their glory to the ground downe flings,
   Where they doe wither, and are fowly mard:
   He flyes about, and with his flaggy wings
   Beates downe both leaves and buds without regard,
Ne ever pittie may relent his malice hard.

40

Yet pittie often did the gods relent,
   To see so faire things mard, and spoyled quight;
   And their great mother *Venus* did lament
   The losse of her deare brood, her deare delight:
   Her hart was pierst with pittie at the sight,
   When walking through the Gardin, them she spyde,
   Yet no'te she find redresse for such despight.
   For all that lives, is subject to that law:
All things decay in time, and to their end do draw.

41

But were it not, that Time their troubler is,
    All that in this delightfull Gardin growes,
    Should happie be, and have immortall blis:
    For here all plentie and all pleasure flowes,
    And sweete love gentle fits emongst them throwes,
    Without fell rancor, or fond gealosie;
    Franckly each paramour his leman knowes,
    Each bird his mate, ne any does envie
Their goodly meriment, and gay felicitie.

42

There is continuall spring, and harvest there
    Continuall, both meeting at one time;
    For both the boughes doe laughing blossomes beare,
    And with fresh colours decke the wanton Prime,
    And eke attonce the heavy trees they clime,
    Which seeme to labour under their fruits lode:
    The whiles the joyous birdes make their pastime
    Emongst the shadie leaves, their sweet abode,
And their trew loves without suspition tell abrode.

43

Right in the middest of that Paradise,
    There stood a stately Mount, on whose round top
    A gloomy grove of mirtle trees did rise,
    Whose shadie boughes sharp steele did never lop,
    Nor wicked beasts their tender buds did crop,
    But like a girlond compassed the hight,
    And from their fruitfull sides sweet gum did drop,
    That all the ground with pretious deaw bedight,
Threw forth most dainty odours, and most sweet delight.

44

And in the thickest covert of that shade,
    There was a pleasant arbour, not by art,
    But of the trees owne inclination made,
    Which knitting their rancke braunches part to part,
    With wanton yvie twyne entrayld athwart,
    And Eglantine, and Caprifole emong,
    Fashiond above within their inmost part,
    That nether *Phœbus* beams could through them throng,
Nor *Aeolus* sharp blast could worke them any wrong.

45

And all about grew every sort of flowre,
　　To which sad lovers were transformd of yore;
　　Fresh *Hyacinthus*, *Phœbus* parmoure,
　　And dearest love,
　　Foolish *Narcisse*, that likes the watry shore,
　　Sad *Amaranthus*, made a flowre but late,
　　Sad *Amaranthus*, in whose purple gore
　　Me seemes I see *Amintas* wretched fate,
To whom sweet Poets verse hath given endlesse date.

46

There wont faire *Venus* often to enjoy
　　Her deare *Adonis* joyous company,
　　And reape sweet pleasure of the wanton boy;
　　There yet, some say, in secret he does ly,
　　Lapped in flowres and pretious spycery,
　　By her hid from the world, and from the skill
　　Of *Stygian* Gods, which doe her love envy;
　　But she her selfe, when ever that she will,
Possesseth him, and of his sweetnesse takes her fill.

47

And sooth it seemes they say: for he may not
　　For ever die, and ever buried bee
　　In balefull night, where all things are forgot;
　　All be he subject to mortialitie,
　　Yet is eterne in mutabilitie,
　　And by succession made perpetuall,
　　Transformed oft, and chaunged diverslie:
　　For him the Father of all formes they call;
Therfore needs mote he live, that living gives to all.

48

There now he liveth in eternall blis,
　　Joying his goddesse, and of her enjoyd:
　　Ne feareth he henceforth that foe of his,
　　Which with his cruell tuske him deadly cloyd:
　　For that wilde Bore, the which him once annoyd,
　　She firmely hath emprisoned for ay,
　　That her sweet love his malice mote avoyd,
　　In a strong rocky Cave, which is they say,
Hewen underneath that Mount, that none him losen may.

49

There now he lives in everlasting joy,
   With many of the Gods in company,
   Which thither haunt, and with the winged boy
   Sporting him selfe in safe felicity:
   Who when he hath with spoiles and cruelty
   Ransackt the world, and in the wofull harts
   Of many wretches set his triumphes hye,
   Thither resorts, and laying his sad darts
Aside, with faire *Adonis* playes his wanton parts.

50

And his true love faire *Psyche* with him playes,
   Faire *Psyche* to him lately reconcyld,
   After long troubles and unmeet upbrayes,
   With which his mother *Venus* her revyld,
   And eke himselfe her cruelly exyld:
   But now in stedfast love and happy state
   She with him lives, and hath him borne a chyld,
   Pleasure, that doth both gods and men aggrate,
Pleasure, the daughter of *Cupid* and *Psyche* late.

51

Hither great *Venus* brought this infant faire,
   The younger daughter of *Chrysogonee*,
   And unto *Psyche* with great trust and care
   Committed her, yfostered to bee,
   And trained up in trew feminitee:
   Who no lesse carefully her tendered,
   Then her owne daughter *Pleasure*, to whom shee
   Made her companion, and her lessoned
In all the lore of love, and goodly womanhead.

52

In which when she to perfect ripenesse grew,
   Of grace and beautie noble Paragone,
   She brought her forth into the worldes vew,
   To be th' ensample of true love alone,
   And Lodestarre of all chaste affectione,
   To all faire Ladies that doe live on ground.
   To Faery court she came, where many one
   Admyrd her goodly haveour, and found
His feeble hart wide launched with loves cruel wound.

53

But she to none of them her love did cast,
　　Save to the noble knight Sir *Scudamore*,
　　To whom her loving hart she linked fast
　　In faithfull love, t' abide for evermore,
　　And for his dearest sake endured sore,
　　Sore trouble of an hainous enimy;
　　Who her would forced have to have forlore
　　Her former love, and stedfast loialty,
As ye may elswhere read that ruefull history.

54

But well I weene, ye first desire to learne,
　　What end unto that fearefull Damozell,
　　Which led so fast from that same foster stearne,
　　Whom with his brethren *Timias* slew, befell:
　　That was to weet, the goodly *Florimell*;
　　Who wandring for to seeke her lover deare,
　　Her lover deare, her dearest *Marinell*,
　　Into misfortune fell, as ye did heare,
And from Prince *Arthur* fled with wings of idle feare.

Canto VII

The witches sonne loves Florimell:
She flyes, he faines to die.
Satyrane saves the Squire of Dames
From Gyants tyrannie.

1

Like as an Hynd forth singled from the heard,
  That hath escaped from a ravenous beast,
  Yet flyes away of her owne feet affeard,
  And every leafe, that shaketh with the least
  Murmure of winde, her terror hath encreast;
  So fled faire *Florimell* from her vaine feare,
  Long after she from perill was releast:
  Each shade she saw, and each noyse she did heare,
Did seeme to be the same, which she escapt whyleare.

2

All that same evening she in flying spent,
  And all that night her course continewed:
  Ne did she let dull sleepe once to relent,
  Nor wearinesse to slacke her hast, but fled
  Ever alike, as if her former dred
  Were hard behind, her readie to arrest:
  And her white Palfrey having conquered
  The maistring raines out of her weary wrest,
Perforce her carried, where ever he thought best.

3

So long as breath, and hable puissance
  Did native courage unto him supply,
  His pace he freshly forward did advaunce,
  And carried her beyond all jeopardy,
  But nought that wanteth rest, can long aby.
  He having through incessant travell spent
  His force, at last perforce a downe did ly,
  Ne foot could further move: The Lady gent
Thereat was suddein strooke with great astonishment.

4

And forst t' alight, on foot mote algates fare,
  A traveller unwonted to such way:
  Need teacheth her this lesson hard and rare,
  That fortune all in equall launce doth sway,
  And mortall miseries doth make her play.

So long she travelled, till at length she came
To an hilles side, which did to her bewray
A litle valley, subject to the same,
All coverd with thick woods, that quite it overcame.

5

Through the tops of the high trees she did descry
A litle smoke, whose vapour thin and light,
Reeking aloft, uprolled to the sky:
Which, chearefull signe did send unto her sight,
That in the same did wonne some living wight.
Eftsoones her steps she thereunto applyde,
And came at last in weary wretched plight
Unto the place, to which her hope did guyde,
To find some refuge there, and rest her weary syde.

6

There in a gloomy hollow glen she found
A little cottage, built of stickes and reedes
In homely wize, and wald with sods around,
In which a witch did dwell, in loathly weedes,
And wilfull want, all carelesse of her needes;
So choosing solitaire to abide,
Far from all neighbours, that her devilish deedes
And hellish arts from people she might hide,
And hurt far off unknowne, whom ever she envide.

7

The Damzell there arriving entred in;
Where sitting on the flore the Hag she found,
Busie (as seem'd) about some wicked gin:
Who soone as she beheld that suddein stound,
Lightly upstarted from the dustie ground,
And with fell looke and hollow deadly gaze
Stared on her awhile, as one astound,
Ne had one word to speake, for great amaze,
But shewd by outward signes, that dread her sence did daze.

8

At last, turning her feare to foolish wrath,
She askt what devill had her thither brought,
And who she was, and what unwonted path
Had guided her, unwelcomed, unsought?
To which the Damzell full of doubtfull thought,
Her mildly answer'd; 'Beldame be not wroth

With silly Virgin by adventure brought
Unto your dwelling, ignorant and loth,
That crave but rowme to rest, while tempest overblo'th.'

9

With that adowne out of her Christall eyne
Few trickling teares she softly forth let fall,
That like two Orient pearles, did purely shyne
Upon her snowy cheeke; and therewithall
She signed soft, that none so bestiall
Nor salvage hart, but ruth of her sad plight
Would make to melt, or pitteously appall;
And that vile Hag, all were her whole delight
In mischiefe, was much moved at so pitteous sight.

10

And gan recomfort her in her rude wyse,
With womanish compassion of her plaint,
Wiping the teares from her suffused eyes,
And bidding her sit downe, to rest her faint
And wearie limbs a while. She nothing quaint
Nor s'deignfull of so homely fashion,
Sith brought she was now to so hard constraint,
Sate downe upon the dusty ground anon,
As glad of that small rest as Bird of tempest gon.

11

Tho gan she gather up her garments rent,
And her loose lockes to dight in order dew,
With golden wreath and gorgeous ornament;
Whom such whenas the wicked Hag did vew,
She was astonisht at her heavenly hew,
And doubted her to deeme an earthly wight,
But of some Goddesse, or of *Dianes* crew,
And thought her to adore with humble spright;
T'adore thing so divine as beauty were but right.

12

This wicked woman had a wicked sonne,
The comfort of her age and weary dayes,
A laesie loord, for nothing good to donne,
But stretched forth in idlenesse alwayes,
Ne ever cast his mind to covet prayse,
Or ply him selfe to any honest trade,
But all the day before the sunny rayes

He us'd to slug, or sleepe in slothfull shade:
Such laesinesse both lewd and poore attonce him made.

13

He comming home at undertime, there found
　The fairest creature that he ever saw,
　Sitting beside his mother on the ground;
　The sight whereof did greatly him adaw,
　And his base thought with terrour and with aw
　So inly smot, that as one, which hath gazed
　On the bright Sunne unwares, doth soone withdraw
　His feeble eyne, with too much brightnesse dazed,
So stared he on her, and stood long while amazed.

14

Softly at last he gan his mother aske,
　What mister wight that was, and whence derived,
　That in so straunge disguizement there did maske,
　And by what accident she there arrived;
　But she, as one nigh of her wits deprived,
　With nought but ghastly lookes him answered,
　Like to a ghost, that lately is revived
　From *Stygian* shores, where late is wandered;
So both at her, and each at other wondered.

15

But the faire Virgin was so meeke and mild,
　That she to them vouchsafed to embace
　Her goodly port, and to their senses vild,
　Her gentle speach applide, that in short space
　She grew familiare in that desert place.
　During which time, the Chorle through her so kind
　And curteise use conceiv'd affection bace,
　And cast to love her in his brutish mind;
No love, but brutish lust, that was so beastly tind.

16

Closely the wicked flame his bowels brent,
　And shortly grew into outrageous fire;
　Yet had he not the hart, nor hardiment,
　As unto her to utter his desire;
　His caytive thought durst not so hight aspire,
　But with soft sighes, and lovely semblaunces,
　He ween'd that his affection entire
　She should aread; many resemblaunces
To her he made, and many kinde remembraunces.

17

Oft from the forrest wildings he did bring,
   Whose sides empurpled were with smiling red,
   And oft young birds, which he had taught to sing
   His mistresse prayses, sweetly caroled,
   Girlonds of flowers sometimes for her faire hed
   He fine would dight; sometimes the squirell wild
   He brought to her in bands, as conquered
   To be her thrall, his fellow servant vild;
All which, she of him tooke with countenance meeke and mild.

18

But past awhile, when she fit season saw
   To leave that desert mansion, she cast
   In secret wize her selfe thence to withdraw,
   For feare of mischiefe, which she did forecast
   Might by the witch or by her sonne compast:
   Her wearie Palfrey closely, as she might,
   Now well recovered after long repast,
   In his proud furnitures she freshly dight,
His late miswandred wayes now to remeasure right.

19

And earely ere the dawning day appeard,
   She forth issewed, and on her journey went;
   She went in perill, of each noyse affeard,
   And of each shade, that did it selfe present;
   For still she feared to be overhent,
   Of that vile hag, or her uncivile sonne:
   Who when too late awaking, well they kent,
   That their faire guest was gone, they both begonne
To make exceeding mone, as they had been undonne.

20

But that lewd lover did the most lament
   For her depart, that ever man did heare;
   He knockt his brest with desperate intent,
   And scratcht his face, and with his teeth did teare
   His rugged flesh, and rent his ragged heare:
   That his sad mother seeing his sore plight,
   Was greatly woe begon, and gan to feare,
   Least his fraile senses were emperisht quight,
And love to frenzy turnd, sith love is franticke hight.

21

All wayes she sought him to restore to plight,
　　With herbs, with charms, with counsel, and with teares,
　　But tears, nor charms, nor herbs, nor counsell might
　　Asswage the fury, which his entrails teares:
　　So strong is passion, that no reason heares.
　　Tho when all other helpes she saw to faile,
　　She turned her selfe backe to her wicked leares
　　And by her devilish arts thought to prevaile,
To bring her backe againe, or worke her finall bale.

22

Eftsoones out of her hidden cave she cald
　　An hideous beast of horrible aspect,
　　That could the stoutest courage have appald;
　　Monstrous mishapt, and all his backe was spect
　　With thousand spots of colours queint elect,
　　Thereto so swift, that it all beasts did pas:
　　Like never yet did living eye detect;
　　But likest it to an *Hyena* was,
That feeds on womens flesh, as others feede on gras.

23

It forth she cald, and gave it streight in charge,
　　Through thicke and thin her to pursew apace,
　　Ne once to stay to rest, or breath at large,
　　Till her he had attaind, and brought in place,
　　Or quite devour her beauties scornefull grace.
　　The Monster swift as word, that from her went,
　　Went forth in hast, and did her footing trace
　　So sure and swiftly, through his perfect sent,
And passing speede, that shortly he her overhent.

24

Whom when the fearefull Damzell nigh espide,
　　No need bid her fast away to flie;
　　That ugly shape so sore her terrifide,
　　That it she shund no lesse then dread to die,
　　And her flit Palfrey did so well apply
　　His nimble feet to her conceived feare,
　　That whilest his breath did strength to him supply,
　　From peril free he her away did beare:
But when his force gan faile, his pace gan wex areare.

25

Which whenas she perceiv'd, she was dismayd
  At that same last extremitie full sore,
  And of her safetie greatly grew afrayd;
  And now she gan approch to the sea shore,
  As it befell, that she could flie no more,
  But yield her selfe to spoile of greedinesse.
  Lightly she leaped, as a wight forlore,
  From her dull horse, in desperate distresse,
And to her feet betooke her doubtfull sickernesse.

26

Not halfe so fast the wicked *Myrrha* fled
  From dread of her revenging fathers hond:
  Nor halfe so fast to save her maidenhed,
  Fled fearefull *Daphne* on th' *Ægæan* strond,
  As *Florimell* fled from that Monster yond,
  To reach the sea, ere she of him were raught:
  For in the sea to drowne her selfe she fond,
  Rather then of the tyrant to be caught:
Thereto fear gave her wings, and need her courage taught.

27

It fortuned (high God did so ordaine)
  As she arrived on the roring shore,
  In minde to leape into the mighty maine,
  A little boate lay hoving her before,
  In which there slept a fisher old and pore,
  The whiles his nets were drying on the sand:
  Into the same she leapt, and with the ore
  Did thrust the shallop from the floting strand:
So safetie found at sea, which she found not at land.

28

The Monster ready on the pray to sease,
  Was of his forward hope deceived quight;
  Ne durst assay to wade the perlous seas,
  But greedily long gaping at the sight,
  At last in vaine was forst to turne his flight,
  And tell the idle tidings to his Dame:
  Yet to avenge his devilish despight,
  He set upon her Palfrey tired lame,
And slew him cruelly, ere any reskew came.

29

And after having him embowelled,
  To fill his hellish gorge, it chaunst a knight
  To passe that way, as forth he travelled;
  It was a goodly Swaine, and of great might,
  As ever man that bloudy field did fight;
  But in vain sheows, that wont yong knights bewitch,
  And courtly services tooke no delight,
  But rather joyd to be, then seemen sich:
For both to be and seeme to him was labour lich.

30

It was to weete the good Sir *Satyrane*,
  That raungd abroad to seeke adventures wilde,
  As was his wont in forrest and in plaine;
  He was all armd in rugged steele unfilde,
  As in the smoky forge it was compilde,
  And in his Scutchin bore a Satyres hed:
  He comming present, where the Monster vilde
  Upon that milke-white Palfreyes carkas fed,
Unto his reskew ran, and greedily him sped.

31

There well perceiv'd he, that it was the horse,
  Whereon faire *Florimell* was wont to ride,
  That of that feend was rent without remorse:
  Much feared he, least ought did ill betide
  To that faire Mayd, the flowre of womens pride;
  For her he dearely loved, and in all
  His famous conquests highly magnifide:
  Besides her golden girdle, which did fall
From her in flight, he found, that did him sore apall.

32

Full of sad feare, and doubtfull agony,
  Fiercely he flew upon that wicked feend,
  And with huge strokes, and cruell battery
  Him forst to leave his pray, for to attend
  Him selfe from deadly daunger to defend:
  Full many wounds in his corrupted flesh
  He did engrave, and muchell bloud did spend,
  Yet might not do him dye, but aye more fresh
And fierce he still appeard, the more he did him thresh.

33

He wist not, how him to despoile of life,
　Ne how to win the wished victory,
　Sith him he saw still stronger grow through strife,
　And him selfe weaker through infirmity;
　Greatly he grew enrag'd, and furiously
　Hurling his sword away, he lightly lept
　Upon the beast, that with great cruelty
　Rored, and raged to be under-kept:
Yet he perforce him held, and strokes upon him hept.

34

As he that strives to stop a suddein flood,
　And in strong banckes his violence enclose,
　Forceth it swell above his wonted mood,
　And largely overflow the fruitfull plaine,
　That all the countrey seemes to be a Maine,
　And the rich furrowes floate, all quite fordonne:
　The wofull husbandman doth lowd complaine,
　To see his whole yeares labor lost so soone,
For which to God he made so many an idle boone.

35

So him he held, and did through might amate:
　So long he held him, and him bet so long,
　That at the last his fiercenesse gan abate,
　And meekely stoup unto the victour strong:
　Who to avenge the implacable wrong,
　Which he supposed donne to *Florimell*,
　Sought by all meanes his dolour to prolong,
　Sith dint of steele his carcas could not quell:
His maker with her charmes had framed him so well.

36

The golden ribband, which that virgin wore
　About her sclender wast, he tooke in hand,
　And with it bound the beast, that lowd did rore
　For great despight of that unwonted band,
　Yet dared not his victour to withstand,
　But trembled like a lambe, fled from the pray,
　And all the way him followd on the strand,
　As he had long bene learned to obay;
Yet never learned he such service, till that day.

37

Thus as he led the Beast along the way,
  He spide far off a mighty Giauntesse,
  Fast flying on a Courser dapled gray,
  From a bold knight, that with great hardinesse
  Her hard pursewd, and sought for to suppresse;
  She bore before her lap a dolefull Squire,
  Lying athwart her horse in great distresse,
  Fast bounden hand and foote with cords of wire,
Whom she did meane to make the thrall of her desire.

38

Which whenas *Satyrane* beheld, in hast
  He left his captive Beast at liberty,
  And crost the nearest way, by which he cast
  Her to encounter ere she passed by:
  But she the way shund nathemore for thy,
  But forward gallopt fast; which when he spyde,
  His might speare he couched warily,
  And at her ran: she having him descryde,
Her selfe to fight addrest, and threw her lode aside.

39

Like as a Goshauke, that in foote doth beare
  A trembling Culver, having spide on hight
  An Egle, that with plumy wings doth sheare
  The subtile ayre, stouping with all his might,
  The quarrey throwes to ground with fell despight,
  And to the battell doth her selfe prepare:
  So ran the Geauntesse unto the fight;
  Her firie eyes with furious sparkes did stare,
And with blasphemous bannes high God in peeces tare.

40

She caught in hand an huge great yron mace,
  Wherewith she many had of life deprived,
  But ere the stroke could seize his aymed place,
  His speare amids her sun-broad shield arrived;
  Yet nathemore the steele a sunder rived,
  All were the beame in bignesse like a mast,
  Ne her out of the stedfast sadle drived,
  But glauncing on the tempred mettall, brast
In thousand shivers, and so forth beside her past.

41

Her Steed did stagger with that puissaunt strooke;
    But she no more was moved with that might,
    Then it had lighted on an aged Oke,
    Or on the marble Pillour, that is pight
    Upon the top of Mount *Olympus* hight,
    For the brave youthly Champions to assay,
    With burning charet wheeles it nigh to smite:
    But who that smites it, mars his joyous play,
And is the spectacle of ruinous decay.

42

Yet therewith sore enrag'd, with sterne regard
    Her dreadfull weapon she to him addrest,
    Which on his helmet martelled so hard,
    That made him low incline his lofty crest,
    And bowd his battred visour to his brest:
    Wherewith he was so stund, that he n'ote ryde,
    But reeled to and fro from East to West:
    Which when his cruell enimy espyde,
She lightly unto him adjoyned side to syde;

43

And on his collar laying puissant hand,
    Out of his wavering seat him pluckt perforse,
    Perforse him pluckt, unable to withstand,
    Or helpe himselfe, and laying thwart her horse,
    In loathly wise like to a carion corse,
    She bore him fast away.   Which when the knight,
    That her pursewed, saw with great remorse
    He nere was touched in his noble spright,
And gan encrease his speed, as she encreast her flight.

44

Whom when as nigh approching she espyde,
    She threw away her burden angrily;
    For she list not the battell to abide,
    But made her selfe more light away to fly:
    Yet her the hardy knight pursewd so nye,
    That almost in the backe he oft her strake:
    But still when him at hand she did espy,
    She turnd, and semblaunce of faire fight did make;
But when he stayd, to flight againe she did her take.

45

By this the good Sir *Satyrane* gan wake
  Out of his dreame, that did him long entraunce,
  And seeing none in place, he gan to make
  Exceeding mone, and curst that cruell chaunce,
  Which reft from him so faire a chevisaunce:
  At length he spide, whereas that wofull Squire,
  Whom he had reskewed from captivaunce
  Of his strong foe, lay tombled in the myre,
Unable to arise, or foote or hand to styre.

46

To whom approching, well he mote perceive
  In that foule plight a comely personage,
  And lovely face, made fit for to deceive
  Fraile Ladies hart with loves consuming rage,
  Now in the blossome of his freshest age:
  He reard him up, and loosd his yron bands,
  And after gan inquire his parentage,
  And how he fell into the Gyaunts hands,
And who that was, which chaced her along the lands.

47

Then trembling yet through feare, the Squire bespake,
  'That Geauntesse *Argante* is behight,
  A daughter of the *Titans* which did make
  Warre against heaven, and heaped hils on hight,
  To scale the skyes, and put *Jove* from his right:
  Her sire *Typhoeus* was, who mad through merth,
  And drunke with bloud of men slaine by his might,
  Through incest, her of his owne mother Earth
Whilome begot, being but halfe twin of that berth.

48

'For at that berth another Babe she bore,
  To weet the mighty *Ollyphant*, that wrought
  Great wreake to many errant knights of yore,
  And many hath to foule confusion brought.
  These twinnes, men say, (a thing far passing thought)
  While in their mothers wombe enclosd they were,
  Ere they into the lightsom world were brought,
  In fleshly lust were mingled both yfere,
And in that monstrous wise did to the world appere.

49

'So liv'd they ever after in like sin,
    Gainst natures law, and good behavioure:
    But greatest shame was to that maiden twin,
    Who not content so fowly to devoure
    Her native flesh, and staine her brothers bowre,
    Did wallow in all other fleshly myre,
    And suffred beasts her body to deflowre:
    So whot she burned in that lustfull fyre,
Yet all that might not slake her sensuall desyre.

50

'But over all the countrey she did raunge,
    To seeke young men, to quench her flaming thrust,
    And feed her fancy with delightfull chaunge:
    Whom so she fittest finds to serve her lust,
    Through her maine strength, in which she most doth trust,
    She with her brings into a secret Ile,
    Where in eternall bondage dye he must,
    Or be the vassall of her pleasures vile,
And in all shameful sort him selfe with her defile.

51

'Me seely wretch she so at vauntage caught,
    After she long in waite for me did lye,
    And meant unto her prison to have brought,
    Her lothsome pleasure there to satisfye;
    That thousand deathes me lever were to dye,
    Then breake the vow, that to faire *Columbell*
    I plighted have, and yet keepe stedfastly:
    As for my name, it mistreth not to tell;
Call me the *Squyre of Dames*, that me beseemeth well.

52

'But that bold knight, whom ye pursuing saw
    That Geauntesse, is not such, as she seemed,
    But a faire virgin, that in martiall law,
    And deedes of armes above all Dames is deemed,
    And above many knights is eke esteemed,
    For her great worth; She *Palladine* is hight:
    She you from death, you me from dread redeemed.
    Ne any may that Monster match in fight,
But she, or such as she, that is so chaste a wight.'

53

'Her well beseemes that Quest' (quoth *Satyrane*)
  'But read, thou *Squyre of Dames*, what vow is this,
  Which thou upon thy selfe hast lately ta'ne?'
  'That shall I you recount' (quoth he) 'ywis,
  So be ye pleasd to pardon all amis.
  That gentle Lady, whom I love and serve,
  After long suit and wearie servicis,
  Did aske me, how I could her love deserve,
And how she might be sure, that I would never swerve.

54

'I glad by any meanes her grace to gaine,
  Bad her commaund my life to save, or spill.
  Eftsoones she bad me, with incessaunt paine
  To wander through the world abroad at will,
  And every where, where with my power or skill
  I might doe service unto gentle Dames,
  That I the same should faithfully fulfill,
  And at the twelve monethes end should bring their names
And pledges; as the spoiles of my victorious games.

55

'So well I to faire Ladies service did,
  And found such favour in their loving hartes,
  That ere the yeare his course had compassid,
  Three hundred pledges for my good desartes,
  And thrice three hundred thanks for my good partes
  I with me brought, and did to her present:
  Which when she saw, more bent to eke my smartes,
  Then to reward my trusty true intent,
She gan for me devise a grievous punishment.

56

'To weet, that I my travell should resume,
  And with like labour walke the world around,
  Ne ever to her presence shuold presume,
  Till I so many other Dames had found,
  The which, for all the suit I could propound,
  Would me refuse their pledges to afford,
  But did abide for ever chast and sound.'
  'Ah gentle Squire' (quoth he) 'tell at one word,
How many foundst thou such to put in thy record?'

57

'In deed, Sir knight' (said he) 'one word may tell
   All, that I ever found so wisely stayd;
   For onely three they were disposd so well,
   And yet three yeares I now abroad have strayd,
   To find them out.' 'Mote I' (then laughing sayd
   The knight) 'inquire of thee what were those three,
   The which thy proffred curtesie denayd?
   Or ill they seemed sure avizd to bee,
Or brutishly brought up, that nev'r did fashions see.'

58

'The first which then refused me' (said hee)
   'Certes was but a common Courtisane,
   Yet flat refusd to have a do with mee,
   Because I could not give her many a Jane.'
   (Thereat full hartely laughed *Satyrane*)
   'The second was an holy Nunne to chose,
   Which would not let me be her Chappellane,
   Because she knew, she said, I would disclose
Her counsell, if she should her trust in me repose.

59

'The third a Damzell was of low degree,
   Whom I in countrey cottage found by chaunce;
   Full little weened I, that chastitee
   Had lodging in so meane a maintenaunce,
   Yet was she faire, and in her countenance
   Dwelt simple truth in seemely fashion.
   Long thus I woo'd her with due observance,
   In hope unto my pleasure to have won;
But was as far at last, as when I first begon.

60

'Safe her, I never any woman found,
   That chastity did for it selfe embrace,
   But were for other causes firme and sound;
   Either for want of handsome time and place,
   Or else for feare of shame and fowle disgrace.
   Thus am I hopelesse ever to attaine
   My ladies love, in such a desperate case,
   But all my dayes am like to wast in vaine,
Seeking to match the chaste with th' unchaste Ladies traine.'

61

'Perdy,' (said Satyrane) 'thou *Squire of Dames*,
  Great labour fondly hast thou hent in hand,
  To get small thankes, and therewith many blames,
  That may emongst *Alcides* labours stand.'
  Thence backe returning to the former land,
  Where late he left the Beast, he overcame,
  He found him not; for he had broke his band,
  And was returnd againe unto his Dame,
To tell what tydings of faire *Florimell* became.

Canto VIII

The Witch creates a snowy Lady,
Like to Florimell,
Who wrongd by Carle by Proteus sav'd,
Is sought by Paridell.

I

So oft as I this history record,
    My heart doth melt with meere compassion,
    To thinke, how causelesse of her owne accord
    This gentle Damzell, whom I write upon,
    Should plonged be in such affliction,
    Without all hope of comfort or reliefe,
    That sure I weene, the hardest hart of stone
    Would hardly find to aggravate her griefe;
For misery craves rather mercie, then repriefe.

2

But that accursed Hag, her hostesse late,
    Had so enranckled her malitious hart,
    That she desyrd th' abridgement of her fate,
    Or long enlargement of her painefull smart.
    Now when the Beast, which by her wicked art
    Late forth she sent, she backe returning spyde,
    Tyde with her golden girdle, it a part
    Of her rich spoyles, whom he had earst destroyd
She weend, and wondrous gladnesse to her hart applyde.

3

And with it running hast'ly to her sonne,
    Thought with that sight him much to have relived;
    Who thereby deeming sure the thing as donne,
    His former griefe with furie fresh revived,
    Much more than earst, and would have algates rived
    The hart out of his brest: for sith her ded
    He surely dempt, himselfe he thought deprived
    Quite of all hope, wherewith he long had fed
His foolish maladie, and long time had misled.

4

With thought whereof, exceeding mad he grew,
    And in his rage his mother would have slaine,
    Had she not fled into a secret mew,
    Where she was wont her Sprights to entertaine
    The maisters of her art: there was she faine

To call them all in order to her ayde,
And them conjure upon eternall paine,
To counsell her, so carefully dismayd,
How she might heale her sonne, whose senses were decayd.

5

By their advise, and her owne wicked wit,
    She there deviz'd a wondrous worke to frame,
    Whose like on earth was never framed yit,
    That even Nature selfe envide the same,
    And grudg'd to see the counterfet should shame
    The thing it selfe.   In hand she boldly tooke
    To make another like the former Dame,
    Another Florimell, in shape and looke
So lively and so like, that many it mistooke.

6

The substance, whereof she the bodie made,
    Was purest snow in massie mould congeald,
    Which she had gathered in a shadie glade
    Of the *Riphœan* hils, to her reveald
    By errant Sprights, but from all men conceald:
    The same she tempred with fine Mercury,
    And virgin wex, that never yet was seald,
    And mingled them with perfect vermily,
That like a lively sanguine it seem'd to the eye.

7

In stead of eyes two burning lampes she set
    In silver sockets, shyning like the skyes,
    And quicke moving Spirit did arret
    To stirre and roll them, like a womans eyes;
    In stead of yellow lockes she did devise,
    With golden wyre to weave her curled head;
    Yet golden wyre was not so yellow thrise
    As *Florimells* faire haire: and in the stead
Of life, she put a Spright to rule the carkasse dead.

8

A wicked Spright yfraught with fawning guile,
    And faire resemblance above all the rest,
    Which with the Prince of Darknesse fell somewhile,
    From heavens blisse and everlasting rest;
    Him needed not instruct, which way were best
    Himselfe to fashion likest *Florimell*,

Ne how to speake, ne how to use his gest,
  For he in counterfeisance did excell,
And all the wyles of wemens wits knew passing well.

9

Him shaped thus, the deckt in garments gay,
  Which *Florimell* had left behind her late,
  That who so then her saw, would surely say,
  It was her selfe, whom it did imitate,
  Or fairer then her selfe, if ought algate
  Might fairer be. And then she forth her brought
  Unto her sonne, that lay in feeble state;
  Who seeing her gan streight upstart, and thought
She was Lady selfe, whom he so long had sought.

10

Tho fast her clipping twixt his armes twaine,
  Extremely joyed in so happie sight,
  And soone forgot his former sickly paine;
  But she, the more to seeme such as she hight,
  Coyly rebutted his embracement light;
  Yet still with gentle countenaunce retained,
  Enough to hold a foole in vaine delight:
  Him long she so with shadowes entertained,
As her Creatresse had in charge to her ordained.

11

Till on a day, as he disposed was
  To walke the woods with that his Idole faire,
  Her to disport, and idle time to pas,
  In th' open freshnesse of the gentle aire,
  A knight that way there chaunced to repaire;
  Yet knight he was not, but a boastfull swaine,
  That deedes of armes had ever in despaire,
  Proud *Braggadocchio*, that in vaunting vaine
His glory did repose, and credit did maintaine.

12

He seeing with that Chorle so faire a wight,
  Decked with many a costly ornament,
  Much merveiled thereat, as well he might,
  And thought that match a fowle disparagement:
  His bloudie speare eftsoones he boldly bent
  Against the silly clowne, who dead through feare,
  Fell streight to ground in great astonishment;

'Villein' (said he) 'this Ladie is my deare,'
Dy, if thou it gainesay: I will away her beare.'

13

The fearefull Chorle durst not gainesay, nor dooe,
But trembling stood, and yielded him the pray;
Who finding litle leasure her to wooe,
On *Tromparts* steed her mounted without stay,
And without reskew led her quite away.
Proud man himselfe then *Braggadocchio* deemed,
And next to none, after that happie day,
Being possessed of that spoyle, which seemed
The fairest wight on ground, and most of men esteemed.

14

But when he saw himselfe free from poursute,
He gan make gentle purpose to his Dame,
With termes of love and lewdnesse dissolute;
For he could well his glozing speaches frame
To such vaine uses, that him best became:
But she thereto would lend but light reward,
As seeming sory, that she ever came
Into his powre, that used her so hard,
To reave her honor, which she more then life prefard.

15

Thus as they two of kindnesse treated long,
There them by chaunce encountred on the way
An armed knight, upon a courser strong,
Whose trampling feet upon the hollow lay
Seemed to thunder, and did nigh affray
That Capons courage: yet he looked grim,
And fain'd to cheare his Ladie in dismay;
Who seem'd for feare to quake in every lim,
And her to save from outrage, meekely prayed him.

16

Fiercely that stranger forward came, and nigh
Approching, with bold words and bitter threat,
Bad that same boaster, as he mote, on high
To leave to him that Lady for excheat,
Or bide him battell without further treat.
That challenge did too peremptory seeme,
And fild his senses with abashment great;
Yet seeing nigh him jeopardy extreme,
He it dissembled well, and light seem'd to esteeme.

17

Saying, 'Thou foolish knight, that weenest with words
  To steale away, that I with blowes have wonne,
  And brought throgh points of many perilous swords:
  But if thee list to see thy Courser ronne,
  Or prove thy selfe, this sad encounter shonne,
  And seeke else without hazard of thy hed.'
  At those proud words that other knight begonne
  To wexe exceeding wroth, and him ared
To turne his steede about, or sure he should be ded.

18

'Sith then' (said *Braggadocchio*) 'needes thou wilt
  Thy dayes abridge, through proofe of puissance,
  Turne we our steedes, that both in equall tilt
  May meete againe, and each take happie chance.'
  This said, they both a furlongs mountenance
  Retyrd their steeds, to ronne in even race:
  But *Braggadocchio*, with his bloudie lance
  Once having turnd, no more returnd his face,
But left his love to losse, and fled him selfe apace.

19

The knight him seeing fly, had no regard
  Him to poursew, but to the Ladie rode,
  And having her from *Trompart* lightly reard,
  Upon his Courser set the lovely lode,
  And with her fled away without abode.
  Well weened he, that fairest *Florimell*
  It was, with whom in company he yode,
  And so her selfe did alwaies to him tell;
So made him thinke him selfe in heaven, that was in hell.

20

But *Florimell* her selfe was farre away,
  Driven to great distresse by fortune straunge,
  And taught the carefull Mariner to play,
  Sith late mischaunce had her compeld to chaunge
  The land for sea, at randon there to raunge:
  Yet there that cruel Queene avengeresse,
  Not satisfide so far her to estraunge
  From courtly blis and wonted happinesse,
Did heape on her new waves of weary wretchednesse.

21

For being fled into the fishers bote,
   For refuge from the Monsters crueltie,
   Long so she on the mighty maine did flote,
   And with the tide drove forward careleslie;
   For th' aire was milde, and cleared was the skie,
   And all his windes *Dan Aeolus* did keepe,
   From stirring up their stormy enmitie,
   As pittying to see her waile and weepe;
But all the while the fisher did securely sleepe.

22

At last when droncke with drowsinesse, he woke,
   And saw his drover drive along the streame,
   He was dismayd, and thrise his brest he stroke,
   For marvell of that accident extreame:
   But when he saw that blazing beauties beame,
   Which with rare light his bote did beautifie,
   He marveild more, and thought he yet did dreame
   Not well awakt, or that some extasie
Assoted had his sence, or dazed was his eie.

23

But when her well avizing, he perceived
   To be no vision, nor fantasticke sight,
   Great comfort of her presence he conceived,
   And felt in his old courage new delight
   To gin awake, and stirre his frozen spright:
   Tho rudely askt her, how she thither came.
   'Ah' (said she) 'father, I note read aright,
   What hard misfortune brought me to the same;
Yet am I glad that here I now in safety am.

24

'But thou good man, sith far in sea we bee,
   And the great waters gin apace to swell,
   That now no more we can the maine-land see,
   Have care, I pray, to guide the cock-bote well,
   Least worse on sea then us onland befell.'
   Thereat th' old man did nought but fondly grin,
   And said, his boat the way could wisely tell:
   But his deceiptfull eyes did never lin,
To looke on her faire face, and marke her snowy skin.

25

The sight whereof in his congealed flesh,
  Infixt such secret sting of greedy lust,
  That the drie withered stocke it gan refresh,
  And kindled heat, that soone in flame forth brust:
  The driest wood is soonest burnt to dust.
  Rudely to her he lept, and his rough hand
  Where ill became him, rashly would have thrust,
  But she with angry scorne him did withstond,
And shamefully reproved for his rudenesse fond.

26

But he, that never good nor maners knew,
  Her sharpe rebuke full litle did esteeme;
  Hard is to teach an old horse amble trew.
  The inward smoke, that did before but steeme,
  Broke into open fire and rage extreme,
  And now he strength gan adde unto his will,
  Forcing to doe, that did him fowle misseeme:
  Beastly he threwe her downe, ne car'd to spill
Her garments gay with scales of fish, that all did fill.

27

The silly virgin strove him to withstand,
  All that she might, and him in vaine revild:
  She strugled strongly both with food and hand,
  To save her honor from that villaine vild,
  And cride to heaven, from humane helpe exild.
  O ye brave knights, that boast this Ladies love,
  Where be ye now, when she is nigh defild
  Of filthy wretch? well may she you reprove
Of falshood or of slouth, when most it may behove.

28

But if that thou, Sir *Satyran*, didst weete,
  Or thou, Sir *Peridure*, her sorie state,
  How soone would yee assemble many a fleete,
  To fetch from sea, that ye at land lose late;
  Towres, Cities, Kingdomes ye would ruinate,
  In your avengement and despiteous rage,
  Ne ought your burning fury mote abate;
  But if Sir Calidore could it presage,
No living creature could his cruelty asswage.

29

But sith that none of all her knights is nye,
　　See how the heavens of voluntary grace,
　　And soveraine favour towards chastity,
　　Doe succour send to her distressed cace:
　　So much high God doth innocence embrace.
　　It fortuned, whilest thus she stifly strove,
　　And the wide sea importuned long space
　　With shrilling shriekes, *Proteus* abroad did rove,
Along the fomy waves driving his finny drove.

30

Proteus is Shepheard of the seas of yore,
　　And hath the charge of *Neptunes* mightie heard;
　　An aged sire with head all frowy hore,
　　And sprinckled frost upon his deawy beard:
　　Who when those pittifull outcries he heard
　　Through all the seas so ruefully resound,
　　His charet swift in haste he thither steard,
　　Which with a teeme of scaly *Phocas* bound
Was drawne upon the waves, that fomed him around.

31

And comming to that Fishers wandring bote,
　　That went at will, withouten carde or sayle,
　　He therein saw that yrkesome sight, which smote
　　Deepe indignation and compassion frayle
　　Into his hart attonce: streight did he hayle
　　The greedy villein from his hoped pray,
　　Of which he now did very litle fayle,
　　And with his staffe, that drives his Heard astray,
Him bet so sore, that life and sence did much dismay.

32

The whiles the pitteous Ladie up did ryse,
　　Ruffled and fowly raid with filthy soyle,
　　And blubbred face with teares of her faire eyes:
　　Her heart nigh broken was with weary toyle,
　　To save her selfe from that outrageous spoyle,
　　But when she looked up, to weet, what wight
　　Had her from so infamous fact assoyld,
　　For shame, but more for feare of his grim sight,
Downe in her lap she hid her face, and loudly shright.

33

Her selfe not saved yet from daunger dred
　　She thought, but chaung'd from one to other feare;
　　Like as a fearefull Partridge, that is fled
　　From the sharpe Hauke, which her attached neare,
　　And fals to ground, to seeke for succour theare,
　　Whereas the hungry Spaniels she does spy,
　　With greedy jawes her readie for to teare;
　　In such distresse and sad perplexity
Was *Florimell*, when *Proteus* she did see thereby.

34

But he endevored with speeches milde
　　Her to recomfort, and accourage bold,
　　Bidding her feare no more her foeman vilde,
　　Nor doubt himselfe; and who he was, her told.
　　Yet all that could not from affright her hold,
　　Ne to recomfort her at at all prevayld;
　　For her faint hart was with the frozen cold
　　Benumbd so inly, that her wits nigh fayld,
And all her senses with abashment quite were quayld.

35

Her up betwixt his rugged hands he reard,
　　And with his frory lips full softly kist,
　　Whiles the cold ysickles from his rough beard,
　　Dropped adowne upon her yvorie brest:
　　Yet he himselfe so busily addrest,
　　That her out of astonishment he wrought,
　　And out of that same fishers filthy nest
　　Removing her, into his charet brought,
And there with many gentle termes her faire besought.

36

But that old leachour, which with bold assault
　　That beautie durst presume to violate,
　　He cast to punish for his hainous fault;
　　Then tooke he him yet trembling sith of late,
　　And tyde behind his charet, to aggrate
　　The virgin whom he had abusde so sore:
　　So drag'd him through the waves in scornfull state,
　　And after cast him up, upon the shore;
But *Florimell* with him unto his bowre he bore.

37

His bowre is in the bottome of the maine,
    Under a mightie rocke, against which do rave
    The roaring billowes in their proud disdaine,
    That with the angry working of the wave,
    Therein is eaten out an hollow cave,
    That seemes rough Masons hand with engines keene
    Had long while laboured it to engrave:
    There was his wonne, ne living wight was seene,
Save one old *Nymph*, hight *Panope* to keepe it cleane.

38

Thither he brought the sory *Florimell*,
    And entertained her the best he might,
    And *Panope* her entertaind eke well,
    As an immortall mote a mortall wight,
    To winne her liking unto his delight:
    With flattering words he sweetly wooed her,
    And offered faire gifts t' allure her sight,
    But she both offers and the offerer
Despysde, and all the fawning of the flatterer.

39

Daily he tempted her with this or that,
    And never suffred her to be at rest:
    But evermore she him refused flat,
    And all his fained kindnesse did detest,
    So firmely she had sealed up her brest.
    Sometimes he boasted that a God he hight:
    But she a mortall creature loved best:
    Then he would make himselfe a mortall wight;
But then she said she lov'd none, but a Faerie knight.

40

Then like a Faerie knight himselfe he drest;
    For every shape on him he could endew:
    Then like a king he as to her exprest,
    And offred kingdoms unto her in vew,
    To be his Leman and his Ladie trew:
    But when all this he nothing saw prevaile,
    With harder meanes he cast her to subdew,
    And with sharpe threates her often did assaile,
So thinking for to make her stubborne courage quaile.

41

To dreadfull shapes he did him selfe transforme,
  Now like a Gyant, now like to a feend,
  Then like a Centaure, then like to a storme,
  Raging within the waves: thereby he weend
  Her will to win unto his wished end.
  But when with feare, nor favour, nor with all
  He else could doe, he saw himselfe esteemd,
  Downe in a Dongeon deepe he let her fall,
And threatned there to make her his eternall thrall.

42

Eternall thraldome was to her more liefe,
  Then losse of chastitie, or chaunge of love:
  Die had she rather in tormenting griefe,
  Then any should of falsenesse her reprove,
  Or loosenesse, that she lightly did remove.
  Most vertuous virgin, glory be thy meed,
  And crowne of heavenly praise with Saints above,
  Where most sweet hymmes of this thy famous deed
Are still emongst them song, that far my rymes exceed.

43

Fit song of Angels caroled to bee;
  But yet what so my feeble Muse can frame,
  Shal be t' advance thy goodly chastitee,
  And to enroll thy memorable name
  In th' heart of every honourable Dame,
  That they thy vertuous deedes may imitate,
  And be partakers of thy endlesse fame.
  Yt yrkes me, leave thee in this wofull state,
To tell of *Satyrane* where I him left of late.

44

Who having ended with that *Squire of Dames*
  A long discourse of his adventures vaine,
  The which himselfe, then Ladies more defames,
  And finding not th' Hyena to be slaine,
  With that same *Squire*, returned back againe
  To his first way. And, as they forward went,
  They spyde a knight faire pricking on the plaine,
  As if he were on some adventure bent,
And in his port appeared manly hardiment.

45

Sir *Satyrane* him towards did addresse,
　　To weet, what wight he was, and what his quest:
　　And comming nigh, eftsoones he gan to gesse
　　Both by the burning hart, which on his brest
　　He bare, and by the colours in his crest,
　　That *Paridell* it was. Tho to him yode,
　　And him saluting, as beseemed best,
　　Gan first inquire of tydings farre abrode;
And afterwardes, on what adventure now he rode.

46

Who thereto answering, said: 'The tydings bad,
　　Which now in Faerie court all men do tell,
　　Which turned hath great mirth, to mourning sad,
　　Is the late ruine of proud *Marinell*,
　　And suddein parture of faire *Florimell*,
　　To find him forth: and after her are gone
　　All the brave knights, that doen in armes excell,
　　To saveguard her, ywandred all alone;
Emongst the rest my lot (unworthy) is to be one.'

47

'Ah gentle knight' (said then Sir *Satyrane*)
　　'Thy labour all is lost, I greatly dread,
　　That hast a thanklesse service on thee ta'ne,
　　And offrest sacrifice unto the dead:
　　For dead, I surely doubt, thou maist aread
　　Henceforth for ever *Florimell* to be,
　　That all the noble knights of *Maydenhead*,
　　Which her ador'd, may sore repent with me,
And all faire Ladies may for ever sory be.'

48

Which words when *Paridell* heard, his hew
　　Gan greatly chaunge, and seem'd dismayd to bee;
　　Then said, 'Faire Sir, how many I weene it trew,
　　That ye doe tell in such uncertaintee?
　　Or speake ye of report, or did ye see
　　Just cause of dread, that makes ye doubt so sore?
　　For perdie else how mote it ever bee,
　　That ever hand should dare for to engore
Her noble bloud? The heavens such crueltie abhore.'

49

'These eyes did see, that they will ever rew
 T' have seene,' (quoth he) 'when as a monstrous beast
 The Palfrey, whereon she did travell, slew,
 And of his bowels made his bloudie feast:
 Which speaking token sheweth at the least
 Her certaine losse, if not her sure decay:
 Besides, that more suspicion encreast,
 I found her golden girdle cast astray,
Distaynd with durt and bloud, as relique of the pray.'

50

'Ay me,' (said *Paridell*) 'the signes be sad,
 And but God turne the same to good soothsay,
 That Ladies safetie is sore to be drad:
 Yet will I not forsake my forward way,
 Till triall doe more certaine truth bewray.'
 'Faire Sir' (quoth he) 'well may it you succeed,
 Ne long shall *Satyrane* behind you stay,
 But to the rest, which in this Quest proceed
My labour adde, and be partaker of their speed.'

51

'Ye noble knights' (said then the *Squire of Dames*)
 'Well may ye speed in so praiseworthy paine:
 But sith the Sunne now ginnes to slake his beames,
 In deawy vapours of the westerne maine,
 And lose the teme out of his weary waine,
 Mote not mislike you also to abate
 Your zealous hast, till morrow next againe
 Both light of heaven, and strength of men relate:
Which if ye please, to yonder castle turne your gate.'

52

That counsell pleased well; so all yfere
 Forth marched to a Castle them before,
 Where soone arriving they restrained were
 Of readie entrance, which ought evermore
 To errant knights be commun: wondrous sore
 Thereat displeasd they were, till that young Squire
 Gan them informe the cause, why that same dore
 Was shut to all, which lodging did desire:
The which to let you weet, will further time require.

Canto IX

Malbecco will no straunge knights host,
For peevish gealousie:
Paridell giusts with Britomart:
Both shew their auncestrie.

1

Redoubted knights, and honorable Dames,
    To whom I levell all my labours end,
    Right sore I feare, least with unworthy blames
    This odious argument my rimes should shend,
    Or ought your goodly patience offend,
    Whiles of a wanton Lady I doe write,
    Which with her loose incontinence doth blend
    The shyning glory of your soveraigne light,
And knighthood fowle defaced by a faithlesse knight.

2

But never let th' ensample of the bad
    Offend the good: for good by paragone
    Of evill, may more notably be rad,
    As white seemes fairer, macht with blacke attone;
    Ne all are shamed by the fault of one:
    For lo in heaven, whereas all goodnesse is,
    Emongst the Angels, a whole legione
    Of wicked Sprights did fall from happy blis;
What wonder then, if one of women all did mis?

3

Then listen Lordings, if ye list to weet
    The cause, why *Satyrane* and *Paridell*
    Mote not be entertaynd, as seemed meet,
    Into that Castle (as that Squire does tell.)
    'Therein a cancred crabbed Carle does dwell,
    That has no skill of Court nor courtesie,
    Ne cares, what men say of him ill or well;
    For all his dayes he drownes in privitie,
Yet has full large to live and spend at libertie.

4

'But all his minde is set on mucky pelfe,
    To hoord up heapes of evill gotten masse,
    For which he others wrongs, and wreckes himselfe:
    Yet is he lincked to a lovely lasse,
    Whose beauty doth her bounty far surpasse,

The which to him both far unequall yeares,
    And also far unlike conditions has;
    For she does joy to play emongst her peares,
And to be free from hard restraint and gealous feares.

5

'But he is old, and withered like hay,
    Unfit faire Ladies service to supply;
    The privie guilt whereof makes him alway
    Suspect her truth, and keepe continuall spy
    Upon her with his other blincked eye;
    Ne suffreth he resort of living wight
    Approch to her, ne keepe her company,
    But in close bowre her mewes from all mens sight,
Depriv'd of kindly joy and naturall delight.

6

'*Malbecco* he, and *Hellenore* she hight,
    Unfitly yokt together in one teeme,
    That is the cause, why never any knight
    Is suffred here to enter, but he seeme
    Such, as no doubt of him he neede misdeeme.'
    Thereat Sir *Satyrane* gan smile, and say;
    'Extremely mad the man I surely deeme,
    That weenes with watch and hard restraynt to stay
A womans will, which is disposed to go astray.

7

'In vaine he feares that which he cannot shonne:
    For who wotes not, that womans subtiltyes
    Can guilen *Argus*, when she list misdonne?
    Is it not yron bandes, nor hundred eyes,
    Nor brasen walls, nor many wakefull spyes,
    That can withhold her wilfull wandring feet;
    But fast good will, with gentle curtesyes,
    And timely service to her pleasures meet
May her perhaps containe, that else would algates fleet.'

8

'Then is he not more mad' (said *Paridell*)
    'That hath himselfe unto such service sold,
    In dolefull thraldome all his dayes to dwell?
    For sure a foole I do him firmely hold,
    That loves his fetters, though they were of gold.
    But why do we devise of others ill,

Whiles thus we suffer this same dotard old,
　　To keepe us out, in scorne of his owne will,
And rather do not ransack all, and him selfe kill?'

9

'Nay let us first' (said *Satyrane*) 'entreat
　　The man by gentle meanes to let us in,
　　And afterwardes affray with cruell threat,
　　Ere that we to efforce it do begin:
　　Then if all fayle, we will by force it win,
　　And eke reward the wretch for his mesprise,
　　As may be worthy of his haynous sin.'
　　That counsell pleasd: then *Paridell* did rise,
And to the Castle gate approcht in quiet wise.

10

Whereat soft knocking, entrance he desyrd.
　　The good man selfe, which then the Porter playd,
　　Him answered, that all were now retyrd
　　Unto their rest, and all the keyes convayd
　　Unto their maister, who in bed was layd,
　　That none him durst awake out of his dreme;
　　And therefore them of patience gently prayd.
　　Then *Paridell* began to chaunge his theme,
And threatned him with force and punishment extreme.

11

But all in vaine; for nought mote him relent,
　　And now so long before the wicket fast
　　They wayted, that the night was forward spent,
　　And the faire welkin fowly overcast,
　　Gan blowen up a bitter stormy blast,
　　With shoure and hayle so horrible and dred,
　　That this faire many were compeld at last,
　　To fly for succour to a little shed,
The which beside the gate for swine was ordered.

12

It fortuned, soone after they were gone,
　　Another knight, whom tempest thither brought,
　　Came to that Castle, and with earnest mone,
　　Like as the rest, late entrance deare besought;
　　But like so as the rest he prayd for nought,
　　For flatly he of entrance was refusd,
　　Sorely thereat he was displeasd, and thought

How to avenge himselfe so sore abusd,
And evermore the Carle of curtesie accusd.

13

But to avoyde th' intollerable stowre,
  He was compeld to seeke some refuge neare,
  And to that shed, to shrowd him from the showre,
  He came, which full of guests he found whyleare,
  So as he was not let to enter there:
  Whereat he gan to wex exceeding wroth,
  And swore, that he would lodge with them yfere,
  Or them dislodge, all were they liefe or loth;
And so defide them each, and so defide them both.

14

Both were full loth to leave that needfull tent,
  And both full loth in darkenesse to debate;
  Yet both full liefe him lodging to have lent,
  And both full liefe his boasting to abate;
  But chiefely *Paridell* his hart did grate,
  To heare him threaten so despightfully,
  As if he did a dogge to kenell rate,
  That durst not barke; and rather had he dy,
Then when he was defide, in coward corner ly.

15

Tho hastily remounting to his steed,
  He forth issew'd: like as a boistrous wind
  Which in th' earthes hollow caves hath long bin hid,
  And shut up fast within her prisons blind,
  Makes the huge element against her kind
  To move, and tremble as it were agast,
  Untill that it an issew forth may find;
  Then forth it breakes, and with his furious blast
Confounds both land and seas, and skyes doth overcast.

16

Their steel-hed speares they strongly coucht, and met
  Together with impetuous rage and forse,
  That with the terrour of their fierce affret,
  They rudely drove to ground both man and horse,
  That each awhile lay like a sencelesse corse.
  But *Paridell* sore brused with the blow,
  Could not arise, the counterchaunge to scorse,
  Till that young Squire him reared from below;
Then drew he his bright sword, and gan about him throw.

17

But *Satyrane* forth stepping, did them stay
  And with faire treatie pacifide their ire,
  Then when they were accorded from the fray,
  Against that Castles Lord they gan conspire,
  To heape on him dew vengeaunce for his hire.
  They bene agreed, and to the gates they goe
  To burne the same with unquenchable fire,
  And that uncurteous Carle their commune foe
To do fowle death to dye, or wrap in grievous woe.

18

Malbecco seeing them resolv'd in deed
  To flame the gates, and hearing them to call
  For fire in earnest, ran with fearfull speed,
  And to them calling from the castle wall,
  Besought them humbly him to beare with all,
  As ignoraunt of servants bad abuse,
  And slacke attendaunce unto straungers call.
  The knights were willing all things to excuse,
Though nought belev'd, and entraunce late did not refuse.

19

They bene ybrought into a comely bowre,
  And serv'd of all things that mote needfull bee;
  Yet secretly their hoste did on them lowre,
  And welcomde more for feare, then charitee;
  But they dissembled, what they did not see,
  And welcomed themselves. Each gan undight
  Their garments wet, and weary armour free,
  To dry them selves by *Vulcanes* flaming light,
And eke their lately bruzed parts to bring in plight.

20

And eke that straunger knight emongst the rest
  Was for like need enforst to disaray:
  Tho whenas vailed was her loftie crest,
  Her golden locks, that were in tramels gay
  Upbounden, did them selves adowne display,
  And raught unto her heeles; like sunny beames,
  That in a cloud their light did long time stay,
  Their vapour vaded, shew their golden gleames,
And through the persant aire shoote forth their azure streames.

21

She also dofte her heavy haberjeon,
  Which the faire feature of her limbs did hyde,
  And her well plighted frock, which she did won
  To tucke about her short, when she did ryde,
  She low let fall, that flowd from her lanck syde
  Downe to her foot, with carelesse modestee.
  Then of them all she plainly was espyde,
  To be a woman wight, unwist to bee,
The fairest woman wight, that ever eye did see.

22

Like as *Minerva*, being late returnd
  From slaughter of the Giaunts conquered;
  Where proud *Encelade*, whose wide nosethrils burnd
  With breathed flames, like to a furnace red,
  Transfixed with her speare downe tombled ded
  From top of *Hemus*, by him heaped hye;
  Hath loosd her helmet from her lofty hed,
  And her *Gorgonian* shield gins to untye
From her lefte arme, to rest in glorious victorye.

23

Which whenas they beheld, they smitten were
  With great amazement of so wondrous sight,
  And each on other, and they all on her
  Stood gazing, as if suddein great affright
  Had them surprised.   At last avizing right,
  Her goodly personage and glorious hew,
  Which they so much mistooke, they tooke delight
  In their first error, and yet still anew
With wonder of her beauty fed their hungry vew.

24

Yet note their hungry vew be satisfide,
  But seeing still the more desir'd to see,
  And ever firmely fixed did abide
  In contemplation of divinitee:
  But most they mervaild at her chevalree,
  And noble prowesse, which they had approved,
  That much they faynd to know who she mote bee;
  Yet none of all them her thereof amoved
Yet every one her likte, and every one her loved.

25

And *Paridell* though partly discontent
   With his late fall, and fowle indignity,
   Yet was soone wonne his malice to relent,
   Through gracious regard of her faire eye,
   And knightly worth, which he too late did try,
   Yet tried did adore.   Supper was dight;
   Then they *Malbecco* prayd of curtesy,
   That of his Lady they might have the sight,
And company at meat, to doe them more delight.

26

But he to shift their curious request,
   Gan causen, why she could not come in place;
   Her crased health, her late recourse to rest,
   And humid evening ill for sicke folkes cace:
   But none of those excuses could take place;
   Ne would they eate, till she in presence came.
   Shee came in presence with right comely grace,
   And fairely them saluted, as became,
And shewd her selfe in all a gentle curteous Dame.

27

They sate to meat, and *Satyrane* his chaunce
   Was her before, and *Paridell* besyde;
   But he him selfe sate looking still askaunce,
   Gainst *Britomart*, and ever closely eyde
   Sir *Satyrane*, that glaunces might not glyde:
   But his blinde eye, that syded *Paridell*,
   All is demeasnure from his sight did hyde:
   On her faire face so did he feede his fill,
And sent close messages of love to her at will.

28

And ever and anone, when none was ware,
   With speaking lookes, that close embassage bore,
   He rov'd at her, and told his secret care:
   For all that art he learned had of yore.
   Ne was she ignoraunt of that lewd lore.
   But in his eye his meaning wisely red,
   And with the like him answerd evermore:
   She sent at him one firie dart, whose hed
Empoisned was with privy lust, and gealous dred.

29

He from that deadly throw made no defence,
    But to the wound his weake heart opened wyde;
    The wicked engine through false influence,
    Past through his eyes, and secretly did glyde
    Into his hart, which it did sorely gryde.
    But nothing new to him was that same paine,
    Ne paine at all; for he so ofte had tryde
    The powre thereof, and lov'd so oft in vaine,
That thing of course he counted, love to entertaine.

30

Thenceforth to her he sought to intimate
    His inward griefe, by meanes to him well knowne,
    Now *Bacchus* fruit out of the silver plate
    He on the table dasht, as overthrowne,
    Or of the fruitfull liquor overflowne,
    And by the dauncing bubbles did divine,
    Or therein write to let his love be showne;
    Which well she red out of the learned line,
A sacrament prophane in mistery of wine.

31

And when so of his hand the pledge she raught,
    The guilty cup she fained to mistake,
    And in her lap did shed her idle draught,
    Shewing desire her inward flame to slake:
    But such close signes they secret way did make
    Unto their wils, and one eyes watch escape;
    Two eyes him needeth, for to watch and wake,
    Who lovers will deceive. Thus was the ape,
By their faire handling, put into *Malbeccoes* cape.

32

Now when of meats and drinks they had their fill,
    Purpose was moved by that gentle Dame,
    Unto those knights adventurous, to tell
    Of deeds of armes, which unto them became,
    And every one his kindred and his name.
    Then *Paridell*, in whom a kindly pryde
    Of gracious speach, and skill his words to frame
    Abounded, being glad of so fit tyde
Him to commend to her, thus spake, of all well eyde.

33

'*Troy*, that art now nought, but an idle name,
And in thine ashes buried low dost lie,
Though whilome far much greater then thy fame,
Before that angry Gods, and cruell skye
Upon thee heapt a direfull destinie,
What boots it boast thy glorious descent,
And fetch from heaven thy great Genealogie,
Sith all thy worthy prayses being blent,
Their off-spring hath embaste, and later glory shent.

34

'Most famous Worthy of the world, by whome
That warre was kindled, which did *Troy* inflame,
And stately towres of Ilion whilome
Brought unto balefull ruine, was by name
Sir *Paris* far renowmd through noble fame,
Who through great prowesse and bold hardinesse,
From *Lacedæmon* fetcht the fairest Dame,
That ever *Greece* did boast, or knight possesse,
Whom *Venus* to him gave for meed of worthinesse.

35

'Faire *Helene*, flowre of beautie excellent,
And girlond of the mighty Conquerours,
That madest many Ladies deare lament
The heavie losse of their brave Paramours,
Which they far off beheld from *Trojan* toures,
And saw the fieldes of faire *Scamander* strowne
With carcases of noble warrioures,
Whose fruitlesse lives were under furrow sowne,
And *Xanthus* sandy bankes with blood all overflowne.

36

'From him my linage I derive aright,
Who long before the ten yeares siege of *Troy*,
Whiles yet on *Ida* he a shepeheard hight,
On faire *Oenone* got a lovely boy,
Whom for remembraunce of her passed joy,
She of his Father *Parius* did name;
Who, after *Greekes* did *Priams* realme destroy,
Gathred the *Trojan* reliques sav'd from flame,
And with them sayling thence, to th' Isle of *Paros* came.

37

'That was by him cald *Paros*, which before
  Hight *Nausa*, there he many yeares did raine,
  And built *Nausicle* by the *Pontick* shore,
  The which he dying left next in remaine
  To *Paridas* his sonne.
  From whom I *Paridell* by kin descend;
  But for faire Ladies love, and glories gaine,
  My native soile have lefte, my dayes to spend
In sewing deeds of armes, my lives and labours end.

38

Whenas the noble *Britomart* heard tell
  Of *Trojan* warres, and *Priams* Citie sackt,
  The ruefull story of Sir *Paridell*,
  She was empassioned at that piteous act,
  With zelous envy of *Greekes* cruell fact,
  Against that nation, from whose race of old
  She heard, that she was lineally extract:
  For noble *Britons* sprong from *Trojans* bold,
And *Troynovant* was built of old *Troyes* ashes cold.

39

Then sighing soft awhile, at last she thus:
  'O lamentable fall of famous towne,
  Which raignd so many yeares victorious,
  And of all *Asie* bore the soveraigne crowne,
  In one sad nigh consumd, and throwen downe:
  What stony hart, that heares thy haplesse fate,
  Is not empierst with deepe compassiowne,
  And makes ensample of mans wretched state,
That floures so fresh at morne, and fades at evening late?

40

'Behold, Sir, how your pitifull complaint
  Hath found another partner of your payne:
  For nothing may impresse so deare constraint,
  As countries cause, and commune foes disdayne.
  But if it should not grieve you, backe agayne
  To turne your course, I would to heare desyre,
  What to *Aeneas* fell; sith that men sayne
  He was not in the Cities wofull fyre
Consum'd, but did him selfe to safetie retyre.'

41

'*Anchyses* some begot of *Venus* faire,'
  (Said he,) 'out of the flames for safegard fled,
  And with a remnant did to sea repaire,
  Where he through fatall errour long was led
  Full many yeares, and weetlesse wandered
  From shore to shore, emongst the Lybicke sands
  Ere rest he found. Much there he suffered,
  And many perils past in forreine lands,
To save his people sad from victours vengefull hands.

42

'At last in *Latium* did he arrive,
  Where he with cruell warre was entertaind
  Of th' inland folke, which sought him backe to drive,
  Till he with old *Latinus* was constraind,
  To contract wedlock: (so the fates ordaind.)
  Wedlock contract in bloud, and eke in blood
  Accomplished, that many deare complaind:
  The rivall slaine, the victour through the flood
Escaped hardly, hardly praisd his wedlock good.

43

'Yet after all, he victour did survive,
  And with *Latinus* did the kingdome part.
  But after, when both nations gan to strive,
  Into their names the title to convart,
  His sonne *Iülus* did from thence depart,
  With all the warlike youth of *Trojans* bloud,
  And in long *Alba* plast his throne apart,
  Where faire it florished and long time stoud,
Till *Romulus* renewing it, to *Rome* remoud.'

44

'There there' (said *Britomart*) a fresh appeard
  The glory of the later world to spring,
  And *Troy* againe out of her dust was reard,
  To sit in second seat of soveraigne king,
  Of all the world under her governing.
  But a third kingdome yet is to arise,
  Out of the *Trojans* scattered of-spring,
  That in all glory and great enterprise,
Both first and second *Troy* shall dare to equalise.

45

'It *Troynovant* is hight, that with the waves
  Of wealthy *Thamis* washed is along,
  Upon whose stubborne neck, whereat he raves
  With roring rage, and sore him selfe does throng,
  That all men feare to tempt his billowes strong,
  She fastned hath her foot, which standes so hy,
  That it a wonder of the world is song
  In forreine landes, of all which passen by,
Beholding it from farre, do thinke it threates the skye.

46

'The *Trojan Brute* did first that Citie found,
  And Hygate made the meare thereof by West,
  And *Overt* gate by North: that is the bound
  Toward the land; two rivers bound the rest.
  So huge a scope at first him seemed best,
  To be the compasse of his kingdomes seat:
  So huge a mind could not in lesser rest,
  Ne in small meares containe his glory great,
That *Albion* had conquered first by warlike feat.'

47

'Ah fairest Lady knight,' (said *Paridell*)
  'Pardon I pray my heedlesse oversight,
  Who had forgot, that whilome I heard tell
  From aged *Mnemon*; for my wits bene light.
  Indeed he said (if I remember right,)
  That of the antique *Trojan* stocke, there grew
  Another plant, that raught to wondrous hight,
  And far abroad his mighty branches threw,
Into the utmost Angle of the world he knew.

48

'For that same *Brute*, whom much he did advaunce
  In all his speach, was *Sylvius* his sonne,
  Whom having slaine, through luckles arrowes glaunce
  He fled for feare of that he had misdonne,
  Or else for shame, so fowle reproch to shonne,
  And with him led to sea an youthly trayne,
  Where wearie wandring they long time did wonne,
  And many fortunes prov'd in th' *Ocean* mayne,
And great adventures found, that now were long to sayne.

49

'At last by fatall course they driven were
  Into an Island spatious and brode,
  The furthest North, that did to them appeare:
  Which after rest they seeking farre abrode,
  Found it the fittest soyle for their abode,
  Fruitfull of all things fit for living foode,
  But wholy wast, and void of peoples trode,
  Save an huge nation of the Geaunts broode,
That fed on living flesh, and druncke mens vitall blood.

50

'Whom he through wearie wars and labours long,
  Subdewd with losse of many *Britons* bold:
  In which the great *Goemagot* of strong
  Corineus, and *Coulin* of *Debon* old
  Were overthrowne, and layd on th' earth full cold,
  Which quaked under their so hideous masse,
  A famous history to be enrold
  In everlasting moniments of brasse,
That all the antique Worthies merits far did passe.

51

'His worke great *Troynovant*, his worke is eke
  Faire *Lincolne*, both renowmed far away,
  That who from East to West will endlong seeke,
  Cannot two fairer Cities find this day,
  Except *Cleopolis*: so heard I say
  Old *Mnemon*. Therefore Sir, I greet you well
  Your countrey kin, and you entirely pray
  Of pardon for the strife, which late befell
Betwixt us both unknowne.' So ended *Paridell*.

52

But all the while, that he these speaches spent,
  Upon his lips hong faire Dame *Hellenore*,
  With vigilant regard, and dew attent,
  Fashioning worlds of fancies evermore
  In her fraile wit, that now her quite forlore:
  The whiles unwares away her wondring eye,
  And greedy eares her weake hart from her bore:
  Which he perceiving, ever privily
In speaking, many false belgardes at her let fly.

53

So long these knights discoursed diversly,
　　Of straunge affaires, and noble hardiment,
　　Which they had past with micke jeopardy,
　　That now the humid night was farforth spent,
　　And heavenly lampes were halfendeale ybrent:
　　Which th' old man seeing well, who too long thought
　　Every discourse and every argument,
　　Which by the houres he measured, besought
Them go to rest. So all unto their bowres were brought.

Canto X

Paridell rapeth Hellenore:
Malbecco her pursewes:
Findes emongst Satyres, whence with him
To turne she doth refuse.

1

The morrow next, so soone as *Phœbus* Lamp
  Bewrayed had the world with early light,
  And fresh *Aurora* had the shady damp
  Out of the goodly heven amoved quight,
  Faire *Britomart* and that same *Faerie* knight
  Uprose, forth on their journey for to wend:
  But *Paridell* complaynd, that his late fight
  With *Britomart* so sore did him offend,
That ryde he could not, till his hurts he did amend.

2

So forth they far'd, but he behind them stayd,
  Maulgre his host, who grudged grievously
  To house a guest, that would be needes obayd,
  And of his owne him left not liberty:
  Might wanting measure moveth surquedry.
  Two things he feared, but the third was death;
  That fierce youngmans unruly maistery;
  His money, which he lov'd as living breath;
And his faire wife, whom honest long he kept uneath.

3

But patience perforce he must abie,
  What fortune and his fate on him will lay,
  Fond is the feare, that findes no remedie;
  Yet warily he watcheth every way,
  By which he feareth evill happen may:
  So th' evill thinkes by watching to prevent;
  Ne doth he suffer her, nor night, nor day,
  Out of his sight her selfe once to absent.
So doth he punish her and eke himselfe torment,

4

But *Paridell* kept better watch, then hee,
  A fit occasion for his turne to finde:
  False love, why do men say thou canst not see,
  And in their foolish fancy feigne thee blind,
  That with thy charmes the sharpest sight doest bind,

And to thy will abuse?   Thou walkest free,
And seest every secret of the mind;
Thou seest all, yet none at all sees thee;
All that is by the working of thy Deitee.

5

So perfect in that art was *Paridell*,
That he *Malbeccoes* halfen eye did wyle,
His halfen eye he wiled wondrous well,
And *Hellenors* both eyes did eke beguyle,
Both eyes and hart attonce, during the whyle
That he there sojourned his woundes to heale;
That *Cupid* selfe it seeing, close did smyle,
To weet how he her love away did steale,
And bad, that none their joyous treason should reveale.

6

The learned lover lost no time nor tyde,
That least advantage mote to him afford,
Yet bore so faire a saile, that none espyde
His secret drift, till he her layd abord.
When so in open space and commune bord,
He fortun'd her to meet, with commune speach
He courted her, yet bayted every word,
That his ungentle hoste n'ote him appeach
Of vile ungentlenesse, or hospitages breach.

7

But when apart (if ever her apart)
He found, then his false engins fast he plyde,
And all the sleights unbosomd in his hart;
He sigh'd, he sobd, he swownd, he perdy dyde,
And cast himselfe on ground her fast besyde:
Tho when againe he him bethought to live,
He wept, and wayld, and false laments belyde,
Saying, but if she Mercie would him give
That he mote algates dye, yet did his death forgive.

8

And otherwhiles with amorous delights,
And pleasing toyes he would her entertaine,
Now singing sweetly, to surprise her sprights,
Now making layes of love and lovers paine,
Bransles, Ballads, virelayes, and verses vaine;
Oft purposes, oft riddles he devysd,

And thousands like, which flowed in his braine,
With which he fed her fancie, and entysd
To take to his new love, and leave her old despysd.

9

And every where he might, and every while
He did her service dewtifull, and sewed
At hand with humble pride, and pleasing guile,
So closely yet, that none but she it vewed,
Who well perceived all, and all indewed.
Thus finely did he his false nets dispred,
With which he many weake harts had subdewed
Of yore, and many had ylike misled:
What wonder then, if she were likewise carried?

10

No fort so fensible, no wals so strong,
But that continuall battery will rive,
Or daily siege through dispurvayance long,
And lacke of reskewes will to parley drive;
And Peace, that unto parley eare will give,
Will shortly yeeld it selfe, and will be made
The vassall of the victors will bylive:
That stratageme had oftentimes assayd
This crafty Paramoure, and now it plaine displayd.

11

For through his traines he her intrapped hath,
That she her love and hart hath wholy sold
To him, without regard of gaine or scath,
Or care of credite, or of husband old,
Whom she hath vow'd to dub a faire Cucquold.
Nought wants but time and place, which shortly shee
Devized hath, and to her lover told.
It pleased well. So well they both agree;
So readie rype to ill, ill wemens counsels bee.

12

Darke was the Evening, fit for lovers stealth,
When chaunst *Malbecco* busie be elsewhere,
She is his closet went, where all his wealth
Lay hid: thereof she countlesse summes did reare,
The which she meant away with her to beare;
The rest she fyr'd for sport, or for despight;
As *Hellene*, when she saw aloft appeare

The *Trojane* flames, and reach to heavens hight
Did clap her hands and joyed at that doleful sight.

13

This second *Hellene*, faire Dame *Hellenore*,
    The whiles her husband ran with sory haste,
    To quench the flames, which she had tyn'd before,
    Laught at his foolish labour spent in waste;
    And ranne into her lovers armes right fast;
    Where streight embraced, she to him did cry,
    And call aloud for helpe, ere helpe were past;
    For loe that Guest would beare her forcibly,
And meant to ravish her, that rather had to dy.

14

The wretched man hearing her call for ayd,
    And readie seeing him with her to fly,
    In his disquiet mind was much dismayd:
    But when againe he backward cast his eye,
    And saw the wicked fire so furiously
    Consume his hart, and scorch his Idoles face,
    He was therewith distressed diversly,
    Ne wist he how to turne, nor to what place;
Was never wretched man in such a wofull cace.

15

Ay when to him she cryde, to her he turnd,
    And left the fire; love money overcame:
    But when he marked, how his money burnd,
    He left his wife; money did love disclame:
    Both was he loth to loose his loved Dame,
    And loth to leave his liefest pelfe behind,
    Yet sith he n'ote save both, he sav'd that same,
    Which was the dearest to his donghill mind,
The God of his desire, the joy of misers blind.

16

Thus whilest all things in troublous uprore were,
    And all men busie to suppresse the flame,
    The loving couple need no reskew feare,
    But leasure had, and libertie to frame
    Their purpost flight, free from all mens reclame;
    And Night, the patronesse of love-stealth faire,
    Gave them safe conduct, till to end they came:
    So beene they gone yfeare, a wanton paire
Of lovers loosely knit, where list them to repaire.

17

Soone as the cruell flames yslaked were,
  Malbecco seeing how his losse did lye,
  Out of the flames, which he had quencht whylere
  Into huge waves of griefe and gealosye
  Full deepe emplonged was, and drowned nye,
  Twixt inward doole and felonous despight;
  He rav'd, he wept, he stampt, he lowd did cry,
  And all the passions, that in man may light,
Did him attonce oppresse, and vex his caytive spright.

18

Long thus he chawd the cud of inward griefe,
  And did consume his gall with anguish sore,
  Still when he mused on his late mischiefe,
  Then still the smart thereof increased more,
  And seem'd more grievous, then it was before:
  At last when sorrow he saw booted nought,
  Ne griefe might not his love to him restore,
  He gan devise how her he reskew mought,
Ten thousand wayes he cast in his confused thought.

19

At last resolving, like a pilgrim pore,
  To search her forth where so she might be fond,
  And bearing with him treasure in close store,
  The rest he leaves in ground: So takes in hond
  To seeke her endlong both by sea and lond.
  Long he her sought, he sought her far and nere,
  And every where that he mote understond,
  Of knights and ladies any meetings were,
And of eachone he met, he tidings did inquere.

20

But all in vaine, his woman was too wise,
  Ever to come into his clouch againe,
  And he too simple ever to surprise
  The jolly *Paridell*, for all his paine.
  One day, as he forpassed by the plaine
  With weary pace, he far away espide
  A couple, seeming well to be his twaine,
  Which hoved close under a forrest side,
As if they lay in wait, or else them selves did hide.

21

Well weened he, that those the same mote bee,
  And as he better did their shape avize,
  Him seemed more their manner did agree;
  For th' one was armed in all warlike wize,
  Whom, to be *Paridell* he did devize;
  And th' other allyclad in garments light,
  Discolour'd like to womanish disguise,
  He did resemble to his Ladie bright;
And ever his faint hart much earned at the sight.

22

And ever faine he towards them would goe,
  But yet durst not for dread approchen nie,
  But stood aloofe, unweeting what to doe;
  Till that prickt forth with loves extremitie,
  That is the father of foule gealosy,
  He closely nearer crept, the truth to weet:
  But, as he nigher drew, he easily
  Might scerne, that it was not his sweetest sweet,
Ne yet her Belamour, the partner of his sheet.

23

But it was scornefull *Braggadocchio*,
  That with his servant *Trompart* hoverd there,
  Sith late he fled from his too earnest foe:
  Whom such when as *Malbecco* spyed clere,
  He turned backe, and would have fled arere;
  Till *Trompart* ronning hastely, him did stay,
  And bad before his soveraine Lord appere:
  That was him loth, yet durst he not gainesay,
And comming him before low louted on the lay.

24

The Boaster at him sternely bent his browe,
  As if he could have kild him him with his looke,
  That to the ground him meekely made to bowe,
  And awfull terror deepe into him strooke,
  That every member of his bodie quooke.
  Said he, 'thou man of nought, what doest thou here,
  Unfitly furnisht with thy bag and booke,
  Where I expected one with shield and spere,
To prove some deeds of armes upon an equall pere.

25

The wretched man at his imperious speach,
  Was all abasht, and low prostrating, said;
  'Good Sir, let not my rudenesse be no breach
  Unto your patience, ne be ill ypaid;
  For I unwares this way by fortune straid,
  A silly Pilgrim driven to distresse,
  That seeke a Lady,'   There he suddein staid,
  And did the rest with grievous sighes suppresse,
While teares stood in his eies, few drops of bitternesse.

26

'What Ladie, man?' (said *Trompart*) 'take good hart,
  And tell thy griefe, if any hidden lye;
  Was never better time to shew thy smart,
  Then now, that noble succour is thee by,
  That is the whole worlds commune remedy.'
  That chearefull word his weake heart much did cheare,
  And with vaine hope his spirits faint supply,
  That bold he said; 'O most redoubted Pere,
Vouchsafe with mild regard a wretches cace to heare.'

27

Then sighing sore, 'It is not long' (said hee)
  'Sith I enjoyd the gentlest Dame alive;
  Of whom a knight, no knight at all perdee,
  But shame of all, that doe for honor strive,
  By treacherous deceipt did me deprive;
  Through open outrage he her bore away,
  And with fowle force unto his will did drive,
  Which all good knights, that armes do bear this day,
Are bound for to revenge, and punish if they may.

28

'And you most noble Lord, that can and dare
  Redresse the wrong of miserable wight,
  Cannot employ your most victorious speare
  In better quarell, then defence of right,
  And for a Ladie gainst a faithlesse knight;
  So shall your glory be advaunced much,
  And all faire Ladies magnifie your might,
  And eke my selfe, albe I simple such,
Your worthy paine shall well reward with guerdon rich.'

29

With that out of his bouget forth he drew
   Great store of treasure, therewith him to tempt;
   But he on it lookt scornefully askew,
   As much disdeigning to be so misdempt,
   Or a war-monger to be basely nempt;
   And said; 'thy offers base I greatly loth,
   And eke thy words uncourteous and unkempt;
   I tread in dust thee and thy money both,
That, were it not for shame,'   So turned from him wroth.

30

But *Trompart*, that his maisters humor knew,
   In lofty lookes to hide an humble mind,
   Was inly tickled with that golden vew,
   And in his eare him rounded close behind:
   Yet stoupt he not, but lay still in the wind,
   Waiting advauntage on the pray to sease;
   Till *Trompart* lowly to the ground inclind,
   Besought him his great courage to appease,
And pardon simple man, that rash did him displease.

31

Bigge lookng like a doughtie Doucepere,
   At last he thus; 'Thou clod of vilest clay,
   I pardon yield, and with thy rudenesse beare;
   But weete henceforth, that all that golden pray,
   And all that else the vaine world vauten may,
   I loath as doung, ne deeme my dew reward:
   Fame is my meed, and glory vertues pray.
   But minds of mortall men are muchell mard,
And mov'd amisse with massie mucks unmeet regard.

32

'And more, I graunt to thy great miserie
   Gratious respect, thy wife shall backe be sent,
   And that vile knight, who ever that he bee,
   Which hath thy Lady reft, and knighthood shent,
   By *Sanglamort* my sword, whose deadly dent
   The blood hath of so many thousands shed,
   I sweare, ere long shall dearely it repent;
   Ne he twixt heaven and earth shall hide his hed,
But soone he shal be found, and shortly doen be ded.

33

The foolish man thereat woxe wondrous blith,
   As if the word so spoken, were halfe donne,
   And humbly thanked him a thousand sith,
   That had from death to life him newly wonne.
   Tho forth the Boaster marching, brave begonne
   His stolen steed to thunder furiously,
   As if he heaven and hell would overronne,
   And all the world confound with cruelty,
That much *Malbecco* joyed in his jollity.

34

Thus long they three together traveiled,
   Through many a wood, and many an uncouth way,
   To seeke his wife, that was far wandered:
   But those two sought nought, but the present pray,
   To weete the treasure, which he did bewray,
   On which their eies and harts were wholly set,
   With purpose, how they might it best betray;
   For sith the houre, that first he did them let
The same behold, therewith their keened desires were whet.

35

It fortuned as they together far'd,
   They spide, where *Paridell* came pricking fast
   Upon the plaine, the which himselfe prepar'd
   To guist with that brave straunger knight a cast,
   As on adventure by the way he past:
   Alone he rode without his Paragone;
   For having filcht her bels, her up he cast
   To the wide world, and let her fly alone,
He nould be clogd. So had he served many one.

36

The gentle Lady, loose at randon left,
   The greene-wood long did walke, and wander wide
   At wilde adventure, like a forlorne weft,
   Till on a day the *Satyres* her espide
   Straying alone withouten groome or guide;
   Her up they tooke, and with them home her led,
   With them as housewife ever to abide,
   To milk their gotes, and make them cheese and bred,
And every one as commune good her handeled.

37

That shortly she *Malbecco* has forgot,
  And eke Sir *Paridell*, all were he deare;
  Who from her went to seeke another lot,
  And now by fortune was arrived here,
  Where those two guilers with *Malbecco* were:
  Soone as the oldman saw Sir *Paridell*,
  He fainted, and was almost dead with feare,
  Ne word he had to speake, his griefe to tell,
But to him louted low, and greeted goodly well.

38

And after asked him for *Hellenore*,
  'I take no keepe of her' (said *Paridell*)
  'She wonneth in the forrest there before.'
  So forth he rode, as his adventure fell;
  The whiles the Boaster from his loftie sell
  Faynd to alight, something amisse to mend;
  But the fresh Swayne would not his leasure dwell,
  But went his way; whom when he passed kend,
He up remounted light, and after faind to wend.

39

'Perdy nay' (said *Malbecco*) 'shall ye not:
  But let him passe as lightly as he came:
  For litle good of him is to be got,
  And mickle perill to be put to shame.
  But let us go to seeke my dearest Dame,
  Whom he hath left in yonder forrest wyld:
  For of her safety in great doubt I am,
  Least salvage beastes her person have despoyld:
Then all the world is lost, and we in vaine have toyld.'

40

They all agree, and forward them addrest:
  'Ah but' (said craftie *Trompart*) 'weete ye well,
  That yonder in that wastefull wildernesse
  Huge monsters haunt, and many dangers dwell;
  Dragons, and Minotaures, and feendes of hell,
  And many wilde woodmen, which robbe and rend
  All travellers; therefore advise ye well,
  Before ye enterprise that way to wend:
One may his journey bring too soone to evill end.'

41

Malbecco stopt in great astonishment,
  And with pale eyes fast fixed on the rest,
  Their counsell crav'd, in daunger imminent.
  Said *Trompart*, 'You that are the most opprest
  With burden of great treasure, I thinke best
  Here for to stay in safetie behind;
  My Lord and I will search the wide forrest.'
  That counsell pleased not *Malbeccoes* mind;
For he was much affraid, himselfe alone to find.

42

'Then is it best' (said he) 'that ye doe leave
  Your treasure here in some securitie,
  Either fast closed in some hollow greave,
  Or buried in the ground from jeopardie,
  Till we returne againe in safetie:
  As for us two, least doubt of us ye have,
  Hence farre away we will blindfolded lie,
  Ne privie be unto your treasures grave.'
It pleased: so he did. Then they march forward brave.

43

Now when amid the thickest woods they were,
  They heard a noyse of many bagpipes shrill,
  And shrieking Hububs them approching near,
  Which all the forrest did with horror fill:
  That dreadfull sound the boasters hart did thrill,
  With such amazement, that in hast he fled,
  Ne ever looked backe good or ill,
  And after him eke fearefull *Trompart* sped;
The old man could not fly, but fell to ground halfe ded.

44

Yet afterwards close creeping as he might,
  He in a bush did hide his fearefull hed,
  The jolly *Satyres* full of fresh delight,
  Came dauncing forth, and with them nimbly led
  Faire *Hellenore* with girlonds all bespred,
  Whom their May-lady they had newly made:
  She proud of that new honour which they red,
  And of their lovely fellowship full glade,
Daunst lively, and her face did with a Lawrell shade.

45

The silly man that in the thicket lay
  Saw all this goodly sport, and grieved sore,
  Yet durst he not against it doe or say,
  But did his hart with bitter thoughts engore,
  To see th' unkindnesse of his *Hellenore*.
  All day they daunced with great lustihed,
  And with their horned feet the greene grasse wore,
  The whiles their Gotes upon the brouzes fed,
Till drouping *Phœbus* gan to hide his golden hed.

46

Tho up they gan their merry pypes to trusse,
  And all their goodly heards did gather round,
  But every *Satyre* first did give a busse
  To *Hellenore*: so busses did abound.
  Now gan the humid vapour shed the ground
  With perly deaw, and th' Earthes gloomy shade
  Did dim the brightnesse of the welkin round,
  That every bird and beast awarned made
To shrowd themselves, while sleepe their sences did invade.

47

Which when *Malbecco* saw, out of his bush
  Upon his hands and feete he crept full light,
  And like a Gote emongst the Gotes did rush,
  That through the helpe of his faire hornes on hight,
  And mighty dampe of misconceiving night,
  And eke through likenesse of his gotish beard,
  He did the better counterfeite aright:
  So home he marcht emongst the horned heard,
That none of all the *Satyres* him espyde or heard.

48

At night, when all they went to sleepe, he vewd,
  Whereas his lovely wife emongst them lay,
  Embraced of a Satyre rough and rude,
  Who all the night did minde his joyous play:
  Nine times he heard him come aloft ere day,
  That all his hart with gealosie did swell;
  But yet that nights ensample did bewray,
  That not for nought his wife them loved so well,
When one so oft a night did ring his matins bell.

49

So closely as he could, he to them crept,
    When wearie of their sport to sleepe they fell,
    And to his wife, that now full soundly slept,
    He whispered in her eare, and did her tell,
    That it was he, which by her side did dwell,
    And therefore prayd her wake, to heare him plaine.
    As one out of a dreame not waked well,
    She turned her, and returned backe againe:
Yet her for to awake he did the more constraine.

50

At last with irkesome trouble she abrayd;
    And then perceiving that it was indeed
    Her old *Malbecco*, which did her upbrayd,
    With loosenesse of her love, and loathly deed,
    She was astonisht with exceeding dreed,
    And would have wakt the *Satyre* by her syde;
    But he her prayd, for mercy, or for meed,
    To save his life, ne let him be descryde,
But hearken to his lore, and all his counsell hyde.

51

Tho gan he her perswade to leave that lewd
    And loathsome life, of God and man abhord,
    And home returne, where all should be renewd
    With perfect peace, and bandes of fresh accord,
    And she receiv'd againe to bed and bord,
    As if no trespasse ever had beene donne:
    But she it all refused at one word,
    And by no meanes would to his will be wonne,
But chose emongst the jolly Satyres still to wonne.

52

He wooed her, till day spring he espyde;
    But all in vaine; and then turnd to the heard,
    Who butted him with hornes on every syde,
    And trode downe in the durt, where his hore beard
    Was fowly dight, and he of death afeard.
    Early before the heavens fairest light
    Out of the ruddy East was fully reard,
    The heardes out of their foldes were loosed quight,
And he emongst the rest crept forth in sory plight.

53

So soone as he the Prison dore did pas,
  He ran as fast as both his feet could beare,
  And never looked, who behind him was,
  Ne scarsely who before: like as a Beare
  That creeping close, amongst the hives to reare
  An hony combe, the wakefull dogs espy,
  And him assayling, sore his carkasse teare,
  That hardly he with life away does fly,
Ne stayes, till safe himselfe he see from jeopardy.

54

Ne stayd he, till he came unto the place,
  Where late his treasure he entombed had,
  Where when he found it not (for *Trompart* bace
  Had it purloyned for his maister bad:)
  With extreme fury he became quite mad,
  And ran away, ran with himselfe away:
  That who so straungely had him seene bestad,
  With upstart haire, and staring eyes dismay,
From Limbo lake him late escaped sure would say.

55

High over hilles and over dales he fled,
  As if the wind him on his winges had borne,
  Ne banck nor bush could stay him, when he sped
  His nimble feet, as treading still on thorne:
  Griefe, and despight, and gealosie, and scorne
  Did all the way him follow hard behind,
  And he himselfe himselfe loath'd so forlorne,
  So shamefully forlorne of womankind;
That as a Snake, still lurked in his wounded mind.

56

Still fled he forward, looking backward still,
  Ne stayd his flight, nor fearefull agony,
  Till that he came unto a rockie hill,
  Over the sea, suspended dreadfully,
  That living creature it would terrify,
  To looke adowne, or upward to the hight:
  From thence he threw himselfe despiteously,
  All desperate of his fore-damned spright,
That seemd no help for him was left in living sight.

57

But through long anguish, and selfe-murdring thought
  He was so wasted and forpined quight,
  That all his substance was consum'd to nought,
  And nothing left, but like an aery Spright,
  That on the rockes he fell so flit and light,
  That he thereby receiv'd no hurt at all,
  But chaunced on a craggy cliff to light;
  Whence he with crooked clawes so long did crall,
That at the last he found a cave with entrance small.

58

Into the same he creepes, and thenceforth there
  Resolv'd to build his balefull mansion,
  In drery darkenesse, and continuall feare
  Of that rockes fall, which ever and anon
  Threates with huge ruine him to fall upon,
  That he dare never sleepe, but that one eye
  Still ope he keepes for that occasion;
  Ne ever rests he in tranquillity,
The roring billowes beat his bowre so boystrously.

59

Ne ever is he wont on ought to feed,
  But toades and frogs, his pasture poysonous,
  Which in his cold complexion do breed
  A filthy bloud, or humour rancorous,
  Matter of doubt and dread suspitious,
  That doth with curelesse care consume the hart,
  Corrupts the stomacke with gall vitious,
  Croscuts the liver with internall smart,
And doth transfixe the soule with deathes eternall dart.

60

Yet can he never dye, but dying lives,
  And doth himselfe with sorrow new sustaine,
  That death and life attonce unto him gives.
  And painefull pleasures turnes to pleasing paine.
  There dwels he ever, miserable swaine,
  Hatefull both to him selfe, and every wight;
  Where he through privy griefe, and horrour vaine,
  Is woxen so deform'd, that he has quight
Forgot he was a man, and *Gealosie* is hight.

Canto XI

1

O hatefull hellish Snake, what furie furst
   Brought thee from balefull house of *Proserpine*,
   Where in her bosome she thee long had nurst,
   And fostred up with bitter milke of tine,
   Fowle Gealosie, that turnest love divine
   To joylesse dread, and mak'st the loving hart
   With hatefull thoughts to languish and to pine,
   And feed it selfe with selfe-consuming smart?
Of all the passions in the mind thou vilest art.

2

O let him far be banished away,
   And in his stead let Love for ever dwell,
   Sweet Love, that doth his golden wings embay
   In blessed Nectar, and pure Pleasures well,
   Untroubled of vile feare, or bitter fell.
   And ye faire Ladies, that your kingdomes make
   In th' harts of men, them governe wisely well,
   And of faire *Britomart* ensample take,
That was as trew in love, as Turtle to her make.

3

Who with Sir *Satyrane*, as earst ye red,
   Forth ryding from *Malbeccoes* hostlesse hous,
   Far off aspyde a young man, the which fled
   From an huge Geaunt, that with hideous
   And hatefull outrage long him chaced thus;
   It was that *Ollyphant*, the brother deare
   Of that *Argante* vile and vitious,
   From whom the *Squire of Dames* were reft whylere;
This all as bad as she, and worse, if worse ought were.

4

For as the sister did in feminine
   And filthy lust exceede all woman kind,
   So he surpassed his sex masculine,
   In beastly use that I did ever finde;
   Whom when as *Britomart* beheld behind

The fearefull boy so greedily pursew,
She was emmoved in her noble mind,
T' employ her puissaunce to his reskew,
And pricked fiercely forward, where she did him vew.

5

Ne was Sir *Satyrane* her far behinde,
But with like fiercenesse did ensew the chace:
Whom when the Gyaunt saw, he soone resinde
His former suit, and from them fled apace;
They after both, and boldly bad him bace,
And each did strive the other to out-goe,
But he them both outran a wondrous space,
For he was long, and swift as any Roe,
And now made better speed, t' escape his feared foe.

6

It was not *Satyrane*, whom he did feare,
But *Britomart* the flowre of chastity;
For he the powre of chast hands might not beare,
But always did their dread encounter fly:
And now so fast his feet he did apply,
That he has gotten to a forrest neare,
Where he is shrowded in security.
The wood they enter, and search every where,
They searched diversely, so both divided were.

7

Faire *Britomart* so long him followed,
That she at last came to a fountaine sheare,
By which there lay a knight all wallowed
Upon the grassy ground, and by him neare
His haberjeon, his helmet, and his speare;
A little off, his shield was rudely throwne,
On which the winged boy in colours cleare
Depeincted was, full easie to be knowne,
And he thereby, where ever it in field was showne.

8

His face upon the ground did groveling ly,
As if he had beene slombring in the shade,
That the brave Mayd would not for courtesy,
Out of his quiet slomber him abrade,
Nor seeme too suddeinly him to invade:
Still as she stood, she heard with grievous throb

Him grone, as if his hart were preeces made,
  And with most painefull pangs to sigh and sob,
That pitty did the Virgins hart of patience rob.

9

At last forth breaking into bitter plaintes
  He said; 'O soveraigne Lord that sit'st on hye,
  And raignst in blis emongst thy blessed Saintes,
  How suffrest thou such shamefull cruelty,
  So long unwreaked of thine enimy?
  Or hast thou, Lord, of good mens cause no heed?
  Or doth thy justice sleepe, and silent ly?
  What booteth then the good and righteous deed,
If goodnesse find no grace, nor righteousnesse no meed?

10

'If good fine grace, and righteousnesse reward,
  Why then is *Amoret* in caytive band,
  Sith that more bounteous creature never far'd
  On foot, upon the face of living land?
  Or if that heavenly justice may withstand
  The wrongfull outrage of unrighteous men,
  Why then is *Busirane* with wicked hand
  Suffred, these seven monethes day in secret den
My Lady and my love so cruelly to pen?

11

'My Lady and my love is cruelly pend
  In dolefull darkenesse from the vew of day,
  Whilest deadly torments do her chast brest rend,
  And the sharpe steele doth rive her hart in tway,
  All for she *Scudamore* will not denay.
  Yet thou vile man, vile *Scudamore* art sound,
  Ne canst her ayde, ne canst her foe dismay;
  Unworthy wretch to tread upon the ground,
For whom so faire a Lady feeles so sore a wound.'

12

There an huge heape of singultes did oppresse
  His strugling soule, and swelling throbs empeach
  His foltring toung with pangs of drerinesse,
  Choking the remnant of his plaintife speach,
  As if his dayes were come to their last reach.
  Which when she heard, and saw the ghastly fit,
  Threatning into his life to make a breach,

Both with great ruth and terrour she was smit,
Fearing least from her cage the wearie soule would flit.

13

Tho stooping downe she him amoved light;
  Who therewith somewhat starting, up gan looke,
  And seeing him behind a stranger knight,
  Whereas no living creature he mistooke,
  With great indignaunce he that sight forsooke,
  And downe againe himselfe disdainefully
  Abjecting th' earth with his faire forhead strooke:
  Which the bold Virgin seeing, gan apply
Fit medcine to his griefe, and spake thus courtesly.

14

'Ah gentle knight, whose deepe conceived griefe
  Well seemes t' exceede the powre of patience,
  Yet if that heavenly grace some good reliefe
  You send, submit you to high providence,
  And ever in your noble hart prepense,
  That all the sorrow in the world is lesse,
  Then vertues might, and values confidence,
  For who nill bide the burden of distresse,
Must not here thinke to live; for life is wretchednesse.

15

'Therefore, faire Sir, do comfort to you take,
  And freely read, what wicked felon so
  Hath outrag'd you, and thrald your gentle make.
  Perhaps this hand may helpe to ease your woe,
  And wreake your sorrow on your cruell foe,
  At least it faire endevour will apply.'
  Those feeling words so neare the quicke did goe,
  That up his head he reared easily,
And, leaning on his elbow, these few words let fly.

16

'What boots it plaine, that cannot be redrest,
  And sow vaine sorrow in a fruitlesse eare,
  Sith powre of hand, nor skill of learned brest,
  Ne worldly price cannot redeeme my deare,
  Out of her thraldome and continuall feare?
  For he the tyraunt, which her hath in ward
  By strong enchauntments and blacke Magicke leare,
  Hath in a dungeon deepe her close embard,
And many dreadfull feends hath pointed to her gard.

17

'There he tormenteth her most terribly,
    And day and night afflicts with mortall paine,
    Because to yield him love she doth deny,
    Once to me yold, not to be yold againe:
    But yet by torture he would her constraine
    Love to conceive in her disdainfull brest;
    Till so she do, she must in doole remaine,
    Ne may by living meanes be thence relest;
What boots it then to plaine, that cannot be redrest?'

18

With this sad hersall of his heavy stresse,
    The warlike Damzell was empassiond sore,
    And said; 'Sir knight, your cause is nothing lesse,
    Then is your sorrow, certes if not more;
    For nothing so much pitty doth implore,
    As gentle Ladies helplesse misery.
    But yet, if please ye listen to my lore,
    I will with proofe of last extremity,
Deliver her fro thence, or with her for you dy.

19

'Ah gentlest knight alive,' (said *Scudamore*)
    'What huge heroicke magnanimity
    Dwels in thy bounteous brest? what couldst thou more,
    If she were thine, and thou as now am I?
    O spare thy happy dayes, and them apply
    To better boot, but let me die that ought;
    More is more losse; one is enough to dy.'
    'Life is not lost,' (said she) 'for which is bought
Endlesse renowm, that more then death is to be sought.'

20

Thus she at length perswaded him to rise,
    And with her wend, to see what new successe
    Mote him befall upon new enterprise;
    His armes, which he had vowed to disprofesse,
    She gathered up and did about him dresse,
    And his forwandred steed unto him got:
    So forth they both yfere make their progresse,
    And march not past the mountenaunce of a shot,
Till they arriv'd, whereas their purpose they did plot.

21

There they dismounting, drew their weapons bold
  And stoutly came unto the Castle gate;
  Whereas no gate they found, them to withhold,
  Nor ward to wait at morne and evening late,
  But in the Porch, that did them sore amate,
  A flaming fire, ymixt with smouldry smoke,
  And stinking Sulphure, that with griesly hate
  And dreadfull horrour did all entraunce choke,
Enforced them their forward footing to revoke.

22

Greatly thereat was *Britomart* dismayd,
  Ne in that stownd wist, how her selfe to beare;
  For daunger vaine it were to have assayd
  That cruell element, which all things feare,
  Ne none can suffer to approchen neare:
  And turning backe to *Scudamour*, thus sayd;
  'What monstrous enmity provoke we heare,
  Foolhardy as th' Earthes children, the which made
Battell against the Gods? so we a God invade.

23

'Daunger without discretion to attempt,
  Inglorious and beastlike is: therefore Sir knight
  Aread what course of you is safest dempt,
  And how he with our foe may come to fight.'
  'This is' (quoth he) 'the dolorous despight,
  Which earst to you I playnd: for neither may
  This fire be quencht by any wit or might,
  Ne yet by any meanes remov'd away,
So mighty be th' enchauntments, which the same do stay.

24

'What is there else, but cease these fruitlesse paines,
  And leave me to my former languishing?
  Faire *Amoret* must dwell in wicked chaines,
  And *Scudamore* here dye with sorrowing.'
  'Perdy not so,' (said she) 'for shameful thing
  It were t' abandon noble chevisaunce,
  For shew of perill, without venturing:
  Rather let try extremities of chaunce,
Then enterprised prayse for dread to disavaunce.'

25

Therewith resolv'd to prove her utmost might,
    Her ample shield she threw before her face,
    And her swords point directing forward right,
    Assayld the flame, the which eftsoones gave place,
    And did it selfe divide with equall space,
    That through she passed; as a thunder bolt
    Perceth the yielding ayre, and doth displace
    The soring clouds into sad showres ymolt;
So to her yold the flames, and did their force revolt.

26

Whom whenas Scudamour saw past the fire
    Safe and untoucht, he likewise gan assay,
    With greedy will and envious desire,
    And bad the stubborne flames to yield him way:
    But cruell *Mulciber* would not obay
    His threatfull pride, but did the more augment
    His mighty rage, and with imperious sway
    Him forst (maulgre) his fiercenesse to relent,
And backe retire, all scorcht and pitifully brent.

27

With huge impatience he inly swelt,
    More for great sorrow, that he could not pas,
    Then for the burning torment, which he felt,
    That with fell woodnesse he effierced was,
    And wilfully him throwing on the gras,
    Did beat and bounse his head and brest ful sore;
    The whiles the Championesse now entred has
    The utmost rowme, and past the foremost dore,
The utmost rowme, abounding with all precious store.

28

For round about, the wals yclothed were
    With goodly arras of great majesty,
    Woven with gold and silke so close and nere,
    That the rich metall lurked privily,
    As faining to be hid from envious eye;
    Yet here, and there, and every where unwares
    It shewd it selfe, and shone unwillingly;
    Like a discolourd Snake, whose hidden snares
Through the greene gras his long bright burnisht back declares.

29

And in those Tapets weren fashioned
    Many faire pourtraicts, and many a faire feate,
    And all of love, and all of lusty-hed,
    As seemed by their semblaunt did entreat;
    And eke all *Cupids* warres they did repeate,
    And cruell battels, which he whilome fought
    Gainst all the Gods, to make his empire great;
    Besides the huge massacres, which he wrought
On mighty kings and kesars, into thraldome brought.

30

Therein was writ, how often thundring *Jove*
    Had felt the point of his hart-percing dart,
    And leaving heavens kingdome, here did rove
    In straunge disguize, to slake his scalding smart;
    Now like a Ram, faire *Helle* to pervart,
    Now like a Bull, *Europa* to withdraw:
    Ah, how the fearefull Ladies tender hart
    Did lively seeme to tremble, when she saw
The huge seas under her t' obay her servaunts law.

31

Soone after that into a golden showre
    Him selfe he chaung'd faire *Danaë* to vew,
    And through the roofe of her strong brasen towre
    Did raine into her lap an hony dew,
    The whiles her foolish garde, that little knew
    Of such deceipt, kept th' yron dore fast bard,
    And watcht, that none should enter nor issew;
    Vaine was the watch, and bootlesse all the ward,
Whenas the God to golden hew him selfe transfard.

32

Then was he turnd into a snowy Swan,
    To win faire *Leda* to his lovely trade:
    O wondrous skill, and sweet wit of the man,
    That her in daffadillies sleeping made,
    From scorching heat her daintie limbes to shade:
    Whiles the proud Bird ruffing his fethers wyde,
    And brushing his faire brest, did her invade;
    She slept, yet twixt her eyelids closely spyde,
How towards her he rusht, and smiled at his pryde.

33

Then shewd it, how the *Thebane Semelee*
  Deceiv'd of gealous *Juno*, did require
  To see him in his soveraigne majestee,
  Armd with his thunderbolts and lightning fire,
  Whence dearely she with death bought her desire.
  But faire *Alcmena* better match did make,
  Joying his love in likenesse more entire;
  Three nights in one, they say, that for her sake
Her then did put, her pleasures lenger to partake.

34

Twise was he seene in soaring Eagles shape,
  And with wide wings to beat the buxome ayre,
  Once, when he with *Asterie* did scape,
  Againe, when as the *Trojane* boy so faire
  He snatcht from *Ida* hill, and with him bare:
  Wondrous delight it was, there to behould,
  How the rude Shepheards after him did stare,
  Trembling through feare, least down he fallen should,
And often to him calling, to take surer hould.

35

In Satyres shape *Antiopa* he snatcht;
  And like a fire, when he *Aegin'* assayd:
  A shepheard, when *Mnemosyne* he catcht:
  And like a Serpent to the *Thracian* mayd.
  Whiles thus on earth great *Jove* these pageaunts playd,
  The winged boy did thrust into his throne,
  And scoffing thus unto his mother sayd,
  'Lo now the heavens obey to me alone,
And take me for their *Jove*, whiles *Jove* to earth is gone.'

36

And thou, faire *Phœbus*, in thy colours bright
  Wast there enwoven, and the sad distresse
  In which that boy thee plonged, for despight,
  That thou bewray'dst his mothers wantonnesse,
  When she with *Mars* was meynt in joyfulnesse:
  For thy he thrild thee with a leaden dart,
  To love faire *Daphne*, which thee loved lesse:
  Lesse she thee lov'd, then was thy just desart,
Yet was thy love her death, and death was thy smart.

37

So lovedst thou the lusty *Hyacinct*,
  So lovedst thou the faire *Coronis* deare:
  Yet both are of thy haplesse hand extinct,
  Yet both in flowres do live, and love thee beare,
  The one a Paunce, the other a sweet breare:
  For griefe whereof, ye mote have lively seene
  The God himselfe rending his golden heare,
  And breaking quite his gyrlond ever greene,
With other signes of sorrow and impatient teene.

38

Both for those two, and for his owne deare sonne,
  The sonne of *Climene* he did repent,
  Who bold to guide the charet of the Sunne,
  Himselfe in thousand peeces fondly rent,
  And all the world with flashing fier brent;
  So like, that all the walles did seeme to flame.
  Yet cruell *Cupid*, not herewith content,
  Forst him eftsoones to follow other game,
And love a Shepheards daughter for his dearest Dame.

39

He loved *Isse* for his dearest Dame,
  And for her sake her cattell fed a while,
  And for her sake a cowheard vile became,
  The servant of *Admetus* cowheard vile,
  Whiles that from heaven he suffered exile.
  Long were to tell each other lovely fit,
  Now like a Lyon, hunting after spoile,
  Now like a stag, now like a faulcon flit:
All which in that faire arras was most lively writ.

40

Next unto him was *Neptune* pictured,
  In his divine resemblance wondrous lyke:
  His face was rugged, and his hoarie hed
  Dropped with brackish deaw; his three-forkt Pyke
  He stearnly shooke, and therewith fierce did stryke
  The raging billowes, that on every syde
  They trembling stood, and made a long broad dyke,
  That his swift charet might have passage wyde,
Which foure great *Hippodames* did draw in temewise tyde.

41

His sea-horses did seeme to snort amayne,
    And from their nosethrilles blow the brynie streame,
    That made the sparckling waves to smoke agayne,
    And flame with gold, but the white fomy creame,
    Did shine with silver, and shoot forth his beame.
    The God himselfe did pensive seeme and sad,
    And hong adowne his head, as he did dreame:
    For privy love his brest empierced had,
Ne ought but deare *Bisaltis* ay could make him glad.

42

He loved eke *Iphimedia* deare,
    And *Aeolus* faire *daughter Arne* hight,
    For whom he turnd him selfe into a Steare,
    And fedd on fodder, to beguile her sight.
    Also to win *Deucalions* daughter bright,
    He turnd him selfe into a Dolphin fayre;
    And like a winged horse he tooke his flight,
    To snaky-locke *Medusa* to repayre,
On whom he got faire *Pegasus*, that flitteth in the ayre.

43

Next *Saturne* was, (but who would ever weene,
    That sullein *Saturne* ever weend to love?
    Yet love is sullein, and *Saturnlike* seene,
    As he did for *Erigone* it prove,)
    That to a *Centaure* did him selfe transmove.
    So proov'd it eke that gratious God of wine,
    When for to compasse *Philliras* hard love,
    He turnd himselfe into a fruitfull vine,
And into her faire bosome made his grapes decline.

44

Long were to tell the amorous assayes,
    And gentle pangues, with which he maked meeke
    The mighty *Mars*, to learne his wanton playes;
    How oft for *Venus*, and how often eek
    For many other Nymphes he sore did shreek,
    With womanish teares, and with unwarlike smarts,
    Privily moystening his horrid cheek.
    There was he painted full of burning darts,
Any many wide woundes launched through his inner parts.

45

Ne did he spare (so cruell was the Elfe)
  His owne deare mother, (ah why should he so?)
  Ne did he spare sometime to pricke himselfe,
  That he might tast the sweet consuming woe,
  Which he had wrought to many others moe.
  But to declare the mournfull Tragedyes,
  And spoiles, wherewith he all the ground did strow,
  More eath to number, with how many eyes
High heaven beholds sad lovers nightly theeveryes.

46

Kings Queenes, Lords Ladies, Knights and Damsels gent
  Were heap'd together with the vulgar sort,
  And mingled with the raskall rablement,
  Without respect of person or of port,
  To shew Dan *Cupids* powre and great effort:
  And round about a border was entrayld,
  Of broken bowes and arrowes shivered short,
  And a long bloudy river through them rayld,
So lively and so like, that living sence it fayld.

47

And at the upper end of that faire rowme,
  There was an Altar built of pretious stone,
  Of passing valew, and of great renowme,
  On which there stood an Image all alone,
  Of massy gold, which with his owne light shone;
  And wings it had with sundry colours dight,
  More sundry colours, then the proud *Pavone*
  Beares in his boasted fan, or *Iris* bright,
When her discolourd bow she spreds through heavens bright.

48

Blindfold he was, and in his cruell fist
  A mortall bow and arrowes keene did hold,
  With which he shot at random, when him list,
  Some headed with sad leand, some with pure gold;
  (Ah man beware, how thou those darts behold)
  A wounded Dragon under him did ly,
  Whose hideous tayle his lefte foot did enfold,
  And with a shaft was shot through either eye,
That no man forth might draw, ne no man remedye.

49

And underneath his feet was written thus,
  Unto the Victor of the Gods this bee:
  And all the people in that ample hous
  Did to that image bowe their humble knee,
  And oft committed fowle Idolatree.
  That wondrous sight faire *Britomart* amazed,
  Ne seeing could her wonder satisfie,
  But ever more and more upon it gazed,
The whiles the passing brightnes her fraile sences dazed.

50

Tho as she backward cast her busie eye,
  To search each secret of that goodly sted,
  Over the dore thus written she did spye
  Be bold: she oft and oft it over-red,
  Yet could not find what sence it figured:
  But what so were therein or writ or ment,
  She was no whit thereby discouraged
  From prosecuting of her first intent,
But forward with bold steps into the next roome went.

51

Much fairer then the former, was that roome,
  And richlier by many partes arayd:
  For not with arras made in painefull loome,
  But with pure gold it all was overlayd,
  Wrought with wilde Antickes, which their follies playd,
  In the rich metall, as they living were:
  A thousand monstrous formes therein were made,
  Such as false love doth oft upon him weare,
For love in thousand monstrous formes doth oft appeare.

52

And all about, glistring walles were hong
  With warlike spoiles, and with victorious prayes,
  Of mighty Conquerours and Captaines strong,
  Which were whilome captived in their dayes
  To cruell love, and wrought their owne decayes:
  Their swerds and speres were broke, and hauberques rent:
  And their proud girlonds of tryumphant bayes
  Troden in dust with fury insolent,
To shew the victors might and mercilesse intent.

53

The warlike Mayde beholding earnestly
  The goodly ordinance of this rich place,
  Did greatly wonder, ne could satisfie
  Her greedy eyes with gazing a long space,
  But more she mervaild that no footings trace,
  Nor wight appear'd, but wastefull emptinesse,
  And solemne silence over all that place:
  Straunge thing it seem'd, that none was to possesse
So rich purveyance, ne them keepe with carefulnesse.

54

And as she lookt about, she did behold,
  How over that same dore was likewise writ,
  Be bold, be bold, and every where *Be bold,*
  That much she muz'd, yet could not construe it
  By any ridling skill, or commune wit.
  At last she spyde at that roomes upper end,
  Another yron dore, on which was writ,
  Be not too bold; whereto though she did bend
Her earnest mind, yet wist not what it might intend.

55

Thus she there waited untill eventyde,
  Yet living creature none she saw appeare:
  And now sad shadowes gan the world to hyde,
  From mortall vew, and wrap in darkenesse dreare;
  Yet nould she d'off her weary armes, for feare
  Of secret daunger, ne let sleepe oppresse
  Her heavy eyes with natures burdein deare,
  But drew her selfe aside in sickernesse,
And her welpointed wepons did about her dresse.

Canto XII

1

Tho whenas chearelesse Night ycovered had
  Fayre heaven with an universall cloud,
  That every wight dismayd with dark
  In silence and in sleepe themselves did shroud,
  She heard a shrilling Trompet sound aloud,
  Signe of nigh battell, or got victory;
  Nought therewith daunted was her courage proud,
  But rather stird to cruell enmity,
Expecting ever, when some foe she might descry.

2

With that, an hideous storme of winde arose,
  With dreadfull thunder and lightning atwixt,
  And an earth-quake, as if it streight would lose
  The worlds foundations from his centre fixt;
  A direfull stench of smoke and sulphure mixt
  Ensewd, whose noyance fild the fearefull sted
  From the fourth houre of night untill the sixt;
  Yet the bold *Britonesse* was nought ydred,
Though much emmov'd, but stedfast still persevered.

3

All suddenly a stormy whirlwind blew
  Throughout the house, that clapped every dore,
  With which that yron wicket open flew,
  As it with mighty levers had bene tore:
  And forth issewd, as on the ready flore
  Of some Theatre, a grave personage,
  That in his hand a branch of laurell bore,
  With comely haveour and count'nance sage,
Yclad in costly garments, fit for tragicke Stage.

4

Proceeding to the midst, he still did stand,
  As if in mind he somewhat had to say,
  And to the vulgar beckning with his hand,
  In signe of silence, as to heare a play,
  By lively actions he gan bewray

Some argument of matter passioned;
Which doen, he backe retyred soft away,
And passing by, his name discovered,
Ease, on his robe in golden letters cyphered.

5

The noble Mayd, still standing, all this vewd,
And merveild at his straunge intendiment;
With that a joyous fellowship issewd
Of Minstrals, making goodly meriment,
With wanton Bardes, and Rymers impudent,
All which together sung full chearefully
A lay of loves delight, with sweet concent:
After whom marcht a jolly company,
In manner of a maske, enranged orderly.

6

The whiles a most delitious harmony,
In full straunge notes was sweetly heard to sound,
That the rare sweetnesse of the melody
The feeble senses wholly did confound,
And the fraile soule in deepe delight nigh dround:
And when it ceast, shrill trompets lowd did bray,
That their report did far away rebound,
And when they ceast, it gan againe to play,
The whiles the maskers marched forth in trim aray.

7

The first was *Fancy*, like a lovely boy,
Of rare aspect, and beautie without peare;
Matchable either to that ympe of *Troy*,
Whom *Jove* did love, and chose his cup to beare,
Or that same daintie lad, which was so deare
To great *Alcides*, that when as he dyde,
He wailed womanlike with many a teare,
And every wood, and every valley wyde
He filled with *Hylas* name; the Nymphes eke *Hylas* cryde.

8

His garment neither was of silke nor say,
But painted plumes in goodly order dight,
Like as the sunburnt *Indians* do aray
Their tawney bodies, in their proudest plight:
As those same plumes, so seemd he vaine and light,
That by his gate might easily appeare;

For still he far'd as dauncing in delight,
  And in his hand a windy fan did beare,
That in the idle aire he mov'd still here and there.

9

And him beside marcht amorous *Desyre*,
  Who seemd of riper yeares, then th' other Swaine,
  Yet was that other swayne this elders syre,
  And gave him being, commune to them twaine:
  His garment was disguised very vaine,
  And his embrodered Bonet at awry;
  Twixt both his hands few sparkes he close did straine,
  Which still he blew, and kindled busily,
That soone they life conceiv'd, and forth in flames did fly.

10

Next after him went *Doubt*, who was yclad
  In a discolour'd cote of straunge disguyse,
  That at his backe a brode Capuccio had,
  And sleeves dependant *Albanese*-wyse:
  He lookt askew with his mistrustfull eyes,
  And nicely trode, as thornes lay in his way,
  Or that the flore to shrinke he did avyse,
  And on a broken reed he still did stay
His feeble steps, which shrunke, when hard theron he lay.

11

With him went *Daunger*, cloth'd in ragged weed,
  Made of Beares skin, that him more dreadfull made,
  Yet his owne face was dreadfull, ne did need
  Straunge horrour, to deforme his griesly shade;
  A net in th' one hand, and a rustie blade
  In th' other was, this Mischiefe, that Mishap;
  With th' one his foes he threatned to invade,
  With th' other he his friends ment to enwrap:
For whom he could not kill, he practizd to entrap.

12

Next him was *Feare*, all arm'd from top to toe,
  Yet thought himselfe not safe enough thereby,
  But feard each shadow moving to and fro,
  And his owne armes when glittering he did spy,
  Or clashing heard, he fast away did fly,
  As ashes pale of hew, and wingy heeld;
  And evermore on daunger fixt his eye,

Gainst whom he alwaies bent a brasen shield,
Which his right hand unarmed fearefully did wield.

13

With him went *Hope* in rancke, a handsome Mayd,
  Of chearefull looke and lovely to behold;
  In silken samite she was light arayd,
  And her faire lockes were woven up in gold;
  She alway smyld, and in her hand did hold
  An holy water Sprinckle, dipt in deowe,
  With which she sprinckled favours manifold,
  On whom she list, and did great liking sheowe,
Great liking unto many, but true love to feowe.

14

And after them *Dissemblance*, and *Suspect*
  Marcht in one rancke, yet an unequall paire:
  For she was gentle and of milde aspect,
  Courteous to all, and seeming debonaire,
  Goodly adorned, and exceeding faire:
  Yet was that all but painted, and purloynd,
  And her bright browes were deckt with borrowed haire:
  Her deeds were forged, and her words false coynd,
And alwaies in her hand two clewes of silke she twynd.

15

But he was foule, ill favoured, and grim,
  Under his eyebrowes looking still askaunce;
  And ever as *Dissemblance* laught on him,
  He lowrd on her with daungerous eyeglaunce;
  Shewing his nature in his countenance;
  His rolling eyes did never rest in place,
  But walkte each where, for feare of hid mischaunce,
  Holding a lattice still before his face,
Through which he stil did peepe, as forward he did pace.

16

Next him went *Griefe*, and *Fury* matcht yfere;
  Griefe all in sable sorrowfully clad,
  Downe hanging his dull head with heavy chere,
  Yet inly being more, then seeming sad:
  A paire of Pincers in his hand he had,
  With which he pinched people to the hart,
  That from thenceforth a wretched life they lad,
  In wilfull languor and consuming smart,
Dying each day with inward wounds of dolours dart.

17

But *Fury* was full ill appareiled
  In rags, that naked nigh she did appeare,
  With ghastly lookes and dreadfull drerihed;
  And from her backe her garments she did teare,
  And from her head oft rent her snarled heare:
  In her right hand a firebrand shee did tosse
  About her head, still roming here and there;
  As a dismayed Deare in chace embost,
Forgetfull of his safety, hath his right way lost.

18

After them went *Displeasure* and *Pleasance*,
  He looking lompish and full sullein sad,
  And hanging downe his heavy countenance;
  She chearfull fresh and full of joyance glad,
  As if no sorrow she ne felt ne drad;
  That evill matched paire they seemd to bee:
  An angry Waspe th' one in a viall had
  Th' other in hers an hony-lady Bee;
Thus marched these six couples forth in faire degree.

19

After all these there marcht a most faire Dame,
  Led of two grysie villeins, th' one *Despight*,
  The other cleped *Cruelty* by name:
  She dolefull Lady, like a dreary Spright,
  Cald by strong charmes out of eternall night,
  Had deathes owne image figurd in her face,
  Full of sad signes, fearfull to living sight;
  Yet in that horror shewd a seemely grace,
And with her feeble feet did move a comely pace.

20

Her brest all naked, as net ivory,
  Without adorne of gold or silver bright,
  Wherewith the Craftesman wonts it beautify,
  Of her dew honour was despoyled quight,
  And a wide wound therein (O ruefull sight)
  Entrenched deepe with knife accursed keene,
  Yet freshly bleeding forth her fainting spright,
  (The worke of cruell hand) was to be seene,
That dyde in sanguine red her skin all snowy cleene.

21

At that wide orifice her trembling hart
   Was drawne forth, and in silver basin layd,
   Quite through transfixed with a deadly dart,
   And in her bloud yet steeming fresh embayd:
   And those two villeins, which her steps upstayd,
   When her weake feete could scarcely her sustaine,
   And fading vitall powers gan to fade,
   Her forward still with torture did constraine,
And evermore encreased her consuming paine.

22

Next after her the winged God himselfe
   Came riding on a Lion ravenous,
   Taught to obay the menage of that Elfe,
   That man and beast with powre imperious
   Subdeweth to his kingdome tyrannous:
   His blindfold eyes he bad a while unbind,
   That his proud spoyle of that same dolorous
   Faire Dame he might behold in perfect kind;
Which seene, he much rejoyced in his cruell mind.

23

Of which fullproud, himselfe up rearing hye,
   He looked round about with sterne disdaine;
   And did survay his goodly company:
   And marshalling the evill ordered traine,
   With that the darts which his right hand did straine.
   Full dreadfully he shooke that all did quake,
   And clapt on hie his coulourd winges twaine,
   That all his many it affraide did make:
Tho blinding him againe, his way he forth did take.

24

Behinde him was *Reproch, Repentance, Shame*;
   Reproch the first, *Shame* next, *Repent* behind:
   Repentance feeble, sorrowful and lame:
   Reproch despightfull, carelesse, and unkind;
   Shame most ill favour, bestiall, and blind:
   Shame lowrd, *Repentance* sighd, *Reproch* did scould;
   Reproch sharpe stings, *Repentance* whips entwind,
   Shame burning brond-yrons in her hand did hold:
All three to each unlike, yet all made in one mould.

25

And after them a rude confused rout
  Of persons flockt, whose names is hard to read:
  Emongst them was sterne *Strife*, and *Anger* stout,
  Unquiet *Care*, and fond *Unthriftihead*,
  Lewd *Losse of Time*, and *Sorrow* seeming dead,
  Inconstant *Chaunge*, and false *Disloyaltie*,
  Consuming *Riotise*, and guilty *Dread*
  Of heavenly vengeance, faint *Infirmitie*,
Vile Povertie, and lastly *Death* with infamie.

26

There were full many moe like maladies,
  Whose names and natures I note readen well;
  So many moe, as there be phantasies
  In wavering wemens wit, that none can tell,
  Or paines in love, or punishments in hell;
  All which disguized marcht in masking wise,
  About the chamber with that Damozell,
  And then returned, having marched thrise,
Into the inner roome, from whence they first did rise.

27

So soone as they were in, the dore streight way
  Fast locked, driven with that stormy blast,
  Which first it opened; and bore all away.
  Then the brave Maid, which all this while was plast
  In secret shade, and saw both first and last,
  Issewed forth, and went unto the dore,
  To enter in, but found it locked fast:
  It vaine she thought with rigorous uprore
For to efforce, when charmes had closed it afore.

28

Where force might not availe, there sleights and art
  She cast to use, both fit for hard emprize;
  For thy from that same roome not to depart
  Till morrow next, she did her selfe avize,
  When that same Maske againe should forth arize.
  The morrow next appeard with joyous cheare,
  Calling men to their daily exercize,
  Then she, as morrow fresh, her selfe did reare
Out of her secret stand, that day for to out weare.

29

All that day she outwore in wandering,
  And gazing on that Chambers ornament,
  Till that againe the second evening
  Her covered with her sable vestiment,
  Wherewith the worlds faire beautie she hath blent:
  Then, when the second watch was almost past,
  That brasen dore flew open, and in went
  Bold *Britomart*, as she had late forecast,
Neither of idle shewes, nor of false charmes aghast.

30

So soone as she was entred, round about
  She cast her eies, to see what was become
  Of all those persons, which she saw without:
  But lo, they streight were vanisht all and some,
  Ne living wight she saw in all that roome,
  Save that same woefull Ladie, both whose hands
  Were bounden fast, that did her ill become,
  And her small wast girt round with yron bands,
Upon a brasen pillour, by the which she stands.

31

And her before the vile Enchaunter sate,
  Figuring straunge characters of his art,
  With living bloud he those characters wrate,
  Dreadfully dropping from her dying hart,
  Seeming transfixed with a cruell dart,
  And all perforce to make her him to love.
  Ah who can love the worker of her smart?
  A thousand charmes he formerly did prove;
Yet thousand charmes could not her stedfast hart remove.

32

Soone as that virgin knight he saw in place,
  His wicked bookes in hast he overthrew,
  Not caring his long labours to deface,
  And fiercely running to that Lady trew,
  A murdrous knife out of his pocket drew,
  The which he thought, for villeinous despight,
  In her tormented bodie to embrew:
  But the stout Damzell to him leaping light,
His cursed hand withheld, and maistered his might.

33

From her, to whom his fury first he ment,
  The wicked weapon rashly he did wrest,
  And turning to her selfe his fell intent,
  Unwares it strooke into her snowie chest,
  That litle drops empurpled her faire brest.
  Exceeding wroth therewith the virgin grew,
  Albe the wound were nothing deepe imprest,
  And fiercely forth her mortall blade she drew,
To give him the reward for such vile outrage dew.

34

So mightily she smote him, that to ground
  He fell halfe dead; next stroke him should have slaine,
  Had not the Lady, which by him stood bound,
  Dernely unto her called to abstaine,
  From doing him to dy. For else her paine
  Should be remedilesse, sith none but hee,
  Which wrought it, could the same recure againe.
  Therewith she stayd her hand, loth stayd to bee;
For life she him envyde, and long'd revenge to see.

35

And to him said, 'Thou wicked man, whose meed
  For so huge mischiefe and vile villany
  Is death, or if that ought do death exceed,
  Be sure, that nought may save thee from to dy,
  But if that thou this Dame doe presently
  Restore unto her health, and former state;
  This doe and live, else die undoubtedly.'
  He glad of life, that lookt for death but late,
Did yield himselfe right willing to prolong his date.

36

And rising up, gan streight to overlooke
  Those cursed leaves, his charmes back to reverse;
  Full dreadfull things out of that balefull booke
  He red, and measur'd many a sad verse,
  That horror gan the virgins hart to perse,
  And her faire locks up stared stiffe on end,
  Hearing him those same bloudy lines reherse;
  And all the while he red, she did extend
Her sword high over him, if ought he did offend.

37

Anon she gan perceive the house to quake,
  And all the dores to rattle round about;
  Yet all that did not her dismaied make,
  Nor slacke her threatfull hand for daungers dout,
  But still with stedfast eye and courage stout
  Abode, to weet what end would come of all.
  At last that mightie chaine, which round about
  Her tender waste was wound, adowne gan fall,
And that great brasen pillour broke in peeces small.

38

The cruell steele, which thrild her dying hart,
  Fell softly forth, as of his owne accord,
  And the wyde wound, which lately did dispart
  Her bleeding brest, and riven bowels gor'd,
  Was closed up, as it had not bene bor'd,
  And every part to safety full sound,
  As she were never hurt, was soone restor'd.
  Tho when she felt her selfe to be unbound,
And perfect hole, prostrate she fell unto the ground.

39

Before faire *Britomart*, she fell prostrate,
  Saying, 'Ah noble knight, what worthy meed
  Can wretched Lady, quit from wofull state,
  Yield you in liew of this your gracious deed?
  Your vertue selfe her owne reward shall breed,
  Even immortall praise and glory wyde,
  Which I your vassall, by your prowesse freed,
  Shall through the world make to be notifyde,
And goodly well advance, that goodly well was tryde.'

40

But *Britomart* uprearing her from ground,
  Said, 'Gentle Dame, reward enough I weene
  For many labours more, then I have found,
  This, that in safety now I have you seene,
  And meane of your deliverance have beene:
  Henceforth faire Lady comfort to you take,
  And put away remembrance of late teene;
  In stead thereof know, that your loving Make,
Hath no lesse griefe endured for your gentle sake.'

41

She much was cheard to heare him mentiond,
  Whom of all living wights she loved best.
  Then laid the whole Championesse strong hond
  Upon th' enchaunter, which had her distrest
  So sore, and with foule outrages opprest:
  With that great chaine, wherewith not long ygo
  He bound that pitteous Lady prisoner, now relest,
  Himselfe she bound, more worthy to be so,
And captive with her led to wretchednesse and wo.

42

Returning backe, those goodly roomes, which erst
  She saw so rich and royally arayd,
  Now vanisht utterly, and cleane subverst
  She found, and all their glory quite decayd,
  That sight of such a chaunge her much dismayd.
  Thence forth descending to that perlous Porch,
  Those dreadfull flames she also found delayd,
  And quenched quite, like a consumed torch,
That erst all entrers wont so cruelly to scorch.

43

At last she came unto the place, where late
  She left Sir *Scudamour* in great distresse,
  Twixt dolour and despight halfe desperate,
  Of his loves succour, of his owne redresse,
  And of the hardie *Britomarts* successe:
  There on the cold earth him now thrown she found,
  In wilfull anguish, and dead heavinesse,
  And to him cald; whose voices knowen sound
Soone as he heard, himself he reared light from ground.

44

There did he see, that most on earth him joyd,
  His dearest love, the comfort of his dayes,
  Whose too long absense him had sore annoyd,
  And wearied his life with dull delayes:
  Straight he upstarted from the loathed layes,
  And to her ran with hasty egernesse,
  Like as a Deare, that greedily embayes
  In the coole soile, after long thirstinesse,
Which he in chace endured hath, now nigh breathlesse.

45

Lightly he clipt her twixt his armes twaine,
  And streightly did embrace her body bright,
  Her body, late the prison of sad paine,
  Now the sweet lodge of love and deare delight:
  But she faire Lady overcommen quight
  Of huge affection, did in pleasure melt,
  And in sweete ravishment pourd out her spright:
  No word they spake, nor earthly thing they felt,
But like two senceles stocks in long embracement dwelt.

46

Had ye them seene, ye would have surely thought,
  That they had beene that faire *Hermaphrodite*,
  Which that rich *Romane* of white marble wrought,
  And in his costly Bath causd to bee site:
  So seemd those two, as growne together quite,
  That *Britomart* halfe envying their blesse,
  Was much empassiond in her gentle sprite,
  And to her selfe oft wisht like happinesse,
In vaine she wisht, that fate n'ould let her yet possesse.

47

Thus doe those lovers with sweet countervayle,
  Each other of loves bitter fruit despoile.
  But now my teme begins to faint and fayle,
  All woxen weary of their journall toyle:
  Therefore I will their sweatie yokes assoyle
  At this same furrowes end, till a new day:
  And ye faire Swayns, after your long turmoyle,
  Now cease your worke, and at your pleasure play;
Now cease your worke; to morrow is an holy day.

Letter of the Authors expounding his
whole intention in the course of this worke: which
for that it giveth great light to the Reader, for
the better understanding is hereunto
annexed.

To the Right noble, and Valorous, Sir Walter Raleigh knight, Lo.
Wardein of the Stanneryes, and her Majesties liefetenaunt of the
County of Cornewayll.

*SIR knowing how doubtfully all Allegories may be construed, and
this booke of mine, which I have entituled the Faery Queene, being
a continued Allegory, or darke conceit, I have thought good aswell
for avoyding of gealous opinions and misconstructions, as also for
your better light in reading thereof, (being so by you commanded,)
to discover unto you the general intention and meaning, which in the
whole course thereof I have fashioned, without expressing of any
particular purposes or by accidents therein occasioned. The generall
end therefore of all the booke is to fashion a gentleman or noble
person in vertuous and gentle discipline: Which for that I conceived
shoulde be most plausible and pleasing, being coloured with an
historicall fiction, the which the most part of men delight to read,
rather for variety of matter, then for profite of the ensample: I chose
the historye of king Arthure, as most fitte for the excellency of his
person, being made famous by many mens former workes, and also
furthest from the daunger of envy, and suspition of present time. In
which I have followed all the antique Poets historicall, first Homere,
who in the Persons of Agamemnon and Ulysses hath ensampled a
good governour and a vertuous man, the one in his Ilias, the other
in his Odysseis: then Virgil, whose like intention was to doe in the
person of Aeneas: after him Ariosto comprised them both in his
Orlando: and lately Tasso dissevered them againe, and formed both
parts in two persons, namely that part which they in Philosophy call
Ethice, or vertues of a private man, coloured in his Rinaldo: the other
named Politice in his Godfredo. By ensample of which excellente
Poets, I labour to pourtraict in Arthure, before he was king, the image
of a brave knight, perfected in the twelve private morall vertues, as
Aristotle hath devised, the which is the purpose of these first twelve
bookes: which if I finde to be well accepted, I may be perhaps
encoraged, to frame the other part of polliticke vertues in his person,
after that hee came to be king. To some I know this Methode will*

seeme displeasaunt, which had rather have good discipline delivered plainly in way of precepts, or sermoned at large, as they use, then thus clowdily enwrapped in Allegoricall devises. But such, me seeme, should be satisfide with the use of these dayes, seeing all things accounted by their showes, and nothing esteemed of, that is not delightfull and pleasing to commune sence. For this cause is Xenophon preferred before Plato, for that the one in the exquisite depth of his judgement, formed a Commune welth such as it should be, but the other in the person of Cyrus and the Persians fashioned a governement such as might best be: So much more profitable and gratious is doctrine by ensample, then by rule. So have I laboured to doe in the person of Arthure: whome I conceive after his long education by Timon, to whom he was by Merlin delivered to be brought up, so soone as he was borne of the Lady Igrayne, to have seene in a dream or vision the Faery Queene, with whose excellent beauty ravished, he awaking resolved to seeke her out, and so being by Merlin armed, and by Timon throughly instructed, he went to seeke her forth in Faerye land. In that Faery Queene I meane glory in my generall intention, but in my particular I conceive the most excellent and glorious person of our soveraine the Queene, and her kingdome in Faery land. And yet in some places els, I doe otherwise shadow her. For considering she beareth two persons, the one of a most royall Queene or Empresse, the other of a most vertuous and beautifull Lady, this latter part in some places I doe expresse in Belphœbe, fashioning her name according to your owne excellent conceipt of Cynthia, (Phœbe and Cynthia being both names of Diana.) So in the person of Prince Arthure I sette forth magnificence in particular, which vertue for that (according to Aristotle and the rest) it is the perfection of all the rest, and conteineth in it them all, therefore in the whole course I mention the deedes of Arthure applyable to that vertue, which I write of in that booke. But of the xii. other vertues, I make xii. other knights the patrones, for the more variety of the history: Of which these three bookes contayn three. The first of the knight of the Redcrosse, in whome I expresse Holynes: The seconde of Sir Guyon, in whome I sette forth Temperaunce: The third of Britomartis a Lady knight, in whome I picture Chastity. But because the beginning of the whole worke seemeth abrupte and as depending upon other antecedents, it needs that ye know the occasion of these three knights seuerall adventures. For the Methode of a Poet historical is not such, as of an Historiographer. For an Historiographer discourseth of affayres orderly as they were donne, accounting as well the times as the actions, but a Poet thrusteth into the middest, even where it most concerneth him, and there recoursing to the thinges fore-paste, and divining of thinges to come, maketh a pleasing Analysis of all. The beginning therefore of my history, if it were to be told by an Historiographer should be the twelfth booke which is the last, where I devise that the Faery Queene kept her Annuall feaste xii. dayes, uppon which xii. severall dayes, the occasions of the xii. severall adventures hapned, which being undertaken by xii. severall knights, are in these xii. books severally handled and discoursed. The first was this. In the beginning of the feast, there presented him selfe a tall clownishe younge man, who falling before the Queene of Faries desired a boone (as the manner then was) which during that feast she might not refuse: which was that hee might have the atchievement of any adventure, which during that feaste should happen, that being graunted, he rested him on the floore, unfitte through his rusticity for a better place. Soone after entred a faire Ladye in mourning weedes, riding on a white Asse, with a dwarfe behind her leading a warlike steed, that bore the Armes of a knight, and his speare in the dwarfes hand. Shee falling before the Queene of Faeries, complayned that her father and mother an ancient King and Queene, had bene by an huge dragon many years shut up in a brasen Castle, who thence suffred them not to yssew: and therefore besought the Faery Queene to assygne her some one of her knights to take on him that exployt. Presently that clownish person upstarting, desired that adventure: whereat the Queene much wondering, and the Lady much gaine-saying, yet he earnestly importuned his desire. In the end the Lady told him that unlesse that armour which she brought would serve him (that is the armour of a Christian man specified by Saint Paul vi. Ephes.) that he could not succeed in that enterprise, which being forthwith put upon him with dewe furnitures thereunto, he seemed the goodliest man in al that company, and was well liked of the Lady. And eftesoones taking on him knighthood, and mounting on that straunge Courser, he went forth with her on that adventure: where beginneth the first booke, vis.

A gentle knight was pricking on the playne. etc.

The second day there came in a Palmer bearing an Infant with bloody hands, whose Parents he complained to have bene slayn by an Enchaunteresse called Acrasia: and therefore craved of the Faery Queene, to appoint him some knight to performe that adventure, which being assigned to Sir Guyon, he presently went forth with that same Palmer: which is the beginning of the second booke and the whole subject thereof. The third day there came in a Groome who complained before the Faery Queene, that a vile Enchaunter, called

Busirane had in hand a most faire Lady called Amoretta, whom he kept in most grievous torment, because she would not yield him the pleasure of her body. Whereupon Sir Scudamour the lover of that Lady presently tooke on him that adventure. But being unable to performe it by reason of the hard Enchauntments, after long sorrow, in the end met with Britomartis, who succoured him, and reskewed his love.

But by occasion hereof, many other adventures are intermedled, but rather as Accidents, then intendments. As the love of Britomart, the overthrow of Marinell, the misery of Florimell, the vertuousnes of Belphœbe, the lasciviousnes of Hellenora, and many the like.

Thus much Sir, I have briefly overronne to direct your understanding to the wel-head of the History, that from thence gathering the whole intention of the conceit, ye may as in a handfull gripe al the discourse, which otherwise may happily seeme tedious and confused. So, humbly craving the continuance of your honorable favour towards me, and th' eternall establishment of your happines, I humble take leave.

23 January 1589
Yours most humbly affectionate
Ed. Spenser.

NOTES

Note: stanza numbers are printed in bold type; biblical quotations are from the Geneva Bible (1560); the following abbreviations have been used: Hamilton (*FQ*, ed. A. C. Hamilton, 1977); *Ger.Lib.* (Tasso, *Gerusalemme Liberata*); *OF* (Ariosto, *Orlando Furioso*); *Met.* (Ovid, *Metamorphoses*); Ripa (Cesare Ripa, *Iconologia*, Rome, 1603); Sp (Spenser); Tervarent (Guy de Tervarent, *Attributs et Symboles dans l'Art Profane 1450–1600*, Geneva, 1958).

BOOK I

PROEM 1 echoes opening of the *Aeneid* telling of Virgil's progress from pastoral poetry to martial epic. 2 invokes Clio, muse of history, conflated with Calliope, muse of epic poetry; *Tanaquill* = wife of Roman king Tarquinius Priscus, type of chastity, here representing Queen Elizabeth (cf. II. x. 76); *Briton Prince* = Arthur. 3 invokes Cupid and the traditional motif, fundamental to the poem, of the reconciliation of Mars and Venus (war and love). 4 celebration of Elizabeth as the *Mirrour* of virtue and truth, like Venus the deity of an *Isle*; and as solar monarch (*Phœbus*).

Canto 1

1 the armour of the Christian man (Ephes. 6, and Sp's *Letter of the Authors*). 2 *dead as living*: Rev. 1:18; *faithfull true*: Christ at Rev. 19:11; *solemne sad*: tendency to melancholy expressed later in encounter with Sansjoy (I. iv, v) and Despair (I. ix) and purged in I.x. See also 2 Cor. 7:10 (*worldlie sorrowe*). 3 *Dragon* = from St George legend, also Satan (Rev. 20:2). 4–5 Una (see st.45) = Oneness, Truth, Elizabeth as head of Anglican church; *Asse* = humility and kingship (Zech. 9:9, Judges 5:10, Matt. 21); *white ... blacke* = Elizabeth's personal colours. The princess saved by St George was depicted with a lamb; *lambe* = innocence and Christ (John 1:29). Una's parents = Adam and Eve (I. vii. 43) symbolising Elizabeth's claim to universal rule. 6 *Dwarfe* = reason, or prudence. 7–9 *pathes:* I. iv. 2 and Matt. 7:13. Book I's action begins, like Dante's *Divine Comedy*, with a dark wood as symbol of chaos, ignorance, and error (Lat. *errare* = to wander). The tree catalogue is a commonplace (Chaucer, *Parl. Fowls*, 176ff.) and Sp exploits traditional attributes. Note emphasis on

pride (st.7,8), hinting at tree of knowledge and myth of the Fall. 13–16 *Errour*, as a general principle enunciated here and also doctrinal error (the *books* of st.20), is based on the archetypal snake woman Echidna whose offspring were destructive to mankind (Hesiod, *Theogony*, 295ff.). The serpent of the Fall myth was often shown with a girl's face and torso. Errour is dark; Redcross is compared to a *Lyon* (17), emblem of the sun as well as wrath and justice (cf. I.iii.7, I.x.28). 21 for the *Nilus* myth see *Met.* 1.416ff; Egypt = evil because of the Jewish captivity. 22–3 the comparison of the baby serpents to *gnattes* anticipates the *flyes* simile of st.38: both are symbols of evil and of the deceiving power of the imagination (Beelzebub = Lord of the Flies). 29 Archimago (see st.43) = depicted as a hermit in accordance with contemp. depictions of *Hypocrisy* (Argt. stanza, and Ripa 200–1): cf. the true hermit Contemplation at I.x. 48ff. He is Roman Catholic (st. 35) and thus to the Elizabethan Protestant, evil. He is the *arch-magician* (Reformation propaganda frequently wrote of Papal and Catholic black magic) and the *arch*etypal *image*-creator, Satanically producing idols in the external world and false images within the imagination. 33 note Redcross's association with the *Sunne* and cf. I.v.2, I.xi.31ff. 36–7 *Morpheus* = god of Dreams; *Pluto* = king of hell, whose *Dame* is Proserpina; *Gorgon* = the primal and unmentionable grandfather of the gods, whom Faustus dares name (Marlowe, *Dr Faustus*, I.iii); *Cocytus* and *Styx* = two of the four infernal rivers: II.v.22n., II.vii.56n. 39 *Tethys*, wife of Oceanus = the sea; *Cynthia* = the moon. 40 alluding to the *gates* of *Odyssey* 19.562ff. and *Aeneid* 6.893ff. 43 *Hecate* = goddess of witches and identif. with *Proserpina* as queen of hell and night. 45–50 Redcross's imagination is tempted by a dream of a false Una collaborating with Venus (goddess of love and lust) accompanied by her companion 3 Graces; *Hymen* = god of marriage; *Flora* = goddess of flowers (and type of Elizabeth) but was also known anciently as a harlot. The false Una is there when he wakes (49), so far are his mental faculties under Archimago's power.

Canto II

1 *wagoner* = Boötes, the Ploughman constellation (cf. Redcross at I.x.66), guiding the *seven* stars of Ursa major; *stedfast starre* = Pole Star. 3–5 another vision that defines Redcross's sin: predominance of anger and lust, the two parts of the tripartite soul that should be controlled by *reason*, which in this case is inoperative. 6–7 *Hesperus* = Venus as morning star (cf. I.xi.33–4, xii.21); *Tithones* = husband of *Morning* (Aurora); *Titan* = the sun. 10 *Proteus* = sea-god capable of infinite metamorphoses and symbol of formlessness, deception, and magic. Cf. III.viii. 12–19 Redcross can overcome faithlessness (Sansfoy) for reasons given in st.18–19, but yields to something only slightly less terrible,

Fidessa (*Duessa* in disguise: st.44), whose parody of Faith manifests itself in the form of the Whore of Babylon (Rev. 17:4), identif. by Protestants as the Catholic Antichrist. Cf. Una at I.i.4–5. Fidessa's father rules, of course, from Rome and she can no longer see Christ (st. 22–4). Redcross will remain with her until canto vii. **25** *Sans joy:* I.iv.38ff.; *Sans loy:* I.iii.33ff. **28–30** *two* trees for doubleness (I.ii.9 and the meaning of Duessa's name) and to recall the trees of life and knowledge. Redcross escapes into a false paradise from the sun's heat which, since it symbolises Christ's judgment, should instead be endured (Malachi 4:4). Cf. I.vii.2ff. and, for the bleeding tree, *Aeneid* 3.22ff. **33** *Fradubio* = Brother Doubt; *Boreas* = north wind, assoc. with Satan. Note the parallel between Fradubio and Redcross. **37** *Frælissa* (Ital. *fralezza*) = Frailty (but *Elisa-Elissa*=Elizabeth), which the *roses* also denote. **40–41** cf. I.vii.47; *origane* (wild marjoram) and *thyme* supposedly cured skin ailments. **43** *well* = Divine grace (John 4:14, Rev. 22:1). Cf. I.xi.29–30,48.

Canto III

3 the wandering woman motif comes from Song of Solomon 3:1ff. and Rev. 12:1–6, the 'woman clothed with the sunne' (cf. st.4) who flees into the wilderness, interpreted in Reformation propaganda as the Protestant church. As Truth, Una can, unlike Redcross, escape into shade (bec. she is unrecognised). She lies down like the FQ herself: I.ix.13–15. **5–7** the lion, emblem of wrath and natural law, succumbs to Una since lions traditionally protect virgins and revere monarchs (New Arden Shakespeare *I Henry IV*, II.iv.267–8). **10–20** the *wench* = *Abessa* (abbess and also absenteeism), her *mother* = *Corceca* (st.18), blind heart (Ephes. 4:18). Together with *Kirkrapine* (17, 22), they represent abuses which Anglicanism had inherited from Catholicism. The lion's defeat of Kirkrapine suggests apocalyptic reform. **16** *Aldeboran* = star in Taurus; *Cassiopeia* = stellified for boasting of her daughter, Andromeda's, beauty. As an Ethiopian, she is black. She parallels Corceca. **26–30** in a world of multiplying darkness even Truth can, for the purposes of narrative at least, be misled. **31** *Orions hound* = Sirius, the heat-bringing Dog Star (Canis major, located to s.e. of *Orion*, bringer of storms); *Nereus* = old man of the sea (*Iliad* 18.141). **33–9** *Sans loy* = absolute lawlessness, symbolically coinciding with, then vanquishing, Archimago who himself originates from chaos. **36** *Lethe* = infernal river of oblivion; the 3 *Furies* perpetually punish guilt. **42–4** the lion's world of natural law yields to the historically prior demon of lawlessness. On another level, is Mother Church the victim of over-zealous reform, in parody of her reunion with Redcross in I.viii?

Canto IV

2 *broad high way*: Matt. 7:13, and cf. I.x.5. **4–5** cf. Alcina's city in *OF*

6.59ff. The *Diall tells* and *tolls* apocalyptically, since this is the (Catholic) house built on sand of Matt. 7:26–7. The *bricke* and *towres* suggest brick-built Babel (Gen. 11:3), though the palace has no *morter*, thus confirming its vulnerability to God's wrath (Ezek. 13:14). 6 *Malvenù* = Ill-come. 7 like Duessa-Fidessa, Lucifera (st.12) is connected with Persia's wealth and paganism. 8 a solar 'mayden Queene' like Eliz. (I Proem 4) and Una (I.iii.4, xii.8, 23); but cf. Is. 47:1 (virgin daughter of Babylon). 9 *Phœbus . . . childe:* Phaëthon stole his father's chariot and nearly destroyed the world. 10 *Dragon:* cf. Whore of Babylon, Rev. 17:3 and Duessa at I.vii.16–18, cf. I.vii.31; *mirrhour:* emblem of Vanity and Lechery. 11 cf. I.i.36–7n. 12 *Lucifera* = Lucifer (Satan) and the proud Nebuchadnezzar, King of Babylon (Is. 14:12). Lucifer is also the morning star, Venus (cf. I.ii.6, xii.21), since Lucifera denies love's powers of illumination and fertility. Politically, Lucifera = machiavellian, a self-elected tyrant (unlike Eliz.) 17 *Flora:* I.i.45–50n.; *Juno* = proud queen of heaven, one of whose emblems is the *peacock*; *Argus: Met.* 1.622ff. 18–36 Lucifera heads the procession of Deadly Sins, ordered according to a traditional trinitarian scheme in which Sloth, Gluttony and Lust = sins of the Flesh; Avarice = the Worldly sin; Envy, Wrath and Pride (*Satan*) = sins of the Devil. The scheme derives from Christ's temptation (e.g. Matt. 4). Sp gives the sins their usual iconographical attributes which derive from classical and biblical sources. 38 Redcross now succumbs to the joylessness born of faithlessness, the worldly (not goodly) source of 2 Cor. 7:8–11. 44, 48 *Morpheus, Stygian:* I.i.36–7n.

Canto v

2 *Phœbus . . . bridegrome:* Ps. 19:4–5. 5 parodies Eliz. at Accession Day tilts. 8 *Gryfon* (half-lion, half-eagle) = emblem of Christ; the Satanic *Dragon* represents Sansjoy. 13 Sansjoy is vanquished but not killed. For the *clowd*, cf. *Aeneid* 5. 808ff. 17 *wine and oyle:* Luke 10:34. 18 the *Crocodile* that supposedly wept for its prey symbolised hypocrisy; the Nile's *seven mouths* were linked with the 7 sins: cf. I.i.21n. 22 *auncient:* Hesiod, *Theogony*, 116ff.; *Dæmogorgon:* I.i.36–7n.; *Nephewes* = grandchildren (Lat. *nepos*). 23 *Aveugle* = blind. 30 Hecate (I.i.43n.) is associated with *dogs* and *wolves*; the *owle* is associated with Night and Death. 31 *Avernus* = the poisonous entrance to hell (*Aeneid* 6.237ff.). 33 *Acheron* = infernal river of grief, *Phlegeton* = river of fire. 34 *Cerberus* = triple-headed canine guardian of hell gate. 35–40 traditional sufferers in hell, e.g. *Odyssey* 11; *Aeneid* 6; *Met.* 4 and 10. 36 *Æsculapius*, god of healing and son of Phœbus (st. 44) = a parody of Christ, concerned with body rather than spirit. For *Hippolytus* (significantly under Diana's protection), see *Aeneid* 7.765ff. 47 *proud king* = Nebuchadnezzar (Daniel 3,4); *Crœsus* = wealthy last king of Lydia; *Antiochus* persecuted the Jews (I Maccabees 1). 48 *Nimrod* = tyrant king, reputed builder of

Babel (Gen. 10,11 and Geneva glosses); *Ninus* founded Nineveh; *mightie Monarch:* Alexander the Great, supposed son of Jupiter *Ammon*, died outside Babylon. **49** *Romulus* founded Rome; *proud*: Tarquinius Superbus, last Roman king; *Lentulus* = proud patrician family; *Scipio* Africanus conquered *Hanniball; Sylla* (Cornelius), vainglorious Roman dictator, fought *Marius; Cæsar* (Julius) defeated *Pompey* at Pharsalia; *Antonius* = Mark Anthony. **50** *Semiramis*, Ninus' wife, lusted after and was killed by her son; *Sthenobœa*, wife of Proetus, vainly loved Bellerophon.

Canto VI

7 *Lyon:* 2 Tim.4:17; *Faunes* and *Satyres* = goat-men and wood-gods representing lower human nature, higher up the hierarchy than Sansloy or the lion. Theologically, they represent a pre-Christian state of religious awareness or the precarious survival of the true faith in an otherwise corrupt world. *Sylvanus* = wood-god, identif. with Faunus and Pan; in one tradition he loved the boy Cyparissus (st.**17**). But note that the *Cypresse* (st.**14**) belongs to Diana (*Aeneid* 3). **13** *olive*, virginal Athena's tree, signifies peace and reconciliation. Cf. I.xii.8. **15** *Bacchus* = god of wine; *Cybele*, the great earth mother, was worshipped drunkenly and noisily; *Dryope* loved Faunus; *Pholoe* was loved by Pan. **16** cf. Aeneas' reaction to Venus disguised as a nymph of Diana at *Aeneid* 1.314ff. (Una combines love and virginity into a 'mystery' of chaste love; like Belphœbe at II.iii she is also Diana as goddess of the refuge of the wood). **18** *Hamadryades* = tree nymphs; *Naiades* = water nymphs. **21** *Satyrane* (st.**28**), son of a satyr and *Thyamis* (Gk. *thymos* = passion) is a wild man who hunts beasts and thus controls his passions. *Labryde* = Gk. *labros*, furious; *Therion* = wild beast (Gk.) **35** Archimago, disguised as a pilgrim who has been to the Spanish shrine of St James (*Jacob)* of Compostela.

Canto VII

2–3 Redcross escapes from the sun's heat into a false paradise: cf. I.ii.29, and Song of Solomon 2:3. He has removed his Christian armour (Ephes. 6). **4–5** the enervating fountain is like that of Salmacis (*Met.* 4.285ff.): cf. I.ii.43, xi.29–30. *Phœbe* = the moon goddess, Diana. **8–10** Orgoglio (Ital. = pride, st.**14**) is, like all Titans/giants, the offspring of Earth and Heaven and rebellious. But *Æolus* = the wind god, so that O. is puffed up with pride. And note the parody of Gen.2:7 (Adam created of earth and made a living soul with the breath of life). If Lucifera = worldly pride, then O. = the demonically corrupt roots of pride itself as a sin. The tree parallels Sylvanus' (vi.**14**), and makes O. a lawless wild man (*Aeneid* 3.665ff, the Cyclops). The Pope was sometimes depicted as a wildman Antichrist. **16** Rev. 17:3, Whore of Babylon interpreted in Geneva glosses as type of Roman Catholicism. **17** *Alcides* (Hercules) killed the manyheaded Lernean hydra, symbol of sin's multiplicity. **29–36** Arthur arrives, bringing grace and exemplifying the inclusive virtue of magnificence. **30** *Ladies head:* Gloriana. The mythical Arthur's shield bore an image of the Virgin Mary; *Hesperus* = Venus as morning star. **31** *Dragon:* another detail from the mythical Arthur, it was a reminder of his father Uther Pendragon. This is also the Welsh (Tudor) dragon. **32** *Almond:* mount Selinus was *palmy* (Aeneid 3.705); the *almond* represents priesthood (Numbers 17:8) and world rule (al-monde). **33** the 'shield of Faith', since the *dia-mond* signifies good faith (Tervarent, col.148). Cf. *OF* 2.55–6, and Minerva's petrifying shield. **37** *Squire:* Timias (Gk. *timē*, honour). Cf. III.i.18, etc. **43** *Phison . . . Gehon:* 3 of the 4 paradisal rivers (Gen. 2:11ff.). **44** *Dragon . . . foure yeres:* Rev. 12:4–6. **46** *order:* Order of Garter, headed by the monarch; its patron saints = St George and the Virgin Mary. *Cleopolis* (cf. I.x.58) = city of glory (Gk. *kleos* = fame, glory).

Canto VIII

4 cf. Joshua 6 (fall of Jericho's walls) and trumpets of Rev. 8,9: **5** ff., the battle is between Christ and Antichrist, 'pure' Protestantism and Roman Catholicism. **10** parodies Exod. 17:5–6 and 1 Cor. 10:2–4. **11** *Cymbria:* in *north* Germany (evil north: I.ii.33n., and Jer. 1:14). **14** *cup:* the Whore's at Rev. 17:4, parody of Christ's blood in Communion. Cf. Circe's cup in *Odyssey* 10 and Fidelia's chalice at I.x.13. **30–4** *Ignaro* = Ignorance (Ephes. 4:17–18). **46–50** the stripping of Duessa echoes Is. 3 (stripping of Zion's proud daughters) and Is. 47 (uncovering of Babylon's daughter). The *fox* = cunning; the *Eagles claw* is from personifications of Deceit (Ripa, pp. 173–5); the *Beares paw* is from Rev. 13:2. Rev. 17:16 anticipates the time when the Whore shall be made 'naked'.

Canto IX

4 *Timon:* Gk. *timē* again (I.vii.37): Arthur talks allegorically. *Rauran* = in Merioneth, a county with strong Tudor connections. The *Dee* divides (and links) north Wales and England. **13–15** the story of the *FQ* is really that of Arthur's quest for the faerie queene, who appears to him here like Diana to Endymion or, more riddlingly, the elf queen to Chaucer's Sir Thopas (*Sir Thopas*, 778ff.) Technically, Arthur's dream is a revelation, that of Redcross at I.i.47ff. an evil illusion. **19** *Diamond:* I.vii.33n.; *liquor pure:* I.xi.30. **29** *rope* and *knife:* traditional emblems of Despair, the sin born of an overwhelming sense of guilt and unworthiness, leading one to deny God's mercy and grace. **33–6** the iconography is suitably infernal and melancholic (cf. I.i.2n.). **38–47** Despair's seductive speech parodies and perverts commonplaces of the 'art of dying' tradition, which drew on ancient and biblical texts and encouraged composure and hope. **38** cf. Romans 6:23, etc. and the trick Faustus plays on himself (*Dr Faustus*, I.i.). **39** echoing Cicero, *De Senectute* 19, etc. **41** *ibid.*, 20. **43** answered at st.**52–3. 53** *chosen:* cf. 2 Thess. 2:13 (*not* Calvinistic).

Canto x

1 *grace:* e.g. Ephes. 2:8–9. **3** *auntient house:* the 'spirituall house' of 1 Peter 2:5 and the Anglican church understood, as it was by subscribing Elizabethans, as the Catholic church restored to its primitive purity. This episode marks Redcross's repentance and recognition of the goal of the Christian pilgrimage; it undoes Lucifera's Babylon by the New Jerusalem (57–8). **4** *Caelia* = Heavenly; mother of Faith, Hope, and Charity. **5** *Humiltá* = the traditional opposite of Pride; *streight and narrow:* Matt. 7:14, cf. st.**10. 12–13** the white robe of purity and eucharistic chalice are emblems of *Christian Faith* (Ripa, p.149): cf. I.viii.14n. *Christall:* faith and purity. *Serpent* = emblem of Christ (John 3:14). **14** *blew:* the heavenly colour; *anchor:* Hebrews 6:18–19. **16** *Charissa:* st.**29–31**n. **20** alludes to Joshua 10:12–13, 2 Kings 20:10–11, Judges 7, Exod. 14:21–31, Matt.21:21. **21–8** Faith produces repentance, whose formal stages are now endured. **28** the *Lyon* of sin (1 Peter 5:8). **29** *kist:* the kiss of greeting and charity (1 Peter 5:14). **30–31** Charity (love) is the supreme, and so last, theological virtue, without which we are 'nothing' (1 Cor. 13:2). The love she represents is traditionally suggested by her suckling of several babies (Ripa, p.64). The *yellow* and *doves*, emblematic of marriage and Venus, confirm her as a supreme statement of love's meaning. **34–5** *Mercie* (Luke 6:36) is a *mother* full of *grace* (*matrone . . . gratious*) **36** *Bead-men* = men of prayer. Contrasting with the 7 sins of I.iv, they exemplify the 7 corporal works of mercy which originate with Matt. 25. **46** cf. I.i.34 and Despair at I.ix. Redcross has now moved from the *active* life to a state of visionary *contemplation* on the traditional mount of meditation and virtue. **47** *Eagle:* cf. I.xi.34n. Believed to be able to gaze at the sun (of righteousness). **53** Sinai (Exod. 24), but cf. Rev. 21:10; *billowes:* Exod. 14. **54** *sacred hill* = Mount of Olives (Matt. 24:3); *pleasaunt Mount* = Parnassus, home of the Muses. The hills signify the progress from old law to new law to a vision of the prophetic and religious power of poetry. **55** *Citie:* New Jerusalem, Rev. 21. **56** *Angels:* Gen. 28:12, Hebr. 12:22. **57** *lam:* John 1:29. **58** *Cleopolis:* I.vii.46n.; *Panthea* (Gk., all the gods), cf. Roman Pantheon. **66** (cf. **61**): *Met.* 15.553ff. tells of the similar discovery by a ploughman of Tages. *George* = from Graeco-Latin *georgos*, ploughman. Redcross is, like Adam, 'of the earth, earthly' (1 Cor. 15:47; cf. st.**52**), and *Adam* means *earthly*.

Canto xi

5 *Muse:* Clio, Muse of history, daughter of Phœbus and Memory, conflated with Calliope, Muse of epic poetry (cf. Proem 2). **7** *second tenor:* supporting voice (from bell ringing). **8–15** the dragon is the Leviathan of Job 41, the dragon of Rev. 12:9, and the dragon of the St George legend and mummers' plays. He is like a *mountaine* because of Rev. 8:8 (*mountain* identif. in Geneva gloss with 'sektes of heretikes'). Cf. the Martian serpent in *Met.* 3.31ff. **11** *stings:* 1 Cor. 15:55–6, 2 Cor. 12:17. **26–7** *armes to leave:* cf. I.vii.2. Redcross now burns like Hercules (*Champion*), type of Christ, poisoned by Deianira with a coat soaked in the blood of the centaur Nessus (*Met.* 9.101ff.). **29** *well of life:* cf. Rev. 22:1 and John 4:14; grace, baptism, and purification are all suggested. **30** *Silo:* John 9:7; Christ was baptised in the *Jordan* (Matt. 3:16); the *Cephise* washed sheep white; the *Hebrus*, traditionally pure, saw Orpheus's death and union with Eurydice (*Met.* 11). **34** another solar eagle myth (x.47), referring to the bird's supposed ability to renew itself by flying to the sun and then immersing itself in water. Allegorised as a myth of regeneration: cf. Ps. 103:4–5. **39** *Five joints:* the 5 senses; and cf. Rev. 17:10. **41** *Cerberus,* cf. I.v.34, was defeated by Hercules. **45** *pestilence:* deliverance is promised in Ps. 91:3, but Redcross is still a backslider (*backeward*). **46–7** the two trees are the tree of life and the tree of knowledge (Gen. 2:9). **48** cf. Rev. 22:2 (and the leaves of the tree served to heale the nations with) and cf. Orgoglio at I.viii.10. **51** answers I.ii.7. **53** the dragon is killed through the mouth to suggest hell's mouth and the destruction of hell (Rev. 20:14). **54** *downe . . . downe:* 'Babylon that great citie is fallen, it is fallen' (Rev. 14:8).

Canto XII

6 cf. the entry into Jerusalem, Matt. 21:8. **18** Redcross and Una are betrothed; their marriage (that of Christ and the true Church) will take place at the end of time, i.e. in the eternal sabbath which succeeds the six ages (*sixe yeares*) of the world. Cf. Hebr. 4:3–4. **21** *morning starre:* cf. I.vii.30 and ii.6–7. Christ is the *Morning Star* at Rev. 22:16 and so is the bride-Church at Song of Solomon 6:10; the phrase is also used of the Virgin Mary. **22** *white . . . spot:* the bride of the Lamb (true church) arrayed for her marriage in Rev. 19:7–8 and 21:2; also the bride in Song of Solomon 4:7 (no spot). This is an apocalyptic vision of the victory of Anglican Protestantism over Rome. **36** cf. the temporary binding of Satan at Rev. 20:2–3. **37–8** recalling Roman marriage customs: see Sp's own *Epithalamion.* **39** *trinall triplicities:* the 9 orders of angels were divided into 3 sets of 3.

BOOK II

PROEM **2** *now found:* i.e. in 1541; *Virginia:* named after Queen Elizabeth upon Ralegh's return from North America in 1584. **5** *Guyon,* named from *gyon,* a wrestler (see Jacobus de Voragine's *Golden Legend;*

Hamilton, I.x.66n); from the paradisal river *Gihon* (I.vii.43), sometimes interpreted as the virtue of *Temperance*; and with hints of the celebrated romance hero *Guy of Warwick*.

Canto I

1 *Architect:* Archimago. 5 *knight:* Sir Guyon. 6 *Huon:* favourite of *Oberon* in medieval romance *Huon of Bordeaux.* 7 *Palmer:* pilgrim who has visited Holy Land (and carries palm leaf as testament to this). Here he = a Christian figure who also embodies reason's power to control the passions. Cf. Archimago at I.i.29. 14–15 i.e., Duessa. 22 cf. I.viii.50. 28 *heavenly Mayd:* Gloriana, with hints of the Marian cult of Elizabeth: see II.ii.40–2. 35–41 *Amavia* (Ital. *amare* + *via*, way of love) loves and tries to redeem *Mortdant* (death-giver, st.55) from his enslavement to the flesh (concupiscence). The Christian depth of her love is shown by her disguise as a palmer (st.52), though since she is human she cannot redeem his mortality. In his death we may see the death of the old Adam (Col. 3:9), but Adam-Mortdant nevertheless bequeathes death and original sin (blood) on the baby. See Robert Reid's brilliant essay in *Studies in Philology* 78 (1981), 370–90. 51 *Acrasia,* the witch of the Bower (II.xii.42ff.), = intemperance (Gk. *a-krasis,* ill-mixture). 53 *Lucina* = *Cynthia* (moon) in her role as goddess of childbirth. 55 *Bacchus* = wine; *Nymphe* = excessively pure water. Mortdant dies from an intemperate clashing of opposites. 58 *squire* = set square, because temperance is the midpoint between extremes (Aristotle, *Nicomachean Ethics*) and the *square* is the symbol of virtue derived from *right reason* symbolised by the *rectangle* (e.g., *Nic. Ethics* 1100B). *Golden* because gold was believed to contain the elements in perfect balance.

Canto II

1–4 baptism promises rebirth but cannot eradicate original sin (Article 9 of the Anglican 39 Articles). Note the analogy with Ezek. 16. 6 *Flora:* I.i.45–50n. 7–10 cf. I.vii.5. The tale is Ovidian in style (e.g. *Met.* 5.572ff., story of Arethusa) but is Sp's invention. *Faunus* = wood-god, symbol of lust. 11 the horse, Brigadore (V.iii.34), has been stolen by Braggadocchio (II.iii.4). Orlando's steed in *OF* = Brigliadoro (golden bridle; both elements suggest temperance, balance, restraint). 14 *Medina* = Middle One. 17 *eldest* = *Elissa* (st.35), Gk. *elasson* = too little. *Huddibras:* Gk. *hydeo* = to name, *brasso* = to shake violently (*name . . . rash*). 18 *youngest* = *Perissa* (st.36), Gk. *perissos* = too much. Temperance as midpoint again. 29 *Erinnys:* the Furies (I.iii.36n.) 31 *Olive:* I.vi.13n. 40–2 praise of Elizabeth as head of Order of the Garter (*Order of Maydenhead*): cf. I.vii.46. *The day that first doth lead the yeare around* is Elizabeth's Accession Day, 17 Nov., celebrated as an annual festival of renewal with jousts, etc. 46 *Orion:* see I.iii.31n. The *hissing snake* is probably the nearly adjacent constellation Hydra (known as the *Dragon*): J. C. Eade, *The Forgotten Sky* (1984) 179, who also suggests a mid-February date for this passage.

Canto III

Arg. *Braggadocchio:* braggart, a *miles gloriosus* in the tradition of Ancient Pistol (Shakespeare's *Henry V*); *Belphœbe* = beautiful (*bella*) Phœbe (moon goddess), a manifestation of Eliz. (Sp in *Letter of the Authors*). She is described at st. 21–31 and temperately combines Diana (huntress, etc.) and Venus (Venerean *roses*, st.22, *Graces*, st.25, etc.). Hence she is greeted as Aeneas greets Venus disguised as Diana at *Aeneid* 1 (I.vi.16n.). **31** *Diana . . . Cynthus: Aeneid* 1.502–3 (Dido was a type of Elizabeth); *Queene . . . Troy:* Penthesilea (*Aeneid* 1.494ff.). **38** *Moone:* Braggadocchio is committed to the moon as planet of Fortune, mutability, and secular honour. Redcross belongs to super-*solar* regions (II.i.32).

Canto IV

1 *skill to ride:* a commonplace (e.g. opening to Sidney's *Apology for Poetry*). **4–5** *Hag:* draws on emblematically conventional descriptions of *Occasio-Fortuna*, in this case suggesting occasion for *wrath*, portrayed in *Furor* (st.6–15). The allegory is simple: here and in canto v Guyon encounters *anger*; in cantos vi and xii he encounters *lust*. This moral progress is sanctioned by Aristotle, *Nicomachean Ethics* 1105A (it is hard to resist anger, harder still to resist pleasure). **18–33** based on story of Ariodante and Ginevra in *OF* 4–5. **20** *Philemon:* the Gk. etymology suggests either *self-love* or *my friend*. **36** *Phaon* = Gk. *phaos*, light. The name is found in 1590 3-book *FQ*. In 1596 it is changed to *Phedon* here and in **Arg.**; *Coradin:* Lat. *cor* (heart) and Gk. *adynamia* (lack of power): Hamilton, II.iv.36n. **41** *Pyrochles:* Gk. *pyr* (flame) + *ochleo* (disturb, annoy), with hints of *kleos* = fame. *Cymochles* = Gk. *kuma* (wave). He symbolises moral instability and also burning (Gk. *kauma*) lust: for water and lust see II.iii.39. The brothers embody the elemental opposites of fire and water and the temperamental opposites of wrath (irascibility) and lust (concupiscence): Plato, *Republic* 434E ff. Hence they derive from *Acrates* (cf. *Acrasia*), *Despight* (Ital. *dispetto* = angry, spiteful, action), *Phlegeton* (the infernal fiery river) and *Herebus*, the underworld. Cf. I.v.22ff. **42** *Atin:* Atē = the Gk. goddess of strife.

Canto V

11 *Saint:* the image of Gloriana (II.i.28). **22** *Stygian:* the infernal river Styx is traditionally 'hateful'. The conjunction of water and fire (cf. st.2) is an emblem of discord. **27** *Acrasia:* II.i.51n. **29** *Yvie* is associated with

wanton and regressive Bacchus; *Eglantine* (wild rose) is Venerean;
Zephyrus is the wind of spring who raped Chloris-Flora. This is a false
paradise of lustful pleasure, so for the rose's *prickles* see Gen. 3:18. Note
the art versus nature theme, and cf. xii.59. **31** the oak was *dedicated* to
Jove, the poplar to *Alcides* (Hercules); but note, Gk. *alkē* = oak, symbol
of strength. *Nemea* = where Hercules slew the Nemean lion.

Canto VI

9 *Phaedria* = joyful (Gk. *phaidros*), a Venerean quality. **16** perverting
Matt. 6:28 and ignoring fallen man's curse of labour (Gen. 3:19). Cf.
Odysseus and the Lotus-eaters in *Odyssey* 9. *Flowre-deluce* = iris,
emblem of chastity. **23** cf. Despair, I.ix.40. **35** cf. I Proem 3. Mars fell in
love with Venus, a union of opposites that was given many ancient and
Renaissance glosses.

Canto VII

3ff.: Guyon's descent to the underworld, a temptation to lay up treasure
on earth (parodying Sermon on the Mount, Matt. 6:19ff.). Mammon (=
riches; cf. Matt. 6:24, Geneva gloss) tempts to the complementary
concupiscible desire to the sexual ones offered by Phædria and Acrasia.
He is described as a blacksmith and as a Saturnian melancholic because
Hades (underworld) signifies *melancholy*. **5** *Mulciber* = Vulcan, the
gods' blacksmith. **8–10** cf. Satan's temptation of Christ to 'all the
kingdomes of the world' (Matt. 4:8). **14** *Caspian, Adrian* (Adriatic):
notoriously stormy. **17** cf. Ovid's account of loss of Golden Age, *Met.*
1.137ff. **21–5** traditional infernal iconography (e.g. *Aeneid* 6.262ff.);
Celeno (st.23) = chief harpy, a rapacious bird woman (*Aeneid* 3.245–6).
28*Arachne* was changed into a spider for her presumption in challenging
Minerva to a weaving contest. **31** *yron dore:* cf. Acts 12:10 (yron gate),
which would equate Mammon with Herod. **35–6** cf. the Cyclopes'
furnaces, *Aeneid* 8.416ff. **41** *Titans:* gigantic offspring of Earth:
cf. III.vii.47. **44–50** *Philotime* (st.49; Gk. *philos* + *time*, lover of honour)
has affinities with Lucifera (I.iv,v) as a mock Gloriana. The pressing
crowds suggest those in Dante's *Inferno* 3. The *chaine* in st. **46** parodies
the chain of love or chain of being. **51–3** *Proserpina* = queen of hell
(I.i.36–7n.); the plants are connected with death or deep sleep: *Heben* =
ebony; *Hellebore* is black and belongs to melancholy Saturn;
Coloquintida = the poisonous gourd of 2 Kings 4:39–40 (Geneva gloss;
Hamilton); *Tetra* = deadly nightshade (*tetrum solanum*); *Samnitis:* not
identified; *Cicuta* (hemlock) killed Socrates, but *Crito* was his *Belamy*. **54**
Atlas daughters = the Hesperides, whose western island garden con-
tained golden apples guarded by a dragon. The *Eubœan* was
Hippomenes (or Meilanion), who slowed Atalanta down by dropping
golden apples which she picked up (*Met.* 10.560ff.). **55** *Acontius* tricked

Cydippe into marriage with an inscribed apple (Ovid, *Heroides* 20,21); *Ate*, goddess of discord, flung the golden apple inscribed 'to the fairest' into the banqueting hall where the marriage of Peleus and Thetis was being celebrated. Juno, Minerva, and Venus quarrelled over which of them it described. Paris judged Venus the victor; Helen was his reward and the Trojan war its consequence: cf. III.ix.36. **56** *Cocytus* = infernal river of lamentation. **57–60** *Tantalus:* cf. I.v.35–40n. **61–2** *Pilate:* John 18:36–8, Matt. 27:23–4. **65** *three dayes:* cf. Christ's 3-day harrowing of hell, echoed in the triple encounter with the dragon, I.xi.

Canto VIII

2 Matt. 4:11, angels to Christ after temptation in wilderness. **5–6** the angel (divine love) is portrayed as a celestial Cupid, whose mother, Venus, frequented mount *Ida. Graces:* cf. I.i.48. **20** *Merlin:* cf. I.vii.36; *Medaewart* = meadow-wort, with hints of the terrible magical power of the witch *Medea* (II.xii.44n.). **21** *Morddure* = hard-biter (Fr. *mordre* + *dur*).

Canto IX

4 *morning starre:* I.xii.21n. **6** *Arthegall* appears in Book III and is the hero of Book V; *Sophy* is never mentioned again (Gk. *sophia* = wisdom). **12** *enemies:* see canto xi; *Seven,* because of the 7 planets and ages of man, signifies earthly life and mortality. **16** *Gnats:* cf. I.i.23 and note Sp's commitment to the Irish landscape. **18** *Alma,* as an adj. = gracious, nourishing (Latin; applied to Ceres and the Virgin Mary); *alma* also = soul (Ital.). She is the rational soul which includes, and is superior to, the sensitive and vegetative souls. Like Belphœbe (II.iii) she combines virgin and Venus, *lily* and *rose.* **21** Alma's castle (the temperate body) is made in part of corrupt earth. Ninus (*Nine*) and Nimrod (who traditionally built the tower of Babel) were often linked, as at I.v.48. The tower was built of *slime* (Gen. 11:3), *Ægyptian* because of the fertile Nile mud (I.i.21n.) and because Cairo was sometimes called Babylon. **22** for a full account see Fowler, *Spenser and the Numbers of Time* (1964). Sp draws on the Pythagorean and Platonic belief, still much alive in the Renaissance, of the symbolic power of numbers. Briefly, he expressed in arithmetical and geometrical terms the mystery of the union of spirit and flesh in the human body. The *circle* = the head (and perfection), the *triangle* = the legs (and imperfection), the *quadrate* = the trunk (and virtue, the Aristotelian meaning of the square). Circle, square, and triangle were also identified with the rational, sensitive, and vegetative souls respectively. *Seven* = mutable, mortal (st.12n.); *nine* = *heavenly* because of the 9 orders of angels (I.xii.39n.) and because in the Ptolemaic system the sphere of fixed stars was ninth counting from, and including, earth. *Diapase* = diapason, octave, i.e., join (*compact*) 7 and 9 and you get harmonious 8 because 8 is the temperate mean between them. 23 *two gates* = mouth and anal passage (st.32). 24 *vine, yvie* = beard and moustache. 25 *Barbican* = outer defences of castle, etc. 27ff. the journey is an ascent following the Platonic moral anatomy of belly (27–32), heart (33–44) and head (45–60): *Timaeus* 69–73. 29 *Mongiball:* Sicilian name for Etna; cf. furnace at II.vii.35–7. 32 *Port Esquiline:* the Esquiline Gate in Rome was an unsavoury sewer and dump haunted by carrion birds. 35 the heart's passions are divided into 4 concupiscible and 5 irascible; cf. Perissa – Elissa in II.ii. 37 *Prays-desire* (st.39) is at the root of Arthur's quest for Gloriana. *Purple* and *gold* = royal (*purple*, as a mixture of red and blue, also belongs to temperance); the *Poplar* belongs to heroic and virtuous Hercules (II.v.31n.). 40–3 *Shamefastnes* (st.43) is Guyon's root virtue, described according to emblematic convention. Aristotle, *Nic. Ethics*, III.vii (1116A), talks of the balance between fear of shame and desire of praise in courageous men. 44 *ten:* anatomically, the spinal vertebrae (Hamilton); numerologically, the number of perfection and law (the commandments). 45 *Cadmus* founded *Thebes*, which was destroyed by *Alexander* in 335 BC; *Hector's* son Astyanax was flung from *Troy's* walls (*Met.* 13.415–17). 47 *heavenly towre:* New Jerusalem (I.x.55–7). 48ff. the 3 rooms and their inhabitants signify the 3 ventricles of the brain recognised as containing Imagination, Reason (Judgment), and Memory, the highest parts of the sensitive soul. 48 *wisest:* Socrates; *Pylian:* wise Nestor, who advised the Greeks during the war against Troy, of which *Priam* was king. 49–52 *Phantastes* (st.52) = Fantasy, Imagination (cf. the *flyes* of 51 and I.i.22–3n. and I.i.38). This is the image-making faculty, melancholic (Saturnian) because Saturn governed visionaries, madmen, etc. 53–4 *goodly reason* modifies Imagination's excesses and works in conjunction with *Memory* (55–8: *Eumnestes* = good memory (Gk.), *Anamnestes* = the reminder (Gk.)). 56 *Nine:* 21n., first to wage war; *Assaracus* = early king of Troy, son of its founder; *Inachus* = river god, first king of Argos. 57 *Nestor* was reputedly 300 at the time of the Trojan war; for Methuselah see Gen. 5:27.

Canto x

Crucial to Sp's apologia for Elizabeth and his conception of the FQ as a dynastic epic. There are complementary cantos in II.iii and ix, each of which draws on Aeneas' vision of his descendants and successors in Aeneid 6. For detailed commentary see Carrie Harper, *The Sources of the British Chronicle History in Spenser's 'Faerie Queene'* (1910). Sp draws on the 'matter of Britain', the tradition found in Geoffrey of Monmouth's 12th-century *History of the Kings of Britain* and other sources that Britain was named after, and settled by, Aeneas' great-grandson Brutus. The original name of Britain is Albion (st.6), originally inhabited by giants who were defeated by Brutus, Trojan by blood (*Assaracs line*, st.9), who founds Troynovant (New Troy) in Britain. His line is followed by that of Dunwallo (st.37–46); the kingdom is then (st.47–63) under the rule of Rome. The climax is the celebration of Arthur's father, Uther Pendragon (st.64–8). 3 *Mæonia:* supposed home of Homer. The giants fought against *Jove* on the *Phlegræan* plain; they had tried to reach heaven by piling mount *Pelion* on *Ossa.* The *daughters* = the Muses. 5 *Island:* traditionally originally connected to the continent but celebrated for its separateness (Virgil, *Eclogues* 1.66). 10: Plymouth *Hogh* (Hoe), where Gogmagog (*Goëmot*) was killed by Brutus' general *Corineus.* 11 *Debon* founded Devonshire; *Coulin . . . Canutus* (cf. III.ix.50): the story is perhaps Sp's invention, but Hercules was reputed to have killed Albion. 12 *Corineus:* Geoffrey, *History* 1.12. The rest seems to be Sp's invention. 13–14 Brutus' 3 sons were *Locrine* (after whom England was called Logres), *Albanact,* who received Scotland (Albania), and *Camber,* who received Wales (Cambria): Geoffrey, *History* 2.1. 15–16 for Humber, king of the Huns, see Geoffrey, *History* 2.1. 17–19: Geoffrey, *History* 2.4–5. 21 *Madan* was *unworthie* because a tyrant. His 2 sons = *Mempricius* and *Manlius; Ebranck* = Ebraucus, the former's son; *Henault* = Hainaut in Belgium. 23 Ebraucus' eldest son = *Brutus Greenshield.* 24 *Scaldis,* river Scheldt in Hainaut; *Henalois* = men of Hainaut, whose prince is *Brunchild. Scuith guiridh* = green shield; *y scuith gogh* = the red shield (Welsh for Tudor propaganda). 25 *Cairleill* = Leill's city (Carlisle); *Cairleon* = Chester. 26 *Cairbadon* = Bath. 27–32 for *Lear,* Sp mainly follows Geoffrey, *History* 2.11–15. 37 i.e. Dunwallo (Geoffrey, *History* 2.17), equivalent as law-giver to *Numa* (st. 39) Pompilius, Rome's second king, who was instructed by the prophetic nymph *Ægeria* (st.42). 46 *Troynovant:* see III.ix.44–6; the *gate* = Ludgate. 50 *Kimbeline:* Geoffrey, *History* 4.11. 53 *Joseph* buried Christ (Matt. 27:57ff.) and supposedly brought the *holy grayle* to Glastonbury. 56 *Semiramis:* I.v.50; *Hypsiphil* ruled Lemnos and was visited by the Argonauts on their quest for the Golden Fleece; *Thomiris* (Tomyris), widow queen of the Massagetae, refused Cyrus the Great's offer of marriage and defeated him in battle. 60 cf. Geoffrey, *History* 5.6–8. Elizabeth was frequently compared to Constantine, the first Christian Roman Emperor. 63 for the *mound* (wall), see IV.xi.36. 68 Uther is Arthur's father, and Arthur does not know his parentage (I.ix.3). 70 Guyon, meanwhile, reads a complementary and mythologically more allusive and elusive account of Elizabeth's ancestry. *Prometheus,* creator of man, also created civilisation. 71 *Quick* = life, alive. For Adonis gardens see III.vi. 72 *Elfin* recalls Bacchus, civiliser of India. *Cleopolis:* I.vii.46n. Subsequent identifications are impossible until st.75: *Elficleos* (Henry VII), *Elferon* (Prince Arthur, d.1502), and *Oberon* (Henry VIII, Elizabeth's father). On *Tanaquill* (st.76) (Elizabeth) see I Proem 2n.

Canto XI

6–7 the *twelve* are divided into *seven* deadly sins, attacking body and soul, and *five* evils which attack the senses, presented in their traditional order of Sight, Hearing, Smell, Taste, Touch. The animals are traditional attributes of the senses to which Sp attaches them. 19 *Spumador* = Golden Foam (Ital. *spuma d'oro*). *Laomedon* = Aeneas' grandfather. 20–3 *Malegar* = *badly sick* (Lat. *male* + *aeger*) and *ill omen* (Ital. *malaugurio*), symbol of original sin as it corrupts the body. The *Tygre* = destructive swiftness, because the Armenian word for *arrow* was *tigris* (P. Valeriano, *Hieroglyphica* (1602) lib.42, p.445). 43 *Joves Bird:* eagle. 45 cf. myth of Antaeus, giant son of Poseidon and Earth, who received renewed strength from his mother when he was thrown to the ground. He was defeated by Hercules.

Canto XII

2ff.: echoing Odysseus' wanderings (*Odyssey* 12), those of Aeneas (*Aeneid* 2,3) and those of Ubaldo and Carlo in *Ger.Lib.* 15. 6 *Tartarus:* hell. 13 *Latona:* story told in *Met.* 6.184ff. 17 *Phædria:* cf. II.vi. 23–4 *Hydre:* many-headed mythological serpent; *whirlpoole:* spouting whale; *Scolopendra:* sea-centipede; *Monoceros:* sea-unicorn (narwhal); *Death:* morse, walrus (Lat. *mors*); *Wasserman:* merman; *Ziffius:* sword-fish; *Rosmarine:* walrus or sea-horse. 26 *Tethys:* I.i.39n. 31 *Heliconian maides:* the Muses. 33 *Zephirus:* spring west wind. 36 *Strich:* screech owl (Lat. *strix*); *Whistler* (plover) portends death; *Harpies:* II.vii.21–5n. 39 cf. Circe's island, *Odyssey* 10. 41 Mercury's *rod* (caduceus) brings peace and harmony, symbolises reason, gives sleep, and guides the souls of the dead. *Orcus* = Pluto–Hades, god of hell. 43 *enclosed:* Song of Solomon 4:12, the garden enclosed as the bride-Church and Virgin Mary. 44–5 for the tale of the Argonauts see Apollonius Rhodius, *Argonautica*. The witch *Medaea* loved and lived with *Jason*. When he abandoned her for *Creusa* she killed her with a poisoned garment. The *boy* is Absyrtus, Medea's brother, killed by her as she and Jason fled with the Golden Fleece from her father, Aeetes. 47–8 *Genius* = god of generation, here perverted. Cf. III.vi.31–3, the good double-sexed Genius *Agdistes*. A *staffe* = emblem of office. 50 *Flora:* I.i.45–50n. 52 *Rhodope* gave birth to a giant sired by Neptune (*Met.* 6.87–9); Apollo chased Daphne in *Tempe*; *Ida:* see viii.5–6n.; *Parnassus:* I.x.54n. 60 *midst:* parodies Rev. 22:1–2. 62 *Jaspar:* parodies Rev. 21:11. 65 transl. from *Ger. Lib.* 15.60; *Cyprian* = Venus, the morning star. 69 *Acrasia:* II.i.51n. 72 *Lover: Verdant* (st. 82), *giver of spring*, a parody Adonis; cf. *Mortdant*, II.i. 74–5 transl. from *Ger.Lib.* 16.14–15; cf. I.ii.37n, for the *Rose*. 77 *Arachne:* II.vii.28n. 86 *Grille* = pig (Gk. *gryllos*), a companion of Odysseus according to Plutarch, 'Whether the Beasts have the Use of Reason' (*Moralia* 985D ff.)

BOOK III

PROEM 2 *Zeuxis*, painter, *Praxiteles*, sculptor, ancient Greek, 5th and 4th cents BC respectively. 4 *servaunt:* Sir Walter Ralegh, *The Ocean's Love to Cynthia;* Sp's prefatory *Letter of the Authors* is addressed to Ralegh.

Canto I

1 *Alma:* II.ix–xi. 2 *Acrasia:* II.xii. 4 *Lion . . . field:* the arms of Britomart's ancestor Brutus, on whom see II.x. 7–8 *Britomart:* Britomartis was anciently identified with Artemis–Diana; the *speare* was an attribute of wise, virginal Minerva (Tervarent, col.230). The name also suggests *British Mars;* and n.b. heroic *Bradamante* in *OF. Venus . . . glas:* for the mirror of Venus, see Tervarent, col.274. 15–16 i.e. Florimell (III.v.8), Ital. *fiore-mela* (flower-honey). Ital. *mela* = apple, emblem of love and Venus. For the *beaten gold* see Ps. 45:9 (Queene in a vesture of gold); *blazing starre:* comet (Gk. *komē* = head hair), symbol of rarity and love as well as ominous. 17 *Foster* = forester, contemp. symbol of lust. 18 *Timias:* I.vii.37 (Gk. *timē*, honour). 34–8 the key myth of Book III: cf. canto vi and *Met.* 10; *Rosemaryes* = remembrance; violets = Venerean; *Pances* (pansies) = thoughts (of death; *pensée*). Adonis was *transmewed* into an anemone. 40 *Lydian:* the mode assoc. with sensuality. 45 a ladder of lechery comprising *looking, talking, jesting, kissing, drinking, night revelry.* 51 *Ceres* = mother goddess of corn; *Lyaeus* = Bacchus (the food and wine essential to love's success): cf. Chaucer, *Parliament of Fowls,* 275–6. 56 *Basci:* kiss your hand. 57 *Malecasta* (Ital. *male* + *casta*) = ill-chaste; *moist daughters:* the Hyades, bringers of rain; suggesting a spring date. 59 *scarlot:* cf. the Whore of Rev. 17:4; *Ermine:* III.ii.25n.

Canto II

4 not *Guyon*, Sp's mistake, but Redcross: cf. st.16. 8 *Arthegall* = *Arthur's equal.* 17–18 *mirrhour:* i.e. glass sphere; *Deheubarth* is used by Holinshed, *Chronicles* 1, for South Wales. 20 *Phao:* light (Gk. *phaos*); *Ptolomaee:* Ptolemy II of Egypt, who arranged the building of the lighthouse on Pharos. 22 cf. Plato, *Phaedrus* 255D (lover as a mirror in which he perceives himself). 25 *Hound* = attribute of Diana as hunting goddess; *Achilles:* great Greek warrior in Trojan war, favourite of Minerva; *Ermilin:* ermine = emblem of royalty and chastity, assoc. with Elizabeth I and Minerva. 30 *Glauce:* mother of Diana; also Gk. *glaux* = owl, attribute of Minerva. 41 *Myrrhe*, mother of Adonis, committed incest with her father (*Met.* 10.311ff.); *Biblis* fell in love with her brother (*Met.* 9.454ff.); *Pasiphaë's* bestial love led to the birth of the Minotaur (*Met.* 9.735ff.). 44 *Cephisus . . . child* = Narcissus, who fell in love with his own reflection, deluded by shadows (*Met.* 3.402ff). 49 herbs which,

inter alia, reduce lust and cause barrenness (Upton in *Variorum Sp.*, 3.221). **50** *three:* anciently rejoiced in by the gods (Virgil, *Eclogues* 8.73–5).

Canto III

4 *Clio* = Muse of history. **6** North *Africans* were believed to be descended from Ishmael (see Genesis). **7** *Maridunum* = sea fort; same as *Cayr-Merdin* (Carmarthen) **8–11** cf. Drayton, *Poly-Olbion* 4.331ff. **13** the names are Sp's addition to Geoffrey, *History* 6.18. The princes of Powys were known as kings of *Mathraval* (in Montgomeryshire): Upton, *Variorum Sp.*, 3.226; *Ambrosius* = Uther's brother (II.x.67), Aurelius Ambrosius. **14** *characters:* cf. John 8:6 and III.xii.31. **20** *Aurora:* I.ii.6–7n. **22** i.e. Britomart's family *Tree*, another statement of the British myth (cf. II.x and III.ix.41–51) culminating in Elizabeth's advent. Cf. the Tree of Jesse (Is. 11:1), a Marian image assimilated into Elizabethan iconography. **27–42** cf. Geoffrey, *History* 8.19–12.17. **32** *Behold the man:* i.e. Malgo (Geoffrey, *History* 11.7). But cf. John 19:5 (And *Pilate* said unto them, Behold the man.). **41** *Armoricke:* Brittany. **42** *woe:* apocalyptic (Rev. 8:13). **45** Welsh kings. **46** *Raven* = emblem of Denmark. **47** *Lyon* = William the Conqueror: Geoffrey, *History* 7.3 (Sp's language is now that of the *Prophecies of Merlin*); also Gen. 49:9–10. **48** *Mona:* Anglesey, birthplace of the first Tudor, Henry VII. **49** *virgin:* Elizabeth I: Sp alludes to the apocalyptic nature of the Protestant fight against Spain. **50** *end is not:* Matt. 24.6 (apocalyptic). **56** *Angela:* rather mysterious Saxon queen, reputedly gave her name to England. **60** *Bladud:* British king of magical powers (cf. II.x.25).

Canto IV

2 the Amazonian queen *Penthesilea* fought with the Trojans, and is mentioned by Virgil (not Homer) at *Aeneid* 1.490ff.; *Debora*, used in the Elizabethan cult, was the judge and prophet who helped arrange Sisera's death in Judges 4; *Camilla* kills *Orsilochus* at *Aeneid* 11.690ff. **8–10** conventionally combining biblical (Ps. 69:1–15) and Petrarchan (*Canzoniere* 189). **17** *Marinell:* a Narcissus and an Adonis figure, associated with the *sea* (Lat./Ital. *mare*) and also reluctant to *marry* (Fr. *mari* = husband; Lat. *nolle* = to be unwilling). **18** Britomart rejects the *gold* because Chastity defeats Avarice (Ripa, 66). **19** *Cymoent:* named as *Cymodoce* at IV.xi.53 (the latter is a daughter of the sea-god Nereus). *Cymoent* cares for her son as Thetis cares for Achilles (*Met.* 13.162ff.); and Gk. *kuma* = wave. *Dumarin:* of the sea (cf. Merlin's home, iii.7). **25** *Proteus:* tricky shape-changer, old man of the sea, sophist, magician: cf. Merlin and, in xi and xii, Busirane. **29** *daffadillyes:* cf. the Narcissus myth; but *daffodils* signify grief because Proserpina was gathering them when she was abducted into the underworld (N. Comes, *Mythologiae* (1567) 3.16; Shakespeare, *Winter's Tale* (New Arden) IV.iv.116ff.).

Another seasonal myth thus enters the book. 30 *Continent:* note the pun, as at st. 10, l.2. 33 *Triton:* Neptune's son, controls sea creatures; *Dolphins:* symbols of love and (because of Arion) salvation. See also Plutarch, *Moralia* 984A ff. 41 *Liagore:* a Nereid in Hesiod's catalogue (*Theogony* 257). Sp tells of her the story recounted of Oenone (Ovid, *Heroides* 5.145ff.). *Apollo* = god of healing; *Paeon* = physician to the gods. 43 *Tryphon:* Sp follows Boccaccio *De gen. deorum* 7.36 in the name and in making him Aesculapius' brother: cf. I.v.36–44. 45 this is *Archimago's* last appearance in the poem. 51 *Hesperus:* I.ii.6–7n. 54 cf. I.ix.13–15. 55 *Cocytus, Herebus:* II.vii.56n., II.iv.41n. 59 cf. I.v.25.

Canto v

5–6 cf. III.i.15–17nn. 8 *Florimell* has a seasonal function as *Flora* (I.i.45–50n.); her relationship with the sea (through Marinell, etc.) suggests an additional, Venerean, role as the Venus Anadyomene (Venus born from the sea): cf. Botticelli's *Birth of Venus.* 15 *three . . . graceless:* a grotesque anti-triad of Graces in contrast to Belphœbe, Amoret, and Florimell, and to suggest the 3 lusts of 1 John 2:16. 27 cf. II.iii. 29 cf. Marinell; Adonis in III.vi; and Mortdant and Verdant (II.i, xii). 32 *Tobacco:* recently introduced (1584) and supposedly curative; Venus gives *Panachaea* to Aeneas at *Aeneid* 12.419; *Polygony* prevents blood flowing and is good for slow-healing wounds and frostbite (*frosen*, st. 31). 51 suggests the *Rose* of virginity, of Venus, and the Tudor rose, combined with the thornless rose which flourished in *Paradize* (st.40; Gen. 3:18), emblem of the Virgin Mary and Elizabeth (E. C. Wilson, *England's Eliza* (1939), 219n.).

Canto vi

2 *Jove, Venus, Phœbus:* astrologically fortunate (Fowler, *Spenser and the Numbers of Time,* 83n.). 3 *Morning dew:* Ps. 110:3, interpreted as referring to Christ's conception; cf. the medieval carol 'I sing of a mayden'. Like Christ, but also like Mary, she is born free from original sin. 4 *Chrysogonee:* Gk. *chrysos* + *gonē*, golden offspring or, more likely, *bearing gold* (also Gk. *gynē* = woman). Gk. *chrysogonos* = used of the Persians, supposedly descendants of Perseus, son of Danaë who was impregnated by Zeus as a golden shower (Aeschylus, *Persians* 79–80). An epithet of Mary in her Litany is *house of gold*; and the sunbeams piercing her womb (st.7) recall an image frequently used of Mary's impregnation (Upton in *Var. Spenser,* 3.250). *Amphisa* = double natured (Gk.). 6 *roses, violets* = love and chastity (though the violet is also Venerean). 7–9 *Nilus:* I.i.21n.; the moon, Apollo's *sister,* governs moisture, menstruation, and birth. The allegorical significance of sun and moon is supported by the echo of Rev. 12:6 where the woman clothed with the sun, having given birth, 'fled into the wildernes'. 11–26 cf.

Moschus, *Idyll* 1, 'Love the Runaway'. **20** *Cytherea* = Venus (from the island by which she was born from the sea). **27** *withouten paine:* like Mary, unlike Eve (Gen. 3:16); *Lucina:* moon as goddess of childbirth. **29** *Paphos*, on Cyprus, assoc. with Venus worship; *Gnidus:* site of Praxitelean statue of Venus. **30** cf. Gen. 1:24, 2:5. The name *Adonis* was associated with *Eden* (= pleasure); *Gardin of Adonis* (st.29) was a phrase signifying place of fruitful and/or fast-growing plants (Plato, *Phaedrus* 276B.). **31** *gates* signify life and death; and suggest the womb (Job 3:10) and double-headed *Janus*, guardian of the gates of the year and identified with Apollo and Diana (Macrobius, *Saturnalia* 1.9; cf. III.vi.7–9n.). *Janus* was a close relative of *Genius* understood as a priest of Nature rather than as a guardian angel. In contrast to II.xii.47–8, this is the nature god Agdistis mentioned in, e.g., Pausanias, *Description of Greece* 7.17. **32–3** cf. Virgil, *Aeneid* 6.713ff. **34** *increase:* Gen. 1:22, 28. **35** *some . . . some:* 1 Cor. 15:39, 'All flesh is not the same flesh'. **42** traditionally the seasons (excluding winter) were simultaneous in Eden and in the Golden Age (Gen. 1:12, *Met.* 1.107–10). **43** *middest:* II.xii.60n.; *mirtle* belongs to Venus, as at v.40. **44** *yvie, Eglantine, Caprifole* (honeysuckle): cf. II.v.29: the first is Bacchic (youth, wine, lust); the other two are Venerean. *Aeolus:* wind-god. **45** *Hyacinthus: Met.* 10.162ff. (accidentally killed by his lover, Phœbus Apollo); *Amaranthus* (Gk., = immortal, unfading), the flower Love-lies-bleeding. It was being gathered by Proserpina's attendants when she was abducted into Hades (Ovid, *Fasti* 4.439): cf. III.iv.29n. In Thomas Watson's *Amyntas* (1585), the eponymous lover dies through grief over Phillis and is changed into an amaranthus. **46–9** *transformed oft* bec. Adonis is, in the Orphic *Hymn to Adonis*, many-formed (cit. Comes, *Mythologiae* (1567), 5.16). Adonis was commonly interpreted as the sun, the killing boar as time and winter, and Venus as the earth, barren or fruitful according to the time of year. **50** *Psyche* (Gk., = Soul) quests for, and is finally married to, *Cupid*. The tale, seen by neo-Platonists as an allegory of the suffering soul's eventual union with the principle of divine love, was originally told in Apuleius, *Golden Ass* 5. Their child, *Pleasure*, is, punningly, the meaning of *Eden*. **53** *Scudamore:* shield of love, Amoret's lover and husband (IV.i., etc.)

Canto VII

1 ff. cf. Angelica in *OF* 1.33ff. **22** *Hyena:* traditionally treacherous and believed to desecrate corpses buried in consecrated ground. Here, Florimell's view of male sexual appetite. **26** *Myrrha:* III.ii.41n.; *Daphne* was pursued by Apollo (*Met.* 1.450ff). **26–7** Florimell turns to the sea; Venus was sea-born (v.8n.). Britomartis was saved by *fishermen* (Diodorus Siculus, *Library*, 5.76.3–4); but *fish* and *fishermen* are associated with lust (A. Alciati, *Emblemata* (Lyons 1551) p.83). The zodiacal sign *Pisces* marks Venus' exaltation (cf. viii.20ff.). 30 *Satyrane:* I.vi.20n. 31 *girdle:* contested for in IV.v., it is the symbol of 'chast love' and originally belonged to Venus (IV.v.3; *Iliad* 14.214ff.). In Latin it is the *cestus*, which suggests *castus* (spotless, chaste). 41 *Olympus:* Sp, like many, thought the Olympic Games were held there. 47–8 as a *Geauntesse, Argante* (pagan warrior in *Ger. Lib.*) is earth-born (Gk. *gē* = earth), not sea-born, and thus 'of the earth, earthly' (1 Cor. 15:47). *Typhoeus* (I.v.35), giant of storm (typhoons), rebelled against Jupiter (I.vii.8–10n.). *Ollyphant* is a mace-bearing 'geaunt' in Chaucer's fragmentary *Tale of Sir Thopas*. These terrible twins parody Belphœbe and Amoret and, more remotely, Apollo and Diana. 51 *Columbell:* dove (Ital.); Venus' bird, emblem of chaste love and lust. 52 *Palladine:* paladin = knight errant (orig. assoc. with Charlemagne); also, *Pallas* = virgin goddess of wisdom. 61 *Alcides:* Hercules (and his 12 labours).

Canto VIII

5–8 *Riphœan hils:* perpetually snowy Scythian mountains. The creation of the phantom Florimell recalls Archimago's machinations in I.i and the story of the 2 Helens, the real one of whom remained in Egypt while a phantom one accompanied Paris to Troy. 11 *Braggadocchio:* II.iii. 28 *Peridure:* one who endures (II.x.44); *Calidore:* the courteous knight of Book VI (but Lat. *calidus* = fierce, fiery). 30 *Proteus:* III.iv.25n.; *Phocas* = seals. The flower maiden now succumbs to the tyrannical force of winter (st.35); she will be released in IV.xii to marry Marinell. 37 for the topography, see Virgil, *Georgics* 4.418ff.; *Panope* is named as a Nereid at IV.xi.49. 41 cf. Archimago at I.ii.10. 45 *Paridell* suggests Trojan *Paris*; his emblem = that of Lechery at I.iv.25; cf. III.xii.20–1n.

Canto IX

3–7 *Malbecco* = evil goat (Ital. *male-becco*), symbol of lust and of horned cuckold. Married to *Hellenore* (Helen-again; Helen-whore), he is Menelaus to Paridell's abducting Paris. A parody of the outbreak of the Trojan war follows. The conjunction of old (man) and young (woman) symbolised disorder. 7 *Argus:* 100-eyed, set by jealous Juno to watch over Io (*Met.* 1.622ff.). 19 *Vulcan:* blacksmith to the gods and Venus's cuckolded husband. 22 *Minerva* (*Bellona* in 1590 text), goddess of war. The reference is to the battle of the giants against the gods. The giant *Enceladus* was reputedly killed by Athena/Minerva's chariot (Pausanias, *Description of Greece*, 8.47.1); but it was Jove who killed Typhoeus on Mount *Hemus*. Minerva bore the *Gorgon*'s head on her shield, symbol of chastity's power over lust; but in Britomart's case there is an additional suggestion of the virtuous armed Venus (E. Wind, *Pagan Mysteries in the Renaissance* (rev.edn 1967) p. 91n.). Cf. I.vii.33. 30 the game, *cottabos*, was played by Helen and Paris (Ovid, *Heroides* 17.75ff.). Sp glances of course at the *mistery* of Communion wine. **33–51**: completes the historical background of the British myth (II.x, III.iii) out of the *Iliad*, *Aeneid*, Geoffrey of Monmouth, etc. **35** *Scamander, Xanthus:* the same Trojan river, anciently often confused. **36** *Priam:* king of Troy. **42** *Latium:* Aeneas' western land, in Italy (*Aeneid* 7, etc.). **47** *Mnemon:* Memory (Gk.) **49–51** cf. II.x.5–12; and I.vii.46n. and I.x.58 for *Cleopolis.*

Canto x

12 *Hellene:* cf. *Aeneid* 6.517–19. **15** Malbecco lusts, the victim of cupidity in both its senses. Cf. III.iv.18n. **19** parodying the Florimell–Marinell story. **31** *Doucepere:* champion, one of Charlemagne's 12 *paladins* (III.vii.52n). **32** *Sanglamort:* bloody death. **33** *stolen* from Guyon at II.iii, returned at V.iii. **43** *bagpipes:* traditionally assoc. with lust. Cf. Una and the satyrs at I.vi. This episode says more about Malbecco than about Hellenore. **55–8** Jealousy is depicted many-eyed (cf. Argus, III.ix.7n.), carrying a *thorny* branch (= self-laceration): Ripa, 181–2, who includes the cockerel among Jealousy's emblems, hence in part the *clawes* of st.57.

Canto xi

1 *Proserpine* = queen of *hell*, assoc. with *serpents* because of her name (*serpere* = to crawl like a serpent (Lat.)): Tervarent, col.344. **3** *Ollyphant:* III.vii.47–8n. **7** *boy:* Cupid, Scudamour's emblem. **10** *Busirane:* Egyptian tyrant assoc. with blood lust and killed by Hercules (*Met.* 9.182–3), identif. with the Pharaoh of Exodus; *seven monethes:* Florimell too is imprisoned for this period (IV.xi.4), suggesting the duration of winter (Proteus, her gaoler, recalls the Egyptian king Proteus: Alexander Ross, *Mystagogus Poeticus* (1648 edn) p.371). **22** *Earthes children:* the giants/Titans (I.vii.8–10n.). **25** *it selfe divide:* as the Red Sea divided to enable the Israelites to escape Busiris' Egyptian bondage (Exod. 14:21ff.). **26** *Mulciber* = Vulcan (III.ix.19n): the *fire* is that of lust or envy (Tervarent, col.183). **28–46** cf. Arachne's tapestry of love's lusts at *Met.* 6.103–28 (and the tapestry in Malecasta's castle, III.i). For the details of Apollo's lusts, see *ibid.* and *Met.* 4.171ff. (st.36), *Met.* 10.162ff. and 2.542ff. (st.37), *Met.* 2.1ff. (st.38), and *Met.* 6.124 (st.39). **40–1** cf. *Aeneid* 1.145ff. **42** cf. *Met.* 6.115–20. **43** *Saturne: Met.* 6.125–126. **45–6** cf. Petrarch's *Triumph of Love.* **47–9** the *Pavone* (peacock) of pride derives its eyes from Argus (x.55–8n.); *Iris* is the rainbow goddess. This is the Cupid of lust and earthly love in contrast to the divine Cupid of II.viii.5. The *Dragon* that traditionally guards virginity is, symbolically, wounded. **54** *Be bold:* the Bluebeard story was known in the Renaissance; this motto appears over the Fox's hall portal (R. Chambers, *Book of Days* (1869) 1.291–2).

Canto XII

2 symbolic of the manifestation of a deity (Exod. 19:16, 1 Kings 19:11–12). **3** *laurell* = the emblem of victory. Sp's masque of Cupid draws on classical (Ovidian), medieval, Petrarchan, and theatrical conventions. The procession of paired masquers depicts the effects of love. **7** *Fancy:* the power of imagination (II.ix.49–52n.); *ympe:* Ganymede (xi.34); Hercules (*Alcides*) loved *Hylas* (Apollonius Rhodius, *Argonautica* 1.1207ff.). **10** *Albanese:* alluding to the Scottish tradition of wearing full-sleeved shirts (*Spenser Newsletter* 16 (1985) 15–16). **13** *Hope:* the secular counterpart of Speranza (I.x.14), just as *Feare* (st.12) is the secular counterpart of Obedience at I.x.17, since obedience here means *fear* of the lord (*timor domini*): Brooks-Davies *Sp's FQ: A Critical Commentary*, p.95. **16** *Griefe ... Pincers:* cf. Amendment's pincers, I.x.26. **17** *Fury:* cf. I.iv.33–4, II.iv.7ff. **18** *hony-lady Bee:* Cupid is linked with bees (his arrows = the stings of love); and note the *honey* in Florimell's name (III.i.15–16n.). **20–1:** the arrow-pierced *hart* is emblematic of love (Tervarent, col.102): cf. II.i.37, III.iv.6. **22–3** Cupid is at the sovereign centre of his triumph (A. D. S. Fowler, *Triumphal Forms* (1970) p.52); he rides on a *lion* to signify love's power (Sp, *Shepheardes Calender*, December, 57–8, love in Leo); love and lions are connected also in Tervarent, col.247. **30–1** the iconography suggests Amoret's fear of the male; the *brass* that predominates (st.29,30) is Venerean (H. C. Agrippa, *3 Books of Occult Philosophy* (1651 edn), 1.28, p.59); the *pillour* signifies both chastity and virtue in general (Tervarent, cols 107–108, s.v. *colonne*). **31** *figuring:* III.iii.14. **36** *reverse:* reversing black magic charms restores normality: e.g. Circe at *Met.* 14.300–1. **42** cf. Guyon's effect on the Bower of Bliss, II.xii.83. **44** *Deare:* the deer/dear pun was common because of the hunt of love *topos*: cf. Petrarch, *Rime*, 190 and Spenser's own *Amoretti*, 67. **46** *Hermaphrodite:* neo-Platonic image of perfect mystical union from Aristophanes' fable in Plato's *Symposium*: Wind, *Pagan Mysteries in the Renaissance* (1967), pp.200–2, 211–14. It also signifies marriage (the 'one flesh' of Gen. 2:24). The *Roman* is unidentified (see Donald Cheney in *Publications of the Modern Language Association of America*, 87 (1972), pp.192–200), but Roman Ovid tells the story of Hermaphroditus in *Met.* 4. 285–388. The notion of growing together like tree trunks (*stocks:* st.45) comes from *Met.* 11.375–7. **47** *Swayns:* Amoret and Scudamour; *pleasure:* cf. III.vi.46–9 above.

GLOSSARY

Abace, abase, to lower, to hang down.

Aband, to abandon.

Abashment, fear.

Abeare, to behave, conduct.

Abet, abett, to aid, support, maintain, asserting falsely.

Abid, abode, remained.

Abie, aby, abye, to pay the penalty of, to atone for, suffer for, abide by.

Abject, to throw or cast down.

Abode, remained, a delay, stay.

Abolish, to wipe out.

Aborde, harbour.

Abouts, about.

Abrade, to rouse, wake up.

Abray (pret. **abrayde**), to start up suddenly, to awake, to quake with sudden fear.

Abusion, abuse, deceit, fraud.

Accloye, to clog up, choke, encumber, hinder.

Accoasting, skimming along near the ground.

Accorage, to encourage.

Accord, to grant, to agree, to reconcile, an agreement.

According, agreeably to, according to, accordingly.

Accoste, to go side by side, to adjoin, border.

Accourting, entertaining (courteously).

Accoy, to coy, caress.

Accoyl, to assemble, gather together.

Accrew, to increase.

Achates (Acates), purchased provisions, cates.

Acquight, acquit, acquite, to deliver, release, acquitted, free.

Adamants, crystals.

Adaw, to adaunt, tame, moderate.

Addeeme, to adjudge.

Addoom, to adjudge.

Address, to prepare, adjust, direct, clothe, arm.

Addrest, ready.

Adjoyne, to approach, join.

Admiraunce, admiration.

Admire, to wonder at.

Adore, to adorn.

Adorne, ornament.

Adowne, down.

Adrad, adred, adredde, afraid, terrified.

Adrad, to be frightened.

Advaunce, to extol.

Adventure, chance, opportunity, to attempt.

Adview, to view.

Advize, advise, to consider, perceive, take thought of, bethink.

Advizement, consideration.

Adward, an award, to award.

Æmuling, emulating, rivalling (æmuled).

Afeard, afraid.

Affear, to frighten.

Affect, affection.

Affection, passion.

Affide, affyde, betrothed, intrusted.

Afflicted, low, humble.

Afford, to consent.

Affrap, to strike, to strike down, to encounter, to assault.

Affray, to terrify, fray, terror.

Affrende, to make friends.

Affret, encounter.

Affront, to confront, encounter, oppose.

Affy, to betroth, espouse, entrust.

Affyaunce, betrothal.

Afore, in front, before.

Aggrace, favour, kindness, goodwill, to make gracious.

Aggrate, to please, delight, charm, treat politely.

Aglet, point, tag.

Agree, to settle, to cause to agree.

Agreeably, alike, in a manner to agree.

Agrise, agrize, agryse, agryze, to cause to shudder, to terrify, to make disgusted.

Agryz'd, having a terrible look, disfigured.

Aguise, aguize, to deck, adorn, fashion, accoutre, to disguise.

Alablaster, alabaster.

Albee, although.

Aleggeaunce, alleviation.

Alew, howling.

Algate, algates, altogether, wholly, by all means, in all ways, at all events.

All, although.

Almes, a free allowance, alms.

Alone (only), without compulsion.

Alow, downwards.

Als, also.

Amaine, violently, by force.

Amate, to daunt, subdue, to stupefy, terrify, to keep company with.

Amaze, amazement.

Amenage, to manage, handle.

Amenaunce, carriage, behaviour.

Amis, amice, a proestly vestment.

Amount, to mount up, ascend.

Amove, to move, remove.

Andvile, anvil.

Annoy, annoyance, grief, hurt.

Antickes, antiques, ancient or fantastic figures.

Apace, fast, copiously.

Appall, to falter, to weaken.

Appay, apay (præt. and p. p. appay'd, appaid), to please, satisfy, pay.

Appeach, to impeach, accuse.

Appease, to cease from.

Appele, to accuse, to offer.

Appellation, appeal.

Apply, to attend to, to bend one's steps to.

Approvaunce, approval.

Approven, to put to the proof, to prove.

Arborett, little grove.

Aread, areed (p. p. ared), to tell, say, declare, describe, inform, teach, interpret, explain, appoint, detect.

Arear, areare, arere, arreare, to the rear, backward, aback.

Aret, arret, to allot, entrust, adjudge.

Arew, in a row, in order.

Arguments, signs, indications.

Arights, rightly.

Arke, box, chest.

Arras, tapestry of Arras.

Arraught (pret. of **arreach**), seized forcibly.

As, as if.

Askaunce, sideways.

Aslake, to slake, abate, appease.

Aslope, on the slope, aside.

Assay, to try, attempt, assail, attack, an attempt, trial, value.

Asseige, to besiege.

Assignment, design.

Assoil, assoyl, to absolve, determine, set free, let loose, renew, remove.

Assott, to befool, to beguile, bewilder.

Assure, to promise, assert confidently.

Asswage, to grow mild.

Assyn, to mark or point out.

Astart, to start up suddenly.

Astond, astound, astonished, stunned.

Astonish, to stun.

Astonying, confounding.

Attach, to seize, take prisoner (attack).

Attaine, attayne, to find, reach, fall in with.

Attaint, to stain, obscure.

Attempt, to tempt.

Attendement, intent.

Attent, attention.

Attone (atone), at one, together, reconciled.

Attone, attons, at once, together.

Attrapt, dressed.

Atween, atweene, between.
Atwixt, between, at intervals.
Aumayl, to enamel.
Avale, to fall, sink, lower, descend, bow down.
Avaunt, depart.
Avauntage, advantage.
Avaunting, advancing (boastfully).
Avenge, revenge.
Avengement, revenge.
Aventred, thrust forward (at a venture).
Aventring, pushing forward.
Avize, avyze, to perceive, consider, regard, view, take note of, reflect, bethink, advise.
Avizefull, observant.
Avoid, to depart, go out.
Avoure, 'to make avoure'=to justify, maintain.
Awarned, made, was made aware.
Awayte, to wait for, watch.
Awhape, to terrify, frighten.
Aygulets (aglets), tags, points of gold.
Aym, direction.

Bace, low.
Bace, 'bad bace'=challenged.
Baffuld, disgraced (as a recreant knight).
Baile, to deliver, custody.
Bains, banns (of marriage).
Bale, grief, sorrow, affliction, trouble; **bales,** ruins; **baleful,** full of bale, destructive, deadly; **balefulnesse,** ruin.
Balke, to disappoint, to deal at cross purposes, a ridge between two furrows.
Ban, banne, to curse (**band,** cursed).
Band, forbid, banish, assemble.
Bane, death, destruction.
Banket, banquet.
Bannerall, a standard (shaped like a swallow's tail).
Barbe, equipments of a horse, horse armour.
Barbican, a watch-tower.
Bard, ornamented with bars (ornaments of a girdle).

Base, low, the lower part.
Baseness, a low humble condition.
Bases, armour for the legs.
Bash, to be abashed.
Bastard, base, lowborn.
Basted, sewed slightly.
Bate, did bite.
Bate, to bait, attack.
Battailous, ready for battle, in order for battle.
Battill (properly to **fatten**), to be of good flavour.
Batton, stick, club.
Bauldricke, belt.
Bay, a standstill, a position in which one is kept at bay.
Baye, to bathe.
Bayes (baies), laurels.
Bayt, bait, artifice, to bait (a bull), to cause to abate, to let rest.
Beades, prayers.
Beadroll, a list.
Beare, bier.
Beath'd, plunged.
Beauperes, fair companions.
Beckes, beaks.
Become, to come to, go to, to suit, to happen.
Bed, bad.
Bedight, dressed, equipped, decked, adorned, 'ill-bedight', disfigured.
Beduck, to dive, dip.
Befell, was fitting, proper.
Beginne, beginning.
Begord, stained with gore.
Behave, to employ, use.
Beheast, behest, command.
Behight, call, name, address, pronounce, promise, command, adjudged, entrusted.
Behoofe, profit.
Behote, to promise; **behott,** promised.
Belaccoyle, kind salutation or greeting.
Belamoure, belamy, a lover.
Belay, adorn.
Belame, fair lady.
Belgard, fair (or kind) looks.
Belyde, counterfeited.

Ben (bene, been), are.
Bend, band.
Bent, long stalks of (**bent**) grass.
Beraft, bereft.
Bere, to bear, bier.
Beseeke, beseech.
Beseene, 'well-beseen', of good appearance, comely.
Beseme, beseeme, to be seemly, to seem fit, to suit, fit, become, appear.
Besitting, befitting.
Bespeake, address.
Bespredd, adorned.
Bestad (bested, bestedded), situated, placed, placed in peril, treated, attended, beset, 'ill-bested'=in a bad plight.
Bestaine, to stain.
Bestow, to place.
Bestrad, bestrided.
Bet, did beat.
Betake (pret. **betooke**), to take (into), to deliver, bestow, betake one's self.
Beteeme, to deliver, give.
Bethinke, to make up one's mind.
Bethrall, to take captive.
Betide, betyde, to befall, to happen to, **betid,** befall, befallen.
Bever, the front part of a helmet (covering the mouth).
Bevy, company (of ladies).
Bewaile, to choose, select.
Bewray, to reveal, betray, accuse.
Bickerment, bickering, strife.
Bid, to pray.
Bide, to bid, offer.
Bilive, bylive, blive, forthwith, quickly.
Bils, battle-axes.
Blame, to blemish, injury, hurt.
Blanckt, confounded, put out of countenance.
Blast, to wither.
Blaze, to blazon forth, proclaim.
Blemishment, a blemish.
Blend (pret. and p. part. **blent**), to mix, confuse, confound, defile, blemish, stain, obscure; **blent,** blinded, obscured, blotted.

Bless, to preserve, deliver, to brandish.
Blesse, bliss.
Blin, to cease.
Blincked, dimmed.
Blind, dark.
Blist, wounded, struck.
Blist, blessed.
Bloosme, blossom, bloom.
Blot, blotten, to defame, blemish.
Blubbred, wet or stained with tears.
Boads, bodes, portends.
Bode, abode.
Bollet, bullet.
Bond, bound.
Boone, prayer, petition.
Boord, bord, to accost, to address, talk with, conversation, go side by side.
Boot, to avail, profit, booty, gain.
Booting, availing.
Bore, borne.
Borde, coast.
Bordraging (pl. **bordrags**), border ravaging, border raid.
Bosse, middle of shield.
Bouget, budget.
Bought, fold.
Boult, to sift, bolt.
Bounse, to beat.
Bountie, bounty, goodness; bounteous, generous, good; bounty-hed, generosity.
Bourne, boundary.
Bout, about.
Bouzing-can, a drinking-can.
Bownd, to lead (by a direct course).
Bowre, chamber, inner room, to lodge, shelter.
Bowrs, muscles (of the shoulder).
Boy, a term of reproach.
Boystrous, rough, rude (as applied to a club).
Brame, sharp passion (cf. O.E. **breme,** severe, sharp).
Bransles, dances, brawls.
Brast, burst.
Brave, fair, beautiful.
Bravely, gallantly, splendidly.
Brawned, muscular, brawny.

Bray, (braie), to cry out suddenly, cry aloud, utter aloud, gasp out.

Braynepan, skull.

Breaded, braided, embroidered.

Breare, brere, briar.

Breech, breeches.

Breede, work, produce.

Breem, boisterous, rough, sharp.

Brenne, to burn.

Brent, burnt.

Brickle, brittle.

Brim, margin of the horizon.

Broch, to commence, broach.

Brode, abroad.

Brond, sword.

Brondiron, sword.

Bronds, embers, **brands.**

Brood, a brooding-place (? an error for **bood**=O.E. **bood** or **abood,** an abode, resting-place; cf. **bode**).

Brooke, to endure, bear **brook.**

Brouzes, twigs.

Brunt, assault.

Brust, burst.

Brutenesse, brutishnesse, brutality, brute-like state.

Bryze, gadfly.

Buckle to, make ready.

Buff (pl. **buffes),** a blow.

Bug, apparition, bugbear, goblin.

Buegle, wild ox.

Bullion, pure gold.

Burdenous, heavy.

Burganet, headpiece, helmet.

Burgein, burgeon, bud.

Busse, kiss.

But-if, unless.

Buxom, obedient, yielding, tractable.

By-and-by, one by one, singly.

Byde, abide; **byding,** abiding, remaining.

Bylive, quickly, also active. See **Blive, belive.**

Bynempt, named, appointed.

Cabinet, cottage, little cabin.

Caitive, caytive, subject, captive, vile, base, menial, rascal.

Call, caul, cowl, cap.

Camis, camus, a light loose robe of some light material (as silk, etc.), chemise.

Can or Gan (an auxiliary of the past tense), did.

Cancred, cankerd, corrupt.

Canon bitt, a smooth round bit (for horses).

Capitayn, captain.

Caprifole, woodbine.

Captivaunce, captivity.

Captived, taken captive, enslaved.

Capuccio, hood (of a cloak), capuchin.

Card, chart.

Care, sorrow, grief, injury; **careful,** sorrowful; **careless,** free from care, uncared for.

Carke, care, sorrow, grief.

Carl, carle, an old man, churl.

Carriage, burden.

Cast, to consider, plot, resolve, purpose, time, period, opportunity; 'nere their utmost cast',=almost dead, a couple.

Castory, colour (red or pink).

Caudron, caldron.

Causen, to assign a cause or reason, explain.

Caved, made hollow.

Centonel, a sentinel.

Certes, certainly.

Cesse, to cease.

Cesure, a breaking off, stop.

Chaffar, to chaffer, exchange.

Chalenge, to claim, to track, follow, accusation.

Chamelot water, camlet watered.

Champain, champian, champion, open country, plain.

Championesse, a female warrior.

Character, image.

Charge, assault, attack.

Charget, chariot.

Chauff, chaufe, to become warm, to be irritated; to **chafe,** rage.

Chaunticleer, the cock.

Chaw, jaw, to chew.

Chayre, chary.

Cheare, chere, countenance, favour, cheer; **chearen,** to cheer up.

Checked, chequered.

Checklaton (O.E. **ciclaton**), a rich kind of cloth.

Cherry, to cherish.

Chevisaunce, enterprise, undertaking, performance, bargain.

Chickens (faithlesse), heathen brood.

Childed, gave birth to a child.

Chimney, fireplace.

Chine, black.

Chorle, churl.

Chynd, cut, divided.

Clarkes, scholars.

Clove, cleft, did cleave.

Cleane, cleene, clene, pure; **clean,** entirely.

Cleep, to call.

Clemence, clemency.

Clew, plot, purpose (properly a hank of thread).

Clift, cliff.

Clombe, climbed, mounted.

Close, secret; **closely,** secretly.

Clouches, clutches.

Cloyd, wounded.

Coast, to approach.

Coch, coach.

Cognizaunce, knowledge, recollection.

Colled, embraced, fondled.

Colour, to hide.

Combrous, laborious, troublesome.

Commen, common, to commune, discourse.

Comment, to relate (falsely).

Commodity, advantage.

Commonly, in common, equally.

Compacte, (?) compacted, concerted.

Compacted, close; **compacture,** a close knitting together.

Companie, companion.

Compare, to collect, procure.

Compasse, circuit.

Compast, contrived; **compast creast,** the round part of the helmet.

Compel, to cite, call to aid.

Complement, perfection (of character), union.

Complish, to accomplish.

Comportaunce, behaviour.

Compound, to agree.

Comprize, to comprehend, understand.

Comprovinciall, to be contained in the same province with.

Compyle, to heap up, frame, settle, reconcile.

Conceiptful, thoughtful.

Concent, to harmonize.

Concert, harmony.

Concrew, to grow together.

Condign, worthy.

Conditions, qualities.

Conduct, conductor, guide, management.

Congé, leave.

Conjure, to conspire.

Consort, company, companion, concert; to combine, unite (in harmony).

Constraint, distress, uneasiness.

Containe, to restrain, control.

Contrive, to wear out, spend.

Controverse, debate, controversy.

Convent, to convene, summon.

Convert, to turn.

Convince, to conquer, overthrow.

Coosen, kindred.

Coportion, an equal portion.

Corage, heart, mind, wrath.

Corbe, corbel, a projecting piece of wood, stone, or iron, placed so as to support a weight of material.

Cordwayne, cordovan leather.

Coronall, a wreath, garland.

Corse, a body, bulk, frame.

Corsive, corrosive.

Cott, a little abode.

Couched, bent, laid (in order).

Could, knew.

Count, an object of interest or account.

Countenance, to make a show of.

Countercast, counterplot.

Counterchaunge, return of a blow.

Counterfesaunce, a counterfeiting.

Counterpoys, to counterbalance.

Countervayle, to oppose, resist.

Couplement, couple.

Coure, to cover, protect.

Courst, chaced.

Couth, could.

Covert, concealed.

Covetise, covetize, covetousness.

Craggy, knotty.

Crake, to boast, boast, boasting.

Crank, a winding.

Crapples, grapples, claws.

Crased helth, impaired health.

Creasted, crested, tufted.

Cremosin, crimson.

Crime, accusation, reproach, fault.

Crisped, curly (hair).

Crooke (cross), gibbet.

Croslet, a little cross.

Cros-cut, to pierce or cut across.

Cruddy, curdled.

Cuffing (or cuffling), striking.

Culver, dove.

Culvering, culverin, a sort of cannon.

Cumbrous, troublesome.

Curats, curiets, cuirasses.

Curelesse, hard to be cured, incurable.

Curtaxe, cutlass.

Dædale, skilful.

Daint, daynt, dainty; (superl. dayntest), dainty; rare, valuable.

Dallie, to trifle; dalliaunce, idle talk, trifling.

Dame, lady.

Damnify, to injure, damage.

Damozel, damsel.

Danisk, Danish.

Darrayne, to prepare, get ready, for battle.

Darred, dazzled, frightened ('a darred lark' is generally explained as a lark caught (? frightened) by means of a looking-glass).

Dayesman, a judge, arbitrator.

Daze, to dazzle, dim, to confound.

Dead-doing, death-dealing.

Deaded, deadened.

Dealth, bestows.

Deare, valuable, precious.

Deare, hurt, injury, sore, sad, sorely.

Dearling, darling.

Deaw, to bedew.

Debate, to contend, strive, battle, strife; debatement, debate.

Debonaire, gracious, courteous.

Decay, to destroy, perish, relax, destruction, ruin, death.

Deceaved, taken by deceit.

Decesse, decease.

Decreed, determined on.

Decrewed, decreased.

Deeme (pret. dempst), to judge, deem; 'deeme his payne'=adjudge his punishment.

Deering-dooers, doers of daring deeds.

Deface, to defeat.

Defame, disgrace, dishonour.

Defaste, defaced, destroyed.

Defeasaunce, defeat.

Defeature, defeat.

Defend, to keep or ward off.

Define, to settle decide.

Deforme, shapeless, deformed.

Defray, to avert (by a proper setlement), appease.

Degendered, degenerated.

Delay, to temper, stop, remove.

Delices, delights; delightsome, delightful.

Delve, dell, hole, cave.

Demayne, demeane, demeasnure, demeanour, bearing, treatment.

Dempt. See Deems.

Denay, to deny.

Dent, dint, blow.

Depainted, depicted.

Depart, to divide, separate, remove, departure.

Depend, to hang down.

Deprave, to defame.

Dernly, secretly, grievously, severely.

Der-doing, performance of daring deeds.

Derring-doe, daring deeds, warlike deeds.

Derth, scarcity.

Deryve, to draw away, transfer.

Descrie, descry, to perceive, discover, reveal.

Descrive, to describe.

Destine, to denote.

Despairefull drift, hopeless cause.

Desperate, despairing.

Despight, anger, malice, a scornful defiance.

Despightful, despiteous, malicious.

Despoyl, to unrobe, undress.

Desse, dais.

Desynde, directed.

Detaine, detention.

Devicefull, full of devices (as masques, triumphs, etc.).

Devise, devize, to guess at, purpose, to describe, talk; devized, painted; devized of, reflected on.

Dew, due; dewfull, due.

Diapase, diapason.

Difference, choice.

Diffused, scattered.

Dight, to order, to arrange, prepare, dress, deck, mark.

Dilute, to spread abroad, enlarge upon.

Dinting, striking.

Dint, scar, dent.

Disaray, disorder.

Disaccord, to withhold consent.

Disadvaunce, to lower, to draw back.

Disadventrous, unfortunate, unsuccessful, unhappy; disadventure, mishap, misfortune.

Disburden, to unburden.

Discharge, to acquit oneself of, account for.

Discide, to cut in two.

Disciple, to discipline.

Disclaim, to expel.

Disclose (pret. discloste), to unfold, transform, set free, disengage.

Discoloured, many-coloured.

Discomfited, disconcerted.

Discommend, to speak disparagingly of.

Discounsell, to dissuade.

Discoure, discure, to discover.

Discourse, shifting.

Discourteise, discourteous.

Discreet, differing.

Discust, thrown or shook off.

Disease, to distress, uneasiness; diseased, ill at ease, afflicted.

Disentrayle, to draw forth, to cause to flow.

Disgrace, deformity.

Disguizement, disguise.

Dishable, to disparage.

Disleall (disloyal), perfidious.

Dislikeful, disagreeable.

Disloignd, separated.

Dismall, fatal.

Dismay, to subdue, defeat, grieve, disquiet, defeat, ruin; dismayfull, terrifying.

Dismayd, mismade, deformed.

Dismayl, to take off a coat of mail.

Dispairful, despairing. See Despairefull.

Disparage, disparagement.

Dispart, to divide.

Dispence, to pay for, expense, abundance.

Dispiteous, cruel.

Display, to spread out, discover.

Disple, to discipline.

Displeasance, displeasaunce, displeasure.

Disport, play, sport.

Disprad, dispred, spread abroad.

Dispraize, to disparage.

Dispredden (pl.), spread out.

Disprofesse, to abandon.

Dispurvayaunce, want of provisions.

Disseise, disseize, dispossess.

Disshivered, shivered to pieces.

Dissolute, weak.

Distayne, to defile.

Distent, beaten out.

Disthronize, to dethrone.

Distinct, marked.

Distraine, to rend.

Distraught, distracted, drawn apart, separated.

Distroubled, greatly troubled.

Dite, dighte, to make ready.

Ditt, ditty, song.

Diverse, distracting, diverting.

Diverst, diverged, turned off.

Divide, to play a florid passage in music.

Divorced, separated by force.

Doale, dole, destruction.

Documents, instructions.

Doe, to cause.

Doffe, to put off.

Dole, doole, sorrow, grief; **doolefull, sorrowful.**

Dolor (dolour), grief.

Dome, doome, doom, judgment, censure.

Don, to put on.

Done, donne, to do; 'of well to **donne'**=of well-doing; **doen,** to cause.

Doomefull, threatening doom.

Dortours, sleeping apartments.

Doted, foolish.

Doubt, fear (also to fear), a matter of doubt; **doubtfull,** fearful.

Drad, dred, dread, dreaded, feared, an object of reverence; **dreddest,** most dread.

Draft, drift, aim, purpose.

Drapet, cloth.

Draught (=draft), stratagem, aim.

Dread, fury; **dreadful,** fearful.

Dreare, drere, dreriment, grief, sorrow, dreadful force; **drerihed, drearyhood, dryrihed,** dreariness, affliction.

Drent, drowned.

Dresse, to dispose, adorn.

Drevill, a slave.

Droome, a drum.

Droupe, to droop.

Drousy-hed, drowsiness.

Drouth, drought.

Drover, a boat.

Drugs, dregs.

Dumpish, heavy.

Duraunce, bondage.

Durefull, enduring.

Duresse, confinement.

Dye, lot, destiny.

Earne, to yearn, to be grieved.

Earst, erst, first, soonest, previously,
at earst, at length.

Easterlings, men of the East (Norwegians, Danes, etc.).

Eath, ethe, easy.

Edge, to sharpen.

Edifye, to build, inhabit.

Eek, eke, to increase.

Effierced, made fierce, inflamed.

Efforce, to oppose.

Efforced, efforst, forced, constrained, compelled (to yield).

Effraid, scared.

Eft, afterwards, again, forthwith, moreover.

Eftsoones, soon after, forthwith.

Eide, seen.

Eld, age, old age.

Elfe, fairy.

Els (elles), else, elsewhere, otherwise.

Embace, embase, to bring or cast down, humiliate, **embaste,** debased, dishonoured.

Embar, to guard, confine.

Embassage, embassy, message.

Embatteil, to arm for battle.

Embaulm, to anoint.

Embay, to bathe.

Embayl, to bind up.

Embosome, to foster.

Emboss, to overwhelm, press hard, to surround, enclose.

Embosse, to adorn, ornament, array.

Embow, to arch over, to curve, bend.

Embowell, to take out the bowels.

Emboyl, to boil (with anger), **emboyled,** heated.

Embrace, to brace, to fasten, or bind, to protect.

Embracement, an embrace.

Embrave, to decorate.

Embrease, embroder, to embroider.

Embrewe, to stain with blood.

Embusied, occupied.

Eme, uncle.

Emeraud, emerald.

Emmove, to move.

Emong, among; **emongest,** amongst.

Empare, empair, to diminish, impair, hurt.

Emparlaunce, treaty.

Empart, assign.

Empassioned, empassionate, moved or touched with passion, feeling.

Empeach, to hinder, prevent, hindrance.

Empeopled, dwelt.

Emperce, empierce, to pierce through (pret. **emperst, empierst**).

Emperill, to endanger.

Empight, fixed, settled.

Emplonged, plunged.

Empoysoned, poisoned.

Emprise, emprize, enterprise, attempt.

Empurpled, purple-dyed.

Enbosome, to fix firmly.

Enchace, enchase, to adorn, embellish, to honour with befitting terms, engrave, dart.

Encheason, reason, cause, occasion.

Encomberment, hindrance.

Endamage, to damage, do harm.

Endangerment, danger.

Endew, to endow.

Endite, to censure.

Endlong, from end to end, continuously.

Endosse, write on the back, endorse.

Endure, to harden.

Enfelon'd, made fell or fierce.

Enfested. See Infest.

Enfierce, to make fierce.

Enforme, to fashion.

Enfouldred, hurled out like thunder and lightning.

Engin, wiles, deceit, contrivance.

Englut, to glut, fill.

Engore, to gore, wound.

Engorge, to devour, glut.

Engraffed, engraft, implanted, fixed.

Engrasp, to grasp.

Engrave, to bury, to cut, pierce.

Engreeve, engrieve, to grieve, to be vexed.

Engroste, made thick.

Enhaunse, to lift up, raise.

Enlargen, enlarge, to set at large, deliver.

Enlumine, to illumine.

Enmove, to move. See **Emmove.**

Enrace, to implant.

Enraunge, to range.

Enraunged, ranged in order.

Enrold, encircled.

Enseames, encloses.

Ensew, ensue, to follow after, pursue; **ensuing,** following.

Ensnarle, to ensnare, entangle.

Entayle, to carve, inlay, (sb.) carving.

Enterdeale, negotiation.

Enterpris, to undertake.

Enterprize, to entertain, take in hand.

Entertain, take, receive (pay); **entertayne, entertainment,** hospitality.

Entertake, to entertain.

Entire, inward, internal; **entyrely,** earnestly, entirely.

Entraile, entrayl, to twist, entwine, interlace.

Entraile, twisting, entanglement.

Entrall, the lowest part, depth (bowels).

Entreat, to treat of, treat.

Enure, to use, practise; **enured,** accustomed, committed habitually.

Envy, to be angry, indignant, to emulate.

Enwallowe, roll about.

Enwombed, pregnant.

Enwrap, to wrap up.

Equipage, array, equipment, to array, equip.

Ermelin, an ermine.

Ermine, skin of the ermine.

Erne, to yearn.

Errant, wandering.

Errour, wandering.

Eschew, escape.

Esloyne, to withdraw.

Espiall, sight, appearance, observation.

Essoyne, to excuse.

Estate, state, rank.

Eterne, eternal; **eternize,** to make eternal.

Ethe, easy.

Eugh, yew; **ewghen,** of yew.

Evangely, gospel.

Evill, poor, unskilful.

Exanimate, lifeless.

Excheat, gain, profit, escheat.
Expire, breathe out, to fulfil a term, put an end to.
Express, to press out.
Extasie, surprise.
Extent, stretched out.
Extirpe, to root out.
Extort, extorted.
Extract, descended.
Extreate, extraction.
Ewfts, efts.
Eyas, newly-fledged young.
Eyne, eyes.

Face, to carry a false appearance.
Fact, feet, deed.
Fail, fayl, to deceive, to cause to fail.
Fain, fayne, glad, eager; **fayned,** desired; **faynes,** delights.
Fain, fayne, to feign, dissemble, to mistake, imagine; 'fained dreadful'=apparently dreadful.
Faitour, faytour, cheat, deceiver, vagabond, villain.
Falsed, falsified, deceived, insecure, weak; **falses,** falsehoods; **falser,** a liar.
Faltring, faltering.
Fantasy, fantazy, fancy, apprehension.
Fare, to go, proceed, act, deal.
Farforth, very far.
Faste, having a face.
Fastnesse, stronghold.
Fate, destined term of life; **fatal,** ordained by fate.
Fault, to offend, be in error.
Favour, feature.
Favourlesse, not showing favour.
Fay, a fairy, faith.
Fear, feare, companion, **to fear,** together.
Fear, fearen, to frighten, 'feard – of,' alarmed by.
Fearfull, timid.
Feastfull, festival.
Feature, fashion, form, character.
Fee, tenure, pay, service, property.
Feeble, enfeebled; **feblesse,** feebleness.

Feeld (golden), an emblazoned field (of a knight's shield).
Feend, fiend, devil.
Feld, let fall, thrown down.
Fell, befell, gall.
Fell, fierce, cruel; **felly,** cruelly; **fellonest,** most fell; **fellonous,** wicked, fell; **fellnesse,** cruelty, fierceness.
Feminitee, womanhood.
Feood, feud, enmity.
Fensible, fit for defence, defensible.
Fere, companion, husband.
Ferme, lodging.
Ferry, a ferry boat.
Fett, to fetch, fetched (rescued).
Fleur-de-luce, the iris. See **Delice.**
Feutre, fewtre, to place the spear in the rest, to prepare for battle.
File, to defile.
File, to polish, smoothe.
Fine, end.
Firm, to fix firmly.
Fit, to be fitting. 'Of loves were fitted' =were suited, furnished with lovers.
Fit, fitt, emotion, passion, grief, a musical strain.
Flaggy, loose.
Flake, a flash.
Flamed, inflamed.
Flatling, flatwise, with the flat side (of the sword).
Flaw, a gust of wind.
Fleet, to sail, float, to flit.
Flex, flax.
Flist, fleet, swift, changing, insubstantial, light.
Flit, flitte, to move, change, flee; **flitting,** fleeting, yielding.
Flore, ground, spot.
Flout, mock, deride.
Flushing, rapidly flowing.
Fodder, grass.
Foen, foes.
Foile, a leaf (of metal).
Folkmote, a meeting, assembly.
Fond, foolish, doting; **fondling,** fool.
Fondly, foolishly.
Fond, found, tried.

Fone, foes.

Food, feud.

Foolhappie, undesigned.

Foolhardise, foolhardiness, folly.

For, notwithstanding.

Fordo, to destroy; **fordonne,** utterly undone, ruined, overcome.

Foreby, forby, hard by, near, with, past.

Forecast, previously determined.

Foredamned, utterly damned.

Forelay, to lay before, or over.

Forelent, given up entirely.

Forelifting, lifting up in front.

Forepast, gone by.

Foreshewed, previously instructed.

Foreside, the side to the fore, external covering.

Forespent, forspent, utterly wasted.

Forestall, to take previous possession of, to hinder, obstruct.

Foretaught, previously taught.

Forged, false.

Forgery, fiction, deceit, a counterfeit or assumed character.

Forgive, to give up.

Forbent, overtaken.

Forhent, gave up.

Forlore, forlorn, utterly lost, abandoned; **forlore** (pret.), deserted, lost (to sense of propriety).

Formally, expressly.

Formerlie, beforehand.

Forpassed, past by or through.

Forpined, pined away.

Forray, to ravage, prey on, a raid.

Forsake, to avoid, renounce.

Forslacke, forsloe, forslow, to delay, waste in sloth, neglect, omit.

Forthink, to repent, be sorry for, to give up.

Forthright, straightway.

Forthy, therefore, because.

Fortilage, a little fortress.

Fortune, to happen.

Fortunize, to make happy.

Fortuneless, unfortunate.

Forwandre, to stray away.

Forwasted, utterly wasted.

Forwearie (forwearied), utterly weary, worn out.

Forwent, left.

Forworne, much worn.

Foster, forester.

Fouldring, thundering.

Found, established.

Foundring, toppling, falling.

Foy, allegiance, faith.

Foyle, repulse, defeat, to defeat, ruin, overthrow.

Foyne, to thrust, push.

Frame, to make, form, support, prepare, direct, to put in shape for motion.

Franchisement, deliverance.

Franck, free, forward.

Francklin, freeman, freeholder.

Franion, a loose woman.

Fray, to frighten, terrify, alarm, affray.

Fret, ornamental border; **fretted,** ornamented with fretwork.

Frett, to consume.

Friend, befriend.

Frigot, a little boat.

Friskes, gambols.

Frize, to freeze.

Fro, from.

Frolicke, 'fa ined her to **frolicke**'= desired her to be cheerful.

Fronts, foreheads.

Frory, frosty, frozen.

Frounce, to fold, plait.

Froward, fromward, at a distance from.

Frowy, stale, musty.

Fry, swarms (of young children).

Fry, to foam.

Fulmined, fulminated.

Funerall, death.

Furniment, furnishing.

Furniture, gear, equipment.

Fylde, felt.

Fyle, polish.

Fyled, kept in files, registered.

Gage, pledge.

Gain, against (as in **gainstrive**).

Gainsay, denial.

Gail, bile.

Gamesome, pleasant.

Gan (can), began, did.

Gard, safeguard, protection.

Garre, to cause, make.

Gate, way, procession.

Gazement, gaze.

Gealosy, gelosy, jealousy.

Geare, gere, gear, dress, equipment, matter, affair.

Geare, to jeer, scoff.

Geason, rare, uncommon.

Gelly, clotted.

Gelt, bribed with gold.

Gelt. This word has been variously explained – by some as a gelding, by others as a **guilty** person. Professor Child explains it as a wild Irishman, **Celt.**

Gelt, castrated.

Gent, gentle, kind, accomplished.

Gere. See Geare.

German, brother.

Gerne, to grin.

Gesse, to deem, think, **guess.**

Gest, deed of arms, gesture, deportment, bearing.

Ghastly, terrible; **ghastlinesse,** terribleness.

Ghess, to guess, deem.

Ghost, spirit, soul.

Giambeux, leggings, greaves.

Gin, engine (of torture), plot, contrivance, snare.

Gin, ginne, to begin.

Giust, tournaments, tilts, to joust, tilt.

Glade, valley, dale.

Glade, to gladden.

Glaive, glave, glayve, a sword.

Glee, pleasure? fee, property.

Glib, a thick bush of hair overhanging the eyes.

Glims, glimpse, indistinct light.

Glinne, glen.

Glitterand, glittering.

Glister, to glitter, shine.

Glode, glided.

Glory, vainglory, boasting.

Glozing, deceitful.

Gnarre, growl, snarl.

Gobbeline, goblin.

Gobbet, morsel, piece.

Gondelay, gondola.

Goodlihed, goodlihead, goodness, goodly appearance.

Gooldes, marigolds.

Gore, to pierce, wound.

Gore-blood, clotted blood.

Gorge, throat.

Gorget, armour for the throat.

Goshawke, a large kind of hawk.

Gossib, kinsman.

Gourmandize, greediness.

Governall, government.

Governaunce, government.

Government, control.

Grace, favour, kindness, to give favour to.

Graile, gravel.

Graine, dye (scarlet).

Grammercy, many thanks.

Grange, dwelling, place.

Graple, to tug.

Graplement, grasp, clutch.

Graste, graced, favoured.

Grate, to scorn.

Grayle, gravel.

Grayle, the holy vessel said to have been used at Our Saviour's Last Supper.

Greave, grove.

Gree, favour, goodwill.

Greete, to congratulate, praise, to assign with praise.

Gren, to grin, snarl.

Grenning, grinning.

Griefull, grievous.

Griesie, thick, sluggish.

Grieslie, grisely, horrible.

Grieved, hurt.

Grin, to gnash the teeth.

Gripe, to grasp.

Griple, gripe, grasp, grasping, greedy.

Gronefull, full of groans.

Groome, man, a young man, a servant.

Grosse, heavy.

Groundhold, ground-tackle (as cables, anchors).

Groveling, with face flat to the ground.

Groynd, growled.

Grudge, grutch, to murmur, growl.

Gryde, cut, pierce through.

Gryesy, grysie, squalid, foggy, moist.

Grufon, gryphon, griffin (a fabulous animal), perhaps used for vulture, eagle.

Grypt, 'through grypt' = **throughgyrd,** pierced through.

Guarish, to heal.

Guerdon, reward.

Guilen, to beguile.

Guiler, guyler, deceiver.

Guilt, guilded.

Guize, manner, mode (of life), custom.

Gust, taste.

Gyeld, guild, courthouse.

Gyre, circle, course.

Gyvd, fettered.

Habergeon, haberjeon, a small coat of mail, armour for the neck and breast.

Habiliment, clothing.

Habitaunce, habitation.

Hable, able, fit.

Hacqueton, a jacket worn under armour.

Hagard, wild, untamed.

Haile, hayl, to drag, haul.

Halfendeale, half part.

Halfen-eye, half ordinary sight., i.e. one eye.

Hand, 'out of **hand**' = at once, 'nigh **hand**' = near.

Handsell, price, reward.

Hap, to happen, fortune, lot.

Happily, haply, by chance.

Happy, successful.

Hard, heard.

Hardiment, hardihood, boldness.

Hardnesse, rudeness.

Hardyhed, hardihood.

Harnesse, weapons.

Harrow, an exclamation of distress, a call for help.

Hartned, encouraged.

Hartlesse, timid.

Haubergh, hauberk, hauberque, hawberk, a coat of mail.

Haught, high, august.

Hault, haughty.

Haulst, embraced.

Haveour, deportment, behaviour.

Hayle, to drag.

Hazardize, danger.

Hazardry, hazard, risk, gaming.

Heard, a keeper of cattle.

Heare, hair; **heavie,** hairy.

Heast, hest, command, behest, name, office (of one who had **taken vows**).

Heben, ebony, of ebony wood.

Hedstall, that part of the bridle which is put on the horse's head.

Heedinesse, heedfulness.

Hefte, raised, threw.

Hell, to cover.

Helme, helmet.

Hend, to seize, grasp.

Henge, hinge.

Hent, took, seized.

Herbars, herbs.

Herneshaw, heron.

Herried, heried, praised, worshipped, honoured.

Hersall, rehearsal.

Herse, ceremonial.

Hether, hither.

Hew, shape, form.

Hew, hacking.

Hide, hastened. See Hye.

Hie, to hasten.

Hight, called, named, entrusted, directed, pronounce worthy, hence determine, choose, appointed.

Hight, 'on **hight**' = aloud.

Hild, held.

Hippodames, sea-horses.

Hole, whole.

Holpen (pp.), helped.

Hond, hand.

Hong, hung.

Honycrock, pot of honey.

Hood, state, manner.

Hopelesse, unexpected.
Hore, hoary.
Horrid, rough.
Hospitage, hospitality.
Hospitale, a place of rest.
Hoste, to entertain, lodge.
Hostlesse, imhospitable.
Hostry, lodging.
Hot, hote, was called.
Housling, sacramental.
Hove, rise, float, hover.
Howre, time; ' **good houre**'=good fortune.
Howres, devotional exercises.
Hoye, vessel, ship.
Hububs, shouts, din.
Humblesse, humility, humbleness.
Hurlyburly, noise of battle.
Hurtle, to rush, dash, hurl, attack, brandish, crowd.
Hurtlesse, innocent.
Husband, farmer.
Hyacine, hyacinth.
Hye, to hasten.
Hylding, base, vile.
Hynde, a servant.

Idle, causeless.
Idole, image.
Ill-faste, having an ill-look; **ill-hedded,** disturbed in the head.
Imbrast, embraced.
Immeasured, unmeasured.
Imp, child, scion, shoot.
Impacable, unappeasible.
Imperceable, not able to be pierced.
Implore, entreaty.
Imply, to enfold, entangle, envelop.
Importable, intolerable.
Importune, violent, savage, full of trouble, to threaten, to solicit.
Importunely, with importunity.
Impresse, to make an impression.
Improvided, unprovided, unlooked for.
In, inne, dwelling, lodging.
In, 'in . . . lyte'=fall upon.
Incontinent, forthwith, immediately.
Indew, to put on.

Indifferent, impartial; **indifferently,** impartially.
Indignaunce, indignation.
Indigne, unworthy.
Indignify, to treat with indignity.
Inferd, offered.
Infest, to make fierce or hostile, hostile.
Influence, the power of the stars.
Informed, formed imperfectly.
Ingate, entrance.
Ingowe, ingot.
Inholder, inhabitant.
Inly, inwardly.
Inquest, quest, adventure.
Inquire, to call.
Insolent, rude.
Inspyre, to breathe.
Insu'th=ensu'th, follows.
Intend, to stretch out, to denote, name, direct one's course.
Intendiment, intention, knowledge.
Intent, purpose.
Interesse, interest.
Interlace, to intermingle, interweave.
Intermedle, to intermix.
Intimate, to communicate.
Intreat, to prevail upon.
Infuse, contusion.
Invade, to come into.
Invent, to find out.
Invest, to put on.
Irkes, wearies.
Irkesome, tired, weary.
Irrenowmed, inglorious.

Jacob's staffe, a pilgrim's staff.
Jade, a horse, a scolding woman.
Jarre, quarrel, variance.
Jeopardie, jeopardy, danger.
Jesses, strips of leather tied round the legs of hawks, with which they are held upon the fist.
Jollie, jolly, handsome, pretty, lively.
Jolliment, jollitee, jollity, joyfulness, prettiness, liveliness.
Jollyhead, jollity.
Jott, speck, small piece.
Journall, diurnal.
Jovial, bright, sunny.

Joy, to rejoice, be glad, enjoy.
Joyaunce, joyfulness, merriment.
Juncates, junkets.

Kaies, keys.
Keepe, heed, care, charge, to take care, protect; 'heedie keepe'= watchful care.
Keight, caught.
Kemd, combed.
Ken, kend, kent, knew, perceived, known.
Kerve, to cut.
Kesar, emperor.
Kest, cast.
Kestrell-kynd, base nature.
Kind, nature, sex, occupation; kindly, natural.
Kirtle, a coat fastened at the waist.
Knee, projection of rocks.
Knife, a sword, dagger.
Kond, knew.
Kynded, begotten.

Lackey, to follow as a servant.
Lad, led.
Lade, to load.
Laid, attacked.
Laire, plain.
Lamping, shining.
Lanck loynes, slender waist.
Langurous, languid.
Lap, lappe, to enfold, entangle.
Lare, pasture.
Large, bountiful.
Launce, balance.
Launch, to pierce.
Laver, a basin.
Lay, field, lea, plain.
Lay, cry.
Lay, to throw up.
Lay, law.
Laystall, a dunghill, a place for the deposit of filth.
Lazar, leper.
Leach, a physician.
Leachcraft, medical skill.
Leake, leaky.
Leare, lore, counsel; **leares,** lessons.
Leasing, lying, falsehood.

Least, lest.
Leave, to raise.
Ledden, dialect, speech.
Lee, river.
Lefte, lifted.
Legierdemain, sleight of hand.
Leke, leaky.
Leman, a lover.
Lend, to give, provide.
Lenger, longer.
Lessoned, instructed.
Lest, to listen.
Let, to hinder; 'let be'=away with, hindrance.
Level, to direct one's course.
Levin, lightning; **levin brond,** thunderbolt.
Lewdly, foolishly.
Lewdnesse, wickedness.
Libbard, leopard.
Lich, like.
Lief, liefe, dear, beloved, willing; 'liefe or sory'=willing or unwilling=lief or loth, (comp.) liefer; (superl.) liefest, 'liefest leife'= dearest loved one.
Liege, lord, master – one to whom faith has been pledged; **liegeman,** a vassal, one who owes homage to a liege lord.
Liful, living, full of life.
Lig, to lie.
Light, easy, ready, to lighten, befall.
Lignage, lynage, lineage.
Like, to please.
Like as, as if.
Likelynesse, likeness.
Lill, to put out the tongue.
Limbeck, retort.
Limehound, a bloodhound, limer.
Lin, to cease.
List, to desire, like; (impers.) please; listful, attentive.
Lite, lyte, alight, befall.
Livelod, livelood, livelihood.
Lively, lifelike, living.
Livelyhed, livelyhead, livelihood, living original, motion of a living being.
Liverey, delivery.

Loathly, loathsome.
Loft, height.
Lome, clay, loam.
Lompish, dull, slow.
Long, to belong.
Loord, lout.
Loos, fame.
Loose, to solve.
Lore, learning, teaching, fashion, speech.
Lore, lorn, left, deserted, lost sight of.
Loring, learning.
Losell, lozell, a loose idle fellow.
Lose, to loosen.
Losen, to set loose; **los'te,** loosed, dissolved.
Lot, fate, share.
Lothfull, unwilling, unpleasant, loathsome.
Loup, loop.
Lout, lowt, to bow, to do obeisance.
Lovely, loving, lovingly; **lovely,** of love.
Lover, an opening in the roof to let out the smoke.
Lug, a perch or rod of land.
Luskishnesse, sluggishness.
Lust, pleasure, desire, to desire, please.
Luster, a glittering, sheen.
Lustlesse, feeble, listless.
Lusty-hedd, pleasure.
Lynage, lineage.
Lyte, to alight, light, befall.

Mace, sceptre.
Mage, magician.
Magnes-stone, the magnet.
Mail, mayl, male, armour.
Maine, mayne, force, ocean; **mainely, maynly,** strongly, violently.
Mainsheat, mainsail.
Maintenaunce, condition.
Maisterdome, maistery, mastery, superiority.
Maistring, superior, controlling.
Make, companion, mate.
Malengine, ill intent, deceit, guile.

Malice (pret. **malist**), regarded with malice, bore ill-will to.
Maligne, to grudge.
Mall, club, mallet, to maul.
Maltalent, ill-will.
Mand, blocked up with men.
Manie, many, company, multitude.
Manner, kind of.
Mantle, to rest with outspread wings.
Mard, spoilt, injured, dishonour.
Marge, margin, bank.
Margent, margin.
Marle, ground, soil.
Marishes, marshes.
Martelled, hammered.
Martyr, to afflict, torment.
Maske, to conceal oneself by means of a mask (as at a masquerade).
Masse, wealth, material.
Massy, massive.
Mate, to stupefy, confound, **amate.**
Matchlesse, not to be matched.
Maugre, maulgre, in spite of, a curse on!, unwillingly.
Maysterdome, superiority.
Maxed, amazed, confounded.
Mazer, a kind of hard wood (probably the maple).
Me, 'he cast me down' (ethic dative).
Mealth, melteth.
Mean, middle, moderate, moderation; means, 'by **meanes,**' because.
Meanesse, humble birth.
Meare, pure, boundary.
Measure, moderation.
Medæwart, meadow-wort.
Measured, sang.
Medling, mixing.
Mell, to intermeddle.
Melling, meddling.
Menage, to manage, guide (a horse); to wield (arms); management.
Mendes, amends.
Mene, means.
Ment, purposed, meant.
Ment, joined, united.
Mercie, mercy, thanks, favour, thank you.
Mercify, to pity.

Merimake, meryment, merry-making, sport.
Mery, pleasant, cheerful.
Mesprise, mesprize, contempt, insolence, mistake.
Mew, to confine, secrete, prison, den.
Mickle, much, great.
Middest, midst, midmost.
Mieve, to move.
Mincing, affected.
Mind, to call to mind.
Mindlesse, unmindful.
Minime, a trifling song, but properly a musical note.
Mininents, trifles, toys.
Mineon, a favourite.
Minisht, diminished.
Mirkesome, dark.
Mis, to sin, err.
Misavized, ill-advised, misinformed.
Misaymed, ill-aimed.
Miscall, to abuse.
Mischalenge, false challenge.
Misconceipt, mistake.
Miscreant, unbeliever.
Miscreated, ill-formed.
Miscreaunce, false faith, misbelief.
Misdeem, to deem amiss, misjudge; **misdeeming,** misleading; **misdempt,** misjudged, misweened.
Misdesert, crime.
Misdid, failed.
Misdiet, over-eating.
Misdight, ill-dressed.
Misdonne, to misdo.
Misdoubting, fearing sadly.
Miser, wretch.
Misfeign, to feign wrongfully.
Misfare, misfortune.
Misfaring, misfortune.
Misguyde, trespass.
Mishappen, happen amiss.
Mishapt, misshaped.
Misleeke, to dislike.
Misregard, misconstruction.
Missay, to say to no purpose, uselessly, abuse, speak ill of.
Misseem, to be unseemly, to misbecome.

Misseeming, unseemly, wrong, deceit.
Misshape, deformity.
Misshapen, deformed.
Mister, sort of, manner of.
Misthought, mistake.
Mistooke, suspected.
Mistrayne, to mislead.
Mistreth, signifies, matters.
Misweene, to think amiss.
Mo, moe, more.
Mold, mole, spot.
Molt, melted.
Mome, blockhead.
Moniment, mark, stamp, record.
Monoceros, sea-unicorn (? swordfish).
Morish, marshy.
Moralize, to cause to be moral.
More, root, plant.
Morion, helmet.
Morrow, morning.
Mortall, deadly.
Mortality, the estate of mortal man.
Most, greatest.
Mot, mote (pl. **moten**), may, must, might.
Mould, to moulder.
Mountenaunce, space, distance.
Mowes, insulting grimaces, **mouths.**
Moyity, half.
Muckell, much, great.
Muck, wealth.
Mucky, sordid, vile.
Munificence (munifience), fortification, defence.
Mured, walled, enclosed.
Muse, to wonder, wonderment.
Must, new wine.
Myndes, resolves.

Namely, especially.
Napron, apron.
Native, natural.
Nathlesse, nathless, none the less, nevertheless.
Nathemoe, nathmore, none the more, never the more.
Ne, nor.
Neat, cattle.

Nempt, named.

Nephews, descendants, grandchildren.

Net, nett, pure, clean.

Nigardise, niggardliness, miserliness.

Nill, will not; will or nill, willing or unwilling; 'nilled', unwilling.

Nimblesse, nimbleness.

Nobilesse, noblesse, nobleness, nobility.

Nominate, to name, affirm.

Noriture, norture, nurture, bringing up.

Norveyses, Norwegians.

Not, note, wot not, know not, knows not. (It sometimes seems to stand for ne mote = could help.)

Nothing, not at all.

Notifye, to proclaim.

Nought, not, of no value.

Nould, would not.

Noule, the head, pate.

Noursle, nousle, to nurse, foster, rear.

Nousling, nestling, burrowing.

Noyance, noyaunce, annoyance.

Noyd, noyed, annoyed.

Noyes, noise.

Noyous, annoying, disagreeable, injurious.

Noysome, hurtful.

Nycely, carefully.

Obliquid, oblique.

Obsequy, funeral rite.

Oddes, advantage.

Of, upon, by; of all, above all.

Offal, that which falls off.

Offend, to harm, hurt.

Ofnew, recently.

Ofspring, origin.

Onely, chief, especial.

Ope, open.

Opprest, taken captive.

Ordain, to set (the battle) in order.

Order, to arrange, rank (of army).

Ordinaunce, arrangement, ordinance, artillery.

Origane, bastard, marjoram.

Other, left.

Otherwise, elsewhere.

Otherwhiles, sometimes.

Ought, owned.

Outbarre, to arrest.

Outgo, to surpass.

Outhyred, let out for hire.

Out-learn, to learn from.

Outrage, violence, outburst.

Outweave, wear out, pass, spend.

Outwell, to gush or well out.

Outwin, to get out.

Outwind (=outwin), to get out.

Outwrest, wrest out, discover.

Outwrought, completed, passed.

Overall, everywhere, all over.

Overbore, overthrew.

Overcame, overspread.

Overcaught, overtook.

Overcraw, to crow over, insult.

Overdight, decked over, covered over, overspread.

Overgive, to give over.

Overgo, to overpower, surpass.

Overhent, overtook, overtaken.

Overkest, overcast.

Overlade, to overwhelm.

Overplast, overhanging.

Over-raught, overtook.

Over-red, read over.

Overpasse, pass over, alleviate.

Overren, to overrun, oppress.

Oversee, to overlook.

Oversight, escape (through having overlooked a danger).

Overswim, to swim over.

Overbore, overthrow.

Overthwart, opposite.

Owe, to own. See Ought.

Owch, a socket of gold to hold precious stones, a jewel.

Owre, ore.

Oystrige, ostrich.

Pace, pase, step, pass, passage.

Packe, to pack off, a burden.

Paine, payne, labour, pains, punishment; 'did him paine'=took pains, exerted himself.

Paire, to impaire.

Paled, 'pinckt upon gold, and **paled part per part,'**='adorned with golden points or eyelets, and regularly intersected with stripes.' In heraldry a shield is said to be **parted per pale** when it is longitudinally divided by a pale or broad bar.

Paled, fenced off.

Pall, to subdue, moderate.

Pall, a cloak of rich material.

Panachæa, panacea.

Pannikell, skull, crown.

Paragon, paragone, companion, equal, rivalry.

Paravaunt, first, beforehand, in front.

Parbreake, vomit.

Pardale, panther.

Parentage, parent.

Part, party, depart.

Partake, to share.

Parture, departure.

Pas, passe (**passing,** surpassing), to surpass, exceed.

Passion, suffering; **passioned,** affected with feeling, be grieved; **passionate,** to express feelingly.

Patronage, defence; **patronesse,** a female defender.

Paunce, pansy.

Pavone, peacock.

Payne, to take pains, exert.

Payse, to poise, balance.

Pealing, appealing.

Peare, pere, equal.

Peasant knight, base knight.

Peaze, blow.

Peece, fabric, fortified place, as a castle, ship, etc.

Peise, to pose, weigh.

Pen, to confine, restrain.

Pendants, ornaments (of wood or stone) hanging down from a Gothic roof.

Penne, feather.

Penurie, want of food.

Percen, to pierce.

Perdu, perdy, pardieu, truly.

Perforce, of necessity.

Perlous, perilous.

Persant, persaunt, piercing.

Personage, personal appearance.

Persue, a track.

Perveyaunce, provision. See **Purveyaunce.**

Pesaunt, a peasant.

Physnomy, countenance.

Pictural, a picture.

Pight, fixed, placed, fastened.

Pill, to spoil, plunder.

Pine, pyne, sorrow, grief, to waste away through torment; '**pined ghost',** a spirit wasted away (through torment); **done to pine,** caused to die.

Pinnoed, pinioned.

Pitteous, compassionate, tenderhearted.

Place, 'of place', of rank.

Plaine, playne, to complain.

Plaintiffe, plaintive.

Platane, plane tree.

Pleasaunce, pleasure, delight, objects affording pleasure.

Pled, pleaded.

Plesh, a shallow pool, plash.

Plight (p. p. **plight**), weave, plait, fold; a plait, fold, condition.

Ply, to move.

Poise, poyse, weight, force.

Point, poynt, to appoint; a whit, 'to poynt'=exactly.

Poke, a pouch.

Poll, to plunder.

Pollicie, statecraft.

Port, portance, portaunce, demeanour, bearing.

Portesse, breviary.

Possesse, to accomplish.

Potshares=potshards, fragments of broken vessels.

Pouldred, powdered, spotted.

Pounce, claws, talons.

Pound, weight, balance; '**new in pound'**=anew in the balance.

Pourtrahed, drawn.

Pourtraict, pourtraiture, portrait, image.

Poynant, piercing, sharp.

Poyse, weight, force.

Practic, practicke, treacherous, deceitful, skilful.

Prancke, to trim, deck, adorn, adjust, a malicious trick.

Praunce, to prance.

Pray, to be the prey of, to make a prey of.

Preace, prease, to press, a press, crowd.

Prefard, preferred.

Prefixt, fixed beforehand.

Prejudize, foresight.

Prepense, to consider.

Presage, to tell or point out, foresee.

Presence, reception-room.

President, precedent.

Prest ready, prepared.

Pretend, to attempt, to stretch out (or over), offer.

Prevent, anticipate.

Price, to pay the price of, atone for, value.

Prick, to ride hard, to spur on quickly; point, centre of target.

Prief, priefe, proof, trial, experiment.

Prieve, to prave.

Prime, pryme, spring time, morning.

Principle, beginning.

Prise, adventure.

Privitee, privitie, private life, intimate relation.

Procure, to arrange, entreat.

Prodigious, ominous.

Professe, to present the appearance of.

Project, to throw forward.

Prolong, to postpone.

Prone, subjected.

Proper, own, peculiar; **proper good,** own property.

Protense, a stretching out.

Prove, to experience, try, feel.

Provokement, a provoking.

Prow, brave; (superl.) **prowest; prowes,** prowess.

Pryse, to pay for. See Price.

Puissant, powerful.

Pumy stones, pumice stones.

Purchase, to obtain, to get, win (honestly or otherwise).

Purchas, purchase, property, booty, robbery.

Purfled, embroidered on the edge.

Purport, disguise.

Purpos, purpose, conversation, discourse; **'to purpose',** to the purpose, to speak as **'purpose diversly'** = to speak of various things.

Purvay, to provide.

Purveyaunce, provision, management, function.

Puttocke, a kite.

Pyne, pain (of hunger), torment.

Pyoning, diggings, work of pioneers.

Quaile, to cast down, defeat, conquer.

Quaint, nice, fastidious.

Qualify, to ease, sooth.

Quarle, quarrel, a square-headed arrow.

Quarrie, quarry, prey, game.

Quart, quarter.

Quayd, quailed, quelled, subdued.

Queane, a worthless woman.

'Queint elect', oddly chosen.

Queint, quenched.

Quell, to kill, to subdue, to perish, to disconcert, frighten.

Quest, expedition, pursuit.

Quick, alive.

Quich, to stir, move.

Quietage, quietness.

Quight, to set free, to requite.

Quilted, padded.

Quib, to sneer at, taunt.

Quire, company.

Quit, quite, quyte, to get free, to requite, repay, to return (a salute), freed, removed; **'quite clame',** to release.

Quooke, quaked.

Rablement, a rabble, troop.

Race, to raze, to cut; **raced,** erazed.

Rad, rode.

Rad, perceived. See Read.

Raft, bereft.

Ragged, rugged.

Raile, rayle, to flow, pour down.

Rain, rayne, to reign, kingdom.

Rakehell, loose, worthless.

Ramp, tear, attack, leap.

Ranck, fiercely.

Randon, random.

Ranke, fiercely.

Rape, rapine.

Rascal, raskall, low, base, worthless.

Rase (pret. **rast**), to erase.

Rash, to tear violently, hack; **rashly,** hastily, suddenly; **rash,** quick.

Rate, to scold.

Rate, allowance, order, state.

Rath, early, soon.

Raught, reached, extended, took.

Ravin, ravine, plunder, prey.

Ravishment, ecstasy.

Ray, to defile, soil.

Ray, array.

Rayle, to flow. See **Raile.**

Rayle, abuse.

Rayne, kingdom.

Read, reede, advice, motto, prophecy.

Read, reed (pret. **rad, red**), to know, declare, explain or advise, discover, perceive, suppose, regard.

Reædifye, to rebuild.

Reallie, to reform.

Reames, realms.

Reare, to raise, take up or away, steal, excite, to rouse.

Reason, proportion.

Reave (pret. **reft, raft**), to bereave, take away (forcibly).

Rebuke, conduct deserving of reproof, rudeness.

Rebutte, to cause to recoil.

Reclayme, to call back.

Recorde, to remember, to call to mind.

Recoure, recower, recure, to recover.

Recourse, to recur, return; '**had recourse**'=did recur, return.

Recoyle, to retire, retreat.

Recuile, recule, to recoil.

Red, redd, declared, described, perceived, saw. See **Read.**

Redisbourse, to repay.

Redoubted, doughty.

Redound, to overflow, flow, be redundant.

Redress, to reunite, remake, to rest.

Reed, to deem; **reede, read,** to advise.

Reek, to smoke.

Reele, to roll.

Refection, refreshment.

Reft, bereft, taken violently away. See **Reave.**

Regalitie, rights of royalty.

Regarde, a subject demanding consideration or attention, value.

Regiment, government, command.

Relate, to bring back.

Release, to break loose from, to give up.

Relent, to give way, to slacken, relax, soften.

Relide, to ally, join.

Relieve, to recover, revive, live again.

Remeasure, to retrace.

Remedilesse, without hope of rescue.

Remercy, to thank.

Remorse, pity.

Rencounter, to encounter, meet in battle.

Renfierced (renfierst), made more fierce or=**renforst**=reinforced.

Renforst, reinforced, enforced, made fresh effort.

Renverse, to reverse, overturn.

Repent, repentance, to grieve.

Repining, a failing (of courage).

Replevie, a law term signifying to take possession of goods claimed, giving security at the same time to submit the question of property to a legal tribunal within a given time.

Report, to carry off.

Reprief, reproof, shame.

Reprive, to deprive of, take away.

Reprive, reprieve.

Reprize, to retake.

Requere, to require, demand.

Request, demand.

Requit, requited, returned.

Reseize, to reinstate, to be repossessed of.

Resemble, to compare.

Resemblaunce, look, regard.

Resiant, resident.

Respect, care, caution.

Respondence, correspondence, reply (in music).

Respyre, to breathe again.

Restlesse, resistless.

Restore, restitution.

Resty, restive.

Retourn, to turn (the eyes) back.

Retraite, picture, portrait.

Retrate, a retreat.

Retyre, retirement.

Revel, a feast.

Revengement, revenge.

Reverse, to return, to cause to return.

Revest, to reclothe.

Revilement, a reviling, abuse.

Revoke, to recall, withdraw.

Revolt, to roll back.

Reu, rue, to pity, to be sorry for, to lament over, repent.

Rew, row.

Ribauld, rybauld, a loose impure person, ribald.

Richesse, riches.

Ridling, skill, skill in explaining riddles.

Rife, ryfe, abundant, abundantly, much, frequent.

Rift, split, broken, gap, fissure, fragment.

Rigor, force; **rigorous,** violent.

Ring, to encircle.

Riotise, riotize, riot, extravagance.

Rivage, bank.

Rive, to split, tear.

Rize, to come to.

Rocke, distaff.

Rode, raid, incursion.

Rode, roadstead, anchorage for ships.

Rong, rang.

Roode, a cross, crucifix.

Rosiere, a rose tree.

Rosmarine, a sea-monster that was supposed to feed on the dew on the tops of the sea rocks.

Rote, a lyre, harp.

Roules, rolls, records.

Rout, crowd, troop.

Rove, to shoot (with a sort of arrow called a rover).

Rowel, the ring of a bit – any small movable ring.

Rowme, place, space.

Rownded, whispered.

Rowndell, a round bubble (of foam).

Rowze, rouze, to shake up.

Royne, to mutter.

Rubin, Rubine, the ruby.

Rue, to grieve.

Ruffed, ruffled; **ruffin,** disordered; **ruffing,** ruffling.

Ruinate, to ruin.

Ruing, pitying.

Ruth, pity.

Ryve, to pierce.

Sacrament, oath of purgation taken by an accused party.

Sacred, accursed.

Sad, firm, heavy, grave.

Saine, to say (pl. **say**).

Sake, cause.

Salew, to salute.

Saliaunce, onslaught.

Salied, leapt, sallied.

Sallows, willows.

Salvage, savage, wild.

Salute, to salute.

Salve, to heal, save, remedy.

Salving, salvation, restoration.

Sam, together.

Samite, silk stuff.

Sanguine, blood-colour.

Sardonian, sardonic.

Saufgard, guard, defence; **savegard,** to protect.

Say, a thin stuff (for cloaks).

Say, assay, proof.

Scald, scabby.

Scand, climbed.

Scarmoges, skirmishes.

Scath, hurt, harm, damage, ruin.

Scatter, to let drop.

Scatterling, a vagrant.

Scerne, to discern.

Schuchin, scutchin, escutcheon, shield, device on a shield.

Scolopendra, fish resembling a centipede.

Scope, dimension; 'aymed scope,' a mark aimed at.

Scorse, to exchange.

Scorse, to chase.

Scould, scowled.

Scriene, scrine, scryne, skreene, a cabinet for papers, a writing desk; entrance of a hall.

Scrike, shriek.

Scruze, to squeeze, crush.

Scryde, descried.

Sdeigne, to disdain.

Sea-shouldring, having shoulders that displace the sea.

Sear, to burn, burning.

Sease, to fasten on, seize.

See, seat.

Seelde, seldom, rare.

Seely, simple, innocent.

Seeming, apparently.

Seemlesse, unseemly.

Seemly, in a seemly manner, comely, apparent.

Seemlyhed, a seemly appearance.

Seene, skilled, experienced.

Seew, to pursue.

Seised, taken possession of.

Seisin, possession.

Selcouth, seldom known, rare, strange.

Sell, seat, saddle.

Semblaunce, semblaunt, semblant, likeness, appearance, phantom, cheer, entertainment.

Sence, feeling.

Seneschall, governor, steward.

Sens, since.

Sensefull, sensible.

Sent, scent, perception.

Serve, to bring to bear upon.

Set by, to esteem.

Severall, diverse.

Sew, to follow, to solicit.

Shade, to shadow, represent.

Shallop, sloop.

Shame, to feel shame, to be ashamed.

Shamefast, modest.

Shamefastnesse, modesty.

Shard, division, boundary, cut.

Share, portion, piece, to cut.

Shayres, shires.

Sheare, to cut, divide.

Sheare, shere, bright, clear.

Sheares, wings.

Shed, to spill life blood, to kill.

Sheene, shene, bright, shining, clear.

Shend (pret. **shent**), to disgrace, defile, abuse, reproach, shame.

Shere, to cleave, divide.

Shere, bright, clear.

Shew, mark, track.

Shine, shyne, a bright light, bright.

Shiver, to quiver.

Shole, shallow.

Shonne, to shun.

Shope, shaped, framed.

Shot, advanced (in years).

Shriech, shriek.

Shrieve, to question (shrive).

Shright, a shriek, to shriek.

Shrill, to give out a ringing, shrill sound.

Shrilling, shrill.

Sib, sibbe, akin, related.

Sich, such.

Sickernesse, security, safety.

Siege, seat.

Sield, cieled.

Sient, scion.

Sight, sighed.

Sign, watchword, representation, picture.

Silly, simple, innocent.

Sin, since.

Singults, sighs.

Sinke, hoard, deposit.

Sited, placed, situated.

Sith, sithe, sythe, time, since.

Sithens, since that time.

Sithes, times.

Sits, is becoming.

Skill, to signify, to be a matter of importance.

Skippet, a little boat.

Slacke, slow.

Slake, to slack.

Slaver, sobber.

Slight, sleight, device, trick.

Slombry, sleepy.

Slug, to live idle.

Sly, subtle, clever.

Smit, smote, smitten.

Smouldry, smouldring, suffocating.

Snag, a knot.

Snaggy, knotted, covered with knots.

Snags, knots.

Snaky-wreathed=(?) snakeywreathed, snake-entwined.

Snar, to snarl.

Snarled, twisted.

Snub, knob (of a club).

Sold, pay, remuneration.

Solemnize, a solemn rite.

Song, sang.

Sooth, truly.

Soothly, soothlich, truly indeed.

Soothsay, prediction, omen.

Sort, company.

Sort, 'in sort', inasmuch as.

Souce, souse, sowse, to swoop on, as a bird does upon his prey, strike, attack, the swoop (of a hawk), blow.

Souse, to immerse.

Southsay, soothsay; **southsayer,** soothsayer.

Sovenaunce, remembrance.

Sownd, to wield; **swond**=**swound,** swoon.

Sowne, a sound.

Sowst, struck.

Soyle, prey.

Space, to walk, roam.

Spalles, the shoulders.

Spangs, spangles.

Sparckle forth, to cause to sparkle.

Spare, sparing, niggardliness, to save.

Sparre, bolt, bar.

Speed, 'evill speed', misfortune.

Sperre, to bolt, shut.

Sperse, to disperse, scatter.

Spies, spyes, keen glances, eyes.

Spight, displeasure, grudge.

Spill, to ravage, destroy.

Spilt, pieced, inlaid.

Spoil, to ravage, carry off.

Sponned, flowed out quickly.

Spot, to blame.

Spoused, espoused, betrothed.

Sprad, spead.

Spray, branch.

Spred, spredden, to spread over, to cover.

Sprent, sprinkled.

Spright, spirit.

Springal, a youth, stripling.

Spring-headed, having heads that spring afresh.

Sprong, sprang.

Spurne, to spur.

Spyall, spy.

Spyre, to shoot forth.

Squire, a square, a rule, a carpenter's measure.

Stadle, a staff, prop.

Stale, decoy, bait.

Stalk, a stride.

Stare, to shine.

Stared, 'up stared', stood up stiffly.

Stark, strong, stiff.

Star-read, knowledge of the stars.

Stay, to hold, hold up, support.

Stayd, caused to stay.

Stayed, constant.

Stayne, to dim, deface.

Stayre, a step.

Stead, sted, stedd, station, place, situation.

Stead, to help, avail, bestead.

Steale, stale, handle.

Steane, a stone (vessel).

Steare, a steer.

Sted, place, condition, steed horse. See **Stead.**

Steedy, steady.

Steely=**steelen,** of steel.

Steemed, esteemed.

Steep, to bathe, stain.

Stelths, thefts.

Steme, to exhale.

Stemme, to rush against.

Stent, to cease, stop.

Sterve, to die.

Stew, a hot steaming place.

Stie, to ascend.

Still, to drop, flow, trickle.

Stint, to stop, cease.

Stir, styre, to stir, move, incite, provoke, to direct, steer.

Stole, a long robe.

Stomachous, angry.

Stomacke, temper.

Stond, attach.

Stonied, astonished, alarmed.

Stound, stownd, stond, a moment of time (a time of) trouble, peril, alarm, assault, a stunning influence, a blow, amazement, stunned.

Stoup, to swoop.

Stout, stubborn, bold.

Stoure, stowre, tumult, disturbance, battle, passion, fit, paroxysm, danger, peril.

Straine, race, lineage.

Straine, strayne, to stretch out.

Straint, grasp, strain.

Strake, strook, a streak.

Straunge, foreign, borrowed.

Strayne, to wield.

Strayt, a street.

Streight, narrow, strait, strict, close.

Streightly, straitly, closely.

Streightnesse, straitness.

Strene, strain, race.

Stresse, distress.

Strich, the screech-owl.

Strif-ful, stryfull, contentious.

Stroken, struck.

Strond, strand.

Stub, stock of a tree.

Sty, to ascend, mount.

Subject, lying beneath.

Submisse, submissive.

Subtile, fine-spun.

Subverst, subverted.

Succeed, to approach.

Successe, succession.

Sue, solicit. See **Sew.**

Sufferaunce, patience, endurance.

Suffised, satisfied.

Sugred, sweet.

Supple, to make supple.

Suppress, to overcome, keep down.

Surbate, to batter.

Surbet, bruised, wearied.

Surcease, to leave off, utterly to cease.

Surcharge, to attack with renewed vigour.

Surcharged, heavily laden.

Surmount, to surpass.

Surplusage, excess.

Surprise, to seize suddenly.

Surquedray, pride, insolence, presumption.

Suspect, suspicion.

Swain, swayn, a labourer, youth, person.

Swart, black.

Swarve, to swerve, retreat.

Swat, did sweat.

Sway, to swing, brandish, wield (arms), force, a rapid motion.

Sweard, sword.

Sweath-bands, swaddling-bands.

Swelt, fainted, swooned, burnt (? swelled).

Swinck, labour, toil.

Swinge, to singe.

Swound, swoon.

Table, a picture.

Tackle (pl. **tackles**), rigging.

Talaunts, talons.

Tare, tore.

Targe, target.

Tarras, terrace.

Tassal gent, the tiersel, or male gosshawk.

Teade, a torch.

Teene (tene), grief, sorrow, pain, affliction. See **Tine.**

Teene (? **leene,** lend, give), to bestow.

Tell, to count; **teld,** told.

Temed, yoked in a team.

Temewise, like a team.

Tempring, controlling, governing.

Tend, to wait on.

Tender, to tend, attend to.

Thee, to prosper, thrive.

Theeveryes, thefts.

Then, than.

Thereto, besides.

Thether, thither.

Thewed, behaved, mannered.

Thewes, qualities, manners.

Thick, a thicket.

Thirst, to thirst, thirst.

Tho, thoe, then.

Thorough, through.

Thother, that other, the other.

Thrall, to take captive, enslave, bring into subjection, constrain, a slave, enslaved.

Threat, to threaten; **threatful,** threatening.

Thresher, a flail.

Thrid, a thread.

Thrill, to pierce; **thrillant,** piercing.

Thristy, thirsty.

Throughly, thoroughly.

Throw, time, while.

Throw, throe, pang, thrust, attack.

Thrust, to thirst, thirst.

Thwart, athwart.

Tickle, uncertain, insecure.

Tide, tyde, time, season, opportunity.

Tight, tied.

Timbered, massive (like timbers).

Tine, affliction.

Tine, to light, kindle, inflame.

Tine or **teen,** sorrow, grief, pain.

Tire, rank, train.

Tire, tyre, attire, dress.

To=for (as in **to frend**).

Tofore, before.

Toole, weapon.

Top, head.

To-rent, rent asunder.

Tort, wrong, injury.

Tortious, injurious, wrongful.

Tossen, brandish, toss.

Totty, tottering, unsteady.

To-torne, torn to pieces.

Tourney, tilt, joust.

Touze, to tease, worry.

Toward, favourable, approaching, near at hand.

To-worne, worn out.

Toy, pastime, sport.

Trace, to walk, track, tract.

Tract, trace, to trace.

Trade, footstep, tread, occupation, conduct.

Traduction, transfer.

Traine, trayne, to drag along, trail, to allure, wile, deceit, snare, trap, track, assembly.

Tramell, a net for the hair, tresses.

Transfard, transformed.

Transmew, to transmute, transform.

Transmove, to transpose.

Trap, to adorn (with trappings).

Traveiled, toiled.

Travell, toil.

Trayled, interwoven, adorned.

Treachour, treachetour, a traitor.

Treague, truce.

Treat, to discourse, hold parley with.

Treen, of trees.

Trenchand, trenchant, cutting.

Trentals, services of 30 masses, which were usually celebrated upon as many different days, for the dead.

Trild, flowed.

Trim, neat, well formed, pleasing.

Trinall, threefold.

Triplicity, quality of being threefold.

Trode, path, footstep.

Troncheon, a headless spear.

Troth, truth.

Troublous, restless.

Trow, to believe.

Truncked, truncated, having the head cut off.

Trusse, to pack up, carry off.

Tryde, proved, essayed.

Trye, tried, purified.

Turmoild, troubled.

Turney, an encounter.

Turribant, turban.

Tway, twaine, two.

Twight, to twit.

Twyfold, twofold.

Tynde, kindled.

Tyne, grief, pain. See **Tine, teen.**

Tyne, to come to grief, to perish.

Tyrannesse, a female tyrant.

Tyranning, acting like a tyrant.

Tyre, to dress, attire.

Tyreling, (?) weary.

Ugly, horrible.

Umbriere, the visor of a helmet.

Unacquainted, unusual, strange.
Unbid, without a prayer.
Unblest, unwounded.
Unbrace, to unfasten.
Uncivile, wild, uncivilised.
Uncouth, unusual, strange.
Undefide, unchallenged.
Underfong, to surprise, circumvent.
Underhand, secretly.
Understand, to learn the cause of (or perhaps to take in hand for purpose of arbitration).
Undertake, to perceive, hear.
Undertime, time of the midday meal.
Undight, to undress, take off ornaments, unloose.
Uneasy, disturbed.
Uneath, unneath, unneathes, uneth, scarcely, with difficulty, uneasily.
Unespyde, unseen.
Unfilde, unpolished.
Ungentle, uncourteous.
Ungentlenesse, base conduct.
Unguilty, not conscious of guilt.
Unhable, incapable.
Unhappie paine, unsuccessful labours (because there was no heir to reap the benefit of their pains).
Unhappy, unfortunate.
Unhastie, slow.
Unheale, unhele, to expose, uncover.
Unheedy, unwary; **unheedily,** unheedingly.
Unherst, 'took from the herse or temporary monument where the knights' arms were hung.'
Unkempt, uncombed, rude.
Unkend, unknown.
Unkind, unnatural.
Unkindly, unnatural.
Unlast, unlaced.
Unlich, unlike.
Unlike, not likely.
Unmannurd, not cultivated.
Unmard, uninjured.
Unmeet, unfit.
Unpurvaide of, unprovided with.
Unred, untold.

Unredrest, without redress, unrescued.
Unreproved, blameless.
Unshed, unparted.
Unspidie, unseen.
Unstayd, unsteady.
Unthrifty, wicked.
Unthriftyhead, unthrift.
Untill, unto.
Untimely, unfortunately.
Unwary, unwary, unexpected.
Unware, unawares, unexpectedly, unknown.
Unweeting, not knowing, unconscious.
Unweldy, unwieldly.
Unwist, unknown.
Unworthy, undeserved.
Unwreaked, unrevenged.
Upbraide, upbraiding, reproach, abuse.
Upbrast, burst open.
Upbray, to upbraid, an upbraiding.
Uphild, upheld.
Upreare, to raise up.
Upstare, to stand up erect.
Up-start, start up.
Upstay, to support.
Uptyde, tied up.
Upwound, knotted.
Urchin, hedgehog.
Usage, behaviour.
Usaunce, usage.
Use, to practise, habits.
Utmost, uttermost, outmost, last.
Utter, outer.

Vade, to go, to vanish.
Vaile, to lay down.
Vaine, frail.
Valew, value, valour, courage.
Valiaunce, valour.
Variable, various.
Vauncing, advancing.
Vaunt, to display.
Vauntage, advantage, opportunity.
Vaut, a vault.
Vauted, vaulted.
Vele, a veil.
Vellanage, villinage, slavery.

Venery, hunting.

Vengeable, revengeful, deserving of revenge.

Vengement, revenge.

Venger, avenger.

Ventayle, the place of the helmet.

Vented, lifted up the visor.

Ventre, to venture.

Ventrous, venturous, bold, adventurous.

Vere, to veer.

Vermeil, vermeill, vermell, vermily, vermilion.

Vertuous, possessing virtue or power.

Vestiment, vestment.

Vild, vile.

Vildly, vilely.

Villein, base-born, low.

Virginal, pertaining to a virgin.

Visnomie, visage.

Vitall, life-giving.

Voide, to avoid, turn aside, to remove.

Voided, cleared.

Wade, to walk, go.

Wag, to move (the limbs).

Wage, a pledge, to pledge.

Waide, weighed, proved.

Waift, a waif, an article found and not claimed by an owner.

Waite, to watch.

Wakefull, watchful.

Walke, to rolle, wag.

Wallowed, grovelling.

Wan, gained, took.

Wan, pale, faint.

Wand, branch of a tree.

Wanton, wild.

Ward, to guard.

ware, wary, cautious.

Wareless, unaware, unexpected, heedless.

War-hable, fit for war.

Wariment, caution.

Warke, work.

War-monger, a mercenary warrior.

Warray, warrey, to make war on, to lay waste.

Warre, worse.

Wasserman, a sea monster in shape like a man.

Wast, to desolate, lay waste.

Wastfull, barren, uninhabited, wild.

Wastness, wilderness.

Water-sprinckle, waterpot.

Wawes, waves.

Wax, wex, to grow.

Way, to weigh, esteem.

Wayd, went on their way, weighed, determined.

Waylfull, lamentable.

Wayment, to lament, lamentation.

Wayne, chariot.

Weare, to pass, spend (the time).

Wearish, mischievous, evil-disposed.

Weasand-pipe, windpipe.

Weather, to expose to the weather.

Weaved, waved, floated.

Weed, clothes, dress.

Weeke, wick.

Weeldelesse, unwieldly.

Ween (pret. **weend**), to suppose, expect, think.

Weet, weeten, to know, learn, understand, perceive. **To weet**=to wit.

Weeting, knowledge.

Weetingly, knowingly.

Weetlesse, unconscious, ignorant.

Weft, a waif.

Wefte, was wafted, avoided, a waif, a thing cast adrift.

Weld, to wield, govern.

Welke, to wane.

Welkin, sky, heavens.

Well, weal, very (**well affectionate**).

Well, to pour; **well-head,** fountain head.

Well-away, an exclamation of great sorrow, alas!

Well-seene, experienced.

Wend, to turn, go.

Went, journey, course.

Wesand, weasand, windpipe.

Wex, to grow, increase, become.

Wex, wax.

Whally, marked with streaks.

What, a thing; **homely what,** homely fare.

Wheare, where, place.
Whelm, to overwhelm.
Whether, which of two.
Whileare, whilere = erewhile, formerly, lately.
Whiles, whilest, whilst.
Whimpled, covered with a wimple.
Whirlpool, a kind of whale.
Whist, silenced.
Whot, hot.
Whylome, formerly.
Wicked, vile (chains).
Wide, round-about.
Wight, person, being.
Wimple, to gather, plait, fold a covering for the neck, veil.
Win(out), get (out), come up to.
Wisard, wizard, wise man.
Wise, wize, mode, manner, guise.
Wist, wiste, knew.
Witch, to bewitch.
Wite, witen, wyte, to blame, twit, reprove.
With-hault, withheld.
Withouten, without.
Wit, mind, intelligence; wittily, wisely, sensibly.
Wo, woe, sad.
Womanhood, womanly feeling.
Won (did won), be wont.
Won, wonne (wonning), dwelling-place, abode, to dwell.
Wondred, marvellous.
Wont, to be accustomed.
Wood, mad, frantic, furious.
Woodnes, madness.
Word, motto.
Wore, passed or spent the time.
Worshippe, honour, reverence.
Worth, to be.
Wot, wote, know, knows.
Wotes, knows; wotest, knowest.
Wowed, wooed.
Woxe, woxen, become, grown.
Wracke, wreck, destruction, violence, to take vengeance; wrackfull, avenging.
Wrast, to wrest.
Wrate, did write.
Wrawling, mewing like a cat.

Wreak, vengeance, ruin, to avenge, take vengeance.
Wreakfull, avenging.
Wreath, to turn.
Wreck, destruction.
Wrest, to wrench, twist, a wrenching, overturning.
Wrest, the wrist.
Wrethe, to twist.
Writ (pl. writtes), writing, a written paper.
Wroke, wroken, avenged.
Wyde, turned away (cf. wide of the mark).
Wyte, to blame.

Y, as a prefix of the past participle, is frequently employed by Spenser, as Yclad, clothed, Yfraught, filled, etc.
Ybent, turned, gone.
Ybet, beaten.
Yblent, blinded, dazzled.
Ybore, born.
Yclad, clad.
Ycleped, called, named.
Ydle, empty.
Ydlesse, idleness.
Ydrad, ydred, dreaded, feared.
Yead, yede, yeed, to go (properly a preterite tense).
Yearne, to earn.
Yfere, together, in company with.
Yfretted, adorned.
Ygo, ygoe, gone, ago.
Yglaunst, glanced, glided.
Yilde, yield.
Yirks, jirks, lashes.
Ylike, alike.
Ymolt, melted.
Ympe, youth. See Imp.
Ympt, joined.
Ynd, India.
Yod, bode, went.
Yold, yielded.
Yond, yonder.
Yond, outrageous, terrible.
Youngling, young of man or beast.
Younker, a youth.
Youthly, youthful.
Yplight, plighted.

Yrkes, wearies.

Yron-braced, sinewed, like iron (of the arm).

Ysame, together.

Ywis, certainly, truly.

Ywrake, ywroke, ywroken, avenged, revenged.

POETRY
IN EVERYMAN

A SELECTION

Silver Poets of the Sixteenth Century

EDITED BY
DOUGLAS BROOKS-DAVIES
A new edition of this famous
Everyman collection **£6.99**

Complete Poems

JOHN DONNE
The father of metaphysical verse in
this highly-acclaimed edition **£4.99**

Complete English Poems, Of Education, Areopagitica

JOHN MILTON
An excellent introduction to
Milton's poetry and prose **£6.99**

Selected Poems

JOHN DRYDEN
A poet's portrait of Restoration
England **£4.99**

Selected Poems

PERCY BYSSHE SHELLEY
'The essential Shelley' in one
volume **£3.50**

Women Romantic Poets 1780-1830: An Anthology

Hidden talent from the Romantic era,
rediscovered for the first time **£5.99**

Poems in Scots and English

ROBERT BURNS
The best of Scotland's greatest lyric
poet **£4.99**

Selected Poems

D. H. LAWRENCE
A newly-edited selection spanning
the whole of Lawrence's literary
career **£4.99**

The Poems

W. B. YEATS
Ireland's greatest lyric poet
surveyed in this ground-breaking
edition **£6.50**

£5.99

£4.99

£3.50

AVAILABILITY

All books are available from your local bookshop or direct from
**Littlehampton Book Services Cash Sales, 14 Eldon Way, LinesideEstate,
Littlehampton, West Sussex BN17 7HE.** PRICES ARE SUBJECT TO CHANGE.

To order any of the books, please enclose a cheque (in £ sterling) made payable to
Littlehampton Book Services, or phone your order through with credit card details (Access,
Visa or Mastercard) on 0903 721596 (24 hour answering service) stating card number and
expiry date. Please add £1.25 for package and postage to the total value of your order.

DRAMA
IN EVERYMAN

A SELECTION

Everyman and Medieval Miracle Plays

EDITED BY A. C. CAWLEY
A selection of the most popular medieval plays **£3.99**

Complete Plays and Poems

CHRISTOPHER MARLOWE
The complete works of this fascinating Elizabethan in one volume **£5.99**

Complete Poems and Plays

ROCHESTER
The most sexually explicit – and strikingly modern – writing of the seventeenth century **£5.99**

Restoration Plays

Five comedies and two tragedies representing the best of the Restoration stage **£7.99**

Female Playwrights of the Restoration: Five Comedies

Rediscovered literary treasures in a unique selection **£5.99**

Poems and Plays

OLIVER GOLDSMITH
The most complete edition of Goldsmith available **£4.99**

Plays, Poems and Prose

J. M. SYNGE
The most complete edition of Synge available **£6.99**

Plays, Prose Writings and Poems

OSCAR WILDE
The full force of Wilde's wit in one volume **£4.99**

A Doll's House/The Lady from the Sea/The Wild Duck

HENRIK IBSEN
A popular selection of Ibsen's major plays **£3.99**

£2.99

£2.99

£2.99

AVAILABILITY

All books are available from your local bookshop or direct from
Littlehampton Book Services Cash Sales, 14 Eldon Way, LinesideEstate, Littlehampton, West Sussex BN17 7HE. PRICES ARE SUBJECT TO CHANGE.

To order any of the books, please enclose a cheque (in £ sterling) made payable to Littlehampton Book Services, or phone your order through with credit card details (Access, Visa or Mastercard) on 0903 721596 (24 hour answering service) stating card number and expiry date. Please add £1.25 for package and postage to the total value of your order.

MEDIEVAL LITERATURE IN EVERYMAN

A SELECTION

Canterbury Tales
GEOFFREY CHAUCER
EDITED BY A. C. CAWLEY
The complete medieval text with translations **£3.99**

Arthurian Romances
CHRÉTIEN DE TROYES
TRANSLATED BY D. D. R. OWEN
Classic tales from the father of Arthurian romance **£5.99**

Everyman and Medieval Miracle Plays
EDITED BY A. C. CAWLEY
A fully representative selection from the major play cycles **£3.99**

Fergus of Galloway: Knight of King Arthur
TRANSLATED BY D. D. R. OWEN
Scotland's own Arthurian romance **£3.99**

The Vision of Piers Plowman
WILLIAM LANGLAND
EDITED BY A. V. C. SCHMIDT
The only complete edition of the B-version available **£4.99**

Sir Gawain and the Green Knight, Pearl, Cleanness, Patience
EDITED BY A. C. CAWLEY
AND J. J. ANDERSON
Four major English medieval poems in one volume **£3.99**

Six Middle English Romances
EDITED BY MALDWYN MILLS
Tales of heroism and piety **£4.99**

Ywain and Gawain, Sir Percyvell of Gales, The Anturs of Arther
EDITED BY MALDWYN MILLS
Three Middle English romances portraying the adventures of Gawain **£5.99**

The Birth of Romance: An Anthology
TRANSLATED BY JUDITH WEISS
The first-ever English translation of these fascinating Anglo-Norman romances **£4.99**

Brut
LAWMAN
TRANSLATED BY ROSAMUND ALLEN
A major new translation of the earliest myths and history of Britain **£7.99**

The Piers Plowman Tradition
EDITED BY HELEN BARR
Four medieval poems of political and religious dissent – widely available for the first time **£5.99**

Love and Chivalry: An Anthology of Middle English Romance
EDITED BY JENNIFER FELLOWS
A unique collection of tales of courtly love and heroic deeds **£5.99**

AVAILABILITY

All books are available from your local bookshop or direct from
Littlehampton Book Services Cash Sales, 14 Eldon Way, LinesideEstate, Littlehampton, West Sussex BN17 7HE. PRICES ARE SUBJECT TO CHANGE.

To order any of the books, please enclose a cheque (in £ sterling) made payable to Littlehampton Book Services, or phone your order through with credit card details (Access, Visa or Mastercard) on 0903 721596 (24 hour answering service) stating card number and expiry date. Please add £1.25 for package and postage to the total value of your order.

ESSAYS, CRITICISM AND HISTORY IN EVERYMAN

A SELECTION

The Embassy to Constantinople and Other Writings
LIUDPRAND OF CREMONA
An insider's view of political machinations in medieval Europe
£5.99

The Rights of Man
THOMAS PAINE
One of the great masterpieces of English radicalism **£4.99**

Speeches and Letters
ABRAHAM LINCOLN
A key document of the American Civil War **£4.99**

Essays
FRANCIS BACON
An excellent introduction to Bacon's incisive wit and moral outlook **£3.99**

Puritanism and Liberty: Being the Army Debates (1647-49) from the Clarke Manuscripts
A fascinating revelation of Puritan minds in action **£7.99**

History of His Own Time
BISHOP GILBERT BURNET
A highly readable contemporary account of the Glorious Revolution of 1688 **£7.99**

Biographia Literaria
SAMUEL TAYLOR COLERIDGE
A masterpiece of criticism, marrying the study of literature with philosophy **£4.99**

Essays on Literature and Art
WALTER PATER
Insights on culture and literature from a major voice of the 1890s **£3.99**

Chesterton on Dickens: Criticisms and Appreciations
A landmark in Dickens criticism, rarely surpassed **£4.99**

Essays and Poems
R. L. STEVENSON
Stevenson's hidden treasures in a new selection **£4.99**

£3.99

£4.99

SAGAS AND OLD ENGLISH
LITERATURE IN EVERYMAN

A SELECTION

Egils saga

TRANSLATED BY
CHRISTINE FELL
A gripping story of Viking exploits in Iceland, Norway and Britain
£4.99

Edda

SNORRI STURLUSON

TRANSLATED BY
ANTHONY FAULKES
The first complete English translation
£5.99

The Fljotsdale Saga and The Droplaugarsons

TRANSLATED BY
ELEANOR HAWORTH
AND JEAN YOUNG
A brilliant portrayal of life and times in medieval Iceland
£3.99

The Anglo-Saxon Chronicle

TRANSLATED BY
G. N. GARMONSWAY
A fascinating record of events in ancient Britain
£4.99

Anglo-Saxon Poetry

TRANSLATED BY
S. A. J. BRADLEY
A widely acclaimed collection
£6.99

AVAILABILITY

All books are available from your local bookshop or direct from
**Littlehampton Book Services Cash Sales, 14 Eldon Way, LinesideEstate,
Littlehampton, West Sussex BN17 7HE.** PRICES ARE SUBJECT TO CHANGE.

To order any of the books, please enclose a cheque (in £ sterling) made payable to
Littlehampton Book Services, or phone your order through with credit card details (Access,
Visa or Mastercard) on 0903 721596 (24 hour answering service) stating card number and
expiry date. Please add £1.25 for package and postage to the total value of your order.

PHILOSOPHY AND RELIGIOUS WRITING IN EVERYMAN

A SELECTION

An Essay Concerning Human Understanding
JOHN LOCKE
A central work in the development of modern philosophy **£4.99**

Philosophical Writings
GOTTFRIED WILHELM LEIBNIZ
The only paperback edition available **£3.99**

Critique of Pure Reason
IMMANUEL KANT
The capacity of the human intellect examined **£6.99**

A Discourse on Method, Meditations, and Principles
RENE DESCARTES
Takes the theory of mind over matter into a new dimension **£4.99**

Philosophical Works including the Works on Vision
GEORGE BERKELEY
An eloquent defence of the power of the spirit in the physical world **£4.99**

The Social Contract and Discourses
JEAN-JAQUES ROUSSEAU
Rousseau's most influential works in one volume **£3.99**

Utilitarianism/OnLiberty/Considerations on Representative Government
J. S. MILL
Three radical works which transformed political science **£4.99**

Utopia
THOMAS MORE
A critique of contemporary ills allied with a visionary ideal for society **£2.99**

Ethics
SPINOZA
Spinoza's famous discourse on the power of understanding **£4.99**

The Buddha's Philosophy of Man
Ten dialogues representing the cornerstone of early Buddhist thought **£4.99**

Hindu Scriptures
The most important ancient Hindu writings in one volume **£6.99**

Apologia Pro Vita Sua
JOHN HENRY NEWMAN
A moving and inspiring account of a Christian's spiritual journey **£5.99**

AVAILABILITY

All books are available from your local bookshop or direct from
Littlehampton Book Services Cash Sales, 14 Eldon Way, LinesideEstate, Littlehampton, West Sussex BN17 7HE. PRICES ARE SUBJECT TO CHANGE.

To order any of the books, please enclose a cheque (in £ sterling) made payable to Littlehampton Book Services, or phone your order through with credit card details (Access, Visa or Mastercard) on 0903 721596 (24 hour answering service) stating card number and expiry date. Please add £1.25 for package and postage to the total value of your order.